**MASONRY INSTITUTE OF AMERICA**

The Masonry Institute of America, founded in 1957 under the name of Masonry Research, is a promotional and technical research organization established to improve and extend the use of masonry. The Masonry Institute of America is supported by California masonry contractors through labor agreement contracts between the unions and contractors.

The Masonry Institute of America is active in California and thoughout the United States promoting new ideas and masonry work, improving national and local building codes, conducting research projects, presenting design, construction and inspection seminars and writing technical and non-technical papers, all for the purpose of improving the masonry industry.

The Masonry Institute of America does not engage in the practice of architectural or engineering design or construction nor does it sell masonry materials.

Masonry Structural Design

About the International Code Council®

The International Code Council is the leading global source of model codes and standards and building safety solutions that include product evaluation, accreditation, technology, codification, consulting, training and certification. The International Code Council's codes, standards and solutions are used to ensure safe, affordable and sustainable communities and buildings worldwide.

The International Code Council family of solutions includes the ICC Evaluation Service (ICC ES), S. K. Ghosh Associates, the International Accreditation Service (IAS), General Code, ICC NTA, ICC Community Development Solutions, Alliance for National & Community Resilience (ANCR) and American Legal Publishing.

Office Locations:
Headquarters:
200 Massachusetts Avenue, NW, Suite 250
Washington, DC 20001
888-ICC-SAFE (888-422-7233)
www.iccsafe.org

Eastern Regional Office
900 Montclair Road
Birmingham, AL 35213

Central Regional Office
4051 Flossmoor Road
Country Club Hills, IL 60478

Western Regional Office
3060 Saturn Street, Suite 100
Brea, CA 92821

MENA Regional Office
Dubai Association Centre Office, One Central
Building 2, Office 8, Dubai World Trade Centre Complex
PO Box 9292, Dubai, UAE

OCEANIA Regional Office
Level 9, Nishi Building
2 Phillip Law Street
Canberra ACT 2601 Australia

Masonry Structural Design

Jennifer Eisenhauer Tanner, Ph.D., P.E.

Third Edition

Cataloging-in-Publication Data is on file with the Library of Congress.

McGraw Hill books are available at special quantity discounts to use as premiums and sales promotions, or for use in corporate training programs. To contact a representative please visit the Contact Us page at www.mhprofessional.com.

Masonry Structural Design, Third Edition

Copyright © 2025 by McGraw Hill LLC. All rights reserved. Printed in the United States of America. Except as permitted under the United States Copyright Act of 1976, no part of this publication may be reproduced or distributed in any form or by any means, or stored in a data base or retrieval system, without the prior written permission of the publisher.

1 2 3 4 5 LBC 29 28 27 26 25

ISBN 978-1-266-17123-9
MHID 1-266-17123-1

The pages within this book were printed on acid-free paper.

Sponsoring Editor Lara Zoble/Olivia Higgins	**Project Manager** Radhika Jolly, KnowledgeWorks Global Ltd.	**Indexer** Edwin Durbin
Production Supervisor Richard Ruzycka	**Copy Editor** Ultra Rajkumari	**Art Director, Cover** Anthony Landi
Acquisitions Coordinator Olivia Higgins	**Proofreader** Manish Tiwari	**Composition** KnowledgeWorks Global Ltd.

Information contained in this work has been obtained by McGraw Hill from sources believed to be reliable. However, neither McGraw Hill nor its authors guarantee the accuracy or completeness of any information published herein, and neither McGraw Hill nor its authors shall be responsible for any errors, omissions, or damages arising out of use of this information. This work is published with the understanding that McGraw Hill and its authors are supplying information but are not attempting to render engineering or other professional services. If such services are required, the assistance of an appropriate professional should be sought.

About the Author

Jennifer Eisenhauer Tanner is a Professor of Civil and Architectural Engineering at the University of Wyoming, Laramie, Wyoming. She was chair of ACI Committee 526, Autoclaved Aerated Concrete and was previously a member of TMS 402 (masonry code) for 12 years. In 2010, she received the ACI Young Member Award for Professional Achievement and was made an ACI Fellow in 2016. Her research interests include laboratory and field testing; concrete and masonry durability, and materials characterization. Her teaching interests include Masonry Design, Concrete Design, Engineering Materials, Structural Analysis, and Earthquake Engineering.

This book is dedicated to
Timothy and Austin Eisenhauer

Contents

Illustrations		xiii
Tables		xxiii
Preface		xxvii
Notice of Use of Copyrighted Material		xxix

1 Basic Structural Behavior and Design of Low-Rise, Bearing Wall Buildings 1
   1.1 Basic Structural Behavior of Low-Rise, Bearing Wall Buildings 1
   1.2 Basic Structural Design of Low-Rise, Masonry Buildings 2

2 Materials Used in Masonry Construction 5
   2.1 Basic Components of Masonry 5
   2.2 Masonry Mortar 10
   2.3 Masonry Grout 18
   2.4 General Information on ASTM Specifications for Masonry Units 19
   2.5 Clay Masonry Units 21
   2.6 Concrete Masonry Units 26
   2.7 Properties of Masonry Assemblages 28
   2.8 Masonry Accessory Materials 28
   2.9 Design of Masonry Structures Requiring Little Structural Calculation 36
   2.10 How to Increase Resistance of Masonry to Water Penetration 43

3 Code Basis for Structural Design of Masonry Buildings 47
   3.1 Introduction to Building Codes in the United States 47
   3.2 Introduction to the Calculation of Design Loading Using the 2024 IBC 51
   3.3 Gravity Loads According to the 2024 IBC 51
   3.4 Wind Loading According to the 2024 IBC 54
   3.5 Earthquake Loading 79
   3.6 Loading Combinations of the 2024 IBC 90
   3.7 Summary of Strength Design Provisions of TMS 402-22 92
   3.8 Summary of Allowable Stress Design Provisions of TMS 402-22 95
   3.9 Additional Information on Code Basis for Structural Design of Masonry Buildings 99

Contents

4 Introduction to TMS 402 Treatment of Structural Design **101**
- 4.1 Basic Mechanical Behavior of Masonry 101
- 4.2 Classification of Masonry Elements 102
- 4.3 Classification of Masonry Elements by Structural Function 102
- 4.4 Classification of Masonry Elements by Design Intent 102
- 4.5 Design Approaches for Masonry Elements 103
- 4.6 How Reinforcement Is Used in Masonry Elements 103
- 4.7 How This Book Classifies Masonry Elements 107

5 Strength Design of Unreinforced Masonry Elements **109**
- 5.1 Strength Design of Unreinforced Panel Walls 109
- 5.2 Strength Design of Unreinforced Bearing Walls 122
- 5.3 Strength Design of Unreinforced Shear Walls 135
- 5.4 Strength Design of Anchor Bolts 141
- 5.5 Required Details for Unreinforced Bearing Walls and Shear Walls 149
- 5.6 Problems 152

6 Strength Design of Reinforced Masonry Elements **155**
- 6.1 Strength Design of Reinforced Beams and Lintels 155
- 6.2 Strength Design of Reinforced Curtain Walls 163
- 6.3 Strength Design of Reinforced Bearing Walls 167
- 6.4 Strength Design of Reinforced Shear Walls 185
- 6.5 Required Details for Reinforced Bearing Walls and Shear Walls 201
- 6.6 Problems 204

7 Allowable-Stress Design of Unreinforced Masonry Elements **207**
- 7.1 Allowable-Stress Design of Unreinforced Panel Walls 207
- 7.2 Allowable-Stress Design of Unreinforced Bearing Walls 220
- 7.3 Allowable-Stress Design of Unreinforced Shear Walls 235
- 7.4 Allowable-Stress Design of Anchor Bolts 241
- 7.5 Required Details for Unreinforced Bearing Walls and Shear Walls 248
- 7.6 Problems 251

8 Allowable-Stress Design of Reinforced Masonry Elements **255**
- 8.1 Review: Behavior of Cracked, Transformed Sections 255
- 8.2 Allowable-Stress Design of Reinforced Beams and Lintels ... 267
- 8.3 Allowable-Stress Design of Curtain Walls 272
- 8.4 Allowable-Stress Design of Reinforced Bearing Walls 277
- 8.5 Allowable-Stress Design of Reinforced Shear Walls 289
- 8.6 Required Details for Reinforced Bearing Walls and Shear Walls 296
- 8.7 Problems 299

Contents

9 Comparison of Design by the Allowable-Stress Approach Versus the Strength Approach 303
    9.1 Comparison of Allowable-Stress and Strength Design of Unreinforced Panel Walls 303
    9.2 Comparison of Allowable Stress Design and Strength Design of Unreinforced Bearing Walls 304
    9.3 Comparison of Allowable Stress Design and Strength Design of Unreinforced Shear Walls 304
    9.4 Comparison of Allowable-Stress and Strength Designs for Anchor Bolts 305
    9.5 Comparison of Allowable-Stress and Strength Designs for Reinforced Beams and Lintels 306
    9.6 Comparison of Allowable-Stress and Strength Designs for Reinforced Curtain Walls 307
    9.7 Comparison of Allowable-Stress and Strength Designs for Reinforced Bearing Walls 307
    9.8 Comparison of Allowable-Stress and Strength Designs for Reinforced Shear Walls 308

10 Lateral Load Analysis of Shear Wall Structures 309
    10.1 Introduction to Lateral Load Analysis of Shear Wall Structures 309
    10.2 Classification of Horizontal Diaphragms as "Rigid" or "Flexible" 309
    10.3 Lateral Load Analysis of Shear Wall Structures with Rigid Floor Diaphragms 311
    10.4 Lateral Load Analysis and Design of Shear Wall Structures with Flexible Floor Diaphragms 327
    10.5 The Simplest of All Possible Analytical Worlds 330
    10.6 Problems 330

11 Design and Detailing of Floor and Roof Diaphragms 333
    11.1 Introduction to Design of Diaphragms 333
    11.2 Introduction to Design of Rigid Diaphragms 333
    11.3 Introduction to Design of Flexible Diaphragms 333
    11.4 Typical Connection Details for Roof and Floor Diaphragms 335

12 Strength Design Example: Low-Rise Building with Reinforced Concrete Masonry 337
    12.1 Introduction 337
    12.2 Design Steps for One-Story Building 337
    12.3 Step 1: Choose Design Criteria 338
    12.4 Calculate Design Roof Load due to Gravity (*ASCE 7-22*) 340
    12.5 Calculate Design Wind Load 340
    12.6 Propose Structural Systems for Gravity and Lateral Load ... 349
    12.7 Step 2: Design Walls for Gravity plus Out-of-Plane Loads ... 349

12.8	Step 3: Design Lintels	363
12.9	Summary So Far	366
12.10	Step 4: Conduct Lateral Force Analysis, Design Roof Diaphragm	367
12.11	Step 5: Design Wall Segments	369
12.12	Step 6: Design and Detail Connections	372

13 Strength Design Example: Four-Story Building with Clay Masonry 373
    13.1 Introduction 373
    13.2 Design Steps for Four-Story Example 373
    13.3 Step 1: Choose Design Criteria, Specify Materials 374
    13.4 Step 2: Design Transverse Shear Walls for Gravity plus Earthquake Loads 381
    13.5 Step 3: Design Exterior Walls for Gravity plus Out-of-Plane Wind 388
    13.6 Overall Comments on Four-Story Building Example 388

14 Structural Design of AAC Masonry 389
    14.1 Introduction to Autoclaved Aerated Concrete (AAC) 389
    14.2 Applications of AAC 393
    14.3 Structural Design of AAC Elements 393
    14.4 Design of Unreinforced Panel Walls of AAC Masonry 397
    14.5 Design of Unreinforced Bearing Walls of AAC Masonry 399
    14.6 Design of Unreinforced Shear Walls of AAC Masonry 408
    14.7 Design of Reinforced Beams and Lintels of AAC Masonry ... 412
    14.8 Design of Reinforced Curtain Walls of AAC Masonry 415
    14.9 Design of Reinforced Bearing Walls of AAC Masonry 416
    14.10 Design of Reinforced Shear Walls of AAC Masonry 425
    14.11 Seismic Design of AAC Structures 437
    14.12 Design Example: Three-Story AAC Shear-Wall Hotel 438
    14.13 References on AAC 465

15 References 467
    15.1 General References 467
    15.2 ASTM Standards 468

    Index 471

Visit *www.mhprofessional.com/masonry* for downloadable spreadsheets and instructor manuals.

Illustrations

Figure 1.1: Basic structural behavior of low-rise, bearing wall buildings. (p. 2)
Figure 1.2: Basic structural configuration of masonry walls. (p. 3)
Figure 1.3: Starting point for reinforcement. (p. 3)
Figure 2.1: Orientations of masonry units in an element. (p. 8)
Figure 2.2: Typical bond patterns in a wall. (p. 8)
Figure 2.3: Wall types, classified by mode of water-penetration resistance. (p. 9)
Figure 2.4: Weathering indices in the United States. (p. 24)
Figure 2.5: Typical application of deformed reinforcement in grouted masonry wall. (p. 29)
Figure 2.6: Typical bed joint reinforcement. (p. 30)
Figure 2.7: Typical use of welded wire reinforcement. (p. 30)
Figure 2.8: Typical use of posttensioning tendons. (p. 31)
Figure 2.9: Typical veneer ties. (p. 32)
Figure 2.10: Typical adjustable pintle ties. (p. 32)
Figure 2.11: Typical connectors. (p. 33)
Figure 2.12: Sample calculation for stiffness of adjustable ties. (p. 33)
Figure 2.13: Placement of flashing at shelf angles in clay masonry veneer. (p. 34)
Figure 2.14: Horizontally oriented expansion joint under shelf angle. (p. 35)
Figure 2.15: Vertically oriented expansion joint. (p. 35)
Figure 2.16: Shrinkage control joint. (p. 36)
Figure 2.17: Example of control joints at openings in concrete masonry. (p. 36)
Figure 2.18: Overall starting point for reinforcement or structures requiring little structural calculation. (p. 38)
Figure 2.19: Example of overall modularity of a masonry structure in plan. (p. 39)
Figure 2.20: Foundation-wall detail. (p. 39)
Figure 2.21: Foundation-wall detail with drainage wall. (p. 40)
Figure 2.22: Detail of intersection between wall and precast concrete roof or floor slab. (p. 40)
Figure 2.23: Detail of wall and wooden roof truss. (p. 41)
Figure 2.24: Detail of drainage wall and open-web joist roof. (p. 41)
Figure 2.25: Elevations showing locations of control joints in CMU wythe, and locations of expansion joints in clay masonry veneer wythe (fixed lintel and loose lintel, respectively). (p. 42)
Figure 2.26: Wall sections at lintels. (p. 43)

Illustrations

Figure 3.1: Schematic of process for development of masonry design codes in the United States. (p. 48)
Figure 3.2: Graph showing permitted live load reduction for roofs. (p. 54)
Figure 3.3: Basic wind speeds for Risk Category II buildings and other structures. (p. 57)
Figure 3.4: External pressure coefficients for main wind force resisting systems. (p. 62)
Figure 3.5: Schematic view of building in Austin, Texas. (p. 64)
Figure 3.6: Basic wind speeds for Risk Category II buildings and other structures. (p. 69)
Figure 3.7: External pressure coefficient for walls. (p. 74)
Figure 3.8: Schematic view of building in Austin, Texas. (p. 75)
Figure 3.9: External pressure coefficient for walls with $h < 60$ ft. (p. 77)
Figure 3.10: Idealized single-degree-of-freedom system. (p. 79)
Figure 3.11: Acceleration response spectrum, smoothed for use in design. (p. 80)
Figure 3.12: Design acceleration response spectrum, for example, problem. (p. 88)
Figure 4.1: Examples of reinforcement in CMU lintels. (p. 104)
Figure 4.2: Examples of reinforcement in clay masonry lintels. (p. 104)
Figure 4.3: Example of placement of reinforcement in a masonry wall made of hollow units. (p. 105)
Figure 4.4: Examples of the placement of hollow units to form pilasters. (p. 106)
Figure 5.1: Example of an unreinforced panel wall. (p. 110)
Figure 5.2: Horizontal section showing connection of a panel wall to a column. (p. 110)
Figure 5.3: Schematic representation of an unreinforced, two-wythe panel wall as two sets of horizontal and vertical crossing strips. (p. 110)
Figure 5.4: Example panel wall to be designed. (p. 112)
Figure 5.5: Idealized cross-sectional dimensions of a nominal $8 \times 8 \times 16$ in. concrete masonry unit. (p. 113)
Figure 5.6: Idealized cross-sectional dimensions of a nominal $8 \times 8 \times 16$ in. concrete masonry unit with face-shell bedding. (p. 115)
Figure 5.7: Idealized cross-sectional dimensions of a nominal $8 \times 8 \times 16$ in. concrete masonry unit with face-shell bedding. (p. 116)
Figure 5.8: Idealization of a panel wall as an assemblage of crossing strips. (p. 119)
Figure 5.9: Idealization of a two-wythe panel wall as an assemblage of two sets of crossing strips. (p. 120)
Figure 5.10: Idealization of bearing walls as vertically spanning strips. (p. 123)
Figure 5.11: Effect of slenderness on the axial capacity of a column or wall. (p. 123)
Figure 5.12: Unreinforced masonry bearing wall with concentric axial load. (p. 124)
Figure 5.13: Assumed linear variation of bearing stresses under the bearing plate. (p. 127)
Figure 5.14: Unreinforced masonry bearing wall with eccentric axial load. (p. 127)
Figure 5.15: Unreinforced masonry bearing wall with eccentric axial load and wind load. (p. 130)
Figure 5.16: Unfactored moment diagrams due to eccentric axial load and wind. (p. 131)
Figure 5.17: Hypothetical unstable resistance mechanism in a wall with openings, involving vertically spanning strips only. (p. 134)
Figure 5.18: Stable resistance mechanism in a wall with openings, involving horizontally spanning strips in addition to vertically spanning strips. (p. 134)
Figure 5.19: Basic behavior of box-type buildings in resisting lateral loads. (p. 135)
Figure 5.20: Design actions for unreinforced shear walls. (p. 136)

Illustrations   xv

Figure 5.21: Example problem for strength design of unreinforced shear wall. (p. 137)
Figure 5.22: Calculation of reaction on roof diaphragm, strength design of unreinforced shear wall. (p. 137)
Figure 5.23: Transmission of forces from roof diaphragm to shear walls. (p. 138)
Figure 5.24: Shear wall with openings. (p. 140)
Figure 5.25: Free body of one wall segment. (p. 140)
Figure 5.26: Common uses of anchor bolts in masonry construction. (p. 141)
Figure 5.27: Idealized conical breakout cones for anchor bolts loaded in tension. (p. 142)
Figure 5.28: Modification of projected breakout area, A_{pt}, by void areas or adjacent anchors. (p. 142)
Figure 5.29: Example involving a single tensile anchor, placed vertically in a grouted cell. (p. 143)
Figure 5.30: Pryout failure (a) and shear breakout failure (b). (p. 145)
Figure 5.31: Design idealization associated with shear breakout failure. (p. 146)
Figure 5.32: Example of wall-to-foundation connection. (p. 149)
Figure 5.33: Example of wall-to-floor connection, planks perpendicular to wall. (p. 150)
Figure 5.34: Example of wall-to-floor connection, planks parallel to wall. (p. 150)
Figure 5.35: Example of wall-to-roof detail. (p. 151)
Figure 5.36: Examples of wall-to-wall connection details. (p. 151)
Figure 6.1: Assumptions used in strength design of reinforced masonry for flexure. (p. 156)
Figure 6.2: Equilibrium of internal stresses and external nominal moment for strength design of reinforced masonry for flexure. (p. 156)
Figure 6.3: Conditions corresponding to balanced reinforcement percentage for strength design. (p. 157)
Figure 6.4: Example of masonry lintel. (p. 158)
Figure 6.5: Example for strength design of a lintel. (p. 159)
Figure 6.6: Example showing placement of bottom reinforcement in lowest course of lintel. (p. 160)
Figure 6.7: Plan view of typical curtain wall construction. (p. 163)
Figure 6.8: Examples of use of curtain walls of clay masonry. (p. 164)
Figure 6.9: Examples of the use of curtain walls with concrete masonry. (p. 165)
Figure 6.10: Anchors holding the ends of curtain wall strips to columns. (p. 167)
Figure 6.11: Effective width of a reinforced masonry bearing wall. (p. 168)
Figure 6.12: Idealized moment-axial force interaction diagram using strength design. (p. 168)
Figure 6.13: Location of neutral axis under balanced conditions, strength design. (p. 169)
Figure 6.14: Three-point moment-axial force interaction (strength basis), calculated by hand. (p. 172)
Figure 6.15: Position of neutral axis at balanced conditions, strength calculation of moment-axial force interaction diagram by spreadsheet. (p. 173)
Figure 6.16: Position of the neutral axis for axial loads less than the balance-point axial load, strength design. (p. 173)
Figure 6.17: Position of the neutral axis for axial loads greater than the balance-point axial load, strength design. (p. 174)

Illustrations

Figure 6.18: Moment-axial force interaction diagram (strength approach), spreadsheet calculation. (p. 176)
Figure 6.19: Reinforced masonry wall loaded by eccentric gravity axial load plus out-of-plane wind load. (p. 178)
Figure 6.20: Unfactored moment diagrams due to eccentric axial load plus wind load. (p. 178)
Figure 6.21: Moment-axial force interaction diagram for out-of-plane example, including the effects of capping for slenderness. (p. 179)
Figure 6.22: Critical strain condition for a masonry wall loaded out of plane. (p. 184)
Figure 6.23: Design actions for reinforced masonry shear walls. (p. 186)
Figure 6.24: V_{nm} as a function of $(M_u/V_u d_v)$. (p. 186)
Figure 6.25: Idealized model used in evaluating the resistance due to shear reinforcement. (p. 187)
Figure 6.26: Maximum permitted nominal shear capacity as a function of $(M_u/V_u d_v)$. (p. 188)
Figure 6.27: Reinforced masonry shear wall to be designed. (p. 188)
Figure 6.28: Unfactored in-plane lateral loads, shear and moment diagrams for reinforced masonry shear wall. (p. 189)
Figure 6.29: Moment-axial force interaction diagram (strength basis) for reinforced shear wall, neglecting slenderness effects. (p. 190)
Figure 6.30: Moment-axial force interaction diagram (strength basis) for reinforced shear wall, including slenderness effects. (p. 193)
Figure 6.31: Critical strain condition for strength design of masonry walls loaded in-plane, and for columns and beams. (p. 198)
Figure 6.32: Example of wall-to-foundation connection. (p. 201)
Figure 6.33: Example of wall-to-floor connection, planks perpendicular to wall. (p. 202)
Figure 6.34: Example of wall-to-floor connection, planks parallel to wall. (p. 202)
Figure 6.35: Example of wall-to-roof detail. (p. 203)
Figure 6.36: Examples of wall-to-wall connection details. (p. 203)
Figure 7.1: Example of an unreinforced panel wall. (p. 208)
Figure 7.2: Horizontal section showing connection of a panel wall to a column. (p. 208)
Figure 7.3: Schematic representation of an unreinforced, two-wythe panel wall as two sets of horizontal and vertical crossing strips. (p. 209)
Figure 7.4: Example panel wall to be designed. (p. 210)
Figure 7.5: Idealized cross-sectional dimensions of a nominal 8 × 8 × 16 in. concrete masonry unit. (p. 211)
Figure 7.6: Idealized cross-sectional dimensions of a nominal 8 × 8 × 16 in. concrete masonry unit with face-shell bedding. (p. 213)
Figure 7.7: Idealized cross-sectional dimensions of a nominal 8 × 8 × 16 in. concrete masonry unit with face-shell bedding. (p. 214)
Figure 7.8: Idealization of a panel wall as an assemblage of crossing strips. (p. 217)
Figure 7.9: Idealization of a two-wythe panel wall as an assemblage of two sets of crossing strips. (p. 218)
Figure 7.10: Idealization of bearing walls as vertically spanning strips. (p. 220)
Figure 7.11: Effect of slenderness on the axial capacity of a column or wall. (p. 221)
Figure 7.12: Unreinforced masonry bearing wall with concentric axial load. (p. 222)
Figure 7.13: Assumed linear variation of bearing stresses under the bearing plate. (p. 225)

Figure 7.14: Unreinforced masonry bearing wall with eccentric axial load. (p. 225)
Figure 7.15: Unreinforced masonry bearing wall with eccentric axial load and wind load. (p. 228)
Figure 7.16: Unfactored moment diagrams due to eccentric axial load and wind. (p. 229)
Figure 7.17: Hypothetical unstable resistance mechanism in a wall with openings, involving vertically spanning strips only. (p. 234)
Figure 7.18: Stable resistance mechanism in a wall with openings, involving horizontally spanning strips in addition to vertically spanning strips. (p. 234)
Figure 7.19: Basic behavior of box-type buildings in resisting lateral loads. (p. 235)
Figure 7.20: Design actions for unreinforced shear walls. (p. 236)
Figure 7.21: Example problem for strength design of unreinforced shear wall. (p. 237)
Figure 7.22: Calculation of reaction on roof diaphragm, allowable-stress design of unreinforced shear wall. (p. 238)
Figure 7.23: Transmission of forces from roof diaphragm to shear walls. (p. 238)
Figure 7.24: Shear wall with openings. (p. 240)
Figure 7.25: Free body of one wall segment. (p. 241)
Figure 7.26: Common uses of anchor bolts in masonry construction. (p. 241)
Figure 7.27: Idealized conical breakout cones for anchor bolts loaded in tension. (p. 242)
Figure 7.28: Modification of projected breakout area, A_{pt}, by void areas or adjacent anchors. (p. 242)
Figure 7.29: Example involving a single tensile anchor, placed vertically in a grouted cell. (p. 243)
Figure 7.30: Pryout failure (a) and shear breakout failure (b). (p. 245)
Figure 7.31: Design idealization associated with shear breakout failure. (p. 246)
Figure 7.32: Example of wall-to-foundation connection. (p. 249)
Figure 7.33: Example of wall-to-floor connection, planks perpendicular to wall. (p. 249)
Figure 7.34: Example of wall-to-floor connection, planks parallel to wall. (p. 250)
Figure 7.35: Example of wall-to-roof detail. (p. 250)
Figure 7.36: Examples of wall-to-wall connection details. (p. 251)
Figure 8.1: States of strain and stress in a cracked masonry section. (p. 256)
Figure 8.2: Location of the neutral axis for particular cases. (p. 257)
Figure 8.3: Slice of a cracked, transformed section showing triangular compressive stress blocks. (p. 258)
Figure 8.4: Slice of a cracked, transformed section showing equilibrium between shear forces and difference in shear forces. (p. 258)
Figure 8.5: Slice of a cracked, transformed section showing equilibrium of the compressive and tensile portions of the slice. (p. 259)
Figure 8.6: Slice of a cracked, transformed section, showing equilibrium of difference in compressive force and difference in tensile force. (p. 260)
Figure 8.7: Tensile portion of a slice, showing equilibrium between bond force and difference in tensile force in reinforcement. (p. 261)
Figure 8.8: Example calculation of the position of the neutral axis. (p. 262)
Figure 8.9: Equilibrium of forces in the cross-section corresponding to allowable stress in the reinforcement. (p. 264)

xviii   Illustrations

Figure 8.10: Equilibrium of forces in the cross-section corresponding to allowable stress in the masonry. (p. 265)
Figure 8.11: Conditions of stress and strain corresponding to allowable-stress balanced reinforcement. (p. 266)
Figure 8.12: Example of masonry lintel. (p. 267)
Figure 8.13: Example for allowable-stress design of a lintel. (p. 268)
Figure 8.14: Example showing placement of bottom reinforcement in lowest course of lintel. (p. 269)
Figure 8.15: Equilibrium of forces on cross-section. (p. 270)
Figure 8.16: Plan view of typical curtain wall construction. (p. 272)
Figure 8.17: Examples of use of curtain walls of clay masonry. (p. 273)
Figure 8.18: Examples of the use of curtain walls with concrete masonry. (p. 274)
Figure 8.19: Anchors holding the ends of curtain wall strips to columns. (p. 277)
Figure 8.20: Effective width of a reinforced masonry bearing wall. (p. 278)
Figure 8.21: Location of neutral axis under allowable-stress balanced conditions. (p. 279)
Figure 8.22: Plot of allowable-stress moment-axial force interaction diagram calculated by hand. (p. 282)
Figure 8.23: Conditions of strain and stress at allowable-stress balanced conditions. (p. 283)
Figure 8.24: Conditions of strain and stress for values of k less than the allowable-stress balanced value. (p. 284)
Figure 8.25: Conditions of strain and stress for values of k greater than the allowable-stress balanced value. (p. 285)
Figure 8.26: Plot of allowable-stress interaction calculated by spreadsheet. (p. 286)
Figure 8.27: Example of reinforced bearing wall loaded out-of-plane. (p. 287)
Figure 8.28: Unfactored moment diagrams due to eccentric axial load plus wind load. (p. 288)
Figure 8.29: Design actions for reinforced masonry shear walls. (p. 289)
Figure 8.30: V_{nm} as a function of $(M_u/V_u d_v)$. (p. 290)
Figure 8.31: Idealized model used in evaluating the resistance due to shear reinforcement. (p. 290)
Figure 8.32: Maximum allowable shear stress as a function of (M/Vd). (p. 291)
Figure 8.33: Reinforced masonry shear wall to be designed. (p. 292)
Figure 8.34: Unfactored in-plane lateral loads, shear and moment diagrams for reinforced masonry shear wall. (p. 292)
Figure 8.35: Plot of allowable-stress moment-axial force interaction diagram calculated by spreadsheet. (p. 294)
Figure 8.36: Example of floor-to-wall connection. (p. 297)
Figure 8.37: Example of wall-to-floor connection, planks perpendicular to wall. (p. 297)
Figure 8.38: Example of wall-to-floor connection, planks parallel to wall. (p. 298)
Figure 8.39: Example of wall-to-roof detail. (p. 298)
Figure 8.40: Examples of wall-to-wall connection details. (p. 299)
Figure 10.1: Example of building with perforated walls. (p. 310)
Figure 10.2: Solution to example problem using Method 1 (finite element method). (p. 312)

Illustrations

Figure 10.3: Shearing deformation of a wall segment. (p. 313)

Figure 10.4: Plan lengths of wall segments for example problem using simplest hand method (Method 2a). (p. 314)

Figure 10.5: Shears in Wall 2 and Wall 4 of example using the simplest hand method (Method 2a). (p. 315)

Figure 10.6: Shears in wall segments of Wall 4 using the simplest hand method (Method 2a). (p. 315)

Figure 10.7: Examples of location of center of rigidity for symmetrical buildings. (p. 316)

Figure 10.8: Examples of location of center of rigidity for unsymmetrical buildings. (p. 316)

Figure 10.9: Decomposition of lateral load into a lateral load applied through the center of rigidity plus pure torsion about the center of rigidity. (p. 316)

Figure 10.10: Location of the center of rigidity in one direction. (p. 317)

Figure 10.11: Free-body diagram of diaphragm showing applied loads and reactions from shear walls. (p. 317)

Figure 10.12: Decomposition of lateral load into lateral load through center of rigidity plus torsion about the center of rigidity. (p. 318)

Figure 10.13: Lateral load applied through the center of rigidity. (p. 319)

Figure 10.14: Pure rotation in plan of a structure with lateral load applied through the center of rigidity. (p. 319)

Figure 10.15: Structure loaded by a combination of load through the center of rigidity plus plan torsion about the center of rigidity. (p. 321)

Figure 10.16: Application of rigid-diaphragm analysis to the structure considered in this section (Method 2b). (p. 322)

Figure 10.17: Location of center of rigidity for the example of this section (Method 2b). (p. 322)

Figure 10.18: Shear forces acting on walls due to direct shear and due to torsion (Method 2b). (p. 324)

Figure 10.19: Combined shear forces acting on walls of example structure (Method 2b). (p. 324)

Figure 10.20: Distribution of shears to segments of the east wall of example structure (Method 2b). (p. 324)

Figure 10.21: Example of perforated wall with segments of unequal height. (p. 325)

Figure 10.22: Plan view of example building with flexible roof diaphragm. (p. 328)

Figure 10.23: Results of example problem, assuming flexible diaphragm. (p. 329)

Figure 10.24: Example of a flexible horizontal diaphragm with more than two points of lateral support. (p. 329)

Figure 11.1: Example of a flexible diaphragm. (p. 334)

Figure 11.2: Example of design of a flexible diaphragm for shear and moment. (p. 334)

Figure 11.3: Example of computation of diaphragm chord forces. (p. 335)

Figure 11.4: Example of a connection detail between a CMU wall and steel joists. (p. 336)

Figure 11.5: Example of a connection detail between a CMU wall and wooden joists. (p. 336)

Figure 12.1: Plan of example single-story building. (p. 338)

Figure 12.2: Elevation of example single-story building. (p. 339)

Figure 12.3: Locations of control joints on North and South facades. (p. 339)

Figure 12.4: Locations of control joints on West facade. (p. 339)
Figure 12.5: Spacing of control joints on East facade. (p. 339)
Figure 12.6: Three-dimensional view of low-rise building. (p. 340)
Figure 12.7: External pressure coefficient for walls with $h < 60$ ft. (p. 346)
Figure 12.8: Assumed variation of bearing stresses under bearing plate. (p. 349)
Figure 12.9: Tributary area of typical bar joist on west wall. (p. 350)
Figure 12.10: West bearing wall of example low-rise building. (p. 350)
Figure 12.11: Unfactored moment diagrams from eccentric dead load and wind load. (p. 351)
Figure 12.12: Design moment-axial force interaction diagram for West wall of example low-rise building. (p. 353)
Figure 12.13: East wall of example low-rise building. (p. 355)
Figure 12.14: Trial design Segment B of East wall as governed by out-of-plane wind load. (p. 355)
Figure 12.15: Design moment-axial force interaction diagram for Wall Segment B of low-rise example building. (p. 355)
Figure 12.16: Design of lintel on east wall for out-of-plane loads. (p. 357)
Figure 12.17: Placement of bar joists adjacent to North and South walls. (p. 358)
Figure 12.18: Cross-section of typical pilaster in north and south walls of example low-rise building. (p. 359)
Figure 12.19: Tributary area supported by typical pilaster. (p. 359)
Figure 12.20: Distribution of bearing stresses under bearing plates of pilasters. (p. 360)
Figure 12.21: Factored moment diagrams due to eccentric dead load and wind on pilasters. (p. 361)
Figure 12.22: Effective depth, d, of pilasters. (p. 361)
Figure 12.23: Strength moment-axial force interaction diagram for typical pilaster. (p. 363)
Figure 12.24: Bearing plate under long-span joists. (p. 363)
Figure 12.25: East façade of low-rise building, showing critical 20-ft lintel. (p. 364)
Figure 12.26: Tributary area supported by bar joists bearing on lintel of east wall. (p. 364)
Figure 12.27: Section through 20-ft lintel of east wall. (p. 365)
Figure 12.28: Reinforcement in east wall of low-rise building. (p. 367)
Figure 12.29: Wind load transmitted to roof diaphragm. (p. 367)
Figure 12.30: Plan view of low-rise building showing wind loads transferred to roof diaphragm. (p. 368)
Figure 12.31: Assumed variation of shear and moment in each segment of east wall. (p. 370)
Figure 13.1: Plan view of typical floor of four-story example building. (p. 374)
Figure 13.2: Plan view of typical floor of four-story example building. (p. 374)
Figure 13.3: Design response spectrum for Charleston, SC. (p. 377)
Figure 13.4: Factored design shears and moments for four-story example building. (p. 381)
Figure 13.5: Effective flange width used for each transverse shear wall. (p. 382)
Figure 13.6: Strength moment-axial force interaction diagram for transverse masonry shear wall. (p. 383)
Figure 14.1: Close-up view of AAC. (p. 390)
Figure 14.2: Examples of AAC elements. (p. 390)

Figure 14.3: Overall steps in manufacture of AAC. (p. 391)
Figure 14.4: AAC residence in Monterrey, Mexico. (p. 393)
Figure 14.5: AAC hotel in Tampico, Mexico. (p. 394)
Figure 14.6: AAC cladding, Monterrey, Mexico. (p. 394)
Figure 14.7: Integrated US design background for AAC elements and structures. (p. 395)
Figure 14.8: Example panel wall to be designed using AAC masonry. (p. 398)
Figure 14.9: Unreinforced AAC masonry bearing wall with concentric axial load. (p. 400)
Figure 14.10: Assumed linear variation of bearing stresses under bearing plate of AAC masonry wall. (p. 402)
Figure 14.11: Unreinforced AAC masonry bearing wall with eccentric axial load. (p. 403)
Figure 14.12: Unreinforced masonry bearing wall with eccentric axial load and wind load. (p. 405)
Figure 14.13: Unfactored moment diagrams due to eccentric axial load and wind. (p. 406)
Figure 14.14: Design actions for unreinforced shear walls. (p. 408)
Figure 14.15: Example problem for strength design of unreinforced shear wall. (p. 409)
Figure 14.16: Calculation of reaction on roof diaphragm, strength design of unreinforced AAC masonry shear wall. (p. 409)
Figure 14.17: Transmission of forces from roof diaphragm to shear walls. (p. 410)
Figure 14.18: Example of masonry lintel. (p. 412)
Figure 14.19: Example for design of an AAC masonry lintel. (p. 413)
Figure 14.20: Example showing placement of bottom reinforcement in lowest course of lintel. (p. 414)
Figure 14.21: Moment-axial force interaction diagram (strength approach), spreadsheet calculation. (p. 416)
Figure 14.22: Reinforced masonry wall loaded by eccentric gravity axial load plus out-of-plane wind load. (p. 418)
Figure 14.23: Unfactored moment diagrams due to eccentric axial load plus wind load. (p. 419)
Figure 14.24: Moment-axial force interaction diagram for out-of-plane example, including the effects of capping for slenderness. (p. 420)
Figure 14.25: Critical strain condition for an AAC masonry wall loaded out of plane. (p. 424)
Figure 14.26: Design actions for reinforced AAC masonry shear walls. (p. 425)
Figure 14.27: Idealized model used in evaluating the resistance due to shear reinforcement. (p. 426)
Figure 14.28: Maximum permitted nominal shear capacity of AAC masonry as a function of $(M_u / V_u d_v)$. (p. 427)
Figure 14.29: Reinforced AAC masonry shear wall to be designed. (p. 428)
Figure 14.30: Unfactored in-plane lateral loads, shear and moment diagrams for reinforced AAC masonry shear wall. (p. 428)
Figure 14.31: Moment-axial force interaction for reinforced AAC shear wall, neglecting slenderness effects. (p. 431)
Figure 14.32: Critical strain condition for design of AAC masonry walls loaded in-plane, and for columns and beams. (p. 435)
Figure 14.33: Plan of three-story hotel example using AAC masonry. (p. 439)
Figure 14.34: Elevation of three-story hotel example using AAC masonry. (p. 439)

Illustrations

Figure 14.35: Design response spectrum for Richmond, VA. (p. 450)

Figure 14.36: Graphs of factored design shears and moments for three-story hotel example using AAC masonry. (p. 453)

Figure 14.37: Typical transverse shear wall of three-story hotel example with AAC masonry. (p. 454)

Figure 14.38: Strength interaction diagram by spreadsheet, AAC transverse shear wall. (p. 456)

Figure 14.39: Plan view of section of exterior wall, three-story example with AAC masonry. (p. 459)

Figure 14.40: Plan view of AAC floor diaphragm, three-story hotel example with AAC masonry. (p. 461)

Figure 14.41: Section of AAC floor diaphragm, three-story hotel example with AAC masonry. (p. 461)

Figure 14.42: Section of panel-to-panel joint or typical grouted key between AAC floor panels. (p. 462)

Figure 14.43: Section of panel-to-bond beam joint, AAC floor diaphragm. (p. 462)

Figure 14.44: Truss model for design of AAC diaphragm. (p. 463)

Figure 14.45: Loaded nodes for design of AAC diaphragm. (p. 463)

Figure 14.46: Unloaded notes for design of AAC diaphragm. (p. 463)

Tables

Table 2.1: Classification of Masonry Units (p. 6)
Table 2.2: Approximate Proportion Requirements for Cement-Lime Mortars from ASTM C270 (p. 13)
Table 2.3: Property Requirements for Cement-Lime Mortars from ASTM C270 (p. 14)
Table 2.4: Approximate Proportion Requirements for Masonry-Cement Mortars from ASTM C270 (p. 14)
Table 2.5: Property Requirements for Masonry-Cement Mortars from ASTM C270 (p. 15)
Table 2.6: Approximate Proportion Requirements for Mortar-Cement Mortars from ASTM C270 (p. 16)
Table 2.7: Property Requirements for Mortar-Cement Mortars from ASTM C270 (p. 16)
Table 2.8: Proportion Requirements for Grout for Masonry (from ASTM C476) (p. 18)
Table 2.9: Summary of ASTM Requirements for Clay Masonry Units (p. 25)
Table 3.1: Minimum Live Loads (L) for Floors (p. 52)
Table 3.2: Table 1607.13.1 of the 2024 IBC (p. 53)
Table 3.3: Wind Directionality Factor, K_d (p. 58)
Table 3.4: Main Wind Force Resisting System and Components and Cladding (p. 60)
Table 3.5: Velocity Pressure Exposure Coefficients, K_h and K_z (p. 61)
Table 3.6: Velocity Pressure Coefficients for Building of Example 1 (p. 65)
Table 3.7: Spreadsheet for Wind Forces, Example 1 (p. 67)
Table 3.8: Wind Directionality Factor, K_d (p. 70)
Table 3.9: Spreadsheet for Components and Cladding Pressures, Windward Side of Example 2 (p. 78)
Table 3.10: Spreadsheet for Components and Cladding Pressures, Leeward Side of Example 2 (p. 78)
Table 3.11: Strength-Reduction Factors (p. 92)
Table 3.12: Summary of Steps for Strength Design of Unreinforced Panel Walls (p. 93)
Table 3.13: Summary of Steps for Strength Design of Unreinforced Bearing Walls (p. 93)
Table 3.14: Summary of Steps for Strength Design of Unreinforced Shear Walls (p. 94)
Table 3.15: Summary of Steps for Strength Design of Reinforced Beams and Lintels (p. 94)
Table 3.16: Summary of Steps for Strength Design of Reinforced Curtain Walls (p. 94)
Table 3.17: Summary of Steps for Strength Design of Reinforced Bearing Walls (p. 95)
Table 3.18: Summary of Steps for Strength Design of Reinforced Shear Walls (p. 95)

Table 3.19: Summary of Steps for Allowable-Stress Design of Unreinforced Panel Walls (p. 96)
Table 3.20: Summary of Steps for Allowable-Stress Design of Unreinforced Bearing Walls (p. 97)
Table 3.21: Summary of Steps for Allowable-Stress Design of Unreinforced Shear Walls (p. 97)
Table 3.22: Summary of Steps for Allowable-Stress Design of Reinforced Beams and Lintels (p. 97)
Table 3.23: Summary of Steps for Allowable-Stress Design of Reinforced Curtain Walls (p. 98)
Table 3.24: Summary of Steps for Allowable-Stress Design of Reinforced Bearing Walls (p. 98)
Table 3.25: Summary of Steps for Strength Design of Reinforced Shear Walls (TMS 402-22) (p. 99)
Table 5.1: Modulus of Rupture (Table 9.1.9.1 of TMS 402-22) (p. 111)
Table 5.2: Section Properties for Clay Masonry Walls (p. 118)
Table 5.3: Section Properties for Concrete Masonry Walls (Face-Shell and Web Thicknesses Consistent with CMHA Tech Note 002, which References ASTM C90-24) (p. 118)
Table 5.4: Section Properties for Concrete Masonry Walls (Face-Shell and Web Thicknesses Consistent with CMHA TEK 002, which References ASTM C90-24) (p. 125)
Table 5.5: Self-Weights of Hollow CMU Walls (p. 125)
Table 5.6: Self-Weights of Fully Grouted CMU Walls (p. 132)
Table 6.1: Physical Properties of Steel Reinforcing Wire and Bars (from Table CC-6.1.3 of *TMS 402-22*) (p. 159)
Table 6.2: Spreadsheet for computing moment-axial force interaction diagram (strength approach) (p. 177)
Table 7.1: Allowable Flexural Tension for Clay and Concrete Masonry, psi (Table 8.2.4.2 of *TMS 402-22*) (p. 209)
Table 7.2: Section Properties for Clay Masonry Walls (p. 215)
Table 7.3: Section Properties for Concrete Masonry Walls (Face-Shell and Web Thicknesses Consistent with CMHA TEK 002, Which References *ASTM C90-06*) (p. 216)
Table 7.4: Section Properties for Concrete Masonry Walls (Face-Shell and Web Thicknesses Consistent with CMHA TEK 002, Which References *ASTM C90-06*) (p. 223)
Table 7.5: Self-Weights of Hollow CMU Walls (p. 223)
Table 7.6: Self-Weights of Fully Grouted CMU Walls (p. 231)
Table 8.1: Physical Properties of Steel Reinforcing Wire and Bars (from Table CC-6.1.3 of *TMS 402-22*) (p. 262)
Table 8.2: Spreadsheet for Calculating Allowable-Stress Interaction Diagram for Wall Loaded Out-of-Plane (p. 286)
Table 9.1: Comparison of Allowable-Stress and Strength Design for Unreinforced Panel Walls (p. 304)
Table 9.2: Comparison of Allowable-Stress and Strength Design for Unreinforced Bearing Walls (p. 304)

Table 9.3: Comparison of Allowable-Stress and Strength Design for Unreinforced Shear Walls (p. 305)

Table 9.4: Comparison of Allowable-Stress and Strength Design for Anchor Bolts, Masonry Controls (p. 305)

Table 9.5: Comparison of Allowable-Stress and Strength Design for Anchor Bolts, Steel Controls (p. 306)

Table 9.6: Comparison of Allowable-Stress and Strength Design for Reinforced Beams and Lintels (as Governed by Flexure) (p. 306)

Table 9.7: Comparison of Allowable-Stress and Strength Design for Reinforced Beams and Lintels (as Governed by Shear) (p. 307)

Table 9.8: Comparison of Allowable-Stress and Strength Design for Reinforced Bearing Walls (Governed by Flexure) (p. 307)

Table 9.9: Comparison of Allowable-Stress and Strength Design for Reinforced Shear Walls (as Governed by Flexure) (p. 308)

Table 9.10: Comparison of Allowable-Stress and Strength Design for Reinforced Shear Walls (as Governed by Shear) (p. 308)

Table 10.1: Comparison of Results Obtained by Each Method for Calculating Shear-Wall Forces by Each Method (p. 326)

Table 10.2: Comparison of Results Obtained by Each Method for Calculating Shear-Wall Forces by Each Method (p. 326)

Table 12.1: Velocity Pressure Coefficients for Low-Rise Example Building (Taken from Table 27.3-1 of *ASCE 7-22*) (p. 341)

Table 12.2: Spreadsheet for Computation of Base Shear for Example Low-Rise Building (MWFRS) (p. 343)

Table 12.3: Spreadsheet for Calculation of Wind Pressure on Windward Side of Low-Rise Example Building (Components and Cladding) (p. 347)

Table 12.4: Spreadsheet for Calculation of Wind Pressure on Leeward Side of Low-Rise Example Building (Components and Cladding) (p. 347)

Table 12.5: Spreadsheet for Calculation of Wind Pressure on Roof of Low-Rise Example Building (Components and Cladding) (p. 348)

Table 12.6: Spreadsheet for Calculating Strength Moment-Axial Force Interaction for West Wall of Low-Rise Building (p. 354)

Table 12.7: Spreadsheet for Calculating Moment-Axial Force Interaction Diagram for Wall Segment B of Low-Rise Example Building (p. 356)

Table 12.8: Spreadsheet for Calculating Strength Moment-Axial Force Interaction Diagram for Typical Pilaster (p. 362)

Table 12.9: Factored Gravity Loads Acting on 20-ft Lintel of East Wall (p. 365)

Table 12.10: Design Shear in Each Segment of East Wall due to Design Wind Load (p. 370)

Table 13.1: Factored Design Lateral Forces for Four-Story Example Building (p. 381)

Table 13.2: Spreadsheet for Calculating Strength Moment-Axial Force Interaction Diagram for Transverse Shear Wall of Four-Story Building Example (p. 384)

Table 14.1: Typical Material Characteristics of AAC in Different Strength Classes (p. 392)

Table 14.2: Dimensions of Plain AAC Wall Units (p. 392)

Table 14.3: Physical Properties of Steel Reinforcing Bars (p. 413)

Table 14.4: Spreadsheet for Computing Moment-Axial Force Interaction Diagram for AAC Bearing Wall (p. 417)

Table 14.5: Calculations for Spreadsheet of Out-of-Plane Example, Including Effects of Capping for Slenderness (p. 421)

Table 14.6: Spreadsheet for Reinforced AAC Shear Wall (p. 432)

Table 14.7: Seismic Design Factors for Ordinary Reinforced AAC Masonry Shear Walls (p. 439)

Table 14.8: Factored Design Shears and Moments for three-Story Hotel Example Using AAC Masonry (p. 453)

Table 14.9: Calculations for Spreadsheet for Typical Transverse Shear Wall of AAC Masonry (p. 457)

Preface

This book came from the merging of material from two masonry courses, each developed by one of the two authors. It covers the design of masonry structures using the 2015 *International Building Code*, the *ASCE 7-10* loading standard, and the *TMS 402-13* and *TMS 602-13* design and construction standards. Although the book was conceived primarily as a textbook for masonry design courses in civil or architectural engineering programs at the undergraduate or graduate level, it is also intended for use in self-study and continuing education by practicing engineers. It emphasizes the strength design of masonry and also includes allowable-stress design.

Chapter 1 of this book begins, not with design calculations, but rather with a basic discussion of how wall-type buildings behave and how those buildings can be detailed and specified using masonry. The reason for this is that until the reader understands how the elements of a masonry building work together structurally, the design of those individual elements will not have a clear purpose. Many categories of masonry buildings require only the most rudimentary structural design, and the first part of this book is intended to show how to detail and specify detail for such buildings correctly.

Chapter 2 then covers the terminology of masonry and masonry materials, followed by an explanation of their basic behavior, and ending with a summary of how to use ASTM specifications for masonry materials.

Chapters 3 and 4 address structural design provisions for masonry elements and structures. In the context of *TMS 402-13*, masonry elements are classified by structural function, and as unreinforced or reinforced. Strength design and allowable-stress design are discussed, along with the loads and loading combinations used for each design approach. To reinforce concepts not always explicitly covered in civil or architectural engineering programs, these chapters include detailed examples of the calculation of design for wind and seismic loads according to the 2015 *IBC* and *ASCE 7-10*, the load standard referenced by that model code.

Chapters 5 and 6 address the strength design of unreinforced and reinforced masonry elements, respectively. Chapters 7 and 8 repeat that presentation for allowable-stress design. In Chapter 9, the strength and allowable-stress provisions of *TMS 402-13* are compared.

In Chapter 10, the lateral load analysis of low-rise wall structures is discussed, and specific recommendations are presented for hand analysis and computer-aided analysis. In Chapter 11, design and detailing of floor and roof diaphragms are discussed.

Chapters 12 and 13 present the preliminary design, using strength procedures, of two representative prototype masonry buildings. The first building is a low-rise commercial building, designed for gravity and wind loads; the second is a four-story hotel, designed for gravity and earthquake loads.

Chapter 14 addresses autoclaved aerated concrete (AAC) masonry, an innovative construction material addressed by the 2015 *IBC, ASCE 7-10, TMS 402-13, TMS 602-13,* and ASTM specifications. Background material on AAC masonry is reviewed, and design examples are presented. Chapter 14 ends with a preliminary design example of a three-story hotel, subjected to gravity and earthquake loads.

Jennifer Eisenhauer Tanner, Ph.D., P.E.
Richard E. Klingner, Ph.D.

Notice of Use of Copyrighted Material

Portions of this publication reproduce sections from *ASCE 7-22*, published by the American Society of Civil Engineers, Reston, VA. Reproduced with permission. All rights reserved. www.asce.org

Portions of this publication reproduce sections from ASTM standards, published by the American Society for Testing and Materials, West Conshohocken, PA. Reproduced with permission. All rights reserved. www.astm.org

Portions of this publication reproduce material supplied by the Brick Industry Association, Reston, VA. Reproduced with permission. All rights reserved. www.bia.org

Portions of this publication reproduce tables and illustrations from the 2024 *International Building Code*, published by the International Code Council, Inc., Washington, D.C. Reproduced with permission. All rights reserved. www.iccsafe.org

Portions of this publication reproduce material supplied by the National Concrete Masonry Association, Herndon, VA. Reproduced with permission. All rights reserved. www.ncma.org

Portions of this publication reproduce material supplied by Xella Mexicana, Monterrey, Mexico. Reproduced with permission. All rights reserved.

Some illustrations were provided by courtesy of Masonry Institute of Michigan.

Cover credits for Top left photo—Jandris Block.

Masonry Structural Design

CHAPTER 1
Basic Structural Behavior and Design of Low-Rise, Bearing Wall Buildings

1.1 Basic Structural Behavior of Low-Rise, Bearing Wall Buildings

This book does not start with the design of masonry elements. Rather, it starts with the behavior of low-rise, bearing wall buildings. The reason for this is that the behavior of masonry structural elements, and the design requirements for those elements, depends on the behavior of the structures comprising those elements.

Low-rise, bearing wall buildings resist lateral loads as shown in Fig. 1.1. This resistance mechanism involves three steps:

- Walls oriented perpendicular to the direction of lateral load transfer those loads to the level of the foundation and the levels of the horizontal diaphragms. The walls are idealized and designed as vertically oriented strips.
- The roof and floors act as horizontal diaphragms, transferring their forces to walls oriented parallel to the direction of lateral load.
- Walls oriented parallel to the direction of applied load must transfer loads from the horizontal diaphragms to the foundation. In other words, they act as shear walls.

This overall mechanism demands that the horizontal roof diaphragm has sufficient strength and stiffness to transfer the required loads.

The addition of vertical loads from sources other than self-weight places the vertical strips in compression and makes the walls bearing walls.

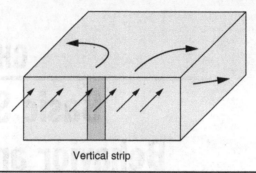

FIGURE 1.1 Basic structural behavior of low-rise, bearing wall buildings.

1.2 Basic Structural Design of Low-Rise, Masonry Buildings

The fundamental design premise of low-rise, masonry buildings is that they are composed of masonry walls only.

THERE ARE NO EMBEDDED STEEL OR CONCRETE FRAME ELEMENTS. THAT'S RIGHT. NONE.

Low-rise, bearing wall masonry buildings are designed for gravity loads and lateral loads. Lateral loads from wind are presumed to act separately in each principal plan direction. Depending on the direction in which they act, walls can be bearing walls or shear walls.

1.2.1 Basic Structural Configuration

Masonry walls are generally composed of hollow masonry units, held together by mortar. Vertical reinforcement is placed in continuous vertical cells, and horizontal reinforcement is placed in horizontal courses (bond beams). Cells with reinforcement, and bond beams, and possibly other cells as well, are filled with grout (a fluid concrete mixture). A typical arrangement is shown in Fig. 1.2 for the case of hollow concrete masonry units. Construction with hollow clay masonry units would be quite similar.

Because the walls are reinforced, design is straightforward and reasonably familiar even to those with little or no experience in masonry design.

- Vertical strips resisting combinations of gravity loads and out-of-plane loads act as reinforced beam-columns. Behavior of reinforced masonry is quite similar to that of reinforced concrete and can be described by a moment-axial force interaction diagram for out-of-plane bending.
- Shear walls act in flexure as cantilever beam-columns. Behavior of reinforced masonry is quite similar to that of reinforced concrete and can be described by a moment-axial force interaction diagram for in-plane bending.

Basic Structural Behavior and Design of Low-Rise, Bearing Wall Buildings

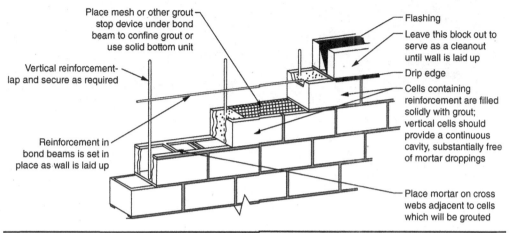

FIGURE 1.2 Basic structural configuration of masonry walls. (*Source*: Figure 1 of CMHA TEK 3-2A.)

1.2.2 Overall Starting Point for Reinforcement

The overall starting point for reinforcement is shown in Fig. 1.3.

Structural design is carried using the strength provisions of the 2022 TMS 402/602 Code and Specification, because that document is referenced by most model codes, and its strength provisions can be easily learned by designers familiar with strength provisions for reinforced concrete.

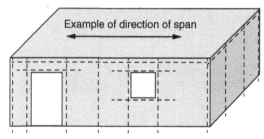

FIGURE 1.3 Starting point for reinforcement.

CHAPTER 2
Materials Used in Masonry Construction

2.1 Basic Components of Masonry

Masonry can be used in a wide variety of architectural applications, including

- Walls (bearing, shear, structural, decorative, bas-relief, mosaic)
- Arches, domes, and vaults
- Beams, columns

Masonry, while often simple and elegant in form, can be complex in behavior. Also, unlike concrete, it cannot be ordered by the cubic yard. To understand its behavior and to be able to specify masonry correctly, we must examine each of its basic components: units, mortar, grout, and accessory materials.

Immediately below, each component (and related concepts) is discussed briefly. In later sections, more details are provided.

2.1.1 Preliminary Discussion of Masonry Units

Masonry units, as noted in Table 2.1, can be classified in a wide variety of ways.

In this book, we shall emphasize the behavior and use of structural masonry units of fired clay or of concrete.

2.1.2 Preliminary Discussion of Masonry Mortar

In the United States, three basic cementitious systems are used for mortar: cement-lime mortar, masonry-cement mortar, and mortar-cement mortar. The first two are widely used; the third has been recently introduced.

Cement-lime mortar is made from different proportions of Portland cement or other cements, hydrated masons' lime, and masonry sand, mixed with water. It can be batched by hand on site using material from bags or batched automatically on site using material from silos.

Mortar-cement mortar is made from different proportions of mortar cement and sand, mixed with water. It may also contain additional Portland cement or other cements. Mortar cement formulations and manufacturing processes are manufacturer-specific. Ingredients are not required to be identified, and usually are not. Mortar cement

TABLE 2.1 Classification of Masonry Units

Unfired Clay Masonry Units	Adobe
Fired clay masonry units	Roofing tile
	Drain tile
	Refractory brick
	Wall tile
	Glazed facing tile (terra cotta, ceramic veneer)
	Structural clay products
	Structural tile
	Facing tile
	Glazed
	Textured
	Floor tile
	Brick (solid, frogged, cored, hollow)
	Facing and building brick
	Glazed brick
	Floor and paving brick
	Industrial
	Paving
	Patio
	Chemical resistant brick
	Sewer brick
	Chimney lining brick
Concrete masonry units	Concrete block (solid, hollow)
Other masonry units	Glass
	Stone (artificial shape)
	Rock (natural shape)

generally consists of Portland cement, pozzolanic cement or slag cement, plasticizing additives, air-entraining additives, water-retention additives, and finely ground limestone (added primarily as a filler, but with some plasticizing and cementitious effect). It differs from masonry cement in that it is formulated specifically for tensile bond strength comparable to that of cement-lime mortar.

2.1.3 Preliminary Discussion of Masonry Grout

Grout is fluid concrete, usually with pea-gravel aggregate. It can be used to fill some or all cells in hollow units, or between wythes.

2.1.4 Preliminary Discussion of Masonry Accessory Materials

Masonry accessory materials include reinforcement, connectors, sealants, flashing, coatings, and vapor barriers.

- Connectors (of galvanized or stainless steel) connect a masonry wall to another wall, or a masonry wall to a frame, or a masonry wall to something else.

- Sealants are used in expansion joints (clay masonry), control joints (concrete masonry), and construction joints.
- Flashing is a flexible waterproof membrane used for drainage walls.
- Coatings include paints and clear water-repellent coatings.
- Moisture barriers and vapor barriers are used as parts of wall systems to retard the passage of water in liquid form and vapor form, respectively.

2.1.5 Preliminary Discussion of Masonry Dimensions

Masonry unit dimensions are typically described in terms of (thickness × height × length). Typically, the length is the largest dimension, the thickness is next, and the height is the smallest dimension.

For example, a typical clay masonry unit has dimensions of 4 × 2.67 × 8 in. These are **nominal dimensions**; that is, the distances occupied by the unit plus one-half a joint width on each side. Joints are normally 3/8-in. thick. The **specified dimensions** of the unit themselves are smaller; in this case, 3-5/8 × 2-¼ × 7-5/8 in. The **actual dimensions** are the measured size and should fall within the specified dimensions, plus or minus the tolerance permitted by the governing material specification.

The sides of a masonry unit are often designated in literature by special names:

- The bed is the side formed by thickness × length.
- The face is the side formed by height × length.
- The head is the side formed by thickness × height (end).

2.1.6 Orientation of Masonry Units in an Element

Masonry units can be placed in a wall or other element in many orientations, as shown in Fig. 2.1 (looking perpendicular to the plane of the element). The stretcher orientation is the most common; and the soldier orientation is often used above or below wall openings.

2.1.7 Bond Patterns

Masonry units can be placed in a wall or other element in many bond patterns (arrangements), as shown in Fig. 2.2 (again, looking perpendicular to the plane of the element). In that figure, the horizontal joints are referred to as bed joints, and the vertical joints are referred to as head joints. In all the bond patterns of that figure, the bed joints are continuous along every course (level) of masonry.

- In running bond, the head joints align in alternate courses and are aligned with the middle of the units in adjacent courses.
- In stack bond, the head joints align in adjacent courses;
- In 1/3 running bond, the head joints align in alternate courses and are aligned one-third of the way along the units in adjacent courses;
- In Flemish bond, units of two different lengths are used.

Many other bond patterns are possible.

Chapter Two

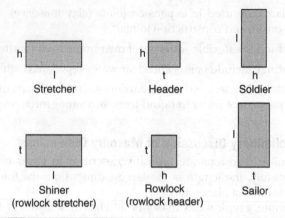

FIGURE 2.1 Orientations of masonry units in an element.

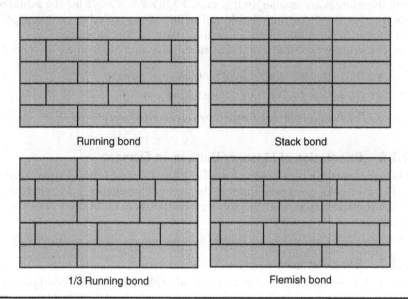

FIGURE 2.2 Typical bond patterns in a wall.

2.1.8 Types of Walls

Masonry is most commonly used in walls. Masonry walls can be classified in many different ways. For now, we shall classify masonry walls according to how they resist water penetration. Using this criterion, masonry walls can be classified as barrier walls or drainage walls. Examples of each type are shown in Fig. 2.3.

- Barrier walls resist water penetration primarily by virtue of their thickness. They may have coatings. They may be single-wythe (one thickness of masonry), or multi-wythe. Multi-wythe barrier walls can have the wythes connected by bonded headers (masonry units placed in header orientation) or by a filled collar joint (space between wythes).

Materials Used in Masonry Construction

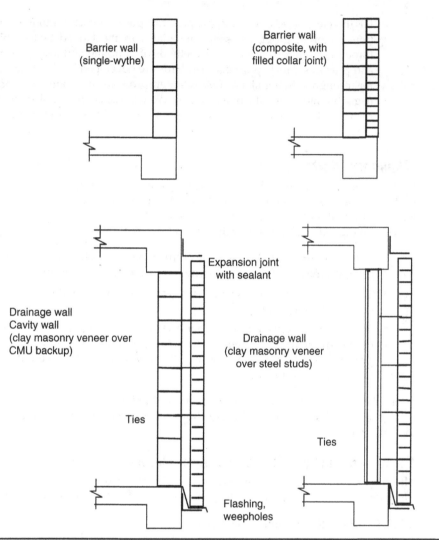

FIGURE 2.3 Wall types, classified by mode of water-penetration resistance.

- Drainage walls resist water penetration by a combination of thickness and drainage details. Drainage walls may also have coatings. Drainage details include an air space (at least 2 in. wide), flashing, and weepholes. Drainage walls can be single-wythe (veneer over steel studs) or multi-wythe (veneer over masonry backup). The latter are often also called "cavity walls."

2.1.9 Overview of How Masonry Is Specified

To further discuss how masonry is specified, it is necessary to recognize the following:

1) Unlike the steel or concrete industries, individual segments of the masonry industry rarely produce a finished masonry assembly.

2) It is therefore necessary to specify/prescribe precisely each component of masonry (units, mortar, grout, accessory materials). In the United States, this is done through standard specifications, methods of sampling and testing, test methods, and practices. Most applicable standards are developed by the American Society for Testing and Materials (ASTM). A few are produced by model code organizations (e.g., the International Code Council). We will focus on ASTM standards, using them as a frame of reference for the specification of masonry elements.

2.2 Masonry Mortar

Masonry mortar holds masonry units together and also holds them apart (compensates for their dimensional tolerances). Mortar for unit masonry is addressed by ASTM C270, which in turn cites other ASTM specifications.

Specifying masonry mortar under ASTM C270 requires three choices:

- The designer must choose a cementitious system. Three options are possible: cement-lime mortar, masonry-cement mortar, or mortar-cement mortar.
- The designer must choose a mortar type, basically related to the proportion of cement in the mortar.
- The designer must choose whether ASTM C270 will be enforced by proportions of the different ingredients, or by the properties of the final mortar. The proportion specification is the default and is assumed to govern if the designer does not state otherwise.

Each choice is discussed in more detail a little later. For now, to help explain the background and significance of these choices, it is useful to discuss the chemistry of masonry mortar.

2.2.1 Introduction to the Chemistry of Masonry Mortar

Masonry mortars can be broadly classified as sand-lime mortars and hydraulic mortars. The former hardens (set) only in the presence of air. The latter can harden under water.

2.2.1.1 Chemistry of Sand-Lime Mortar

Since the time of the Romans, masonry mortar has been made from a mixture of lime and sand. Limestone is first calcined (heated) to produce quicklime (calcium oxide). The chemical formulas for this reaction, and its corresponding verbal explanation, are shown here:

$$\text{limestone} + \text{heat} = \text{calcium oxide} + \text{carbon dioxide}$$
$$(\text{quicklime})$$
$$CaCO_3 = CaO + CO_2$$

To form mortar, the quicklime is mixed with water to produce hydrated lime, plus large amounts of heat:

$$\text{calcium oxide} + \text{water} = \text{calcium hydroxide} + \text{heat}$$
$$(\text{quicklime}) \quad (\text{hydrated lime})$$
$$CaO + H_2O = Ca(OH)_2 + \text{heat}$$

Finally, exposure to the atmosphere converts the calcium hydroxide to calcium carbonate. This reaction takes place over several years:

$$\text{calcium hydroxide} + \text{air} = \text{calcium carbonate} + \text{water}$$
$$\text{(hydrated lime)} \quad \text{(carbon dioxide)} \quad \text{(limestone)}$$
$$Ca(OH)_2 + CO_2 = CaCO_3 + H_2O$$

Sand-lime mortar is found in many historic buildings. It hardens very slowly, but also has the ability to deform slowly over time without cracking. Sand-lime mortar is not a hydraulic-cement mortar because the last step in its hardening process (conversion of calcium hydroxide to calcium carbonate) occurs only in the presence of air.

2.2.1.2 Chemistry of Hydraulic-Cement Mortars

Hydraulic cements harden as a result of a chemical reaction of minerals with water. Hydraulic cements have been used since prehistoric times. Their cementitious ingredients include pozzolanic cements, gypsum cements, Portland cements, and other cements.

2.2.1.2.1 Chemistry of Pozzolanic Cements These were discovered by the Greeks. The word "pozzolan" comes from a site in Italy (Pozzuoli, near the volcano Vesuvius) where these minerals were found and used by the Romans. A pozzolan possesses little or no cementitious properties on its own but reacts with calcium hydroxide and water to form cementitious compounds. An example of a natural pozzolan is quartz, whose chemical formula ($SiO_2 \cdot XH_2O$) denotes silica (silicon dioxide) combined chemically with water. When finely ground quartz is mixed with hydrated lime (calcium hydroxide, or $Ca(OH)_2$), the following reaction occurs:

$$SiO_2 \cdot XH_2O + Ca(OH)_2 = Ca_{1-3}SiO_3 \cdot H_2O$$
$$\text{(calcium silicate, a natural cement)}$$

2.2.1.2.2 Chemistry of Gypsum Cement ("Plaster of Paris") Gypsum reacts much faster with water than do lime or pozzolans. Pure gypsum sets in about 5 minutes. Commercial gypsum (such as Hydrostone®) sets in about 45 minutes because it has a retarder with it.

Gypsum rock is calcined (heated) like limestone but requires less energy:

$$CaSO_4 \cdot 2H_2O + \text{heat} = CaSOH_4 \cdot \tfrac{1}{2}H_2O + 3/2H_2O$$
$$\text{(gypsum rock)} \quad \text{(plaster of Paris)}$$

When water is added to the calcined gypsum, it reverts to its original state:

$$CaSO_4 \cdot \tfrac{1}{2}H_2O + 3/2H_2O = CaSOH_4 \cdot 2H_2O + \text{heat}$$
$$\text{(plaster of Paris)} \quad \text{(gypsum rock)}$$

The resulting cement is very strong and stiff as concrete. Its main disadvantage is that it expands slowly over time as it absorbs water from the outside air. This produces large splitting forces if the gypsum is restrained.

In the calcining operation, if the gypsum rock is heated too much, the following undesirable reaction results, producing a powder that is not useful for building:

$$CaSO_4 \cdot 2H_2O + heat = CaSOH_4 + 2H_2O$$
(gypsum rock)   (anhydrite)

2.2.1.2.3 Chemistry of Portland Cement Portland cement is a particular class of hydraulic cement. It was first manufactured in England in the early 1800s and was so named because its color was thought to resemble that of a natural limestone from the Isle of Portland.

Hardened Portland cement is the result of the hydration of four principal chemical constituents:

Name	Chemical Formula	Abbreviated Name
Tricalcium silicate	$3CaO \cdot SiO_2$	C_3S
Dicalcium silicate	$2CaO \cdot SiO_2$	C_2S
Tricalcium aluminate	$3CaO \cdot Al_2O_3$	C_3A
Tetracalcium aluminoferrite	$4CaO \cdot Al_2O_3 \cdot Fe_2O_3$	C_4AF

Dry (unhydrated) cement consists of these compounds in powdered form. When water is added, the compounds combine with water in an exothermic (heat producing) reaction, to form calcium hydroxide (about 25% by weight) and calcium silicate hydrate (about 50% by weight).

2.2.1.2.4 Chemistry of Other Hydraulic Cements In recent years, Portland cement has increasingly been used in combination with other hydraulic cements, particularly pozzolanic cements and slag cements. Each has its own ASTM specification. Pozzolanic cements combine with calcium hydroxide to produce calcium silicate hydrate. Slag cements (usually produced from ground granulated blast-furnace slag, or GGBF slag), are combinations of silicates and aluminosilicates. Slag cements, when hydrated, produce primarily calcium silicate hydrates as well.

2.2.2 Cementitious Systems Used in Modern Masonry Mortar

Modern masonry mortar is composed of cementitious agents (Portland cement or other hydraulic cements and hydrated lime, or masonry cement, or mortar cement), sand, and water. Each of these can be referred to as a cementitious system. Three cementitious systems are defined by ASTM C270:

- cement and lime
- masonry cement
- mortar cement

The first of these (cement and lime) is self-explanatory. The second and third (masonry cement and mortar cement) are generally mixtures of Portland or blended cement and plasticizing materials (such as hydrated lime or finely ground limestone), together with other materials introduced to enhance performance. These other materials generally include air-entraining and water-retention additives, intended to improve freeze-thaw durability, workability, and water retention. These are discussed further in this chapter.

2.2.3 Types of Masonry Mortar

ASTM C270 defines, for all cementitious systems, different mortar types. In general, these are distinguished by the proportion of cement in the mortar. Types of masonry mortar are designated by ASTM C270 as shown below. The letters M, N, S, and O represent every second letter of the phrase, "mason work":

$$M, S, N, O \quad (\text{M a S o N w O r K})$$

Toward the "M" end of the spectrum, mortars have a higher volume proportion of cement; toward the "N" end, a lower proportion. This designation was selected intentionally (rather than, e.g., "A, B, C, D") to avoid the implication that a "Type A" mortar would always be the best.

2.2.4 Characteristics of Different Types of Masonry Mortar

Type M: High compressive strength and tensile bond strength
Type S: Moderate compressive and tensile bond strength
Type N: Low compressive strength and tensile bond strength
Type O: Very low compressive and tensile bond strength
Type K: No longer used

Type S mortar is a good all-purpose mortar.

Now let's look at how mortar is specified using each cementitious system. Specification is either by proportion or by property. Specification by proportion is the default. If the specifier does not say "by property," the specification is assumed to be by proportion.

2.2.5 Cement-Lime Mortar

Approximate proportion requirements for cement-lime mortar are shown in Table 2.2. The proportions given in that table are near the mid-points of the ranges of proportions required by ASTM C270. When specifying a mortar by the proportion specifications of ASTM C270, it is not necessary to specify the proportions, only the mortar type.

TABLE 2.2 Approximate Proportion Requirements for Cement-Lime Mortars from ASTM C270

Mortar Type	Portland Cement or Other Cements	Hydrated Lime	Mason's Sand (2-1/4 to 3 times volume of cementitious materials)
M	1	≤1/4	3
S	1	1/2	4-1/2
N	1	1	6
O	1	2	9

ASTM C270 refers in turn to other ASTM specifications:

ASTM C207:	Hydrated lime for masonry purposes
Type N:	No oxide limits (Type NA is air-entrained)
Type S:	Oxide limits (Type SA is air-entrained)
ASTM C144:	Aggregate for masonry mortar (sand gradations)

Even if sand doesn't meet grading limits, it can still pass "by use" (if mortar made with it can pass the property specifications of ASTM C270).

Property requirements for cement-lime mortar from ASTM C270 are repeated in Table 2.3.

2.2.6 Masonry-Cement Mortar

Approximate proportion specifications for masonry-cement mortar are given in Table 2.4. The proportions given in that table are near the mid-points of the ranges of proportions required by ASTM C270. When specifying a mortar by the proportion specifications of ASTM C270, it is not necessary to specify the proportions, only the mortar type.

The most common types are single-bag mixes (the first four lines of the table). However, Types M and S masonry-cement mortar can also be made by adding Portland cement to Type N masonry cement.

TABLE 2.3 Property Requirements for Cement-Lime Mortars from ASTM C270

Mortar Type	Compressive Strength, psi	Water Retention	Maximum Air Content
M	2500	75%	12%
S	1800	75%	12%
N	750	75%	14% (12% if reinforced)
O	350	75%	14% (12% if reinforced)

Note: These property requirements apply only to laboratory-prepared mortar, with a flow of about 110. They are not requirements for field mortar. See the end of this section for an explanation of flow.

TABLE 2.4 Approximate Proportion Requirements for Masonry-Cement Mortars from ASTM C270

Mortar Type	Portland Cement Or Blended Cement	Masonry Cement Type M	Masonry Cement Type S	Masonry Cement Type N	Mason's Sand (2-¼ to 3 times volume of cementitious materials)
M		1			3
S			1		3
N				1	3
O				1	3
M	1			1	6
S	½			1	4-½

Materials Used in Masonry Construction

TABLE 2.5 Property Requirements for Masonry-Cement Mortars from ASTM C270

Masonry-Cement Mortar Type	Property Requirements for Masonry-Cement Mortar		
	Compressive Strength, psi	Water Retention	Maximum Air Content
M	2500	75%	18%
S	1800	75%	18%
N	750	75%	20% (18% if reinforced)
O	350	75%	20% (18% if reinforced)

Note: These property requirements apply only to laboratory-prepared mortar, with a flow of about 110. They are not requirements for field mortar.

Property requirements for masonry-cement mortar from ASTM C270 are repeated in Table 2.5.

2.2.7 Mortar-Cement Mortar

Approximate proportion specifications for mortar-cement mortar are given in Table 2.6. The proportions given in that table are near the mid-points of the ranges of proportions required by ASTM C270. When specifying a mortar by the proportion specifications of ASTM C270, it is not necessary to specify the proportions, only the mortar type.

By far the most common types are single-bag mixes (the first four lines of the table). Types M and S mortar-cement mortar can also be made, however, by adding Portland cement to Type N mortar cement.

Property requirements for mortar-cement mortar from ASTM C270 are repeated in Table 2.5.

2.2.8 Characteristics of Fresh Mortar

The most important characteristic of fresh mortar is workability, generally defined as the ability to be easily spread on masonry units using a trowel. In the context of ASTM C270, workability is defined measured very simply, in terms of flow. A standard-shaped, circular sample of mortar 4 in. in diameter is placed on a flow table, which is then dropped 25 times. The flow of that mortar is defined as the increase in diameter of the sample, divided by the original diameter and multiplied by 100. Thus, if the final diameter is 8 in., the flow is $(8 - 4)/4$, or 100. Laboratory-mixed mortars have a flow of about 110 ± 5; field mortars, about 130 to 150. Field mortars should be retempered (water added) as necessary to maintain workability but should not be used beyond 2-½ hours after mixing. Workability can also be measured with a cone penetrometer.

According to ASTM C270, mortar can be specified by proportion (the default) or by property. If mortar is specified by proportion, the following characteristics of fresh mortar are controlled indirectly as a result of complying with the required proportions. If mortar is specified by property, they are controlled directly:

1) Retentivity: This is the ratio of the flow after suction to the initial flow. Flow after suction is measured using mortar from which some of the water has been removed using a standard vacuum apparatus. In one other specification, the mortar is spread on a masonry unit and allowed to sit for 1 minute. According to ASTM C270, mortar is required to have a retentivity of at least 75%.

TABLE 2.6 Approximate Proportion Requirements for Mortar-Cement Mortars from ASTM C270

Mortar Type	Portland Cement	Mortar Cement Type M	Mortar Cement Type S	Mortar Cement Type N	Mason's Sand (2-¼ to 3 times volume of cementitious materials)
M		1			3
S			1		3
N				1	3
O				1	3
M	1			1	6
S	½			1	4-½

TABLE 2.7 Property Requirements for Mortar-Cement Mortars from ASTM C270

Mortar-Cement Mortar Type	Compressive Strength, psi	Water Retention	Maximum Air Content
M	2500	75%	12%
S	1800	75%	12%
N	750	75%	14% (12% if reinforced)
O	350	75%	14% (12% if reinforced)

Note: These property requirements apply only to laboratory-prepared mortar, with a flow of about 110. They are not requirements for field mortar.

2) Air content: Percent air by volume (ASTM C91). Cement-lime mortar and mortar-cement mortar usually have a maximum permissible air content of 12%. Masonry-cement mortar usually has a maximum permitted air content of 18% if used in reinforced masonry.

2.2.9 Characteristics of Hardened Mortar

Characteristics of hardened mortar include compressive strength and tensile bond strength. Only the first is controlled by ASTM C270.

If mortar is specified by the property specification of ASTM C270, compressive strength is controlled directly. It is measured using 2-in. mortar cubes, made with laboratory-flow mortar, cured for 28 days at 100% relative humidity and 70°F. It typically ranges from 500 to 3000 psi. It does not significantly affect the compressive strength of masonry assemblages. ASTM C270 requires minimum compressive strengths of 2500, 1800, 750, and 350 psi for Type M, S, N, and O mortar, respectively.

If mortar is specified by the proportion specification of ASTM C270, compressive strength is controlled indirectly. Masonry-cement mortar meeting the proportion specification usually has a compressive strength slightly greater than the minimum value specified in the property specification. Cement-lime mortar meeting the proportion specification usually has a compressive strength considerably greater than the minimum value specified in the property specification.

2.2.10 Other Characteristics of Hardened Mortar

One other characteristic of hardened mortar is tensile bond strength (the tensile strength of the bond between mortar and units). Cement-lime mortar has traditionally satisfied practical requirements for tensile bond strength. Tensile bond strength is not specified directly for cement-lime mortar nor for masonry-cement mortar. It is addressed directly in the specification for mortar-cement mortar. Strictly speaking, it can be measured only in conjunction with units and is therefore not a property of the hardened mortar alone. Nevertheless, certain characteristics of the mortar itself contribute to good tensile bond strength regardless of the type of unit used. High tensile bond strength can be obtained using cement-lime mortar or mortar-cement mortar. It is also enhanced by the use of mortars with air content below 12%.

2.2.11 Note on Cement-Lime Mortars versus Masonry-Cement Mortars

At times in the past, and to some extent even to this day, controversy has existed within the masonry technical community over the comparative performance of cement-lime mortar and masonry-cement mortar. Each cementitious system has advantages and disadvantages. Each has demonstrated general suitability for use and also general cost-effectiveness for suppliers and users.

Masonry cement complies with the physical property requirements of ASTM C91. Because the standard specifications are based on properties rather than ingredients, specific formulations of masonry cement vary from manufacturer to manufacturer. Ingredients and formulations are not required to be disclosed, and generally are not. Masonry cement is generally delivered to the jobsite in prepackaged form. It consists of a mixture of Portland or blended cement and plasticizing materials (such as hydrated lime or finely ground limestone) together with other materials introduced to enhance performance. These other materials generally include air-entraining and water-retention additives, intended to improve freeze-thaw durability, workability, and water retention.

The primary advantage of cement-lime mortar is its high tensile bond strength. Its disadvantages are the additional complexity of mixing three ingredients, and some lack of workability (stickiness) if not retempered. The first disadvantage can be overcome by single-bag or silo mixes. The second can sometimes be overcome by retempering.

The advantages of masonry-cement mortar are its relative simplicity of batching and its good workability. It has a "fluffy" consistency (because of its entrained air), which leads to good productivity. Its lower tensile bond strength is accounted for by lower allowable stresses in design codes. In part because of these lower bond strengths, and in part because of tradition, masonry cement is prohibited in structural masonry zones of high seismic risk in the United States.

Considerable anecdotal evidence, and some controlled experimental evidence, indicates that other things being equal, walls laid with cement-lime mortar leak less than walls with masonry-cement mortar. In the author's judgment, this is true. It is also true, however, that acceptably water-resistant walls can be constructed using either cementitious system, and the cementitious system is not the most important choice to make when specifying masonry. The proper type of wall (drainage vs. barrier) and proper drainage details, if applicable, are more important.

From the viewpoint of cement producers, masonry cement is probably a profitable "niche" product. A 70-lb bag of masonry cement typically contains about 40% or less (28 lb or less) of Portland cement or other cements, and about 40 lb of ground limestone. The rest is air-entraining additives, and possibly additives for water-retention and plasticity. A 70-lb bag of masonry cement (28 lb cement, 40 lb limestone, and additives) commonly sells for the same price as a 94-lb bag of Portland cement.

Mortar cement was introduced in the 1990s to preserve the construction advantages and potential profitability of masonry cement, while at the same time increasing the tensile bond strength of the resulting mortar to values comparable to those of cement-lime mortar. Mortar cement is regarded by building codes as the equivalent of cement-lime mortar and is permitted in all seismic zones of the United States.

2.3 Masonry Grout

Masonry grout is essentially fluid concrete. It is used to fill spaces in masonry, and to surround reinforcement and anchors. It is specified using ASTM C476 (Grout for Masonry).

Grout for masonry is composed of Portland cement, sand, and (for coarse grout) pea gravel. It is permitted to contain a small amount of hydrated masons' lime but usually does not. It is permitted to be specified by proportion or by compressive strength. Neither of these is the default.

2.3.1 Proportion Specifications for Grout for Masonry

The proportion requirements of ASTM C476 for grout for masonry are repeated in Table 2.8. Note that hydrated lime is permitted but not required.

2.3.2 Properties of Fresh Grout

The most important property of fresh grout is its ability to flow. Masonry grout should be placed with a slump of 8 to 11 in. so that it will flow freely into the cells of the masonry. Because of its high water-cement ratio at time of grouting, masonry grout undergoes considerable plastic shrinkage as the excess water is absorbed by the surrounding units. To prevent the formation of voids due to this process, the grout is consolidated during placement, and reconsolidated after initial plastic shrinkage. Grouting admixtures containing plasticizers and water-retention agents can also be useful in the grouting process.

2.3.3 Properties of Hardened Grout

The most important property of hardened grout is its compressive strength. If grout is specified by compressive strength, that strength must be at least 2000 psi. If it is specified

TABLE 2.8 Proportion Requirements for Grout for Masonry (from ASTM C476)

Grout Type	Portland Cement	Hydrated Lime	Mason's Sand	Pea Gravel
Fine	1	≤1/10	2-¼ to 3	—
Coarse	1	≤1/10	2-¼ to 3	1 to 2

by proportion, its compressive strength is controlled indirectly to at least that value, by the ingredients used.

Because of its high water-cement ratio at the time of grouting, masonry grout cast into impermeable molds has a very low compressive strength, which is not representative of its strength under field conditions, when the surrounding units absorb water from it. For this reason, ASTM C1019 (Sampling and Testing Grout) requires that the compression specimen be cast using permeable molds. The most common way of preparing such a mold is to arrange masonry units so that they enclose a rectangular solid whose base is 2 in^2, and whose height is equal to the height of the units. The rectangular solid is surrounded by paper towels or filter paper, so that the compressive specimen's water-cement ratio is similar to that of grout in the actual wall.

2.3.4 Self-Consolidating Grout

Based on TMS 402-13, self-consolidating grout is permitted to be used in masonry. Self-consolidating grout is a highly fluid and stable grout, typically with admixtures, that remains homogeneous when placed and does not require puddling or vibration for consolidation. This type of grout has the ability to flow easily into even small voids in the masonry, and to surround reinforcement without the need for mechanical consolidation. This ability is imparted by a combination of super-plasticizing admixtures and aggregate characteristics. Test methods associated with self-consolidating grout are provided in ASTM C1611.

2.4 General Information on ASTM Specifications for Masonry Units

Definitions of terms are given in ASTM C1180 (Standard Terminology of Mortar and Grout for Unit Masonry) and in ASTM C1232 (Standard Terminology of Masonry).

2.4.1 General Information on ASTM Specifications for Clay or Shale Masonry Units

ASTM specifications for clay or shale masonry units are summarized below:

ASTM C62:	Building Brick (Solid Masonry Units Made from Clay or Shale)
ASTM C216:	Facing Brick (Solid Masonry Units Made from Clay or Shale)
ASTM C410:	Industrial Floor Brick
ASTM C652:	Hollow Brick (Hollow Masonry Units Made from Clay or Shale)
ASTM C902:	Pedestrian and Light Traffic Paving Brick
ASTM C1272:	Heavy Vehicular Paving Brick

ASTM specifications for methods of sampling and testing clay or shale masonry units are given in ASTM C67 (Sampling and Testing Brick and Structural Clay Tile) and in ASTM C1006 (Splitting Tensile Strength of Masonry Units).

2.4.2 General Information on ASTM Specifications for Concrete Masonry Units

ASTM specifications for concrete masonry units are summarized below:

C55:	Concrete Building Brick
C90:	Hollow Load-Bearing Concrete Masonry Units
C129:	Hollow Non–Load-Bearing Concrete Masonry Units
C139:	Concrete Masonry Units for Construction of Catch Basins and Manholes
C744:	Prefaced Concrete and Calcium Silicate Masonry Units
C936:	Solid Concrete Interlocking Paving Units
C1319:	Concrete Grid Paving Units
C1372:	Dry-Cast Segmental Retaining Wall Units

ASTM specifications for methods of sampling and testing concrete masonry units are given in ASTM C140, which references ASTM C426 (Drying Shrinkage).

2.4.3 General Information on ASTM Specifications for Masonry Assemblages

ASTM specifications for standard methods of test for masonry assemblages are summarized below:

ASTM E 72:	Strength Tests of Panels for Building Construction (lateral load by air bag)
ASTM E514:	Water Permeance of Masonry
ASTM E518:	Flexural Bond Strength of Masonry (modulus of rupture)
ASTM E519:	Diagonal Tension (Shear) in Masonry Assemblages
ASTM C1072:	Measurement of Masonry Flexural Bond Strength (bond wrench)
ASTM C1314:	Measurement of Compressive Strength of Masonry Prisms to Determine Compliance with f'_m
ASTM C1357:	Evaluating Masonry Bond Strength
ASTM C1717:	Conducting Strength Tests of Masonry Wall Panels

2.4.4 Concluding Remarks on ASTM Specifications for Masonry

The above apparently bewildering list of applicable ASTM specifications covers almost every possible aspect of masonry mortar, units, and assemblages. While the ASTM specifications can help organize the field, they may have indirect rather than direct relationships with the performance of the finished masonry. To shed more light on this point, we must investigate the desired performance characteristics of masonry materials and study the relation between those characteristics and the ASTM specifications.

2.5 Clay Masonry Units

2.5.1 Geology Associated with Clay Masonry Units

Clay masonry units are formed of clay, a sedimentary mineral. Clay is found in the form of surface clay, shale (naturally compressed and hardened clay), or fire clay (deeper clays). In the United States, clay is found primarily in central Texas and the east coast, although small amounts are found in sedimentary deposits throughout the country.

2.5.2 Chemistry Associated with Clay Masonry Units

Clays and shales are about 65% silicon oxide and 20% aluminum oxide. They may also contain varying amounts of other metallic oxides (manganese, phosphorus, calcium, magnesium, sodium, potassium, and vanadium). These metallic oxides give a fired clay units a distinctive color, decrease the unit's vitrification temperature and also affect its appearance and durability. For example, small amounts of chromite, added to light-colored (buff) clay, give it a gray color; small amounts of manganese, added to buff clay, give it a brown color.

2.5.3 Manufacturing of Clay Masonry Units

Three processes are in use today for manufacturing clay masonry units:

1) Soft mud process: Clay containing 20% to 30% water by weight is molded. This process is used occasionally in the United States but more often in Europe.

2) Stiff mud process: Clay containing 12% to 15% water by weight is mixed, forced through a die, and cut with wire. This is the most common process in the United States.

3) Dry press process: Mix clay containing 7% to 10% water by weight, form in hydraulic press. This process is rare. It is used, for example, to make fire brick.

After forming, various surface textures can be imparted to the unit: wire-cut; rug (heavy scratches); matte (light scratches); or sand finished. The clay units are then placed on specially insulated railway cars, and subjected to the firing process. This involves six basic steps:

1) Preheating: The "green" units are dried at about 350°F, in drying ovens heated by exhaust gases from the kiln. During this process, the units shrink.

   The units then move into a tunnel kiln, which is kept relatively cool at the entrance, hot in the middle, and cooler again at the exit. The heat comes from burning fuel within the kiln itself. Over a period of 12 hours to as long as 3 days, the units pass from the entrance to the hottest section, and then to the cooler exit. Temperatures in the different sections are regulated to produce different results. The units pass through the following steps:

2) Dehydration: The units continue to dry at temperatures from 300 to about 800°F.

3) Oxidation: At temperatures from about 800 to 1800°F, organic material burns.

4) Vitrification (or incipient vitrification): At temperatures of 1600 to 2400°F, the clay begins to vitrify. Silicates in the clay begin to fuse, binding the unvitrified clay particles together. This point is termed "incipient fusion." The temperature used depends on the type of clay. Most clays will undergo incipient fusion at about 2000°F. The purest clays, which are used for refractory brick, are fired at temperatures up to 2400°F.

5) Control of Oxygen: The color of metallic oxides can be changed by feeding additional air into the kiln at this point to promote an oxidizing environment, or by intentionally withholding air to produce a reducing environment. The latter is termed "flashing."

6) Cooling: The units are then slowly cooled.

2.5.4 Visual and Serviceability Characteristics of Clay Masonry Units

The following characteristics are covered by ASTM C62 (Standard Specification for Building Brick) or by ASTM C216 (Standard Specification for Facing Brick):

- Dimensional tolerances
- Durability
- Freeze-thaw resistance
- Appearance

Different ASTM requirements for clay masonry units are summarized in a table at the end of this section, and are described in more detail below.

1) Dimensional tolerances for building brick (ASTM C62) vary with nominal dimensions but are typically ±¼ in. For facing brick (ASTM C216), corresponding typical required tolerances are ±8/32 in. for Type FBS ("face brick, standard") and ±5/32 inch for Type FBX ("face brick, extra"). Tolerances are also specified for distortion.

2) Durability is controlled indirectly in terms of boiling-water absorption. Units are dried at 230 to 239°F, placed in boiling water for 5 hours, then reweighed. Boiling water absorption equals weight gain divided by original dry weight.

   Boiling-water absorption is taken as a general index of durability. Building brick (ASTM C62) must have a boiling-water absorption (average of 5 units) of at most 17% for Grade SW ("severe weathering"), and at most 22% for Grade MW ("moderate weathering"). No limit is imposed for Grade NW ("normal weathering"). Facing brick (ASTM C216) must have corresponding boiling-water absorptions of 17% (Grade SW) and 22% (Grade MW). Grade NW does not exist under ASTM C216.

3) Freeze-thaw resistance is controlled indirectly in terms of a "saturation coefficient," defined as follows:
   a) Cold-water absorption (24 hours): Units are dried at 230 to 239°F, placed in cold water for 24 hours, then reweighed. Cold water absorption equals weight gain divided by original dry weight.
   b) Boiling-water absorption (5 hours): After the cold-water absorption test described above, units are placed in boiling water for an additional 5 hours,

and again weighed. Boiling-water absorption equals weight gain (cold plus boiling-water absorption) divided by original dry weight.

   c) Saturation coefficient (c/b ratio): Cold water absorption (24 hours) divided by boiling water absorption (5 hours).

The saturation coefficient is a measure of the additional void space available in the units after saturation by cold water. A saturation coefficient of 1.0 indicates no additional void space. The lower the saturation coefficient, the more additional void space. This is taken as a rough index of resistance to freeze-thaw degradation (additional void space is available for the freezing water).

Building brick (ASTM C62) must have a saturation coefficient (average of 5 units) of at most 0.78 for Grade SW ("severe weathering"), and at most 0.88 for Grade MW ("moderate weathering"), and at most 1.0 (no limit), for Grade NW ("normal weathering"). Facing brick (ASTM C216) must have corresponding saturation coefficients of 0.78 (Grade SW) and 0.88 (Grade MW). Grade NW does not exist under ASTM C216.

4) Appearance is not addressed by ASTM C62 (Building Brick). ASTM C216 (Facing Brick) addresses chippage and efflorescence potential.

   a) Chippage: Under ASTM C216, up to 10% of units complying with Grade FBS can have chips up to 1 in. in size; for Grade FBX, the corresponding percentage is 5%.

   b) Efflorescence: This is a white or colored chemical residue on the surface of the masonry. It is produced by water-soluble compounds within or in contact with the masonry. If water gains access into the masonry in sufficient amounts, and comes in contact with the water-soluble compounds for a sufficient time, it dissolves those compounds into positive and negative ions. The water containing the dissolved compounds (in ionic form) moves through the masonry and evaporates; the dissolved ions combine to form deposits. If these deposits form on the surface of the masonry, they are called "efflorescence". If they form within the pores of the masonry near the surface, they are called "crypto-florescence." The positive ions are usually potassium, sodium, or calcium. The negative ions are usually sulfates, chlorides, or hydroxides. In general, because the positive and negative ions are present in all masonry, efflorescence is reduced by limiting the amount of water in contact with the masonry, and by limiting the passage of water to the surface of the masonry.

When required to be tested, facing brick (ASTM C216) are required to show "no efflorescence." Efflorescence testing (in accordance with ASTM C67) uses distilled water and is not a complete check for efflorescence.

2.5.5 Mechanical Characteristics of Clay Masonry Units

The compressive strength varies from about 1200 to 30,000 psi. It is typically 8000 to 15,000 psi. Building brick (ASTM C62) must have a minimum compressive strength (average of 5 units, tested flatwise) of 1500 psi for Grade NW, 2500 psi for Grade MW, and 3000 psi for Grade SW. Building brick (ASTM C216) must have corresponding compressive strengths of 2500 psi for Grade MW, and 3000 psi for Grade SW. Grade NW does not exist under ASTM C216.

2.5.6 Specification of Clay Masonry Units

Clay masonry units are specified in accordance with the required appearance and durability (refer to the summary table at the end of this section).

- The required appearance determines whether the units need to conform to C62 or to C216. Under C216, the required dimensional tolerances determines the Type (FBS or FBX).
- The required durability and freeze-thaw resistance determine whether the units need to conform to Grade NW, MW, or SW. The required durability and freeze-thaw resistance depend on the "weathering index" (product of the average annual number of freezing cycle days and the average annual winter rainfall in inches), defined in detail in ASTM C62 and depicted in the map of Figure 1 of that specification (Fig. 2.4). "Negligible" weathering regions have weathering indices of less than 50; "moderate" weathering regions have weathering indices between 50 and 500; and "severe" weathering regions have weathering indices in excess of 500.

Under ASTM C62 (Building Brick), Grade NW brick are recommended for interior use only. Grade MW brick are permitted for use in "severe" weathering regions. Grade SW brick are recommended for use in "severe" weathering regions, and whenever brick are in contact with the ground, or laid in horizontal surfaces, or likely to be permeated with water.

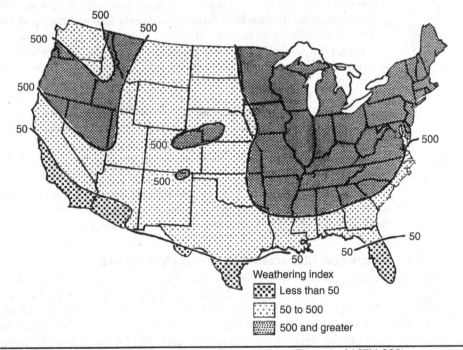

FIGURE 2.4 Weathering indices in the United States (*Source:* Figure 1 of ASTM C62).

Under ASTM C216 (Facing Brick), there are no Grade NW brick. Grade MW brick are permitted for use in "severe" weathering regions. Grade SW brick are required for use whenever the weathering index is greater than or equal to 500, and whenever brick in other than vertical surfaces are in contact with soil.

Requirements of ASTM C62 and C216 for clay units are summarized in Table 2.9.

2.5.7 Other Characteristics of Clay Masonry Units

The following other characteristics of clay masonry units are not addressed by ASTM specifications:

1) Color: Metallic oxides give different units their characteristic color. Colors are commonly judged by eye from sample panels. Systems for color tolerance exist but are not widely used.

2) Tensile strength: Parallel to the grain (in the direction of extrusion), this is typically 20% to 30% of the corresponding compressive strength. Perpendicular to the grain, it is typically 10% to 20% of the corresponding compressive strength.

TABLE 2.9 Summary of ASTM Requirements for Clay Masonry Units

Characteristic	Requirement According to ASTM C62	Requirement According to ASTM C216
Dimensional tolerance	±¼ in.	Type FBS ±¼ in. Type FBX ±5/32 in.
Chippage	No requirements	Type FBS 10% Type FBX 5%
Efflorescence	No requirements	Required to show "not effloresced" by ASTM C67 (distilled water, units only)
Compressive strength	Grade NW: 1500 psi Grade MW: 2500 psi Grade SW: 3000 psi	Grade MW: 2500 psi Grade SW: 3000 psi
Durability (boiling water absorption)	Grade NW no requirement Grade MW ≤ 22% Grade SW ≤ 17%	Grade MW ≤ 22% Grade SW ≤ 17%
Saturation coefficient (c/b ratio)	Grade NW ≤ 1.0 Grade MW ≤ 0.88 Grade SW ≤ 0.78	Grade MW ≤ 0.88 Grade SW ≤ 0.78
Design criteria	Grade NW interior use only Grade MW permitted for WI ≤ 500 Grade SW recommended for WI > 500	Grade MW permitted for WI ≤ 500 Grade SW required for WI > 500

3) Initial rate of absorption (IRA): This is defined as the number of grams of water absorbed in 1 min/30 in² of bed area. An ideal range is 10 to 30. Many clay masonry units used in Texas have IRAs exceeding 30. Units with an IRA greater than 30 should be wetted briefly before laying. A simple field test for IRA is as follows: Place 20 drops of water in a quarter-sized area. If it takes longer than 1.5 minutes for the water to be absorbed, the units do not need to be wetted before laying.

4) Tensile bond strength (strength between mortar and units): This is typically about 100 psi when cement-lime mortar or mortar-cement mortar are used, and about 50 psi or less when masonry-cement mortar is used. Tensile bond strength is increased by compatibility between mortar and units: Units with high IRA should be used with mortar having high water retention (high lime content); low IRA units should be used with low-retentivity mortar.

5) Modulus of elasticity: 1.4 to 5×10^6 psi.

6) Freeze-thaw expansion: Clay units exposed to cycles of freezing and thawing undergo permanent expansion (mean, standard deviation, and 97-percentile value of 118, 96, and 300 µε, respectively).

7) Moisture expansion: Clay units exposed to moisture undergo permanent expansion caused by adsorption of water into unvitrified clay molecules (mean, standard deviation, and 97-percentile values of 200, 190, and 540 µε, respectively).

8) Coefficient of thermal expansion: 3 to 4 µε/°F.

2.6 Concrete Masonry Units

2.6.1 Materials and Manufacturing of Concrete Masonry Units

Concrete masonry units are formed from zero-slump concrete, sometimes using lightweight aggregate. The concrete mixture is usually vibrated under pressure in multiple-block molds. After stripping the molds, the units are usually cured under atmospheric conditions in a chamber that is maintained at warm and humid conditions by the presence of the curing units. Atmospheric steam or high-pressure steam (autoclaving) can also be used for curing. Concrete units normally have a much higher void ratio than clay units, making determination of (c/b) ratios unnecessary.

2.6.2 Visual and Serviceability Characteristics of Concrete Masonry Units

The following visual and serviceability characteristics are addressed by ASTM C90 (Standard Specification for Hollow Load-Bearing Concrete Masonry Units):

1) Dimensional tolerances: ASTM C90 prescribes maximum dimensional tolerances of ±1/8 in. Thicknesses of face shells and webs are specified.

2) Chippage: According to ASTM C90, up to 5% of a shipment may contain units with chips up to 1 in. in size.

Other visual and serviceability characteristics, such as color, are not addressed by ASTM C90. Color is gray or white, unless metallic oxide pigments are used.

2.6.3 Mechanical Characteristics of Concrete Masonry Units

The following mechanical characteristics are covered by ASTM C90, ASTM C140, and ASTM C426:

1) Compressive strength is typically 1500 to 3000 psi on the net area (actual area of concrete). ASTM C90 requires a minimum compressive strength (average of 3 units) of 2000 psi, measured on the net area.

2) Absorption (used to measure void volume) is evaluated in the following manner. The unit is immersed in cold water for 24 hours. It is weighed immersed (weight F), and weighed in air while still wet (weight E). It is then dried for at least 24 hours at a temperature of 212 to 239°F, and again weighed (weight C). Absorption in lb/ft^3 is calculated as $[(E - C) / (E - F)] \times 62.4$. Maximum permissible absorption is 18 lb/ft^3 for lightweight units (<105 lb/ft^3 oven-dried weight), 15 lb/ft^3 for medium-weight units (105–125 lb/ft^3), and 13 lb/ft^3 for normal-weight units (>125 lb/ft^3).

3) Shrinkage of concrete masonry units due to drying and carbonation is 300 to 600 µε. In general, shrinkage is controlled by controlling the concrete mix used to make the units, and by limiting the moisture content of the units between the time of production and when they are placed in the wall.

  The concrete masonry industry formerly produced Type I (moisture-controlled) units, which due to a combination of inherent characteristics and packaging were designed to shrink less, and Type II units (nonmoisture-controlled). This distinction was not as successful as originally hoped because it was difficult to control the condition of Type I units in the field. As a result, ASTM C90 now does not refer to Type I and Type II units. All C90 units must demonstrate a potential drying shrinkage of less than 0.065% (650 µε), which was the shrinkage requirement that formerly applied to Type II units.

2.6.4 Other Characteristics of Concrete Masonry Units

The following characteristic are not covered by ASTM specifications:

1) Surface texture can be smooth, slump block, split-face block, ribbed block, various patterns, polished face.

2) Tensile strength is about 10% of compressive strength.

3) Tensile bond strength (strength between mortar and CMU) is typically about 40 to 75 psi when Portland cement-lime mortar is used, and about 35 psi or less when masonry-cement mortar is used.

4) Initial rate of absorption (IRA) is typically 40 to 160 g/min/30 in^2 of bed area. It is much less than this in units with integral water-repellent admixtures. In contrast to clay units, the tensile bond strength of concrete masonry units is not sensitive to initial rate of absorption. For this reason, specifications for concrete masonry units do not require determination of IRA.

5) Modulus of elasticity is typically 1 to 3×10^6 psi.

6) Coefficient of thermal expansion is typically: 4 to 5 µε/F.

2.7 Properties of Masonry Assemblages

The following characteristics of masonry assemblages are covered by ASTM Specifications E72, C1072, C1388, C1389, C1390, C1391, C1357, and C1314.

1) Compressive strength: This is often denoted by f_m. Using ASTM C1314, it is measured using stack-bonded prisms whose maximum ratio of height divided by least lateral dimension is between 1.3 and 5. For example:
   a) Hollow concrete masonry units measuring 8 × 8 × 16 in., tested as a 2-high prism, would have a height of about 16 in. and a minimum lateral dimension of about 8 in., for a ratio of height to least lateral dimension of about 2.
   b) Modular clay units measuring 4 × 2-2/3 × 8 in., tested as a 6-high prism, would have a height of about 16 in. and a minimum base dimension of about 4 in., for a ratio of height to least lateral dimension of about 4.

   The compressive strength of a clay masonry prism is less than that of the mortar or the unit tested alone. This is because clay masonry prisms typically fail due to transverse splitting. The mortar is usually more flexible than the units. Under compression perpendicular to the bed joints, it expands laterally, placing the units in transverse biaxial tension. The prism cracks perpendicular to the bed joints (parallel to the direction of the applied load).

   Because concrete masonry prisms typically have mortar and units of similar strengths and elasticity, these tend to fail like a concrete cylinder.

2) Tensile bond strength can be measured by tests on wall specimens (E72), by modulus of rupture tests on masonry beams (E518), by bond wrench tests (C1072), or by crossed-brick couplet tests. Results from these tests are not equal. Strict protocols for bond-wrench testing are specified in C1357.

3) Shear strength can be measured by diagonal compression tests (E519).

4) Water permeability is measured in terms of the amount of water passing through a wall under a standard pressure gradient, simulating the effects of wind-driven rain (E514).

2.8 Masonry Accessory Materials

Masonry accessory materials include reinforcement, connectors, sealants, flashing, coatings, and vapor barriers and moisture barriers. Each of these is described further below.

Reinforcement	
Connectors (galvanized or stainless steel)	Ties (connect a masonry wall to another wall)
	Anchors (connect a masonry wall to a frame)
	Fasteners (connect something else to a masonry wall)
Sealants	Expansion joints (clay masonry)
	Control joints (concrete masonry)
	Construction joints
Flashing	
Coatings	Paints
	Water-repellent coatings
Vapor barriers and moisture barriers	

2.8.1 Reinforcement

Reinforcement consists of the following:

- Steel deformed reinforcing bars meeting the requirements of ASTM A615 (billet steel) or A996 (rail and axle steel), or ASTM A706 (low-alloy weldable steel)
- Joint reinforcement (ASTM A951)
- Deformed reinforcing wire (ASTM A496)
- Steel welded wire reinforcement for concrete (ASTM A497)
- Steel prestressing strand (ASTM A416)

Typical uses of each type of reinforcement are shown in Figs. 2.5–2.8. Figure 2.5 shows deformed reinforcing bars in a grouted masonry wall. Figure 2.6 shows joint reinforcement. Figure 2.7 shows welded wire reinforcement in the topping of a floor slab connected to a masonry wall. Figure 2.8 shows posttensioning tendons in a masonry wall.

2.8.2 Connectors

Connectors are addressed by the following ASTM specifications.

- ASTM F1554 (plate, headed, and bent bar anchors)
- ASTM A325 (high-strength bolt anchors)
- ASTM A1008 (sheet steel anchors and ties)
- ASTM A185 (steel wire mesh ties)

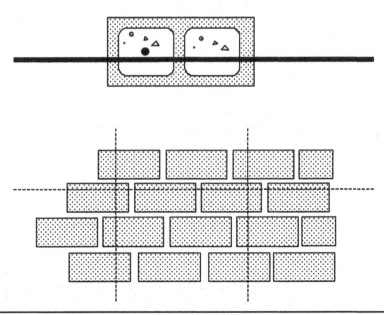

FIGURE 2.5 Typical application of deformed reinforcement in grouted masonry wall.

FIGURE 2.6 Typical bed joint reinforcement (*Source*: Figure 2 of NCMA TEK 12-01A).

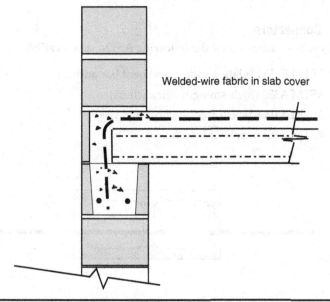

FIGURE 2.7 Typical use of welded wire reinforcement.

- ASTM A82 (steel wire ties and anchors)
- ASTM A167 (stainless steel sheet anchors and ties)
- ASTM A193-B7 (high-strength threaded rod anchors)
- ASTM A641, A153, or A653 (galvanized steel connectors)

Typical uses of each type of connector are shown in Figs. 2.9–2.11. Figure 2.9 shows typical veneer ties. Figure 2.10 shows typical adjustable pintle ties. Figure 2.11 shows typical connectors.

Materials Used in Masonry Construction 31

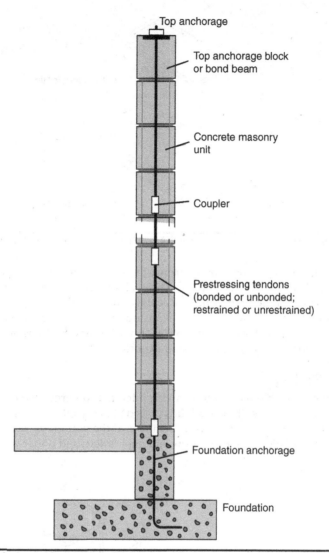

FIGURE 2.8 Typical use of posttensioning tendons.

Adjustable ties are useful for accommodating differences in elevation of bed joints. As shown in Fig. 2.12, adjustable ties can be very flexible if they are used at large eccentricities (difference in elevation of bed joints).

2.8.3 Sealants

Sealants are used to prevent the passage of water at places where gaps are intentionally left in masonry walls. Three basic kinds of gaps (joints) are used:

- Expansion joints are used in clay masonry to accommodate expansion.
- Control joints are used in concrete masonry to conceal cracking due to shrinkage.
- Construction joints are placed between different sections of a structure.

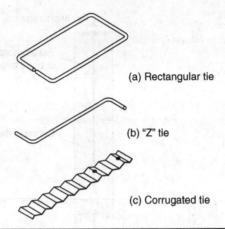

FIGURE 2.9 Typical veneer ties (*Source*: BIA Technical Note 44B Figure 2).

Sealants are most commonly formulated using synthetic polymers such as silicone, neoprene, latex, or butyl rubber. Their elastic properties include compressibility, expressed as the ratio of (minimum thickness/original thickness). Because the polymers comprising them deteriorate under exposure to ultraviolet light and ozone, the normal life of sealants in exterior exposures is about 7 years. Sealants should be replaced at intervals approximately equal to their expected life.

2.8.4 Flashing

Flashing is a flexible waterproof barrier, intended to permit water that has penetrated the outer wythe to reexit the wall. It is placed at every interruption of the vertical drainage cavity, including the following locations: at the bottom of each story level (on shelf angles or foundations); over window and door lintels; and under window and door sills.

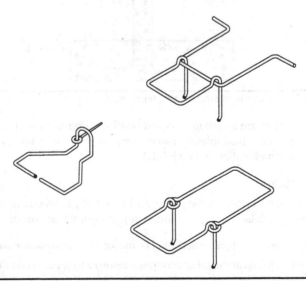

FIGURE 2.10 Typical adjustable pintle ties (*Source*: BIA Technical Note 44B Figure 7).

Materials Used in Masonry Construction 33

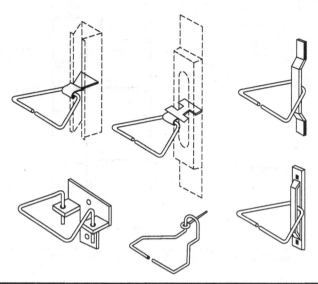

FIGURE 2.11 Typical connectors (*Source*: BIA Technical Note 44B Figure 6).

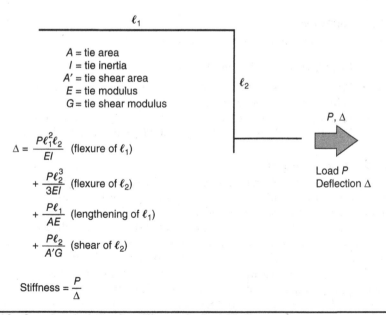

FIGURE 2.12 Sample calculation for stiffness of adjustable ties.

34 Chapter Two

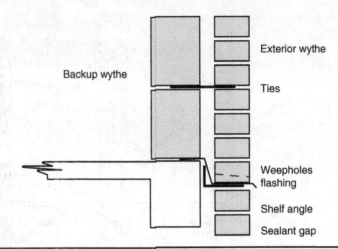

FIGURE 2.13 Placement of flashing at shelf angles in clay masonry veneer.

Flashing is made of stainless steel, copper, plastic-coated aluminum, plastic, rubberized asphalt, EPDM (ethylene-propylene-diene monomer), or PVC (polyvinyl chloride). Metallic flashing lasts much longer than plastic flashing. Nonmetallic flashings are subject to tearing. Modern self-adhering flashing of rubberized asphalt is a good compromise between durability and ease of installation.

Flashing should be applied above shelf angles, above door and window openings, and below door and window openings. Flashing should be lapped, and ends of flashing should be defined by end dams (flashing turned up at ends). Directly above the level of the flashing, weepholes should be provided at 24-in. spacing.

2.8.5 Coatings

Coatings include paints and water-repellent coatings.

- Paint is less durable than the masonry it covers.
- Water-repellent coatings cannot bridge wide cracks. They tend to trap water behind them, causing freeze-thaw damage behind the coating and also cryptoflorescence. They are generally unnecessary for clay masonry, and generally less effective than integral water-repellent admixtures for concrete masonry.

2.8.6 Vapor Barriers

Vapor barriers are waterproof membranes (usually polyethylene or PVC). They are intended to prevent the passage of water in vapor or liquid form, and thereby prevent interstitial condensation within the air space of a drainage wall.

In warm climates, warm air from the outside of the building can pass through the outer wythe of a cavity wall and condense within the interior wythe. The vapor barrier is therefore placed against the exterior face of the interior wythe.

In cold climates, warm air from the inside of the building will pass through the inner wythe of a cavity wall and condense within the cavity. The vapor barrier should therefore be placed against the interior face of the exterior wythe. In practice, this conflicts with the above requirements for warm climates.

As a result, vapor barriers are often placed on the exterior face of the interior wythe anyway, as a compromise.

2.8.7 Moisture Barriers

Moisture barriers are membranes that prevent the passage of water in liquid form but permit the passage of water in vapor form. One example is Tyvek®. They are intended to keep liquid water out of walls. They do not prevent interstitial condensation within the air space of a drainage wall.

2.8.8 Movement Joints

Three basic kinds of movement joints are used in masonry construction: expansion joints, control joints, and construction joints.

1) Expansion joints, shown in Figs. 2.14 and 2.15, are used in clay masonry to accommodate expansion. In the figures below, the backer rod is shown separated from the sealant, so that they can be distinguished. In reality, they are in contact.

2) Control joints, shown in Fig. 2.16, are used in concrete masonry to conceal cracking due to shrinkage.

   Control joints are placed at openings in concrete masonry. As shown in Fig. 2.17, the joints are "dog-legged" so that the lintel can be supported by the masonry on both sides of the opening, and also it can be restrained against uplift by vertical reinforcement at the edges of the opening.

3) Construction joints are placed between different sections of a structure.

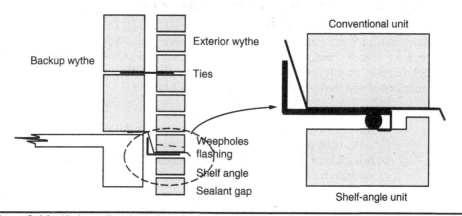

FIGURE 2.14 Horizontally oriented expansion joint under shelf angle.

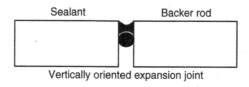

FIGURE 2.15 Vertically oriented expansion joint.

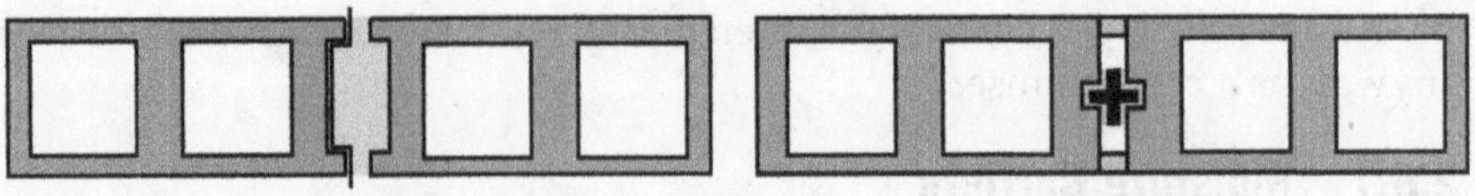

FIGURE 2.16 Shrinkage control joint.

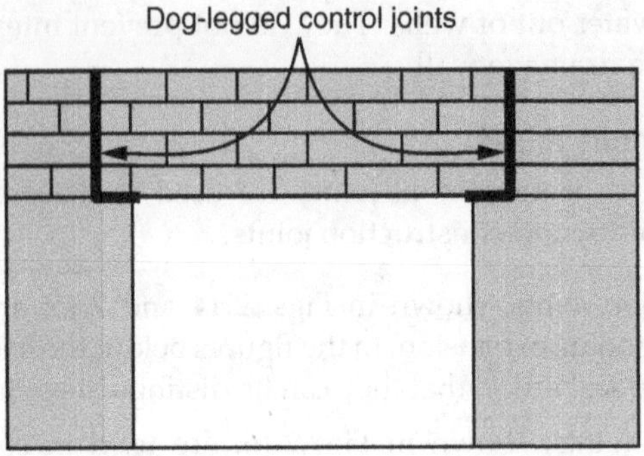

FIGURE 2.17 Example of control joints at openings in concrete masonry.

2.9 Design of Masonry Structures Requiring Little Structural Calculation

2.9.1 Design Steps for Structures Requiring Little Structural Calculation

Many masonry structures require little structural calculation. Their primary design steps are layout, design involves primarily structural layout, detailing, and material specification. In this section, those steps are outlined. This section can be viewed as a summary of material previously presented in Chapter 1.

1) Lay out overall structural configuration:
   a) Modularity: Adjust the plan dimensions to the nominal dimensions of the units to be used.
   b) Selection of the overall structural system: Locate walls in plan.
   c) Architectural details: Locate windows and doors.
2) Specify type of wall system according to desired level of water-penetration resistance. In areas of severe driving rain, specify a drainage wall, or a fully grouted barrier wall with a thickness of at least 8 in. If a drainage wall is specified, it should have at least a 2-in. cavity and be provided with drainage details (flashing and weepholes). Further details of water-penetration resistance are addressed at the end of this chapter.
3) Specify masonry units:
   a) Specification of clay units: Decide whether building brick (ASTM C62), facing brick (ASTM C216), or some other kind of unit (e.g., ASTM C652, hollow brick) is required. Specify the grade of unit (SW, MW, or NW) based on the weathering index at the building's geographic location.

b) Specification of concrete units: Decide whether conventional hollow units (ASTM C90) or some other type of unit is required.

4) Specify mortar: Specify an ASTM C270 mortar, Type S or Type N (normally by proportion), and either cement-lime, masonry cement, or mortar cement. The proportion specification is normally preferable to the property specification because it avoids the additional cost of testing and the additional difficulty of having to decide what to do if the test results do not comply with the required values. The property specification permits some savings in material costs, in return for increases in costs due to testing. Although it is theoretically not required, it is useful to insert the words "by proportion" in the specification as additional protection against inadvertent and possibly improper mortar testing. If tensile bond strength is important, use either cement-lime mortar or mortar-cement mortar. While water-penetration resistance can be enhanced by using cement-lime mortar, this choice is probably not as important as choosing a properly specified drainage wall.

5) Specify grout: Normally, specify a coarse grout, conforming to the proportion specifications of ASTM C476 (one part Portland cement or other cements, three parts sand, and two parts pea gravel). The amount of water should be sufficient to obtain a slump of about 11 in.

6) Specify accessories: For simple structures with single-wythe walls, the only accessories will be deformed reinforcement, conforming to ASTM A615 (new steel). This is simply prescribed (e.g., #4 bars @ 48 in. on centers) based on seismic design category or other considerations. Joint reinforcement could also be specified.
   a) For hollow units of concrete or clay, vertical reinforcement is placed in the continuous vertical cells, and horizontal reinforcement is placed in bond beam units (units with depressed webs).
   b) For solid units of concrete or clay, deformed reinforcement (vertical or horizontal) can be placed only in grouted spaces between wythes. Bed-joint reinforcement can be placed in the bed joints of a single-wythe wall.
   c) Specify connectors, flashing, and sealants.

7) Specify construction details:
   a) Foundation dowels.
   b) Splices between foundation dowels and vertical reinforcement (required lap length depends on bar diameter).
   c) Foundation details: See below.
   d) Roof connection details: See below.

8) Construction process:
   a) Decide whether to wet clay units: Check if the IRA exceeds 30, or use a field test (see if 20 drops of water, placed in a quarter-sized circle, are absorbed in 90 seconds or less). If the IRA exceeds 30, or if the drops are absorbed in the field test, wet the units briefly before laying.
   b) Place units in running or stack bond. Tool joints using concave tooling.
   c) Place reinforcement.
   d) Pour grout (clean cells, mist the cells with water, grout by high-lift or low-lift procedures).
   e) If possible, cure the masonry by keeping it damp.

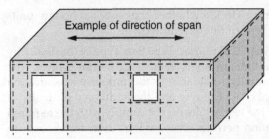

FIGURE 2.18 Overall starting point for reinforcement or structures requiring little structural calculation.

2.9.2 Overall Starting Point for Reinforcement

An overall starting point for reinforcement for structures requiring little structural calculation is shown in Fig. 2.18. Structural design is discussed extensively in later chapters of this book.

2.9.3 Examples of Construction Details for Masonry Structures Requiring Little Structural Calculation

Examples of construction details for masonry structures requiring little calculation are given in the sections and figures below. These details are generic in nature. Then can be supplemented by the details provided in NCMA and BIA technical notes.

1) Overall modularity:
   a) Overall modularity of the CMU wythe will be satisfied provided that the interior nominal dimensions of the CMU wythe are an even number of ft, and the units have a nominal thickness of 8 in. The exterior dimensions of each CMU wythe will be an even number of ft, plus two times 8 in. (two nominal CMU wythes). Any such exterior dimension can be laid out without cutting CMU, because the interior dimension is an even number of ft (some number of 16-in. units plus perhaps one 8-in. half-unit), and the exterior dimension is obtained by adding another nominal dimension of 16 in.
   b) Overall modularity of the clay wythe will be satisfied given the above, plus a 2-in. nominal air space and nominal 4-in. clay units. The exterior nominal dimensions of each clay wythe will be an even number of ft (see above), plus two times 8 in. (two nominal 8-in. CMU wythes), plus two times 2 in. (two nominal 2-in. air spaces), plus two times 4 in. (two nominal 4-in. clay wythes). Any such exterior dimension is an even number of ft, plus 16 in. plus 4 in. plus 8 in., or an even number of ft plus 28 in. This exterior dimension can always be made with nominal 8-in. units plus a nominal 4-in. half-unit.

   Overall modularity in this example is shown in Fig. 2.19.

2) Connections between floor slab and walls.
   Connections between floor slab and walls are exemplified by Figs. 2.20 and 2.21.

3) Connections between walls and roof.
   Examples of connections between walls and roof are exemplified by Figs. 2.22–2.24.

Materials Used in Masonry Construction 39

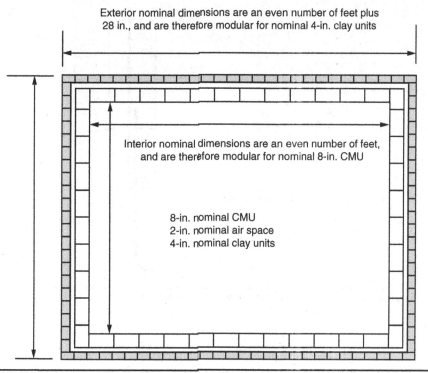

FIGURE 2.19 Example of overall modularity of a masonry structure in plan.

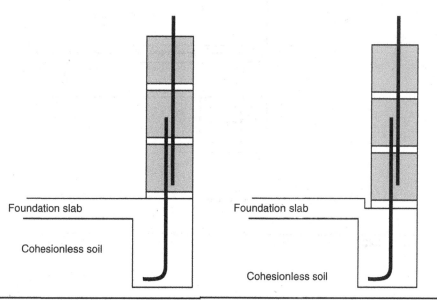

FIGURE 2.20 Foundation-wall detail.

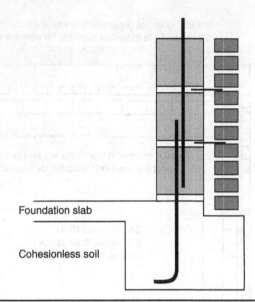

FIGURE 2.21 Foundation-wall detail with drainage wall.

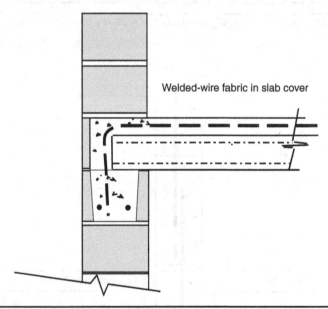

FIGURE 2.22 Detail of intersection between wall and precast concrete roof or floor slab.

Materials Used in Masonry Construction

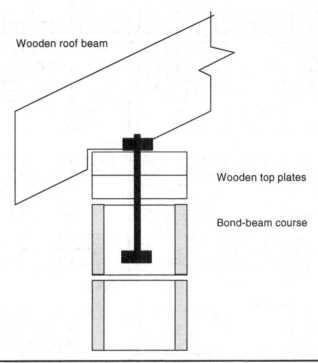

FIGURE 2.23 Detail of wall and wooden roof truss.

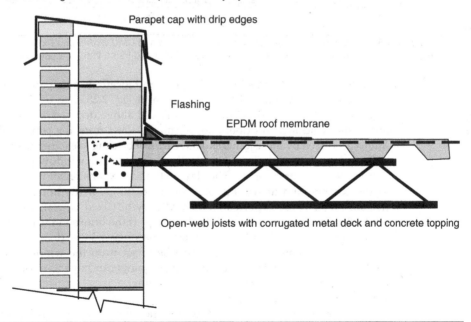

FIGURE 2.24 Detail of drainage wall and open-web joist roof.

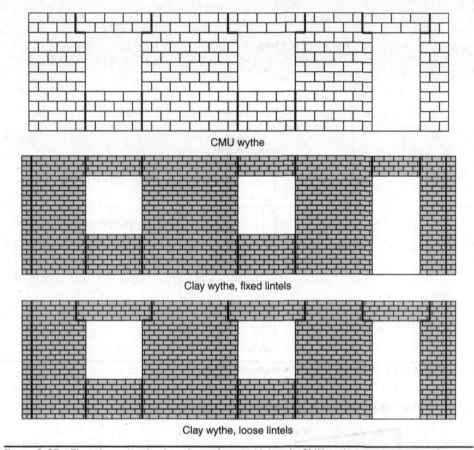

Figure 2.25 Elevations showing locations of control joints in CMU wythe, and locations of expansion joints in clay masonry veneer wythe (fixed lintel and loose lintel, respectively).

4) Locations of control joints in CMU wythe, and locations of expansion joints in clay wythe. An example of these is shown in Fig. 2.25. The CMU wythe has control joints above and below windows, and above doors. The control joints above the windows and doors are normally offset from the jams so that the lintels produced by these joints can have 8 in. of bearing at each end. The control joints below the windows are normally even with the window jams because there is no need for an offset. The clay wythe has expansion joints within 18 in. of the corners, and at window and door openings. If the lintels in the clay masonry wythe are supported on the CMU wythe (fixed lintels), the expansion joints at openings can be even with the jambs. If the lintels in the clay masonry wythe are supported only by the clay masonry wythe (loose lintels), the expansion joints above openings must be offset from the window and door jambs so that the lintels produced by these joints can have 8 in. of bearing at each end, just like the lintels in the CMU wythe.

5) Wall sections at windows.

Details of wall sections at windows are shown in Fig. 2.26. The left and right figures correspond to fixed lintels and loose lintels, respectively.

Materials Used in Masonry Construction

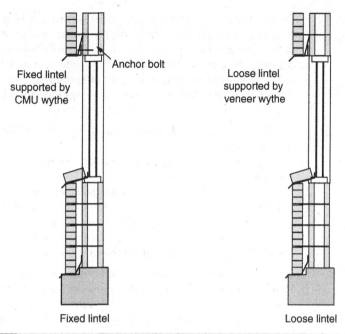

FIGURE 2.26 Wall sections at lintels.

The details are identical except that in the fixed-lintel detail, the lintel is supported by the CMU wythe (note the anchor bolt), whereas for the loose-lintel detail, the lintel is supported by the veneer wythe. In each case, the window head has weepholes in the veneer, and flashing with end dams. The window foot has an inclined masonry or precast concrete sill, with flashing and weepholes underneath. The wall has weepholes and flashing at the top of the foundation. In these details, the roof connection or parapet are not shown.

Sections at doors are the same, except that the door sill is at foundation level.

2.10 How to Increase Resistance of Masonry to Water Penetration

Water penetration resistance of masonry depends on wall type, workmanship, and materials. In this section, additional information is presented on each of these.

1) Specification and design:
   a) Specify and design wall types appropriate for the severity of driving rain expected in the geographic location of the building. In areas of severe driving rain, specify a drainage wall, or a fully grouted barrier wall with a thickness of at least 8 in.
   b) If a drainage wall is specified, specify and design to reduce water penetration through the outer wythe.

i) Don't let the outer wythe crack under service loads. If masonry cement is used, consider the effect of its lower tensile bond strength in determining whether the veneer will crack. If steel studs are used, consider the effect of their flexibility in determining whether the veneer will crack. Follow industry recommendations that the out-of-plane deflection of the studs not exceed their span divided by 600.
   ii) Specify proper sealant joints in outer wythe.
  c) If a cavity wall is specified, specify and design to keep the cavity open and properly drained.
   i) Specify proper weepholes and flashing to keep water out of cavity and direct it outward if it gets in.
   ii) Specify hot-dip galvanized or stainless-steel ties.
   iii) Specify a cavity at least 2 in. wide. Keep the cavity clean by beveling the back of the joint, using a board to catch mortar droppings, or both.
   iv) Use a vapor barrier on the exterior face of the interior wythe, to prevent interstitial condensation within the inner wythe.
  d) Design and detail to accommodate differential movement.
   i) Provide horizontally oriented expansion joints in clay masonry walls under shelf angles. Over time, clay masonry typically expands about 300 $\mu\varepsilon$, due to permanent moisture expansion and freeze-thaw expansion. In contrast, concrete and concrete masonry shrink, typically about 600 $\mu\varepsilon$. These opposite tendencies combine to produce differential strain of about 1000 $\mu\varepsilon$. Over a 12-ft (144-in.) story height, that corresponds to a differential deformation of 0.144 in. In other words, a gap of 0.144 in. under a shelf angle would be expected to close completely during the life of a building. Because the gap must be filled with sealant that can compress to about half its original thickness, the gap must be twice the 0.144 in., or 0.29 in. A gap of 3/8 in. is typically used. If a sufficient gap is not used, the veneer will be loaded vertically, and can spall, crack, or even buckle under the load.
   ii) Provide vertically oriented expansion joints in clay masonry walls near corners. Expansion of clay masonry, restrained at building corners, causes moments about vertical axes near the corners. Vertically oriented expansion joints prevent such moments and resulting cracking.
   iii) Use bond breaker between clay masonry walls and concrete foundations, slabs and roofs. Expansion of clay masonry (about 300 $\mu\varepsilon$) and shrinkage of concrete (about 600 $\mu\varepsilon$) combine to give differential strain of 1000 $\mu\varepsilon$. If restrained, this differential strain can crack the concrete foundation.
   iv) Use control joints at door and window openings of concrete masonry walls. These will prevent tensile stresses from restrained shrinkage.
   v) If composite brick-block masonry walls are used, consider the effect of restrained differential movement on interfacial stresses and wall deformations.
2) Construction
  a) Use compatible combinations of mortar and clay units. Clay units with high IRA should be wetted and used with high-retentivity mortar.

Materials Used in Masonry Construction

b) Mix and batch mortar properly: Measure ingredients accurately by volume. To distribute them thoroughly in the mix, combine cementitious ingredients with part of the sand and part of the water. If all the water is added at the beginning, the initial mix will be too fluid, and the cementitious ingredients will again not combine well. The following mixing sequence is taken from ASTM C780 (field mortar):

    Add all cement and lime + ½ sand + ¾ water
    Mix 2 minutes
    Add remaining sand and water
    Mix 3 to 8 minutes

c) Clean and roughen the foundation before laying the first course.
d) Lay units within 1 minute of spreading the mortar bed.
e) Lay units without excessive tapping.
f) Use full bed and head joints.
g) Use concave-tooled joints. In particular, use raked joints for interior masonry only.
h) Retemper mortar as required to maintain workability. Do not use mortar more than 2-½ hours after initial mixing.
i) After laying, keep masonry walls damp to help the mortar cure properly.

CHAPTER 3
Code Basis for Structural Design of Masonry Buildings

3.1 Introduction to Building Codes in the United States

The United States has no national design code, primarily because the US Constitution has been interpreted as delegating building code authority to the states, some of which in turn delegate it to municipalities and other local governmental agencies. Design codes used in the United States are developed by a complex process involving technical experts, industry representatives, code users, and building officials. As it applies to the development of design provisions for masonry, this process is shown in Fig. 3.1 and is then described:

1. Consensus design provisions and specifications for materials or methods of testing are first drafted in mandatory language by technical specialty organizations, operating under consensus rules approved by the American National Standards Institute (ANSI), or (in the case of American Society for Testing and Materials [ASTM]) rules that are similar in substance. Those consensus rules vary from organization to organization, but include requirements for the following:

    a. Balance of interests (producer, user, and general interest).

    b. Written balloting of proposed provisions, with prescribed requirements for a successful ballot.

    c. Resolution of negative votes. Negative votes must be discussed and found non-persuasive before a ballot item can pass. A single negative vote, if found persuasive, can prevent an item from passing.

    d. Public comment. After being approved within the technical specialty organization, the mandatory-language provisions must be published for review and comment by the general public. All comments are responded to, but do not necessarily result in further modification.

2. These consensus design and construction provisions are adopted, usually by reference and sometimes in modified form, by model code organizations and take the form of model codes.

Chapter Three

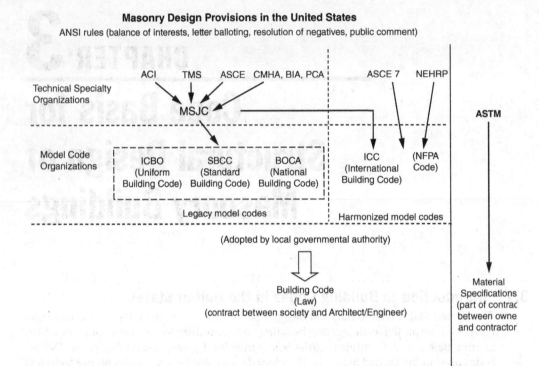

FIGURE 3.1 Schematic of process for development of masonry design codes in the United States.

3. These model codes are adopted, sometimes in modified form, by local governmental agencies (such as states, cities, or counties). Upon adoption, but not before, they acquire legal standing as building codes.

3.1.1 Technical Specialty Organizations

Technical specialty organizations are open to designers, contractors, product suppliers, code developers, and end users. Their income (except for Federal Emergency Management Agency [FEMA], a US government agency) is derived from member dues and the sale of publications. Technical specialty organizations active in the general area of masonry include the following:

   a. American Society for Testing and Materials (ASTM): Through its many technical committees, ASTM develops consensus specifications for materials and methods of test. Although some model code organizations use their own such specifications, most refer to ASTM specifications.

   b. American Concrete Institute (ACI): Through its many technical committees, this group publishes a variety of design recommendations dealing with different aspects of concrete design. ACI Committee 318 develops design provisions for concrete structures. ACI was one of the three initial sponsors of the Masonry Standards Joint Committee (MSJC).

Code Basis for Structural Design of Masonry Buildings 49

    c. American Society of Civil Engineers (ASCE): Until 2016, ASCE was a joint sponsor of many ACI technical committees dealing with concrete or masonry. ASCE served as the third of the three sponsoring societies of the MSJC (see above). ASCE publishes ASCE 7-22 (2022), which prescribes design loadings and load factors for all structures, independent of material type.

    d. The Masonry Society (TMS): Through its technical committees, this group influences different aspects of masonry design. From 1978 to 2016, TMS was one of the three sponsors (along with the ACI and the ASCE) of the MSJC, which was responsible for producing and maintaining the masonry design standard for the United States. From 2002 through 2016, TMS was the lead sponsor of the MSJC. Starting in 2016, TMS became the sole sponsor of that committee, and the masonry design standard was redesignated as TMS 402, after the name of the TMS committee responsible for maintaining it. The corresponding specification was redesignated as TMS 602. TMS also publishes a *Masonry Designers' Guide* to accompany the TMS design standard.

3.1.2 Industry Organizations

    e. Portland Cement Association (PCA): This marketing and technical support organization is composed of cement producers. Its technical staff participates in technical committee work.

    f. Concrete Masonry Hardscape Association (CMHA—Formerly National Concrete Masonry Association [NCMA]): This marketing and technical support organization is composed of producers of concrete masonry units. Its technical staff participates in technical committee work and also produces technical bulletins which can influence consensus design provisions.

    g. Brick Industry Association (BIA): This marketing, distributing, and technical support organization is composed of clay brick and tile producers and distributors. Its technical staff participates in technical committee work and also produces technical bulletins which can influence consensus design provisions.

    h. National Lime Association (NLA): This marketing and technical support organization is composed of hydrated lime producers. Its technical staff participates in technical committee work.

    i. Expanded Shale Clay and Slate Institute (ESCSI): This marketing and technical support organization is composed of producers. Its technical staff participates in technical committee meetings.

    j. International Masonry Institute (IMI): This is a union contractor-craftworker collaborative supported by dues from union masons. Its technical staff participates in technical committee meetings.

    k. Mason Contractors' Association of America (MCAA): This organization is composed of union and nonunion mason contractors. Its technical staff participates in technical committee meetings.

3.1.3 Governmental Organizations

Federal Emergency Management Agency (FEMA): FEMA has jurisdiction over the National Earthquake Hazard Reduction Program (NEHRP) and develops and periodically updates the NEHRP provisions, a set of recommendations for earthquake-resistant design. Those documents includes provisions for masonry design. The document was pioneered by ATC 3-06, issued in 1978 by the Applied Technology Council under contract to the National Bureau of Standards. The NEHRP provisions are now published at six-year intervals by the Building Seismic Safety Council (BSSC) under contract with the National Institute of Building Sciences (NIBS). BSSC is not a consensus organization. Its recommended design provisions are intended for consideration and possible adoption by consensus organizations. Its latest recommendations, the 2020 NEHRP *Recommended Provisions* (NEHRP 2020), address the determination of design seismic loadings on structures and with the design of structures (including masonry structures) for those loadings. The role of the NEHRP Provisions is evolving slightly, with the next edition anticipated to reference existing standards (ASCE 7 for loads, TMS 402 for masonry design, etc.) much more and to emphasize the development of innovative design and construction suggestions for consensus design and construction standards.

3.1.4 Model-Code Organizations

Model-code organizations are composed primarily of building officials, although designers, contractors, product suppliers, code developers, and end users can also be members. Their income is derived from dues and the sale of publications. Historically, the United States had three legacy model-code organizations:

n. International Conference of Building Officials (ICBO): In the past, this group developed and published the Uniform Building Code (UBC).

o. Southern Building Code Congress International (SBCCI): In the past, this group developed and published the Standard Building Code (SBC).

p. Building Officials and Code Administrators International (BOCA): In the past, this group developed and published the National Building Code (NBC).

In the past, certain model codes were used more in certain areas of the country. The *Uniform Building Code* was used throughout the western United States and in the state of Indiana. It was used in California until January of 2008, in the slightly modified form of the California Building Code. The *Standard Building Code* was used in the southern part of the United States. The *National Building Code* was used in the eastern and northeastern United States.

In 1996, intensive efforts began in the United States to harmonize the three model building codes. The primary harmonized model building code is called the International Building Code (IBC). It has been developed by the International Code Council (ICC) and is composed primarily of building code officials of the three legacy model code organizations. The first edition of the IBC (2000) was published in May 2000. In most cases, it references consensus design provisions and specifications. It is intended to take effect when adopted by local jurisdictions and to replace the three legacy model building codes. Its latest edition was published in 2024. The IBC has been adopted or is scheduled for adoption in most governmental jurisdictions of the United States. Another model code, adopted in only a few jurisdictions, is published by the National Fire Protection Association (NFPA 5000).

 q. International Code Council (ICC): This group develops and publishes the IBC.

 r. National Fire Protection Association (NFPA): This group develops and publishes NFPA 5000.

3.2 Introduction to the Calculation of Design Loading Using the 2024 IBC

Design loadings for buildings in general, including masonry buildings, are prescribed by the legally adopted building code. In most parts of the United States, the legally adopted building code is based on the IBC. In the following sections of this chapter, background information and sample calculations are presented for each of the principal IBC-mandated design loadings:

- Gravity loads (dead load and live load)
- Wind loads
- Earthquake loads

These loads are used in many design examples in subsequent chapters of this book.

Many designers are familiar with the layout of ASCE 7 and are accustomed to using loadings and load combinations taken directly from ASCE 7, even though this is strictly legal only in jurisdictions without a legally adopted building code. For most common loading combinations, differences between the loading combinations of the 2024 IBC and ASCE 7-22 are not significant.

3.3 Gravity Loads According to the 2024 IBC

3.3.1 Dead Load According to the 2024 IBC

Dead load is due to the weight of the structure itself, plus permanently attached components. Calculation of dead loads is not discussed further at this point. It is discussed in specific examples, as are IBC loading combinations including dead load.

3.3.2 Floor Live Load According to the 2024 IBC

Live load is prescribed by the 2024 IBC. The loading provisions of the 2024 IBC are discussed here using the section numbers taken from that document. The 2024 IBC itself uses loads that are almost identical to those prescribed by ASCE 7-22. In the future, the IBC will tend more and more to reference ASCE 7 loads directly. Minimum live loads (L) for floors (from Table 1607.1 of the 2024 IBC) are given in Table 3.1.

By Section 1607.9.1 of the 2024 IBC, live loads are permitted to be reduced based on the tributary area over which those live loads act. Live loads in public assembly areas (balconies, corridors, and stairs) are not permitted to be reduced. The live-load reduction

TABLE 3.1 Minimum Live Loads (L) for Floors

Occupancy or Use	Uniform (psf)	Concentrated (lb)
4. Assembly areas w/moveable seats	100	—
5. Balconies (exterior) and decks	Same as occupancy served	
9. Corridors, except as otherwise indicated	100	
26. Offices	50	2000
27. Residential	40	
27. Residential, corridors, and public areas of hotels	100	
29. Ordinary flat roofs	20	300
30. School classrooms	40	1000
30. School corridors above first floor	80	1000
30. School corridors, first floor	100	1000
35. Stairs and exits	100	
35. Stairs and exits, 1- and 2-family dwellings	40	
37. Stores, retail, first floor	100	1000
37. Stores, retail, upper floors	75	1000

Source: Table 1607.1 of the 2024 IBC.

factor, shown below, applies to elements for which the product $K_{LL} A_T$ equals or exceeds 400 ft².

$$L = L_o \left(0.25 + \frac{15}{\sqrt{K_{LL} A_T}} \right)$$

where L = Reduced design live load per square foot of area supported by the member
L_o = Unreduced design live load per square foot of area supported by the member (see Table 1607.1)
K_{LL} = Live element factor (see Table 1607.13.1)
A_T = Tributary area, in square feet

L shall not be less than 0.50 L_o for members supporting one floor and L shall not be less than 0.40 L_o for members supporting or more floors in a building.

Live load reduction factors are given in Table 1607.13.1 of the 2024 IBC, reproduced as Table 3.2.

3.3.3 Example of Floor Live-Load Reduction According to the 2024 IBC

Consider an interior beam of an office floor with a tributary area of 400 ft² (K_{LL} = 2).

$$L = L_o \left(0.25 + \frac{15}{\sqrt{K_{LL} A_T}} \right) = L_o \left(0.25 + \frac{15}{\sqrt{2 \times 400}} \right) = 0.78 L_o$$

Code Basis for Structural Design of Masonry Buildings

TABLE 3.2 Table 1607.13.1 of the 2024 IBC

Element	K_{LL}
Interior columns	4
Exterior columns without cantilever slabs	4
Edge columns with cantilever slabs	3
Corner columns with cantilever slabs	2
Edge beams without cantilever slabs	2
Interior beams	2

All other members not identified above including:
  Edge beams with cantilever slabs
  Cantilever beams
  One-way slabs
  Two-way slabs
  Members without provisions for continuous shear transfer normal to their span
	1

The lower limit of 0.50 does not govern, and

$$L = 0.78\, L_o.$$

3.3.4 Example of a Wall Live-Load Reduction According to the 2024 IBC

Consider an interior wall supporting 10 floors, each with tributary area 400 ft² (assume $K_{LL} = 4$).

$$L = L_o\left(0.25 + \frac{15}{\sqrt{K_{LL}\, A_T}}\right) = L_o\left(0.25 + \frac{15}{\sqrt{4 \times (10 \times 400)}}\right) = 0.37\, L_o$$

The 0.40 limit governs, and

$$L = 0.40\, L_o.$$

3.3.5 Roof Live Load According to the 2024 IBC

In accordance with Section 1607.11.2 of the 2024 IBC, the minimum roof live load for most roofs is 20 psf. Roof live loads are permitted to be reduced in accordance with the following:

$$L_r = L_0 R_1 R_2$$

where L_r = reduced roof live load per square foot
L_0 = unreduced roof live load per square foot
R_1 = see graph below
R_2 = 1.0 for flat roofs

The minimum reduced roof live load is 12 psf. The reduction is shown graphically in Fig. 3.2.

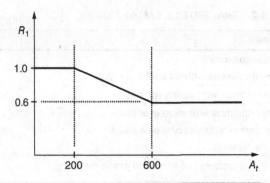

FIGURE 3.2 Graph showing permitted live load reduction for roofs. (*Source:* Section 1607.11.2 of the 2024 IBC.)

3.4 Wind Loading According to the 2024 IBC

According to Section 1609.1.1 of the 2024 IBC, wind loading is to be calculated using the provisions of *Minimum Design Loads for Buildings and Other Structures* (ASCE 7-22), or the simplified alternate all-heights method in Section 1609.6 of the 2024 IBC. ASCE Chapter 26 covers general requirements for both the main wind force resisting system (MWFRS) and for components and cladding (C&C). The determination of design forces on the main wind force-resisting system using the directional procedure is covered in ASCE Chapter 27. A simplified method for low-rise buildings is contained in ASCE Chapter 28. Specialty elements such as roof overhangs are covered in ASCE Chapter 29. ASCE Chapter 30 addresses a simplified method for the design of C&C. Finally, wind-tunnel procedures are covered in ASCE Chapter 31.

We are interested in two types of design wind loads.

- The first type is used to calculate the design base shear and base overturning moment on a building due to wind pressure. These wind loads are referred to as "Main Wind-Force Resisting System loads," commonly abbreviated as "MWFRS loads."

- The second type is used to calculate the local design pressures acting on sections of a building envelope. These wind loads are referred to as "Components and Cladding" loads, commonly abbreviated as "C&C loads."

Section 26.1.2 of ASCE 7-22 gives the following general procedures for computing each type of wind load.

Section 26.1.2.1: Main Wind Force Resisting System (MWFRS)

1. Directional Procedure for buildings of all heights as specified in Chapter 27;
2. Envelope Procedure for low-rise buildings as specified in Chapter 28;
3. Directional Procedure for building appurtenances (rooftop structures and rooftop equipment) and other structures (such as solid freestanding walls and solid freestanding signs, chimneys, tanks, open signs, lattice frameworks, and trussed towers) as specified in Chapter 29; or

Code Basis for Structural Design of Masonry Buildings 55

4. Wind Tunnel Procedure for all buildings and all other structures as specified in Chapter 31.

Section 26.1.2.2: Components and Cladding (C&C)
1. Analytical Procedures provided in Parts 1 through 6, as appropriate, of Chapter 30 or
2. Wind Tunnel Procedure as specified in Chapter 31.

The six analytical procedures are as follows (Section 30.1.1):

1. Part 1 is applicable to an enclosed or partially enclosed:
   - Low-rise building (see definition in Section 26.2)
   - Building with $h \leq 60$ ft (18.3 m)

   The building has a flat roof, gable roof, multispan gable roof, hip roof, monoslope roof, stepped roof, or sawtooth roof and the wind pressures are calculated from a wind pressure equation.

2. Part 2 is a simplified approach and is applicable to an enclosed:
   - Low-rise building (see definition in Section 26.2)
   - Building with $h \leq 60$ ft (18.3 m)

   The building has a flat roof, gable roof, or hip roof and the wind pressures are determined directly from a table.

3. Part 3 is applicable to an enclosed or partially enclosed:
   - Building with $h > 60$ ft (18.3 m)

   The building has a flat roof, pitched roof, gable roof, hip roof, mansard roof, arched roof, or domed roof and the wind pressures are calculated from a wind pressure equation.

4. Part 4 is a simplified approach and is applicable to an enclosed:
   - Building with $h \leq 160$ ft (48.8 m)

   The building has a flat roof, gable roof, hip roof, monoslope roof, or mansard roof and the wind pressures are determined directly from a table.

5. Part 5 is applicable to an open building of all heights having a pitched free roof, monoslope free roof, or trough free roof.

6. Part 6 is applicable to building appurtenances such as roof overhangs and parapets and rooftop equipment.

In this textbook, we shall calculate MWFRS loads using the directional procedure (Chapter 27 of ASCE 7-22), and we shall calculate C&C loads using Part (3) of Chapter 30 of ASCE 7-22. These procedures are generally applicable to a wide range of buildings, and the simplified procedures are based on them.

3.4.1 Summary of Directional Procedure of ASCE 7-22 for MWFRS Loads

The steps of the Directional Procedure of ASCE 7-22 for MWFRS loads are outlined in Table 27.2-1 of that document. In each step, the table and section numbers refer to ASCE 7-22 unless indicated otherwise:

Step 1: Determine risk category of building or other structure, see Table 1.5-1.

Step 2: Determine the basic wind speed, V, for the applicable risk category, see Figure 26.5-1A, B, or C.

Step 3: Determine wind load parameters:
- Wind directionality factor, K_d; see Section 26.6 and Table 26.6-1
- Exposure category; see Section 26.7
- Topographic factor, K_{zt}; see Section 26.8 and Table 26.8-1
- Gust effect factor, G; see Section 26.11
- Enclosure classification; see Section 26.12
- Internal pressure coefficient, GC_{pi}; see Section 26.13 and Table 26.13-1

Step 4: Determine velocity pressure exposure coefficient, K_z or K_h; see Table 26.10-1.

Step 5: Determine velocity pressure q_z or q_h; Equation 27.3-1.

Step 6: Determine external pressure coefficient, C_p or C_N:
- Figure 27.3-1 for walls and flat, gable, hip, monoslope, or mansard roofs
- Figure 27.3-2 for domed roofs
- Figure 27.3-3 for arched roofs
- Figure 27.3-4 for monoslope roof, open building
- Figure 27.3-5 for pitched roof, open building
- Figure 27.3-6 for troughed roof, open building
- Figure 27.3-7 for a long-ridge/valley wind load case for monoslope, pitched or troughed roof, open building

Step 7: Calculate wind pressure, p, on each building surface.
- Equation 27.3-1 for rigid buildings
- Equation 27.3-2 for flexible buildings
- Equation 27.3-3 for open buildings

Now let's discuss each step in more detail:

Step 1: Determine risk category of building or other structure, see Table 1.5-1.

The default risk category, Risk Category II, applies to most buildings.

Step 2: Determine the basic wind speed, V, for the applicable risk category, see Figure 26.5-1A, B, or C.

For buildings in Risk Category II, use Figure 26.5-1A. Basic wind speeds are described in terms of a 3-s gust speed (average speed over a 3-s window). In earlier codes, wind speeds were often described in terms of "fastest mile wind speed" (the speed with which a group of hypothetical air particles would travel a distance of 1 mile).

In ASCE 7-22, for structures assigned to Risk Category II, the basic wind speed is associated with an annual probability of exceedance of 0.0014 (return period of 700 years).

For wind speeds in Texas based on ASCE 7-22, refer to Fig. 3.3 (adapted from Figure 26.5-1A of ASCE 7-22).

Step 3: Determine wind load parameters:
- Wind directionality factor, K_d; see Section 26.6 and Table 26.6-1
- Exposure category; see Section 26.7
- Topographic factor, K_{zt}; see Section 26.8 and Table 26.8-1
- Gust effect factor, G; see Section 26.9
- Enclosure classification; see Section 26.10
- Internal pressure coefficient, GC_{pi}; see Section 26.11 and Table 26.11-1

Code Basis for Structural Design of Masonry Buildings 57

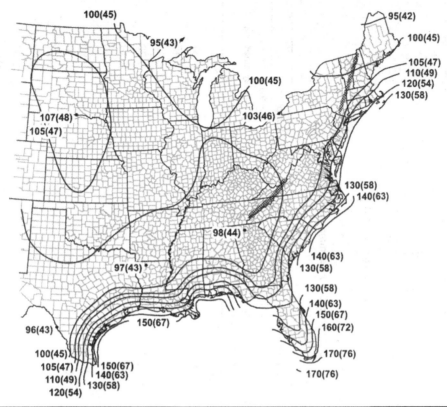

FIGURE 3.3 Basic wind speeds for Risk Category II buildings and other structures. (*Source:* Adapted from Figure 26.5-1A of ASCE 7-22.)

The wind directionality factor K_d is determined using ASCE Equation 26.8-1 $K_{zt} = (1 + K_1 K_2 K_3)^2$.

The exposure category is determined using Section 26.7. One first determines the surface roughness category in the two 45-degree upwind sectors.

- Surface Roughness B: Urban and suburban areas, wooded areas, or other terrain with numerous closely spaced obstructions having the size of single-family dwellings or larger.
- Surface Roughness C: Open terrain with scattered obstructions having heights generally less than 30 ft (9.1 m). This category includes flat open country and grasslands.
- Surface Roughness D: Flat, unobstructed areas and water surfaces. This category includes smooth mud flats, salt flats, and unbroken ice.

A surface roughness category that extends a large multiple of the building height in the upwind direction requires an exposure category equal to that surface roughness category. The most common exposure category is Exposure Category C. These specifically include hurricane zones.

➤ The topographic factor, K_{zt}, is determined using Section 26.8 and Table 26.8-1.

Table 3.3 Wind Directionality Factor, K_d

Diagrams

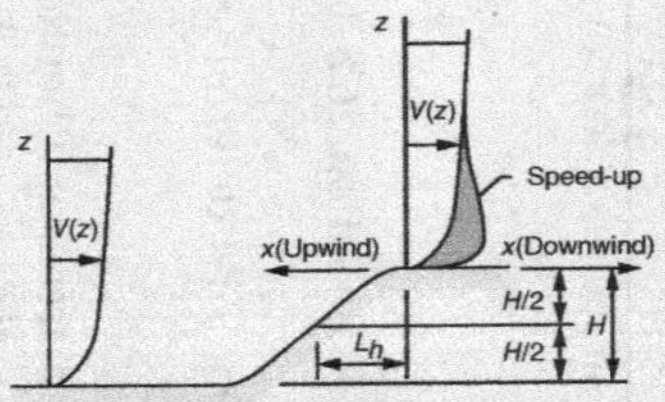

Escarpment

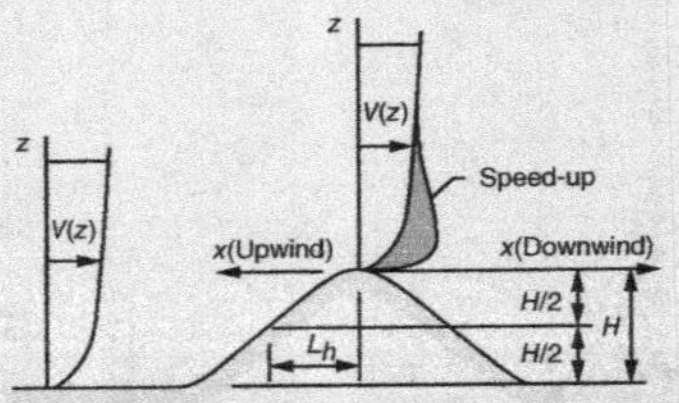

2-D Ridge or 3-D Axisymmetrical Hill

Topographic Multipliers[a,b,c,d]

	K_1 Multiplier				K_2 Multiplier			K_2 Multiplier		
H/L_h	2D Ridge	2D Escarpment	3D Axisymmetrical Hill	x/L_h	2D Escarpment	All Other Cases	z/L_h	2D Ridge	2D Escarpment	3D Axisymmetrical Hill
0.20	0.29	0.17	0.21	0.00	1.00	1.00	0.00	1.00	1.00	1.00
0.25	0.36	0.21	0.26	0.50	0.88	0.67	0.10	0.74	0.78	0.67
0.30	0.43	0.26	0.32	1.00	0.75	0.33	0.20	0.55	0.61	0.45
0.35	0.51	0.30	0.37	1.50	0.63	0.00	0.30	0.41	0.47	0.30
0.40	0.58	0.34	0.42	2.00	0.50	0.00	0.40	0.30	0.37	0.20
0.45	0.65	0.38	0.47	2.50	0.38	0.00	0.50	0.22	0.29	0.14
0.50	0.72	0.43	0.53	3.00	0.25	0.00	0.60	0.17	0.22	0.09
				3.50	0.13	0.00	0.70	0.12	0.17	0.06
				4.00	0.00	0.00	0.80	0.09	0.14	0.04
							0.90	0.07	0.11	0.03
							1.00	0.05	0.08	0.02
							0.50	0.01	0.02	0.00
							2.00	0.00	0.00	0.00

Source: Table 26.6-1 of ASCE 7-22.

Code Basis for Structural Design of Masonry Buildings

The topographic factor applies to structures located on a hill (higher than the surrounding terrain in all directions), ridge (higher than the surrounding terrain in two opposite directions), or escarpment (higher than the surrounding terrain in one direction only):

$$K_{zt} = (1 + K_1 K_2 K_3)^2$$

Values of K_1, K_2, and K_3 are given in Figure 26.8-1 of ASCE 7-22. The default condition is $K_{zt} = 1.0$.

> The gust effect factor, G, is defined in Section 26.9 of ASCE 7-22.

For rigid structures, the gust effect factor, G, is taken as 0.85 or is calculated by an equation.

For flexible structures, the gust effect factor, G_f, is calculated by an equation.

> Enclosure classification is defined in Section 26.12 of ASCE 7-22, and additional requirements for protection of glazed openings are provided in Section 26.12.3.

Classify the building as enclosed, partially enclosed, or open as defined in Section 26.2. In these definitions,

A_o = total area of openings in a wall that receives positive external pressure
A_g = gross area of that wall in which A_o is identified
A_{oi} = the sum of the areas of openings in the building envelope (walls and roof) not including A_o
A_{gi} = the sum of the gross surface areas of the building envelope (walls and roof) not including A_g

- Open buildings have each wall at least 80% open ($A_o \geq 0.80 A_g$).
- Partially enclosed buildings satisfy the following conditions:

$$\begin{cases} A_o \geq 1.10 A_{oi} \\ A_o > \text{smaller of} \begin{cases} 4\text{ ft}^2 \\ 0.01 A_g \end{cases} \\ \dfrac{A_{oi}}{A_{gi}} \leq 0.20 \end{cases}$$

- Enclosed buildings are those that do not comply with the requirements for open or partially enclosed buildings.

> The internal pressure coefficient, GC_{pi}, is determined using Section 26.13 and Table 26.13-1 of ASCE 7-22.

Step 4: Determine the velocity pressure exposure coefficients, K_z or K_h, using Table 3.5 (Table 27.3-1 of ASCE 7-22).

Step 5: Determine velocity pressure, q_z or q_h, using Equation 27.3-1

Using Section 26.10, the velocity pressure is calculated by ASCE 7-22, Equation 26.10-1.

$$q_z = 0.00256 K_z K_{zt} K_e V^2$$

where K_e = ground elevation factor defined in Section 26.8
K_z = velocity pressure exposure coefficient defined in Section 26.10.1

Chapter Three

TABLE 3.4 Main Wind Force Resisting System and Components and Cladding

Enclosure Classification	Criteria for Enclosure Classification	Internal Pressure	Internal Pressure Coefficient (GC_{pi})
Enclosed buildings	A_o is less than the smaller of $0.01A_g$ or 4 ft² (0.37 m²), and $A_{oi}/A_{gi} \leq 0.2$	Moderate	+0.18 −0.18
Partially enclosed buildings	$A_o > 1.1A_{oi}$, and $A_o >$ the lesser of $0.01A_g$ or 4 ft² (0.37 m²), and $A_{oi}/A_{gi} \leq 0.2$	High	+0.55 −0.55
Partially open buildings	A building that does not comply with Enclosed, Partially Enclosed, or Open classifications	Moderate	+0.18 −0.18
Open buildings	Each wall is at least 80% open	Negligible	0.00

Notes:
1. Plus and minus signs signify pressures acting toward and away from the internal surfaces, respectively.
2. Values of (GC_{pi}) shall be used with q_z or q_h as specified.
3. Two cases shall be considered to determine the critical load requirements for the appropriate condition:
   (a) A positive value of (GC_{pi}) applied to all internal surfaces, or
   (b) A negative value of (GC_{pi}) applied to all internal surfaces.

K_{zt} = topographic factor defined in Section 26.8.2
V = basic wind speed defined in Section 26.5

Step 6: Determine external pressure coefficient, C_p or C_N

> Figure 27.3-1 for walls and flat, gable, hip, monoslope, or mansard roofs
> Figure 27.3-2 for domed roofs
> Figure 27.3-3 for arched roofs
> Figure 27.3-4 for monoslope roof, open building
> Figure 27.3-5 for pitched roof, open building
> Figure 27.3-6 for troughed roof, open building
> Figure 27.3-7 for a long-ridge/valley wind load case for monoslope, pitched or troughed roof, open building

Because the most common case is addressed by Figure 27.3-1, which is reproduced as Fig. 3.4.

Step 7: Calculate wind pressure, p, on each building surface.

> Equation 27.3-1 for rigid buildings
> Equation 27.3-2 for flexible buildings
> Equation 27.3-3 for open buildings

Because Equation 27.3-1 addresses the most common case, it is provided below. For main wind force resisting systems of rigid systems,

$$p = qK_d GC_p - q_i K_d (GC_{pi})$$

where $q = q_z$ for windward walls evaluated at height z above the ground
$= q_h$ for leeward walls, side walls, and roofs, evaluated at height h

TABLE 3.5 Velocity Pressure Exposure Coefficients, K_h and K_z

Height above Ground Level, z or h		Exposure		
ft	(m)	B	C	D
0–15	0–4.6	0.57 (0.70)*	0.85	1.03
20	6.1	0.62 (0.70)*	0.90	1.08
25	7.6	0.66 (0.70)*	0.94	1.12
30	9.1	0.70	0.98	1.16
40	12.2	0.74	1.04	1.22
50	15.2	0.79	1.09	1.27
60	18.3	0.83	1.13	1.31
70	21.3	0.86	1.17	1.34
80	24.4	0.90	1.21	1.38
90	27.4	0.92	1.24	1.40
100	30.5	0.95	1.26	1.43
120	36.6	1.00	1.31	1.48
140	42.7	1.04	1.34	1.52
160	48.8	1.08	1.39	1.55
180	54.9	1.11	1.41	1.58
200	61.0	1.14	1.44	1.61
250	76.2	1.21	1.51	1.68
300	91.4	1.27	1.57	1.73
350	106.7	1.33	1.62	1.78
400	121.9	1.38	1.66	1.82
450	137.2	1.42	1.70	1.86
500	152.4	1.46	1.74	1.89

*Use 0.70 in Chapter 28, Exposure B, when $z < 30$ ft (9.1 m).

Notes:
1. The velocity pressure exposure coefficient K_z may be determined from the following formula:

   For $z < 15$ ft $\quad K_z = 2.41 (15/z_g)^{2/\alpha}$
   For $z < 4.6$ m $\quad K_z = 2.41 (4.6/z_g)^{2/\alpha}$
   For 15 ft (4.6 m) $\leq z \leq z_g$ $\quad K_z = 2.41 (z/z_g)^{2/\alpha}$
   For $z_g < z \leq 3{,}280$ ft
   (1,000 m) $\quad K_z = 2.41$

2. α and z_g are tabulated in Table 26.11-1.
3. Linear interpolation for intermediate values of height z is acceptable.
4. Exposure categories are defined in Section 26.7.

Source: Table 27.3-1 of ASCE 7-22.

Diagrams

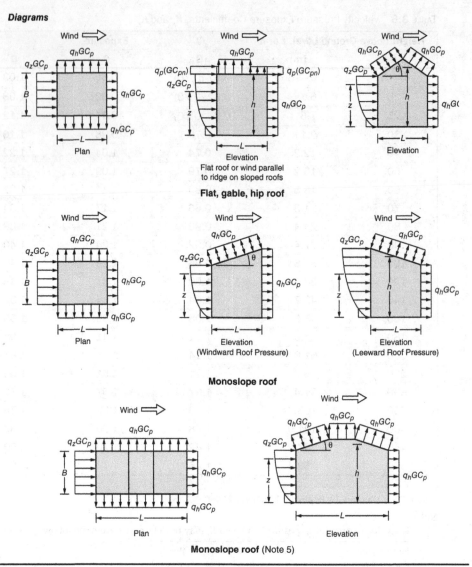

FIGURE 3.4 External pressure coefficients for main wind force resisting systems. (*Source:* Figure 27.4-1 of ASCE 7-22.)

$q_i = q_h$ for windward walls, side walls, leeward walls, and roofs of enclosed buildings and for negative internal pressure evaluation in partially enclosed buildings

$= q_z$ for positive internal pressure evaluation in partially enclosed buildings where height z is defined as the level of the highest opening in the building that could affect the positive internal pressure. For buildings sited in wind-borne debris regions, glazing that is not impact-resistant or protected with an impact-resistant covering shall be treated as an opening

Code Basis for Structural Design of Masonry Buildings 63

Wall Pressure Coefficients, C_p

Surface	L/B	C_p	Use with
Windward wall	All values	0.8	q_z
Leeward wall	0–1	−0.5	q_h
	2	−0.3	q_h
	≥4	−0.2	q_h
Sidewall	All values	−0.7	q_h
Parapet	All values	See Section 27.3.4 for GC_{pn}	q_p

Roof Pressure Coefficients, C_p, for use with q_h

		Windward								Leeward		
		Angle, θ								Angle, θ		
Wind Direction	h/L	10°	15°	20°	25°	30°	35°	45°	60°	60°<θ≤80° >80°	10°	15°	≥20°
Normal to Ridge for θ ≥ 10°	≤0.25	−0.7	−0.5	−0.3	−0.2	−0.2	0.0ª						
		−0.18	0.0ª	0.2	0.3	0.3	0.4	0.4	0.6	0.01θ 0.8	−0.3	−0.5	−0.6
	0.5	−0.9	−0.7	−0.4	−0.3	−0.2	−0.2	0.0ª					
		−0.18	−0.18	0.0ª	0.2	0.2	0.3	0.4	0.6	0.01θ 0.8	−0.5	−0.5	−0.6
	≥1.0	−1.3ᵇ	−1.0	−0.7	−0.5	−0.3	−0.2	0.0ª					
		−0.18	−0.18	−0.18	0.0ª	0.2	0.2	0.3	0.6	0.01θ 0.8	−0.7	−0.6	−0.6

Wind Direction	h/L	Horizontal Distance from Windward Edge	C_p
Normal to Ridge for θ ≥ 10° and Parallel to Ridge for all θ	≤0.5	0 to h/2	−0.9, −0.18
		h/2 to h	−0.9, −0.18
		h to 2h	−0.5, −0.18
		>2h	−0.3, −0.18
	≥1.0	0 to h/2	−1.3ᵇ, −0.18
		> h/2	−0.7, −0.18

ªValue is provided for interpolation purposes.
ᵇValue can be reduced linearly, with area over which it is applicable as follows:

FIGURE 3.4 (Continued)

in accordance with Section 26.10.3. For positive internal pressure evaluation, q_i may conservatively be evaluated at height h ($q_i = q_h$)

K_d = wind directionality factor from Section 26.6
G = gust effect factor from Section 26.9
C_p = external pressure coefficient from Figures 27.4-1, 27.4-2, and 27.4-3
GC_{pi} = internal pressure coefficient from Table 26.11-1

q and q_i shall be evaluated using exposure defined in Section 26.7.3. Pressure shall be applied simultaneously on windward and leeward walls and on roof surfaces as defined in Figure 27.3-1.

3.4.2 Example 1 (Wind Loading on Main Wind Force Resisting System)

Using the procedures of ASCE 7-22, compute the design base shear due to wind for the building of Fig. 3.5, located in the suburbs of Austin, Texas.

The critical direction will be NS because the walls on the north and south sides have greater area and the shear walls in the north and south directions have less area.

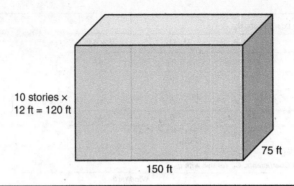

FIGURE 3.5 Schematic view of building in Austin, Texas.

Step 1: Determine risk category of building or other structure, see Table 1.5-1.

Assume that the default risk category, Risk Category II, applies to this building.

Step 2: Determine the basic wind speed, V, for the applicable risk category, see Figure 26.5-1A, B, or C

Because this building is in Risk Category II, use Figure 26.5-1A. For Austin, Texas, the basic wind speed is 100 miles per hour.

Step 3: Determine wind load parameters:

➤ Wind directionality factor, K_d; see Section 26.6 and Table 26.6-1

$$K_d = 0.85$$

➤ Exposure category; see Section 26.7

Assume a long upwind stretch of Surface Roughness B (urban and suburban areas, wooded areas, or other terrain with numerous closely spaced obstructions having the size of single-family dwellings or larger) and corresponding Exposure Category B.

➤ Topographic factor, K_{zt}; see Section 26.8 and Table 26.8-1

Assume $K_{zt} = 1.0$ (no hills, ridges, or escarpments).

➤ Ground elevation factor, K_e; see Section 26.9

Elevation of Austin, Texas, is 500 ft. Use $K_e = 0.98$ (interpolate between elevations of 0 and 1000 ft).

➤ Gust effect factor, G; see Section 26.11

Because this structure's period of vibration is much shorter than the characteristic period of wind gusts, it is considered rigid, and the gust effect factor G can be taken as 0.85.

➤ Enclosure classification; see Section 26.12

Because this structure has few openings and because glazing is impact-resistant, it is classified as enclosed.

➤ Internal pressure coefficient, GC_{pi}; see Section 26.13 and Table 26.13-1

Because this structure is enclosed, from Table 26.11-1, the internal pressure coefficient (GC_{pi}) is ±0.18.

Step 4: Determine the velocity pressure exposure coefficient, K_z or K_h, using Table 27.3-1 of ASCE 7-22.

From Table 27.3-1 of ASCE 7-22, for Exposure Category B, relevant table cells are reproduced as Table 3.6.

Step 5: Determine velocity pressure q_z or q_h using Equation 26.10-1.

$$q_z = 0.00256\, K_z K_{zt} K_e V^2$$
$$K_e = 0.98$$
$$V = 100 \text{ miles/hr}$$
$$K_{zt} = 1.0$$
$$q_z = 25.09\, K_z \text{ lb/ft}^2$$

Note that the above expression for q_z has the velocity pressure exposure coefficient K_z embedded in it.

Step 6: Determine external pressure coefficient, C_p or C_N.

The external pressure coefficients C_p for main wind force resisting systems are given in Figure 27.3-1 of ASCE 7-22 for walls and flat roofs.

From the plan views in Figure 27.3-1 of ASCE 7-22, the windward pressure is $q_z GC_p$. The leeward pressure is $q_h GC_p$. The difference between the q_z and the q_h is that the former varies as a function of the height above ground level, while the latter is uniform over the height of the building and is evaluated using the height of the building.

TABLE 3.6 Velocity Pressure Coefficients for Building of Example 1

Height above Ground Level, z	K_h, K_z
1–15	0.57
20	0.62
25	0.66
30	0.70
40	0.74
50	0.79
60	0.83
70	0.86
80	0.90
90	0.92
100	0.95
120	1.00

Source: Taken from Table 26.10-1 of ASCE 7-22.

For wind blowing in the NS direction, $L/B = 0.5$. From Figure 27.3-1 (cont'd), on the windward side of the building, the external pressure coefficient C_p is 0.8. On the leeward side of the building, it is –0.5.

Step 7: Calculate wind pressure, p, on each building surface.

Use Equation 27.3-1 for MWFRS and rigid systems.

$$p = qK_d GC_p - q_i K_d (GC_{pi})$$

where $q = q_z$ for windward walls evaluated at height z above the ground
$ = q_h$ for leeward walls, side walls, and roofs, evaluated at height h
$q_i = q_h$ for windward walls, side walls, leeward walls, and roofs of enclosed buildings and for negative internal pressure evaluation in partially enclosed buildings
$ = q_z$ for positive internal pressure evaluation in partially enclosed buildings where height z is defined as the level of the highest opening in the building that could affect the positive internal pressure. For buildings sited in wind-borne debris regions, glazing that is not impact-resistant or protected with an impact-resistant covering shall be treated as an opening in accordance with Section 26.12.3. For positive internal pressure evaluation, q_i may conservatively be evaluated at height h ($q_i = q_h$)
G = gust effect factor from Section 26.11.5
C_p = external pressure coefficient from Figures 27.3-1, 27.3-2, and 27.3-3
GC_{pi} = internal pressure coefficient from Table 26.13-1

q and q_i shall be evaluated using exposure defined in Section 26.7.3. Pressure shall be applied simultaneously on windward and leeward walls and on roof surfaces as defined in Figures 27.3-1, 27.3-2, and 27.3-3.

Because the building is enclosed, the internal pressures on the windward and leeward sides are of equal magnitude and opposite direction, produce zero net base shear, and therefore need not be considered.

On the windward side of the building,

$$p = q_z K_d GC_p$$

$$p = (25.09\ K_z) K_d GC_p$$

Because C_p is positive in sign, this pressure is positive in sign, indicating that the pressure acts inward against the windward wall. If the wind comes from the south, for example, the force on the windward wall acts toward the north. These values are shown in the "Windward Side" columns of the spreadsheet in Table 3.7.

On the leeward side of the building,

$$p = q_h K_d GC_p$$

$$p = (25.09\ K_h)\ K_d GC_p$$

Because C_p is negative in sign, this pressure is negative in sign, indicating that the pressure acts outward against the leeward wall. If the wind comes from the south, for example, the force on the leeward wall acts toward the north. These values are shown in the "Leeward Side" columns of the spreadsheet in Table 3.7.

TABLE 3.7 Spreadsheet for Wind Forces, Example 1

Building Floor	Height above Ground (ft)	Tributary Area (ft²)	K_z	q_z (psf)	Kd	G	C_p	p (psf)	Force (kip)	K_h	q_h (psf)	Kd	G	C_p	p (psf)	Force (kip)
Roof	120	900	1	25.09	0.85	0.85	0.8	14.5	13.1	1	25.1	0.85	0.85	−0.5	−9.06	−8.2
10	108	1800	0.97	24.34	0.85	0.85	0.8	13.6	24.6	1	25.1	0.85	0.85	−0.5	−9.06	−16.3
9	96	1800	0.94	23.58	0.85	0.85	0.8	12.8	23.1	1	25.1	0.85	0.85	−0.5	−9.06	−16.3
8	84	1800	0.91	22.83	0.85	0.85	0.8	12	21.6	1	25.1	0.85	0.85	−0.5	−9.06	−16.3
7	72	1800	0.87	21.83	0.85	0.85	0.8	11	19.8	1	25.1	0.85	0.85	−0.5	−9.06	−16.3
6	60	1800	0.83	20.82	0.85	0.85	0.8	9.99	18.0	1	25.1	0.85	0.85	−0.5	−9.06	−16.3
5	48	1800	0.78	19.57	0.85	0.85	0.8	8.82	15.9	1	25.1	0.85	0.85	−0.5	−9.06	−16.3
4	36	1800	0.72	18.06	0.85	0.85	0.8	7.52	13.5	1	25.1	0.85	0.85	−0.5	−9.06	−16.3
3	24	1800	0.66	16.56	0.85	0.85	0.8	6.32	11.4	1	25.1	0.85	0.85	−0.5	−9.06	−16.3
2	12	1800	0.57	14.3	0.85	0.85	0.8	4.71	8.5	1	25.1	0.85	0.85	−0.5	−9.06	−16.3
Ground	0	900	0.57	14.3	0.85	0.85	0.8	4.71	4.2	1	25.1	0.85	0.85	−0.5	−9.06	−8.2
Total force									173.5							−163.1

Windward Side / Leeward Side

67

The design base shear due to wind load is the summation of 173.5 kips acting inward on the upwind wall and 163.1 kips acting outward on the downwind wall for a total of 336.7 kips.

Summary of Part 3 of Chapter 30 of ASCE 7-22 for C&C Loads

The steps of the Directional Procedure of ASCE 7-22 for C&C loads are outlined in Table 30.6-127.2-1:

Step 1: Determine risk category, see Table 1.5-1.

Step 2: Determine the basic wind speed, V, for applicable risk category, see Figure 26.5-1A, B, or C.

Step 3: Determine wind load parameters:
- Wind directionality factor, K_d; see Section 26.6 and Table 26.6-1
- Exposure category B, C, or D; see Section 26.7
- Topographic factor, K_{zt}; see Section 26.8 and Figure 26.8-1
- Ground elevation factor, K_e; see Section 26.9
- Gust effect factor, G; see Section 26.11
- Enclosure classification; see Section 26.12
- Internal pressure coefficient, GC_{pi}; see Section 26.13 and Table 26.13-1

Step 4: Determine velocity pressure exposure coefficient, K_z or K_h, see Table 30.3-1.

Step 5: Determine velocity pressure, q_h; Equation 30.3-1.

Step 6: Determine external pressure coefficient, GC_p.
- Walls and flat roofs ($\theta < 10$ deg), see Figure 30.6-1
- Gable and hip roofs, see Figure 30.4-2 per Note 6 of Figure 30.6-1
- Arched roofs, see Figure 27.4-3, footnote 4
- Domed roofs, see Figure 30.4-7

Step 7: Calculate wind pressure, p, Equation 30.6-1.

Many of these steps are identical or almost identical to those used in the calculation of MWFRS forces. A few, however, are quite different. For this reason, calculation steps for MWFRS and C&C have been kept separate, with a separate example for C&C as well.

Now let's discuss each step in more detail.

Step 1: Determine risk category of building or other structure, see Table 1.5-1.

The default risk category, Risk Category II, applies to most buildings.

Step 2: Determine the basic wind speed, V, for the applicable risk category, see Figure 26.5-1A, B, or C.

For buildings in Risk Category II, use Figure 26.5-1A. For Risk Category II structures, the basic wind speed is associated with a return period of 700 years, or an annual probability of exceedance of 0.0014. Basic wind speeds are described in terms of a 3-s gust speed (average speed over a 3-s window).

Refer to Fig. 3.6 (adapted from Figure 26.5-1A of ASCE 7-22).

Step 3: Determine wind load parameters:
- Wind directionality factor, K_d; see Section 26.6 and Table 26.6-1
- Exposure category; see Section 26.7

Code Basis for Structural Design of Masonry Buildings 69

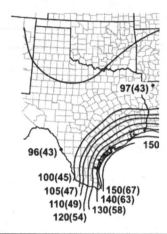

FIGURE 3.6 Basic wind speeds for Risk Category II buildings and other structures. (*Source:* Adapted from Figure 26.5-1A of ASCE 7-22.)

➤ Topographic factor, K_{zt}; see Section 26.8 and Table 26.8-1
➤ Gust effect factor, G; see Section 26.9
➤ Enclosure classification; see Section 26.10
➤ Internal pressure coefficient, GC_{pi}; see Section 26.11 and Table 26.11-1
➤ The wind directionality factor K_d is determined using Table 3.3 (Section 26.6 and Table 26.6-1 of ASCE 7-22).
➤ The exposure category is determined using Section 26.7. One first determines the surface roughness category in the two 45-degree upwind sectors.

Surface Roughness B: Urban and suburban areas, wooded areas, or other terrain with numerous closely spaced obstructions having the size of single-family dwellings or larger.

Surface Roughness C: Open terrain with scattered obstructions having heights generally less than 30 ft (9.1 m). This category includes flat open country and grasslands.

Surface Roughness D: Flat, unobstructed areas and water surfaces. This category includes smooth mud flats, salt flats, and unbroken ice.

A surface roughness category that extends a large multiple of the building height in the upwind direction requires an exposure category equal to that surface roughness category. The most common exposure category is Exposure Category C. In ASCE 7-22 open stretches of water are considered Surface Roughness D, and require Exposure Category D. These specifically include hurricane zones.

➤ The topographic factor, K_{zt}, is determined using Section 26.8 and Table 26.8-1. The topographic factor applies to structures located on a hill (higher than the surrounding terrain in all directions), ridge (higher than the surrounding terrain in two opposite directions), or escarpment (higher than the surrounding terrain in one direction only):

$$K_{zt} = (1 + K_1 K_2 K_3)^2$$

TABLE 3.8 Wind Directionality Factor, K_d

Structure Type	Directionality Factor K_d
Buildings	
Main wind force resisting system	0.85
Components and cladding	0.85
Arched roofs	0.85
Circular domes	1.0*
Chimneys, tanks, and similar structures	
Square	0.90
Hexagonal	0.95
Octagonal	1.0*
Round	1.0*
Solid freestanding walls, roof top equipment, and solid freestanding and attached signs	0.85
Open signs and single-plane open frames	0.85
Trussed towers	
Triangular, square, rectangular	0.85
All other cross sections	0.95

*Directionality factor $K_d = 0.95$ shall be permitted for round or octagonal structures with non-axisymmetric structural systems.
Source: Table 26.6-1 of ASCE 7-22.

Values of K_1, K_2, and K_3 are given in Figure 26.8-1 of ASCE 7-22. The default condition is $K_{zt} = 1.0$.

➤ The gust effect factor, G, is defined in Section 26.9 of ASCE 7-22.
For rigid structures, the gust effect factor, G, is taken as 0.85 or is calculated by an equation.
For flexible structures, the gust effect factor, G_f, is calculated by an equation.

➤ Enclosure classification is defined in Section 26.2 of ASCE 7-22, and additional requirements for protection of glazed openings are provided in Section 26.10.
Classify the building as enclosed, partially enclosed, or open as defined in Section 26.2. In these definitions,

A_o = total area of openings in a wall that receives positive external pressure
A_g = gross area of that wall in which A_o is identified
A_{oi} = the sum of the areas of openings in the building envelope (walls and roof) not including A_o
A_{gi} = the sum of the gross surface areas of the building envelope (walls and roof) not including A_g

- Open buildings have each wall at least 80% open ($A_o \geq 0.80 A_g$).

Code Basis for Structural Design of Masonry Buildings

- Partially enclosed buildings satisfy the following:

$$\begin{cases} A_o \geq 1.10 A_{oi} \\ A_o > \text{smaller of } \begin{cases} 4 \text{ ft}^2 \\ 0.01 A_g \end{cases} \\ \dfrac{A_{oi}}{A_{gi}} \leq 0.20 \end{cases}$$

- Enclosed buildings are those that do not comply with the requirements for open or partially enclosed buildings.
  - The internal pressure coefficient, GC_{pi}, is determined using Section 26.11 and Table 26.11-1 of ASCE 7-22.

Step 4: Determine velocity pressure exposure coefficient, K_z or K_h, using Table 30.3-1 of ASCE 7-22. This step is different for C&C loads compared to MWFRS loads. The table is different for each.

Step 5: Determine velocity pressure, q_h, using Equation 30.-1.

$$q_z = 0.00256 \, K_z K_{zt} K_d V^2$$

where K_d = wind directionality factor defined in Section 26.6
K_z = velocity pressure exposure coefficient defined in Section 30.3.1

ASCE 7-22 TABLE 26.13-1 Main Wind Force Resisting System and Components and Cladding (All Heights): Internal Pressure Coefficient (GC_{pi}), for Enclosed, Partially Enclosed, Partially Open, and Open Buildings (Walls and Roof).

Enclosure Classification	Criteria for Enclosure Classification	Internal Pressure	Internal Pressure Coefficient (GC_{pi})
Enclosed buildings	A_o is less than the smaller of $0.01 A_g$ or 4 ft² (0.37 m²), and $A_o/A_{gi} \leq 0.2$	Moderate	+0.18 −0.18
Partially enclosed buildings	$A_o > 1.1 A_{oi}$, and $A_o >$ the lesser of $0.01 A_g$ or 4 ft² (0.37 m²), and $A_o/A_{gi} \leq 0.2$	High	+0.55 −0.55
Partially open buildings	A building that does not comply with Enclosed, Partially Enclosed, or Open classifications	Moderate	+0.18 −0.18
Open buildings	Each wall is at least 80% open	Negligible	0.00

Notes:
1. Plus and minus signs signify pressures acting toward and away from the internal surfaces, respectively.
2. Values of (GC_{pi}) shall be used with q_z or q_h as specified.
3. Two cases shall be considered to determine the critical load requirements for the appropriate condition:
   (a) A positive value of (GC_{pi}) applied to all internal surfaces, or
   (b) A negative value of (GC_{pi}) applied to all internal surfaces.

ASCE 7-22 TABLE 26.10-1 Velocity Pressure Exposure Coefficients, K_h and K_z

| Height above Ground Level, z or h || Exposure |||
ft	(m)	B	C	D
0–15	0–4.6	0.57 (0.70)*	0.85	1.03
20	6.1	0.62 (0.70)*	0.90	1.08
25	7.6	0.66 (0.70)*	0.94	1.12
30	9.1	0.70	0.98	1.16
40	12.2	0.74	1.04	1.22
50	15.2	0.79	1.09	1.27
60	18.3	0.83	1.13	1.31
70	21.3	0.86	1.17	1.34
80	24.4	0.90	1.21	1.38
90	27.4	0.92	1.24	1.40
100	30.5	0.95	1.26	1.43
120	36.6	1.00	1.31	1.48
140	42.7	1.04	1.34	1.52
160	48.8	1.08	1.39	1.55
180	54.9	1.11	1.41	1.58
200	61.0	1.14	1.44	1.61
250	76.2	1.21	1.51	1.68
300	91.4	1.27	1.57	1.73
350	106.7	1.33	1.62	1.78
400	121.9	1.38	1.66	1.82
450	137.2	1.42	1.70	1.86
500	152.4	1.46	1.74	1.89

*Use 0.70 in Chapter 28, Exposure B, when z < 30 ft (9.1 m).

Notes:
1. The velocity pressure exposure coefficient K_z may be determined from the following formula:

   For z < 15 ft $K_z = 2.41 (15/z_g)^{2/\alpha}$
   For z < 4.6 m $K_z = 2.41 (4.6/z_g)^{2/\alpha}$
   For 15 ft (4.6 m) $\leq z \leq z_g$ $K_z = 2.41 (z/z_g)^{2/\alpha}$
   For $z_g < z \leq 3,280$ ft
       (1,000 m) $K_z = 2.41$

2. α and z_g are tabulated in Table 26.11-1.
3. Linear interpolation for intermediate values of height z is acceptable.
4. Exposure categories are defined in Section 26.7.

Code Basis for Structural Design of Masonry Buildings

K_{zt} = topographic factor defined in Section 26.8
V = basic wind speed defined in Section 26.5
q_h = velocity pressure calculated using Equation 30.3-1 at height h

Step 6: Determine external pressure coefficient, GC_p.

- Walls and flat roofs (θ < 10 deg); see Figure 30.6-1
- Gable and hip roofs; see Figure 30.4-2 per Note 6 of Figure 30.6-1
- Arched roofs; see Figure 27.4-3, footnote 4
- Domed roofs; see Figure 30.4-7

Because the most common case is addressed by Figure 30.6-1, which is reproduced as Fig. 3.7.

Note that the title of the figure is in white letters on a black background.

In computing the effective area of the cladding element, it is permitted to use an effective area equal to the product of the span and an effective width not less than one-third the span.

Step 7: Calculate wind pressure, p, Equation 30.6-1

For C&C of buildings with $h > 60$ ft:

$$p = qK_d GC_p - q_i K_d (GC_{pi})$$

where
$q = q_z$ for windward walls calculated at height z above the ground
$\quad = q_h$ for leeward walls, side walls, and roofs evaluated at height h
$q_i = q_h$ for windward walls, side walls, leeward walls, and roofs of enclosed buildings and for negative internal pressure evaluation in partially enclosed buildings
$\quad = q_z$ for positive internal pressure evaluation in partially enclosed buildings where height z is defined as the level of the highest opening in the building that could affect the positive internal pressure. For positive internal pressure evaluation, q_i may conservatively be evaluated at height h ($q_i = q_h$)
GC_p = external pressure coefficient given in 30.3 or 30.4 depending on building height and roof characteristics
GC_{pi} = internal pressure coefficient given in Table 26.13-1

q and q_i shall be evaluated using exposure defined in Section 26.10.

3.4.3 Example 2 (Wind Loading on Components and Cladding)

Using the procedures of ASCE 7-22, compute the design wind pressure on a cladding element near the corner of the top floor of the building of Example 1 as illustrated in Fig. 3.8.

Step 1: Determine risk category of building or other structure, see Table 1.5-1.

Assume that the default risk category, Risk Category II, applies to this building.

Step 2: Determine the basic wind speed, V, for the applicable risk category, see Figure 26.5-1A, B, or C

Because this building is in Risk Category II, use Figure 26.5-1A. For Austin, Texas, the basic wind speed is 100 miles per hour.

74 Chapter Three

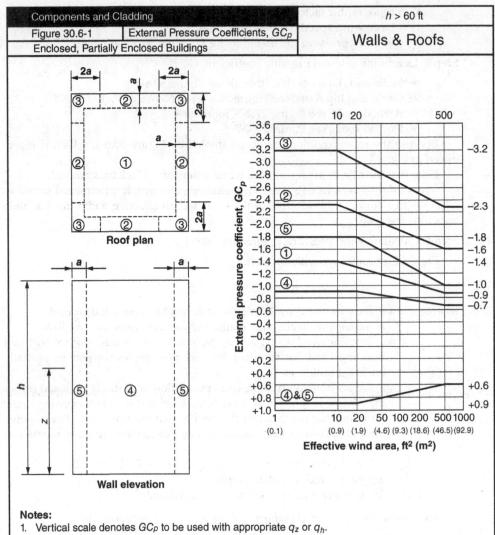

FIGURE 3.7 External pressure coefficient for walls. (*Source*: Adapted from Figure 30.6-1 of ASCE 7-22.)

Code Basis for Structural Design of Masonry Buildings

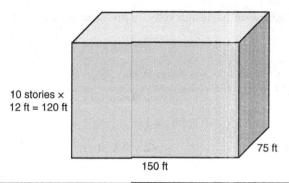

FIGURE 3.8 Schematic view of building in Austin, Texas.

Step 3: Determine wind load parameters:

➢ Wind directionality factor, K_d; see Section 26.6 and Table 26.6-1

$$K_d = 0.85$$

➢ Exposure category, see Section 26.7

Assume a long upwind stretch of Surface Roughness B (urban and suburban areas, wooded areas, or other terrain with numerous closely spaced obstructions having the size of single-family dwellings or larger), and corresponding Exposure Category B.

➢ Topographic factor, K_{zt}; see Section 26.8 and Table 26.8-1

Assume $K_{zt} = 1.0$ (no hills, ridges, or escarpments)

➢ Ground elevation factor, K_e; see Section 26.9

Elevation of Austin, Texas, is 500 ft. Use $K_e = 0.98$ (interpolate between elevations of 0 and 1,000 ft)

➢ Gust effect factor, G, see Section 26.11

Because this structure's period of vibration is much shorter than the characteristic period of wind gusts, it is considered rigid, and the gust effect factor, G, can be taken as 0.85.

➢ Enclosure classification; see Section 26.12

Because this structure has few openings, and because glazing is impact-resistant, it is classified as enclosed.

➢ Internal pressure coefficient, GC_{pi}; see Section 26.13 and Table 26.13-1

Because this structure is enclosed, from Table 26.13-1, the internal pressure coefficient (GC_{pi}) is ±0.18.

Step 4: Determine velocity pressure exposure coefficient, K_z or K_h, using Table 26.10-1.

For Exposure Category B, at a height of 120 ft above the ground, K_z equals 1.0.

Step 5: Determine design velocity pressure, q_h, using Equation 26.10-3.

$$q_z = 0.00256 \, K_z K_{zt} K_e V^2$$

$$K_e = 0.98$$

$$V = 100 \, \text{miles/hr}$$

$$K_{zt} = 1.0$$

$$q_z = 25.09 \, K_z \, \text{lb/ft}^2$$

Note that the above expression for q_z has the velocity pressure exposure coefficient K_z embedded in it.

Step 6: Determine external pressure coefficient, GC_p.

➢ Walls; see Figure 30.4-1
➢ Flat roofs (θ < 10 deg), gable, and hip roofs; see Figure 30.3-2
➢ Arched roofs; see Figure 30.3-8, footnote 4
➢ Domed roofs; see Figure 30.3-7

The external pressure coefficients for C&C GC_p are given in Figure 30.4-1 of ASCE 7-22.

In computing the effective area of the cladding element, it is permitted to use an effective area equal to the product of the span and an effective width not less than one-third the span.

Assume a panel with a span equal to the story height of 12 ft minus a spandrel depth of 2 ft or 10 ft. Assume an effective width of one-third of that span, or 3.33 ft. The resulting effective area is 33.3 ft². From Figure 30.4-1, a panel in Zone 5 has a positive pressure coefficient of 0.85, and a negative pressure coefficient of –1.7.

Step 7: Calculate wind pressure, p, Equation 30.4-1

Since this is a building with $h > 60$ ft:

$$p = qK_d(GC_p) - q_iK_d(GC_{pi})$$

Windward Side of Building
On the windward side of the building, the maximum inward pressure will be produced on the cladding due to the combination of GC_p acting inward (positive sign) and GC_{pi} acting outward (negative sign).

$q = q_z$ evaluated at the height of the element, or 120 ft
$q_i = q_h$ evaluated at the height of the building, or 120 ft
$(GC_p) = 0.85$ (Figure 30.4-1), see Fig. 3.9
$(GC_{pi}) = \pm 0.18$ (Table 26.13-1)

$$p = q \, K_d(GC_p) - q_i K_d \, (GC_{pi})$$

$$p = q_z \, K_d(GC_p) - q_h K_d \, (GC_{pi})$$

$$p = (25.09 \, K_z) \, K_d G \, C_p - (25.09 \, K_h) \, K_d G \, C_{pi}$$

Code Basis for Structural Design of Masonry Buildings 77

Diagrams

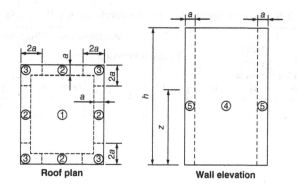

Notation
a = 10% of least horizontal dimension, but not less than 3 ft (0.9 m).
h = Mean roof height, ft (m), except that eave height shall be used for $\theta \leq 10°$.
z = Height above ground, ft (m).
θ = Angle of plane of roof from horizontal, degrees.

External Pressure Coefficients

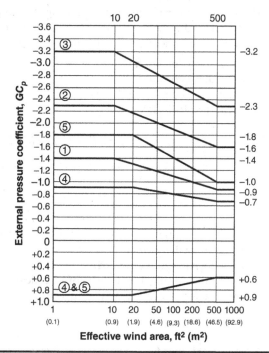

FIGURE 3.9 External pressure coefficient for walls with $h < 60$ ft. (*Source*: Adapted from Figure 30.4-1 of ASCE 7-22.)

TABLE 3.9 Spreadsheet for Components and Cladding Pressures, Windward Side of Example 2

Building Floor	Height above Ground (ft)	Maximum Inward Pressure (Windward Wall)										Total
		External Pressure				Internal Pressure					
		K_z	q_z (psf)	GC_p	$p_{outside}$ (psf)	K_h	q_h (psf)	G	C_p	p_{inside} (psf)	p_{total} (psf)
Roof	120	1	25.09	0.85	18.13	1	25.09	0.85	−0.18	−3.26	21.39

$K_d = 0.85$.

These values are shown in the spreadsheet of Table 3.9. The maximum inward pressure is the sum of 18.13 psf on the outside plus 3.26 psf on the inside for a total of 21.39 psf acting inward.

Leeward Side of Building
On the leeward side of the building, the maximum outward pressure will be produced on the cladding due to the combination of GC_p acting outward (negative sign) and GC_{pi} also acting outward (positive sign).

$q = q_h$, or 120 ft
$q_i = q_h$, or 120 ft
$(GC_p) = -1.7$ (Figure 30.4-1)
$(GC_{pi}) = \pm 0.18$ (Table 26.11-1)

$$p = q\, K_d(GC_p) - q_i K_d(GC_{pi})$$
$$p = q_z K_d(GC_p) - q_h K_d(GC_{pi})$$
$$p = (25.09\, K_z) K_d GC_p - (25.09\, K_h) K_d GC_{pi}$$

These values are shown in the spreadsheet of Table 3.10. The maximum outward pressure is the sum of −36.25 psf on the outside plus 3.26 psf on the inside for a total of 36.51 psf acting outward.

The cladding must therefore be designed for a pressure of 21.4 lb/ft² acting inward and 39.5 lb/ft² acting outward.

TABLE 3.10 Spreadsheet for Components and Cladding Pressures, Leeward Side of Example 2

Building Floor	Height above Ground (ft)	Maximum Inward Pressure (Leeward Wall)										Total
		External Pressure				Internal Pressure					
		K_z	q_z (psf)	GC_p	$p_{outside}$ (psf)	K_h	q_h (psf)	G	C_p	p_{inside} (psf)	p_{total} (psf)
Roof	120	1	25.09	−1.7	−36.25	1	25.09	0.85	0.18	3.26	−39.51

$K_d = 0.85$.

3.5 Earthquake Loading

Design earthquake loads are calculated according to Section 1613 of the 2024 IBC. That section essentially references ASCE 7-22. Seismic design criteria are given in Chapter 11 of ASCE 7-22. The seismic design provisions of ASCE 7-22 begin in Chapter 12, which prescribes basic requirements (including the requirement for continuous load paths) (Section 12.1); selection of structural systems (Section 12.2); diaphragm characteristics and other possible irregularities (Section 12.3); seismic load effects and combinations (Section 12.4); direction of loading (Section 12.5); analysis procedures (Section 12.6); modeling procedures (Section 12.7); and specific design approaches. Four procedures are prescribed: an equivalent lateral force procedure (Section 12.8); a modal response-spectrum analysis (Section 12.9); a simplified alternative procedure (Section 12.14); and a seismic response history procedure (Chapter 16). The equivalent lateral-force procedure is described here, because it is relatively simple, and is permitted in most situations. The simplified alternative procedure is permitted in only a few situations. The other procedures are permitted in all situations and are required in only a few situations.

3.5.1 Background on Earthquake Loading

The basic approach to earthquake design is to idealize a building as a single-degree-of-freedom system—that is, a system whose configuration in space can be defined using a single variable (Fig. 3.10).

The equation of equilibrium for this system is

$$M\ddot{u} + 2\xi\omega M\dot{u} + \omega^2 M u = -M\ddot{u}_g(t)$$

where $\omega = \sqrt{K/M}$, and ξ is an equivalent viscous damping coefficient, whose value is chosen so that the energy dissipation of the system in the elastic range will be similar to that of the original structure.

For a given ground motion, the solution to the above equation can be calculated step by step using computer programs. The response of a structure depends on the strength of the ground motion and also on the relationship between the characteristic frequencies of ground motion, and the frequency of the structure.

Of particular interest are the maximum values of the seismic response, which can be graphed in the form of a response spectrum, whose ordinates indicate the maximum

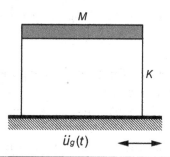

FIGURE 3.10 Idealized single-degree-of-freedom system.

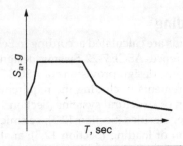

FIGURE 3.11 Acceleration response spectrum, smoothed for use in design.

response as a function of the period of vibration of the structure. For example, the acceleration response spectrum gives the values of absolute acceleration (which can be multiplied by mass to give the maximum inertial forces that act on the structure) in terms of period. An example of an acceleration response spectrum smoothed for use in design is given in Figure 3.11.

Using a response spectrum, the maximum response of a structure can be calculated for a particular earthquake with little effort. Such response spectra, smoothed as shown above, can be used to calculate design forces as part of the process of seismic design.

In modern design codes, these design spectra are modified to address the effects of inelastic response, structural overstrength, and multimodal response.

3.5.2 Determine Seismic Ground Motion Values

1. Determine S_{MS}, the mapped MCE (maximum considered earthquake), 5% damped, spectral response acceleration parameter at short periods as defined in Section 11.4.3 of ASCE 7-22, at the USGS website at http://earthquake.usgs.gov/designmaps, or through the ASCE load calculator.

2. Determine S_{M1}, the mapped MCE, 5% damped, spectral response acceleration parameter at a period of 1 s as defined in Section 11.4.3.

3. Determine the site class (A through F, a measure of soil response characteristics and soil stability) in accordance with Section 20.2 and Table 20.2-1.

4. Determine the design response acceleration parameter for short periods, S_{DS}, and for a 1-s period, S_{D1}, using Equations 11.4-1 and 11.4-2, respectively.

5. If required, determine the design response spectrum curve as prescribed by Section 11.4.5.2.

3.5.3 Determine Seismic Base Shear Using the Equivalent Lateral Force Procedure

6. Determine the structure's importance factor, I, and occupancy category using Section 11.5.

7. Determine the structure's seismic design category using Section 11.6.

8. Calculate the structure's seismic base shear using Sections 12.8.1 and 12.8.2.

3.5.4 Distribute Seismic Base Shear Vertically and Horizontally

9. Distribute seismic base shear vertically using Section 12.8.3.
10. Distribute seismic base shear horizontally using Section 12.8.4.

Now let's discuss each step in more detail, combining with an example for Charleston, South Carolina.

Step 1: Determine S_{MS}, the mapped MCE (maximum considered earthquake), 5% damped, spectral response acceleration parameter at short periods as defined in Section 11.4.3.

Step 2: Determine S_{M1}, the mapped MCE, 5% damped, spectral response acceleration parameter at a period of 1 s as defined in Section 11.4.3.

Determine the parameters S_{MS} and S_{M1} from the 0.2-s and 1-s spectral response maps shown in Figures 22-1 through 22-7 of ASCE 7-22.

With the exception of some parts of the western United States (where design earthquakes have a deterministic basis), those maps generally correspond to accelerations with a 2% probability of exceedance within a 50-year period. The earthquake associated with such accelerations is sometimes described as a "2500-year earthquake." To see why, let p be the unknown annual probability of exceedance of that level of acceleration:

The probability of exceedance in a particular year is:	p
The probability of non-exceedance in a particular year is:	$(1-p)$
The probability of non-exceedance in 50 consecutive years is:	$(1-p)^{50}$
The probability of exceedance within a 50-year period is:	$[1-(1-p)^{50}]$
Solve for p, the annual probability of exceedance. Set the probability of exceedance within the 50-year period equal to the given 2%:	$[1-(1-p)^{50}] = 0.02$ $(1-p)^{50} = 0.98$ $p = 1 - 0.98^{(1/50)}$ $p = 4.04 \times 10^{-4}$
The return period is the reciprocal of the annual probability of exceedance:	$1/p = 2475$
The approximate return period is:	2500 years

82 **Chapter Three**

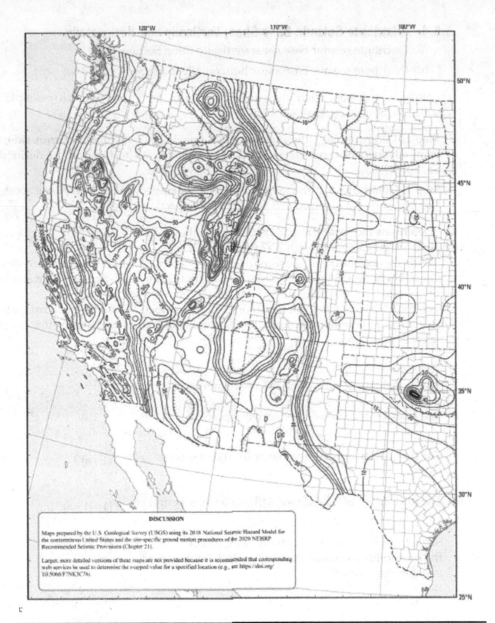

ASCE 7-22 FIGURE 22-1 S_{MS} for the default site conditions for the conterminous United States.

Code Basis for Structural Design of Masonry Buildings 83

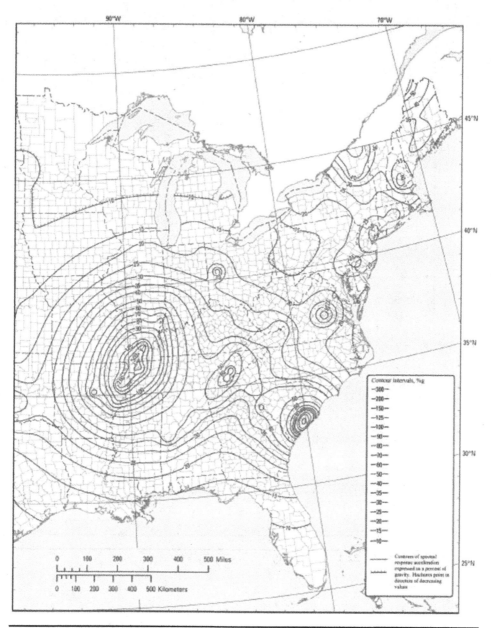

ASCE 7-22 FIGURE 22-1 (Continued)

84 Chapter Three

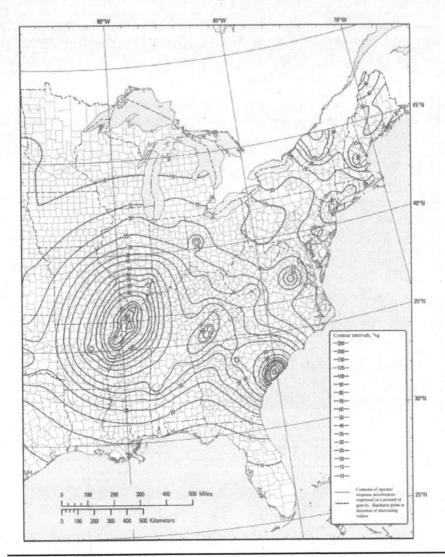

ASCE 7-22 Figure 22-1 (Continued)

Code Basis for Structural Design of Masonry Buildings 85

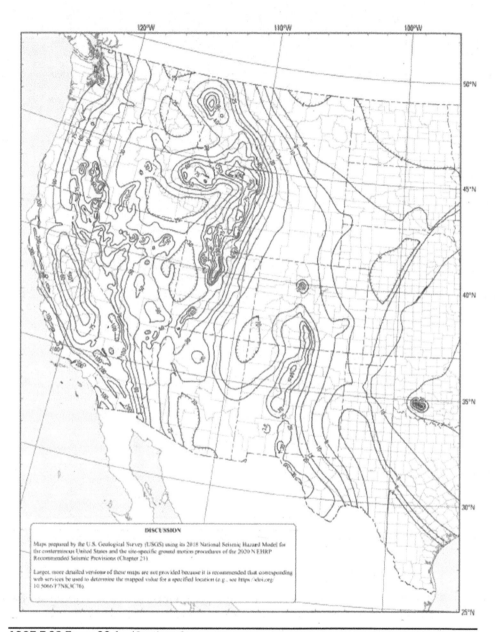

ASCE 7-22 FIGURE 22-1 *(Continued)*

86   Chapter Three

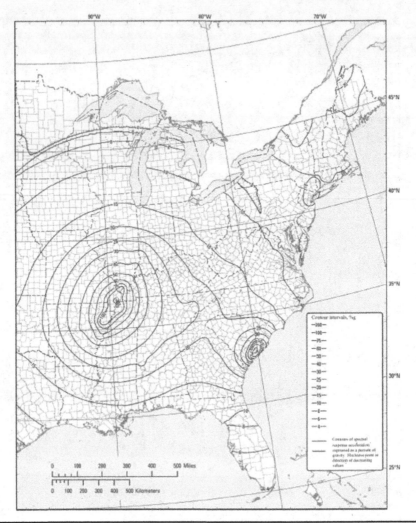

ASCE 7-22 Figure 22-2 S_{MS} for the default site conditions for the conterminous United States.

For Charleston, South Carolina, for example, $S_{MS} = 2.00g$, and $S_{M1} = 0.75g$.

Step 3: Determine the site class (A through F, a measure of soil response characteristics and soil stability) in accordance with Section 20.2 and Table 20.2-1.

Assume Site Class D (stiff soil).

Step 4: Determine the design response acceleration parameter for short periods, S_{DS}, and for a 1-s period, S_{D1}, using Equations 11.4-1 and 11.4-2, respectively.

The design response acceleration is two-thirds of the maximum considered acceleration:

$$S_{DS} = \frac{2}{3} \cdot S_{MS} \qquad (11.4\text{-}1)$$

$$S_{D1} = \frac{2}{3} \cdot S_{M1} \qquad (11.4\text{-}2)$$

Code Basis for Structural Design of Masonry Buildings 87

With the exception of some parts of the western United States (where design earthquakes have a deterministic basis), these design spectral ordinates correspond to an earthquake with a 10% probability of exceedance within a 50-year period. Such an earthquake is sometimes described as a "500-year earthquake." To see why, let p be the unknown annual probability of exceedance of that level of acceleration:

The probability of exceedance in a particular year is:	p
The probability of non-exceedance in a particular year is:	$(1-p)$
The probability of non-exceedance in 50 consecutive years is:	$(1-p)^{50}$
The probability of exceedance within a 50-year period is:	$[1-(1-p)^{50}]$
Solve for p, the annual probability of exceedance. Set the probability of exceedance within the 50-year period equal to the given 10%:	$[1-(1-p)^{50}]=0.10$
	$(1-p)^{50}=0.90$
	$p = 1 - 0.90^{(1/50)}$
	$p = 2.10 \times 10^{-3}$
The return period is the reciprocal of the annual probability of exceedance:	$1/p = 475$
The approximate return period is:	500 years

Continuing with our example for Charleston, South Carolina, the design response acceleration for short periods is:

$$S_{DS} = \frac{2}{3} \cdot S_{MS} = \frac{2}{3} \cdot 2.00g = 1.33g$$

and the design response acceleration for a 1-s period is:

$$S_{D1} = \frac{2}{3} \cdot S_{M1} = \frac{2}{3} \cdot 0.75g = 0.50g$$

Step 5: If required, determine the design response spectrum curve as prescribed by Section 11.4.5.2.

Because the equivalent lateral force procedure is being used, the response spectrum curve is not required. Nevertheless, for pedagogical completeness, it is developed here.

First, define $T_0 \equiv 0.2 \frac{S_{D1}}{S_{DS}}$ and $T_S \equiv \frac{S_{D1}}{S_{DS}}$.

Then for our case,

$$T_0 \equiv 0.2 \frac{S_{D1}}{S_{DS}} = 0.2 \left(\frac{0.50g}{1.33g} \right) = 0.08 \text{ sec}$$

$$T_S \equiv \frac{S_{D1}}{S_{DS}} = \left(\frac{0.50g}{1.33g} \right) = 0.38 \text{ sec}$$

- For periods less than or equal to T_0, the design spectral response acceleration, S_a, is given by Equation 11.4-5:

$$S_a = S_{DS}\left(0.4 + 0.6\frac{T}{T_0}\right) \quad (11.4\text{-}5)$$

- For periods greater than T_0 and less than or equal to T_S, the design spectral response acceleration, S_a, is equal to S_{DS}.
- For periods greater than T_S and less than or equal to T_L (from Figures 22-15 through 22-20), the design spectral response acceleration, S_a, is given by Equation 11.4-6. In our case, $T_L = 8$ s.

$$S_a = \frac{S_{D1}}{T} \quad (11.4\text{-}6)$$

- For periods greater than T_L, the design spectral response acceleration, S_a, is given by Equation 11.4-7:

$$S_a = \frac{S_{D1} T_L}{T^2} \quad (11.4\text{-}7)$$

The resulting design acceleration response spectrum is given in Fig. 3.12.

Step 6: Determine the structure's importance factor, I, and occupancy category using Section 11.5.

Assume that the structure is assigned an Occupancy Category II. This corresponds to an Importance Factor of 1.0.

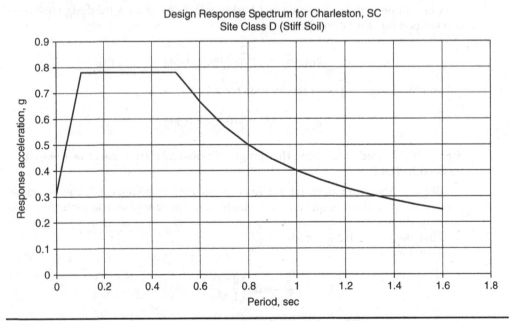

FIGURE 3.12 Design acceleration response spectrum, for example, problem.

Code Basis for Structural Design of Masonry Buildings

ASCE 7-22 TABLE 11.6-1 Seismic Design Category Based on Short Period Response Acceleration Parameter

Value of S_{DS}	Risk Category I, II, or III	Risk Category IV
$S_{DS} < 0.167$	A	A
$0.167 \leq S_{DS} < 0.33$	B	C
$0.33 \leq S_{DS} < 0.50$	C	D
$0.50 \leq S_{DS}$	D	D

Step 7: Determine the structure's seismic design category using Section 11.6.

Tables 11.6-1 and 11.6-2 must be checked, and the higher seismic design category from those two tables applies.

In our case, S_{DS} is 1.33, and S_{D1} is 0.50. Because S_{DS} exceeds 0.50 (Table 11.6-1) and S_{D1} exceeds 0.20 (Table 11.6-2), the structure is assigned to Seismic Design Category D.

Step 8: Calculate the structure's seismic base shear using Sections 12.8.1 and 12.8.2.

Step 9: Distribute seismic base shear vertically using Section 12.8.3.

Step 10: Distribute seismic base shear horizontally using Section 12.8.4.

These last three steps are structure-dependent. They depend on the seismic response modification coefficient assigned to the structural system, on the structure's plan structural irregularities, on the structure's vertical structural irregularities, and on the structure's redundancy.

Plan structural irregularities include the following:

- Plan eccentricities between the center of mass and the center of stiffness
- Reentrant corners
- Out-of-plane offsets
- Nonparallel systems

These can increase seismic response.

Vertical structural irregularities include the following:

- Stiffness irregularity
- Mass irregularity

ASCE 7-22 TABLE 11.6-2 Seismic Design Category Based on 1 s Period Response Acceleration Parameter

Value of S_{D1}	Risk Category I, II, or III	Risk Category IV
$S_{D1} < 0.067$	A	A
$0.067 \leq S_{D1} < 0.133$	B	C
$0.133 \leq S_{D1} < 0.20$	C	D
$0.20 \leq S_{D1}$	D	

- Vertical geometric irregularity
- In-plane discontinuity in vertical lateral-force-resisting elements
- Discontinuity in capacity—weak story

These can also increase seismic response.

Structures with low redundancy have a higher probability of failure, which is compensated for by increasing design seismic forces.

The above characteristics depend on the particular building, and are not addressed further here. They are addressed in an example problem at the end of this book.

3.6 Loading Combinations of the 2024 IBC

3.6.1 Strength Loading Combinations of the 2024 IBC (Section 1605.2.1)

Strength loading combinations from Section 1605.2.1 of the 2024 IBC are given here:

1. $1.4(D + F)$
2. $1.2(D + F + T) + 1.6(L + H) + 0.5(L_r \text{ or } S \text{ or } R)$
3. $1.2D + 1.6(L_r \text{ or } S \text{ or } R) + (L \text{ or } 0.8W)$
4. $1.2D + 1.0W + f_1 L + 0.5(L_r \text{ or } S \text{ or } R)$
5. $1.2D + 1.0E + f_1 L + f_2 S$
6. $0.9D + 1.0W + 1.6H$
7. $0.9D + 1.0E + 1.6H$

where f_1 = 1.0 for floors in places of public assembly, for live loads in excess of 100 pounds per square foot, and for parking garage live load, and
= 0.5 for other live loads

f_2 = 0.7 for roof configurations (such as saw tooth) that do not shed snow off the structure, and
= 0.2 for other roof configurations

and

D = dead load
E = combined effect of horizontal and vertical earthquake induced forces as defined in Section 12.4.2 of ASCE 7
F = load due to fluids with well-defined pressures and maximum heights
H = load due to lateral earth pressure, ground water pressure, or pressure of bulk materials
L = live load, except roof live load, including any permitted live load reduction
L_r = roof live load including any permitted live load reduction
R = rain load
S = snow load
T = self-straining force arising from contraction or expansion resulting from temperature change, shrinkage, moisture change, creep in component materials, movement due to differential settlement, or combinations thereof
W = wind load due to wind pressure

3.6.2 Basic Allowable-Stress Loading Combinations of the 2024 IBC (Section 1605.3.1)

Basic allowable-stress loading combinations from Section 1605.3.1 of the 2024 IBC are given here:

1. $D + F$
2. $D + H + F + L + T$
3. $D + H + F + (L_r$ or S or $R)$
4. $D + H + F + 0.75 (L + T) + 0.75 (L_r$ or S or $R)$
5. $D + H + F + (W$ or $0.7E)$
6. $D + H + F + 0.75 (W$ or $0.7E) + 0.75L + 0.75 (L_r$ or S or $R)$
7. $0.6D + W + H$
8. $0.6D + 0.7E + H$

where D = dead load
E = combined effect of horizontal and vertical earthquake induced forces as defined in Section 12.4.2 of ASCE 7
F = load due to fluids with well-defined pressures and maximum heights
H = load due to lateral earth pressure, ground water pressure, or pressure of bulk materials
L = live load, except roof live load, including any permitted live load reduction
L_r = roof live load including any permitted live load reduction.
R = rain load
S = snow load
T = self-straining force arising from contraction or expansion resulting from temperature change, shrinkage, moisture change, creep in component materials, movement due to differential settlement or combinations thereof
W = wind load due to wind pressure

Note on 1/3 Stress Increase

The allowable-stress provisions of the 2008 TMS/MSJC Code permitted allowable stresses to be increased by 1/3 for loading combinations involving wind or earthquake, for load standards that do not specifically prohibit such increase.

This 1/3 increase was based on experience only. No data exist to justify it based on rate effects, and because dead load always acts, there is no statistical justification for a reduction in wind or earthquake loading in combination with dead load. The 1/3 stress increase was in effect simply an extra increase in allowable stress for wind or earthquake loads. It might be justified in some cases by historically low allowable stresses for flexural reinforcement, but it does not seem justified in general. It was removed from the MSJC Code in 2011; at the same time, appropriate adjustments were made to allowable stresses.

The 2024 IBC specifically prohibits use of the 1/3 increase in conjunction with basic allowable-stress loading combinations (IBC 2024, Section 1605.3.1.1), while permitting use of the 1/3 stress increase in conjunction with the alternative allowable-stress loading combinations (IBC 2024, Section 1605.3.2). ASCE 7-22 specifically prohibits the use of the 1/3 increase. Because it is permitted in only limited circumstances, the 1/3 increase is not used in this book.

3.7 Summary of Strength Design Provisions of TMS 402-22

In Chapters 5 and 6 of this book, the strength design of masonry elements is discussed in detail. In this section, strength design provisions are summarized.

3.7.1 Strength Loading Combinations from Section 1605.2.1 of the 2024 IBC

Strength loading combinations from Section 1605.2.1 of the 2024 IBC are repeated here:

1. $1.4(D + F)$
2. $1.2(D + F + T) + 1.6(L + H) + 0.5(L_r \text{ or } S \text{ or } R)$
3. $1.2D + 1.6(L_r \text{ or } S \text{ or } R) + (L \text{ or } 0.8W)$
4. $1.2D + 1.6W + f_1 L + 0.5(L_r \text{ or } S \text{ or } R)$
5. $1.2D + 1.0E + f_1 L + f_2 S$
6. $0.9D + 1.6W + 1.6H$
7. $0.9D + 1.0E + 1.6H$

where $f_1 = 1.0$ for floors in places of public assembly, for live loads in excess of 100 pounds per square foot, and for parking garage live load, and
$\quad\quad = 0.5$ for other live loads
$\quad f_2 = 0.7$ for roof configurations (such as saw tooth) that do not shed snow off the structure, and
$\quad\quad = 0.2$ for other roof configurations

3.7.2 Strength-Reduction Factors from TMS 402-22, Section 9.1.4

Strength-reduction factors, taken from Section 9.1.4 of TMS 402-22, are summarized in Table 3.11.

TABLE 3.11 Strength-Reduction Factors

Combination of Actions	Strength-Reduction Factor
Combinations of flexure and axial load in reinforced masonry (tension controlled)	0.90
Combinations of flexure and axial load in reinforced masonry (compression controlled)	0.65
Shear	0.80
Anchor bolts, strength controlled by steel	0.90
Anchor bolts, strength controlled by masonry breakout, crushing, or pryout	0.50
Anchor bolts, strength controlled by pullout	0.65
Bearing	0.60

Source: Taken from Section 9.1.4 of TMS 402-22.

TABLE 3.12 Summary of Steps for Strength Design of Unreinforced Panel Walls

Design Step	Reference (TMS 402-22, TMS 602-22)
For most boundary conditions, assume all load will be taken by the vertical strip in the interior wythe. Check that strip for maximum stresses. Because axial stresses are zero, maximum compressive stress will not govern, nor will axial capacity reduced by slenderness effects. Because masonry is unreinforced, maximum tensile stresses will govern. So only tensile stresses need to be checked.	Code 9.1.4 Code 9.2.3 Code Table 9.1.9.1 Specification Table 1, Table 2
Check one-way shear (usually will not govern)	Code 9.1.4 Code 9.2.6

Source: TMS 402-22.

3.7.3 Summary of Steps for Strength Design of Unreinforced Panel Walls

Using TMS 402-22, steps for strength design of panel walls are summarized in Table 3.12.

3.7.4 Summary of Steps for Strength Design of Unreinforced Bearing Walls

Using TMS 402-22, steps for strength design of unreinforced bearing walls are summarized in Table 3.13.

3.7.5 Summary of Steps for Strength Design of Unreinforced Shear Walls

Using TMS 402-22, steps for strength design of unreinforced bearing walls are summarized in Table 3.14.

3.7.6 Summary of Steps for Strength Design of Reinforced Beams and Lintels

Using TMS 402-22, steps for strength design of reinforced beams and lintels are summarized in Table 3.15.

TABLE 3.13 Summary of Steps for Strength Design of Unreinforced Bearing Walls

Design Step	Reference (TMS 402-22, TMS 602-22)
Usually, all load is taken by vertical strips. Check typical vertical strip for slenderness-dependent axial capacity, maximum compressive stresses, and maximum tensile stresses.	Code 9.1.4 Code 9.2.3 Specification Table 1, Table 2
Check one-way shear (usually will not govern)	Code 9.1.4 Code 9.2.6

Source: TMS 402-22.

TABLE 3.14 Summary of Steps for Strength Design of Unreinforced Shear Walls

Design Step	Reference (TMS 402-22, TMS 602-22)
Check in-plane flexural capacity.	Code 9.1.4 Code 9.2.3 Specification Table 1, Table 2
Check in-plane shear capacity. Verify ability of roof diaphragm to transfer horizontal reactions to shear walls.	Code 9.1.4 Code 9.2.6

Source: TMS 402-22.

TABLE 3.15 Summary of Steps for Strength Design of Reinforced Beams and Lintels

Design Step	Reference (TMS 402-22, TMS 602-22)
Check that depth is sufficient to ensure that shear can be resisted by masonry alone, without shear reinforcement.	Code 9.1.4 Code 9.3.3.1.2 Specification Table 1, Table 2
Compute required flexural reinforcement, approximating internal lever arm as $0.9d$. Revise if necessary. $M_n \approx A_s f_y \, 0.9 d$ Check nominal moment versus cracking capacity. Check maximum reinforcement.	Code 9.1.4 Code 9.3.2 Code 9.3.3.2.2 Code 9.3.2.4

Source: TMS 402-22.

3.7.7 Summary of Steps for Strength Design of Reinforced Curtain Walls

Using TMS 402-22, steps for strength design of reinforced curtain walls are summarized in Table 3.16.

TABLE 3.16 Summary of Steps for Strength Design of Reinforced Curtain Walls

Design Step	Reference (TMS 402-22, TMS 602-22)
All load must be taken by horizontal strips. Check that strip for stresses. Usually, reinforcement will be needed. Estimate required reinforcement using $jd = d - d'$, then recalculate if necessary: $M_n = A_s f_y (d - d')$	Code 9.1.4 Code 9.3.2 Specification Table 1, Table 2
Check one-way shear (usually will not govern)	Code 9.1.4 Code 9.3.3.1.2.1

Source: TMS 402-22.

TABLE 3.17 Summary of Steps for Strength Design of Reinforced Bearing Walls

Design Step	Reference (TMS 402-22, TMS 602-22)
Usually, all load is taken by vertical strips. Verify ability of roof diaphragm to transfer horizontal reactions from those strips. Check typical vertical strip for stresses using column interaction diagram.	Code 9.1.4 Code 9.3.2 Specification Table 1, Table 2
Check one-way shear out of plane (usually will not govern).	Code 9.1.4 Code 9.3.3.1.2

Source: TMS 402-22.

3.7.8 Summary of Steps for Strength Design of Reinforced Bearing Walls

Using TMS 402-22, steps for strength design of reinforced bearing walls are summarized in Table 3.17.

3.7.9 Summary of Steps for Strength Design of Reinforced Shear Walls

Using TMS 402-22, steps for strength design of reinforced shear walls are summarized in Table 3.18.

3.8 Summary of Allowable Stress Design Provisions of TMS 402-22

In Chapters 7 and 8 of this book, the allowable-stress design of masonry elements is discussed in detail. In this section, allowable-stress design provisions are summarized.

3.8.1 Allowable-Stress Loading Combinations from Section 1605.3.1 of the 2024 IBC

Allowable-stress loading combinations from Section 1605.3.1 of the 2024 IBC are repeated below:

1. $D + F$

TABLE 3.18 Summary of Steps for Strength Design of Reinforced Shear Walls

Design Step	Reference (TMS 402-22, TMS 602-22)
Check for in-plane flexure plus axial loads.	Code 9.1.4 Code 9.2.2
Check maximum reinforcement.	Code 9.3.3.2.4 Specification Table 1, Table 2
Check in-plane shear capacity.	Code 9.1.4
Verify ability of roof diaphragm to transfer horizontal reactions to shear walls.	Code 9.3.3.1.2

Source: TMS 402-22.

2. $D + H + F + L + T$
3. $D + H + F + (L_r \text{ or } S \text{ or } R)$
4. $D + H + F + 0.75 (L + T) + 0.75 (L_r \text{ or } S \text{ or } R)$
5. $D + H + F + (W \text{ or } 0.7E)$
6. $D + H + F + 0.75 (W \text{ or } 0.7E) + 0.75L + 0.75 (L_r \text{ or } S \text{ or } R)$
7. $0.6D + W + H$
8. $0.6D + 0.7E + H$

3.8.2 Summary of Steps for Allowable-Stress Design of Unreinforced Panel Walls

Using TMS 402-22, steps for allowable-stress design of unreinforced panel walls are summarized in Table 3.19.

3.8.3 Summary of Steps for Allowable-Stress Design of Unreinforced Bearing Walls

Using TMS 402-22, steps for allowable-stress design of unreinforced bearing walls are summarized in Table 3.20.

3.8.4 Summary of Steps for Allowable-Stress Design of Unreinforced Shear Walls

Using TMS 402-22, steps for allowable-stress design of unreinforced bearing walls are summarized in Table 3.21.

3.8.5 Summary of Steps for Allowable-Stress Design of Reinforced Beams and Lintels

Using TMS 402-22, steps for allowable-stress design of reinforced beams and lintels are summarized in Table 3.22.

TABLE 3.19 Summary of Steps for Allowable-Stress Design of Unreinforced Panel Walls

Design Step	Reference (TMS 402-22, TMS 602-22)
For most boundary conditions, assume all load will be taken by the vertical strip in the interior wythe. Check that strip for stresses. Because axial stresses are zero, f_a/F_a will always be zero, and buckling will never govern. Because masonry is unreinforced, tensile stresses will govern. So only tensile stresses need to be checked.	Code 8.2.4.2 Code Table 8.2.4.2
Check one-way shear (usually will not govern) $f_v = \dfrac{VQ}{I_n b} = \dfrac{3}{2} \dfrac{V}{A_n}$	Code Equation 8-15 Code 8.2.6

Source: TMS 402-22.

TABLE 3.20 Summary of Steps for Allowable-Stress Design of Unreinforced Bearing Walls

Design Step	Reference (TMS 402-22, TMS 602-22)
Usually, all load is taken by vertical strips. Check typical vertical strip for compressive stresses. Use unity equation: $$\frac{f_a}{F_a} + \frac{f_b}{F_b} \leq 1$$ F_a depends on slenderness and f'_m. F_b is $(1/3)\, f'_m$.	Code Equation 8-9 Code Equations 8-11, 8-12 Specification Table 1, Table 2 Code Equation 8-13
Check that strip for tensile stresses.	Code Table 8.2.4.2
Check that strip for buckling.	Code Equation 8-14
Check one-way shear out of plane (usually will not govern) $$f_v = \frac{VQ}{I_n b} = \frac{3}{2}\frac{V}{A_n}$$	Code Equation 8-15 Code 8.2.6

Source: TMS 402-22.

TABLE 3.21 Summary of Steps for Allowable-Stress Design of Unreinforced Shear Walls

Design Step	Reference (TMS 402-22, TMS 602-22)
Check for in-plane shear: $$f_v = \frac{VQ}{I_n b} = \frac{3}{2}\frac{V}{A_n}$$	Code Equation 8-15 Code 8.2.6 Specification Table 1, Table 2
Verify ability of roof diaphragm to transfer horizontal reactions to shear walls.	
Check for in-plane flexure plus axial loads: $$f_t = \frac{Mc}{I} - \frac{P}{A} \leq F_t$$	Code 8.2.4.2

Source: TMS 402-22.

TABLE 3.22 Summary of Steps for Allowable-Stress Design of Reinforced Beams and Lintels

Design Step	Reference (TMS 402-22, TMS 602-22)
Check that depth is sufficient to ensure that shear can be resisted by masonry alone, without shear reinforcement.	Code 8.2.6 Specification Table 1, Table 2
Compute required flexural reinforcement, approximating internal lever arm as $0.9d$. Revise if necessary. $$M \approx A_s F_s \left(\frac{7}{8}\right) d$$	Code 8.3.2

Source: TMS 402-22.

TABLE 3.23 Summary of Steps for Allowable-Stress Design of Reinforced Curtain Walls

Design Step	Reference (TMS 402-22, TMS 602-22)
All load must be taken by horizontal strips. Check that strip for stresses. Usually, reinforcement will be needed. Estimate required reinforcement using $k = 3/8$, $j = 7/8$, then calculate k and j and check: $$f_s = \frac{M_o}{A_s jd} \qquad f_m = \frac{2M_o}{jkbd^2}$$ $f_s \leq F_s \qquad f_m \leq F_m$ Allowable stress in masonry is $(1/3) f'_m$.	Code 8.3.3.2 Code 8.3.2 Specification Table 1, Table 2
Check one-way shear (usually will not govern): $$f_v = \frac{V}{A_{nv}}$$	Code Equation 8-19 Code 8.3.5

Source: TMS 402-22.

3.8.6 Summary of Steps for Allowable-Stress Design of Reinforced Curtain Walls

Using TMS 402-22, steps for allowable-stress design of reinforced curtain walls are summarized in Table 3.23.

3.8.7 Summary of Steps for Allowable-Stress Design of Reinforced Bearing Walls

Using TMS 402-22, steps for strength design of reinforced bearing walls are summarized in Table 3.24.

TABLE 3.24 Summary of Steps for Allowable-Stress Design of Reinforced Bearing Walls

Design Step	Reference (TMS 402-22, TMS 602-22)
Usually, all load is taken by vertical strips. Verify ability of roof diaphragm to transfer horizontal reactions from those strips. Check typical vertical strip for stresses using column interaction diagram. Allowable stress in masonry is $(1/3) f'_m$.	Code 8.3.2 Code 8.3.4 Specification Table 1, Table 2
Check one-way shear out of plane (usually will not govern) $$f_v = \frac{V}{A_{nv}}$$	Code Equation 8-19 Code 8.3.5

Source: TMS 402-22.

TABLE 3.25 Summary of Steps for Strength Design of Reinforced Shear Walls (TMS 402-22)

Design Step	Reference (TMS 402-22, TMS 602-22)
Check for in-plane shear: $f_v = \dfrac{V}{A_{nv}}$ Verify ability of roof diaphragm to transfer horizontal reactions to shear walls.	Code Equation 8-19 Code 8.3.5.1.3 (default case) or Code 8.3.5.1.4 (steel resists all shear) Specification Table 1, Table 2
Check for in-plane flexure plus axial loads. See "Reinforced Bearing Walls" above.	Code 8.3.4.1 Code 8.3.3 Code 8.3.4.2.2

3.8.8 Summary of Steps for Allowable-Stress Design of Reinforced Shear Walls

Using TMS 402-22, steps for strength design of reinforced shear walls are summarized in Table 3.25.

3.9 Additional Information on Code Basis for Structural Design of Masonry Buildings

In this section are given the complete names and addresses of United States technical specialty organizations, industry organizations, governmental organizations, and model-code organizations.

3.9.1 Technical Specialty Organizations Related to Masonry

American Concrete Institute
38800 Country Club Drive
Farmington Hills, MI 48331
www.aci-int.org

American Institute of Steel Construction
130 East Randolph, Suite 2000,
Chicago, IL 60601
www.aisc.org

American Society of Civil Engineers
1801 Alexander Bell Drive
Reston, VA 20191
www.asce.org

TMS (The Masonry Society)
www.masonrysociety.org

3.9.2 Industry Organizations Related to Masonry

Brick Industry Association
www.bia.org

International Masonry Institute
www.imiweb.org

Concrete Masonry Hardscapes Association—Formerly National Concrete Masonry Association
www.ncma.org

Prestressed Concrete Institute
www.pci.org

Mason Contractors Association of America
www.masoncontractors.org

Portland Cement Association
www.cement.org

3.9.3 Model Code Development Organizations

International Code Council Headquarters
www.iccsafe.org

National Fire Protection Association
www.nfpa.org

3.9.4 Specification Development Organizations

American Society for Testing and Materials, Inc.
www.astm.org

3.9.5 Governmental Organizations

Building Seismic Safety Council
https://www.nibs.org/bssc

3.9.6 Other Organizations

American National Standards Institute, Inc.
www.ansi.org

CHAPTER 4

Introduction to TMS 402 Treatment of Structural Design

4.1 Basic Mechanical Behavior of Masonry

Masonry is a composite material, comprising units, mortar, grout, and accessory materials. Because of this, its mechanical behavior is complex. Using nonlinear finite-element analysis, addressing the behavior of constituent materials and of the interface relationships between them, it is possible to describe the force-deformation behavior of masonry elements.

For design, however, this approach is neither practical nor necessary. For design purposes, masonry is normally idealized as an isotropic material, with nonlinear stress-strain behavior in compression (much like concrete), and linear stress-strain behavior in tension. Compressive capacity is governed by crushing (often characterized by complex local behavior), and tensile capacity, by the bond strength between units and mortar.

The crushing strength of masonry can be evaluated by compression tests on masonry prisms. Design of masonry elements is based on a specified compressive strength of masonry, f'_m, whose role is analogous to that of the specified compressive strength of concrete, f'_c, in concrete design. The specified compressive strength of masonry is the basis for design and forms part of the contract documents. Those contract documents require verification that the masonry complies with the specified compressive strength, either by compression tests of prisms or by conservative relationships involving the compressive strengths of the units and the type of mortar. These are addressed in the *TMS 402 Code* and the *TMS 602 Specification* for masonry.

One advantage of using the conservative relationships involving the compressive strengths of the units and the type of mortar (the so-called "unit strength method" from Tables 1 and 2 of the *TMS 602 Specification*) is that it is possible to verify compliance with the specified compressive strength f'_m with no project-specific material testing whatsoever. The compressive strength of the units is verified by the manufacturer as part of quality control and compliance with the unit specification. The mortar can be specified by proportion, and compliance with that specification is verified by verifying proportions (no mortar testing). The grout can be specified by proportion, and compliance with that specification is verified by verifying proportions (no grout testing). The minimum probable strength of the masonry is then obtained from Table 1 or Table 2 of the *TMS 602 Specification*. Material tests can be performed for quality control or to verify compliance with a specified strength, but they are not necessary if the designer chooses specification criteria that do not require testing.

Masonry elements requiring structural calculation are designed using the specified compressive strength, verified as noted above, and prescribed tensile bond strengths based on extensive experimental investigation.

4.2 Classification of Masonry Elements

Masonry elements can be designed in at least two ways:

- According to their structural function.
- According to the approach used to design them.

4.3 Classification of Masonry Elements by Structural Function

- *Nonload-bearing masonry*: Supports vertical loads from self-weight only, plus possibly loads from out-of-plane wind or earthquake.
- *Load-bearing masonry*: Supports vertical loads from roof or overlying floors, plus possibly loads from in-plane shear, plus possibly loads from out-of-plane wind or earthquake.
- *Participating elements*: Masonry walls that are part of the seismic force resisting system.

Although these two types of masonry can be approached using exactly the same tools of engineering mechanics, they have been distinguished historically.

4.4 Classification of Masonry Elements by Design Intent

- *Unreinforced masonry*: It is designed assuming that flexural tensile stresses are resisted by masonry, and that the presence of any reinforcement is neglected in design. "Unreinforced masonry" can therefore actually have reinforcement in it, for structural integrity or by prescription. That reinforcement, however, is neglected in design calculations. Design is carried out in the linear elastic range.
- *Reinforced masonry*: It is designed assuming that flexural tensile stresses cannot be resisted by masonry and are resisted by reinforcement only. Shear stresses can be resisted by masonry or by reinforcement, singly or in combination. Design can be carried out by allowable stress design, or by strength design. Using this definition, unreinforced masonry can actually have reinforcement (for integrity or to meet prescriptive requirements).

4.5 Design Approaches for Masonry Elements

- *Strength design*: In strength design, design actions (axial forces, shears and moments) are computed using service loads, and are then increased by load factors. The factored design actions are then compared with nominal member strengths, decreased by strength-reduction factors (ϕ-factors).

$$\text{service actions} \times \text{LF} \leq \phi \times \text{nominal capacity}$$

- *Allowable-stress design*: In allowable-stress design, stresses corresponding to service loads are compared with allowable stresses. Historically, because early versions of legacy model codes used design loads that were calibrated for service levels, their allowable-stress design provisions used unfactored loads. More recently, as design loads are calibrated for strength levels, it is necessary to introduce allowable-stress load factors into allowable-stress loading combinations. In this book, the words "allowable-stress" are used to describe those load factors to avoid possible confusion with the load factors used for strength design. The allowable stresses are material strengths, reduced by a factor of safety. Factors of safety for masonry typically range from 2.5 to 4.

$$\text{stresses from service loads} \leq \frac{\text{failure stresses}}{\text{safety factor}}$$

The two design approaches (strength design and allowable-stress design) can each have the same result and also the same level of safety (measured in terms of probability of failure under service loads). In strength design, the probability of failure depends on the quotient of the load factor and the capacity reduction factor (ϕ-factor). In allowable-stress design, the probability of failure is controlled directly by the factor of safety applied to failure stresses and also (in modern codes) by allowable-stress load factors.

Most modern codes are based on strength design because it gives a more uniform factor of safety against collapse.

- *Veneer design*: According to Chapter 13 of the *TMS 402 Code*, masonry veneer is designed prescriptively through control of connector type and spacing. Design of veneer is not discussed further in this book.

- *Glass-block masonry design*: Design of glass unit masonry is addressed by Chapter 14 of the *TMS 402 Code*. It is not discussed further in this book.

- *AAC masonry design*: Design of autoclaved aerated concrete (AAC) masonry is addressed by Chapter 11 of the *TMS 402 Code*. It is covered in detail in the last chapter of this book.

4.6 How Reinforcement Is Used in Masonry Elements

4.6.1 How Reinforcement Is Used in Masonry Beams and Lintels

These require horizontal reinforcement placed in hollow bond-beam units, or in fully grouted cavities between wythes of solid clay masonry units. Examples of these are shown in Figs. 4.1 and 4.2, respectively. As noted in later sections dealing with the

104 Chapter Four

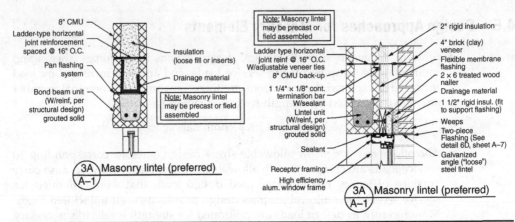

FIGURE 4.1 Examples of reinforcement in CMU lintels. (*Source:* http://www.mim-online.org/engineers/masonry-lintels, Masonry Institute of Michigan.)

design of masonry beams and lintels, it is not necessary to use so-called "trough units" in concrete masonry; ordinary stretcher units can be used if supported by a shoring board.

4.6.2 How Reinforcement Is Used in Masonry Curtain Walls

Masonry curtain walls are normally single-wythe, made of clay masonry units. Reinforcement is oriented horizontally and is placed in bed joints. The reinforcement can be bed-joint reinforcement or smooth (No. 2) bars. Deformed bars cannot be used because the outer diameter of their deformations normally exceeds the specified width of a bed joint (3/8 in.). Also, the *TMS 402 Code* requires that deformed reinforcement be surrounded by grout.

4.6.3 How Reinforcement Is Used in Masonry Walls

When solid units are used, masonry walls are reinforced horizontally with bed joint reinforcement. Alternatively, the wall can be constructed in two wythes and a curtain

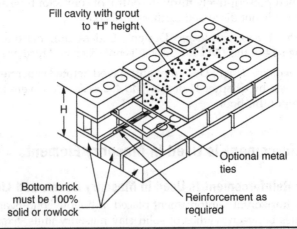

FIGURE 4.2 Examples of reinforcement in clay masonry lintels. (*Source:* Figure 7 of BIA Technical Note 7B.)

Introduction to TMS 402 Treatment of Structural Design

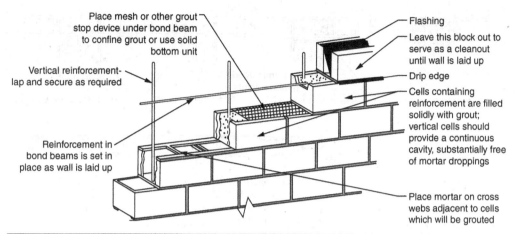

FIGURE 4.3 Example of placement of reinforcement in a masonry wall made of hollow units. (*Source:* Figure 1 of CMHA TEK 3-2A.)

of reinforcement is placed between the wythes, and grout is then poured between the wythes.

In other countries (but rarely in the United States), masonry walls laid with solid units are reinforced by continuous horizontal and vertical elements of reinforced concrete. This type of masonry is sometimes referred to as "confined masonry."

When masonry walls are made of hollow units, vertical reinforcement is placed in grouted cells, and horizontal reinforcement either consists of bed-joint reinforcement, placed in the bed joints, or deformed horizontal reinforcement, placed in bond-beam units or units with cut-out webs. An example of this is shown in Fig. 4.3.

4.6.4 How Reinforcement Is Used in Masonry Columns and Pilasters

In the context of the *TMS 402 Code*, a column is an isolated element, meeting certain dimensional restrictions, that carries axial load and moment. A pilaster is an element that forms part of a wall and projects out from the plane of the wall. Masonry columns and pilasters can be made with solid units or hollow units. If solid units are used, they are formed to make a box. A cage of reinforcement is placed in the box, which is then filled with grout or concrete. In such applications, the solid masonry units are essentially used as stay-in-place cover and formwork with structural function. If hollow units are used, they are laid in an overlapping pattern. Reinforcement is placed in the cells, which are then filled with grout. Examples of the placement of hollow units to form pilasters are shown in Fig. 4.4.

4.6.5 Nomenclature Associated with Reinforced Masonry

As we have discussed, "unreinforced masonry" may actually have reinforcement in it but is designed ignoring the structural action of that reinforcement. Nominal reinforcement is placed at corners, around openings, and in bond beams at the tops of walls, primarily for general structural integrity.

Whenever reinforcement is considered in design, the masonry is in general referred to as "reinforced." Because masonry is a regional tradition in the United States, however,

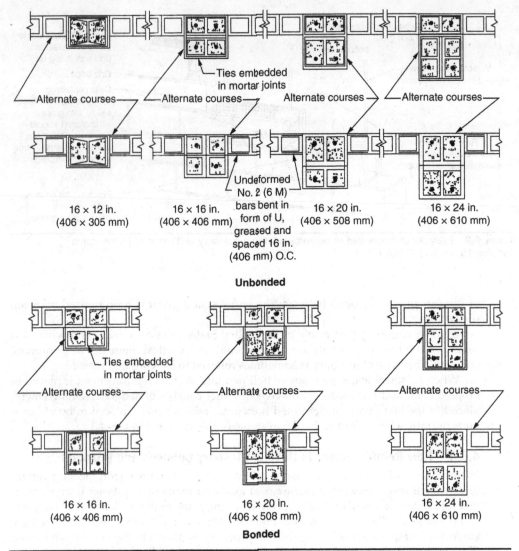

FIGURE 4.4 Examples of the placement of hollow units to form pilasters. (*Source:* Figure 1 of NCMA TEK 17-4B.)

some terms associated with reinforced masonry have historically meant different things in different parts of the country.

- East of Denver (approximately), masonry with bed-joint reinforcement only (such curtain wall), has historically been referred to as "partially reinforced" masonry. This term was introduced to make this type of reinforced masonry seem less intimidating to masons who were not used to using any reinforcement at all. As explained below, this term has historically meant something completely different west of Denver.

- West of Denver, in regions where the Uniform Building Code formerly dominated, seismic resistance has traditionally been very important. After significant damage and deaths of school children in the Long Beach earthquake of 1933, masonry construction was revived only on the condition that it be reinforced similarly to the reinforced concrete shear walls of the time. That new type of masonry construction, referred to as "reinforced masonry," required that the combined percentage of horizontal and vertical wall reinforcement be not less than 0.002, and that the percentage of reinforcement in each single direction (horizontal and vertical) be not less than one-third of this total, or 0.0007. That is,

$$\rho_h + \rho_v \geq 0.002$$
$$\rho_h \geq 0.0007$$
$$\rho_v \geq 0.0007$$

West of Denver, masonry so reinforced has historically been referred to as "fully reinforced masonry."

- West of Denver, masonry with reinforcement not meeting those requirements has historically been referred to as "partially reinforced masonry."

When a relatively small amount of reinforcement is used, it can be placed in individually grouted cells, confining elements of reinforced concrete, bed joints, and bond beams. When relatively larger amounts of reinforcement are required, it is often more cost-effective to grout the wall completely.

4.7 How This Book Classifies Masonry Elements

In this book, masonry elements are distinguished first by strength design versus allowable-stress design; then by whether they are designed as unreinforced or reinforced; and finally by their structural function.

4.7.1 Structural Design of Unreinforced Masonry Elements by the Strength Approach

4.7.1.1 Nonbearing Elements

- Unreinforced panel walls

4.7.1.2 Bearing Elements

- Unreinforced bearing walls with eccentric gravity load
- Unreinforced bearing walls with eccentric gravity load plus out-of-plane load
- Effect of openings on bearing walls
- Unreinforced shear walls

4.7.2 Structural Design of Reinforced Masonry Elements by the Strength Approach

- Reinforced beams and lintels
- Curtain walls with horizontal reinforcement only
- Reinforced bearing walls with eccentric gravity load
- Reinforced bearing walls with eccentric gravity load plus out-of-plane load
- Effect of openings on bearing walls
- Reinforced shear walls

4.7.3 Elements Designed by the Allowable-Stress Approach

4.7.4 Structural Design of Unreinforced Masonry Elements by the Strength Approach

4.7.4.1 Nonbearing Elements

- Unreinforced panel walls

4.7.4.2 Bearing Elements

- Unreinforced bearing walls with eccentric gravity load
- Unreinforced bearing walls with eccentric gravity load plus out-of-plane load
- Effect of openings on bearing walls
- Unreinforced shear walls

4.7.5 Structural Design of Reinforced Masonry Elements by the Strength Approach

- Reinforced beams and lintels
- Curtain walls with horizontal reinforcement only
- Reinforced bearing walls with eccentric gravity load
- Reinforced bearing walls with eccentric gravity load plus out-of-plane load
- Effect of openings on bearing walls
- Reinforced shear walls

In each case, we shall use both the strength provisions and the allowable-stress provisions of the *TMS 402 Code*. We shall compare the results of those provisions.

4.7.6 Design of Overall Buildings by the Strength Approach

Design of individual elements is followed by strength design of overall buildings, with one example of a low-rise building and one example of a high-rise building.

4.7.7 Design of Autoclaved Aerated Concrete Masonry

Finally, a chapter is devoted to autoclaved aerated concrete masonry, an innovative construction material.

CHAPTER 5
Strength Design of Unreinforced Masonry Elements

5.1 Strength Design of Unreinforced Panel Walls

5.1.1 Examples of Use of Unreinforced Panel Walls

Panel walls commonly comprise the masonry envelope surrounding reinforced concrete or steel frames. In the context of TMS 402-22, a panel wall would be termed a "multiwythe, noncomposite" wall. An example of an unreinforced panel wall is shown in Fig. 5.1.

The outer wythes of panel walls must span horizontally. They cannot span vertically, because of the open expansion joint under each shelf angle. Support conditions for the horizontally spanning outer wythe can be simple or continuous. An example of the connection of a panel wall to a column is shown in the horizontal section of Fig. 5.2. A simple support condition would be achieved by inserting a vertically oriented expansion joint in the clay masonry wythe on both sides of the column.

The inner wythes of panel walls can span horizontally and vertically.

As a result, it is convenient to visualize panel walls as being composed of sets of vertical and horizontal crossing strips in each wythe. This is shown schematically in Fig. 5.3.

At the end of this section, it will be shown that

- Because of their aspect ratio, the inner wythe can almost always be considered to span in the vertical direction only.
- It is simple and only slightly conservative to design single-wythe panel walls as though the vertical strips resisted all out-of-plane load.
- It is simple and only slightly conservative to design two-wythe panel walls as though the vertical strips of the inner wythe resisted all out-of-plane load.

5.1.2 Flexural Design of Panel Walls Using Strength Provisions of *TMS 402-22*

According to the strength provisions of TMS 402-22, nominal flexural capacity of unreinforced masonry is computed assuming linear stress-strain relationships. Nominal flexural capacity corresponds to a maximum flexural compressive stress of $0.80 f'_m$, or a

110   Chapter Five

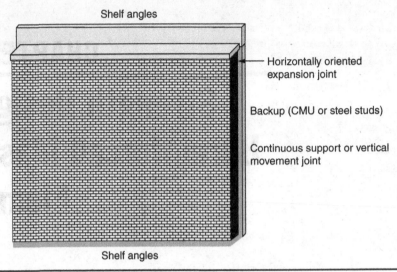

Figure 5.1   Example of an unreinforced panel wall.

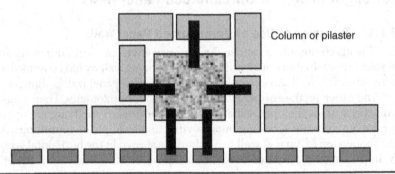

Figure 5.2   Horizontal section showing connection of a panel wall to a column.

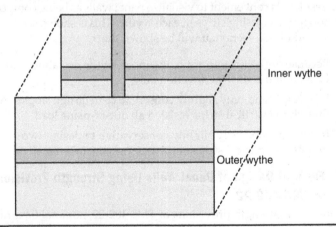

Figure 5.3   Schematic representation of an unreinforced, two-wythe panel wall as two sets of horizontal and vertical crossing strips.

maximum flexural tensile stress equal to the modulus of rupture. Because the modulus of rupture is much lower than $0.80 f'_m$, it governs. Design actions are factored, and design capacities are computed using those nominal capacities and the appropriate strength-reduction factor.

5.1.2.1 Load Factors

Load factors are as discussed previously. As prescribed in Section 1605.2 of the 2024 IBC, the two loading combinations involving wind are:

1. $1.2D + 1.0W + f_1 L + 0.5 (L_r$ or S or $R)$
2. $0.9D + 1.0W + 1.6H$

Of these, the second will usually govern. Both combinations have a load factor for W of 1.0.

5.1.2.2 Modulus of Rupture

For strength design, the nominal flexural strength is to be computed using the modulus of rupture values given in Table 9.1.9.1 of TMS 402-22. Those values are intended to be 2.5 times the corresponding allowable stresses of TMS 402-22. TMS 402-22 provides different nominal capacities for flexural tension normal to bed joints, and parallel to bed joints in running bond. Capacities are higher parallel to bed joints in running bond because of the interlocking of units laid in that bond pattern. Allowable flexural tension is zero parallel to bed joints in stack bond, unless they are resisted by a continuous grout section parallel to the bed joints.

TABLE 5.1 Modulus of Rupture (Table 9.1.9.1 of TMS 402-22)

	PCL or Mortar Cement		Masonry Cement or Air-Entrained PCL	
Masonry Type	M or S	N	M or S	N
Normal to bed joints				
Solid units	133	100	80	51
Hollow units[1]				
Ungrouted	84	64	51	31
Fully grouted	163	158	153	145
Parallel to bed joints in running bond				
Solid units	267	200	160	100
Hollow units				
Ungrouted and partially grouted	167	127	100	64
Fully grouted	267	200	160	100
Parallel to bed joints in stack bond				
Continuous grout section parallel to bed joints	335	335	335	335
Other	0	0	0	0

5.1.2.3 Strength-Reduction Factors

Strength-reduction factors are as discussed previously. For combinations of flexure and axial load in unreinforced masonry, $\phi = 0.60$ (Section 9.1.4.3 of TMS 402-22).

5.1.3 Example: Strength Design of a Single-Wythe Panel Wall Using Solid Units

Check the design of the panel wall shown in Fig. 5.4, for a wind load w of 32 lb/ft², using PCL mortar, Type N, and units with a nominal thickness of 8 in.

The panel wall will be designed as unreinforced masonry. The design follows the following steps, using a nominal thickness of 8 in. The panel could be designed as a two-way panel. Nevertheless, because of its aspect ratio, the vertical strips will carry practically all the load. Therefore, design it as a one-way panel, consisting of a series of vertically spanning, simply supported strips.

Calculate the maximum factored design bending moment and corresponding factored design flexural tensile stress in a strip 1-ft wide, with a nominal thickness of 8 in.:

$$M_{u\,max} = \frac{w_u \ell^2}{8} = \frac{1.0 \times 32 \text{ lb/ft} (8 \text{ ft})^2}{8} \times 12 \text{ in./ft} = 3072 \text{ lb-in.}$$

$$f_t = \frac{Mc}{I} = \frac{3072 \text{ lb-in.} \times (7.625/2) \text{ in.}}{\left[12 \text{ in.} \times (7.625 \text{ in.})^3 / 12\right]} = 26.4 \text{ lb/in}^2$$

The factored flexural tensile stress, 26.4 lb/in², is less than the modulus of rupture normal to bed joints for solid units and Type N PCL mortar (100 lb/in²), reduced by a

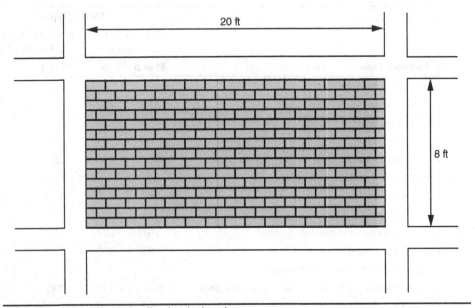

FIGURE 5.4 Example panel wall to be designed.

strength-reduction factor of 0.6, or 60 lb/in². The design is therefore satisfactory. We should also check one-way (beam) shear. An example of this is given later.

5.1.4 Example: Strength Design of a Single-Wythe Panel Wall Using Hollow Units

Check the design of the panel wall of the example of Section 5.1.3 for a wind load w of 32 lb/ft², using PCL mortar, Type N, and assuming hollow units with face shells and cross-webs mortared.

The panel wall will be designed as unreinforced masonry. The design follows the following steps, using a nominal thickness of 8 in. The panel could be designed as a two-way panel. Nevertheless, because of its aspect ratio, the vertical strips will carry practically all the load. Therefore, design it as a one-way panel, consisting of a series of vertically spanning, simply supported strips.

Calculate the maximum bending moment and corresponding flexural tensile stress in a strip 1-ft wide, with a nominal thickness of 8 in. Assume that the head joints are only 1.25-in. thick. All length dimensions are in inches. These dimensions are shown in Fig. 5.5. The wall thicknesses given below are consistent with the dimensions assumed in NCMA TEK 14-13B (Concrete Masonry Wall Weights). They are not necessarily the minimum wall thicknesses permitted by ASTM C90.

Illustrate the computation of section properties for this cross-section:

$$A = A_{solid} - A_{cells} - A_{head\,joint}$$

$$A = (16)(7.63) - (15.63 - 3 \cdot 1.00)(7.63 - 2 \cdot 1.25) - 0.37(7.63 - 2 \cdot 1.25)$$

$$A = 122.1 - 64.8 - 1.9 = 55.4 \text{ in}^2 \quad \text{for a 16-in. wide strip}$$

$$A = 55.4 \text{ in}^2 \left(\frac{12 \text{ in.}}{16 \text{ in.}}\right) = 41.5 \text{ in}^2 \quad \text{for a 12-in. wide strip}$$

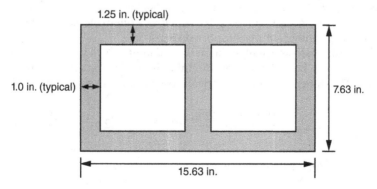

FIGURE 5.5 Idealized cross-sectional dimensions of a nominal 8 × 8 × 16 in. concrete masonry unit.

$$I = I_{solid} - I_{cells} - I_{head\,joint}$$

$$I = \frac{(16)(7.625)^3}{12} - \frac{(15.625 - 3 \cdot 1.00)(7.625 - 2 \cdot 1.25)^3}{12} - \frac{0.375(7.625 - 2 \cdot 1.25)^3}{12}$$

$$I = 591.1 - 141.6 - 4.2 = 445.3 \text{ in}^4 \text{ per 16 in. of width}$$

$$I = 445.3 \left(\frac{12}{16}\right) = 334.0 \text{ in}^4 \text{ per 12 in. of width}$$

$$c = \frac{7.625}{2} = 3.81 \text{ in.}$$

For the 12-in. wide strip,

$$M_{u\,max} = \frac{w_u \ell^2}{8} = \frac{1.0 \times 32 \text{ lb/ft } (8 \text{ ft})^2}{8} \times 12 \text{ in./ft} = 3072 \text{ lb-in.}$$

$$f_t = \frac{Mc}{I} = \frac{3072 \text{ lb-in.} \times 3.81 \text{ in.}}{334.0 \text{ in}^3} = 35.0 \text{ lb/in}^2$$

The factored flexural tensile stress, 35.0 lb/in², does not exceed the modulus of rupture normal to bed joints for hollow units and Type N PCL mortar (64 lb/in²), reduced by the strength-reduction factor of 0.6 (38.4 lb/in²). This design is satisfactory. If it had not worked, the mortar could have changed to Type S (modulus of rupture 84 lb/in²).

5.1.5 Example: Strength Design of a Single-Wythe Panel Wall Using Hollow Units, Face-Shell Bedding Only

Check the design of the panel wall of Section 5.1.3 assuming face-shell bedding only (mortar on the face shells of the units only).

The panel wall will be designed as unreinforced masonry. The design follows the following steps, using a nominal thickness of 8 in. The panel could be designed as a two-way panel. Nevertheless, because of its aspect ratio, the vertical strips will carry practically all the load. Therefore, design it as a one-way panel, consisting of a series of vertically spanning, simply supported strips.

The critical stresses will occur on the bed joint, which is the horizontal plane through the masonry where the section modulus is minimum. All length dimensions are in inches. The dimensions of this critical cross-section are shown in Fig. 5.6.

$$I = I_{faceshells} = \frac{(1.25 \text{ in.})^3 \times 12 \text{ in.}}{12} \times 2 + 2\,(1.25 \times 12 \text{ in}^2)\left(\frac{7.625 - 1.25}{2}\right)^2$$

$$= 309.2 \text{ in}^4 \text{ per ft of width}$$

$$S = \frac{I}{c} = \frac{309.2}{3.81} = 81.2 \text{ in}^3 \text{ per ft of width}$$

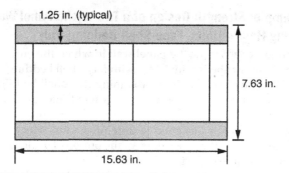

FIGURE 5.6 Idealized cross-sectional dimensions of a nominal 8 × 8 × 16 in. concrete masonry unit with face-shell bedding.

For the 12-in. wide strip,

$$M_{u\,max} = \frac{w_u \ell^2}{8} = \frac{1.0 \times 32 \text{ lb/ft } (8 \text{ ft})^2}{8} \times 12 \text{ in./ft} = 3072 \text{ lb-in.}$$

$$f_t = \frac{M}{S} = \frac{3072 \text{ lb-in.}}{81.2 \text{ in}^3} = 37.9 \text{ lb/in}^2$$

The calculated flexural tensile stress, 37.9 lb/in², is less than the modulus of rupture normal to bed joints for hollow units and Type N PCL mortar (64 lb/in²), reduced by the strength-reduction factor of 0.6 (38.4 lb/in²). The design is satisfactory.

5.1.6 Example: Strength Design of a Single-Wythe Panel Wall Using Hollow Units, Fully Grouted

Check the design of the panel wall of Section 5.1.3 for a wind load w of 32 lb/ft², using PCL mortar, Type N, and assuming hollow units, fully grouted.

As in the example of Section 5.1.3, assume vertically spanning, simply supported strips. Calculate the maximum bending moment and corresponding flexural tensile stress in a strip 12-in. wide, with a nominal thickness of 8 in.:

$$M_{u\,max} = \frac{w_u \ell^2}{8} = \frac{1.0 \times 32 \text{ lb/ft } (8 \text{ ft})^2}{8} = 3072 \text{ lb-in.}$$

$$f_t = \frac{Mc}{I} = \frac{3072 \text{ lb-in.} \cdot \left(7.625/2\right) \text{ in.}}{\left[12 \text{ in.} \cdot (7.625 \text{ in.})^3 / 12\right]} = 26.4 \text{ lb/in}^2$$

The calculated flexural tensile stress, 26.4 lb/in², is less than the modulus of rupture normal to bed joints for fully grouted hollow units and Type N PCL mortar (158 lb/in²), reduced by an strength-reduction factor of 0.6 (94.8 lb/in²). The design is therefore satisfactory.

5.1.7 Example: Strength Design of a Two-Wythe Panel Wall Using Hollow Units, Face-Shell Bedding Only

Check the design of a two-wythe panel wall in which the outer wythe is modular clay units and the inner wythe is 8-in. CMU with face-shell bedding. The wall has the panel wall of the example of Section 5.1.5, assuming face-shell bedding only (mortar on the face shells of the units only). The wall has a wind load w of 32 lb/ft², and uses PCL mortar, Type N.

The panel wall will be designed as unreinforced masonry, assuming that the vertical strips of the inner wythe resist 100% of the out-of-plane load. The design is therefore identical to the example of Section 5.1.5.

The critical stresses will occur on the bed joint, which is the horizontal plane through the masonry where the section modulus is minimum. This idealized horizontal cross-section is shown in Fig. 5.7.

$$I = I_{faceshells} = 309.2 \text{ in}^4 \text{ per ft of width}$$

$$S = \frac{I}{c} = \frac{309.2}{3.81} = 81.17 \text{ in}^3 \text{ per ft of width}$$

For the 12-in. wide strip,

$$M_{u\,max} = \frac{w_u \ell^2}{8} = \frac{1.0 \times 32 \text{ lb/ft} (8 \text{ ft})^2}{8} \times 12 \text{ in./ft} = 3072 \text{ lb-in.}$$

$$f_t = \frac{M}{S} = \frac{3072 \text{ lb-in.}}{81.17 \text{ in}^3} = 37.9 \text{ lb/in}^2$$

The calculated flexural tensile stress, 37.9 lb/in², is less than the modulus of rupture normal to bed joints for hollow units and Type N PCL mortar (64 lb/in²), reduced by the strength-reduction factor of 0.6 (38.4 lb/in²).

5.1.8 Strength Checks of One-Way Shear for Unreinforced Panel Walls

The examples of Section 5.1.3 through Section 5.1.7 in this chapter dealt with design of unreinforced panel walls for flexure. In theory, we should also check one-way shear. In practice, an example shows that shear does not come close to governing the design.

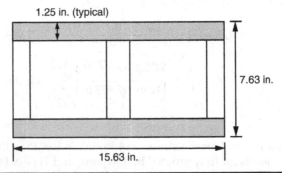

Figure 5.7 Idealized cross-sectional dimensions of a nominal 8 × 8 × 16 in. concrete masonry unit with face-shell bedding.

According to the strength provisions of TMS 402-22 (Section 9.2.6), for hollow units in running bond, nominal shear strength V_n is the least of:

$$\begin{cases} 3.8\sqrt{f'_m}\, A_{nv} \\ 300 A_{nv} \\ 56 A_{nv} + 0.45 N \end{cases}$$

The third criterion is

$56 A_{nv} + 0.45 P_u$ for running bond masonry not grouted solid
$56 A_{nv} + 0.45 P_u$ for stack bond masonry with open-end units, grouted solid
$90 A_{nv} + 0.45 P_u$ for running bond masonry grouted solid
$23 A_{nv}$ for other stack bond masonry

The strength-reduction factor for shear is 0.80 (TMS 402-22, Section 9.1.4.5).

5.1.9 Example: Strength Check of Shear Capacity for Unreinforced Panel Walls

Check the effect of shear in the example of Section 5.1.7.

With f'_m of 2000 psi/in² and masonry in running bond, and conservatively neglecting the beneficial effects of axial load, the third of the above equations governs, and $V_n = 56 A_n$.

On a strip 1-ft wide, the factored wind load of 32 lb/ft² produces a factored design shear of

$$V_u = \frac{q_u L}{2} = \frac{1.0 \times 32 \text{ lb/ft} \cdot (8 \text{ ft})}{2} = 128 \text{ lb}$$

The design shear capacity is the nominal capacity on two face shells, each 1.25 in. in width, reduced by the strength-reduction factor for shear (0.8):

$$\phi V_n = 0.8 \times 56 \text{ lb/in}^2 \times (2 \times 1.25 \text{ in.}) \times 12 \text{ in.} = 1344 \text{ lb}$$

This is far greater than the factored design shear, and one-way shear does not govern the design.

5.1.10 Overall Comments on Strength Design of Unreinforced Panel Walls

- Nonload-bearing masonry, without calculated reinforcement, can easily resist wind loads. It approaches its capacity only in the case of ungrouted hollow masonry. In this case, the lower allowable flexural tensile stress for masonry cement mortar can be critical in design.
- If noncalculated reinforcement is included, it will not act until the masonry has cracked.
- Elements such as the ones we have calculated in this section can be designed in many cases by prescription.

TABLE 5.2 Section Properties for Clay Masonry Walls

Unit	Area, in² per ft	Moment of inertia, in⁴ per ft
4-in. modular, fully bedded	43.5	47.6

5.1.11 Section Properties for Masonry Walls

Section properties for masonry walls are summarized in Tables 5.2 and 5.3.

5.1.12 Theoretical Derivation of the Strip Method (Hillerborg 1996)

In the preceding examples, we have used the simplifications that single-wythe panel walls can be designed assuming that all of the load is resisted by vertically spanning strips, and that two-wythe panel walls can be designed assuming that all of the load is resisted by vertically spanning strips of the inner wythe.

It is now appropriate to consider the theoretical basis for this simplification. We first consider the simplification of wythes as crossing strips using the strip method, and then derive additional simplifications based on the relative stiffnesses of those strips.

Consider the differential equation for the out-of-plane deflection of an elastic plate with a uniformly distributed, out-of-plane load:

$$\frac{\partial^4 w}{\partial x^4} + \frac{\partial^4 w}{\partial x^2 \partial y^2} + \frac{\partial^4 w}{\partial y^4} = \frac{-q}{D}$$

where w = out-of-plane deflection
q = uniformly distributed load

TABLE 5.3 Section Properties for Concrete Masonry Walls (Face-Shell and Web Thicknesses Consistent with CMHA Tech Note 002, which References ASTM C90-24)

Unit	Face-Shell Thickness, in.	Web Thickness, in.	Area, in² per ft	Moment of Inertia, in⁴ per ft
4-in. hollow CMU, fully bedded	3/4	3/4	21.6	39.4
4-in. hollow CMU, face-shell bedded			18.0	38.0
6-in. hollow CMU, fully bedded	1	1	32.2	139
6-in. hollow CMU, face-shell bedded			24.0	130
8-in. hollow CMU, fully bedded	1-1/4	1	41.5	334
8-in. hollow CMU, face-shell bedded			30.0	309
10-in. hollow CMU, fully bedded	1-1/4	1-1/8	48.0	606
10-in. hollow CMU, face-shell bedded			30.0	530
12-in. hollow CMU, fully bedded	1-1/4	1-1/8	53.1	972
12-in. hollow CMU, face-shell bedded			30.0	811

and

$$D = \frac{EI}{(1-v^2)} = \frac{Et^3}{12(1-v^2)}$$

(EI is calculated per unit width, and Poisson effects are included)
Conservatively, ignore twisting moments:

$$\frac{\partial^4 w}{\partial x^4} + \frac{\partial^4 w}{\partial y^4} = \frac{-q}{D} = -\left(\frac{q_x}{D} + \frac{q_y}{D}\right)$$

This is the differential equation for independent x and y strips (beams). The two sets of strips can be designed independently, provided that equilibrium is satisfied at every point:

$$q_x + q_y = q$$

5.1.13 Distribution of Out-of-Plane Load to Vertical and Horizontal Strips of a Single-Wythe Panel Wall

Earlier in this section, it was stated that single-wythe panel walls can be designed as though out-of-plane load were carried by the vertical strips alone. Now let's show why that's true. Consider the single-wythe panel shown in Fig. 5.8.

Assume that the panel resists out-of-plane loading as an assemblage of crossing strips, in the x direction (horizontally on the page) and the y direction (vertically on the page). At the very end of this section, it will be shown that such an assumption is legitimate ("strip method").

Now impose compatibility of out-of-plane deflections on the strips—that is, that the crossing x and y strips must have equal out-of-plane displacements. For a simply supported strip with uniformly distributed loading q, the center-line displacement is

$$\Delta_{center} = \frac{5qL^4}{384EI}$$

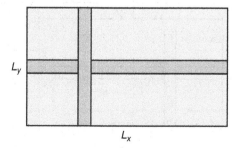

Figure 5.8 Idealization of a panel wall as an assemblage of crossing strips.

For equal deflections of the x and y strips,

$$\frac{5q_x L_x^4}{384EI} = \Delta_{center} = \frac{5q_y L_y^4}{384EI}$$

And because those strips have equal moduli and moments of inertia,

$$\frac{q_x}{q_y} = \frac{L_y^4}{L_x^4}$$

The span of the vertical strips, L_y, is the distance from the top of a floor slab to the underside of the slab or beam above, typically about 10 ft. The span of the horizontal strips, L_x, is the distance from the face of a column to the face of the adjacent column, typically about 20 ft. So

$$\frac{q_x}{q_y} = \frac{L_y^4}{L_x^4} = \left(\frac{10}{20}\right)^4 = 0.063$$

The horizontal strips will carry only about 6% of the out-of-plane load. If it is conservatively assumed that the vertical strips will carry 100% of the out-of-plane load, and the horizontal strip will carry zero load, the design work is halved, and the results will be conservative.

5.1.14 Distribution of Out-of-Plane Load to Vertical and Horizontal Strips of a Two-Wythe Panel Wall

The above analysis can easily be extended to the case of a two-wythe panel wall, with an outer wythe of clay masonry and an inner wythe of concrete masonry as shown in Fig. 5.9.

As before, assume that each wythe of the panel resists out-of-plane loading as an assemblage of crossing strips, in the x direction (horizontally on the page) and the y direction (vertically on the page). At the very end of this section, it will be shown that such an assumption is legitimate ("strip method").

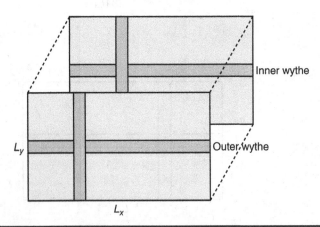

Figure 5.9 Idealization of a two-wythe panel wall as an assemblage of two sets of crossing strips.

Strength Design of Unreinforced Masonry Elements 121

Let's also assume that the inner wythe is of hollow, ungrouted, 8-in. CMU laid in face-shell bedding, and that the outer wythe is of solid modular units (nominal thickness of 4 in.).

From Example #3, we know that the moment of inertia of the hollow CMU is 444.9 in^4 per 16 in. of width, or 333.7 in^4 per foot of width. It is proper to compute the average flexural stiffness of the wall using the moment of inertia of the hollow unit rather than the moment of the face-shell bedding only because the bed joints occupy only a small portion of the volume of the wall.

The moment of inertia of the modular outer wythe, per foot of width, is

$$I = \frac{bt^3}{12} = \frac{(12 \text{ in.})(3.625 \text{ in.})^3}{12} = 47.6 \text{ in}^4 \text{ per ft of width}$$

Assume that the ties between wythes are axially rigid, so that the two wythes have equal out-of-plane deflection.

The total load q must be equilibrated by the summation of the load resisted by each strip of each wythe

$$(q_x + q_y)_{exterior} + (q_x + q_y)_{interior} = q$$

Because the vertical strips in the exterior wythe are simply supported at the bottom and free at the top (expansion joint, they carry no load):

$$(q_x)_{exterior} + (q_x + q_y)_{interior} = q$$

Now impose compatibility of out-of-plane deflections on the strips,

$$\Delta_{x\,exterior} = \frac{5 q_{x\,exterior} L_{x\,exterior}^4}{384 E_{x\,exterior} I_{x\,exterior}} = \frac{5 q_{x\,exterior} 20^4}{384 E_{x\,exterior} \times 47.6}$$

$$\Delta_{x\,interior} = \frac{5 q_{x\,interior} L_{x\,interior}^4}{384 E_{x\,interior} I_{x\,interior}} = \frac{5 q_{x\,interior} 20^4}{384 E_{x\,interior} \times 334.0}$$

$$\Delta_{y\,interior} = \frac{5 q_{y\,interior} L_{y\,interior}^4}{384 E_{y\,interior} I_{y\,interior}} = \frac{5 q_{y\,interior} 10^4}{384 E_{y\,interior} \times 334.0}$$

Equate those deflections, cancel out the common term of (5/384), and assume that all E's are the same:

$$\frac{q_{x\,exterior} 20^4}{47.6} = \frac{q_{x\,interior} 20^4}{334.0} = \frac{q_{y\,interior} 10^4}{334.0}$$

$$3361 q_{x\,exterior} = 479.0 q_{x\,interior} = 29.94 q_{y\,interior}$$

Express $q_{x\,exterior}$ and $q_{x\,interior}$ in terms of $q_{y\,interior}$:

$$q_{x\,exterior} = 0.00891 \, q_{y\,interior}$$

$$q_{x\,interior} = 0.0625 \, q_{y\,interior}$$

Now recall that the loads resisted by each strip must equilibrate the total load:

$$(q_x)_{\text{exterior}} + (q_x + q_y)_{\text{interior}} = q$$

$$(0.00891 + 0.0625 + 1.0)q_{y\,\text{interior}} = q$$

Solve for $q_{y\,\text{interior}}$ in terms of q:

$$q_{y\,\text{interior}} = \frac{q}{1.0714} = 0.933\,q$$

Finally, express the load carried by each set of strips in terms of q:

$$q_{y\,\text{interior}} = 0.93\,q$$

$$q_{x\,\text{interior}} = 0.06\,q$$

$$q_{x\,\text{exterior}} = 0.008\,q$$

Clearly, it is conservative and very reasonable to assume that the vertical strips of the interior wythe resist 100% of the out-of-plane load, and the other strips resist no load.

5.2 Strength Design of Unreinforced Bearing Walls

5.2.1 Basic Behavior of Unreinforced Bearing Walls

Load-bearing masonry (without calculated reinforcement) must be designed for the effects of:

1) Gravity loads from self-weight, plus gravity loads from overlying roof or floor levels
2) Moments from eccentric gravity load, or out-of-plane wind or earthquake
3) In-plane shear

For now, we shall study Loadings (1) and (2). Later, we shall study Loading (3), in the general context of design of masonry shear walls.

For Loadings (1) and (2), we shall design unreinforced, load-bearing masonry as a series of vertically spanning strips (Fig. 5.10), subjected to gravity loads (possibly eccentric) and out-of-plane wind or earthquake.

The only aspect of behavior that we haven't studied so far is the effect of slenderness on the load-carrying capacity of a column or wall. This effect is shown in Fig. 5.11.

At low values of slenderness, a masonry column in compression exhibits material failure. At high values of slenderness, it exhibits stability failure.

For masonry design, the effective length coefficient, k, is usually equal to 1.

5.2.2 Steps in Strength Design of Unreinforced Bearing Walls

In TMS 402-22, design of unreinforced bearing walls is similar to the design of panel walls, except that axial load must be considered. In Section 9.3.2 of TMS 402-22, no explicit equations are given for computing flexural strength. The usual assumption of

Strength Design of Unreinforced Masonry Elements

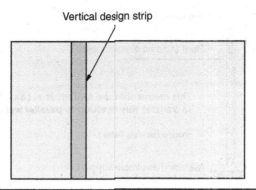

FIGURE 5.10 Idealization of bearing walls as vertically spanning strips.

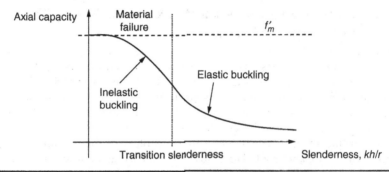

FIGURE 5.11 Effect of slenderness on the axial capacity of a column or wall.

plane sections is invoked, and tensile and compressive stresses in masonry are to be assumed proportional to strain.

Nominal capacities in masonry are reached at an extreme fiber tension equal to the modulus of rupture (Table 9.1.9.1 of TMS 402-22), and at a compressive stress of $0.80 f'_m$.

Compressive capacity is given by Equations 9-11 and 9-12 of TMS 402-22:

For $\dfrac{kh}{r} = \dfrac{h}{r} \leq 99$,

$$P_n = 0.80 \left\{ 0.80 A_n f'_m \left[1 - \left(\dfrac{h}{140r} \right)^2 \right] \right\}$$

and for $\dfrac{kh}{r} = \dfrac{h}{r} > 99$,

$$P_n = 0.80 \left[0.80 A_n f'_m \left(\dfrac{70r}{h} \right)^2 \right]$$

The strength reduction factor, ϕ, is equal to 0.60 (Section 9.1.4.2 of TMS 402-22). Unlike the allowable-stress provisions, the strength provisions of TMS 402-22 require a direct stability check using a moment magnifier.

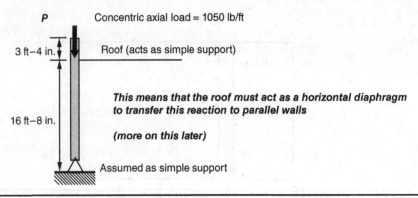

FIGURE 5.12 Unreinforced masonry bearing wall with concentric axial load.

5.2.3 Example: Strength Design of Unreinforced Bearing Wall with Concentric Axial Load

The bearing wall shown in Fig. 5.12 has an unfactored, concentric axial load of 1050 lb/ft. Using hollow concrete masonry units with face-shell bedding, design the wall. In Fig. 5.12, the wall is shown as simply supported at its base. This assumption is discussed further in Example 5.2.3. At this point, it is sufficient to emphasize that the assumption has nothing to do with whether the wall is actually cracked at that point. It is a simplifying assumption introduced as part of the design process.

According to the 2024 IBC, and in the context of these example problems (dead load, wind load and roof live load), the following loading combinations must be checked for strength design:

1. $1.2D + 1.0W + f_1 L + 0.5 \, (L_r \text{ or } S \text{ or } R)$
2. $0.9D + 1.0W + 1.6H$

The second of these is usually critical because roof live load must be considered off as well as on.

To apply those loading combinations, let us assume that the total unfactored wall load of 1050 lb/ft represents 700 lb/ft of dead load and 350 lb/ft of live load.

Table 5.4, repeated from Section 5.1.11, gives section properties for masonry units.

Table 5.5, taken from CMHA TEK 002, gives the self-weight of hollow CMU walls, assuming units with a density of 115 lb/ft³ and face-shell bedding.

At each horizontal plane through the wall, the following conditions must be met:

- Maximum compressive stress from factored axial loads must not exceed the slenderness-dependent values in Equations 9-12 or 9-13 as appropriate, reduced by a ϕ-factor of 0.60.
- Maximum compressive stress from factored loads (including a moment magnifiers) must not exceed $0.80 \, f'_m$ in the extreme compression fiber, reduced by a ϕ-factor of 0.60.
- Maximum tension stress from factored loads (including a moment magnifier) must not exceed the modulus of rupture in the extreme tension fiber, reduced by the ϕ-factor of 0.60.

Strength Design of Unreinforced Masonry Elements 125

TABLE 5.4 Section Properties for Concrete Masonry Walls (Face-Shell and Web Thicknesses Consistent with CMHA TEK 002, which References ASTM C90-24)

Unit	Face-Shell Thickness, in.	Web Thickness, in.	Area, in² per ft	Moment of Inertia, in⁴ per ft
4-in. hollow CMU, fully bedded	3/4	3/4	21.6	39.4
4-in. hollow CMU, face-shell bedded			18.0	38.0
6-in. hollow CMU, fully bedded	1	1	32.2	139
6-in. hollow CMU, face-shell bedded			24.0	130
8-in. hollow CMU, fully bedded	1-1/4	1	41.5	334
8-in. hollow CMU, face-shell bedded			30.0	309
10-in. hollow CMU, fully bedded	1-1/4	1-1/8	48.0	606
10-in. hollow CMU, face-shell bedded			30.0	530
12-in. hollow CMU, fully bedded	1-1/4	1-1/8	53.1	972
12-in. hollow CMU, face-shell bedded			30.0	811

TABLE 5.5 Self-Weights of Hollow CMU Walls

Nominal Thickness, in.	Weight per ft²
4	18
6	26
8	33
10	38
12	42

For each condition, the more critical of the two possible loading combinations must be checked. Because there is no wind load, this example will be worked using that loading combination $1.2D + 1.6L$.

In theory, we must check various points on the wall. In this problem, however, the wall has only axial load, which increases from top to bottom due to the wall's self-weight. Therefore, we need to check only at the base of the wall:

Try 8-in. nominal units and a specified compressive strength, f'_m, of 2000 lb/in². This can be satisfied using units with a net-area compressive strength of 2000 lb/in², and Type S PCL mortar. Work with a strip with a width of 1 ft (measured along the length of the wall in plan). Stresses are calculated using the critical section, consisting of the bedded area only (TMS 402-22, Section 4.4.1).

At the base of the wall, the factored axial force is

$$P_u = 1.2(700 \text{ lb}) + 1.6(350 \text{ lb}) + 1.2(20 \text{ ft} \times 33 \text{ lb/ft}) = 2192 \text{ lb}$$

To calculate stiffness-related parameters for the wall, we use the average cross-section, corresponding to the fully bedded section in the table (TMS 402-22, Section 4.4.1).

$$r = \sqrt{\frac{I}{A}} = \sqrt{\frac{334 \text{ in}^4}{41.5 \text{ in}^2}} = 2.84 \text{ in.}$$

$$\frac{kh}{r} = \frac{16.67 \text{ ft} \times 12 \text{ in./ft}}{2.84 \text{ in.}} = 70.5$$

This is less than the transition slenderness of 99, so the nominal axial capacity is based on the curve that is an approximation to inelastic buckling:

$$\phi P_n = \phi 0.80 \left\{ 0.80 A_n f'_m \left[1 - \left(\frac{h}{140r} \right)^2 \right] \right\}$$

$$\phi P_n = 0.60 \times 0.80 \times \left\{ 0.80 \times 30.0 \text{ in}^2 \times 2000 \text{ lb/in}^2 \left[1 - \left(\frac{16.67 \text{ ft} \times 12 \text{ in./ft}}{140 \times 2.84 \text{ in}^2} \right)^2 \right] \right\}$$

$$\phi P_n = 23{,}040 \text{ lb} \times 0.746 = 17{,}188 \text{ lb}$$

The factored axial load, P_u, 2192 lb, is far less than this, and this part of the design is satisfactory.

Now check the net compressive stress. Because the load is concentric, there is no bending stress. At the base of the wall,

$$f_a = \frac{P_u}{A} = \frac{1.2(700 \text{ lb}) + 1.6(350 \text{ lb}) + 1.2(20 \text{ ft} \times 33 \text{ lb/ft})}{30 \text{ in}^2} = \frac{2192 \text{ lb}}{30 \text{ in}^2} = 73.1 \text{ lb/in}^2$$

$$f_a = 73.1 \text{ lb/in}^2$$

The maximum permitted compressive stress is

$$0.60 \cdot 0.80 f'_m = 0.60 \times 0.80 \times 2000 \text{ lb/in}^2 = 960 \text{ lb/in}^2$$

The maximum compressive stress is much less than this, and the design is satisfactory for this also.

Clearly, because this example involves concentric axial loads only, the first criterion (axial capacity reduced by slenderness effects) is more severe than the second (maximum compressive stress from axial loads and bending moments).

Because the wall has concentric axial load, there is no net tensile stress, and that criterion does not have to be checked.

Because the axial load is concentric, there is no moment, and the magnified moment does not have to be checked. The design is satisfactory.

Strength Design of Unreinforced Masonry Elements 127

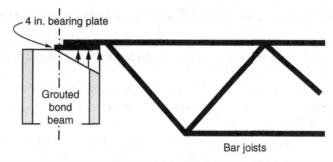

FIGURE 5.13 Assumed linear variation of bearing stresses under the bearing plate.

It would probably be possible to achieve a satisfactory design with a smaller nominal wall thickness. To maintain continuity in the example problems that follow, however, the design will stop at this point.

Although TMS 402-22, Section 4.2.3 has no explicit minimum eccentricity requirements for walls, the leading coefficient of 0.80 for nominal axial compressive capacity effectively imposes a minimum eccentricity of about $0.1\,t$.

5.2.4 Example: Strength Design of Unreinforced Bearing Wall with Eccentric Axial Load

Now consider the same bearing wall of the previous example but make the gravity load eccentric.

Suppose that the load is applied over a 4-in. bearing plate, and assume that bearing stresses vary linearly under the bearing plate as shown in Fig. 5.13.

Then the eccentricity of the applied load with respect to the centerline of the wall is

$$e = \frac{t}{2} - \frac{\text{plate}}{3} = \frac{7.63 \text{ in.}}{2} - \frac{4 \text{ in.}}{3} = 2.48 \text{ in.}$$

The wall is as shown in Fig. 5.14.

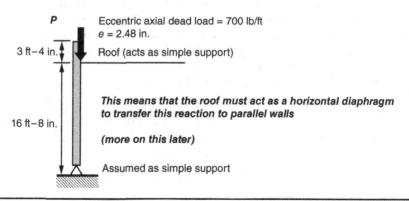

FIGURE 5.14 Unreinforced masonry bearing wall with eccentric axial load.

At each horizontal plane through the wall, the following conditions must be met:

- Maximum compressive stress from factored axial loads must not exceed the slenderness-dependent values in Equations 9-11 or 9-12 as appropriate, reduced by a ϕ-factor of 0.60.
- Maximum compressive stress from factored loads (including a moment magnifiers) must not exceed $0.80\,f'_m$ in the extreme compression fiber, reduced by a ϕ-factor of 0.60.
- Maximum tension stress from factored loads (including a moment magnifier) must not exceed the modulus of rupture in the extreme tension fiber, reduced by the ϕ-factor of 0.60.

For each condition, the more critical of the two possible loading combinations must be checked. Because there is no wind load, this example will be worked using that loading combination $1.2D + 1.6L$.

We must check various points on the wall. Critical points are just below the roof reaction (moment is high and axial load is low, so maximum tension may govern); and at the base of the wall (axial load is high, so maximum compression may govern). Check each of these locations.

As before, the base of the wall is assumed to be simply supported. This assumption has nothing to do with the probable relationship between the maximum stresses acting in the wall at that level and the failure stresses of the material, nor with the rotational flexibility of the foundation. The assumption is made for convenience in the design process, and it is based on the lower-bound principle of structural mechanics. According to that principle, any structural solution that satisfies equilibrium and constitutive relationships, but not necessarily kinematics, corresponds to a collapse capacity that is less than or equal to the actual collapse capacity and is therefore conservative (safe) for design. A design solution that assumes a simple support at the base satisfies statics; it satisfies constitutive relationships (because the failure stresses are nowhere exceeded); but it does not necessarily satisfy the kinematic condition of rotational continuity at the base. This design solution also simplifies the design process because it makes the structure statically determinate. As illustrated in the advanced examples at the end of this chapter, a design carried out using this assumption would have a slightly greater collapse load than that assumed and would therefore be safe.

As before, try 8-in. nominal units, and a specified compressive strength, f'_m, of 2000 lb/in². This can be satisfied using units with a net-area compressive strength of 2000 lb/in², and Type S PCL mortar. Work with a strip with a width of 1 ft (measured along the length of the wall in plan). Stresses are calculated using the critical section, consisting of the bedded area only (TMS 402-22, Section 4.4.1):

Just below the roof reaction, the axial force is

$$P_u = 1.2(700 \text{ lb}) + 1.6(350 \text{ lb}) + 1.2(3.33 \text{ ft} \times 33 \text{ lb/ft}) = 1532 \text{ lb}$$

To calculate stiffness-related parameters for the wall, we use the average cross-section, corresponding to the fully bedded section in the table (TMS 402-22, Section 4.4.1).

$$r = \sqrt{\frac{I}{A}} = \sqrt{\frac{334 \text{ in}^4}{41.5 \text{ in}^2}} = 2.84 \text{ in.}$$

$$\frac{kh}{r} = \frac{16.67 \cdot 12 \text{ in.}}{2.84 \text{ in.}} = 70.5$$

Strength Design of Unreinforced Masonry Elements

This is less than the transition slenderness of 99, so the nominal axial capacity is based on the curve that is an approximation to inelastic buckling:

$$\phi P_n = \phi 0.80 \left\{ 0.80 A_n f'_m \left[1 - \left(\frac{h}{140r} \right)^2 \right] \right\}$$

$$\phi P_n = 0.60 \times 0.80 \times \left\{ 0.80 \times 30.0 \text{ in}^2 \times 2000 \text{ lb/in}^2 \left[1 - \left(\frac{16.67 \text{ ft} \times 12 \text{ in./ft}}{140 \times 2.84 \text{ in}^2} \right)^2 \right] \right\}$$

$$\phi P_n = 23{,}040 \text{ lb} \times 0.746 = 17{,}188 \text{ lb}$$

Because the factored axial force is much less than slenderness-dependent nominal capacity, reduced by the appropriate ϕ factor, the axial force check is satisfied.

Now check the net compressive stress. Because the loading is eccentric, there is bending stress:

$$f_{compression} = \frac{P_u}{A} + \frac{M_u c}{I}$$

The factored design axial load, P_u, is computed above. The factored design moment, M_u, is given by

$$M_u = P_u e = (1.2 \times 700 + 1.6 \times 350) \text{ lb} \times 2.48 \text{ in.} = 3472 \text{ lb-in.}$$

$$f_{compression} = \frac{P_u}{A} + \frac{M_u c}{I}$$

$$f_{compression} = \frac{1532 \text{ lb}}{30 \text{ in}^2} + \frac{3472 \text{ lb-in.} \left(7.63/2 \right)}{309 \text{ in}^4} = 51.1 + 42.9 \text{ lb/in}^2 = 93.9 \text{ lb/in}^2$$

$$0.60 \times 0.80 f'_m = 0.60 \times 0.80 \times 2000 \text{ lb/in}^2 = 960 \text{ lb/in}^2$$

The net compressive stress does not exceed the prescribed value. Clearly, because this example involves eccentric axial loads, the first criterion (axial load reduced by slenderness effects) is less severe than the second (maximum compressive stress from axial loads and bending moments).

Because the bending stress from factored design moments (42.9 lb/in²) is less than the axial stress from factored axial load (51.1 lb/in²), there is no net tension, and the third criterion (net tension) is automatically satisfied.

Section 9.2.4.3.4 of TMS 402-22 requires that magnified moments be checked. For this wall, the ratio of (h/r) is 70.5, which exceeds 45. Therefore, a magnifier must be calculated.

$$\psi = \frac{1}{1 - \dfrac{P_u}{A_n f'_m \left(\dfrac{70r}{h} \right)^2}} = \frac{1}{1 - \dfrac{1532 \text{ lb}}{41.5 \text{ in}^2 \times 2000 \dfrac{\text{lb}}{\text{in}^2} \left(\dfrac{70}{70.5} \right)^2}} = 1.02$$

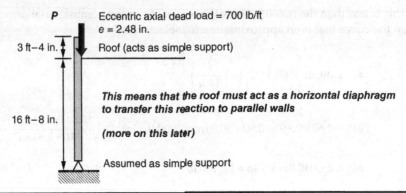

FIGURE 5.15 Unreinforced masonry bearing wall with eccentric axial load and wind load.

This is very close to 1.0 and does not affect the previous checks.

The other critical section could be at the base of the wall, where the checks of all three criteria are identical to those of Example 5.2.3, with the addition of the moment magnifier. All are satisfied, and the design of the wall illustrated in Fig. 5.15 is therefore satisfactory.

5.2.5 Example: Strength Design of Unreinforced Bearing Wall with Eccentric Axial Load plus Wind

Now consider the same bearing wall of the previous example but add a uniformly distributed wind load of 40 lb/ft².

The wall is as shown in Fig. 5.15.

At each horizontal plane through the wall, the following conditions must be met:

- Maximum compressive stress from factored axial loads must not exceed the slenderness-dependent values in Equations 9-12 or 9-13 as appropriate, reduced by a ϕ-factor of 0.60.

- Maximum compressive stress from factored loads (including a moment magnifiers) must not exceed $0.80 f'_m$ in the extreme compression fiber, reduced by a ϕ-factor of 0.60.

- Maximum tension stress from factored loads (including a moment magnifier) must not exceed the modulus of rupture in the extreme tension fiber, reduced by the ϕ-factor of 0.60.

For each condition, the more critical of the two possible loading combinations must be checked. Because there is wind load, and because the two previous examples showed little problem with the first two criteria, the third criterion (net tension) may well be critical. For this criterion, the critical loading condition could be either $1.2D + 1.6L$, or $0.9D + 1.0W$. Both loading conditions must be checked.

We must check various points on the wall. Critical points are just below the roof reaction (moment is high and axial load is low, so net tension may govern); at the mid-height of the wall, where moment from eccentric gravity load and wind load are highest; and at the base of the wall (axial load is high, so the maximum compressive stress may govern). Check each of these locations:

Strength Design of Unreinforced Masonry Elements

To avoid having to check a large number of loading combinations and potentially critical locations, it is worthwhile to assess them first and check only the ones that will probably govern.

Due to wind only, the unfactored moment at the base of the parapet (roof level) is

$$M = \frac{wL^2_{parapet}}{2} = \frac{40 \text{ lb/ft} \times 3.33^2 \text{ ft}^2}{2} \times 12 \text{ in./ft} = 2661 \text{ lb-in.}$$

The maximum moment is close to that occurring at mid-height. The moment from wind load is the superposition of one-half moment at the upper support due to wind load on the parapet only, plus the midspan moment in a simply supported beam with that same wind load:

$$M_{midspan} = -\frac{2661}{2} + \frac{wL^2}{8} = -\frac{1663 \text{ lb-in.}}{2} + \frac{40 \text{ lb/ft} \times 16.67^2 \text{ ft}^2}{8} \times 12 \text{ in./ft} = 15,343 \text{ lb-in.}$$

The unfactored moment due to eccentric axial load is

$$M_{gravity} = Pe = 1050 \text{ lb} \times 2.48 \text{ in.} = 2604 \text{ lb-in.}$$

Unfactored moment diagrams due to eccentric axial load and wind are as shown in Fig. 5.16.

From the example of Section 5.2.4, we know that loading combination $1.2D + 1.6L$ was not close to critical directly underneath the roof. Because the wind-load moments directly underneath the roof are not very large, they will probably not be critical either. The critical location will probably be at mid-height; the critical loading condition will probably be $0.9D + 1.0W$; and the critical criterion will probably be net tension, because this masonry wall is unreinforced.

As before, try 8-in. nominal units, and a specified compressive strength, f'_m, of 2000 lb/in^2. This can be satisfied using units with a net-area compressive strength of 2000 lb/in^2, and Type S PCL mortar. Work with a strip with a width of 1 ft (measured along the length of the wall in plan). Stresses are calculated using the critical section, consisting of the bedded area only (TMS 402-22 Section 4.4.1):

Now check the net tensile stress. At the mid-height of the wall, the axial force due to $0.9D$ is:

$$P_u = 0.9(700 \text{ lb}) + 0.9(3.33 \text{ ft} + 8.33 \text{ ft}) \times 33 \text{ lb/ft} = 976.3 \text{ lb}$$

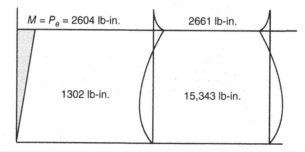

Figure 5.16 Unfactored moment diagrams due to eccentric axial load and wind.

At the mid-height of the wall, the factored design moment, M_u, is given by

$$M_u = P_{u\,eccentric}\frac{e}{2} + M_{u\,wind} = \left(\frac{1}{2}\right)0.9 \cdot 700 \text{ lb} \times 2.48 \text{ in.} + 1.0 \times 15{,}343 \text{ lb-in.} = 16{,}124 \text{ lb-in.}$$

$$f_{tension} = -\frac{P_u}{A} + \frac{M_u c}{I}$$

$$f_{tension} = -\frac{976.3 \text{ lb}}{30 \text{ in}^2} + \frac{16{,}124 \text{ lb-in.}\left(7.63/2\right)}{309 \text{ in}^4} = -32.5 + 199.1 \text{ lb/in}^2 = 166.6 \text{ lb/in}^2$$

$$0.60 f_r = 0.60 \times 84 \text{ lb/in}^2 = 50.4 \text{ lb/in}^2$$

The maximum tensile stress exceeds the prescribed value, and the design is not satisfactory. It will be necessary to grout the wall. The wall weight will increase somewhat, increasing the stress from factored dead load; the factored wind moments will remain unchanged; the section modulus of the wall will increase; and the modulus of rupture of the wall will increase from 84 to 163 lb/in².

Recheck the wall as grouted:

Table 5.6, taken from CMHA Tech Note 002, gives the self-weight of fully grouted CMU walls, assuming units with a density of 115 lb/ft³. Units with a nominal thickness of 4 in. are not shown because their cells are too narrow to permit consolidation of grout.

$$P_u = 0.9(700 \text{ lb}) + 0.9(3.33 \text{ ft} + 8.33 \text{ ft}) \times 81 \text{ lb/ft} = 1480 \text{ lb}$$

$$M_u = P_u\frac{e}{2} + M_{u\,wind} = \left(\frac{1}{2}\right)0.9 \times 700 \text{ lb} \times 2.48 \text{ in.} + 1.0 \times 15{,}343 \text{ lb-in.} = 16{,}124 \text{ lb-in.}$$

$$f_{tension} = -\frac{P_u}{A} + \frac{M_u c}{I}$$

$$f_{tension} = -\frac{1480 \text{ lb}}{7.63 \times 12 \text{ in}^2} + \frac{16{,}124 \text{ lb-in.}\left(7.63/2\right) \text{ in.}}{\left(\dfrac{12 \times 7.63^3 \text{ in}^4}{12}\right)} = -16.2 + 138.5 \text{ lb/in}^2 = 122.3 \text{ lb/in}^2$$

$$0.60 f_r = 0.60 \cdot 163 \text{ lb/in}^2 = 97.8 \text{ lb/in}^2$$

The wall would have to be thickened to 10 in. or reinforced.

Finally, the moment magnifier would have to be checked. Because we know that we have to thicken the wall in any event, and the moment magnifier would make the above checks worse, the calculation is not done here.

TABLE 5.6 Self-Weights of Fully Grouted CMU Walls

Nominal Thickness, in.	Weight per ft²
6	60
8	81
10	103
12	125

5.2.6 Comments on the Above Examples for Strength Design of Unreinforced Bearing Walls

1) In retrospect, it probably would not have been necessary to check all three criteria at all locations. With experience, a designer could realize that the location with highest wind moment would govern and could therefore check only the mid-height of the wall.

2) The addition of wind load to Example 5.2.4, to produce Example 5.2.5, changes the critical location from just under the roof, to the mid-height of the simply supported section of the wall. The wind load of 40 lb/ft² in Example 5.2.5 produces maximum tensile stresses above the allowable values for ungrouted masonry and makes it necessary to grout the wall, thicken it, or reinforce it.

5.2.7 Extension of the Above Concepts to Masonry Walls with Openings

In the previous examples, we have studied the behavior of bearing walls of unreinforced masonry, idealized as a series of vertical strips, simply supported at the level of the floor slab, and at the level of the roof. This section considers the effects of openings on bearing wall design. For design purposes, the fundamental point is that openings are normally occupied by doors or windows, which are loaded just as the wall would be. Therefore, the presence of openings does not change the total out-of-plane load on the wall nor does it change the maximum out-of-plane moment in the wall. A wall with vertical span ℓ, plan length ℓ_2, and uniformly distributed out-of-plane pressure q_u will have a total maximum out-of-plane moment of $\frac{q_u \ell_2 \ell^2}{8}$. Often a plan length of one foot is used, corresponding to $\ell_2 = 1$.

The presence of openings does reduce the amount of masonry available to resist that moment, however, and therefore increases the maximum flexural tensile stress in the remaining masonry. For example, if one-half the plan length of a masonry wall is occupied by openings, the remaining half of its plan length is masonry, and for the same total out-of-plane moment, the maximum flexural tensile stress in that remaining masonry is twice what it would be if those openings did not exist.

The fundamental point noted above addresses out-of-plane bending in vertical strips only. To address horizontal bending as well, it is useful to develop a design approach involving horizontal as well as vertical strips. This is a lower-bound approach, quite similar to the strip method for design of slabs. It is conservative for design.

1) In Fig. 5.17, load applied above the window and door openings clearly cannot be resisted by vertical strips, because those vertical strips have only one point of lateral support (at the roof level).

2) For that reason, the wall must be idealized as horizontal strips above and below the openings, supported by vertical strips on both sides of the openings, as shown in Fig. 5.18.

3) Each set of horizontal strips, idealized as simply supported, must be supported by the adjacent vertical strips. For example, the horizontal strips above the door are supported by Strip A and Strip B. The window and door are considered to transfer loads applied to them, via horizontal strips, to the vertical strips on either side of the openings.

134 Chapter Five

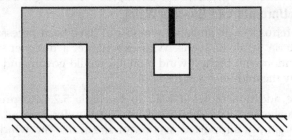

FIGURE 5.17 Hypothetical unstable resistance mechanism in a wall with openings, involving vertically spanning strips only.

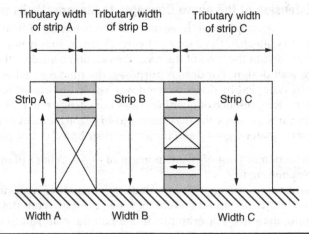

FIGURE 5.18 Stable resistance mechanism in a wall with openings, involving horizontally spanning strips in addition to vertically spanning strips.

4) Therefore, Strip A has to support, spanning vertically, the out-of-plane loads acting directly on it, plus the out-of-plane loads acting on the left half of the horizontal strips above the door. In other words, Strip A has to resist the out-of-plane loads acting on what might be termed a "tributary width," which extends from the left-hand edge of Strip A itself, to the midspan of the horizontal strips above the door. In the same way, Strips B and C have to resist the loads corresponding to Tributary Widths B and C, respectively.

5) For example, if Strip B has to resist the loads acting over Tributary Width B, this represents an increase in the design loads on Strip B. That strip must resist the loads that normally would be applied to it (if no openings had existed), multiplied by the ratio of Tributary Width B, divided by Width B:

$$\text{Actions in Strip } B = \text{Initial Actions} \left(\frac{\text{Tributary Width } B}{\text{Width } B} \right)$$

6) The same applies to vertical loads because these also must be transferred from horizontal to vertical strips.

7) In any event, the presence of openings can be considered to increase the initial actions in the vertical strips adjacent to the openings. Aside from this increase, the design of those elements proceeds exactly as before.

5.2.8 Final Comment on the Effect of Openings in Unreinforced Masonry Bearing Walls

As the summation of the plan lengths of openings in a bearing wall exceeds about one-half the plan length of the wall, even the higher allowable stresses (or moduli of rupture) corresponding to fully grouted walls will be exceeded, and it will generally become necessary to use reinforcement. Design of reinforced masonry bearing walls is addressed later in this book.

5.3 Strength Design of Unreinforced Shear Walls

5.3.1 Basic Behavior of Unreinforced Shear Walls

Wall-type structures resist lateral loads as shown in Fig. 5.19.

This resistance mechanism involves three steps:

- Walls oriented perpendicular to the direction of lateral load transfer those loads to the level of the foundation and the levels of the horizontal diaphragms. The walls are idealized and designed as vertically oriented strips.
- The roof and floors act as horizontal diaphragms, transferring their forces to walls oriented parallel to the direction of lateral load.
- Walls oriented parallel to the direction of applied load must transfer loads from the horizontal diaphragms to the foundation. In other words, they act as shear walls.

As noted previously in the sections dealing with unreinforced bearing walls, this overall mechanism demands that the horizontal roof diaphragm have sufficient strength

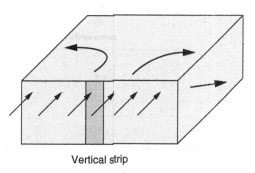

FIGURE 5.19 Basic behavior of box-type buildings in resisting lateral loads.

and stiffness to transfer the required loads. This is discussed again in a later section of this book dealing with horizontal diaphragms.

The rest of this section addresses the design of shear walls. We shall see that in almost all cases, the design itself is very simple, because the cross-sectional areas of the masonry walls so large that nominal stresses are quite low.

5.3.2 Design Steps for Unreinforced Shear Walls

Unreinforced masonry shear walls must be designed for the effects of:

1) Gravity loads from self-weight, plus gravity loads from overlying roof or floor levels

2) Moments and shears from in-plane shear loads

Actions are shown in Fig. 5.20. Either allowable-stress design or strength design can be used.

When strength design is used, TMS 402-22 requires that maximum tensile stresses from in-plane flexure, alone or in combination with axial loads, not exceed the in-plane modulus of rupture from Table 9.1.9.1 of TMS 402-22.

Shear must also be checked. From Section 9.2.6 of TMS 402-22, for hollow units in running bond, nominal shear strength is the least of:

$$\begin{cases} 3.8\sqrt{f'_m}\, A_{nv} \\ 300 A_{nv} \\ 56 A_{nv} + 0.45 N \end{cases}$$

The third criterion is

$56 A_{nv} + 0.45\, N$ for running bond masonry not grouted solid
$56 A_{nv} + 0.45\, N$ for stack bond masonry with open-end units, grouted solid
$90 A_{nv} + 0.45\, N$ for running bond masonry grouted solid
$23 A_{nv}$ for other stack bond masonry

The strength-reduction factor for shear is 0.80 (TMS 402-22 Section 9.1.4.5).

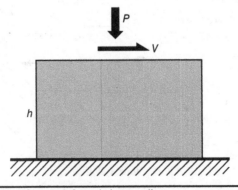

FIGURE 5.20 Design actions for unreinforced shear walls.

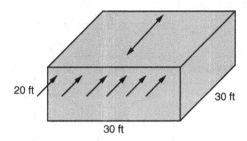

FIGURE 5.21 Example problem for strength design of unreinforced shear wall.

5.3.3 Example: Strength Design of Unreinforced Masonry Shear Wall

Consider the simple structure of Fig. 5.21, the same one whose bearing walls have been designed previously in this book. Use nominal 8-in. concrete masonry units, f'_m = 2000 lb/in², and Type S PCL mortar. The roof applies a gravity load of 1050 lb/ft to the walls; the walls measure 16 ft, 8 in. height to the roof, and have an additional 3 ft, 4 in. parapet. The walls are loaded with a wind load of 32 lb/ft². The roof acts as a one-way system, transmitting gravity loads to the front and back walls. At this stage, all loads are unfactored; load factors will be applied later.

Now design the shear wall. Try an 8-in. wall, ungrouted, with face-shell bedding only. The critical section for shear is just under the roof, where axial load in the shear walls is least, coming from the parapet only.

As a result of the wind loading, the reaction transmitted to the roof diaphragm is as calculated using Fig. 5.22:

$$\text{Reaction} = \frac{32 \text{ lb/ft}^2 \times \left(\dfrac{20^2 \text{ ft}^2}{2}\right)}{16.67 \text{ ft}} = 384 \text{ lb/ft}$$

Total roof reaction acting on one side of the roof is

$$\text{Reaction} = 384 \text{ lb/ft} \times 30 \text{ ft} = 11{,}520 \text{ lb}$$

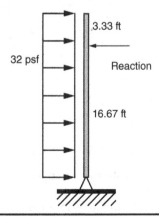

FIGURE 5.22 Calculation of reaction on roof diaphragm, strength design of unreinforced shear wall.

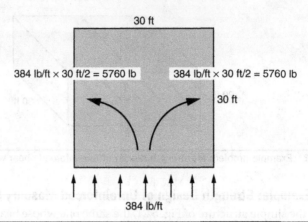

FIGURE 5.23 Transmission of forces from roof diaphragm to shear walls.

This is divided evenly between the two shear walls, so the shear per wall is 5760 lb.

In Fig. 5.23, for simplicity, the lateral load is shown as if it acted on the front wall alone. In reality, it also acts on the back wall, so that the structure is subjected to pressure on the front wall, and suction on the back wall.

The horizontal diaphragm reaction transferred to each shear wall is 384 lb/ft, multiplied by the building width of 30 ft, and then divided equally between the two shear walls, for a total of 5760 lb per shear wall.

Using the conservative loading case of 0.9D + 1.0W,

$$V_u = 1.0 V_{\text{unfactored}} = 1.0 \times 5760 \text{ lb} = 5760 \text{ lb}$$

Compute the axial force in the wall at that level. To be conservative, use the loading combination 0.9D + 1.0W. The force acting normal to the shear-transfer plane is

$$N_u = 0.9 \times 3.33 \text{ ft} \times 33 \text{ lb/ft}^2 \times 30 \text{ ft} = 2967 \text{ lb}$$

The nominal shear capacity at that level is

$$V_{nm} = \min \begin{cases} 3.8\sqrt{f'_m} A_{nv} = 3.8 \times 44.72 \text{ lb/in}^2 \times (30 \text{ ft} \times 30 \text{ in}^2/\text{ft}) = 152{,}947 \text{ lb} \\ 300 A_{nv} = 300 \times (30 \text{ ft} \times 30 \text{ in}^2/\text{ft}) = 270{,}000 \text{ lb} \\ 56 A_{nv} + 0.45 N_u = 56 \times (30 \text{ ft} \times 30 \text{ in}^2/\text{ft}) + 0.45 \times 2967 \text{ lb} = 51{,}735 \text{ lb} \end{cases}$$

$$V_{nm} = 51{,}735 \text{ lb}$$

The design shear capacity is

$$\phi V_n = 0.80 \times 51{,}735 \text{ lb} = 41{,}388 \text{ lb}$$

The design shear capacity far exceeds the factored design shear of 5760 lb, and the wall is satisfactory for shear.

Now check for the net flexural tensile stress. The critical section is at the base of the wall, where in-plane moment is maximum. Because the roof spans between the front and back walls, the distributed gravity load on the roof does not act on the side walls, and their axial load comes from self-weight only. Again, use the conservative loading combination of $0.9D + 1.0W$:

$$f_{tension} = \frac{M_u c}{I} - \frac{P_u}{A} = \frac{V_u hc}{I} - \frac{P_u}{A} \leq \phi f_r$$

$$f_{tension} = \frac{1.0 \times 5760 \text{ lb} \times 16.67 \text{ ft} \times 12 \text{ in./ft} \left(\dfrac{30 \text{ ft} \times 12 \text{ in./ft}}{2}\right)}{\left[\dfrac{2 \times 1.25 \text{ in.} \times (30 \text{ ft} \times 12 \text{ in./ft})^3}{12}\right]} - \frac{0.9 \times 20 \text{ ft} \times 33 \text{ lb/ft}}{30 \text{ in}^2}$$

$$f_{tension} = 1.0 \times 21.33 \text{ lb/in}^2 - 0.9 \times 22.00 \text{ lb/in}^2$$

$$f_{tension} = 21.33 \text{ lb/in}^2 - 19.80 \text{ lb/in}^2$$

$$f_{tension} = 1.53 \text{ lb/in}^2$$

The net tension in the wall is less than the modulus of rupture for Type S PCL mortar and hollow units (84 lb/in²) times the ϕ-factor of 0.6 (in other words, 50.4 lb/in²), and the design is satisfactory.

When the wind blows against the side walls, these walls transfer their loads to the roof diaphragm, and the front and back walls act as shear walls. The side walls must be checked for this loading direction also, following the procedures of previous examples in this book.

In-plane, the (h/r) value for this shear wall is much less than the triggering value of 45, and the moment magnifier can be taken as 1.0 (TMS 402-22 Section 9.2.4.3).

5.3.4 Comments on Example Problem with Strength Design of Unreinforced Shear Walls

Clearly, unreinforced masonry shear walls, whether designed by allowable stress or strength design procedures, have tremendous shear capacity because of their large cross-sectional area. If this area is reduced by openings, then shear capacities will decrease, and in-plane flexural capacities as governed by net flexural tension may decrease even faster.

5.3.5 Comments on Behavior and Design of Wall Buildings in General

Wall buildings are very efficient structurally, because the same element can act as part of the building envelope, as a vertically spanning structural element perpendicular to the direction of applied lateral load, and as a shear wall parallel to the direction of applied lateral load. If the wall building is made of a material that is aesthetically pleasing, like masonry, even more efficiency is achieved. Wall buildings are also very efficient from the viewpoint of design. The ultimate objective is design, not analysis.

The basic steps that are discussed here, in the context of simple, one-story shear wall buildings, can be applied to multi-story shear wall buildings as well. At the roof level and at each floor level, horizontal diaphragms receive reactions from vertically spanning strips, and transfer those reactions to shear walls. Each shear wall acts essentially as a free-standing, statically determinate cantilever, with axial loads and in-plane lateral loads applied at each floor level. At each floor level, the shear wall must simply be designed for shear, and for combined axial force and moment.

Design of shear wall buildings is typically much easier than the design of frames, which are statically indeterminate and must usually be analyzed using computer programs.

5.3.6 Extension to Design of Unreinforced Masonry Shear Walls with Openings

Consider the structure shown in Fig. 5.24. The wall is identical to that addressed in the previous examples, with the exception of two openings, each measuring 9 ft in plan. These openings divide the wall into three smaller wall segments.

Assume that the applied shear is divided equally among the three wall segments; that points of inflection exist at the mid-height of each wall segment; and that axial forces in the wall are negligible. Then the moments and shears can be determined by statics where L is the 10-ft height of the wall segments. A free body of one wall segment is shown in Fig. 5.25.

The rest of the design proceeds as before. The shear area of the wall segments is reduced in proportion to the plan length of each segment, compared to the plan length

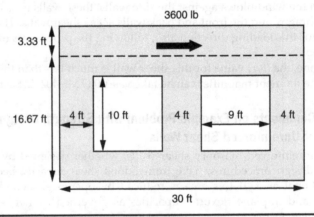

Figure 5.24 Shear wall with openings.

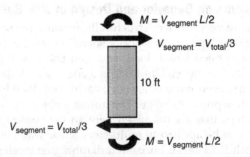

Figure 5.25 Free body of one wall segment.

of the original unperforated wall. The moment of inertia of the segments, however, is considerably less than the moment of inertia of the original unperforated wall.

5.4 Strength Design of Anchor Bolts

In masonry construction, anchor bolts are most commonly used to anchor roof or floor diaphragms to masonry walls. As shown in Fig. 5.26, vertically oriented anchor bolts can be placed along the top of a masonry wall to anchor a roof diaphragm resting on the top of the wall. Alternatively, horizontally oriented anchor bolts can be placed along the face of a masonry wall to anchor a diaphragm through a horizontal ledger. In these applications, anchor bolts are subjected to combinations of tension and shear. In this section, the behavior of anchors under those loadings is discussed, and the strength-design provisions of TMS 402-22 are reviewed.

5.4.1 Behavior and Design of Anchor Bolts Loaded in Tension

Anchor bolts loaded in tension can fail by breakout of a roughly conical body of masonry, or by yield and fracture of the anchor bolt steel. Bent-bar anchor bolts (such as J-bolts or L-bolts) can also fail by straightening of the bent portion of the anchor bolt, followed by pullout of the anchor bolt from the masonry. Nominal tensile capacity as governed by masonry breakout is evaluated using a design model based on a uniform tensile stress of $4\sqrt{f'_m}$ acting perpendicular to the inclined surface of an idealized breakout body consisting of a right circular cone (Fig. 5.27). The capacity associated with that stress state is identical with the capacity corresponding to a uniform tensile stress of $4\sqrt{f'_m}$ acting perpendicular to the projected area of the right circular cone.

Nominal tensile capacities for anchors as governed by masonry breakout are identical for headed and bent-bar anchors, and are given by Equation 9-1 of TMS 402-22.

$$B_{anb} = 4A_{pt}\sqrt{f'_m} \qquad \text{TMS 402-22, Equations 9-1}$$

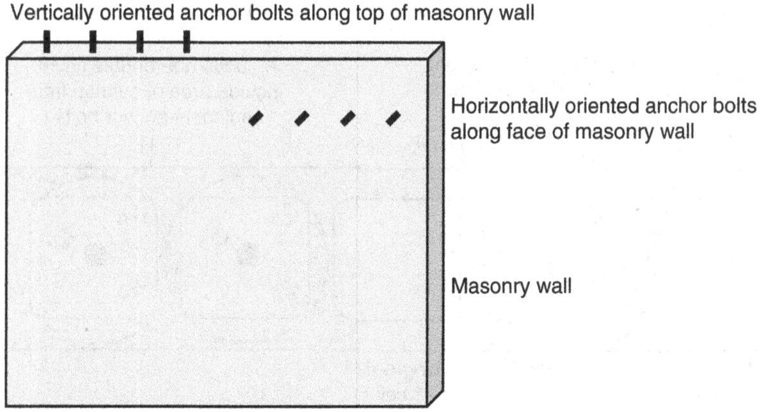

FIGURE 5.26 Common uses of anchor bolts in masonry construction.

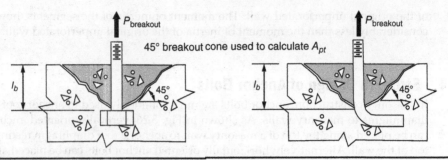

Figure 5.27 Idealized conical breakout cones for anchor bolts loaded in tension.

In Equation 6-5, the projected tension area A_{pt} is evaluated in accordance with Section 6.3.2 of TMS 402-22:

$$A_{pt} = \pi\, l_b^2 \qquad \text{TMS 402-22, Equation 6-5}$$

As required by Section 6.3 of TMS 402-22, the effective embedment length, l_b, for headed anchors is the length of the embedment measured perpendicular from the masonry surface to the compression bearing surface of the anchor head. As required by Section 6.3.5 of TMS 402-22, the effective embedment for a bent-bar anchor bolt, l_b, is the length of embedment measured perpendicular from the masonry surface to the compression bearing surface of the bent end, minus one anchor bolt diameter. These are shown in Fig. 5.27. As shown in Fig. 5.28, the projected area must be reduced for the effect of overlapping projected circular areas, and for the effect of any portion of the project area falling in an open cell or core.

Nominal tensile capacities for anchors as governed by steel and masonry crushing are given by Equations 9-2 and Equation 9-5 of TMS 402-22. In those equations, A_b is the effective tensile stress area of the anchor bolt, including the effect of threads.

$$B_{ans} = A_b f_u \qquad \text{TMS 402-22, Equation 9-2}$$

$$B_{vnc} = 1750 \sqrt[4]{f'_m A_b} \qquad \text{TMS 402-22, Equation 9-5}$$

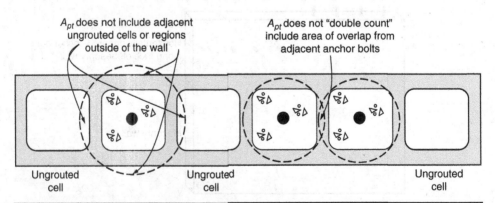

Figure 5.28 Modification of projected breakout area, A_{pt}, by void areas or adjacent anchors.

The nominal tensile capacity of bent-bar anchor bolts as governed by pullout is given by Equation 9-3 of TMS 402-22.

$$B_{anp} = 1.5 f'_m e_b d_b + [300\pi(l_b + e_b + d_b)d_b] \quad \text{TMS 402-22, Equation 9-3}$$

In that equation, the first term represents capacity due to the hook, and the second term represents capacity due to adhesion along the anchor shank. Article 3.2A of TMS 602-22 requires that anchor shanks be cleaned of material that could interfere with that adhesion.

The failure mode with the lowest design capacity governs.

5.4.2 Example: Strength Design of a Single Anchor Loaded in Tension

Using strength design, compute the design tensile capacity of a 1/2-in. diameter, A307 bent-bar anchor with a 1-in. hook, embedded vertically in a grouted cell of a nominal 8-in. wall with a specified compressive strength, f'_m, of 2000 lb/in². Assume that the bottom of the anchor hook is embedded a distance of 4.5 in. This example might represent a tensile anchor used to attach a roof diaphragm to a wall.

First, compute the effective embedment, l_{br}. In accordance with Section 6.3 of TMS 402-22, this is equal to the total embedment of 4.5 in., minus the diameter of the anchor (to get to the inside of the hook), and minus an additional anchor diameter, or 3.5 in. As shown in Fig. 5.29, the projected tensile breakout area has a radius of 3.5 in. (diameter of 7 in.). Because the masonry wall has a specified thickness of 7.63 in., the projected tensile breakout area is not affected by adjacent ungrouted cells or regions outside of the wall.

$$A_{pt} = \pi l_b^2 \quad \text{TMS 402-22, Equation 6-5}$$
$$A_{pt} = \pi (3.5 \text{ in.})^2$$
$$A_{pt} = 38.5 \text{ in}^2$$

Calculate the nominal capacity due to tensile breakout of masonry.

$$B_{anb} = 4 A_{pt} \sqrt{f'_m} \quad \text{TMS 402-22, Equation 9-1}$$
$$B_{anb} = 4 \times 38.5 \text{ in}^2 \sqrt{2000} \text{ lb/in}^2$$
$$B_{anb} = 6887 \text{ lb}$$

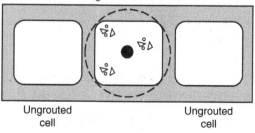

FIGURE 5.29 Example involving a single tensile anchor, placed vertically in a grouted cell.

144 Chapter Five

Now obtain the design capacity by multiplying the nominal capacity by the corresponding strength-reduction factor from Section 9.1.4.1 of TMS 402-22:

$$\phi B_{anb} = 0.5 \times 6887 \text{ lb} \quad \text{TMS 402-22, Section 9.1.4.1}$$

$$\phi B_{anb} = 3444 \text{ lb}$$

Now compute the nominal tensile capacity as governed by steel fracture. In this computation, A_b is the effective tensile stress area of the anchor bolt, including the effect of threads.

$$A_b = \frac{\pi}{4}\left(d_o - \frac{0.9743}{n_t}\right)^2 \quad \text{TMS 402-22, Equation 6-7}$$

where d_o = nominal anchor diameter, in.
n_t = number of threads per inch

For anchors with nominal diameters typically used in masonry, the effective tensile stress area can be approximated with sufficient accuracy as 0.75 times the nominal area. That approximation is used in this and other anchor bolt problems here. Use an ultimate strength for A307 steel of 60 ksi.

$$B_{ans} = A_b f_u \quad \text{TMS 402-22, Equation 9-2}$$

$$B_{ans} = 0.75 \times 0.20 \text{ in}^2 \times 60{,}000 \text{ lb/in}^2$$

$$B_{ans} = 9000 \text{ lb}$$

Now obtain the design capacity by multiplying the nominal capacity by the corresponding strength-reduction factor from Section 9.1.4.1 of TMS 402-22:

$$\phi B_{ans} = 0.75 \times 9000 \text{ lb} \quad \text{TMS 402-22, Section 9.1.4.1}$$

$$\phi B_{anb} = 6750 \text{ lb}$$

The nominal tensile capacity of bent-bar anchor bolts as governed by pullout is given by Equation 9-3 of TMS 402-22.

$$B_{anp} = 1.5 f'_m e_b d_b + [300\pi(l_b + e_b + d_b)d_b] \quad \text{TMS 402-22, Equation 9-3}$$

$$B_{anp} = 1.5 \times 2000 \text{ lb/in}^2 \times 1.0 \text{ in.} \times 0.5 \text{ in.}$$

$$+ [300\pi(3.5 \text{ in.} + 1.0 \text{ in.} + 0.5 \text{ in.})\,0.5 \text{ in.}]$$

$$B_{anp} = 1500 \text{ lb} + 2356 \text{ lb}$$

$$B_{anp} = 3856 \text{ lb}$$

Now obtain the design capacity by multiplying the nominal capacity by the corresponding strength-reduction factor from Section 9.1.4.1 of TMS 402-22:

$$\phi B_{anp} = 0.65 \times 3856 \text{ lb} \quad \text{TMS 402-22, Section 9.1.4.1}$$

$$\phi B_{anp} = 2506 \text{ lb}$$

Strength Design of Unreinforced Masonry Elements

The governing design tensile capacity is the lowest of that governed by masonry breakout (3444 lb), fracture of the anchor shank (6750 lb), and pullout (2506 lb). Pullout governs, and the design tensile capacity is 2506 lb.

If this problem had involved an anchor with deeper embedment (so that the projected tensile breakout area would have been affected by adjacent ungrouted cells or regions outside of the wall), only the anchor capacity as governed by tensile breakout would have been affected, due to a reduced projected tensile breakout area.

Similarly, if this problem had involved adjacent anchors with overlapping tensile breakout areas, only the anchor capacity as governed by tensile breakout would have been affected, again due to a reduced projected tensile breakout area.

5.4.3 Behavior and Design of Anchor Bolts Loaded in Shear

Anchor bolts loaded in shear, and located without a nearby free edge in the direction of load, can fail by local crushing of the masonry under bearing stresses from the anchor bolt; by pryout of the head of the anchor in a direction opposite to the direction of applied load, or by yield and fracture of the anchor bolt steel. Anchor bolts loaded in shear, and located near a free edge in the direction of load, can also fail by breakout of a roughly semi-conical volume of masonry in the direction of the applied shear. Pryout and shear breakout are shown in Part (a) and Part (b), respectively, of Fig. 5.30.

Nominal shear capacity as governed by pryout is taken as twice the nominal tensile breakout capacity, based on the same empirical evidence used in ACI 318. Nominal shear capacity as governed by masonry breakout is evaluated using a design model based on a uniform tensile stress of $4\sqrt{f'_m}$ acting perpendicular to the inclined surface of an idealized breakout body consisting of a right circular semi-cone (Fig. 5.31).

The capacity associated with that stress state is identical with the capacity corresponding to a uniform tensile stress of $4\sqrt{f'_m}$ acting perpendicular to the projected area of the right circular semi-cone.

The nominal shear breakout capacity of an anchor is given by Equation 9-4 of TMS 402-22. In evaluating that equation, the projected area of the breakout semi-cone is given by Equation 6-6 of TMS 402-22.

$$B_{vnb} = 4A_{pv}\sqrt{f'_m} \qquad \text{TMS 402-22, Equation 9-4}$$

$$A_{pv} = \frac{\pi l_{be}^2}{2} \qquad \text{TMS 402-22, Equation 6-6}$$

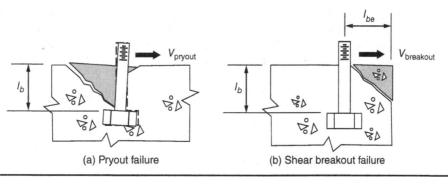

(a) Pryout failure (b) Shear breakout failure

FIGURE 5.30 Pryout failure (a) and shear breakout failure (b).

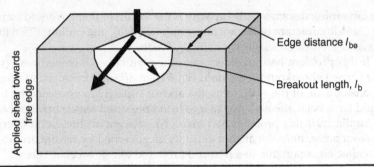

FIGURE 5.31 Design idealization associated with shear breakout failure.

Nominal capacities of anchors loaded in shear are given by Equation 9-4 for masonry breakout, by Equation 9-5 for masonry crushing, by Equation 9-6 for shear pryout, and by Equation 9-7 for shear strength. In Equations 9-5 and 9-7 of TMS 402-22 (masonry breakout and for the anchor in shear, respectively), the effective tensile stress area of the bolt (including the effect of threads) is to be used, unless threads are excluded from the shear plane.

$$B_{vnc} = 1750 \sqrt[4]{f'_m A_b} \qquad \text{TMS 402-22, Equation 9-5}$$

$$B_{vnpry} = 2.0 B_{anb} = 8 A_{pt} \sqrt{f'_m} \qquad \text{TMS 402-22, Equation 9-6}$$

$$B_{vns} = 0.6 A_b f_u \qquad \text{TMS 402-22, Equation 9-7}$$

The failure mode with the lowest design capacity governs.

5.4.4 Example: Strength Design of a Single Anchor Loaded in Shear

Using strength design, compute the design shear capacity of a 1/2-in. diameter, A307 bent-bar anchor with a 1-in. hook, embedded horizontally in a grouted cell of a nominal 8-in. wall with a specified compressive strength, f'_m, of 2000 lb/in². Assume that the bottom of the anchor hook is embedded a distance of 4.5 in., and that the anchor is located far from free edges in the direction of applied shear. This might represent an anchor used to attach a ledger to a masonry wall. Because free edges are not a factor, shear breakout does not apply.

First, compute the effective embedment, l_b. In accordance with Section 6.2 of TMS 402-22, this is equal to the total embedment of 4.5 in., minus the diameter of the anchor (to get to the inside of the hook), and minus an additional anchor diameter, or 3.5 in. The projected tensile breakout area has a radius of 3.5 in. (diameter of 7 in.).

$$A_{pv} = \frac{\pi l_{be}^2}{2} \qquad \text{TMS 402-22, Equation 6-6}$$

$$A_{pv} = \frac{\pi \, 3.5 \text{ in}^2}{2}$$

$$A_{pv} = 19.24 \text{ in}^2$$

Strength Design of Unreinforced Masonry Elements

First, compute the allowable capacity of the anchor as governed by masonry breakout.

$$B_{nvb} = 4A_{pv}\sqrt{f'_m} \quad \text{TMS 402-22, Equation 9-4}$$

$$B_{nvb} = 4 \times 19.4 \text{ in}^2 \sqrt{2000 \text{ psi}} = 3342 \text{ lb}$$

Now obtain the design capacity by multiplying the nominal capacity by the corresponding strength-reduction factor from Section 9.1.4.1 of TMS 402-22:

$$\phi B_{vnc} = 0.5 \times 3{,}342 \text{ lb} \quad \text{TMS 402-22, Section 9.1.4.1}$$

$$\phi B_{vnc} = 1721 \text{ lb}$$

Next, compute the nominal capacity of the anchor as governed by masonry crushing.

$$B_{vnc} = 1750 \sqrt[4]{f'_m A_b} \quad \text{TMS 402-22, Equation 9-5}$$

In this computation, A_b is the effective tensile stress area of the anchor bolt, including the effect of threads.

$$A_b = \frac{\pi}{4}\left(d_o - \frac{0.9743}{n_t}\right)^2 \quad \text{TMS 402-22, Equation 6-7}$$

where d_o = nominal anchor diameter, in.
n_t = number of threads per inch

For anchors with nominal diameters typically used in masonry, the effective tensile stress area can be approximated with sufficient accuracy as 0.75 times the nominal area. That approximation is used in this and other anchor bolt problems here.

$$B_{vnc} = 1750\sqrt[4]{f'_m A_b} \quad \text{TMS 402-22, Equations 6-7 and 9-5}$$

$$B_{vnc} = 1750\sqrt[4]{2000 \text{ lb/in}^2 \times (0.75 \times 0.20 \text{ in}^2)}$$

$$B_{vnc} = 7283 \text{ lb/in}^2$$

Now obtain the design capacity by multiplying the nominal capacity by the correspond strength-reduction factor from Section 9.1.4.1 of TMS 402-22:

$$\phi B_{vnc} = 0.5 \times 7283 \text{ lb} \quad \text{TMS 402-22, Section 9.1.4.1}$$

$$\phi B_{vnc} = 3{,}642 \text{ lb}$$

Next, compute the nominal capacity of the anchor as governed by pryout.

$$B_{vnpry} = 2.0 B_{anb} = 8 A_{pt}\sqrt{f'_m} \quad \text{TMS 402-22, Equation 9-6}$$

Because nominal pryout capacity is a multiple of the nominal tensile breakout capacity, we must compute the nominal tensile breakout capacity.

$$B_{anb} = 4A_{pt}\sqrt{f'_m} \quad \text{TMS 402-22, Equations 9-1}$$
$$B_{anb} = 4 \times 38.5 \text{ in}^2 \sqrt{2000} \text{ lb/in}^2$$
$$B_{anb} = 6887 \text{ lb}$$

Continue with the pryout calculation:

$$B_{vnpry} = 2.0 B_{anb} \quad \text{TMS 402-22, Equation 9-6}$$
$$B_{vnpry} = 2.0 \times 6887 \text{ lb}$$
$$B_{vnpry} = 13{,}774 \text{ lb}$$

Now obtain the design capacity by multiplying the nominal capacity by the corresponding strength-reduction factor from Section 9.1.4.1 of TMS 402-22:

$$\phi B_{vnpry} = 0.5 \times 13{,}774 \text{ lb} \quad \text{TMS 402-22, Section 9.1.4.1}$$
$$\phi B_{vnpry} = 6887 \text{ lb}$$

Next, compute the nominal capacity of the anchor as governed by fracture of the anchor shank. Use an ultimate strength for A307 steel of 60 ksi.

$$B_{vns} = 0.6 A_b f_u \quad \text{TMS 402-22, Equations 6-7 and 9-7}$$
$$B_{vns} = 0.6 \times (0.75 \times 0.20 \text{ in}^2) \times 60{,}000 \text{ lb/in}^2$$
$$B_{vns} = 5400 \text{ lb}$$

Now obtain the design capacity by multiplying the nominal capacity by the corresponding strength-reduction factor from Section 9.1.4.1 of TMS 402-22:

$$\phi B_{vns} = 0.65 \times 5400 \text{ lb} \quad \text{TMS 402-22, Section 9.1.4.1}$$
$$\phi B_{vns} = 3510 \text{ lb}$$

The governing design shear capacity is the lowest of that governed by masonry breakout (1721 lb) masonry crushing (3642 lb), pryout (6887 lb), and yield and fracture of the anchor shank (3510 lb). Because the anchor is not close to a free edge, shear breakout does not apply. Masonry breakout, and the design shear capacity is 1721 lb.

If this problem had involved an anchor loaded toward a free edge, then shear breakout would have had to be checked.

5.4.5 Behavior and Design of Anchor Bolts Loaded in Combined Tension and Shear

Design capacities of anchor bolts in combined tension and shear are given by the interaction equation of Equation 9-8 of TMS 402-22.

$$\left(\frac{b_{af}}{\phi B_{an}}\right)^{\frac{5}{3}} + \left(\frac{b_{vf}}{\phi B_{vn}}\right)^{\frac{5}{3}} \leq 1 \quad \text{TMS 402-22, Equation 9-8}$$

5.5 Required Details for Unreinforced Bearing Walls and Shear Walls

Bearing walls that resist out-of-plane lateral loads, and shear walls, must be designed to transfer lateral loads to the floors above and below. Examples of such connections are shown below. These connections would have to be strengthened for regions subject to strong earthquakes or strong winds. Section 1604.8.2 of the 2024 IBC has additional requirements for anchorage of diaphragms to masonry walls. Section 12.11 of ASCE 7-22 has additional requirements for anchorage of structural walls for structures assigned to Seismic Design Categories C and higher.

5.5.1 Wall-to-Foundation Connections

As shown in Fig. 5.32, CMU walls (or the inner CMU wythe of a drainage wall) must be connected to the concrete foundation. Bond breaker should be used only between the outer veneer wythe and the foundation.

5.5.2 Wall-to-Floor Details

Example of a wall-to-floor detail are shown in Figs. 5.33 and 5.34. In the latter detail (floor or roof planks oriented parallel to walls), the planks are actually cambered. They are shown on the outside of the walls so that this camber does not interfere with the coursing of the units. Some designers object to this detail because it could lead to spalling of the cover. If it is modified so that the planks rest on the face shells of the walls, then the thickness of the topping must vary to adjust for the camber, and form boards must be used against both sides of the wall underneath the planks, so that the concrete or grout that is cast into the bond beam does not run out underneath the cambered beam.

5.5.3 Wall-to-Roof Details

An example of a wall-to-roof detail is shown in Fig. 5.35.

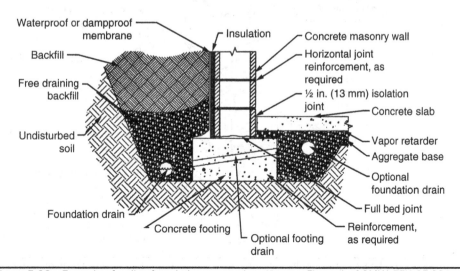

Figure 5.32 Example of wall-to-foundation connection. (*Source:* Figure 1 of CMHA TEK 05-03.)

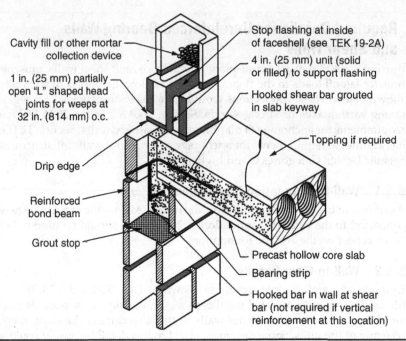

FIGURE 5.33 Example of wall-to-floor connection, planks perpendicular to wall. (*Source:* Figure 14 of CMHA TEK 05-07A.)

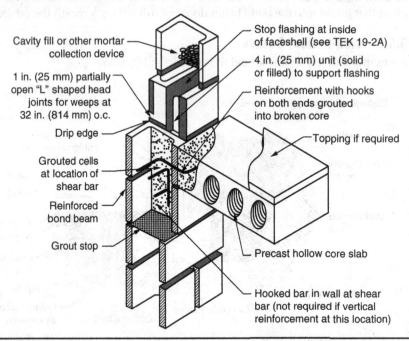

FIGURE 5.34 Example of wall-to-floor connection, planks parallel to wall. (*Source:* Figure 15 of CMHA TEK 05-07A.)

Strength Design of Unreinforced Masonry Elements **151**

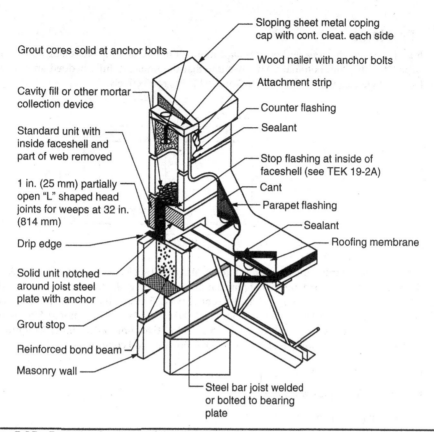

FIGURE 5.35 Example of wall-to-roof detail. (*Source:* Figure 11 of CMHA TEK 05-07A.)

5.5.4 Typical Details of Wall-to-Wall Connections

Typical details of wall-to-wall connections are shown in Fig. 5.36.

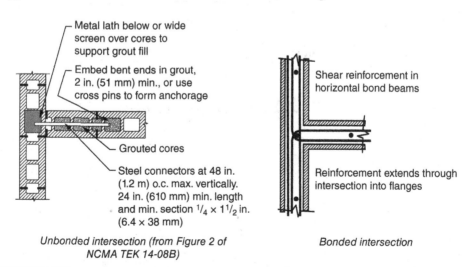

FIGURE 5.36 Examples of wall-to-wall connection details.

5.6 Problems

5.1 Determine the area and out-of-plane moment of inertia for a 1-foot long strip of a wall constructed with 10-in. nominal CMU. Assume that the units are fully bedded and have specified face- and web-shell thicknesses of 1.25 and 1.125 in., respectively.

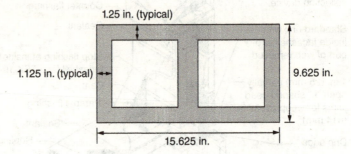

5.2 Design a simply supported ungrouted bearing wall subjected to eccentric axial loads of 500 lb dead and 250 lb live load per foot of plan length, combined with out-of-plane wind load of 25 psf. All loads are unfactored. The axial-load eccentricity is 2.5 in. and the story height is 10 ft. Assume a specified compressive strength of masonry of 2000 psi and Type S PCL mortar. Start with nominal 6-in. CMU and the self-weight from Table 5.5 (26 lb/ft² for ungrouted units). Continue until you find a satisfactory nominal thickness. Use the following load conditions.

a. Gravity loads alone.

b. Gravity loads plus wind load.

The wall is as shown below:

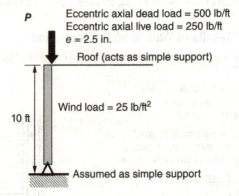

Strength Design of Unreinforced Masonry Elements

5.3 In the building shown below, the roof is assumed to span longitudinally between the two gable walls. The 1-foot strip of CMU shown below is subjected to unfactored eccentric gravity loads of 800 lb dead load and 200 lb live load at the building apex, whose height is 16 ft. The eccentricity is 3 in. Include self-weight. The wall is also subjected to an out-of-plane wind load whose magnitude is not specified. A ceiling provides horizontal restraint at the mid-height of each gable wall. As an initial design assumption, idealize this vertical strip assuming zero moment at the building apex, the ceiling, and the base. Assume ungrouted units; 8-in. nominal thickness; f'_m = 2000 psi; and Type S PCL mortar.

Part 1 Considering gravity loads only, check the existing design for compliance with TMS 402-22.

Part 2 Repeat Part 1 including wind load. Calculate the maximum unfactored wind load the vertical strip can support.

The wall is as shown below:

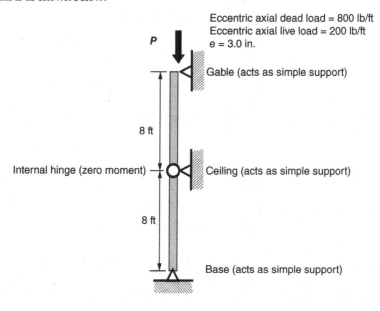

*5.4 Repeat Problem 5.3 using a single two-span beam. This assumes a continuous beam-column at the height of the ceiling and at the base. Comment on how the maximum permissible wind load changes.

Part 1 Considering gravity loads only, check the existing design for compliance with TMS 402-22.

Part 2 Repeat Part 1 including wind load. Calculate the maximum unfactored wind load the vertical strip can support.

The wall is as shown below:

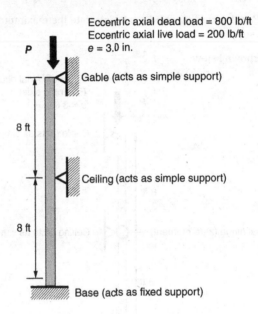

5.5 Extend the problem of Fig. 5.21 to a two-story building. Change the typical story height to 10 ft. Gravity loads on a typical floor are equal to those on the roof. Try a nominal 8-in. CMU wall, ungrouted, with face-shell bedding and Type S PCL mortar. Use a specified masonry compressive strength of 2000 psi. Assume a unit density of 115 lb/ft^3, and use the self-weight from Table 5.5 (33 lb/ft^2). If this does not work, list an alternate way to solve the problem using 8-in. units.

---

*Denotes problems intended for graduate students.

CHAPTER 6
Strength Design of Reinforced Masonry Elements

6.1 Strength Design of Reinforced Beams and Lintels

6.1.1 Background on Strength Design of Reinforced Masonry Beams for Flexure

Strength design of reinforced masonry beams follows the same steps used for reinforced concrete beams. The basic assumptions (Section 9.3.2 of *TMS 402-22*) are shown in Fig. 6.1.

Strain in the masonry is assumed to have a maximum useful value of 0.0025 for concrete masonry and 0.0035 for clay masonry. Tension reinforcement is assumed to be somewhere on the yield plateau. Because axial load is zero, flexural capacity is equal to either the tension force or the compression force on the cross-section, multiplied by the internal lever arm (the distance between the tensile and compressive forces).

$$M_n = A_s f_y \left(d - \frac{\beta_1 c}{2} \right)$$

But the depth of the compressive stress block is known from equilibrium of axial forces:

$$T = C$$

$$A_s f_y = 0.80 f'_m \beta_1 c b$$

$$\beta_1 c = \frac{A_s f_y}{0.80 f'_m b}$$

156 Chapter Six

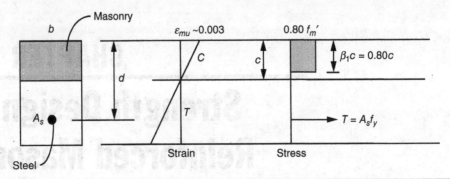

FIGURE 6.1 Assumptions used in strength design of reinforced masonry for flexure.

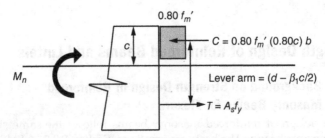

FIGURE 6.2 Equilibrium of internal stresses and external nominal moment for strength design of reinforced masonry for flexure.

Now define $\rho \equiv \dfrac{A_s}{bd}$ and $\omega \equiv \rho\left(\dfrac{f_y}{f'_m}\right)$. Then

$$M_n = A_s f_y \left(d - \dfrac{\beta_1 c}{2}\right)$$

$$M_n = A_s f_y \left(d - \dfrac{A_s f_y}{2 \times 0.80 f'_m b}\right)$$

$$M_n = \rho b d f_y \left(d - \dfrac{\rho b d f_y}{2 \times 0.80 f'_m b}\right)$$

$$M_n = \rho b d f_y \left(\dfrac{f'_m}{f'_m}\right)\left(d - \dfrac{\rho b d f_y}{2 \times 0.80 f'_m b}\right)$$

$$M_n = \omega b d f'_m \left(d - \dfrac{\omega d}{1.6}\right)$$

Strength Design of Reinforced Masonry Elements

And finally,

$$M_n = \omega b d^2 f'_m (1 - 0.63\omega)$$

This closed-form expression permits solving for the required dimensions if the steel percentage is known. The variable ω is sometimes referred to as the "tensile reinforcement index." For design of masonry beams, where dimensions are known, it is usually easier simply to use $M_n = A_s f_y \left(d - \dfrac{\beta_1 c}{2} \right)$. For additional simplicity, the internal lever arm $\left(d - \dfrac{\beta_1 c}{2} \right)$ can be approximated as $0.9\,d$.

The steel percentage is constrained by the requirement that the steel be on the yield plateau when the masonry reaches its maximum useful strain. For this condition to be satisfied, the steel must yield before the masonry reaches its maximum useful strain. In other words, the steel percentage must be less than the balanced steel percentage, at which the steel yields just as the masonry reaches its maximum useful strain.

The balanced steel percentage for strength design can be derived based on the strains in steel and masonry:

First, locate the neutral axis under balanced conditions:

$$\frac{\varepsilon_{mu}}{\varepsilon_y} = \frac{c}{d-c}$$

$$c\varepsilon_y = \varepsilon_{mu}(d-c)$$

$$c(\varepsilon_y + \varepsilon_{mu}) = \varepsilon_{mu} d$$

$$c = d \left(\frac{\varepsilon_{mu}}{\varepsilon_y + \varepsilon_{mu}} \right)$$

Next, compute the compressive force under those conditions, and compute balanced steel area as the steel area, acting at yield, that is necessary to equilibrate that compressive force:

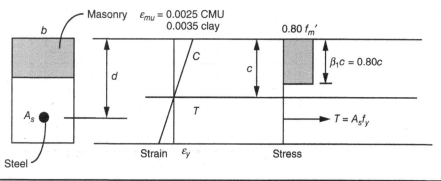

Figure 6.3 Conditions corresponding to balanced reinforcement percentage for strength design.

$$T = C$$

$$A_{sb}f_y = 0.80 f'_m \beta_1 cb$$

$$A_{sb}f_y = 0.80 f'_m \beta_1 bd \left(\frac{\varepsilon_{mu}}{\varepsilon_y + \varepsilon_{mu}} \right)$$

$$\rho_b = 0.80 \left(\frac{f'_m}{f_y} \right) \beta_1 \left(\frac{\varepsilon_{mu}}{\varepsilon_y + \varepsilon_{mu}} \right)$$

If the reinforcement ratio is less than the balanced reinforcement ratio, the steel will be on the yield plateau. When using an assumed internal lever arm of $0.9\,d$, designers do not explicitly check if the steel has yielded. Because lightly reinforced or deep-beams will nearly always satisfy this condition, the simplifying assumption is used in this textbook.

6.1.2 Steps in Strength Design of Reinforced Beams and Lintels

The most common reinforced masonry beam is a lintel. Lintels are beams that support masonry over openings. Strength design of reinforced beams and lintels follows the steps given below:

1) Shear design:
   a) Calculate the factored design shear, and compare it with the corresponding resistance. Revise the lintel depth if necessary.

2) Flexural design:
   a) Calculate the factored design moment.
   b) Calculate the required flexural reinforcement. Check that it fits within minimum and maximum reinforcement limitations.

In many cases, the depth of the lintel is determined by architectural considerations. In other cases, it is necessary to determine the number of courses of masonry that will work as a beam. For example, consider the lintel in Fig. 6.4.

The depth of the beam, and hence the area that is effective in resisting shear, is determined by the number of courses it comprises of. Because it is not very practical to put shear reinforcement in masonry beams, the depth of the beam may be determined

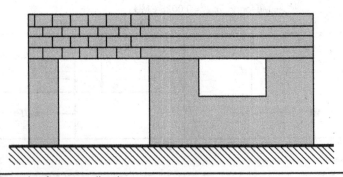

FIGURE 6.4 Example of masonry lintel.

TABLE 6.1 Physical Properties of Steel Reinforcing Wire and Bars (from Table CC-6.1.3 of *TMS 402-22*)

Designation	Diameter, in.	Area, in²
Wire		
W1.1 (11 gage)	0.121	0.011
W1.7 (9 gage)	0.148	0.017
W2.1 (8 gage)	0.162	0.020
W2.8 (3/16 wire)	0.187	0.027
W4.9 (1/4 wire)	0.250	0.049
Bars		
#3	0.375	0.11
#4	0.500	0.20
#5	0.625	0.31
#6	0.750	0.44
#7	0.875	0.60
#8	1.000	0.79
#9	1.128	1.00
#10	1.270	1.27
#11	1.410	1.56

by this. In other words, the beam design may start with the number of courses that are needed so that shear can be resisted by masonry alone.

6.1.3 Physical Properties of Steel Reinforcing Wire and Bars

Physical properties of steel reinforcing wire and bars are given in Table 6.1.

Cover requirements are given in Section 6.1.5 of *TMS 402-22*. Minimum cover for joint reinforcement (exterior exposure) is 5/8 in.

6.1.4 Example: Lintel Design According to Strength Provisions

Suppose that we have a uniformly distributed load of 850 lb/ft, applied at the level of the roof of the structure shown in Fig. 6.5. Design the lintel.

According to Table 2 of *TMS 602-22*, for Type M or S mortar and concrete units with a specified strength of 2000 lb/in² (the minimum specified strength for ASTM C90 units), the compressive strength of the masonry can conservatively be taken as 2000 psi

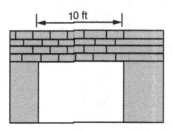

FIGURE 6.5 Example for strength design of a lintel.

(the so-called "unit strength method"). If the compressive strength is evaluated by prism testing, a higher value can probably be used. Take the specified compressive strength of the masonry as $f'_m = 2000$ lb/in².

Assume fully grouted concrete masonry with a nominal thickness of 8 in., a weight of 81 lb/ft², and a specified compressive strength of 2000 lb/in². Use Type S PCL mortar. The lintel has a span of 8 ft, and a total depth (height of parapet plus distance between the roof and the lintel) of 4 ft. These are shown in the schematic figure below. Assume that 700 lb/ft of the roof load is D, and the remaining 350 lb/ft is L. The governing loading combination is $1.2D + 1.6L$. Our design presumes that the entire depth of the lintel is grouted.

First check whether the depth of the lintel is sufficient to avoid the use of shear reinforcement. Because the opening may have a movement joint on either side, again use a span equal to the clear distance, plus one-half of a half-unit on each side. So, the span is 10 ft plus 8 in., or 10.67 ft.

$$M_u = \frac{w_u l^2}{8} = \frac{[(700 + 4\,\text{ft} \times 81\,\text{lb/ft}) \times 1.2 + 350\,\text{lb/ft} \times 1.6] \times 10.67^2\,\text{ft}^2 \times 12\,\text{in./ft}}{8}$$

$$= 305{,}479\,\text{lb-in.}$$

$$V_u = \frac{w_u l}{2} = \frac{[(700 + 4\,\text{ft} \times 81\,\text{lb/ft}) \times 1.2 + 350\,\text{lb/ft} \times 1.6] \times 10.67\,\text{ft}}{2} = 9543\,\text{lb}$$

The bars in the lintel will probably be placed in the lower part of an inverted bottom course.

The effective depth d is calculated using the minimum cover of 1.5 in. (Section 6.1.5 of TMS 402-22), plus one-half the diameter of an assumed #8 bar (Fig. 6.6).

Because this is a reinforced element, shearing capacity is calculated using Section 9.3.3.1.2.1 of TMS 402-22:

$$V_{nm} = \left[4.0 - 1.75\left(\frac{M_u}{V_u d_v}\right)\right] bd_v \sqrt{f'_m} + 0.25 P_u$$

As $(M_u/V_u d_v)$ increases, V_{nm} decreases. Because $(M_u/V_u d_v)$ need not be taken greater than 1.0 (Section 9.3.3.1.2.1 of TMS 402-22), the most conservative (lowest) value of V_{nm} is obtained with $(M_u/V_u d_v)$ equal to 1.0. Also, factored design axial load, P_u, is zero:

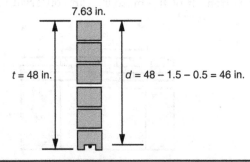

FIGURE 6.6 Example showing placement of bottom reinforcement in lowest course of lintel.

$$V_{nm} = [4.0 - 1.75(1.0)]bd_v\sqrt{f'_m}$$

$$V_{nm} = 2.25bd_v\sqrt{f'_m}$$

The nominal in-plane shear stress, V_n, is the summation of the nominal capacity of the masonry and nominal capacity of the shear reinforcement:

$$V_n = (V_{nm} + V_{ns})\gamma_g$$

In this case, we shall have no shear reinforcement, so $V_{ns} = 0$. Because our masonry is fully grouted, $\gamma_g = 1$ and our shear strength is the nominal capacity of the masonry.

$$V_u = 9543 \text{ lb} \leq \phi V_n = 0.8 \times 2.25 \times 7.63 \text{ in.} \times 48 \text{ in.} \times \sqrt{2000} \text{ lb/in}^2 = 29,462 \text{ lb}$$

Also, according to Equation 9-17 of *TMS 402-22*,

$$V_n \leq 4bd_v\sqrt{f'_m}$$

$$V_n \leq 4 \times 7.625 \text{ in.} \times 48 \text{ in} \sqrt{2000 \text{ psi}} = 65,470 \text{ lb}$$

This does not govern, and the shear design is acceptable.

Now check the required flexural reinforcement using an assumed lever arm of $0.9d$:

$$M_n = A_s f_y (\text{lever arm})$$

$$M_n \approx A_s f_y \times 0.9d$$

In our case,

$$M_n^{\text{required}} = \frac{M_u}{\phi} = \frac{M_u}{0.9} = \frac{305,479 \text{ lb-in.}}{0.9} = 339,421 \text{ lb-in.}$$

$$A_s^{\text{required}} \approx \frac{M_n^{\text{required}}}{0.9df_y} = \frac{339,421 \text{ lb-in.}}{0.9 \times 46 \text{ in.} \times 60,000 \text{ lb/in}^2} = 0.137 \text{ in}^2$$

This is satisfied with a #4 bar in the lowest course (of concrete masonry units). The corresponding nominal flexural capacity is computed as illustrated below.

$$a = \frac{A_s f_y}{0.8 f'_m b} = \frac{0.2 \text{ in}^2 \times 60,000 \text{ psi}}{0.8 \times 2000 \text{ psi} \times 7.625 \text{ in.}} = 0.984 \text{ in.}$$

$$M_n = 0.2 \text{ in}^2 \times 60,000 \frac{\text{lb}}{\text{in}^2} \times \left(46 \text{ in.} - \frac{0.984}{2 \text{ in.}}\right) = 546,098 \text{ lb-in.}$$

Because the lintel is 4 ft tall and lightly reinforced, the strain in the tensile steel will yield and meet the maximum area of flexural tensile reinforcement prescribed in *TMS 402-22* Section 9.3.3.2.4. Here we review the required calculations.

$$c = \frac{a}{\beta_1} = \frac{0.984 \text{ in.}}{0.8} = 1.23 \text{ in.}$$

$$\varepsilon_s = \frac{d-c}{c} \times \varepsilon_{mu} = \frac{46 \text{ in.} - 1.23 \text{ in.}}{1.23 \text{ in.}} \times 0.0035 = 0.127$$

$$\varepsilon_s > \varepsilon_{ty} + 0.003 = \frac{60,000 \text{ psi}}{29,000,000 \text{ psi}} + 0.003 = 0.00507$$

The section is indeed tension controlled and we meet the requirements of *TMS 402-22* Section 9.1.4. Thus, the corresponding strength reduction factor is 0.9.

$$\phi M_n = 0.9 \times 546,098 \text{ kip-in.} = 491,489 \text{ lb-in.}$$

$$M_u = 172,377 \text{ lb-in.} < \phi M_n = 491,489 \text{ lb-in.}$$

Also include two #4 bars at the level of the roof (bond beam reinforcement). The flexural design is quite simple.

Section 9.3.3.2.2.1 of *TMS 402-22* requires that the nominal flexural strength of a beam not be less than 1.3 times the nominal cracking capacity, calculated using the modulus of rupture from Section 9.1.9.2 of *TMS 402-22*. In our case, the nominal cracking moment for the 4-ft deep section is

$$M_{cr} = Sf_r = \frac{bt^2}{6} f_r = \frac{7.625 \text{ in.} \times 48^2 \text{ in}^2}{6} \times 267 \frac{\text{lb}}{\text{in}^2} = 781,776 \text{ lb-in.}$$

This value, multiplied by 1.3, is 1,063,309 lb-in., which exceeds the nominal capacity of this lintel with the provided #4 bar. Flexural reinforcement must be increased to

$$A_s \approx A_s \frac{1.3 M_{cr}}{M_n} = 0.2 \text{ in}^2 \left(\frac{1,063,309 \text{ lb-in}}{546,098 \text{ lb-in.}} \right) = 0.372 \text{ in}^2$$

Under typical circumstances, the area of tensile reinforcement would need to be increased. However, Section 9.3.4.2.2.2 of *TMS 402-22* need not be met if the amount of tensile reinforcement is at least one-third greater than required by analysis (Section 9.3.3.2.2.2 of *TMS 402-22*). Because in this case $M_n/M_u = 546,098/305,479 = 1.79$, we do not need to increase the area of tensile reinforcement.

Finally, Section 9.3.3.2.4 of *TMS 402-22* imposes maximum flexural reinforcement limitations that are based on a series of critical strain gradients. These generally do not govern for members with little or no axial load, like this lintel. They may govern for members with significant axial load, such as tall shear walls.

6.1.5   Comments on Arching Action

1) Using the traditional assumption that distributed loads act only within a beam length defined by 45-degree lines from the ends of the distributed load, it would have been possible to take advantage of so-called "arching action" to reduce the gravity load for which the lintel must be designed. Nevertheless, this measure is hardly necessary, because the required area of reinforcement is quite small in any case.

2) Even though it would have been possible to refine the flexural design (for example, by reducing the required depth of the lintel, or including the mid-depth reinforcement in the bond beam in the calculation of flexural resistance), this additional design effort would not have been cost-effective. The goal is to simplify the design process, and the final layout of reinforcement.

6.2 Strength Design of Reinforced Curtain Walls

6.2.1 Background on Curtain Walls

In the first part of the structural design section of this book, we began with the design of panel walls, which can be designed as unreinforced masonry, and which span primarily in the vertical direction to transmit out-of-plane loads to the structural system. Panel walls are nonload-bearing masonry, because they support gravity loads from self-weight only.

At this point, it is appropriate for us to study another type of nonload-bearing masonry, the curtain wall. Like panel walls, curtain walls carry gravity load from self-weight only, and transmit out-of-plane loads to a structural frame. Unlike panel walls, however, curtain walls can be more than one story high, and span horizontally rather than vertically. Typical curtain wall construction is shown in Fig. 6.7.

A single wythe of masonry spans horizontally between columns, which support the roof. This type of construction can be used for industrial buildings, gymnasiums, theaters, and other buildings of similar configuration.

In previous sections dealing with panel walls, we have seen that because those walls are unreinforced, their design is governed by the flexural tensile strength of masonry. In the previous example, using reasonable unfactored wind loads of about 32 lb/ft^2, the flexural tensile stresses in vertically spanning panel walls were comfortably within allowable values.

If we tried to use the same principles to design horizontally spanning curtain walls, however, they wouldn't work. In the figure above, the horizontal span between columns is at least 20 ft, about twice the typical vertical span of panel walls. Since moments increase as the square of the span, doubling the span would increase the flexural tensile stresses by a factor of four. Even considering that allowable flexural tensile stresses parallel to bed joints in running bond are about twice as high as those normal to the bed joints (reflecting the interlocking nature of running bond), the calculated flexural tensile stresses in the direction of span would exceed the allowable values.

The most reasonable solution to this problem is to reinforce the masonry horizontally. Single-wythe curtain walls are commonly used for industrial buildings, where water-penetration resistance is not a primary design consideration.

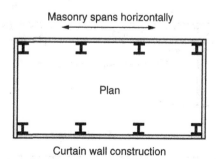

FIGURE 6.7 Plan view of typical curtain wall construction.

6.2.2 Examples of Use of Curtain Walls—Clay Masonry

Examples of use of curtain walls with clay masonry are shown in Fig. 6.8.

6.2.3 Examples of Use of Curtain Walls—Concrete Masonry

Examples of use of curtain walls with concrete masonry are shown in Fig. 6.9.

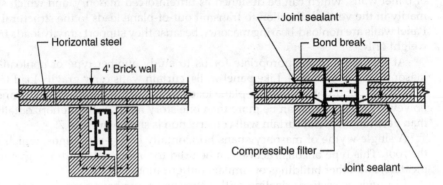

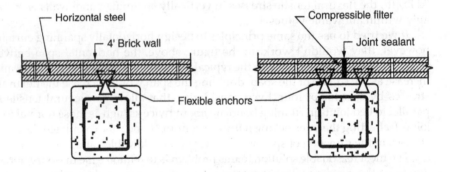

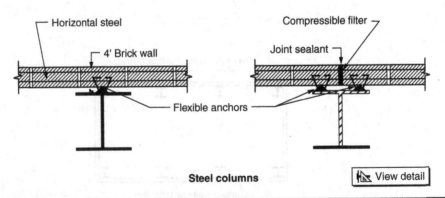

FIGURE 6.8 Examples of use of curtain walls of clay masonry. (*Source:* Figure 6 of BIA Technical Note 17L.)

Strength Design of Reinforced Masonry Elements

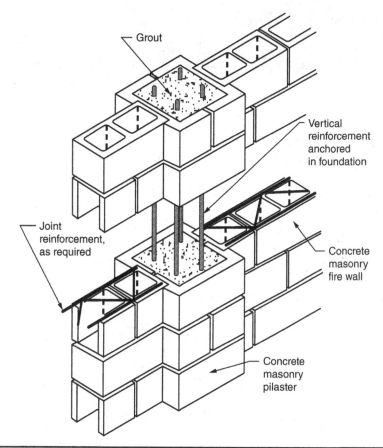

FIGURE 6.9 Examples of the use of curtain walls with concrete masonry. (*Source:* Figure 1 of CMHA TEK 05-08B.)

6.2.4 Structural Action of Curtain Walls

Curtain walls act as horizontal strips to transfer out-of-plane loads to vertical supporting members such as steel or reinforced concrete columns, or masonry pilasters (masonry columns partially embedded in the wall).

6.2.5 Example: Strength Design of a Reinforced Curtain Wall

A curtain wall of standard modular clay units spans 20 ft between columns and is simply supported at each column. It has reinforcement consisting of W4.9 wire each face, every course. The curtain wall is subjected to a wind pressure w = 20 lb/ft². Design the curtain wall. As an initial assumption, use f'_m = 2,500 lb/in². Referring to Table 1 of *TMS 602-22*, this would require clay units with a compressive strength of at least 6600 psi, and Type S mortar.

The load factor for wind load W is 1.0 (ASCE 7-22, Section 2.3.2).

The strength-reduction factor for flexure is 0.90 (Section 9.1.4.4 of *TMS 402-22*), and for shear, 0.80 (Section 9.1.4.5 of *TMS 402-22*).

For a 1-ft strip,

$$M_u = \frac{q_u L^2}{8} = \frac{1.0 \times 32 \frac{\text{lb}}{\text{ft}} \times (20 \text{ ft})^2}{8} \times 12 \text{ in./ft} = 19,200 \text{ lb-in.}$$

$$V_u = \frac{q_u L}{2} = \frac{1.0 \times 32 \text{ lb/ft} \times (20 \text{ ft})}{2} = 320 \text{ lb}$$

6.2.5.1 Flexural Design
We shall begin by approximating the internal lever arm as $0.9\,d$.

$$d = t - \text{cover} - \frac{d_b}{2} = 3.63 - 0.63 - 0.125 = 2.87 \text{ in.}$$

$$M_n \approx A_s f_y (0.9d) = 0.049 \text{ in}^2 \times \left(\frac{12 \text{ in.}}{2.67 \text{ in.}}\right) \times 60,000 \text{ lb/in}^2 \times 0.9 \times 2.87 \text{ in.} = 34,130 \text{ lb-in.}$$

$$M_u = 19,200 \text{ lb-in.} \le \phi \quad M = 0.9 \times 34,130 \text{ lb-in.} = 30,717 \text{ lb-in.}$$

For comparison, calculate the exact depth of the compressive stress block.

$$a = \frac{A_s f_y}{0.85 f'_m b} = \frac{0.049 \text{ in}^2 \times 60,000 \text{ lb/in}^2}{0.85 \times 2500 \text{ psi} \times 12 \text{ in.}} = 0.518 \text{ in.}$$

$$M_n = A_s f_y \left(d - \frac{a}{2}\right) = 0.049 \text{ in}^2 \times \left(\frac{12 \text{ in.}}{2.67 \text{ in.}}\right) \times 60,000 \frac{\text{lb}}{\text{in}^2}$$

$$\times \left(2.87 \text{ in.} - \frac{0.518 \text{ in.}}{2}\right) = 34,449 \text{ lb-in.}$$

$$M_u = 19,200 \text{ lb-in.} \le \phi \quad M = 0.9 \times 34,449 \text{ lb-in.} = 31,049 \text{ lb-in.}$$

The factored nominal flexural capacity is slightly larger, this confirms that the design assumption of $0.9\,d$ is conservative. Next, we check that the steel had yielded.

$$c = \frac{a}{\beta_1} = \frac{0.518 \text{ in.}}{0.8} = 0.648 \text{ in.}$$

$$\varepsilon_s = \frac{d-c}{c} \times \varepsilon_{mu} = \frac{2.87 \text{ in.} - 0.648 \text{ in.}}{0.648 \text{ in.}} \times 0.0035 = 0.012$$

$$\varepsilon_s > \varepsilon_{ty} + 0.003 = \frac{60,000 \text{ psi}}{29,000,000 \text{ psi}} + 0.003 = 0.00507$$

The strain in the steel has exceeded yield strain and is tension controlled justifying a strength reduction factor of 0.9. Our design is satisfactory.

6.2.5.2 Shear Design
From Section 9.3.3.1.2.1 of TMS 402-22,

$$V_{nm} = \left[4.0 - 1.75\left(\frac{M_u}{V_u d_v}\right)\right] b d_v \sqrt{f'_m} + 0.25 P_u$$

Strength Design of Reinforced Masonry Elements

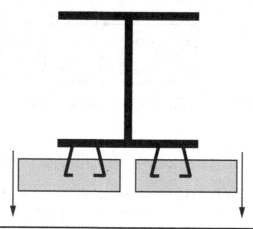

FIGURE 6.10 Anchors holding the ends of curtain wall strips to columns.

As $(M_u/V_u d_v)$ increases, V_{nm} decreases. Because $(M_u/V_u d_v)$ need not be taken greater than 1.0 (*TMS 402-22* Section 9.3.3.1.2.1), the most conservative (lowest) value of V_{nm} is obtained with $(M_u/V_u d_v)$ equal to 1.0. Also, the factored design axial load, P_u, is zero:

$$V_{nm} = [4.0 - 1.75(1.0)]bd_v\sqrt{f'_m}$$

$$V_{nm} = 2.25 bd_v\sqrt{f'_m}$$

$$V_u = 320 \text{ lb} \le \phi V_{nm} = 0.8 \times 2.25 \times 12 \text{ in.} \times 3.63 \text{ in.} \times \sqrt{2500} \text{ lb/in}^2 = 3924 \text{ lb}$$

and the design is acceptable.

6.2.6 Design of Anchors for Curtain Wall

The design of the curtain wall would have to finish with the design of anchors holding the ends of the curtain wall strips, to the columns (Fig. 6.10).

For example, if anchors are spaced at 12 in. vertically, the load per anchor is

$$\text{Anchor load} = \frac{q_u bL}{2} = \frac{32 \text{ lb/ft}^2 \times 1 \text{ ft} \times 20 \text{ ft}}{2} = 320 \text{ lb}$$

6.3 Strength Design of Reinforced Bearing Walls

6.3.1 Introduction to Strength Design of Reinforced Bearing Walls

In this section, we shall study the behavior and design of reinforced masonry wall elements subjected to combinations of axial force and out-of-plane flexure. In the context of engineering mechanics, they are beam-columns. In the context of *TMS 402*, however, a "column" is an isolated masonry element rarely found in real masonry construction.

Masonry beam-columns, like those of reinforced concrete, are designed using moment-axial force interaction diagrams. Combinations of axial force and moment

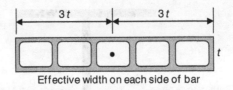

FIGURE 6.11 Effective width of a reinforced masonry bearing wall.

lying inside the diagram represent permitted designs; combinations lying outside represent prohibited ones.

Unlike reinforced concrete, however, reinforced masonry beam-columns rarely take the form of isolated rectangular elements with four longitudinal bars and transverse ties. The most common form for a reinforced masonry beam-column is a wall, loaded out-of-plane by eccentric gravity load, alone or in combination with wind.

For example, Fig. 6.11 shows a portion of a wall, with a total effective width of $6t$ prescribed by Section 5.1.2 of *TMS 402-22*. Other effective widths are possible for other situations.

6.3.2 Background on Moment-Axial Force Interaction Diagrams by the Strength Approach

Using the strength approach, we seek to construct interaction diagrams that represent combinations of axial and flexural capacity. This can be done by hand, or with the help of a spreadsheet.

6.3.3 Background on Strength Interaction Diagrams by Hand

By hand, we can compute three points (pure compression, pure flexure, and the balance point). We then draw a straight line between pure compression and the balance point, and either a straight line or an appropriate curve between the balance point and pure flexure. This approach is commonly applied to reinforced concrete columns (Fig. 6.12).

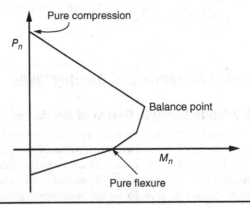

FIGURE 6.12 Idealized moment-axial force interaction diagram using strength design.

6.3.3.1 Pure Compression

$$P_0 = 0.80 \times 0.80 f'_m (A_g - A_{st}) + A_{st} f_y$$

As in ACI 318, the leading factor of 0.80 in effect imposes a minimum design eccentricity.

6.3.3.2 Pure Flexure

As before, the possible contribution of compressive reinforcement is small and can be neglected.

$$\rho = \frac{A_s}{bd}$$

$$\omega = \rho \left(\frac{f_y}{f'_m} \right)$$

$$M_n = A_s f_y \left(d - \frac{\beta_1 c}{2} \right) = \omega b d^2 f'_m (1 - 0.63\omega)$$

6.3.3.3 Balance Point

First, locate the neutral axis (Fig. 6.13):

$$\frac{c}{d-c} = \frac{\varepsilon_{mu}}{\varepsilon_y}$$

$$c = d \left(\frac{\varepsilon_{mu}}{\varepsilon_{mu} + \varepsilon_y} \right)$$

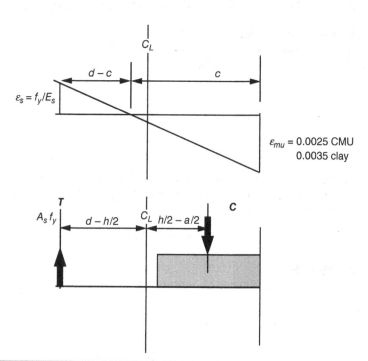

FIGURE 6.13 Location of neutral axis under balanced conditions, strength design.

Next, calculate the corresponding tensile and compressive forces:

$$T = A_s f_y$$

$$C = 0.80 f'_m (\beta_1 c) b$$

$$P_n = C - T$$

$$M_n = T\left(d - \frac{h}{2}\right) + C\left(\frac{h}{2} - \frac{\beta_1 c}{2}\right)$$

6.3.4 Example: Moment-Axial Force Interaction Diagram by the Strength Approach (Hand Calculation)

Construct the moment-axial force interaction diagram by the strength approach for a nominal 8-in. CMU wall, fully grouted, with $f'_m = 2000$ lb/in² and reinforcement consisting of #5 bars at 48 in., placed in the center of the wall. Compute the interaction diagram per foot of wall length.

For the case of a wall with reinforcement at mid-depth, the reference axis for moment is located at the plastic centroid (geometric centroid) of the cross section, which is also at mid-depth. This leads to results that appear considerably different from what we are used to for a symmetrically reinforced column. For example, using the geometric centroid (the level of the reinforcement) as the reference axis, the contribution of the reinforcement to the moment is always zero. In what is apparently even stranger, the balanced-point axial force does not coincide with the maximum moment capacity. As a result, hand calculations are useful for some reinforced masonry beam-columns, but not all.

6.3.4.1 Pure Compression

Because the compressive reinforcement in the wall is not supported laterally, it is not counted when computing the capacity.

$$P_0 = 0.80 \times 0.80 f'_m (A_g - A_{st}) + A_{st} f_y$$

$$P_n = 0.80 \times 0.80 \times 2000 \text{ lb/in}^2 \times (7.63 \text{ in.} \times 48 \text{ in.} - 0.31 \text{ in}^2) + 0.31 \text{ in}^2 \times 0 \text{ lb/in}^2$$

$$P_n = 468,390 \text{ lb}$$

Per foot of wall length, the design capacity will be the above value, divided by 4 (the length of the wall in feet), and multiplied by the strength reduction factor of 0.65 for strains in the steel less than e_y:

$$\phi P_n = 76,113 \text{ lb}$$

6.3.4.2 Pure Flexure

As before, neglect the influence of compressive reinforcement:

$$d = \left(\frac{1}{2}\right) 7.63 \text{ in.} = 3.81 \text{ in.}$$

$$\rho = \frac{A_s}{bd} = \frac{0.31 \text{ in}^2}{48 \text{ in.} \times 3.81 \text{ in.}} = 1.70 \times 10^{-3}$$

Strength Design of Reinforced Masonry Elements

$$\omega = \rho\left(\frac{f_y}{f'_m}\right) = (1.70 \times 10^{-3}) \times \left(\frac{60,000}{2000}\right) = 0.0509$$

$$M_n = \omega b d^2 f'_m (1 - 0.63\omega)$$

$$M_n = 0.0678 \times 48 \text{ in.} \times 3.81^2 \text{ in}^2 \times 2000 \text{ lb/in}^2 \times (1 - 0.63 \times 0.0509)$$

$$M_n = 68,659 \text{ lb-in.}$$

Per foot of wall length, the design capacity is the above value, divided by 4 and multiplied by the strength reduction factor that is based on the strain in the tensile steel. In this case, it is 0.9:

$$\phi M_n = 15,448 \text{ lb-in.}$$

6.3.4.3 Balance Point

First, locate the neutral axis:

$$c = d\left(\frac{\varepsilon_{mu}}{\varepsilon_{mu} + \varepsilon_y}\right)$$

$$c = d\left(\frac{0.0025}{0.0025 + 0.00207}\right)$$

$$c = 0.547 d$$

$$c = 0.547 \times 3.81 \text{ in.} = 2.086 \text{ in.}$$

The value of β_1 is prescribed in Section 9.3.2 (g) of *TMS 402-22* as 0.80:

$$T = A_s f_y = 0.31 \text{ in}^2 \times 60,000 \text{ lb/in}^2 = 18,600 \text{ lb}$$

$$C = 0.80 f'_m (\beta_1 c) b = 0.80 f'_m (0.80 \times 0.547 d) b$$

$$C = 0.80 \times 2000 \text{ lb/in}^2 (0.80 \times 0.547 \times 3.81 \text{ in.}) \times 48 \text{ in.} = 128,045 \text{ lb}$$

$$P_n = C - T = 109,445 \text{ lb}$$

$$M_n = T\left(d - \frac{h}{2}\right) + C\left(\frac{h}{2} - \frac{\beta_1 c}{2}\right)$$

$$M_n = 18,600 \text{ lb}(3.81 - 3.81) \text{ in.} + 128,045 \text{ lb}\left(\frac{7.63}{2} - \frac{0.80 \times 2.086}{2}\right) \text{in.}$$

$$M_n = 0 \text{ lb-in.} + \text{lb-in.} = 381,651 \text{ lb-in.}$$

Per foot of wall length, the design capacities are the above values, divided by 4 and multiplied by the strength reduction factor of 0.65:

$$\phi P_n = 17,784 \text{ lb}$$

$$\phi M_n = 62,018 \text{ lb-in.}$$

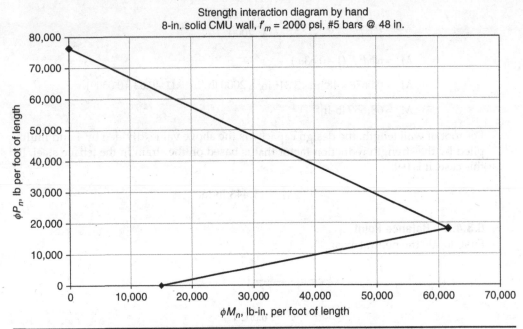

Figure 6.14 Three-point moment-axial force interaction (strength basis), calculated by hand.

6.3.4.4 Plot of Strength Interaction Diagram by Hand

The strength-based moment-axial force interaction diagram calculated above is plotted in Fig. 6.14.

As we shall shortly see, the points that we have calculated are correct. The form of the diagram is misleading, however, because the balance point is actually not the point of maximum moment. It is incorrect to draw the diagram with a straight line from the balance point to the pure-compression point. The balance point becomes the point of maximum moment as the reinforcement is placed farther apart than about 70% of the thickness of the wall.

6.3.5 Strength Interaction Diagrams by Spreadsheet

To calculate strength interaction diagrams using a spreadsheet, we first calculate the position of the neutral axis corresponding to the balance point (Fig. 6.15).

$$\frac{c}{d-c} = \frac{\varepsilon_{mu}}{\varepsilon_y}$$

$$c = d\left(\frac{\varepsilon_{mu}}{\varepsilon_{mu} + \varepsilon_y}\right)$$

For values of c less than that balanced value, the steel will yield before the masonry reaches its maximum useful strain. Combinations of axial force and moment corresponding to nominal capacity can then be calculated, as can the corresponding moment (Fig. 6.16).

Strength Design of Reinforced Masonry Elements 173

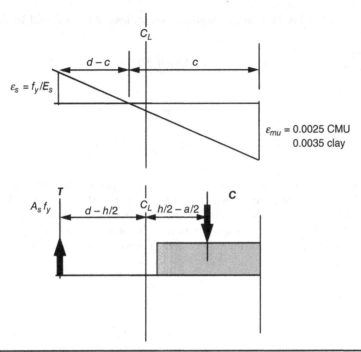

FIGURE 6.15 Position of neutral axis at balanced conditions, strength calculation of moment-axial force interaction diagram by spreadsheet.

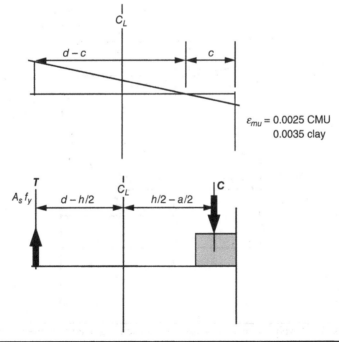

FIGURE 6.16 Position of the neutral axis for axial loads less than the balance-point axial load, strength design.

Given the position of the neutral axis, c, less than or equal to the balance-point value:

$$C = 0.80c(0.80f'_m)b$$

$$T = A_s f_y$$

$$P_n = C - T$$

$$M_n = T\left(d - \frac{h}{2}\right) + C\left(\frac{h}{2} - \frac{\beta_1 c}{2}\right)$$

Similarly, for values of c greater than the balance-point value, the steel will still be elastic when the masonry reaches its maximum useful strain. Compute the strain (and corresponding stress) in the steel by proportion, and find combinations of axial force and moment corresponding to each position of the neutral axis (Fig. 6.17).

Given the position of the neutral axis, c, greater than or equal to the balance-point value:

$$\frac{\varepsilon_s}{\varepsilon_{mu}} = \frac{d-c}{c}$$

$$\varepsilon_s = \varepsilon_{mu}\left(\frac{d-c}{c}\right)$$

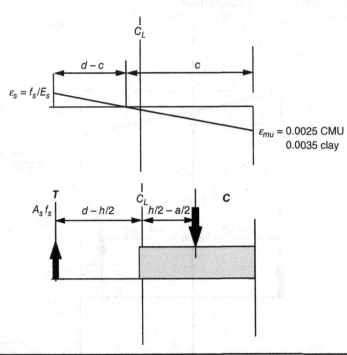

FIGURE 6.17 Position of the neutral axis for axial loads greater than the balance-point axial load, strength design.

$$f_s = E_s \varepsilon_s$$

$$C = 0.80c\,(0.80 f'_m)b$$

$$T = A_s f_s$$

$$P_n = C - T$$

$$M_n = T\left(d - \frac{h}{2}\right) + C\left(\frac{h}{2} - \frac{\beta_1 c}{2}\right)$$

In the above expression, β_1, is the ratio between the depth of the compressive stress block and the distance from the neutral axis to the extreme compression fiber. It is also denoted as "a" in technical references dealing with reinforced concrete, so $a = 0.80c$.

This calculation is limited by the pure compression resistance, calculated as noted above and reduced by a slenderness-dependent factor (*TMS 402-22*, Sections 9.3.3.1.1 and 9.3.4.4):

$$P_n = 0.80 \times \left[0.80 f'_m (A_n - A_{st}) + A_{st} f_y\right]$$

As in ACI 318-22, the factor of 0.80 in effect imposes a minimum design eccentricity.

The slenderness-dependent factor is applied to nominal capacity under pure axial load as shown below:

For $h/r \leq 99$,

$$P_n = 0.80 \times \left[0.80 f'_m (A_n - A_{st}) + A_{st} f_y\right]\left[1 - \left(\frac{h}{140\,r}\right)^2\right]$$

For $h/r > 99$,

$$P_n = 0.80 \times \left[0.80 f'_m (A_n - A_{st}) + A_{st} f_y\right]\left(\frac{70\,r}{h}\right)^2$$

Because out-of-plane walls are checked for magnified moments in accordance with Section 9.3.4.4 of *TMS 402-22*, the slenderness-dependent reduction factor is applied only to the pure compression capacity.

6.3.6 Example: Moment-Axial Force Interaction Diagram by the Strength Approach (spreadsheet calculation)

Construct the moment-axial force interaction diagram by the strength approach for a nominal 8-in. CMU wall, fully grouted, with $f'_m = 2000$ lb/in² and reinforcement consisting of #5 bars at 48 in., placed in the center of the wall.

The effective width of the wall is $6t$, or 48 in. The spreadsheet and corresponding interaction diagram are shown below. As noted in the above example, the results are interesting. Because the reinforcement is located at the geometric centroid of the section, the balance-point axial load (about 17,800 lb) does not correspond to the maximum moment capacity. The diagram is also valid for partially grouted walls, provided that the compressive stress block is entirely within the face shell.

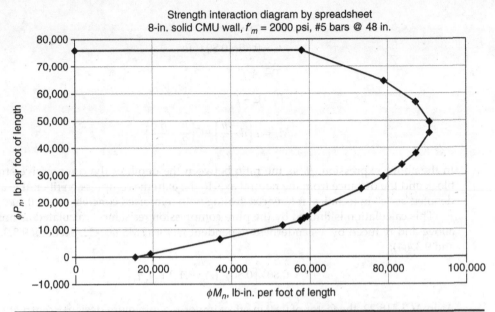

FIGURE 6.18 Moment-axial force interaction diagram (strength approach), spreadsheet calculation.

6.3.6.1 Plot of Strength Interaction Diagram by Spreadsheet

The moment-axial force interaction diagram (strength basis) as plotted by spreadsheet is shown in Fig. 6.18. The change in slope between axial loads of 13,200 and 17,800 lb is due to the phi factor changing from 0.9 to 0.65 based on the strain in the reinforcing bar as defined by Table 9.1.4 of TMS 402. Because the h/r ratio for the wall is not known, no reductions for slenderness are applied.

Relevant cells from the spreadsheet are reproduced in Table 6.2.

6.3.7 Example: Strength Design of Masonry Walls Loaded Out of Plane

Once we have developed the moment-axial force interaction diagram by the strength approach, the actual design simply consists of verifying that the combination of factored design axial force and moment lies within the diagram of nominal axial and flexural capacity, reduced by strength-reduction factors. Because the (h/r) ratio for the wall is known, it is used to reduce the nominal axial capacity under pure axial load. Because secondary moments are calculated, other nominal capacities are not so reduced.

Consider the bearing wall designed previously as unreinforced, shown in Fig. 6.19. It has an eccentric axial load plus out-of-plane wind load of 40 lb/ft². The eccentric axial load is 1050 lb/ft, of which 700 lb/ft is dead load, and 350 lb/ft is live load.

At each horizontal plane through the wall, the following condition must be met:

- combinations of factored axial load and moment must lie within the moment-axial force interaction diagram, reduced by strength-reduction factors and capped by the slenderness-dependent reduction factor.

Because flexural capacity increases with increasing axial load, the critical loading combination is probably $0.9D + 1.0W$.

TABLE 6.2 Spreadsheet for Computing Moment-Axial Force Interaction Diagram (Strength Approach)

Example of spreadsheet for calculating strength moment-axial force interaction diagram for solid masonry wall								
Reinforcement at mid-depth								
Specified thickness	7.625							
ε_{mu}	0.0025							
f'_m	2000							
f_y	60000							
E_s	29000000							
ε_y	0.00207							
d	3.8125							
(c/d) balanced	0.54717							
Tensile reinforcement area	0.31							
Effective width	48							
Because compression reinforcement is not supported, it is not counted								
	C/d	c	C_{mas}	ε_s	f_s	ϕ	ϕ Mn	ϕ Pn
Pure axial load						0.65	0	76064
Points controlled by masonry	2	7.625	468480	0.00125	0	0.65	58048	76128
	1.7	6.48125	398208	0.00103	0	0.65	78945	64709
	1.5	5.71875	351360	0.00083	0	0.65	87071	57096
	1.3	4.95625	304512	0.00058	0	0.65	90554	49483
	1.2	4.575	281088	0.00042	0	0.65	90554	45677
	1	3.8125	234240	0.00000	0	0.65	87071	38064
	0.9	3.43125	210816	−0.00028	−8056	0.65	83589	33852
	0.8	3.05	187392	−0.00063	−18125	0.65	78945	29538
	0.7	2.66875	163968	−0.00107	−31071	0.65	73140	25080
	0.54717	2.086085	128169	−0.00207	−60000	0.65	62026	17805
Points controlled by steel	0.54717	2.086085	128169	−0.00207	−60000	0.65	62026	17805
	0.5	1.90625	117120	−0.00250	−60000	0.69	61255	16894
	0.4	1.525	93696	−0.00375	−60000	0.79	59269	14833
	0.37	1.410625	86669	−0.00426	−60000	0.83	58579	14164
	0.33	1.258125	77299	−0.00508	−60000	0.90	57556	13207
	0.3	1.14375	70272	−0.00583	−60000	0.90	53047	11626
	0.2	0.7625	46848	−0.01000	−60000	0.90	36972	6356
	0.1	0.38125	23424	−0.02250	−60000	0.90	19290	1085
	0.0794	0.302713	18599	−0.02899	−60000	0.90	15447	0

178 Chapter Six

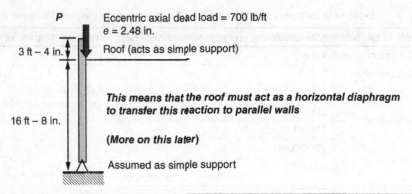

FIGURE 6.19 Reinforced masonry wall loaded by eccentric gravity axial load plus out-of-plane wind load.

From our previous experience, we know that the critical point on the wall is at the midspan of the lower portion.

Due to wind only, the unfactored moment at the base of the parapet (roof level) is

$$M_{u\,wind} = \frac{w_u L^2_{parapet}}{2} = \frac{40\,\frac{lb}{ft} \times 3.33^2\,ft^2}{2} \times 12\,in./ft = 2661\,lb\text{-}in.$$

The maximum moment is close to that occurring at mid-height. The moment from wind load is the superposition of one-half moment at the upper support due to wind load on the parapet only, plus the midspan moment in a simply supported beam with that same wind load:

$$M_{u\,midspan} = -\frac{2661}{2} + \frac{w_u L^2}{8} = -\frac{2661}{2} + \frac{40\,lb/ft \times 16.67^2\,ft^2}{8} \times 12\,in./ft = 15,343\,lb\text{-}in.$$

The unfactored moment due to eccentric axial load is

$$M_{gravity} = Pe = 1050\,lb \times 2.48\,in. = 2604\,lb\text{-}in.$$

Unfactored moment diagrams due to eccentric axial load and wind are as shown in Fig. 6.20:

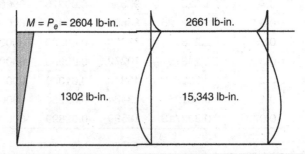

FIGURE 6.20 Unfactored moment diagrams due to eccentric axial load plus wind load.

Strength Design of Reinforced Masonry Elements 179

Check the adequacy of the wall with 8-in. nominal units, a specified compressive strength, f'_m, of 2000 lb/in², and #5 bars spaced at 48 in. All design actions are calculated per foot of width of the wall.

At the mid-height of the wall, the axial force due to $0.9D$ is:

$$P_u = 0.9(700 \text{ lb}) + 0.9(3.33 \text{ ft} + 8.33 \text{ ft}) \times 81 \text{ lb/ft} = 1480 \text{ lb}$$

At the mid-height of the wall, the factored design moment, M_u, is given by:

$$M_u = P_u \frac{e}{2} + M_{uwind} = \left(\frac{1}{2}\right) 0.9 \times 700 \text{ lb} \times 2.48 \text{ in.} + 1.0 \times 15,343 \text{ lb-in.} = 16,124 \text{ lb-in.}$$

The pure compression resistance of the wall is reduced by a slenderness-dependent factor (*TMS 402-22*, Section 9.3.3.1.1). That has the effect of "capping" the moment-axial force interaction diagram.

In each foot of wall, the design actions are $P_u = 1480$ lb, and $M_u = 16,124$ lb-in. That combination lies within the interaction diagram of design capacities capped for slenderness (Fig. 6.21) as illustrated by the square marker, and the design is satisfactory.

Because this out-of-plane wall is checked for magnified moments in accordance with Section 9.3.4.4 of *TMS 402-22*, the slenderness-dependent reduction factor is applied only to the compression capacity under pure axial load, and not to the remaining nominal axial capacities.

Relevant cells from the spreadsheet of Fig. 6.21 are reproduced in the following table:

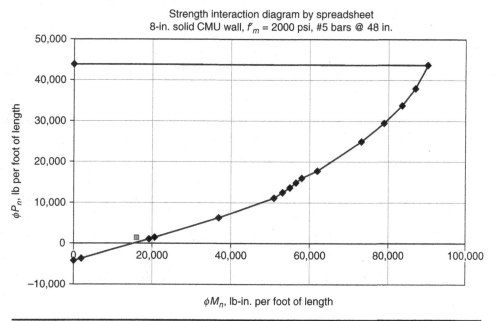

FIGURE 6.21 Moment-axial force interaction diagram for out-of-plane example, including the effects of capping for slenderness.

Chapter Six

Spreadsheet for out-of-plane wall example, including slenderness								
Reinforcement at mid-depth								
Specified thickness	7.625					h	200	
ε_{mu}	0.0025					r	2.20	
f'_m	2000					h/r	90.9	
f_y	60000					Slenderness factor	0.579	
E_s	29000000							
ε_y	0.00207							
d	3.8125							
(c/d) balanced	0.54717							
Tensile reinforcement area	0.31							
Effective width	48							
Because compression reinforcement is not supported, it is not counted								
	c/d	c	C_{mas}	ε_s	f_s	ϕ	ϕ Mn	ϕ Pn
Pure axial load								
Points controlled by masonry	1.1566	4.409538	270922	0.00034	0	0.65	0	44024
	1.15	4.384375	269376	0.00033	0	0.65	90119	43774
	1	3.8125	234240	0.00000	0	0.65	87071	38064
	0.9	3.43125	210816	−0.00028	−8056	0.65	83589	33852
	0.8	3.05	187392	−0.00063	−18125	0.65	78945	29538
	0.7	2.66875	163968	−0.00107	−31071	0.65	73140	25080
	0.54717	2.086085	128169	−0.00207	−60000	0.65	62026	17805
Points controlled by steel	0.54717	2.086085	128169	−0.00207	−60000	0.65	62026	17805
	0.5	1.90625	117120	−0.00250	−60000	0.65	58048	16010
	0.45	1.715625	105408	−0.00306	−60000	0.69	56508	14886
	0.4	1.525	93696	−0.00375	−60000	0.73	54927	13747
	0.35	1.334375	81984	−0.00464	−60000	0.79	53095	12520
	0.3	1.14375	70272	−0.00583	−60000	0.86	50954	11167
	0.2	0.7625	46848	−0.01000	−60000	0.90	36972	6356
	0.10748	0.409768	25176	−0.02076	−60000	0.90	20668	1480
	0.1	0.38125	23424	−0.02250	−60000	0.90	19290	1085
	0.01	0.038125	2342	−0.24750	−60000	0.90	2001	−3658
	0.001	0.003813	234	−2.49750	−60000	0.90	201	−4132

Strength Design of Reinforced Masonry Elements

The strength provisions of *TMS 402-22* also require a check of the possible effects of secondary moments for reinforced walls loaded out of plane (*TMS 402-22*, Sections 9.3.4.4 and 9.3.4.5).

In accordance with those sections, Equation 9-21 of *TMS 402-22* can be used to calculate the maximum moment, including possible secondary moments. That maximum moment is then compared with the interaction diagram. Equation 9-21 of *TMS 402-22* is based on a member simply supported at top and bottom, which is the case here:

$$M_u = \frac{w_u h^2}{8} + P_{uf}\left(\frac{e_u}{2}\right) + P_u \delta_u$$

As calculated above, for each ft of wall length, the first two terms in this equation total 16,124 lb-in., and P_u equals 1480 lb. In accordance with *TMS 402-22* Section 9.3.5.4, δ_u is to be calculated using Equations 9-23 and 9-24 of *TMS 402-22*.

For this problem, the cracked moment of inertia for *TMS 402-22* Section 9.3.4.4.5 is calculated using Equation 9-28 of *TMS 402-22*. Section properties are per foot of plan length. The location of the neutral axis is obtained from the moment-axial force interaction spreadsheet, at an axial load of 1480 lb. The same location could have been obtained using Equation 9-29 of *TMS 402-22*.

$$I_{cr} = n\left(A_s + \frac{P_u}{f_y}\frac{t_{sp}}{2d}\right)(d-c)^2 + \frac{bc^3}{3}$$

$$n = \frac{E_s}{E_m} = \frac{29 \times 10^6 \text{ lb/in}^2}{900 f'_m} = \frac{29 \times 10^6 \text{ lb/in}^2}{900 \times 2000 \text{ lb/in}^2} = 16.11$$

$$I_{cr} = 16.11\left(\frac{0.31 \text{ in}^2}{4} + \frac{1480 \text{ lb}}{60,000 \text{ lb/in}^2} \times \frac{7.63 \text{ in.}}{2 \times 7.63 \text{ in.}/2}\right)\left(\frac{7.63 \text{ in.}}{2} - 0.410 \text{ in.}\right)^2$$

$$+ \frac{12 \times 0.410^3 \text{ in}^4}{3}$$

$$I_{cr} = 19.08 \text{ in}^4 + 0.28 \text{ in}^4 = 19.36 \text{ in}^4$$

$$f_{cracking} = f_r = \frac{M_{cr} I_g}{t/2} - \frac{P}{A}$$

$$M_{cr} = \left(f_r + \frac{P}{A}\right)\left(\frac{I_g}{t/2}\right) = \left(163 \text{ lb/in}^2 + \frac{1480 \text{ lb}}{12 \times 7.63 \text{ in}^2}\right)\left(\frac{12 \text{ in.} \times 7.63^3 \text{ in}^3}{12 \times 7.63/2 \text{ in.}}\right) = 20,861 \text{ lb-in.}$$

Because the cracking moment used in those equations is calculated without strength-reduction factors, it exceeds the factored design moment. Nevertheless, it is believed prudent to assume that reinforced masonry is cracked at all bed joints. This is conservative.

$$\delta_u = \frac{5M_u h^2}{48 E_m I_{cr}}$$

$$\delta_{u1} = \frac{5 \times 16,124 \text{ lb-in.} \times (16.67 \text{ ft} \times 12 \text{ in.}/\text{ft})^2}{48(900 \times 2000 \text{ lb/in}^2)(19.36 \text{ in}^4)} = 1.93 \text{ in.}$$

$$M_{u2} = 16,124 \text{ lb-in.} + 1480 \times (1.93) \text{ lb-in.} = 18,978 \text{ lb-in.}$$

Check convergence:

$$\delta_{u2} = \frac{5(18{,}978 \text{ lb-in.})(16.67 \text{ ft} \times 12 \text{ in./ft})^2}{48(900 \times 2000 \text{ lb/in}^2)(19.36 \text{ in}^4)} = 2.27 \text{ in.}$$

$$M_{u3} = 16{,}124 \text{ lb-in.} + 1480 \times (2.27) = 19{,}483 \text{ lb-in.}$$

Because the moment is changing by less than 3%, it can be assumed to have converged.

Alternately, a moment magnifier approach to considering secondary moments can be used as prescribed in Section 9.3.5.4.3.

$$M_u = \Psi M_{u,0}$$

Equation 9-31 defines the moment magnifier, and additional quantities are calculated using Equations 9-32 and 9-33.

$$\Psi = \frac{1}{1 - \frac{P_u}{P_e}}$$

$$P_e = \frac{\pi^2 E_m I_{\text{eff}}}{h^2}$$

As with the iterated moment, we shall use $I_{\text{eff}} = I_{cr}$. This is conservative and consistent with the iterative procedure.

$$P_e = \frac{\pi^2 E_m I_{\text{eff}}}{h^2} = \frac{\pi^2 900 \cdot 2000 \text{ psi} \cdot 19.36 \text{ in}^4}{16.67 \text{ ft} \cdot \frac{12 \text{ in.}}{\text{ft}}} = 8595 \text{ lb}$$

$$\Psi = \frac{1}{1 - \frac{1480 \text{ lb}}{8595 \text{ lb}}} = 1.208$$

$$M_u = 1.208 \cdot 16{,}124 \text{ lb-in} = 19{,}478 \text{ lb-in}$$

This calculated value is very close to that of the previous approach and is simpler to compute.

The combination of factored axial force and factored moment (including secondary moments) remains within the moment-axial force interaction diagram, and the design is still satisfactory.

Although shear will not control, it is calculated here to illustrate the process. We use superposition of the wind and gravity loads.

$$V_u = \frac{40 \frac{\text{lb}}{\text{ft}} \times 20 \text{ ft} \cdot 10 \text{ ft}}{16.67 \text{ ft}} + \frac{2604 \text{ lb-in}}{16.67 \text{ ft} \times 12 \text{ in/ft}} = 493 \text{ lb}$$

Shearing capacity of a reinforced masonry member is calculated using Section 9.3.3.1.2.1 of *TMS 402-22*:

$$V_{nm} = \left[4.0 - 1.75\left(\frac{M_u}{V_u d_v}\right)\right] A_n \sqrt{f'_m} + 0.25 P_u$$

As $(M_u/V_u d_v)$ increases, V_{nm} decreases. Because $(M_u/V_u d_v)$ need not be taken greater than 1.0 (TMS 402-22, Section 9.3.3.1.2.1), the most conservative (lowest) value of V_{mm} is obtained with $(M_u/V_u d_v)$ equal to 1.0. In this calculation, P_u, is conservatively neglected:

$$V_{nm} = [4.0 - 1.75(1.0)]A_{nv}\sqrt{f'_m}$$

$$V_{nm} = 2.25 A_{nv}\sqrt{f'_m} = 2.25 \cdot 12 \text{ in.} \cdot 7.63 \text{ in.} \cdot \sqrt{2000} \text{ psi} = 9.21 \text{ kip}$$

$$\phi V_n = 0.8 \cdot 9.21 \text{ kip} = 7.37 \text{ kip} > V_u = 0.48 \text{ kip}$$

Finally, the strength provisions of TMS 402-22 also require a check of out-of-plane deflections for reinforced walls loaded out of plane (Section 9.3.4.5).

In accordance with those sections, TMS 402-22 Equation 9-23 or 9-24 is used to calculate the midheight deflection at service loads by replacing M_u with M_{serv}. Those equations are based on a member simply supported at top and bottom, which is the case here. In this problem, the service-level moment is taken as 0.6 times the strength-level moment, because 0.6 is the service-level load factor in ASCE 7-22 allowable-stress loading combinations. In this problem, service level moments are less than cracking moments, so Equation 9-23 applies.

$$\delta_s = \frac{5 M_{ser} h^2}{48 E_m I_g}$$

$$I_g = \frac{bt^3}{12} = \frac{12 \text{ in.} \times 7.63^3 \text{ in}^3}{12} = 444 \text{ in}^4$$

$$\delta_s = \frac{5 \times 0.6 \times 16{,}124 \text{ lb-in.} \times (16.67 \text{ ft} \times 12 \text{ in.}/\text{ft.})^2}{48(900 \times 2000 \text{ lb/in}^2)(444 \text{ in}^4)} = 0.05 \text{ in.}$$

This service deflection is far smaller than $0.007 h$ (equal to 0.007 times 16.67 ft, or 1.40 in.). The out-of-plane deflection requirement is satisfied.

6.3.8 Minimum and Maximum Reinforcement Ratios for Out-of-plane Flexural Design of Masonry Walls by the Strength Approach

The strength design provisions of TMS 402-22 include requirements for minimum and maximum flexural reinforcement. In this section, the implications of those requirements for the out-of-plane flexural design of masonry walls are addressed.

6.3.8.1 Minimum Flexural Reinforcement by TMS 402-22

TMS 402-22 has no requirements for minimum flexural reinforcement for out-of-plane design of masonry walls.

6.3.8.2 Maximum Flexural Reinforcement by TMS 402-22

TMS 402-22 has a maximum reinforcement requirement (Section 9.3.3.2.4) that is intended to ensure ductile behavior over a range of axial loads. As compressive axial load increases, the maximum permissible reinforcement percentage decreases. For compressive axial loads above a critical value, the maximum permissible reinforcement percentage drops to zero, and design is impossible unless the cross-sectional area of the element is increased.

For walls subjected to out-of-plane forces, for columns, and for beams, the provisions of *TMS 402-22* set the maximum permissible reinforcement based on a critical strain condition in which the masonry is at its maximum useful strain, and the extreme tension reinforcement is set at 0.005.

The critical strain condition for walls with a single layer of concentric reinforcement and loaded out-of-plane is shown in Fig. 6.22, along with the corresponding stress state. The parameters for the equivalent rectangular stress block are the same as those used for conventional flexural design. The height of the equivalent rectangular stress block is $0.80 f'_m$, and the depth is $0.80 c$. The tensile reinforcement is assumed to be at f_y. Equilibrium is evaluated under nominal moment and axial force.

Locate the neutral axis using the critical strain condition:

$$\frac{\varepsilon_{mu}}{0.005} = \frac{c}{d-c}$$

$$c = d\left(\frac{\varepsilon_{mu}}{0.005 + \varepsilon_{mu}}\right)$$

Compute the tensile and compressive forces acting on the section, assuming concentric reinforcement with a percentage of reinforcement $\rho = \frac{A_s}{bd}$, where $d = \frac{t}{2}$.

The compressive force in the masonry is given by

$$C_{masonry} = 0.80 f'_m 0.80 cb$$

The tensile force in the reinforcement is given by

$$T_{steel} = \rho b d f_y$$

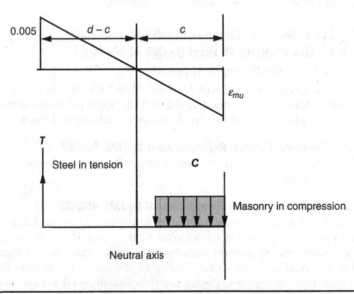

Figure 6.22 Critical strain condition for a masonry wall loaded out of plane.

Equilibrium of axial forces requires

$$P_n = C - T$$

$$\frac{P_u}{\phi} = C - T$$

$$\frac{P_u}{\phi} = 0.80 f'_m 0.80 cb - \rho db f_y$$

$$\frac{P_u}{\phi} = 0.80 f'_m 0.80 d \left(\frac{\varepsilon_{mu}}{0.005 + \varepsilon_{mu}} \right) b - \rho db f_y$$

$$\rho = \frac{0.80 f'_m 0.80 d \left(\frac{\varepsilon_{mu}}{0.005 + \varepsilon_{mu}} \right) b - \frac{P_u}{\phi}}{bd f_y}$$

$$\rho = \frac{0.80 f'_m 0.80 \left(\frac{\varepsilon_{mu}}{0.005 + \varepsilon_{mu}} \right) - \frac{P_u}{bd\phi}}{f_y}$$

So

$$\rho_{max} = \frac{0.64 f'_m \left(\frac{\varepsilon_{mu}}{0.005 \varepsilon_y + \varepsilon_{mu}} \right) - \frac{P_u}{bd\phi}}{f_y}$$

6.4 Strength Design of Reinforced Shear Walls

6.4.1 Introduction to Strength Design of Reinforced Shear Walls

In this section, we shall study the behavior and design of reinforced masonry shear walls. The discussion follows the same approach used previously for unreinforced masonry shear walls.

6.4.2 Design Steps for Strength Design of Reinforced Shear Walls

Reinforced masonry shear walls must be designed for the effects of:

1) Gravity loads from self-weight, plus gravity loads from overlying roof or floor levels.
2) Moments and shears from in-plane shear loads.

Actions are shown in Fig. 6.23.

Flexural capacity of reinforced shear walls using strength procedures is calculated using moment-axial force interaction diagrams as discussed in the section on masonry walls loaded out-of-plane. In contrast to the elements addressed in that section, a shear wall is subjected to flexure in its own plane rather than out-of-plane. It therefore usually has multiple layers of flexural reinforcement. Computation of moment-axial force interaction diagrams for shear walls is much easier using a spreadsheet.

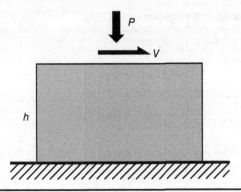

FIGURE 6.23 Design actions for reinforced masonry shear walls.

From *TMS 402-22*, Section 9.3.3.1.2.1, nominal shear strength is the summation of shear strength from masonry and shear strength from shear reinforcement:

$$V_n = (V_{nm} + V_{ns})\gamma_g$$

From *TMS 402-22*, Section 9.3.3.1.2.1,

$$V_{nm} = \left[4.0 - 1.75\left(\frac{M_u}{V_u d_v}\right)\right] A_{nv}\sqrt{f'_m} + 0.25 P_u$$

As $(M_u/V_u d_v)$ increases, V_{nm} decreases (Fig. 6.24). Because $(M_u/V_u d_v)$ need not be taken greater than 1.0 (*TMS 402-22*, Section 9.3.3.1.2.1), the most conservative (lowest) value of V_{nm} is obtained with $(M_u/V_u d_v)$ equal to 1.0.

Just as in reinforced concrete design, this model assumes that shear is resisted by reinforcement crossing a hypothetical failure surface oriented at 45 degrees, as shown in Fig. 6.25.

The nominal resistance from reinforcement is taken as the area associated with each set of shear reinforcement, multiplied by the number of sets of shear reinforcement crossing the hypothetical failure surface, multiplied by the specified yield strength of

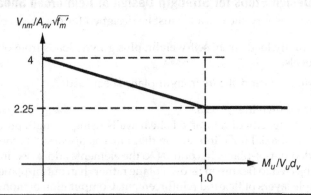

FIGURE 6.24 V_{nm} as a function of $(M_u/V_u d_v)$.

Strength Design of Reinforced Masonry Elements

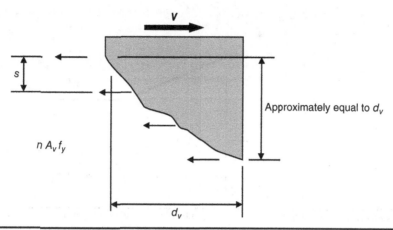

FIGURE 6.25 Idealized model used in evaluating the resistance due to shear reinforcement.

the shear reinforcement. Because the hypothetical failure surface is assumed to be inclined at 45 degrees, its projection along the length of the member is approximately equal to d_v, and number of sets of shear reinforcement crossing the hypothetical failure surface can be approximated by (d_v/s):

$$V_{ns} = A_v f_y n$$

$$V_{ns} = A_v f_y \left(\frac{d_v}{s}\right)$$

The actual failure surface may be inclined at a larger angle with respect to the axis of the wall, however. Also, all reinforcement crossing the failure surface may not yield. For both these reasons, the assumed resistance is decreased by an efficiency factor of 0.5. From *TMS 402-22*, Section 9.3.3.1.2.2,

$$V_{ns} = 0.5 \left(\frac{A_v}{s}\right) f_y d_v$$

Finally, because shear resistance really comes from a truss mechanism in which horizontal reinforcement is in tension, and diagonal struts in the masonry are in compression, crushing of the diagonal compressive struts is controlled by limiting the total shear resistance V_n, regardless of the amount of shear reinforcement (Fig. 6.26):

For $(M_u / V_u d_v) > 0.25$,

$$V_n \leq \left(6 A_{nv} \sqrt{f'_m}\right) \gamma_g;$$

and for $(M_u / V_u d_v) < 1.00$,

$$V_n \leq \left(4 A_{nv} \sqrt{f'_m}\right) \gamma_g.$$

Interpolation is permitted between these limits.

If these upper limits on V_n are not satisfied, the cross-sectional area of the section must be increased.

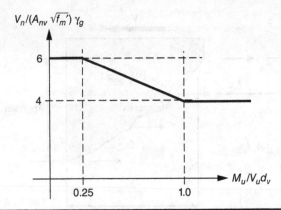

FIGURE 6.26 Maximum permitted nominal shear capacity as a function of $(M_u/V_u d_v)$.

6.4.3 Example: Strength Design of Reinforced Clay Masonry Shear Wall

Consider the masonry shear wall shown in Fig. 6.27.

Design the wall. Unfactored in-plane lateral loads at each floor level are due to earthquake, and are shown in Fig. 6.28, along with the corresponding shear and moment diagrams.

Assume an 8-in. nominal clay masonry wall, fully grouted, with Type S PCL mortar. The total plan length of the wall is 24 ft (288 in.), and its thickness is 7.5 in. Assume an effective depth d of 285 in.

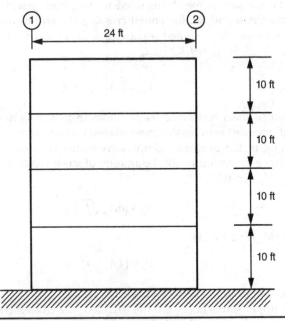

FIGURE 6.27 Reinforced masonry shear wall to be designed.

Strength Design of Reinforced Masonry Elements 189

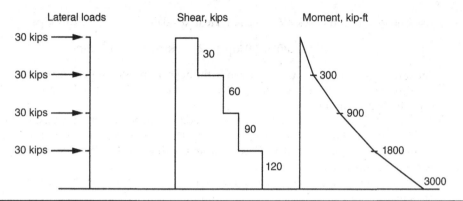

FIGURE 6.28 Unfactored in-plane lateral loads, shear and moment diagrams for reinforced masonry shear wall.

	Clay Masonry
Unit Strength	6600
Mortar	Type S
f'_m (psi)	2500 (unit strength method)
Reinforcement = Grade 60; $E_s = 29 \times 10^6$ psi	

Unfactored axial loads on the wall are given in the following table.

Level (Top of wall)	DL, kips	LL, kips
4	90	15
3	180	35
2	270	55
1	360	75

Use 2022 IBC strength design Load Combination 7: $0.9D + 1.0E$
Check shear for assumed wall thickness. By Section 9.3.4.1.2 of *TMS 402-22*,

$$V_n = (V_{nm} + V_{ns})\gamma_g$$

$M_u = 3000 \times 12 \times 1000$ lb-in. $= 36.0 \times 10^6$ lb-in.
$V_u = 120{,}000$ lb $d_v = 288$ in.

$$\frac{M_u}{V_u d_v} = \frac{36 \times 10^6 \text{ lb-in.}}{120{,}000 \text{ lb } (288 \text{ in.})} = 1.04$$

$$V_{nm} = \left[4.0 - 1.75\left(\frac{M_u}{V_u d_v}\right)\right] A_{nv}\sqrt{f'_m} + 0.25 P_u$$

$V_{nm} = [4.0 - 1.75(1.0)]\, 7.5 \text{ in.} \times 288 \text{ in.} \left(\sqrt{2500} \text{ psi}\right) + 0.25(0.9 \times 360{,}000 \text{ lb})$

$V_{nm} = 242.9$ kips $+ 81.0$ kips $= 323.9$ kips

$V_n \le \left(4 A_{nv}\sqrt{f'_m}\right)\gamma_g = 4 \times 7.5 \text{ in.} \times 288 \text{ in.} \left(\sqrt{2500} \text{ psi}\right) = 432$ kips

Assume $V_{ns} = 0$, and check $\phi V_n > V_u$. For shear, $\phi = 0.80$. $V_n = V_{nm} = 323.9$ kips

$$\phi V_n = 0.80(323.9 \text{ kips}) = 259.1 \text{ kips} \geq V_u = 120 \text{ kips}$$

Shear design is satisfactory so far, even without shear reinforcement. Capacity design as required by *TMS 402-22*, Section 7.3.2.5.1.2 will be checked once the nominal flexural capacity is determined.

Now check flexural capacity using a spreadsheet-generated moment-axial force interaction diagram. For Seismic Design Category D, minimum prescriptive horizontal and vertical reinforcement ($\rho = 0.0007$) is consistent with #5 bars @ 48 in. Neglecting slenderness effects, the diagram is shown in Fig. 6.29.

Relevant cells from the spreadsheet are reproduced below with selected intermediate steps.

Now include slenderness effects based on *TMS 402-22*, Section 9.3.3.1.1.

For $h/r \leq 99$,

$$P_n = 0.80 \times \left[0.80 f'_m (A_g - A_{st}) + A_{st} f_y\right] \left[1 - \left(\frac{h}{140r}\right)^2\right]$$

For $h/r > 99$,

$$P_n = 0.80 \times \left[0.80 f'_m (A_n - A_{st}) + A_{st} f_y\right] \left(\frac{70r}{h}\right)^2$$

According to *TMS 402-22* Commentary 9.3.3.1.1, slenderness is calculated using the weak-axis radius of gyration, and an effective unbraced out-of-plane length equal to the

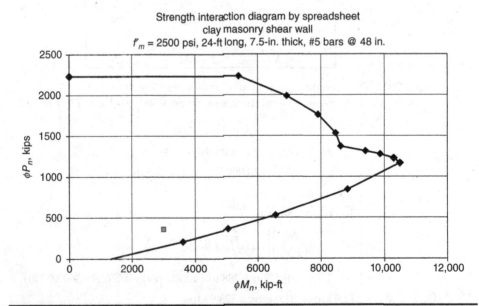

FIGURE 6.29 Moment-axial force interaction diagram (strength basis) for reinforced shear wall, neglecting slenderness effects.

Spreadsheet for calculating strength moment-axial force interaction diagram for clay masonry shear wall

Depth	288
ε_{mu}	0.0035
f'_m	2.5
f_y	60
E_s	29000
ε_y	0.002069
d	285
(c/d) balanced	0.628483
Width	7.5
Steel layers are counted from the extreme compression fiber to the extreme tension fiber	
Distances are measured from the extreme compression fiber	
Reinforcement is assumed to be placed at 4-ft intervals	
Compression in masonry and reinforcement is taken as positive	
Stress in compressive reinforcement is set to zero, because the reinforcement is not laterally supported	

Row of Reinforcement	Distance	Area
1	3.00	0.31
2	51.00	0.31
3	99.00	0.31
4	147.00	0.31
5	195.00	0.31
6	237.00	0.31
7	285.00	0.31

	c/d	c	C_{mas}	$f_s(1)$	$f_s(2)$	$f_s(3)$	$f_s(4)$	$f_s(5)$	$f_s(6)$	$\varepsilon_y(7)$	$f_y(7)$	ϕ	M_n	P_n	ϕM_n	ϕP_n
Pure axial load												0.65	0	3453	0	2244
Points controlled by masonry	1.01	287.9	3454	0.0	0.0	0.0	0.0	0.0	0.0	0.0000	0.00	0.65	8307	3454	5400	2245
	0.9	256.5	3078	0.0	0.0	0.0	0.0	0.0	0.0	−0.0004	−11.28	0.65	10660	3075	6929	1998
	0.8	228.0	2736	0.0	0.0	0.0	0.0	0.0	−4.0	−0.0009	−25.38	0.65	12140	2727	7891	1772
	0.7	199.5	2394	0.0	0.0	0.0	0.0	0.0	−19.1	−0.0015	−43.50	0.65	13012	2375	8458	1543
	0.628483	179.1	2149	0.0	0.0	0.0	0.0	−9.0	−32.8	−0.0021	−60.00	0.65	13269	2118	8625	1377
Points controlled by steel	0.628483	179.1	2149	0.0	0.0	0.0	0.0	−9.0	−32.8	−0.0021	−60.00	0.65	13269	2118	8625	1377
	0.55	156.8	1881	0.0	0.0	0.0	0.0	−24.8	−52.0	−0.0029	−60.00	0.72	13120	1839	9397	1317
	0.5	142.5	1710	0.0	0.0	0.0	−3.2	−37.4	−60.0	−0.0035	−60.00	0.77	12810	1660	9854	1277
	0.45	128.3	1539	0.0	0.0	0.0	−14.8	−52.8	−60.0	−0.0043	−60.00	0.83	12322	1481	10278	1235
	0.4	114.0	1368	0.0	0.0	0.0	−29.4	−60.0	−60.0	−0.0053	−60.00	0.90	11662	1303	10495	1173
	0.3	85.5	1026	0.0	0.0	−16.0	−60.0	−60.0	−60.0	−0.0082	−60.00	0.90	9816	947	8834	852
	0.2	57.0	684	0.0	0.0	−60.0	−60.0	−60.0	−60.0	−0.0140	−60.00	0.90	7285	591	6557	532
	0.1462	41.7	500	0.0	−22.7	−60.0	−60.0	−60.0	−60.0	−0.0204	−60.00	0.90	5628	400	5065	360
	0.1	28.5	342	0.0	−60.0	−60.0	−60.0	−60.0	−60.0	−0.0315	−60.00	0.90	4012	230	3610	207
	0.01	2.85	34	−5.34	−60.0	−60.0	−60.0	−60.0	−60.0	−0.3465	−60.00	0.90	620	−79	558	−71

story height, or 120 in. This approach is quite conservative because it neglects any out-of-plane restraint of the compressive region of the wall due to the adjacent tension region.

The moment-axial force interaction diagram including the effects of slenderness is shown in Fig. 6.30, and the spreadsheet is shown immediately following the graph.

At a factored axial load of $0.9\,D$, or 0.9×360 kips = 324 kips, the design flexural capacity of this wall is about 4,730 kip-ft, and the design is satisfactory for flexure.

We have designed the wall for the calculated design shear, which is normally sufficient. Now suppose that the wall is a special reinforced masonry shear wall (required in areas of high seismic risk), so that the capacity design requirements of TMS 402-22, Section 7.3.2.5.1.2 apply.

First try to meet the capacity design provisions of that section. At an axial load of 324 kips, the nominal flexural capacity of this wall is the design flexural capacity of 4730 kip-ft, divided by the strength reduction factor for flexure of 0.9, or 5256 kip-ft. The ratio of this nominal flexural capacity to the factored design moment is 5256 divided by 3000, or 1.752. Including the additional factor of 1.25 to account for overstrength and the start of strain-hardening of the reinforcement produces a ratio of 2.19. Also, V_n need not exceed $2.5\,V_u$:

$$\phi V_n \geq 2.45\,V_u$$

$$V_n \geq \frac{2.19}{\phi} V_u = \frac{2.19}{0.8} V_u = 2.73\,V_u > 2.5\,V_u$$

$$V_n = 323.9 \text{ kip} \geq 2.5\,V_u = 2.5 \times 120 = 300 \text{ kips}$$

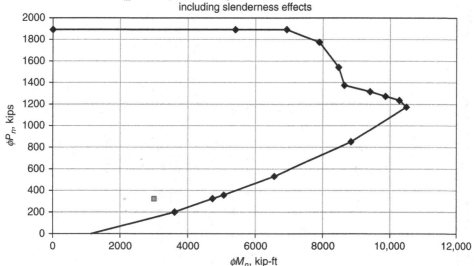

FIGURE 6.30 Moment-axial force interaction diagram (strength basis) for reinforced shear wall, including slenderness effects.

Spreadsheet for calculating strength moment-axial force interaction diagram for clay masonry shear wall

depth	288		h	120	
ε_{mu}	0.0035		r	2.1651	
f'_m	2.5		h/r	55.426	
f_y	60		factor	0.8433	
E_s	29000				
ε_y	0.002069				
d	285				
(c/d) balanced	0.628483				
width	7.5				
				Mu	300 kip-ft
				Pu	324 kip

steel layers are counted from the extreme compression fiber to the extreme tension fiber
distances are measured from the extreme compression fiber
reinforcement is assumed to be placed at 4-ft intervals
compression in masonry and reinforcement is taken as positive
stress in compressive reinforcement is set to zero, because the reinforcement is not laterally supported

Row of Reinforcement	Distance	Area
1	3.00	0.31
2	51.00	0.31
3	99.00	0.31
4	147.00	0.31
5	195.00	0.31
6	237.00	0.31
7	285.00	0.31

	c/d	c	C_{mas}	$f_s(1)$	$f_s(2)$	$f_s(3)$	$f_s(4)$	$f_s(5)$	$f_s(6)$	$\varepsilon_y(7)$	$f_s(7)$	ϕ	M_n	P_n	ϕM_n	ϕP_n
Pure axial load	1.01	287.9	3454	0.0	0.0	0.0	0.0	0.0	0.0	0.0000	0.00	0.65	0	2911	0	1892
	0.9	256.5	3078	0.0	0.0	0.0	0.0	0.0	0.0	−0.0004	−11.28	0.65	8307	2912	5400	1893
	0.8	228.0	2736	0.0	0.0	0.0	0.0	0.0	0.0	−0.0009	−25.38	0.65	10660	2912	6929	1893
	0.7	199.5	2394	0.0	0.0	0.0	0.0	0.0	−4.0	−0.0015	−43.50	0.65	12140	2727	7891	1772
Points controlled by masonry	0.628483	179.1	2149	0.0	0.0	0.0	0.0	0.0	−19.1	−0.0021	−60.00	0.65	13012	2375	8458	1543
	0.628483	179.1	2149	0.0	0.0	0.0	0.0	−9.0	−32.8	−0.0021	−60.00	0.65	13269	2118	8625	1377
Points controlled by steel	0.628483	179.1	2149	0.0	0.0	0.0	0.0	−9.0	−32.8	−0.0021	−60.00	0.65	13269	2118	8625	1377
	0.55	156.8	1881	0.0	0.0	0.0	0.0	−24.8	−52.0	−0.0029	−60.00	0.72	13120	1839	9397	1317
	0.5	142.5	1710	0.0	0.0	0.0	−3.2	−37.4	−60.0	−0.0035	−60.00	0.77	12810	1660	9854	1277
	0.45	128.3	1539	0.0	0.0	0.0	−14.8	−52.8	−60.0	−0.0043	−60.00	0.83	12322	1481	10278	1235
	0.4	114.0	1368	0.0	0.0	0.0	−29.4	−60.0	−60.0	−0.0053	−60.00	0.90	11662	1303	10495	1173
	0.3	85.5	1026	0.0	0.0	−16.0	−60.0	−60.0	−60.0	−0.0082	−60.00	0.90	9816	947	8834	852
	0.2	57.0	684	0.0	0.0	−60.0	−60.0	−60.0	−60.0	−0.0140	−60.00	0.90	7285	591	6557	532
	0.1462	41.7	500	0.0	−22.7	−60.0	−60.0	−60.0	−60.0	−0.0204	−60.00	0.90	5628	400	5065	360
	0.1353	38.6	463	0.0	−32.7	−60.0	−60.0	−60.0	−60.0	−0.0224	−60.00	0.90	5256	360	4730	324
	0.1	28.5	342	0.0	−60.0	−60.0	−60.0	−60.0	−60.0	−0.0315	−60.00	0.90	4012	230	3610	207
	0.01	2.85	34	−5.34	−60.0	−60.0	−60.0	−60.0	−60.0	−0.3465	−60.00	0.90	620	−79	558	−79

The wall is satisfactory without shear reinforcement. Prescriptive seismic reinforcement for Seismic Design Category D will probably require #5 bars horizontally @ 24 in., however. We have vertical reinforcement of #5 bars @ 48 in., corresponding to a reinforcement ratio of:

$$\rho_{vertical} = \frac{0.31 \text{ in}^2}{48 \text{ in.} \times 7.5 \text{ in.}} = 0.000861$$

Section 7.3.2.5(d) of *TMS 402-22* requires that the summation of vertical and horizontal reinforcement ratios be at least 0.002. This can be satisfied by specifying horizontal reinforcement consisting of #5 bars @ 24 in.

$$\rho_{horizontal} = \frac{0.31 \text{ in}^2}{24 \text{ in.} \times 7.5 \text{ in.}} = 0.00172$$

$$\rho_{vertical} + \rho_{horizontal} = 0.000861 + 0.00172 = 0.00258$$

Check the shear capacity using that prescriptive reinforcement.

$$V_n = V_{nm} + V_{ns} = 323.9 \text{ kips} + \left(\frac{1}{2}\right) A_v f_y \frac{d}{s} = 323.9 + \left(\frac{1}{2}\right) 0.31 \text{ in}^2 \times 60,000 \text{ psi} \times \left(\frac{285 \text{ in.}}{24 \text{ in.}}\right)$$

$$V_n = 323.9 \text{ kips} + 110.4 \text{ kips} = 434.3 \text{ kips}$$

Prescriptive seismic reinforcement is sufficient for shear. Use #5 bars at 24 in.

Check ρ, assuming that the wall is classified as a special reinforced masonry shear wall ($\alpha = 4$) based on Table 9.3.5.6.1 of *TMS 402-22*. In the equation below, the code commentary equation for walls with uniformly distributed steel of *TMS 402-22*, Section 9.3.5.6.1, has been divided by b to produce a general equation for ρ_{max}. See derivation and discussion in Section 6.4.4 of this book.

$$\rho_{max} = \frac{0.64 f'_m \left(\frac{\varepsilon_{mu}}{\alpha \varepsilon_y + \varepsilon_{mu}}\right) - \frac{P}{bd}}{f_y \left(\frac{\alpha \varepsilon_y - \varepsilon_{mu}}{\alpha \varepsilon_y + \varepsilon_{mu}}\right)}$$

$$\rho_{max} = \frac{0.64 f'_m \left(\frac{\varepsilon_{mu}}{4\varepsilon_y + \varepsilon_{mu}}\right) - \frac{P}{bd}}{f_y \left(\frac{4\varepsilon_y - \varepsilon_{mu}}{4\varepsilon_y + \varepsilon_{mu}}\right)}$$

In accordance with *TMS 402-22*, Section 9.3.3.2.4, the governing axial load combination is $D + 0.75 L + 0.525 Q_E$, and the axial load is $(360,000 + 0.75 \times 75,000 \text{ lb})$, or 416,250 lb.

$$\rho_{max} = \frac{0.64 f'_m \left(\frac{\varepsilon_{mu}}{4\varepsilon_y + \varepsilon_{mu}}\right) - \frac{P}{bd_v}}{f_y \left(\frac{4\varepsilon_y - \varepsilon_{mu}}{4\varepsilon_y + \varepsilon_{mu}}\right)}$$

$$\rho_{max} = \cfrac{0.64(2500\text{ psi})\left[\cfrac{0.0035}{4(0.00207)+0.0035}\right] - \cfrac{416,250\text{ lb}}{(7.50\text{ in.})(288\text{ in.})}}{(60,000\text{ psi})\left[\cfrac{4(0.00207)-0.0035}{4(0.00207)+0.0035}\right]}$$

$$\rho_{max} = 0.0116$$

Check maximum area of flexural reinforcement per 48 in. of wall length:

$$A_{smax} = \rho_{max}(b \times d) = 0.0115(7.5\text{ in.} \times (288\text{ in.})) = 25.1\text{ in}^2$$

Our design has 0.31 in² every 48 in. for a total of 7(0.31 in²) = 2.17 in² significantly less than 21.5 in² and our design is satisfactory.

Alternately, the exact code equation could be used to evaluate the steel area per unit length of the wall.

$$\frac{A_{smax}}{d_v} = \cfrac{0.64 f'_m b \left(\cfrac{\varepsilon_{mu}}{4\varepsilon_y + \varepsilon_{mu}}\right) - \cfrac{P}{d_v}}{f_y\left(\cfrac{4\varepsilon_y - \varepsilon_{mu}}{4\varepsilon_y + \varepsilon_{mu}}\right)}$$

$$\frac{A_{smax}}{d_v} = \cfrac{0.64(2500\text{ psi})(7.5\text{ in})\left(\cfrac{0.0035}{4(0.00207)+0.0035}\right) - \cfrac{416,250\text{ lb}}{(288\text{ in})}}{60,000\text{ psi}\left(\cfrac{4(0.00207)-0.0035}{4(0.00207)+0.0035}\right)}$$

$$\frac{A_s}{d_v} = 0.0872\text{ in.}$$

Our design has 0.31 in² per 48 in for a ratio of $\dfrac{A_s}{\text{spacing}} = \dfrac{0.31\text{ in}^2}{48\text{ in.}} = 0.00646\text{ in.} < 0.0872\text{ in.}$

Again, the area of steel provided is well below the maximum area of steel permitted of TMS 402-22, Section 9.3.5.6.1.

Summary: Use #5 @ 48 in. vertically, #5 @ 24 in. horizontally.

6.4.4 Minimum and Maximum Reinforcement Ratios for Flexural Design of Masonry Shear Walls by the Strength Approach

6.4.4.1 Minimum Flexural Reinforcement by *TMS 402-22*

TMS 402-22 has no global requirements for minimum flexural reinforcement for shear walls.

6.4.4.2 Maximum Flexural Reinforcement by *TMS 402-22*

TMS 402-22 has a maximum reinforcement requirement (Section 9.3.5.6.1) that is intended to ensure ductile behavior over a range of axial loads. As compressive axial load increases, the maximum permissible reinforcement percentage decreases. For compressive axial loads above a critical value, the maximum permissible reinforcement percentage drops to zero, and design is impossible unless the cross-sectional area of the element is increased.

198　Chapter Six

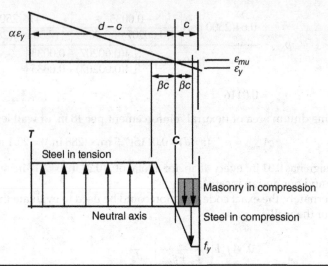

FIGURE 6.31 Critical strain condition for strength design of masonry walls loaded in-plane, and for columns and beams.

For walls subjected to in-plane forces, for columns, and for beams, the provisions of *TMS 402-22* set the maximum permissible reinforcement based on a critical strain condition in which the masonry is at its maximum useful strain, and the extreme tension reinforcement is set at a multiple of the yield strain, where the multiple depends on the expected curvature ductility demand on the wall. For "special" reinforced masonry shear walls, the multiple is 4; for "intermediate" walls, it is 3. For walls not required to undergo inelastic deformations, no upper limit is imposed.

The critical strain condition for walls loaded in-plane, and for columns and beams, is shown in Fig. 6.31, along with the corresponding stress state. The multiple is termed "α." The parameters for the equivalent rectangular stress block are the same as those used for conventional flexural design. The height of the stress block is $0.80 f'_m$, and the depth is $0.80\,c$. The stress in yielded tensile reinforcement is assumed to be f_y. Compression reinforcement is included in the calculation based on the assumption that protecting the compression toe will permit the masonry there to provide lateral support to the compression reinforcement. This assumption, while perhaps reasonable, is not consistent with that used for calculation of moment-axial force interaction diagrams.

Locate the neutral axis using the critical strain condition:

$$\frac{\varepsilon_{mu}}{0.005} = \frac{c}{d-c}$$

$$c = d\left(\frac{\varepsilon_{mu}}{0.005 + \varepsilon_{mu}}\right)$$

Compute the tensile and compressive forces acting on the section, assuming uniformly distributed flexural reinforcement, with a percentage of reinforcement $\rho = \dfrac{A_s}{bd}$. On each side of the neutral axis, the distance over which the reinforcement is in the elastic range is βc, where β is given by proportion as $\beta = \dfrac{\varepsilon_y}{\varepsilon_{mu}}$.

Strength Design of Reinforced Masonry Elements

The compressive force in the masonry is given by

$$C_{masonry} = 0.80 f'_m 0.80 cb$$

The compressive force in the reinforcement is given by

$$C_{steel} = \rho\beta cbf_y \left(\frac{1}{2}\right) + \rho(1-\beta)cbf_y$$

$$C_{steel} = \rho\left(\frac{\varepsilon_y}{\varepsilon_{mu}}\right)cbf_y\left(\frac{1}{2}\right) + \rho\left[1 - \left(\frac{\varepsilon_y}{\varepsilon_{mu}}\right)\right]cbf_y$$

The tensile force in the reinforcement is given by

$$T_{steel} = \rho\beta cbf_y\left(\frac{1}{2}\right) + \rho(d-c-\beta c)bf_y$$

$$T_{steel} = \rho\left(\frac{\varepsilon_y}{\varepsilon_{mu}}\right)cbf_y\left(\frac{1}{2}\right) + \rho\left[d-c-\left(\frac{\varepsilon_y}{\varepsilon_{mu}}\right)c\right]bf_y$$

Equilibrium of axial forces requires

$$P_n = C - T$$

$$\frac{P_u}{\phi} = C - T$$

$$\frac{P_u}{\phi} = 0.80 f'_m 0.80 cb$$

$$+ \rho\left(\frac{\varepsilon_y}{\varepsilon_{mu}}\right)cbf_y\left(\frac{1}{2}\right) + \rho\left[1 - \left(\frac{\varepsilon_y}{\varepsilon_{mu}}\right)\right]cbf_y$$

$$- \rho\left(\frac{\varepsilon_y}{\varepsilon_{mu}}\right)cbf_y\left(\frac{1}{2}\right) - \rho\left[d-c-\left(\frac{\varepsilon_y}{\varepsilon_{mu}}\right)c\right]bf_y$$

$$\frac{P_u}{\phi} = 0.80 f'_m 0.80 cb + \rho\left[1-\left(\frac{\varepsilon_y}{\varepsilon_{mu}}\right)\right]cbf_y - \rho\left[d-c-\left(\frac{\varepsilon_y}{\varepsilon_{mu}}\right)c\right]bf_y$$

$$\frac{P_u}{\phi} = 0.80 f'_m 0.80 cb + \rho(2-d)cbf_y$$

$$\frac{P_u}{\phi} = 0.80 f'_m 0.80 d\left(\frac{\varepsilon_{mu}}{\alpha\varepsilon_y + \varepsilon_{mu}}\right)b + 2\rho cbf_y - \rho dbf_y$$

$$\frac{P_u}{\phi} = 0.80 f'_m 0.80 d\left(\frac{\varepsilon_{mu}}{\alpha\varepsilon_y + \varepsilon_{mu}}\right)b + 2\rho d\left(\frac{\varepsilon_{mu}}{\alpha\varepsilon_y + \varepsilon_{mu}}\right)bf_y - \rho dbf_y$$

$$\frac{P_u}{\phi} = 0.80 f'_m 0.80 d\left(\frac{\varepsilon_{mu}}{\alpha\varepsilon_y + \varepsilon_{mu}}\right)b + \rho b df_y\left[\left(\frac{2\varepsilon_{mu}}{\alpha\varepsilon_y + \varepsilon_{mu}}\right) - 1\right]$$

$$\rho b d f_y \left[1 - \left(\frac{2\varepsilon_{mu}}{\alpha\varepsilon_y + \varepsilon_{mu}}\right)\right] = 0.80 f'_m 0.80 d \left(\frac{\varepsilon_{mu}}{\alpha\varepsilon_y + \varepsilon_{mu}}\right) b - \frac{P_u}{\phi}$$

$$\rho = \frac{0.80 f'_m 0.80 d \left(\dfrac{\varepsilon_{mu}}{\alpha\varepsilon_y + \varepsilon_{mu}}\right) b - \dfrac{P_u}{\phi}}{b d f_y \left[1 - \left(\dfrac{2\varepsilon_{mu}}{\alpha\varepsilon_y + \varepsilon_{mu}}\right)\right]} = \frac{0.80 f'_m 0.80 \left(\dfrac{\varepsilon_{mu}}{\alpha\varepsilon_y + \varepsilon_{mu}}\right) - \dfrac{P_u}{bd\phi}}{f_y \left[1 - \left(\dfrac{2\varepsilon_{mu}}{\alpha\varepsilon_y + \varepsilon_{mu}}\right)\right]}$$

$$\rho = \frac{0.80 f'_m 0.80 \left(\dfrac{\varepsilon_{mu}}{\alpha\varepsilon_y + \varepsilon_{mu}}\right) - \dfrac{P_u}{bd\phi}}{f_y \left[\left(\dfrac{\alpha\varepsilon_y + \varepsilon_{mu}}{\alpha\varepsilon_y + \varepsilon_{mu}}\right) - \left(\dfrac{2\varepsilon_{mu}}{\alpha\varepsilon_y + \varepsilon_{mu}}\right)\right]} = \frac{0.80 f'_m 0.80 \left(\dfrac{\varepsilon_{mu}}{\alpha\varepsilon_y + \varepsilon_{mu}}\right) - \dfrac{P_u}{bd\phi}}{f_y \left(\dfrac{\alpha\varepsilon_y - \varepsilon_{mu}}{\alpha\varepsilon_y + \varepsilon_{mu}}\right)}$$

So

$$\rho = \frac{0.64 f'_m \left(\dfrac{\varepsilon_{mu}}{\alpha\varepsilon_y + \varepsilon_{mu}}\right) - \dfrac{P_u}{bd\phi}}{f_y \left(\dfrac{\alpha\varepsilon_y - \varepsilon_{mu}}{\alpha\varepsilon_y + \varepsilon_{mu}}\right)}$$

The derived equation can be compared to the code commentary equation for walls with uniformly distributed steel, Section 9.3.5.6.1 shown below. The code equation has been divided by b to produce a general equation for A_s per linear ft. One difference is the use of P_u and ϕ. TMS 402-22 does not use a factored load because the governing load combination ($D + 0.75 L + 0.525 Q_E$) has a leading coefficient of 1 for dead load and a potentially variable strength reduction factor, ϕ. Another difference is the use of d_v rather than d that is simpler and makes little difference.

$\dfrac{A_s}{d_v} = \dfrac{0.64 \left(\dfrac{\varepsilon_{mu}}{\alpha\varepsilon_y + \varepsilon_{mu}}\right) - \dfrac{P}{d_v}}{f_y \left(\dfrac{\alpha\varepsilon_y - \varepsilon_{mu}}{\alpha\varepsilon_y + \varepsilon_{mu}}\right)}$	TMS 402-22 Section 9.3.5.6.1 code commentary for walls with uniformly distributed steel

6.4.5 Additional Comments on the Design of Reinforced Shear Walls

Reinforced masonry shear walls, like unreinforced ones, are relatively easy to design by either strength or allowable-stress approaches. Although shear capacities per unit area is small, the available area is large.

With either strength or allowable-stress approaches, it is rarely necessary to use shear reinforcement. In this sense, the best shear design strategy for shear walls is like that for shear design of beams—use enough cross-sectional area to eliminate the need for shear reinforcement. Seismic requirements may still dictate some shear reinforcement, however.

6.5 Required Details for Reinforced Bearing Walls and Shear Walls

Bearing walls that resist out-of-plane lateral loads, and shear walls, must be designed to transfer lateral loads to the floors above and below. Examples of such connections are shown below. These connections would have to be strengthened for regions subject to strong earthquakes or strong winds. Section 1604.8.2 of the 2022 IBC has additional requirements for anchorage of diaphragms to masonry walls. Section 12.11 of ASCE 7-22 has additional requirements for anchorage of structural walls for structures assigned to Seismic Design Categories C and higher.

6.5.1 Wall-to-Foundation Connections

As shown in Fig. 6.32, CMU walls (or the inner CMU wythe of a drainage wall) must be connected to the concrete foundation. Bond breaker should be used only between the outer veneer wythe and the foundation.

6.5.2 Wall-to-Floor Details

Examples of a wall-to-floor detail are shown in Figs. 6.33 and 6.34. In the latter detail (floor or roof planks oriented parallel to walls), the planks are actually cambered. They are shown on the outside of the walls so that this camber does not interfere with the coursing of the units. Some designers object to this detail because it could lead to spalling of the cover. If it is modified so that the planks rest on the face shells of the walls, then the thickness of the topping must vary to adjust for the camber and form boards must be used against both sides of the wall underneath the planks so that the concrete or grout that is cast into the bond beam does not run out underneath the cambered beam.

6.5.3 Wall-to-Roof Details

An example of a wall-to-roof detail is shown in Fig. 6.35.

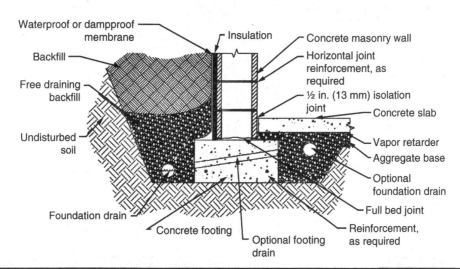

Figure 6.32 Example of wall-to-foundation connection. (*Source:* Figure 1 of CMHA TEK 05-03.)

202 Chapter Six

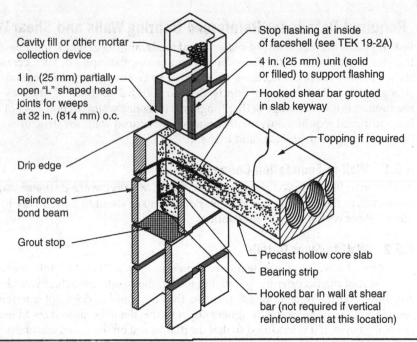

Figure 6.33 Example of wall-to-floor connection, planks perpendicular to wall. (*Source:* Figure 14 of CMHA TEK 05-07A.)

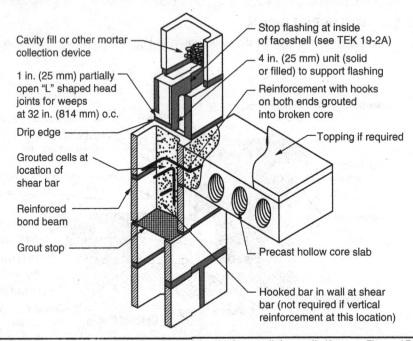

Figure 6.34 Example of wall-to-floor connection, planks parallel to wall. (*Source:* Figure 15 of CMHA TEK 05-07A.)

6.5.4 Typical Details of Wall-to-Wall Connections

Typical details of wall-to-wall connections are shown in Fig. 6.36.

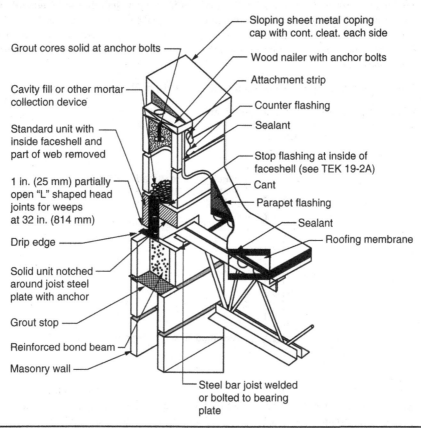

FIGURE 6.35 Example of wall-to-roof detail. (*Source:* Figure 11 of CMHA TEK 05-07A.)

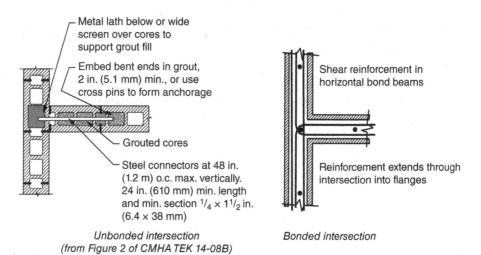

FIGURE 6.36 Examples of wall-to-wall connection details. (*Source:* Figure 2 of CMHA TEK 14-08B.)

6.6 Problems

6.1 Design a simply supported, fully grouted, reinforced bearing wall subjected to eccentric axial loads of 500 lb dead and 250 lb live load per foot of plan length, combined with out-of-plane wind load of 25 psf. All loads are unfactored. The axial-load eccentricity is 2.5 in. and the story height is 10 ft. Assume a specified compressive strength of masonry of 2000 psi. Use nominal 8-in. CMU and the self-weight from Table 5.6 (81 lb/ft² for fully grouted units). Use the following load conditions.

Part 1 Considering gravity loads only, check the existing design for compliance with *TMS 402-22*.

Part 2 Repeat Part 1 including wind load.

The wall is as shown below:

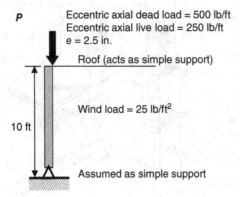

6.2 In the building shown below, the roof is assumed to span longitudinally between the two gable walls. The 1-ft strip of CMU shown below is subjected to unfactored eccentric gravity loads of 800 lb dead load and 200 lb live load at the building apex, whose height is 16 ft. The eccentricity is 3 in. Include self-weight. The wall is also subjected to an out-of-plane wind load whose magnitude is not specified. A ceiling provides horizontal restraint at the mid-height of each gable wall. As an initial design assumption, idealize this vertical strip assuming zero moment at the building apex, the ceiling, and the base. The wall is fully grouted, with 8-in. units, reinforcement consisting of #4 bars at 48 in., and f'_m = 2000 psi.

Part 1 Considering gravity loads only, check the existing design for compliance with *TMS 402-22*.

Part 2 Repeat Part 1 including wind load. Calculate the maximum unfactored wind load the vertical strip can support.

The wall is as shown below:

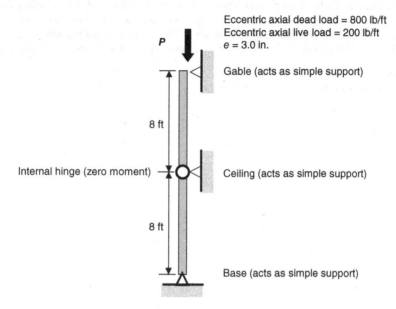

*6.3 Repeat Problem 6.2 using a single two-span beam. This assumes a continuous beam-column at the height of the ceiling and at the base. Comment on how the maximum permissible wind load changes.

Part 1 Considering gravity loads only, check the existing design for compliance with *TMS 402-22*.

Part 2 Repeat Part 1 including wind load. Calculate the maximum unfactored wind load the vertical strip can support.

The wall is as shown below:

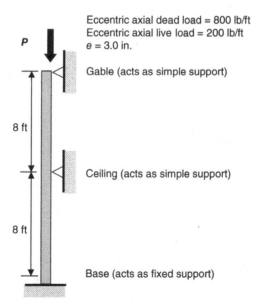

Chapter Six

6.4 Extend the problem of Fig. 5.21 to a two-story building. Change the typical story height to 10 ft. Gravity loads on a typical floor are equal to those on the roof. Try a nominal 8-in. CMU wall, ungrouted, with face-shell bedding and Type S PCL mortar. Use a specified masonry compressive strength of 2000 psi. Assume a unit density of 115 lb/ft^3, and use the self-weight from Table 5.4 (33 lb/ft^2). If this does not work, list an alternate way to solve the problem using 8-in. units.

*6.5 Using the design of Problem 6.4, and continuing the same load at each diaphragm level, how many stories could the building have?

---

*Denotes problems intended for graduate students.

CHAPTER 7
Allowable-Stress Design of Unreinforced Masonry Elements

7.1 Allowable-Stress Design of Unreinforced Panel Walls

7.1.1 Examples of Use of Unreinforced Panel Walls

Panel walls commonly comprise the masonry envelope surrounding reinforced concrete or steel frames. In the context of *TMS 402-22*, a panel wall would be termed a "multi-wythe, non-composite" wall. An example of an unreinforced panel wall is shown in Fig. 7.1.

The outer wythes of panel walls must span horizontally. They cannot span vertically, because of the open expansion joint under each shelf angle. Support conditions for the horizontally spanning outer wythe can be simple or continuous. An example of the connection of a panel wall to a column is shown in the horizontal section of Fig. 7.2. A simple support condition would be achieved by inserting a vertically oriented expansion joint in the clay masonry wythe on both sides of the column.

The inner wythes of panel walls can span horizontally and vertically.

As a result, it is convenient to visualize panel walls as being composed of sets of vertical and horizontal crossing strips in each wythe. This is shown schematically in Fig. 7.3.

At the end of this section, it will be shown that:

- Because of their aspect ratio, the inner wythe can almost always be considered to span in the vertical direction only.
- It is simple and only slightly conservative to design single-wythe panel walls as though the vertical strips resisted all out-of-plane load.
- It is simple and only slightly conservative to design two-wythe panel walls as though the vertical strips of the inner wythe resisted all out-of-plane load.

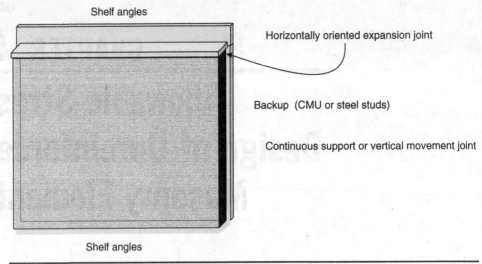

FIGURE 7.1 Example of an unreinforced panel wall.

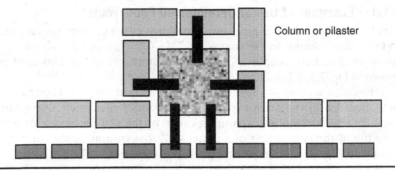

FIGURE 7.2 Horizontal section showing connection of a panel wall to a column.

7.1.2 Flexural Design of Panel Walls Using Allowable-Stress Provisions of *TMS 402-22*

According to the allowable-stress provisions of *TMS 402-22*, allowable flexural capacity of unreinforced masonry is computed assuming linear stress-strain relationships. Allowable flexural capacity corresponds to a maximum flexural compressive stress of $\left(\frac{1}{3}\right)f'_m$ (*TMS 402-22* Section 8.2.4.1(c)). The allowable stress in flexural tension is much lower (Table 7.1), and governs the design.

TMS 402-22 provides different allowable stresses for flexural tension normal to bed joints, and parallel to bed joints in running bond. Allowable stresses are higher parallel to bed joints in running bond, because of the interlocking of units laid in that bond pattern. Allowable flexural tension is zero parallel to bed joints in stack bond, unless they are resisted by a continuous grout section parallel to the bed joints.

The allowable stresses in Table 8.2.4.2 apply to out-of-plane and in-plane bending.

Allowable-Stress Design of Unreinforced Masonry Elements

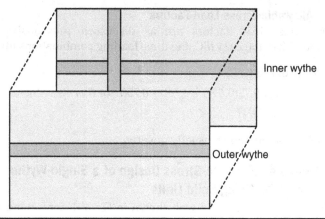

FIGURE 7.3 Schematic representation of an unreinforced, two-wythe panel wall as two sets of horizontal and vertical crossing strips.

TABLE 7.1 Allowable Flexural Tension for Clay and Concrete Masonry, psi (Table 8.2.4.2 of TMS 402-22)

Direction of Flexural Tensile Stress and Masonry Type	PCL or Mortar Cement M or S	PCL or Mortar Cement N	Masonry Cement or Air-Entrained PCL M or S	Masonry Cement or Air-Entrained PCL N
Normal to bed joints				
Solid units	53	40	32	20
Hollow units[1]	33	25	20	12
Ungrouted	86	84	81	77
Fully grouted				
Parallel to bed joints in running bond				
Solid units	106	80	64	40
Hollow units	66	50	40	25
Ungrouted and partially grouted	106	80	64	40
Fully grouted				
Parallel to bed joints in masonry not laid in running bond	133	133	133	133
Continuous grout section parallel to bed joints	0	0	0	0
Other				

[1]For partially grouted masonry, allowable stresses shall be determined on the basis of linear interpolation between fully grouted hollow units and ungrouted hollow units based on amount (percentage) of grouting.

7.1.2.1 Allowable-Stress Load Factors

Allowable-stress load factors are as discussed previously. As prescribed in Section 1605.3.2 of the 2024 *IBC*, the three loading combinations involving wind are:

$D + (0.6W \text{ or } 0.7E)$

$D + H + F + 0.75(0.6W) + 0.75L + 0.75(L_r \text{ or } S \text{ or } R)$

$0.6D + 0.6W + H$

Of these, Combination 8 usually governs.

7.1.3 Example: Allowable-Stress Design of a Single-Wythe Panel Wall Using Solid Units

Check the design of the panel wall shown in Fig. 7.4, for a wind load w of 32 lb/ft², using portland cement limestone (PCL) mortar, Type N, and units with a nominal thickness of 8 in.

The panel wall will be designed as unreinforced masonry. The design follows the steps below, using a nominal thickness of 8 in. The panel could be designed as a two-way panel. Nevertheless, because of its aspect ratio, the vertical strips will carry practically all the load. Therefore, design it as a one-way panel, consisting of a series of vertically spanning, simply supported strips.

Calculate the maximum bending moment and corresponding flexural tensile stress in a strip 1-ft wide, with a nominal thickness of 8 in.:

$$M_{max} = \frac{w\ell^2}{8} = \frac{0.6 \times 32 \text{ lb/ft }(8 \text{ ft})^2}{8} \times 12 \text{ in./ft} = 1843 \text{ lb-in.}$$

$$f_t = \frac{Mc}{I} = \frac{1843 \text{ lb-in.} \times \left(\frac{7.625}{2}\right) \text{ in.}}{\left[12 \text{ in.} \times \left(\frac{7.625 \text{ in.}}{12}\right)^3\right]} = 15.9 \text{ lb/in}^2$$

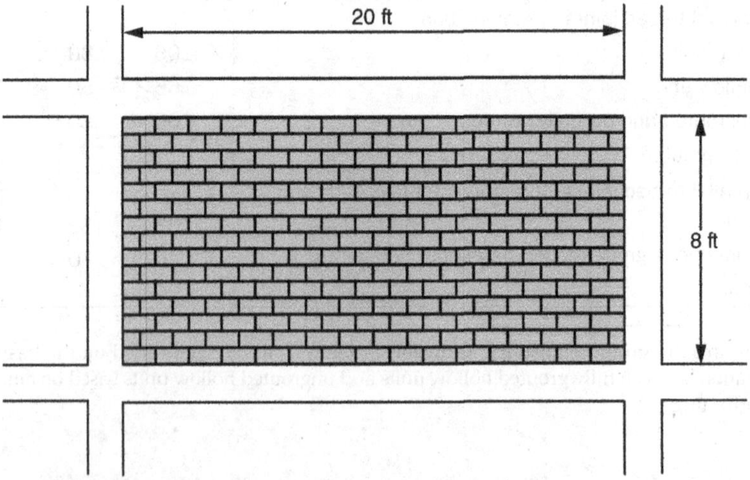

FIGURE 7.4 Example panel wall to be designed.

The calculated flexural tensile stress, 15.9 lb/in², is less than the allowable flexural tensile stress normal to bed joints for solid units and Type N PCL mortar (40 lb/in²). The design is therefore satisfactory. We should also check one-way (beam) shear. An example of this is given later.

7.1.4 Example: Allowable-Stress Design of a Single-Wythe Panel Wall Using Hollow Units

Check the design of the panel wall of the example of the preceding section for a wind load q of 32 lb/ft², using PCL mortar, Type N, and assuming hollow units with face shells and cross-webs mortared.

The panel wall will be designed as unreinforced masonry. The design follows the following steps, using a nominal thickness of 8 in. The panel could be designed as a two-way panel. Nevertheless, because of its aspect ratio, the vertical strips will carry practically all the load. Therefore, design it as a one-way panel, consisting of a series of vertically spanning, simply supported strips.

Calculate the maximum bending moment and corresponding flexural tensile stress in a strip 1-ft wide, with a nominal thickness of 8 in. Assume that the head joints are only 1.25-in. thick. All length dimensions are in inches. These dimensions are shown in Fig. 7.5. The wall thicknesses given below are consistent with the dimensions assumed in CMHA TEK 002 (Concrete Masonry Wall Weights). They are not necessarily the minimum wall thicknesses permitted by *ASTM C90*.

Illustrate the computation of section properties for this cross-section:

$$A = A_{solid} - A_{cells} - A_{head\,joint}$$

$$A = (16)(7.63) - (15.63 - 3 \cdot 1.00)(7.63 - 2 \cdot 1.25) - 0.37(7.63 - 2 \cdot 1.25)$$

$$A = 122.1 - 64.8 - 1.9 = 55.4 \text{ in}^2 \quad \text{for a 16-in. wide strip}$$

$$A = 55.4 \text{ in}^2 \left(\frac{12 \text{ in.}}{16 \text{ in.}}\right) = 41.5 \text{ in}^2 \quad \text{for a 12-in. wide strip}$$

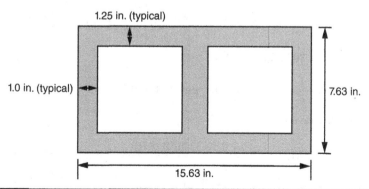

FIGURE 7.5 Idealized cross-sectional dimensions of a nominal 8 × 8 × 16 in. concrete masonry unit.

$$I = I_{solid} - I_{cells} - I_{head\,joint}$$

$$I = \frac{(16)(7.625)^3}{12} - \frac{(15.625 - 3 \cdot 1.00)(7.625 - 2 \cdot 1.25)^3}{12} - \frac{0.375(7.625 - 2 \cdot 1.25)^3}{12}$$

$$I = 591.1 - 141.6 - 4.2 = 445.3 \text{ in}^4 \text{ per 16 in. of width}$$

$$I = 445.3\left(\frac{12}{16}\right) = 334.0 \text{ in}^4 \text{ per 12 in. of width}$$

$$c = \frac{7.625}{2} = 3.81 \text{ in.}$$

For the 12-in. wide strip,

$$M_{max} = \frac{w\ell^2}{8} = \frac{0.6 \times 32 \text{ lb/ft }(8 \text{ ft})^2}{8} \times 12 \text{ in./ft} = 1843 \text{ lb-in.}$$

$$f_t = \frac{Mc}{I} = \frac{1843 \text{ lb-in.} \times 3.81 \text{ in.}}{334 \text{ in}^4} = 21.0 \text{ lb/in}^2$$

The calculated flexural tensile stress, 21.0 lb/in², is less than the allowable flexural tensile stress normal to bed joints for hollow units and Type N PCL mortar (25 lb/in²). The design is satisfactory.

7.1.5 Example: Design of a Single-Wythe Panel Wall Using Hollow Units, Face-Shell Bedding Only

Check the design of the panel wall of the previous example assuming face-shell bedding only (mortar on the face shells of the units only).

The panel wall will be designed as unreinforced masonry. The design follows the following steps, using a nominal thickness of 8 in. The panel could be designed as a two-way panel. Nevertheless, because of its aspect ratio, the vertical strips will carry practically all the load. Therefore, design it as a one-way panel, consisting of a series of vertically spanning, simply supported strips.

The critical stresses will occur on the bed joint, which is the horizontal plane through the masonry where the section modulus is minimum. All length dimensions are in inches. The dimensions of this critical cross-section are shown in Fig. 7.6.

$$I = I_{faceshells} = \frac{(1.25 \text{ in.})^3 \times 12 \text{ in.}}{12} \times 2 + 2(1.25 \times 12 \text{ in}^2)\left(\frac{7.625 - 1.25}{2}\right)^2$$

$$= 309.2 \text{ in}^4 \text{ per ft of width}$$

$$S = \frac{I}{c} = \frac{309.2}{3.81} = 81.2 \text{ in}^3 \text{ per ft of width}$$

For the 1-ft wide strip,

$$M_{max} = \frac{w\ell^2}{8} = \frac{0.6 \times 32 \text{ lb/ft }(8 \text{ ft})^2}{8} \times 12 \text{ in./ft} = 1843 \text{ lb-in.}$$

$$f_t = \frac{M}{S} = \frac{1843 \text{ lb-in.}}{81.2 \text{ in}^3} = 22.7 \text{ lb/in}^2$$

Allowable-Stress Design of Unreinforced Masonry Elements 213

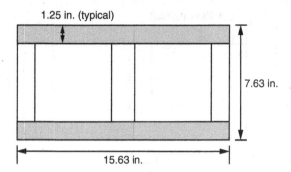

FIGURE 7.6 Idealized cross-sectional dimensions of a nominal 8 × 8 × 16 in. concrete masonry unit with face-shell bedding.

The calculated flexural tensile stress, 22.7 lb/in², is less than the allowable flexural tensile stress normal to bed joints for hollow units and Type N PCL mortar (25 lb/in²). The design is satisfactory.

7.1.6 Example: Allowable-Stress Design of a Single-Wythe Panel Wall using Hollow Units, Fully Grouted

Check the design of the panel wall of the example of the preceding section for a wind load q of 32 lb/ft², using PCL mortar, Type N, and assuming hollow units, fully grouted.

As in the previous examples, assume vertically spanning, simply supported strips. Calculate the maximum bending moment and corresponding flexural tensile stress in a strip 1-ft wide, with a nominal thickness of 8 in.:

$$M_{max} = \frac{w\ell^2}{8} = \frac{0.6 \times 32 \text{ lb/ft }(8 \text{ ft})^2}{8} \times 12 \text{ in./ft} = 1843 \text{ lb-in.}$$

$$f_t = \frac{Mc}{I} = \frac{1843 \text{ lb-in.} \times \left(\frac{7.625}{2}\right) \text{in.}}{\left[12 \text{ in.} \times \frac{(7.625 \text{ in.})^3}{12}\right]} = 15.9 \text{ lb/in}^2$$

The calculated flexural tensile stress, 15.9 lb/in², is less than the allowable flexural tensile stress normal to bed joints for fully grouted hollow units and Type N PCL mortar (80 lb/in²). The design is therefore satisfactory.

7.1.7 Example: Design of a Two-Wythe Panel Wall Using Hollow Units, Face-Shell Bedding Only

Check the design of a two-wythe panel wall in which the outer wythe is modular clay units and the inner wythe is 8-in. CMU with face-shell bedding. The wall has the panel wall of Example #3 assuming face-shell bedding only (mortar on the face shells of the units only). The wall has a wind load q of 32 lb/ft², and uses PCL mortar, Type N.

The panel wall will be designed as unreinforced masonry, assuming that the vertical strips of the inner wythe resist 100% of the out-of-plane load. The design is therefore identical to the design of Section 7.1.5.

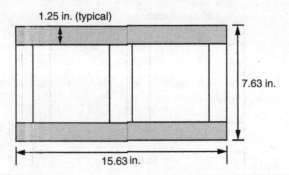

FIGURE 7.7 Idealized cross-sectional dimensions of a nominal 8 × 8 × 16 in. concrete masonry unit with face-shell bedding.

This idealized horizontal cross-section is shown in Fig. 7.7.

$$I = I_{faceshells} = 309.2 \text{ in}^4 \text{ per ft of width}$$

$$S = \frac{I}{c} = \frac{309.2}{3.81} = 81.2 \text{ in}^3 \text{ per ft of width}$$

For the 12-in. wide strip,

$$M_{max} = \frac{w\ell^2}{8} = \frac{0.6 \times 32 \text{ lb/ft } (8 \text{ ft})^2}{8} \times 12 \text{ in./ft} = 1843 \text{ lb-in.}$$

$$f_t = \frac{M}{S} = \frac{1843 \text{ lb-in.}}{87.8 \text{ in}^3} = 21.0 \text{ lb/in}^2$$

The calculated flexural tensile stress, 21.0 lb/in², is less than the allowable flexural tensile stress normal to bed joints for hollow units and Type N PCL mortar (25 lb/in²). The design is satisfactory. Addition of the outer wythe does not change the design of the panel wall.

7.1.8 Allowable-Stress Checks of One-Way Shear

The above examples dealt with design of panel walls for flexure. In theory, we should also check one-way shear. In practice, an example shows that shear does not come close to governing the design.

According to *TMS 402-22*, allowable one-way shear for unreinforced masonry flexural elements is prescribed by Section 2.2.5:

$$f_v = \frac{VQ}{I_n b}$$

and allowable in-plane shear stresses, F_v, shall not exceed any of:

$$F_v = \begin{cases} 1.5\sqrt{f'_m} \\ 120 \text{ psi} \\ v + 0.45(N_v + A_v) \end{cases}$$

in the third equation, v has the following values:

- 37 psi   for running bond masonry not fully grouted
- 37 psi   for masonry not laid in running bond, constructed of open-end units, and fully grouted
- 60 psi   for running bond masonry fully grouted
- 15 psi   for masonry not laid in running bond, constructed of other than open end units, and fully grouted

7.1.9 Example: Allowable-Stress Check of Shear Stress for Unreinforced Panel Walls

Check the effect of shear in the example immediately above.

With f'_m of 2000 lb/in² and masonry in running bond, and conservatively neglecting the beneficial effects of axial load, the third of the above equations governs, and $F_v = 37$ psi.

The wind load of 20 lb/ft² produces shears on a strip 12-in. wide, of

$$V = \frac{wL}{2} = \frac{0.6 \times 32 \text{ lb/ft} \times (8 \text{ ft})}{2} = 76.8 \text{ lb}$$

$$f_v = \frac{VQ}{Ib} = \left(\frac{3}{2}\right)\left(\frac{V}{A}\right) = \left(\frac{3}{2}\right)\left(\frac{76.8 \text{ lb}}{2 \times 12 \text{ in.} \times 1.25 \text{ in.}}\right) = 3.8 \text{ lb/in}^2$$

This is far less than the allowable shear stress, and one-way shear does not govern the design.

7.1.10 Overall Comments on Allowable-Stress Design of Unreinforced Panel Walls

- Non-load-bearing masonry, without calculated reinforcement, can easily resist wind loads. It approaches its capacity only in the case of ungrouted hollow masonry. In this case, the lower allowable flexural tensile stress for masonry cement mortar can be critical in design.
- If non-calculated reinforcement is included, it will not act until the masonry has cracked.
- Elements such as the ones we have calculated in this section can be designed in many cases by prescription.

7.1.11 Section Properties for Masonry Walls

Section properties for masonry walls are summarized in Tables 7.2 and 7.3.

TABLE 7.2   Section Properties for Clay Masonry Walls

Unit	Area in² per ft	Moment of Inertia in⁴ per ft
4-in. modular, fully bedded	43.5	47.6

TABLE 7.3 Section Properties for Concrete Masonry Walls (Face-Shell and Web Thicknesses Consistent with CMHA TEK 002, Which References *ASTM C90-06*)

Unit	Face-Shell Thickness, in.	Web Thickness, in.	Area in² per ft	Moment of Inertia in⁴ per ft
4-in. hollow CMU, fully bedded	3/4	3/4	21.6	39.4
4-in. hollow CMU, face-shell bedded			18.0	38.0
6-in. hollow CMU, fully bedded	1	1	32.2	139
6-in. hollow CMU, face-shell bedded			24.0	130
8-in. hollow CMU, fully bedded	1-1/4	1	41.5	334
8-in. hollow CMU, face-shell bedded			30.0	309
10-in. hollow CMU, fully bedded	1-1/4	1-1/8	48.0	606
10-in. hollow CMU, face-shell bedded			30.0	530
12-in. hollow CMU, fully bedded	1-1/4	1-1/8	53.1	972
12-in. hollow CMU, face-shell bedded			30.0	811

7.1.12 Theoretical Derivation of the Strip Method (Hillerborg 1996)

In the preceding examples, we have used the simplifications that single-wythe panel walls can be designed assuming that all of the load is resisted by vertically spanning strips, and that two-wythe panel walls can be designed assuming that all of the load is resisted by vertically spanning strips of the inner wythe.

It is now appropriate to consider the theoretical basis for this simplification. We first consider the simplification of wythes as crossing strips using the strip method, and then derive additional simplifications based on the relative stiffnesses of those strips.

Consider the differential equation for the out-of-plane deflection of an elastic plate with a uniformly distributed, out-of-plane load:

$$\frac{\partial^4 w}{\partial x^4} + \frac{\partial^4 w}{\partial x^2 \partial y^2} + \frac{\partial^4 w}{\partial y^4} = \frac{-q}{D}$$

where w = out-of-plane deflection
q = uniformly distributed pressure
and

$$D = \frac{EI}{(1-v^2)} = \frac{Et^3}{12(1-v^2)}$$

(EI is calculated per unit width, and Poisson effects are included)
Conservatively, ignore twisting moments:

$$\frac{\partial^4 w}{\partial x^4} + \frac{\partial^4 w}{\partial y^4} = \frac{-q}{D} = -\left(\frac{q_x}{D} + \frac{q_y}{D}\right)$$

This is the differential equation for independent x and y strips (beams). The two sets of strips can be designed independently, provided that equilibrium is satisfied at every point:

$$q_x + q_y = q$$

7.1.13 Distribution of Out-of-Plane Load to Vertical and Horizontal Strips of a Single-Wythe Panel Wall

Earlier in this section, it was stated that single-wythe panel walls can be designed as though out-of-plane load were carried by the vertical strips alone. Now let's show why that's true. Consider the single-wythe panel shown in Fig. 7.8.

Assume that the panel resists out-of-plane loading as an assemblage of crossing strips, in the x direction (horizontally on the page) and the y direction (vertically on the page). At the very end of this section, it will be shown that such an assumption is legitimate ("strip method").

Now impose compatibility of out-of-plane deflections on the strips—that is, that the crossing x and y strips must have equal out-of-plane displacements. For a simply supported strip with uniformly distributed loading q, the center-line displacement is:

$$\Delta_{center} = \frac{5qL^4}{384EI}$$

For equal deflections of the x and y strips,

$$\frac{5q_x L_x^4}{384EI} = \Delta_{center} = \frac{5q_y L_y^4}{384EI}$$

And because those strips have equal moduli and moments of inertia,

$$\frac{q_x}{q_y} = \frac{L_y^4}{L_x^4}$$

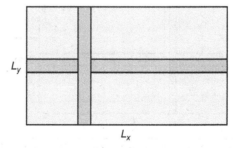

FIGURE 7.8 Idealization of a panel wall as an assemblage of crossing strips.

The span of the vertical strips, L_y, is the distance from the top of a floor slab to the underside of the slab or beam above, typically about 10 ft. The span of the horizontal strips, L_x, is the distance from the face of a column to the face of the adjacent column, typically about 20 ft. So

$$\frac{q_x}{q_y} = \frac{L_y^4}{L_x^4} = \left(\frac{10}{20}\right)^4 = 0.063$$

The horizontal strips will carry only about 6% of the out-of-plane load. If it is conservatively assumed that the vertical strips will carry 100% of the out-of-plane load, and the horizontal strip will carry zero load, the design work is halved, and the results will be conservative.

7.1.14 Distribution of Out-of-Plane Load to Vertical and Horizontal Strips of a Two-Wythe Panel Wall

The above analysis can easily be extended to the case of a two-wythe panel wall (Fig. 7.9), with an outer wythe of clay masonry and an inner wythe of concrete masonry.

As before, assume that each wythe of the panel resists out-of-plane loading as an assemblage of crossing strips, in the x direction (horizontally on the page) and the y direction (vertically on the page). At the very end of this section, it will be shown that such an assumption is legitimate ("strip method").

Also assume that the inner wythe is of hollow, ungrouted, 8-in. CMU laid in face-shell bedding, and that the outer wythe is of solid modular units (nominal thickness of 4 in.).

From Example #3, we know that the moment of inertia of the hollow CMU is 444.9 in^4 per 16 in. of width, or 333.7 in^4 per foot of width. It is proper to compute the average flexural stiffness of the wall using the moment of inertia of the hollow unit rather than the moment of the face-shell bedding only, because the bed joints occupy only a small portion of the volume of the wall.

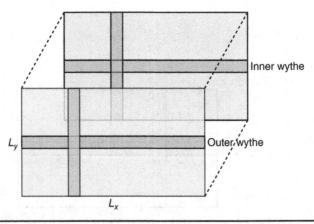

Figure 7.9 Idealization of a two-wythe panel wall as an assemblage of two sets of crossing strips.

Allowable-Stress Design of Unreinforced Masonry Elements

The moment of inertia of the modular outer wythe, per foot of width, is:

$$I = \frac{bt^3}{12} = \frac{(12 \text{ in.})(3.625 \text{ in.})^3}{12} = 47.6 \text{ in}^4 \text{ per ft of width}$$

Assume that the ties between wythes are axially rigid, so that the two wythes have equal out-of-plane deflection.

The total load q must be equilibrated by the summation of the load resisted by each strip of each wythe:

$$(q_x + q_y)_{\text{exterior}} + (q_x + q_y)_{\text{interior}} = q$$

Because the vertical strips in the exterior wythe are simply supported at the bottom and free at the top (expansion joint, they carry no load:

$$(q_x)_{\text{exterior}} + (q_x + q_y)_{\text{interior}} = q$$

Now impose compatibility of out-of-plane deflections on the strips,

$$\Delta_{x\text{ exterior}} = \frac{5q_{x\text{ exterior}} L_{x\text{ exterior}}^4}{384 E_{x\text{ exterior}} I_{x\text{ exterior}}} = \frac{5q_{x\text{ exterior}} 20^4}{384 E_{x\text{ exterior}} \times 47.6}$$

$$\Delta_{x\text{ interior}} = \frac{5q_{x\text{ interior}} L_{x\text{ interior}}^4}{384 E_{x\text{ interior}} I_{x\text{ interior}}} = \frac{5q_{x\text{ interior}} 20^4}{384 E_{x\text{ interior}} \times 334.0}$$

$$\Delta_{y\text{ interior}} = \frac{5q_{y\text{ interior}} L_{y\text{ interior}}^4}{384 E_{y\text{ interior}} I_{y\text{ interior}}} = \frac{5q_{y\text{ interior}} 10^4}{384 E_{y\text{ interior}} \times 334.0}$$

Equate those deflections, cancel out the common term of (5/384), and assume that all E's are the same:

$$\frac{q_{x\text{ exterior}} 20^4}{47.6} = \frac{q_{x\text{ interior}} 20^4}{334.0} = \frac{q_{y\text{ interior}} 10^4}{334.0}$$

$$3361\, q_{x\text{ exterior}} = 479.0\, q_{x\text{ interior}} = 29.94\, q_{y\text{ interior}}$$

Express $q_{x\text{ exterior}}$ and $q_{x\text{ interior}}$ in terms of $q_{y\text{ interior}}$:

$$q_{x\text{ exterior}} = 0.00891\, q_{y\text{ interior}}$$

$$q_{x\text{ interior}} = 0.0625\, q_{y\text{ interior}}$$

Now recall that the loads resisted by each strip must equilibrate the total load:

$$(q_x)_{\text{exterior}} + (q_x + q_y)_{\text{interior}} = q$$

$$(0.00897 + 0.0625 + 1.0) q_{y\text{ interior}} = q$$

Solve for $q_{y\text{ interior}}$ in terms of q:

$$q_{y\text{ interior}} = \frac{q}{1.0715} = 0.933 q$$

Finally, express the load carried by each set of strips in terms of q:

$$q_{y\,\text{interior}} = 0.93q$$

$$q_{x\,\text{interior}} = 0.06q$$

$$q_{x\,\text{exterior}} = 0.008q$$

Clearly, it is conservative and very reasonable to assume that the vertical strips of the interior wythe resist 100% of the out-of-plane load, and the other strips resist no load.

7.2 Allowable-Stress Design of Unreinforced Bearing Walls

7.2.1 Basic Behavior of Unreinforced Bearing Walls

Load-bearing masonry (without calculated reinforcement) must be designed for the effects of:

1) Gravity loads from self-weight, plus gravity loads from overlying roof or floor levels.
2) Moments from eccentric gravity load, or out-of-plane wind or earthquake.
3) In-plane shear.

For now, we shall study Loadings (1) and (2). Later, we shall study Loading (3), in the general context of design of masonry shear walls.

For Loadings (1) and (2), we shall design unreinforced, load-bearing masonry as a series of vertically spanning strips (Fig. 7.10), subjected to gravity loads (possibly eccentric) and out-of-plane wind or earthquake.

The only aspect of behavior that we haven't studied so far is the effect of slenderness on the load-carrying capacity of a column or wall. This effect is shown in Fig. 7.11.

At low values of slenderness, a masonry column in compression exhibits material failure. At high values of slenderness, it exhibits stability failure.

For masonry design, the effective length coefficient, k, is usually equal to 1.

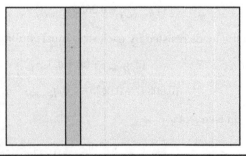

FIGURE 7.10 Idealization of bearing walls as vertically spanning strips.

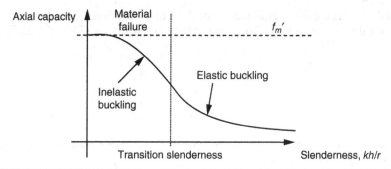

FIGURE 7.11 Effect of slenderness on the axial capacity of a column or wall.

7.2.2 Steps in Allowable-Stress Design of Unreinforced Bearing Walls

Allowable-stress codes usually address slenderness effects by decreasing the allowable axial stress with increasing slenderness. Equations 8-16 and 8-17 (Section 8.2.4.1) of TMS 402-22, for example, require that for $\frac{kh}{r} = \frac{h}{r} \leq 99$,

$$F_a = \left(\frac{1}{4}\right) f'_m \left[1 - \left(\frac{h}{140r}\right)^2\right]$$

and for $\frac{kh}{r} = \frac{h}{r} > 99$,

$$F_a = \left(\frac{1}{4}\right) f'_m \left(\frac{70}{\frac{h}{r}}\right)^2$$

These two equations give a curve that looks very much like that shown above, with a transition between inelastic and elastic buckling at a slenderness value of 99.

Combinations of axial force and bending are addressed by a so-called "unity equation" (TMS 402-22, Equation 8-14):

$$\frac{f_a}{F_a} + \frac{f_b}{F_b} \leq 1$$

where f_a = calculated axial stress (P/A)
 F_a = allowable axial stress as specified above
 f_b = calculated bending stress (M/S)
 F_b = allowable bending stress, $(f'_m/3)$

Next, TMS 402-22 requires that the extreme-fiber tensile stress not exceed the out-of-plane allowable stress from Table 8.2.4.2:

$$f_t = \frac{Mc}{I} - \frac{P}{A} \leq F_t$$

Finally, in addition to the slenderness-dependent allowable axial stress in the unity equation, TMS 402-22 imposes another stability requirement. The axial load in the bearing wall must not exceed one-quarter of the Euler buckling load, decreased by a penalty factor that becomes very significant at high eccentricities (*TMS 402-22, Equation 8-15*):

$$P \leq \frac{P_e}{4}$$

$$P_e = \frac{\pi^2 E_m I}{h^2}\left(1 - 0.577\frac{e}{r}\right)^3$$

where e = actual eccentricity of the applied compressive load (not M_{max} divided by P at the section under consideration).

This equation is effectively equivalent to assuming that the masonry units are stacked one on top of the other without any mortar. For units with a rectangular cross-section, for which $r = t/\sqrt{12}$, at an eccentricity of ($t/2$) (load applied at the edge of the units), the penalty factor becomes equal to zero, and so does the allowable axial load. This equation was developed as a conservative alternative to moment magnifier methods, which were regarded as too complex. TMS is working to develop moment magnifier methods that will be user-friendly and not so conservative.

7.2.3 Example: Allowable Stress Design of Unreinforced Bearing Wall with Concentric Axial Load

The bearing wall shown in Fig. 7.12 has a concentric axial load of 1050 lb/ft, due to dead plus live load. Using hollow concrete masonry units with face-shell bedding, design the wall. The governing load combination for allowable-stress design in the 2024 *IBC* is $D + L$.

Table 7.4, repeated from Section 7.1.11, gives section properties for concrete masonry units.

Table 7.5, taken from CMHA TEK 002, gives the self-weight of hollow CMU walls, assuming units with a density of 115 lb/ft³ and face-shell bedding.

At each horizontal plane through the wall, the following conditions must be met:

- Combination of axial and flexural compressive stresses must not violate the unity equation.

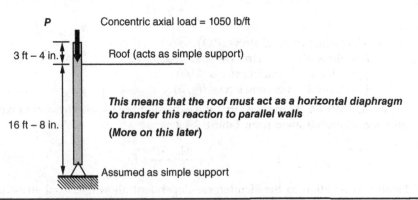

Figure 7.12 Unreinforced masonry bearing wall with concentric axial load.

Allowable-Stress Design of Unreinforced Masonry Elements

TABLE 7.4 Section Properties for Concrete Masonry Walls (Face-Shell and Web Thicknesses Consistent with CMHA TEK 002, Which References *ASTM C90-06*)

Unit	Face-Shell Thickness, in.	Web Thickness, in.	Area in² per ft	Moment of Inertia in⁴ per ft
4-in. hollow CMU, fully bedded	3/4	3/4	21.6	39.4
4-in. hollow CMU, face-shell bedded			18.0	38.0
6-in. hollow CMU, fully bedded	1	1	32.2	139
6-in. hollow CMU, face-shell bedded			24.0	130
8-in. hollow CMU, fully bedded	1-1/4	1	41.5	334
8-in. hollow CMU, face-shell bedded			30.0	309
10-in. hollow CMU, fully bedded	1-1/4	1-1/8	48.0	606
10-in. hollow CMU, face-shell bedded			30.0	530
12-in. hollow CMU, fully bedded	1-1/4	1-1/8	53.1	972
12-in. hollow CMU, face-shell bedded			30.0	811

TABLE 7.5 Self-Weights of Hollow CMU Walls

Nominal Thickness, in.	Weight per ft²
4	18
6	26
8	33
10	38
12	42

- Net tension stress must not exceed the allowable flexural tension.
- Separate stability check must be satisfied.

In theory, we must check various points on the wall. In this problem, however, the wall has only axial load, which increases from top to bottom due to the wall's self-weight. Therefore, we need to check only at the base of the wall.

Try 8-in. nominal units, and a specified compressive strength, f'_m, of 2000 lb/in². This can be satisfied using units with a net-area compressive strength of 2000 lb/in², and Type S PCL mortar. Work with a strip with a width of 1 ft (measured along the length of the wall in plan). Stresses are calculated using the critical section, consisting of the bedded area only (*TMS 402-22*, Section 4.3.1):

At the base of the wall, the axial stress is

$$f_a = \frac{P}{A} = \frac{1050 \text{ lb} + 20 \text{ ft} \times 33 \text{ lb/ft}}{30 \text{ in}^2} = \frac{1710 \text{ lb}}{30 \text{ in}^2} = 57.0 \text{ lb/in}^2$$

To calculate stiffness-related parameters for the wall, we use the average cross-section, corresponding to the fully bedded section in the table (TMS 402-22, Section 4.3.2).

$$r = \sqrt{\frac{I}{A}} = \sqrt{\frac{334 \text{ in}^4}{41.5 \text{ in}^2}} = 2.84 \text{ in.}$$

$$\frac{kh}{r} = \frac{h}{r} = \frac{16.67 \times 12 \text{ in.}}{2.84 \text{ in.}} = 70.5$$

This is less than the transition slenderness of 99, so the allowable stress is based on the curve that is an approximation to inelastic buckling:

$$F_a = 0.25 f'_m \left[1 - \left(\frac{h}{140\,r}\right)^2\right]$$

$$F_a = 0.25 \times 2000 \text{ lb/in}^2 \left[1 - \left(\frac{16.67 \text{ ft} \times 12 \text{ in./ft}}{140 \times 2.84 \text{ in.}}\right)^2\right]$$

$$= 500 \text{ lb/in}^2 \times 0.746 = 373 \text{ lb/in}^2$$

Now check the unity equation. Because the load is concentric, there is no bending stress:

$$\frac{f_a}{F_a} + \frac{f_b}{F_b} \leq 1$$

$$\frac{f_a}{F_a} = \frac{68.6 \text{ lb/in}^2}{373 \text{ lb/in}^2} = 0.18 \leq 1$$

and the unity equation is satisfied.

Because the wall has concentric axial load, there is no net tensile stress, and that equation does not have to be checked.

Now check the stability equation. Because the load is concentric, the eccentricity is zero, and the penalty term has a value of 1.

$$P_e = \frac{\pi^2 E_m I}{h^2}\left(1 - 0.577 \frac{e}{r}\right)^3$$

$$P_e = \frac{\pi^2 \times 900 \times 2000 \text{ lb/in}^2 \times 334 \text{ in}^4}{(16.67 \text{ ft} \times 12 \text{ in./ft})^2} = 148{,}281 \text{ lb}$$

$$\frac{P_e}{4} = 27{,}070 \text{ lb}$$

Because the calculated axial force per foot of length, 2010 lb, is much less than the allowable value of 27,070 lb, the design is satisfactory.

It would probably be possible to achieve a satisfactory design with a smaller nominal wall thickness. To maintain continuity in the example problems that follow, however, the design will stop at this point.

TMS 402-22 has no minimum eccentricity requirements for walls.

7.2.4 Example: Allowable-Stress Design of Unreinforced Bearing Wall with Eccentric Axial Load

Now consider the same bearing wall of the previous example, but make the gravity load eccentric. As before, the governing load combination in the 2024 *IBC* for allowable-stress design is $D + L$.

First, review the calculation of the gravity load itself. Suppose that it comes from a uniformly distributed roof dead load of 50 lb/ft² and live load of 20 lb/ft², acting on a 30-ft span. The reaction on the wall per foot of plan length is then:

$$\text{Wall load/ft} = \frac{ql}{2} = \frac{(50+20)\text{ lb/ft}^2 \times 30 \text{ ft}}{2} = 1050 \text{ lb/ft}$$

Now consider how it is applied to the wall. Suppose that the load is applied over a 4-in. bearing plate, and assume that bearing stresses vary linearly under the bearing plate as shown in Fig. 7.13.

Then the eccentricity of the applied load with respect to the centerline of the wall is

$$e = \frac{t}{2} - \frac{\text{plate}}{3} = \frac{7.63 \text{ in.}}{2} - \frac{4 \text{ in.}}{3} = 2.48 \text{ in.}$$

The wall is as shown in Fig. 7.14:

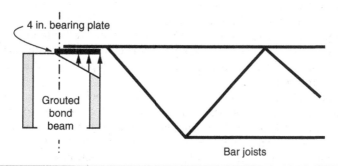

FIGURE 7.13 Assumed linear variation of bearing stresses under the bearing plate.

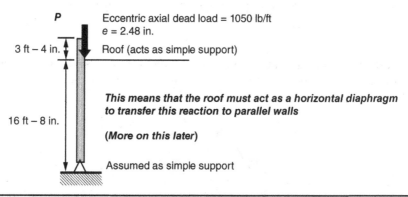

FIGURE 7.14 Unreinforced masonry bearing wall with eccentric axial load.

Chapter Seven

At each horizontal plane through the wall, the following conditions must be met:

- Combination of axial and flexural compressive stresses must not violate the unity equation.
- Net tension stress must not exceed the allowable flexural tension.
- Separate stability check must be satisfied.

We must check various points on the wall. Critical points are just below the roof reaction (moment is high and axial load is low, so net tension may govern); and at the base of the wall (axial load is high, so the unity equation or the stability equation may govern). Check each of these locations on the wall.

The base of the wall is assumed to be simply supported. This assumption has nothing to do with the probable relationship between the maximum stresses acting in the wall at that level and the failure stresses of the material, nor with the rotational flexibility of the foundation. The assumption is made for convenience in the design process, and it is based on the lower-bound principle of structural mechanics. According to that principle, any structural solution that satisfies equilibrium and constitutive relationships, but not necessarily kinematics, corresponds to a collapse capacity that is less than or equal to the actual collapse capacity and is therefore conservative (safe) for design. A design solution that assumes a simple support at the base satisfies statics; it satisfies constitutive relationships (because the failure stresses are nowhere exceeded); but it does not necessarily satisfy the kinematic condition of rotational continuity at the base. This design solution also simplifies the design process, because it makes the structure statically determinate. As illustrated in the advanced examples at the end of this chapter, a design carried out using this assumption would have a slightly greater collapse load than that assumed, and would therefore be safe.

As before, try 8-in. nominal units, and a specified compressive strength, f'_m, of 2000 lb/in². This can be satisfied using units with a net-area compressive strength of 2000 lb/in², and Type S PCL mortar. Work with a strip with a width of 1 ft (measured along the length of the wall in plan). Stresses are calculated using the critical section, consisting of the bedded area only (TMS 402-22, Section 4.3.1):

Just below the roof reaction,

$$f_a = \frac{P}{A} = \frac{1050 \text{ lb} + 3.33 \text{ ft} \times 33 \text{ lb/ft}}{30 \text{ in}^2} = \frac{1160 \text{ lb}}{30 \text{ in}^2} = 38.7 \text{ lb/in}^2$$

To calculate stiffness-related parameters for the wall, we use the average cross-section, corresponding to the fully bedded section in the table (TMS 402-22, Section 4.3.2).

$$r = \sqrt{\frac{I}{A}} = \sqrt{\frac{334 \text{ in}^4}{41.5 \text{ in}^2}} = 2.84 \text{ in.}$$

$$\frac{kh}{r} = \frac{h}{r} = \frac{16.67 \text{ ft} \times 12 \text{ in./ft}}{2.84 \text{ in.}} = 70.5$$

Allowable-Stress Design of Unreinforced Masonry Elements

This is less than the transition slenderness of 99, so the allowable stress is based on the curve that is an approximation to inelastic buckling:

$$F_a = 0.25 f'_m \left[1 - \left(\frac{h}{140r}\right)^2\right]$$

$$F_a = 0.25 \times 2000 \text{ lb/in}^2 \left[1 - \left(\frac{16.67 \text{ ft} \times 12 \text{ in./ft}}{140 \times 2.84 \text{ in.}}\right)^2\right] = 500 \text{ lb/in}^2 \times 0.746 = 373 \text{ lb/in}^2$$

Now there is bending stress:

$$M = Pe = 1050 \text{ lb} \times 2.48 \text{ in.} = 2604 \text{ lb-in.}$$

$$f_b = \frac{Mc}{I} = \frac{2604 \text{ lb-in.} \times \left(\frac{7.63}{2}\right) \text{ in.}}{309 \text{ in}^4} = 32.15 \text{ lb/in}^2$$

$$F_b = \frac{f'_m}{3} = \frac{2000 \text{ lb/in}^2}{3} = 667 \text{ lb/in}^2$$

Now check the unity equation.

$$\frac{f_a}{F_a} + \frac{f_b}{F_b} \le 1$$

$$\frac{38.7 \text{ lb/in}^2}{373 \text{ lb/in}^2} + \frac{32.15 \text{ lb/in}^2}{667 \text{ lb/in}^2} = 0.104 + 0.048 = 0.152 \le 1$$

and the unity equation is satisfied.

Because the bending stress (32.15 lb/in²) is less than the axial stress (38.7 lb/in²), there is no net tensile stress, and that equation does not have to be checked.

Now check the stability equation. Because the load is eccentric, the penalty term has a value less than 1. The eccentricity is the actual eccentricity of the applied axial load:

$$e = 2.48 \text{ in.}$$

$$P_e = \frac{\pi^2 E_m I}{h^2}\left(1 - 0.577\frac{e}{r}\right)^3$$

$$P_e = \frac{\pi^2 \times 900 \times 2000 \text{ lb/in}^2 \times 334 \text{ in}^4}{(16.67 \times 12 \text{ in.})^2}\left(1 - 0.577 \times \frac{2.48}{2.84}\right)^3 = 148,281 \times 0.122 = 18,090 \text{ lb}$$

$$\frac{P_e}{4} = 4523 \text{ lb}$$

Because the calculated axial force per foot of length, 1160 lb, is less than the allowable value of 4523 lb, the stability check is also satisfied.

The other critical section is at the base of the wall. The checks of the unity equation, net flexural tensile stress, and stability are identical to those of the previous example, and are satisfied. The design is therefore satisfactory. The increase in effective eccentricity from the previous example to this example makes a significant difference in this problem.

7.2.5 Example: Allowable-Stress Design of Unreinforced Bearing Wall with Eccentric Axial Load plus Wind

Now consider the same bearing wall of the previous example, but add a uniformly distributed wind load of 40 lb/ft². The governing allowable-stress loading combination from the 2024 *IBC* is $0.6\,D + 0.6\,W$. Assume that 700 lb/ft of the 1050 lb/ft is due to D, and 350 to L.

The wall is as shown in Fig. 7.15.

At each horizontal plane through the wall, the following conditions must be met:

- Combination of axial and flexural compressive stresses must not violate the unity equation.
- Net tension stress must not exceed the allowable flexural tension.
- Separate stability check must be satisfied.

We must check various points on the wall. Critical points are just below the roof reaction (moment is high and axial load is low, so net tension may govern); and at the base of the wall (axial load is high, so the unity equation or the stability equation may govern). Check each of these locations on the wall.

To avoid having to check a large number of loading combinations and potentially critical locations, it is worthwhile to assess them first, and check only the ones that will probably govern.

Due to wind only, the unfactored moment on a 1-ft strip at the base of the parapet (roof level) is

$$M = \frac{wL^2}{2} = \frac{40\text{ lb/ft} \times 3.33^2 \text{ ft}^2}{2} \times 12\text{ in./ft} = 2661 \text{ lb-in.}$$

The maximum moment is close to that occurring at mid-height. The moment on a 1-ft strip from wind load is the superposition of one-half moment at the upper support due

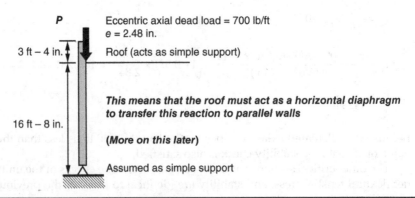

Figure 7.15 Unreinforced masonry bearing wall with eccentric axial load and wind load.

Allowable-Stress Design of Unreinforced Masonry Elements

to wind load on the parapet only, plus the midspan moment in a simply supported beam with that same wind load:

$$M_{midspan} = -\frac{2661}{2} + \frac{wL^2}{8} = -\frac{2661}{2} + \frac{40 \text{ lb/ft} \times 16.67^2 \text{ ft}^2}{8} \times 12 \text{ in./ft} = 15{,}343 \text{ lb-in.}$$

The unfactored moment due to eccentric axial dead load is

$$M_{gravity} = Pe = 700 \text{ lb} \times 2.48 \text{ in.} = 1736 \text{ lb-in.}$$

Unfactored moment diagrams due to eccentric axial dead load and wind load are as shown in Fig. 7.16.

As before, try 8-in. nominal units, and a specified compressive strength, f'_m, of 2000 lb/in². This can be satisfied using units with a net-area compressive strength of 2000 lb/in², and Type S PCL mortar. Work with a strip with a width of 1 ft (measured along the length of the wall in plan). Stresses are calculated using the critical section, consisting of the bedded area only (TMS 402-22 Section 4.3.1).

Just below the roof reaction,

$$f_a = \frac{0.6P}{A} = \frac{0.6 \times 700 \text{ lb} + 0.6 \times 3.33 \text{ ft} \times 33 \text{ lb/ft}}{30 \text{ in}^2} = \frac{486 \text{ lb}}{30 \text{ in}^2} = 16.20 \text{ lb/in}^2$$

To calculate stiffness-related parameters for the wall, we use the average cross-section, corresponding to the fully bedded section in the table (TMS 402-22 Section 4.3.2).

$$r = \sqrt{\frac{I}{A}} = \sqrt{\frac{334 \text{ in}^4}{41.5 \text{ in}^2}} = 2.84 \text{ in.}$$

$$\frac{kh}{r} = \frac{h}{r} = \frac{16.67 \text{ ft} \times 12 \text{ in./ft}}{2.84 \text{ in.}} = 70.5$$

This is less than the transition slenderness of 99, so the allowable stress is based on the curve that is an approximation to inelastic buckling:

$$F_a = 0.25 f'_m \left[1 - \left(\frac{h}{140r}\right)^2\right]$$

$$F_a = 0.25 \times 2000 \text{ lb/in}^2 \left[1 - \left(\frac{16.67 \text{ ft} \times 12 \text{ in./ft}}{140 \times 2.84 \text{ in.}}\right)^2\right] = 500 \text{ lb/in}^2 \times 0.746 = 373 \text{ lb/in}^2$$

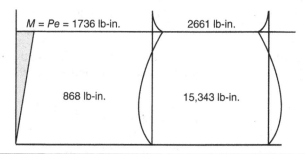

FIGURE 7.16 Unfactored moment diagrams due to eccentric axial load and wind.

Bending stress comes from wind load plus eccentric gravity load:

$$M = Pe + \text{wind} = 0.6 \times 700 \text{ lb} \times 2.48 \text{ in.} + 0.6 \times 2661 \text{ lb-in.} = 2638 \text{ lb-in.}$$

$$f_b = \frac{Mc}{I} = \frac{2638 \text{ lb-in.} \times \left(\frac{7.63}{2}\right) \text{ in.}}{309 \text{ in}^4} = 32.57 \text{ lb/in}^2$$

$$F_b = \frac{f'_m}{3} = \frac{2000 \text{ lb/in}^2}{3} = 667 \text{ lb/in}^2$$

Now check the unity equation.

$$\frac{f_a}{F_a} + \frac{f_b}{F_b} \leq 1$$

$$\frac{16.20 \text{ lb/in}^2}{373 \text{ lb/in}^2} + \frac{32.57 \text{ lb/in}^2}{667 \text{ lb/in}^2} = 0.043 + 0.049 = 0.092 \leq 1$$

and the unity equation is satisfied.

The bending stress (32.57 lb/in²) exceeds the axial stress (16.20 lb/in²). The net tensile stress (16.37 lb/in²) is less than the allowable stress of 33 lb/in² for flexural tensile stresses normal to the bed joint in ungrouted hollow masonry, with Type S PCL mortar. Net tensile stresses are satisfactory.

Now check the stability equation. The check is exactly as before.

$$e = 2.48 \text{ in.}$$

$$P_e = \frac{\pi^2 E_m I}{h^2}\left(1 - 0.577\frac{e}{r}\right)^3$$

$$P_e = \frac{\pi^2 \times 900 \times 2000 \text{ lb/in}^2 \times 334 \text{ in}^4}{(16.67 \times 12 \text{ in})^2}\left(1 - 0.577 \times \frac{2.48}{2.84}\right)^3 = 148,281 \times 0.122 = 18,090 \text{ lb}$$

$$\frac{P_e}{4} = 4523 \text{ lb}$$

Because the calculated axial force per foot of length, 1210 lb, is less than the allowable value of 4523 lb, the stability check is also satisfied.

Now check the wall at mid-height:

$$f_a = \frac{P}{A} = \frac{0.6 \times 700 \text{ lb} + 0.6 \times (3.33 + 8.33) \text{ ft} \times 33 \text{ lb/ft}}{30 \text{ in}^2} = \frac{650.9 \text{ lb}}{30 \text{ in}^2} = 21.70 \text{ lb/in}^2$$

To calculate stiffness-related parameters for the wall, we use the average cross-section, corresponding to the fully bedded section in the table (*TMS 402-22* Section 4.3.2).

$$r = \sqrt{\frac{I}{A}} = \sqrt{\frac{334 \text{ in}^4}{41.5 \text{ in}^2}} = 2.84 \text{ in.}$$

$$\frac{kh}{r} = \frac{h}{r} = \frac{16.67 \times 12 \text{ in.}}{2.84 \text{ in.}} = 70.5$$

This is less than the transition slenderness of 99, so the allowable stress is based on the curve that is an approximation to inelastic buckling:

$$F_a = 0.25 f'_m \left[1 - \left(\frac{h}{140r}\right)^2\right]$$

$$F_a = 0.25 \times 2000 \text{ lb/in}^2 \left[1 - \left(\frac{16.67 \times 12 \text{ in.}}{140 \times 2.84 \text{ in.}}\right)^2\right] = 500 \text{ lb/in}^2 \times 0.746 = 373 \text{ lb/in}^2$$

Bending stress comes from the net moment shown above, assuming that the wind is directed so that moments from eccentric gravity load are added to moments from wind:

$$M = P\left(\frac{e}{2}\right) + \text{wind} = 0.6 \times 868 + 0.6 \times 15{,}343 \text{ lb-in.} = 9727 \text{ lb-in.}$$

$$f_b = \frac{Mc}{I} = \frac{9727 \text{ lb-in.} \times \left(\frac{7.63}{2}\right) \text{in.}}{309 \text{ in}^4} = 120.1 \text{ lb/in}^2$$

$$F_b = \frac{f'_m}{3} = \frac{2000 \text{ lb/in}^2}{3} = 667 \text{ lb/in}^2$$

Now check the unity equation.

$$\frac{f_a}{F_a} + \frac{f_b}{F_b} \leq 1$$

$$\frac{21.70 \text{ lb/in}^2}{373 \text{ lb/in}^2} + \frac{120.1 \text{ lb/in}^2}{667 \text{ lb/in}^2} = 0.058 + 0.180 = 0.238 \leq 1$$

and the unity equation is satisfied.

The bending stress (120.1 lb/in²) exceeds the axial stress (21.70 lb/in²). The net tensile stress (120.1 lb/in² − 21.70 lb/in² − 98.40 lb/in²) exceeds the allowable stress of 33 lb/in² for flexural tensile stresses normal to the bed joint in ungrouted hollow masonry, with Type S PCL mortar. It will be necessary to grout the wall or make it thicker. Try grouting the wall. The section modulus will increase, and the allowable stress will also increase from 33 lb/in² to 86 lb/in². Recheck the wall as grouted.

Table 7.6, taken from CMHA TEK 002, gives the self-weight of fully grouted CMU walls, assuming units with a density of 115 lb/ft³. Units with a nominal thickness

TABLE 7.6 Self-Weights of Fully Grouted CMU Walls

Nominal Thickness, in.	Weight per ft²
6	60
8	81
10	103
12	125

of 4 in. are not shown because their cells are too narrow to permit consolidation of grout.

$$f_a = \frac{P}{A} = \frac{0.6 \times 700 \text{ lb} + 0.6 \times (3.33 + 8.33) \text{ ft} \times 81 \text{ lb/ft}}{30 \text{ in}^2} = \frac{986.7 \text{ lb}}{30 \text{ in}^2} = 32.89 \text{ lb/in}^2$$

To calculate stiffness-related parameters for the wall, we use the average cross-section, corresponding to the gross section (TMS 402-22 Section 4.3.2).

$$r = \sqrt{\frac{I}{A}} = \sqrt{\frac{bt^3/12}{bt}} = \frac{t}{\sqrt{12}} = \frac{7.63 \text{ in.}}{\sqrt{12}} = 2.20 \text{ in.}$$

$$\frac{kh}{r} = \frac{h}{r} = \frac{16.67 \times 12 \text{ in.}}{2.20 \text{ in.}} = 90.9$$

This is less than the transition slenderness of 99, so the allowable stress is based on the curve that is an approximation to inelastic buckling:

$$F_a = 0.25 f'_m \left[1 - \left(\frac{h}{140r} \right)^2 \right]$$

$$F_a = 0.25 \times 2000 \text{ lb/in}^2 \left[1 - \left(\frac{16.67 \times 12 \text{ in.}}{140 \times 2.20 \text{ in.}} \right)^2 \right] = 500 \text{ lb/in}^2 \times 0.578 = 289 \text{ lb/in}^2$$

Bending stress comes from the net moment shown above, assuming that the wind is directed so that moments from eccentric gravity load are added to moments from wind:

$$M = P\left(\frac{e}{2}\right) + \text{wind} = 0.6 \times 868 + 0.6 \times 15{,}343 \text{ lb-in.} = 9727 \text{ lb-in.}$$

$$f_b = \frac{Mc}{I} = \frac{Mc}{\left(\frac{bt^3}{12}\right)} = \frac{9727 \text{ lb-in.} \times \left(\frac{7.625}{2}\right) \text{in.}}{\left(\frac{12 \times 7.625^3}{12}\right) \text{in}^4} = 83.65 \text{ lb/in}^2$$

$$F_b = \frac{f'_m}{3} = \frac{2000 \text{ lb/in}^2}{3} = 667 \text{ lb/in}^2$$

The bending stress (83.65 lb/in²) exceeds the axial stress (32.89 lb/in²). The net tensile stress (83.65 lb/in² − 32.89 lb/in² = 50.76 lb/in²) is less than the allowable stress of 86 lb/in² for flexural tensile stresses normal to the bed joint in fully grouted masonry, with Type S PCL mortar.

Now check the unity equation.

$$\frac{f_a}{F_a} + \frac{f_b}{F_b} \le 1$$

$$\frac{32.89 \text{ lb/in}^2}{289 \text{ lb/in}^2} + \frac{83.65 \text{ lb/in}^2}{667 \text{ lb/in}^2} = 0.114 + 0.125 = 0.239 \le 1$$

and the unity equation is satisfied.

Now check the stability equation. Because the wall is fully grouted, the radius of gyration changes.

$$r = \sqrt{\frac{I}{A}} = \sqrt{\frac{bt^3/12}{bt}} = \frac{t}{\sqrt{12}} = \frac{7.63 \text{ in.}}{\sqrt{12}} = 2.20 \text{ in.}$$

The eccentricity is the actual eccentricity of the lateral load.

$e = 2.48$ in.

$$P_e = \frac{\pi^2 E_m I}{h^2}\left(1 - 0.577\frac{e}{r}\right)^3$$

$$P_e = \frac{\pi^2 \times (900 \times 2000 \text{ lb/in}^2) \times 334 \text{ in}^4}{(16.67 \text{ ft} \times 12 \text{ in./ft})^2}\left(1 - 0.577 \times \frac{2.48}{2.20}\right)^3 = 148{,}281 \text{ lb} \times 0.0430 = 6376 \text{ lb}$$

$$\frac{P_e}{4} = 1594 \text{ lb}$$

Because the calculated axial force per foot of length, 986.7 lb, is less than the allowable value of 1594 lb, the stability check is also satisfied. Note the counter-intuitive nature of the stability check. Because it assumes zero flexural tensile strength (inconsistent with the design for net flexural tension), grouting the wall decreases the radius of gyration, and actually decreases the calculated allowable axial capacity.

The other potentially critical section, at the base of the wall, would have to be checked as well, and does not govern, because the eccentricity of applied axial load is zero at the base of the wall.

7.2.6 Comments on the Above Examples for Allowable-Stress Design of Unreinforced Bearing Walls

1) In retrospect, it probably would not have been necessary to check all three criteria at all locations. With experience, a designer could realize that the location with highest wind moment would govern and could therefore check only the mid-height of the wall.

2) The addition of wind load to the second example, to produce the third example, changes the critical location from just under the roof, to the mid-height of the simply supported section of the wall. The wind load of 25 lb/ft² in the third example produces maximum tensile stresses above the allowable values for ungrouted masonry, and makes it necessary to grout the wall, thicken it, or reinforce it.

7.2.7 Extension of the Above Concepts to Masonry Walls with Openings

In the above examples, we have studied the behavior of bearing walls of unreinforced masonry, idealized as a series of vertical strips, simply supported at the level of the floor slab, and at the level of the roof. Let's see how this changes in the case of bearing walls with openings.

1) In Fig. 7.17, load applied above the window and door openings clearly cannot be resisted by vertical strips, because those vertical strips have only one point of lateral support (at the roof level).

Chapter Seven

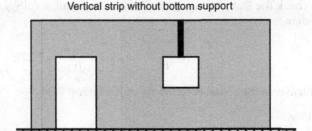

FIGURE 7.17 Hypothetical unstable resistance mechanism in a wall with openings, involving vertically spanning strips only.

2) For that reason, the wall must be idealized as horizontal strips above and below the openings, supported by vertical strips on both sides of the openings, as shown in Fig. 7.18.

3) Each set of horizontal strips, idealized as simply supported, must be supported by the adjacent vertical strips. For example, the horizontal strips above the door are supported by Strip A and Strip B. The window and door are considered to transfer loads applied to them, via horizontal strips, to the vertical strips on either side of the openings.

4) Therefore, Strip A has to support, spanning vertically, the out-of-plane loads acting directly on it, plus the out-of-plane loads acting on the left half of the horizontal strips above the door. In other words, Strip A has to resist the out-of-plane loads acting on what might be termed a "tributary width," which extends from the left-hand edge of Strip A itself, to the midspan of the horizontal strips above the door. In the same way, Strips B and C have to resist the loads corresponding to Tributary Widths B and C, respectively.

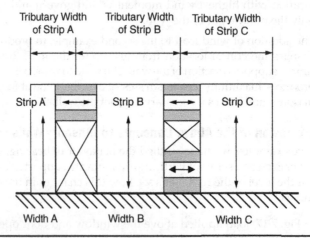

FIGURE 7.18 Stable resistance mechanism in a wall with openings, involving horizontally spanning strips in addition to vertically spanning strips.

5) For example, if Strip B has to resist the loads acting over Tributary Width B, this represents an increase in the design loads on Strip B. That strip must resist the loads that normally would be applied to it (if no openings had existed), multiplied by the ratio of Tributary Width B, divided by Width B:

$$\text{Actions in Strip B} = \text{Initial Actions}\left(\frac{\text{Tributary Width B}}{\text{Width B}}\right)$$

6) The same applies to vertical loads, because these also must be transferred from horizontal to vertical strips.

7) In any event, the presence of openings can be considered to increase the initial actions in the vertical strips adjacent to the openings. Aside from this increase, the design of those elements proceeds exactly as before.

7.2.8 Final Comment on the Effect of Openings in Unreinforced Masonry Bearing Walls

As the summation of the plan lengths of openings in a bearing wall exceeds about one-half the plan length of the wall, even the higher allowable stresses (or moduli of rupture) corresponding to fully grouted walls will be exceeded, and it will generally become necessary to use reinforcement. Design of reinforced masonry bearing walls is addressed later in this book.

7.3 Allowable-Stress Design of Unreinforced Shear Walls

7.3.1 Basic Behavior of Unreinforced Shear Walls

Wall-type structures resist lateral loads as shown in Fig. 7.19.
This resistance mechanism involves three steps:

- Walls oriented perpendicular to the direction of lateral load transfer those loads to the level of the foundation and the levels of the horizontal diaphragms. The walls are idealized and designed as vertically oriented strips.

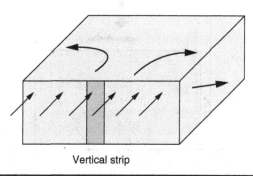

Figure 7.19 Basic behavior of box-type buildings in resisting lateral loads.

- The roof and floors act as horizontal diaphragms, transferring their forces to walls oriented parallel to the direction of lateral load.
- Walls oriented parallel to the direction of applied load must transfer loads from the horizontal diaphragms to the foundation. In other words, they act as shear walls.

As noted previously in the sections dealing with unreinforced bearing walls, this overall mechanism demands that the horizontal roof diaphragm have sufficient strength and stiffness to transfer the required loads. This is discussed again in a later section of this book dealing with horizontal diaphragms.

The rest of this section addresses the design of shear walls. We shall see that in almost all cases, the design itself is very simple, because the cross-sectional areas of the masonry walls so large that nominal stresses are quite low.

7.3.2 Design Steps for Unreinforced Shear Walls

Unreinforced masonry shear walls must be designed for the effects of:

1) Gravity loads from self-weight, plus gravity loads from overlying roof or floor levels; and
2) Moments and shears from in-plane shear loads.

Actions are shown in Fig. 7.20. Either allowable-stress design or strength design can be used.

TMS 402-22 specifies allowable flexural tensile stresses for unreinforced masonry in Table 8.2.4.2, which applies equally to in-plane and out-of-plane bending.

$$f_{tension} = \frac{M}{S} - \frac{P}{A} = \frac{Vh}{S} - \frac{P}{A} \leq F_t$$

Shearing capacity is calculated using Section 8.2.6 of *TMS 402-22*. Shear stresses are calculated by

$$f_v = \frac{VQ}{I_n b}$$

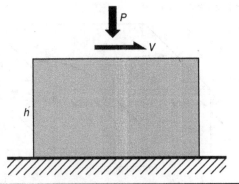

Figure 7.20 Design actions for unreinforced shear walls.

Allowable-Stress Design of Unreinforced Masonry Elements

and allowable in-plane shear stresses, F_v, shall not exceed any of

$$F_v = \begin{cases} 1.5\sqrt{f'_m} \\ 120\,\text{psi} \\ v + 0.45(N_v/A_v) \end{cases}$$

in the third equation,

v = 37 psi for masonry in running bond that is not grouted solid.
 = 37 psi for masonry in other than running bond with open-end units grouted solid.
 = 60 psi for masonry in running bond that is grouted solid.

7.3.3 Design Example: Allowable-Stress Design of Unreinforced Masonry Shear Wall

Consider the simple structure of Fig. 7.21, the same one whose bearing walls have been designed previously in this course. Use nominal 8-in. concrete masonry units, f'_m = 2000 lb/in², and Type S PCL mortar. This requires CMU with a specified compressive strength of 2000 lb/in², the default minimum of *ASTM C90*. The roof applies a gravity load of 1050 lb/ft to the walls; the walls measure 16 ft, 8 in. height to the roof, and have an additional 3 ft, 4 in. parapet. The walls are loaded with a wind load of 32 lb/ft². The roof acts as a one-way system, transmitting gravity loads to the front and back walls. The critical allowable-stress load combination of the 2024 *IBC* is $0.6 D + 0.6 W$.

Now design the shear wall. Try an 8-in. wall with face-shell bedding only. The critical section for shear is just under the roof, where axial load in the shear walls is least, coming from the parapet only.

As a result of the wind loading, the reaction transmitted to the roof diaphragm is as calculated using Fig. 7.22:

$$\text{Reaction} = \frac{32\,\text{lb/ft}^2 \times \left(\dfrac{20^2\,\text{ft}^2}{2}\right)}{16.67\,\text{ft}} = 384\,\text{lb/ft}$$

Total roof reaction acting on one side of the roof is

$$\text{Reaction} = 384\,\text{lb/ft} \times 30\,\text{ft} = 11{,}520\,\text{lb}$$

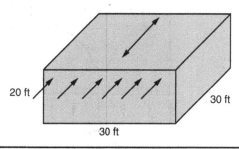

FIGURE 7.21 Example problem for strength design of unreinforced shear wall.

Chapter Seven

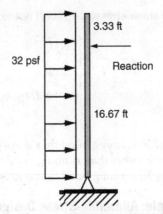

FIGURE 7.22 Calculation of reaction on roof diaphragm, allowable-stress design of unreinforced shear wall.

This is divided evenly between the two shear walls, so the shear per wall is 5760 lb.

In Fig. 7.23, for simplicity, the lateral load is shown as if it acted on the front wall alone. In reality, it also acts on the back wall, so that the structure is subjected to pressure on the front wall, and suction on the back wall.

The horizontal diaphragm reaction transferred to each shear wall is 384 lb/ft, multiplied by the building width of 30 ft, and then divided equally between the two shear walls, for a total of 5760 lb per shear wall.

Using the conservative loading case of $0.6D + 0.6W$,

$$V = 0.6\,V_{\text{unfactored}} = 0.6 \times 5760 \text{ lb} = 3456 \text{ lb}$$

Compute the axial force in the wall at that level. To be conservative, use the loading combination $0.6D + 0.6W$. The force acting normal to the shear-transfer plane is

$$N = 0.6 \times 3.33 \text{ ft} \times 33 \text{ lb/ft}^2 \times 30 \text{ ft} = 1978 \text{ lb}$$

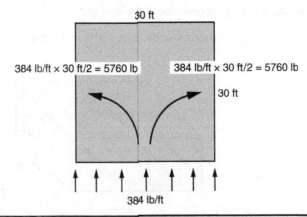

FIGURE 7.23 Transmission of forces from roof diaphragm to shear walls.

The maximum shear stress at that level is

$$f_v = \frac{VQ}{I_n b} = \left(\frac{3}{2}\right)\frac{V}{A} = \left(\frac{3}{2}\right)\frac{3456 \text{ lb}}{30 \text{ in}^2/\text{ft} \times 30 \text{ ft}} = 5.76 \text{ lb/in}^2$$

and the allowable in-plane shear stresses, F_v, is the smallest of:

$$F_v = \begin{cases} 1.5\sqrt{f'_m} = 1.5\sqrt{2000} = 67.1 \text{ lb/in}^2 \\ 120 \text{ psi} \\ v + 0.45(N_v/A_v) = 37 \text{ lb/in}^2 + 0.45\left(\frac{1978 \text{ lb}}{30 \times 30 \text{ in}^2}\right) = 38.0 \text{ lb/in}^2 \end{cases}$$

The lowest allowable shear stress, 38.0 lb/in², far exceeds the maximum shear stress of 5.76 lb/in², and the design is satisfactory for shear.

Now check the net flexural tensile stress. The critical section is at the base of the wall, where in-plane moment is a maximum. Because the roof spans between the front and back walls, the distributed gravity load on the roof does not act on the side walls, and their axial load comes from self-weight only:

$$f_{tension} = \frac{Mc}{I} - \frac{P}{A} = \frac{Vhc}{I} - \frac{P}{A} \leq F_t$$

$$f_{tension} = \frac{3456 \text{ lb} \times 16.67 \text{ ft} \times 12 \text{ in./ft}\left(\frac{30 \text{ ft} \times 12 \text{ in./ft}}{2}\right)}{\left[\frac{2 \times 1.25 \text{ in.} \times (30 \text{ ft} \times 12 \text{ in./ft})^3}{12}\right]} - \frac{20 \text{ ft} \times 33 \text{ lb/ft}}{30 \text{ in}^2}$$

$$f_{tension} = 12.80 \text{ lb/in}^2 - 22.00 \text{ lb/in}^2 = -9.20 \text{ lb/in}^2$$

The net flexural tension is actually compression and is certainly less than the allowable flexural tension from Table 8.2.4.2 of *TMS 402-22*. The design is satisfactory.

When the wind blows against the side walls, these walls transfer their loads to the roof diaphragm, and the front and back walls act as shear walls. The side walls must be checked for this loading direction also, following the procedures of previous example problems.

7.3.4 Comments on Example Problem with Allowable-Stress Design of Unreinforced Shear Walls

Clearly, unreinforced masonry shear walls, whether designed by allowable stress or strength design procedures, have tremendous shear capacity because of their large cross-sectional area. If this area is reduced by openings, then shear capacities will decrease, and in-plane flexural capacities as governed by net flexural tension may decrease even faster.

7.3.5 Comments on Behavior and Design of Wall Buildings in General

Wall buildings are very efficient structurally, because the same element can act as part of the building envelope, as a vertically spanning structural element perpendicular to the direction of applied lateral load, and as a shear wall parallel to the direction of applied lateral load. If the wall building is made of a material that is aesthetically pleasing, like masonry, even more efficiency is achieved. Wall buildings are also very efficient from the viewpoint of design. The ultimate objective of design is design, not analysis.

The basic steps that are discussed here, in the context of simple, one-story shear wall buildings, can be applied to multi-story shear wall buildings as well. At the roof level and at each floor level, horizontal diaphragms receive reactions from vertically spanning strips, and transfer those reactions to shear walls. Each shear wall acts essentially as a free-standing, statically determinate cantilever, with axial loads and in-plane lateral loads applied at each floor level. At each floor level, the shear wall must simply be designed for shear, and for combined axial force and moment.

Design of shear wall buildings is typically much easier than the design of frames, which are statically indeterminate and must usually be analyzed using computer programs.

7.3.6 Extension to Design of Unreinforced Masonry Shear Walls with Openings

Consider the structure shown in Fig. 7.24. The wall is identical to that addressed in the previous examples, with the exception of two openings, each measuring 9 ft in plan. These openings divide the wall into three smaller wall segments.

Assume that the applied shear is divided equally among the three wall segments; that points of inflection exist at the mid-height of each wall segment; and that axial forces in the wall are negligible. Then the moments and shears can be determined by statics, where L is the 10-ft height of the wall segments. A free body of one wall segment is shown in Fig. 7.25.

The rest of the design proceeds as before. The shear area of the wall segments is reduced in proportion to the plan length of each segment, compared to the plan length of the original unperforated wall. The moment of inertia of the segments, however, is considerably less than the moment of inertia of the original unperforated wall.

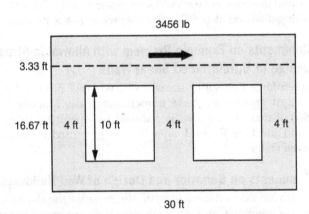

FIGURE 7.24 Shear wall with openings.

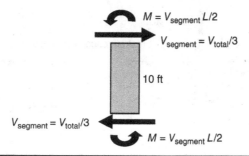

FIGURE 7.25 Free body of one wall segment.

7.4 Allowable-Stress Design of Anchor Bolts

In masonry construction, anchor bolts are most commonly used to anchor roof or floor diaphragms to masonry walls. As shown in Fig. 7.26, vertically oriented anchor bolts can be placed along the top of a masonry wall to anchor a roof diaphragm resting on the top of the wall. Alternatively, horizontally oriented anchor bolts can be placed along the face of a masonry wall to anchor a diaphragm through a horizontal ledger. In these applications, anchor bolts are subjected to combinations of tension and shear. In this section, the behavior of anchors under those loadings is discussed, and *TMS 402-22* allowable-stress design provisions are reviewed.

7.4.1 Behavior and Design of Anchor Bolts Loaded in Tension

Anchor bolts loaded in tension can fail by breakout of a roughly conical body of masonry, or by fracture of the anchor bolt steel. Bent-bar anchor bolts (such as J-bolts or L-bolts) can also fail by straightening of the bent portion of the anchor bolt, followed by pullout of the anchor bolt from the masonry. Allowable tensile capacity as governed by masonry breakout is evaluated using a design model based on a uniform tensile stress of $1.25\sqrt{f'_m}$ acting perpendicular to the inclined surface of an idealized breakout body

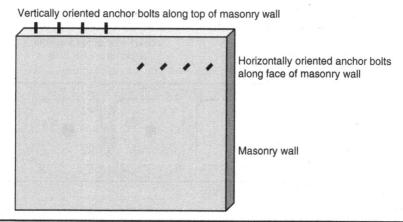

FIGURE 7.26 Common uses of anchor bolts in masonry construction.

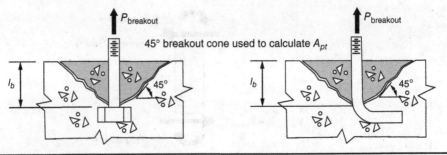

FIGURE 7.27 Idealized conical breakout cones for anchor bolts loaded in tension.

consisting of a right circular cone (Fig. 7.27). The capacity associated with that stress state is identical with the capacity corresponding to a uniform tensile stress of $1.25\sqrt{f'_m}$ acting perpendicular to the projected area of the right circular cone.

Allowable tensile capacities for anchors as governed by masonry breakout are identical for headed and bent-bar anchors, and are given by Equation 6-5 and Equation 8-1 of *TMS 402-22*.

$$B_{ab} = 1.25 A_{pt}\sqrt{f'_m} \qquad \text{TMS 402-22, Equation 8-1}$$

In Equation 8-1, the projected area A_{pt} is evaluated in accordance with Equation 6-5 of *TMS 402-22*:

$$A_{pt} = \pi l_b^2 \qquad \text{TMS 402-22, Equation 6-5}$$

As required by Section 6.3.2 of *TMS 402-22*, the effective embedment length, l_b, for headed anchors is the length of the embedment measured perpendicular from the masonry surface to the compression bearing surface of the anchor head. As required by Section 6.3.5 of *TMS 402-22*, The effective embedment for a bent-bar anchor bolt, l_b, is the length of embedment measured perpendicular from the masonry surface to the compression bearing surface of the bent end, minus one anchor bolt diameter. These are shown in Fig. 7.27. As shown in Fig. 7.28, the projected area must be reduced for

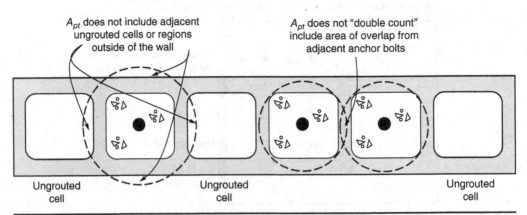

FIGURE 7.28 Modification of projected breakout area, A_{pt}, by void areas or adjacent anchors.

the effect of overlapping projected circular areas, and for the effect of any portion of the project area falling in an open cell or core.

Allowable tensile capacities for anchors as governed by steel fracture are also identical for headed and bent-bar anchors, and are given by Equation 6-5 and Equation 8-2 of *TMS 402-22*. In those equations, A_b is the effective tensile stress area of the anchor bolt, including the effect of threads.

$$B_{as} = 0.5\, A_b f_y \qquad \text{TMS 402-22, Equation 8-2}$$

The allowable tensile capacity of bent-bar anchor bolts as governed by pullout is given by Equation 8-3 of *TMS 402-22*.

$$B_{ap} = 0.6 f'_m e_b d_b + [120\pi(l_b + e_b + d_b)d_b] \qquad \text{TMS 402-22, Equation 8-3}$$

In that equation, the first term represents capacity due to the hook, and the second term represents capacity due to adhesion along the anchor shank. Article 3.2A of TMS 602-22 requires that anchor shanks be cleaned of material that could interfere with that adhesion.

The failure mode with the lowest allowable capacity governs.

7.4.2 Example: Allowable-Stress Design of a Single Anchor Loaded in Tension

Using allowable-stress design, compute the allowable tensile capacity of a 1/2-in. diameter, A307 bent-bar anchor with a 1-in. hook, embedded vertically in a grouted cell of a nominal 8-in. wall with a specified compressive strength, f'_m, of 2000 lb/in². Assume that the bottom of the anchor hook is embedded a distance of 4.5 in. This example might represent a tensile anchor used to attach a roof diaphragm to a wall.

First, compute the effective embedment, l_b. In accordance with Section 6.3.4 of *TMS 402-22*, this is equal to the total embedment of 4.5 in., minus the diameter of the anchor (to get to the inside of the hook), and minus an additional anchor diameter, or 3.5 in. As shown in Fig. 7.29, the projected tensile breakout area has a radius of 3.5 in. (diameter of 7 in.). Because the masonry wall has a specified thickness of 7.63 in., the

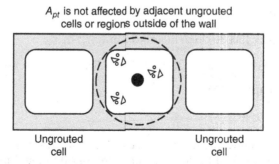

FIGURE 7.29 Example involving a single tensile anchor, placed vertically in a grouted cell.

projected tensile breakout area is not affected by adjacent ungrouted cells or regions outside of the wall.

$$A_{pt} = \pi l_b^2$$

$$A_{pt} = \pi (3.5 \text{ in.})^2 \qquad \text{TMS 402-22, Equation 6-5}$$

$$A_{pt} = 38.5 \text{ in}^2$$

Calculate the allowable capacity due to tensile breakout of masonry.

$$B_{ab} = 1.25 A_{pt} \sqrt{f'_m}$$

$$B_{ab} = 1.25 \times 38.5 \text{ in}^2 \sqrt{2000 \text{ lb/in}^2} \qquad \text{TMS 402-1, Equation 8-1}$$

$$B_{ab} = 2152 \text{ lb}$$

Now compute the allowable tensile capacity as governed by steel fracture. In this computation, A_b is the effective tensile stress area of the anchor bolt, including the effect of threads.

$$A_b = \frac{\pi}{4}\left(d_o - \frac{0.9743}{n_t}\right)^2 \qquad \text{TMS 402-22, Equation 6-7}$$

where d_o = nominal anchor diameter, in.
n_t = number of threads per inch

For anchors with nominal diameters typically used in masonry, the effective tensile stress area can be approximated with sufficient accuracy as 0.75 times the nominal area. That approximation is used in this and other anchor bolt problems here. Use an ultimate strength for A307 steel of 60 ksi.

$$B_{as} = 0.5 A_b f_u$$

$$B_{as} = 0.5 \times 0.75 \times 0.20 \text{ in}^2 \times 60{,}000 \text{ lb/in}^2 \qquad \text{TMS 402-22, Equations 6-7 and 8-2}$$

$$B_{ans} = 4500 \text{ lb}$$

The allowable tensile capacity of bent-bar anchor bolts as governed by pullout is given by Equation 8-3 of *TMS 402-22*.

$$B_{ap} = 0.6 f'_m e_b d_b + [120\pi(l_b + e_b + d_b)d_b]$$

$$B_{ap} = 0.6 \times 1500 \text{ lb/in}^2 \times 1.0 \text{ in.} \times 0.5 \text{ in.}$$

$$\qquad + [120\pi(3.5 \text{ in.} + 1.0 \text{ in.} + 0.5 \text{ in.})\, 0.5 \text{ in.}] \qquad \text{TMS 402-22, Equation 8-3}$$

$$B_{ap} = 450 \text{ lb} + 942 \text{ lb}$$

$$B_{ap} = 1392 \text{ lb}$$

The governing allowable tensile capacity is the lowest of that governed by masonry breakout (2152 lb), yield of the anchor shank (4500 lb), and pullout (1392 lb). Pullout governs, and the allowable tensile capacity is 1392 lb.

If this problem had involved an anchor with deeper embedment (so that the projected tensile breakout area would have been affected by adjacent ungrouted cells or regions outside of the wall), only the anchor capacity as governed by tensile breakout would have been affected, due to a reduced projected tensile breakout area.

Similarly, if this problem had involved adjacent anchors with overlapping tensile breakout areas, only the anchor capacity as governed by tensile breakout would have been affected, again due to a reduced projected tensile breakout area.

7.4.3 Behavior and Design of Anchor Bolts Loaded in Shear

Anchor bolts loaded in shear, and located without a nearby free edge in the direction of load, can fail by local crushing of the masonry under bearing stresses from the anchor bolt; by pryout of the head of the anchor in a direction opposite to the direction of applied load, or by yield and fracture of the anchor bolt steel. Anchor bolts loaded in shear, and located near a free edge in the direction of load, can also fail by breakout of a roughly semi-conical volume of masonry in the direction of the applied shear. Pryout and shear breakout are shown in Part (a) and Part (b), respectively, of Fig. 7.30.

Allowable shear capacity as governed by pryout is taken as twice the allowable tensile breakout capacity, based on the same empirical evidence used in ACI318. Allowable shear capacity as governed by masonry breakout is evaluated using a design model based on a uniform tensile stress of $1.25\sqrt{f'_m}$ acting perpendicular to the inclined surface of an idealized breakout body consisting of a right circular semi-cone (Fig. 7.31).

The capacity associated with that stress state is identical with the capacity corresponding to a uniform tensile stress of $1.25\sqrt{f'_m}$ acting perpendicular to the projected area of the right circular semi-cone.

The nominal shear breakout capacity of an anchor is given by Equation 8-4 of *TMS 402-22*. In evaluating that equation, the projected area of the breakout semi-cone is given by Equation 6-6 of *TMS 402-22*.

$$B_{vb} = 1.25\, A_{pv}\sqrt{f'_m} \quad \text{TMS 402-22, Equation 8-4}$$

$$A_{pv} = \frac{\pi\, l_{be}^2}{2} \quad \text{TMS 402-22, Equation 6-6}$$

Allowable capacities of anchors loaded in shear are given by Equation 8-4 for masonry breakout, by Equation 8-5 for masonry crushing, by Equation 8-6 for shear pryout, and

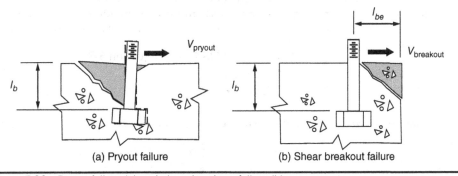

FIGURE 7.30 Pryout failure (a) and shear breakout failure (b).

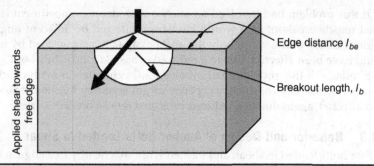

FIGURE 7.31 Design idealization associated with shear breakout failure.

by Equation 8-7 of *TMS 402-22* for the anchor in shear. In Equations 8-5 and 8-7 of *TMS 402-22* (masonry crushing and shear strength, respectively), the effective tensile stress area of the bolt (including the effect of threads) is to be used, unless threads are excluded from the shear plane.

$$B_{vc} = 580 \sqrt[4]{f'_m A_b} \quad \text{TMS 402-22, Equations 6-7 and 8-5}$$
$$B_{vpry} = 2.0\, B_{nb} = 2.5\, A_{pt} \sqrt{f'_m} \quad \text{TMS 402-22, Equation 8-6}$$
$$B_{vs} = 0.25\, A_b f_u \quad \text{TMS 402-22, Equation 8-7}$$

The failure mode with the lowest allowable capacity governs.

7.4.4 Example: Allowable-Stress Design of a Single Anchor Loaded in Shear

Using allowable-stress design, compute the allowable shear capacity of a 1/2-in. diameter, A307 bent-bar anchor with a 1-in. hook, embedded horizontally in a grouted cell of a nominal 8-in. wall with a specified compressive strength, f'_m, of 2000 lb/in². Assume that the bottom of the anchor hook is embedded a distance of 4.5 in., and that the anchor is located far from free edges in the direction of applied shear. This might represent an anchor used to attach a ledger to a masonry wall. Because free edges are not a factor, shear breakout does not apply.

First compute the effective embedment, l_b. In accordance with Section 6.3.4 of *TMS 402-22*, this is equal to the total embedment of 4.5 in., minus the diameter of the anchor (to get to the inside of the hook), and minus an additional anchor diameter, or 3.5 in. The projected tensile breakout area has a radius of 3.5 in. (diameter of 7 in.).

$$A_{pv} = \pi l_{be}^2 \quad \text{TMS 402-22, Equation 6-5}$$
$$A_{pt} = \pi (3.5 \text{ in.})^2$$
$$A_{pt} = 38.5 \text{ in}^2$$

First, compute the allowable capacity of the anchor as governed by masonry breakout.

$$B_{vb} = 1.25 A_{pv} \sqrt{f'_m} \quad \text{TMS 402-22, Equation 8-4}$$

$$B_{vb} = 1.25 \times 19.4 \text{ in}^2 \sqrt{2000 \text{ psi}} = 1076 \text{ lb}$$

Allowable-Stress Design of Unreinforced Masonry Elements

Next, compute the allowable capacity of the anchor as governed by masonry crushing.

$$B_{vc} = 580 \sqrt[4]{f'_m A_b} \qquad \text{TMS 402-22, Equation 8-5}$$

In this computation, A_b is the effective tensile stress area of the anchor bolt, including the effect of threads.

$$A_b = \frac{\pi}{4}\left(d_o - \frac{0.9743}{n_t}\right)^2 \qquad \text{TMS 402-22, Equation 6-7}$$

where d_o = nominal anchor diameter, in.
n_t = number of threads per inch

For anchors with nominal diameters typically used in masonry, the effective tensile stress area can be approximated with sufficient accuracy as 0.75 times the nominal area. That approximation is used in this and other anchor bolt problems here.

$$B_{vc} = 580 \sqrt[4]{f'_m A_b} \qquad \text{TMS 402-22, Equations 6-7 and 8-5}$$
$$B_{vc} = 580 \sqrt[4]{2000 \text{ lb/in}^2 \times (0.75 \times 0.20 \text{ in}^2)}$$
$$B_{vc} = 2414 \text{ lb}$$

Next, compute the allowable capacity of the anchor as governed by pryout.

$$B_{vpry} = 2.0 B_{ab} = 2.5 A_{pt}\sqrt{f'_m} \qquad \text{TMS 402-22, Equation 8-6}$$

Because allowable pryout capacity is a multiple of the allowable tensile breakout capacity, we must compute the allowable tensile breakout capacity.

$$B_{ab} = 1.25 A_{po}\sqrt{f'_m} \qquad \text{TMS 402-22, Equations 6-6 and 8-4}$$
$$B_{ab} = 1.25 \times 38.5 \text{ in}^2 \sqrt{2000 \text{ lb/in}^2}$$
$$B_{ab} = 2152 \text{ lb}$$

Continue with the pryout calculation:

$$B_{vpry} = 2.0 B_{ab} \qquad \text{TMS 402-22, Equation 8-6}$$
$$B_{vpry} = 2.0 \times 2152 \text{ lb}$$
$$B_{vpry} = 4304 \text{ lb}$$

Next, compute the allowable capacity of the anchor as governed by yield and fracture of the anchor shank.

$$B_{vs} = 0.25 A_b f_y \qquad \text{TMS 402-22, Equation 8-7}$$
$$B_{vs} = 0.25 \times (0.75 \times 0.20 \text{ in}^2) \times 60{,}000 \text{ lb/in}^2$$
$$B_{vs} = 2250 \text{ lb}$$

The governing allowable shear capacity is the lowest of that governed by masonry breakout (1076 lb), masonry crushing (2414 lb), pryout (4304 lb), and fracture of the anchor shank (2250 lb). Because the anchor is not close to a free edge, shear breakout does not apply. Masonry breakout governs, and the allowable shear capacity is 1076 lb.

If this problem had involved an anchor loaded toward a free edge, then shear breakout would have had to be checked.

7.4.5 Behavior and Design of Anchor Bolts Loaded in Combined Tension and Shear

Design capacities of anchor bolts in combined tension and shear are given by the linear interaction equation of Equation 8-8 of TMS 402-22.

$$\left(\frac{b_a}{B_a}\right)^{\frac{5}{3}} + \left(\frac{b_v}{B_v}\right)^{\frac{5}{3}} \leq 1 \qquad \text{TMS 402-22, Equation 8-8}$$

7.5 Required Details for Unreinforced Bearing Walls and Shear Walls

Bearing walls that resist out-of-plane lateral loads, and shear walls, must be designed to transfer lateral loads to the floors above and below. Examples of such connections are shown below. These connections would have to be strengthened for regions subject to strong earthquakes or strong winds. Section 1604.8.2 of the 2024 *IBC* has additional requirements for anchorage of diaphragms to masonry walls. Section 12.11 of ASCE 7-15 introduced additional requirements for anchorage of structural walls for structures assigned to Seismic Design Categories C and higher.

7.5.1 Wall-to-Foundation Connections

As shown in Fig. 7.32, CMU walls (or the inner CMU wythe of a drainage wall) must be connected to the concrete foundation. Bond breaker should be used only between the outer veneer wythe and the foundation.

7.5.2 Wall-to-Floor Details

Examples of a wall-to-floor detail are shown in Figs. 7.33 and 7.34. In the latter detail (floor or roof planks oriented parallel to walls), the planks are actually cambered. They are shown on the outside of the walls so that this camber does not interfere with the coursing of the units. Some designers object to this detail because it could lead to spalling of the cover. If it is modified so that the planks rest on the face shells of the walls, then the thickness of the topping must vary to adjust for the camber, and form boards must be used against both sides of the wall underneath the planks, so that the concrete or grout that is cast into the bond beam does not run out underneath the cambered beam.

7.5.3 Wall-to-Roof Details

An example of a wall-to-roof detail is shown in Fig. 7.35.

7.5.4 Typical Details of Wall-to-Wall Connections

Typical details of wall-to-wall connections are shown in Fig. 7.36.

Allowable-Stress Design of Unreinforced Masonry Elements 249

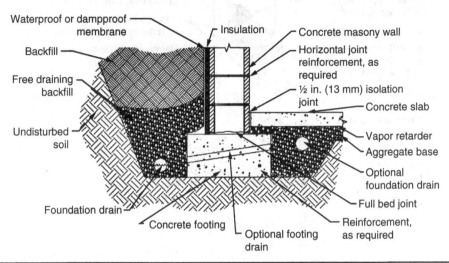

FIGURE 7.32 Example of wall-to-foundation connection (Figure 1 of CMHA TEK 05-07A).

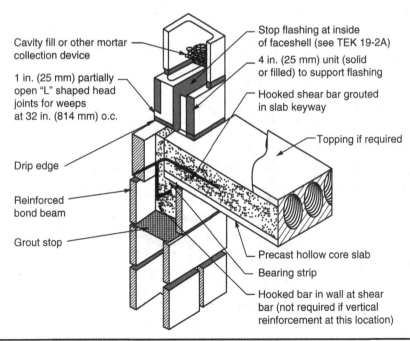

FIGURE 7.33 Example of wall-to-floor connection, planks perpendicular to wall (Figure 14 of CMHA TEK 05-07A).

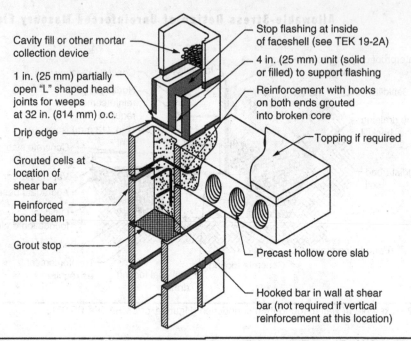

Figure 7.34 Example of wall-to-floor connection, planks parallel to wall (Figure 15 of NCMA TEK 05-07A).

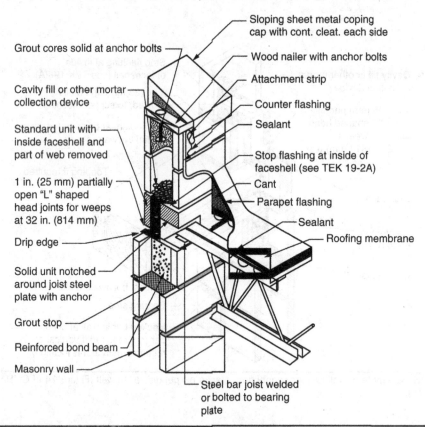

Figure 7.35 Example of wall-to-roof detail (Figure 11 of NCMA TEK 05-07A).

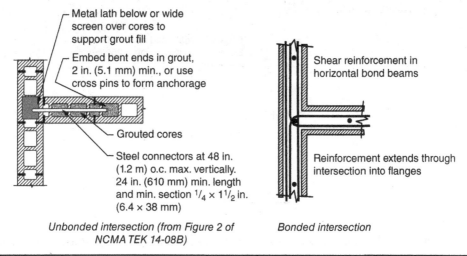

FIGURE 7.36 Examples of wall-to-wall connection details.

7.6 Problems

7.1 Determine the area and out-of-plane moment of inertia for a 1-ft long strip of a wall constructed with 10-in. nominal CMU. Assume that the units are fully bedded and have specified face- and web-shell thicknesses of 1.25 and 1.125 in., respectively.

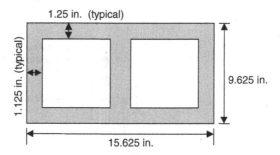

7.2 Design a simply supported ungrouted bearing wall subjected to eccentric axial loads of 500 lb dead and 250 lb live load per foot of plan length, combined with out-of-plane wind load of 25 psf. All loads are unfactored. The axial-load eccentricity is 2.5 in. and the story height is 10 ft. Assume a specified compressive strength of masonry of 2000 psi and Type S PCL mortar. Start with nominal 6-in. CMU and the self-weight from Table 7.5 (26 lb/ft² for ungrouted units). Continue until you find a satisfactory nominal thickness. Use the following load conditions.

Part 1. Considering gravity loads only, check the existing design for compliance with *TMS 402-22*.

Part 2. Repeat Part 1 including wind load.

The wall is as shown below:

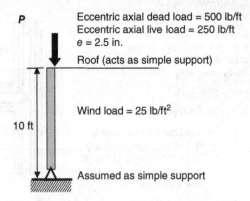

7.3 In the building shown below, the roof is assumed to span longitudinally between the two gable walls. The 1-ft strip of CMU shown below is subjected to unfactored eccentric gravity loads of 800 lb dead load and 200 lb live load at the building apex, whose height is 16 ft. The eccentricity is 3 in. Include self-weight. The wall is also subjected to an out-of-plane wind load whose magnitude is not specified. A ceiling provides horizontal restraint at the mid-height of each gable wall. As an initial design assumption, idealize this vertical strip assuming zero moment at the building apex, the ceiling, and the base. Assume ungrouted units; 8-in. nominal thickness; f'_m = 2000 psi; and Type S PCL mortar.

Part 1. Considering gravity loads only, check the existing design for compliance with *TMS 402-22*.

Part 2. Repeat Part 1 including wind load. Calculate the maximum unfactored wind load the vertical strip can support.

The wall is as shown below:

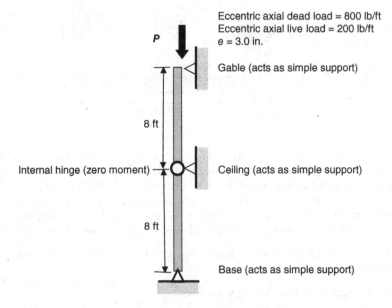

*7.4 Repeat Problem 5.3 using a single two-span beam. This assumes a continuous beam-column at the height of the ceiling and at the base. Comment on how the maximum permissible wind load changes.

Part 1. Considering gravity loads only, check the existing design for compliance with *TMS 402-22*.

Part 2. Repeat Part 1 including wind load. Calculate the maximum unfactored wind load the vertical strip can support.

The wall is as shown below:

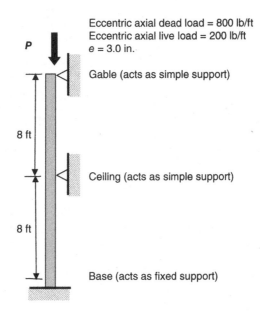

7.5 Extend the problem of Fig. 7.21 to a two-story building. Change the typical story height to 10 ft. Gravity loads on a typical floor are equal to those on the roof. Try a nominal 8-in. CMU wall, ungrouted, with face-shell bedding and Type S PCL mortar. Use a specified masonry compressive strength of 2000 psi. Assume a unit density of 115 lb/ft³, and use the self-weight from Table 5.4 (33 lb/ft²). If this does not work, list an alternate way to solve the problem using 8-in. units.

*7.6 Using the design of Prob. 5.5, and continuing the same load at each diaphragm level, how many stories could the building have?

---

*Denotes problems intended for graduate students.

CHAPTER 8

Allowable-Stress Design of Reinforced Masonry Elements

Before studying the allowable-stress design of reinforced masonry elements, it is useful to review the behavior of reinforced masonry elements in the linear elastic range. This is accomplished in the first section of this lecture. Later sections then address the allowable-stress design of beams, lintels, reinforced bearing walls, and reinforced shear walls.

8.1 Review: Behavior of Cracked, Transformed Sections

8.1.1 Review: Flexural Behavior of Cracked, Transformed Sections

The basic principles of the flexural behavior of cracked, transformed sections are developed using kinematics, stress-strain relations and equilibrium, as shown in Fig. 8.1.

The cracked masonry section must satisfy kinematics (plane sections remain plane), stress-strain relationships, and statics.

Kinematics	Stress–Strain Relation	Statics
$\varepsilon_m = \varepsilon_s$	$f_m = E_m \varepsilon_m$	$\sum f\, dA = 0$
$\varepsilon = \phi y$	$f_s = E_s \varepsilon_s$	$\sum fy\, dA = M$

Axial equilibrium of the section locates the neutral axis of the cracked, transformed section as shown below:

$$b \int_0^{kd} f_m dy + A'_s f'_s + A_s f_s = 0$$

$$b \int_0^{kd} \phi E_m y\, dy + A'_s E_s \phi y'_1 + A_s E_s \phi y_1 = 0$$

$$E_m \phi \left[b \int_0^{kd} y\, dy + (n-1) A'_s y'_1 + n A_s y_1 \right] = 0$$

256 Chapter Eight

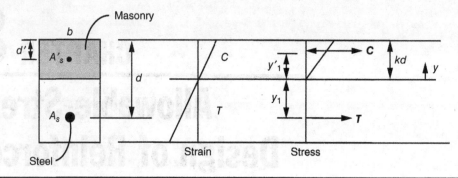

FIGURE 8.1 States of strain and stress in a cracked masonry section.

$$n \equiv \frac{E_s}{E_m} \text{ (modular ratio)}$$

$$E_m \phi \neq 0$$

$$b \int_0^{kd} y\, dy + (n-1) A'_s y'_1 + n A_s y_1 = 0$$

In other words, the neutral axis is located at the geometric centroid of the cracked, transformed section. We shall later develop closed-form expressions for that location.

A derivation quite similar to the foregoing can be carried out for moment equilibrium:

$$b \int_0^{kd} f_m y\, dy + A'_s y'_1 f'_s + A_s y_1 f_s = M_o$$

$$b \int_0^{kd} \phi E_m y^2\, dy + A'_s E_s \phi y'^2_1 + A_s E_s \phi y^2_1 = M_o$$

$$E_m \phi \left[b \int_0^{kd} y^2\, dy + (n-1) A'_s y'^2_1 + n A_s y^2_1 \right] = M_o$$

The quantity in brackets represents the centroidal moment of inertia of the cracked, transformed section. Continuing,

$$\boxed{\begin{array}{c} E_m \phi I_{c,t} = M_o \\ \phi = \dfrac{M}{E I_{c,t}} \end{array}}$$

But

$$\varepsilon = y\phi$$

$$f_s = E_s \varepsilon = E_s y \phi = n E_m y \phi = \frac{n M_o y}{I_{c,t}} = f_s$$

$$f_m = E_m \varepsilon = E_m y \phi = \frac{M_o y}{I_{c,t}} = f_m$$

And in summary,

$$\boxed{\begin{aligned} f_s &= \frac{nM_o y}{I_{c,t}} \\ f_m &= \frac{M_o y}{I_{c,t}} \end{aligned}}$$

8.1.2 Location of the Neutral Axis for Particular Cases

Now examine the location of the neutral axis. The neutral axis is located using the information shown in Fig. 8.2:

$$\rho \equiv \frac{A_s}{bd} \qquad \rho' \equiv \frac{A'_s}{bd}$$

The neutral axis is located at the centroid of the cracked, transformed section:

$$(bkd)\left(\frac{kd}{2}\right) + (n-1)A'_s(kd - d') = nA_s(d - kd)$$

$$\left(\frac{d}{2}\right)k^2 + (n-1)\rho'(kd - d') = n\rho(d - kd)$$

$$\left(\frac{d}{2}\right)k^2 + [n\rho + (n-1)\rho']\,dk - \left[n\rho + (n-1)\rho'\left(\frac{d'}{d}\right)\right]d = 0$$

$$k^2 + 2[n\rho + (n-1)\rho']\,k - 2\left[n\rho + (n-1)\rho'\left(\frac{d'}{d}\right)\right] = 0$$

Using the quadratic formula, and noting that only positive areas of reinforcement have physical meaning:

$$k = \frac{-2[n\rho + (n-1)\rho'] \pm \sqrt{4[n\rho + (n-1)\rho']^2 + 8\left[n\rho + (n-1)\rho'\left(\frac{d'}{d}\right)\right]}}{2}$$

$$k = -[n\rho + (n-1)\rho'] + \sqrt{[n\rho + (n-1)\rho']^2 + 2\left[n\rho + (n-1)\rho'\left(\frac{d'}{d}\right)\right]}$$

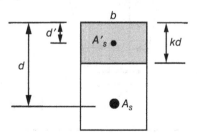

FIGURE 8.2 Location of the neutral axis for particular cases.

Neglecting the compressive reinforcement,

$$k = -n\rho + \sqrt{n^2\rho^2 + 2n\rho}$$

8.1.3 Review: Shear Behavior of Cracked, Transformed Sections

Now examine the shear behavior of a cracked, transformed section. Consider a slice of a beam, with a maximum compressive stress f_b on one side, and a maximum compressive stress $f_b + \dfrac{df_b}{dx}dx$ on the other side (Fig. 8.3).

Now cut the slice at a distance y_1 from the neutral axis, as shown in Fig. 8.4.

$$\tau\, dx\, b = \int_{y_1}^{y_{max}} \frac{df_b}{dx} dx\, b\, dy$$

but

$$f_b = \frac{My}{I}$$

So

$$\frac{df_b}{dx} = \frac{dM}{dx}\frac{y}{I} = \frac{Vy}{I}$$

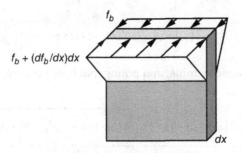

FIGURE 8.3 Slice of a cracked, transformed section showing triangular compressive stress blocks.

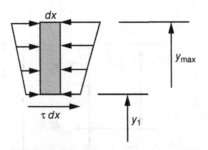

FIGURE 8.4 Slice of a cracked, transformed section showing equilibrium between shear forces and difference in shear forces.

and

$$\tau\,dx\,b = \int_{y_1}^{y_{max}} by\,dy\,\frac{V}{I}$$

Finally,

$$\tau = \frac{V\int_{y_1}^{y_{max}} by\,dy}{Ib}$$

$$\tau = \frac{VQ}{Ib}$$

Now consider the special case of a cracked, transformed section. Shear is greatest at the neutral axis. Examine the equilibrium of the compressive and tensile portions of the slice (Fig. 8.5).

Axial equilibrium of the compressive block requires

$$\tau b\,dx = b\int_0^{kd}\frac{df_b}{dx}\,dx\,dy$$

but

$$b\int_0^{kd}\frac{df_b}{dx}\,dx\,dy = \frac{df_s}{dx}\,dx\,A_s$$

So

$$\tau b\,dx = \frac{df_s}{dx}\,dx\,A_s = \frac{d\left(\frac{M}{A_s jd}\right)}{dx}\,dx\,A_s = \left(\frac{dM}{dx}\right)\frac{dx}{jd} = \frac{V}{jd}\,dx$$

And finally,

$$\boxed{\tau = \frac{V}{bjd}}$$

FIGURE 8.5 Slice of a cracked, transformed section showing equilibrium of the compressive and tensile portions of the slice.

8.1.4 Review: Bond Behavior of Cracked, Transformed Sections

Now examine the bond behavior of a cracked, transformed section. Consider a slice of a beam, with a maximum steel stress f_s on the far side, and a maximum steel stress $f_s + \frac{df_s}{dx}dx$ on the other side, as shown in Fig. 8.6.

The far side of the slice has a moment M; the near side has a moment $M + \frac{dM}{dx}dx$.

Far side of slice	Near side of slice
$A_s f_s = \dfrac{M}{jd}$	$A_s\left(f_s + \dfrac{df_s}{dx}dx\right) = \dfrac{M + \dfrac{dM}{dx}dx}{jd}$

For the near side of the slice,

$$A_s\left(f_s + \frac{df_s}{dx}dx\right) = \frac{\left(M + \frac{dM}{dx}dx\right)}{jd}$$

$$A_s f_s + A_s \frac{df_s}{dx}dx = \frac{M}{jd} + \frac{dM}{dx}\frac{dx}{jd}$$

The first term on the left-hand side is equal to the first term on the right-hand side, so they cancel:

$$A_s \frac{df_s}{dx}dx = \frac{dM}{dx}\frac{dx}{jd}$$

$$\boxed{\frac{df_s}{dx} = \frac{V}{A_s jd}}$$

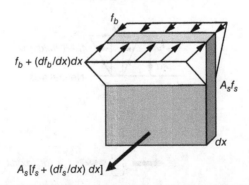

FIGURE 8.6 Slice of a cracked, transformed section, showing equilibrium of difference in compressive force and difference in tensile force.

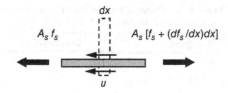

FIGURE 8.7 Tensile portion of a slice, showing equilibrium between bond force and difference in tensile force in reinforcement.

However, this change in steel stress requires a bond stress u, acting over the perimeter of the bar, Σ_o, times the length, dx. This is shown in Fig. 8.7.

Imposing horizontal equilibrium,

$$A_s f_s + A_s \frac{df_s}{dx} dx = A_s f_s + u\Sigma_o dx$$

$$A_s \frac{df_s}{dx} dx = u\Sigma_o dx$$

$$u = \frac{A_s}{\Sigma_o} \frac{df_s}{dx} = \frac{A_s}{\Sigma_o} \frac{dM}{dx} \frac{1}{A_s jd}$$

So

$$\boxed{u = \frac{V}{\Sigma_o jd}}$$

8.1.5 Physical Properties of Steel Reinforcing Wire and Bars

Physical properties of steel reinforcing wire and bars are given in Table 8.1.

Cover requirements are given in Section 6.1.5 of *TMS 402-22*. Minimum cover for joint reinforcement (exterior exposure) is 5/8 in.

8.1.6 Example: Location of the Neutral Axis (Cracked, Transformed Section)

For a 4-in. modular clay masonry wall with two W1.7 wires every course, loaded out of plane, what is the effect on the location of the neutral axis if compressive reinforcement is neglected? Assume Type S mortar, and units with a compressive strength of 6600 psi. See Fig. 8.8. Because the section is loaded out of plane, the depth of the section is measured horizontally on the page, and the width is measured vertically. The effective width per bar is 2.67 in.

According to Table 1 of *TMS 602-22*, for Type M or S mortar and clay units with a strength of 6600 psi, the compressive strength of the masonry can conservatively be taken as 2500 psi (the so-called "unit strength method"). If the compressive strength is evaluated by prism testing, a higher value can probably be used. Take the specified compressive strength of the masonry as $f'_m = 2500$ psi.

Then according to Section 4.2.2 of *TMS 402-22*, for clay masonry,

$$E_m = 700 f'_m = 700 \times 2500 \text{ lb/in}^2 = 1.75 \times 10^6 \text{ lb/in}^2$$

TABLE 8.1 Physical Properties of Steel Reinforcing Wire and Bars (from Table CC-6.1.3 of *TMS 402-22*)

Designation	Diameter, in.	Area, in^2
Wire		
W1.1 (11 gage)	0.121	0.011
W1.7 (9 gage)	0.148	0.017
W2.1 (8 gage)	0.162	0.020
W2.8 (3/16 wire)	0.187	0.027
W4.9 (1/4 wire)	0.250	0.049
Bars		
#3	0.375	0.11
#4	0.500	0.20
#5	0.625	0.31
#6	0.750	0.44
#7	0.875	0.60
#8	1.000	0.79
#9	1.128	1.00
#10	1.270	1.27
#11	1.410	1.56

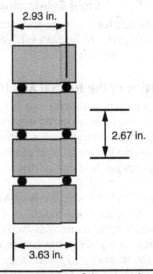

FIGURE 8.8 Example calculation of the position of the neutral axis.

The modular ratio n is given by

$$n = \frac{E_s}{E_m} = \frac{29 \times 10^6}{1.75 \times 10^6} = 16.6$$

$$t = 3.63$$

$$d = 3.63 - \frac{5}{8} - \frac{0.148}{2} = 2.93 \text{ in.}$$

$$d' = \frac{5}{8} + \frac{0.148}{2} = 0.70 \text{ in.}$$

$$\rho = \rho' = \frac{A_s}{bd} = \frac{0.0172}{2.93 \cdot 8/3} = 0.00220$$

First, compute the location of the neutral axis neglecting the effect of compressive reinforcement.

$$k = -n\rho + \sqrt{(n\rho)^2 + 2n\rho} = 0.236$$

Now compute the location of the neutral axis including the effect of compressive reinforcement:

$$k = -[n\rho + (n-1)\rho'] + \sqrt{[n\rho + (n-1)\rho']^2 + 2\left[n\rho + (n-1)\rho'\left(\frac{d'}{d}\right)\right]} = 0.237$$

Therefore, compressive reinforcement does not significantly affect the location of the neutral axis.

For most sections, a good initial assumption is that k (the location of the neutral axis) is close to 3/8, and therefore j (the internal lever arm) is close to 7/8.

$$kd \approx \frac{3}{8}d$$

$$jd = d - \frac{kd}{3} \approx \frac{7}{8}d$$

8.1.7 Example: Allowable Flexural Capacity of the Cross-Section

Now compute the allowable flexural capacity of the cross-section considered above. The allowable flexural capacity could be governed by the maximum flexural tensile stress in the reinforcement, or by the maximum flexural compressive stress in the masonry.

Using the allowable-stress approach, computed stresses are denoted by the lower-case letter f. For example, f_s is the computed stress in the reinforcement, and f_b is the computed bending stress in the masonry. Allowable stresses are denoted by the upper-case letter F. For example, F_s is the allowable stress in the reinforcement, and F_b is the allowable flexural compressive stress in the masonry.

In accordance with Section 8.3.3.2 of *TMS 402-22*, the allowable stress in drawn wire reinforcement is 30,000 lb/in². In accordance with Section 8.3.4.2.2 of *TMS 402-22*, the allowable flexural compressive stress in masonry is $(0.45) f'_m$.

264 Chapter Eight

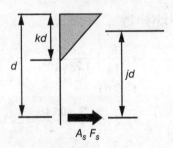

FIGURE 8.9 Equilibrium of forces in the cross-section corresponding to allowable stress in the reinforcement.

First consider the allowable moment capacity as governed by the allowable stress in the reinforcement, F_s (Fig. 8.9): The moment is the allowable tensile force in the reinforcement, multiplied by the internal lever arm:

$$\boxed{M = A_s F_s jd}$$

In our case,

$$k = 0.24$$

$$j = 1 - \frac{k}{3} = 1 - \frac{0.24}{3} = 0.92$$

$$M = A_s F_s jd = 0.0172 \text{ in}^2 \times 30{,}000 \text{ lb/in}^2 \times 0.92 \times 2.93 \text{ in.}$$

$$M = 1391 \text{ lb-in./course}$$

$$M = 1391 \text{ lb-in./course} \times \left(\frac{3 \text{ courses}}{8 \text{ in.}}\right) \times 12 \text{ in./ft}$$

$$M = 6259 \text{ lb-in. per foot of width}$$

Now consider the allowable moment capacity as governed by the allowable stress in the masonry, F_b (Fig. 8.10). The moment is the allowable compressive force in the masonry, multiplied by the internal lever arm:

$$M = \left(\frac{1}{2} \times F_b bkd\right)(jd)$$

$$\boxed{M = \frac{1}{2} F_b jkbd^2}$$

In our case,

$$M = \frac{1}{2} bjkd^2 F_b$$

$$M = \frac{1}{2} \times 12 \text{ in.} \times 0.92 \times 0.24 \times 2.93^2 \text{ in}^2 \times 0.45 \times 2500 \text{ psi}$$

$$M = 12{,}795 \text{ lb-in. per foot of width}$$

Allowable-Stress Design of Reinforced Masonry Elements

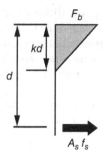

FIGURE 8.10 Equilibrium of forces in the cross-section corresponding to allowable stress in the masonry.

Because the allowable moment as governed by the allowable stress in the reinforcement is less than the allowable moment as governed by the allowable stress in the masonry, the former governs.

Another way of working the same problem is to compute the stress in the masonry when the stress in the allowable reinforcement equals the allowable stress. For any steel stress f_s (not necessarily the allowable stress), equilibrium of axial forces in the beam gives

$$(f_b bkd)\left(\frac{1}{2}\right) = A_s f_s$$

$$f_b = \frac{2A_s f_s}{bkd}$$

But from above,

$$A_s = \frac{M}{jdf_s}$$

So

$$f_b = \frac{2\left(M/f_s jd\right)f_s}{bkd} = \frac{2M}{jkbd^2}$$

In our case,

$$f_b = \frac{2M}{jkbd^2} = \frac{2 \times 6259 \text{ lb-in.}}{0.24 \times 0.92 \times 12 \text{ in.} \times 2.93^2 \text{ in}^2} = 550 \text{ lb/in}^2$$

This is less than the allowable stress of $0.45 f'_m$, and the design is satisfactory.

8.1.8 Allowable-Stress Balanced Reinforcement

For allowable-stress design, the concept of balanced reinforcement exists but has little physical significance. The allowable-stress balanced steel area is simply the steel area at which the masonry and steel simultaneously reach their respective allowable stresses.

Because the factors of safety are different for steel and masonry, and because the assumed stress distribution in masonry is linear rather than an equivalent rectangular stress block, the allowable-stress balanced steel area does not mark a transition between ductile and brittle behavior. It is a reference point, however, between behavior governed by allowable stresses in reinforcement, and behavior governed by allowable stresses in masonry.

The balanced steel percentage for allowable-stress design can be derived based on the strains in steel and masonry, as shown in Fig. 8.11.

First, locate the neutral axis under allowable-stress balanced conditions:

$$\frac{\varepsilon_m}{\varepsilon_s} = \frac{(F_b/E_m)}{(F_s/E_s)} = \frac{k_b d}{d - k_b d}$$

$$\left(\frac{F_b}{E_m}\right)(d - k_b d) = \left(\frac{F_s}{E_s}\right)k_b d$$

$$\frac{E_s}{E_m} \equiv n$$

$$\left(\frac{F_b}{E_m}\right)d - \left(\frac{F_b}{E_m}\right)k_b d = \left(\frac{F_s}{nE_m}\right)k_b d$$

$$k_b\left(\frac{F_b}{E_m} + \frac{F_s}{nE_m}\right) = \left(\frac{F_b}{E_m}\right)$$

$$k_b = \frac{F_b}{F_b + F_s/n}$$

And finally,

$$\boxed{k_b = \frac{n}{(F_s/F_b) + n}}$$

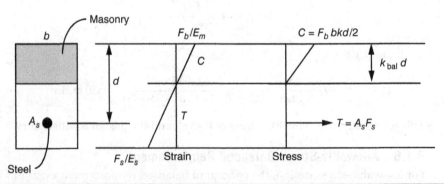

FIGURE 8.11 Conditions of stress and strain corresponding to allowable-stress balanced reinforcement.

The corresponding steel percentage, ρ_b, is given by

$$T = C$$

$$A_s F_s = \left(\frac{1}{2}\right) F_b bkd$$

$$\rho_b bd F_s = \left(\frac{1}{2}\right) F_b bkd$$

$$\rho_b = \left(\frac{1}{2}\right) k_b \left(\frac{F_b}{F_s}\right)$$

8.2 Allowable-Stress Design of Reinforced Beams and Lintels

8.2.1 Steps in Allowable-Stress Design of Reinforced Beams and Lintels

The most common reinforced masonry beam is a lintel, as shown in Fig. 8.12. Lintels are beams that support masonry over openings.

Allowable-stress design of reinforced beams and lintels follows the basic steps given below:

1) Shear design:
   a) Calculate the ASD factored design shear, and compare it with the corresponding resistance. Revise the lintel depth if necessary.
2) Flexural design:
   a) Calculate the ASD factored design moment.
   b) Calculate the required flexural reinforcement. Check that it fits within minimum and maximum reinforcement limitations.

In many cases, the depth of the lintel is determined by architectural considerations. In other cases, it is necessary to determine the number of courses of masonry that will work as a beam.

The depth of the beam, and hence the area that is effective in resisting shear, is determined by the number of courses that comprise it. Because it is not very practical

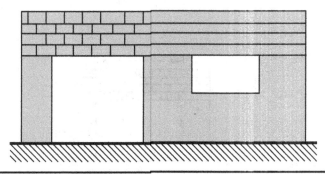

FIGURE 8.12 Example of masonry lintel.

to put shear reinforcement in masonry beams, the depth of the beam may be determined by this. In other words, the beam design may start with the number of courses that are needed so that shear can be resisted by masonry alone.

8.2.2 Example: Lintel Design according to Allowable-Stress Provisions

Suppose that we have a uniformly distributed load of 1050 lb/ft, applied at the level of the roof of the structure shown in Fig. 8.13. Design the lintel.

According to Table 8.2.4.2 of *TMS 602-22*, for Type M or S mortar and concrete masonry units with a specified strength of 2000 psi (the minimum specified strength for ASTM C90 units), the compressive strength of the masonry can conservatively be taken as 2000 psi (the so-called "unit strength method"). If the compressive strength is evaluated by prism testing, a higher value can probably be used. Take the specified compressive strength of the masonry as $f'_m = 2000$ psi.

Assume fully grouted concrete masonry with a nominal thickness of 8 in. and a weight of 81 lb/ft². Use Type S PCL mortar. The lintel has a span of 10 ft, and a total depth (height of parapet plus distance between the roof and the lintel) of 4 ft. These are shown in the following schematic figure. Our design presumes that the entire height of the lintel is grouted.

First check whether the depth of the lintel is sufficient to avoid the use of shear reinforcement. The opening may have a movement joint placed on either or both sides, at a distance of one-half the unit length from the opening. The lintel therefore bears on two bearing areas, each of length 8 in. Conservatively, the span of the lintel is taken as the clear distance, plus one-half of 8 in. on each side. So the span is 10 ft plus 8 in., or 10.67 ft.

$$M = \frac{wl^2}{8} = \frac{(1050 \text{ lb/ft} + 4 \text{ ft} \times 81 \text{ lb/ft}^2) \times \left(\frac{1 \text{ ft}}{12 \text{ in.}}\right) \times (10.67 \text{ ft} \times 12 \text{ in./ft})^2}{8} = 234,643 \text{ lb-in.}$$

$$V = \frac{wl}{2} = \frac{(1050 \text{ lb/ft} + 4 \text{ ft} \times 81 \text{ lb/ft}^2) \times 10.67 \text{ lb}}{2} = 7330 \text{ lb}$$

Shearing capacity is calculated using Section 8.3.5.1 of *TMS 402-22*. Shear stresses are calculated by

$$f_v = \frac{V}{A_{nv}}$$

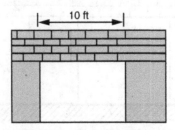

FIGURE 8.13 Example for allowable-stress design of a lintel.

Allowable-Stress Design of Reinforced Masonry Elements

The allowable in-plane shear stress, F_v, is the summation of an allowable shear stress in masonry and an allowable stress in shear reinforcement:

$$F_v = (F_{vm} + F_{vs})\gamma_g$$

In this case, we shall have no shear reinforcement, so $F_{vs} = 0$. Because our masonry is fully grouted, $\gamma_g = 1$.

$$F_{vm} = \frac{1}{2}\left[4.0 - 1.75\left(\frac{M}{Vd_v}\right)\right]\sqrt{f'_m} + 0.25\frac{P}{A_n}$$

As (M/Vd) increases, F_{vm} decreases. Because (M/Vd) need not be taken greater than 1.0 (TMS 402-22 of Section 8.3.5.1.3), the most conservative (lowest) value of F_{vm} is obtained with (M/Vd) equal to 1.0.

In our case, the bars in the lintel will be placed in the lower part of an inverted bottom course as shown in Fig. 8.14.

The effective depth d is calculated using the minimum cover of 1.5 in. (Section 6.1.5 of TMS 402-22), plus one-half the diameter of an assumed #8 bar.

$$f_v = \frac{V}{A_{nv}} = \frac{7330 \text{ lb}}{7.63 \times 48 \text{ in}^2} = 20.0 \text{ lb/in}^2$$

Also, axial load, P, is zero:

$$F_{vm} = \frac{1}{2}[4.0 - 1.75(1.0)]\sqrt{f'_m}$$
$$F_{vm} = 1.13\sqrt{f'_m}$$
$$F_{vm} = 1.13\sqrt{2000} \text{ lb/in}^2 = 50.5 \text{ lb/in}^2$$

This exceeds the calculated shear stress, and our design is satisfactory so far.

Also, according to Equation 8-22 of TMS 402-22,

$$F_v \leq 2\sqrt{f'_m}\,\gamma_g$$

This does not govern, and the shear design is acceptable. The depth is satisfactory to avoid the use of shear reinforcement.

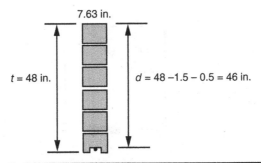

FIGURE 8.14 Example showing placement of bottom reinforcement in lowest course of lintel.

Now check the required flexural reinforcement, using the approximate value $j = 7/8$:

$$A_s^{\text{required}} = \frac{M}{F_s jd} = \frac{234{,}643 \text{ lb-in.}}{30{,}000 \text{ lb/in}^2 \times \left(\frac{7}{8} \times 46 \text{ in.}\right)} = 0.19 \text{ in}^2$$

Because of the depth of the beam, this can be satisfied with a #4 bar. Also include two #4 bars at the level of the roof (bond beam reinforcement). The flexural design is quite simple. Because j is approximated as 7/8, the required steel area calculated above is not exact. The calculation could be refined by solving for the actual value of j.

TMS 402-22 has no minimum reinforcement requirements for allowable-stress design of flexural members, and its maximum reinforcement requirements apply only to special reinforced masonry shear walls subjected to in-plane loading (TMS 402-22 of Section 8.3.4.4).

Although the compressive stress in the masonry will probably not govern if the beam is deep enough not to need shear reinforcement, it is checked here for completeness. Equilibrium of forces on the cross-section is shown in Fig. 8.15.

First calculate the position of the neutral axis. Neglecting compressive reinforcement, the position of the neutral axis is given by

$$n \equiv \frac{E_s}{E_m}, \quad \text{and} \quad \rho \equiv \frac{A_s}{bd}$$

$$k = -n\rho + \sqrt{n^2\rho^2 + 2n\rho} \approx \frac{3}{8}$$

$$j = 1 - \frac{k}{3} \approx \frac{7}{8}$$

For a given moment, the tensile stress in the tensile reinforcement is

$$M = A_s f_s jd$$

$$f_s = \frac{M}{A_s jd}$$

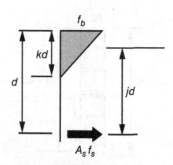

Figure 8.15 Equilibrium of forces on cross-section.

And the maximum compressive stress in the masonry is given as follows

$$(f_b bkd)\left(\frac{1}{2}\right) = A_s f_s$$

$$f_b = \frac{2A_s f_s}{bkd}$$

$$A_s f_s = \frac{M}{jd}$$

$$f_b = \frac{2M}{bjdkd} = \frac{2M}{bjkd^2}$$

In this case, which involves concrete masonry,

$$n \equiv \frac{E_s}{E_m} = \frac{E_s}{900 f'_m} = \frac{29 \times 10^6 \text{ psi}}{900 \times 2000 \text{ psi}} = 16.11$$

$$\rho \equiv \frac{A_s}{bd} = \frac{0.20 \text{ in}^2}{7.63 \times 46 \text{ in}^2} = 0.570 \times 10^{-4}$$

$$n\rho = 0.00918$$

$$k = -n\rho + \sqrt{n^2 \rho^2 + 2n\rho} = 0.127$$

$$j = 1 - \frac{k}{3} = 0.958$$

$$f_s = \frac{M}{A_s jd} = \frac{234{,}643 \text{ lb-in.}}{0.20 \text{ in}^2 \times 0.952 \times 46 \text{ in.}} = 26{,}629 \text{ lb/in}^2 \leq 30{,}000 \text{ lb/in}^2 \quad \text{OK}$$

$$f_b = \frac{2M}{bjkd^2} = \frac{2 \times 234{,}643 \text{ lb-in.}}{7.63 \text{ in.} \times 0.145 \times 0.952 \times (46 \text{ in.})^2} = 240 \text{ lb/in}^2 \leq 0.45\, f'_m = 675 \text{ lb/in}^2 \quad \text{OK}$$

The design is therefore satisfactory. Note also that the approximate values of 3/8 and 7/8 could have been used for k and j, respectively. The calculated stresses would have been conservative because the actual values were smaller than the assumed values.

8.2.3 Comments on Arching Action

1) Using the traditional assumption that distributed loads act only within a beam length defined by 45-degree lines from the ends of the distributed load, it would have been possible to take advantage of so-called "arching action" to reduce the gravity load for which the lintel must be designed. Nevertheless, this measure is hardly necessary, because the required area of reinforcement is quite small in any case.

2) Even though it would have been possible to refine the flexural design (e.g., by reducing the required depth of the lintel, or including the mid-depth reinforcement in the bond beam in the calculation of flexural resistance), this additional design effort would not have been cost-effective. The goal is to simplify the design process, and the final layout of reinforcement.

8.3 Allowable-Stress Design of Curtain Walls

8.3.1 Background on Curtain Walls

In the first part of the structural design section of this book, we began with the design of panel walls, which can be designed as unreinforced masonry, and which span primarily in the vertical direction to transmit out-of-plane loads to the structural system. Panel walls are nonload-bearing masonry because they support gravity loads from self-weight only.

At this point, it is appropriate for us to study another type of nonload-bearing masonry, the curtain wall. Like panel walls, curtain walls carry gravity load from self-weight only and transmit out-of-plane loads to a structural frame. Unlike panel walls, however, curtain walls can be more than one story high, and span horizontally rather than vertically. Typical curtain wall construction is shown in Fig. 8.16.

A single wythe of masonry spans horizontally between columns, which support the roof. This type of construction can be used for industrial buildings, gymnasiums, theaters, and other buildings of similar configuration.

In previous sections dealing with panel walls, we have seen that because those walls are unreinforced, their design is governed by the flexural tensile strength of masonry. In previous examples with panel walls, using reasonable unfactored wind loads of about 20 lb/ft^2, the flexural tensile stresses in vertically spanning panel walls were comfortably within allowable values.

If we tried to use the same principles to design horizontally spanning curtain walls, however, they wouldn't work. In the figure above, the horizontal span between columns is at least 20 ft, about twice the typical vertical span of panel walls. Since moments increase as the square of the span, doubling the span would increase the flexural tensile stresses by a factor of 4. Even considering that allowable flexural tensile stresses parallel to bed joints in running bond are about twice as high as those normal to the bed joints (reflecting the interlocking nature of running bond), the calculated flexural tensile stresses in the direction of span would exceed the allowable values.

The most reasonable solution to this problem is to reinforce the masonry horizontally. Single-wythe curtain walls are commonly used for industrial buildings, where water-penetration resistance is not a primary design consideration.

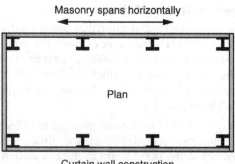

Figure 8.16 Plan view of typical curtain wall construction.

8.3.2 Examples of Use of Curtain Walls—Clay Masonry

Examples of use of curtain walls with clay masonry are shown in Fig. 8.17.

8.3.3 Example of Use of Curtain Walls—Concrete Masonry

Examples of use of curtain walls with concrete masonry are shown in Fig. 8.18.

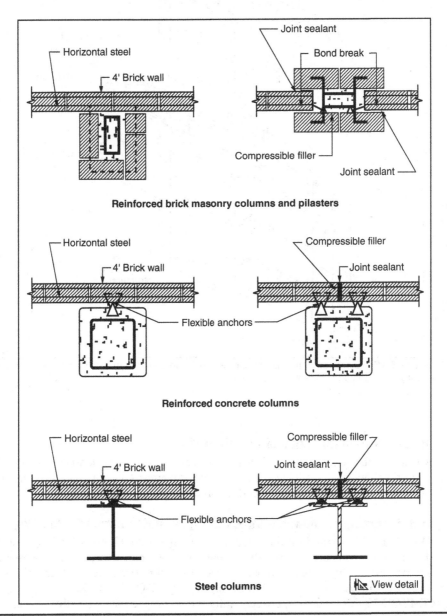

FIGURE 8.17 Examples of use of curtain walls of clay masonry. (*Source:* BIA Tech-Note 17L, "Panel and Curtain Walls.")

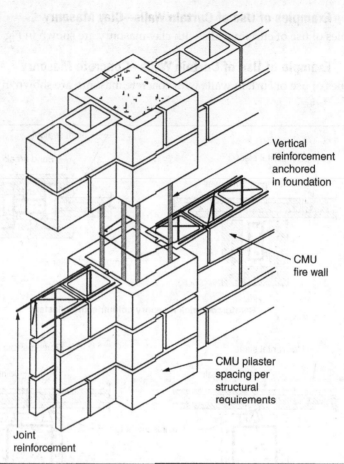

Figure 8.18 Examples of the use of curtain walls with concrete masonry. (*Source:* CMHA Tek 5-8A, "Details for Concrete Masonry Fire Walls.")

8.3.4 Structural Action of Curtain Walls

Curtain walls act as horizontal strips to transfer out-of-plane loads to vertical supporting members such as steel or reinforced concrete columns, or masonry pilasters (masonry columns partially embedded in the wall).

8.3.5 Example: Allowable-Stress Design of a Reinforced Curtain Wall

A curtain wall of standard modular clay units spans 20 ft between columns and is simply supported at each column. It has reinforcement consisting of W4.9 wire each face, every course. The curtain wall is subjected to a wind pressure $q = 32$ lb/ft². Design the curtain wall. As an initial assumption, use $f'_m = 2500$ lb/in². Referring to Table 1 of *TMS 602-22*, this would require clay units with a compressive strength of at least 6600 psi, and Type S mortar. Because we are designing a 1-ft wide strip, the uniformly distributed load, w, is the same as the wind pressure, q.

Allowable-Stress Design of Reinforced Masonry Elements

Maximum bending moment:

$$M = \frac{wL^2}{8}$$

Maximum shear:

$$V = \frac{wL}{2}$$

The governing loading combination has an allowable-stress load factor of 0.6 for wind load.

For a 1-ft strip,

$$M = \frac{wL^2}{8} = \frac{0.6 \times 32 \text{ lb/ft} \times (20 \text{ ft})^2}{8} \times 12 \text{ in./ft} = 11{,}520 \text{ lb-in.}$$

$$V = \frac{wL}{2} = \frac{0.6 \times 32 \text{ lb/ft} \times (20 \text{ ft})}{2} = 192 \text{ lb}$$

Stresses in reinforcement and masonry due to flexure are shown below. Because wires are located in every bed joint, b is taken as the nominal height of a clay masonry unit.

$$d = t - \text{cover} - \frac{d_b}{2} = 3.63 - 0.63 - 0.13 = 2.87 \text{ in.}$$

$$\rho = \frac{A_s}{bd} = \frac{0.049 \text{ in}^2}{2.67 \text{ in.} \times 2.87 \text{ in.}} = 0.00639$$

$$n = \frac{E_s}{E_m} = \frac{29 \times 10^6 \text{ psi}}{700 \times 2500 \text{ psi}} = 16.57$$

$$k = -n\rho + \sqrt{(n\rho)^2 + 2n\rho}$$

$$j = 1 - \frac{k}{3}$$

$$k = 0.366$$

$$j = 0.878$$

The moment above is for a 12-in. wide section of masonry. For flexural reinforcement spaced at 2.67 in., it is convenient to compute the moment on a 2.67-in. wide section.

$$f_s = \frac{M}{A_s jd} = \frac{11{,}520 \text{ lb-in.} \times \left(\frac{2.67 \text{ in.}}{12 \text{ in.}}\right)}{0.049 \text{ in}^2 \times 0.878 \times 2.87 \text{ in.}} = 20{,}759 \text{ lb/in}^2$$

$$f_b = \frac{2M}{jkbd^2} = \frac{2 \times 11{,}520 \text{ lb-in.} \times \left(\frac{2.67}{12}\right)}{0.878 \times 0.366 \times 2.67 \text{ in.} \times 2.87^2 \text{ in}^2} = 725 \text{ lb/in}^2$$

This analysis shows that the stress in reinforcement, 20.8 kips/in², is less than or equal to the allowable stress of 30 kips/in² (*TMS 402-22*, Section 8.3.3.2). The stress in the masonry, 725 lb/in², is less than or equal to the allowable flexural compressive stress of 0.45 f'_m, or 1125 lb/in² (TMS 402-22, Section 8.3.4.2.2).

Because this is a reinforced element subject to flexural tension, shearing capacity is calculated using Section 8.3.5.1.1 of TMS 402-22. Shear stresses are calculated by

$$f_v = \frac{V}{A_{nv}}$$

The allowable in-plane shear stress, F_v, is the summation of an allowable shear stress in masonry and an allowable stress in shear reinforcement:

$$F_v = (F_{vm} + F_{vs})\gamma_g$$

In this case, we shall have no shear reinforcement, so $F_{vs} = 0$.

$$F_{vm} = \frac{1}{2}\left[4.0 - 1.75\left(\frac{M}{Vd}\right)\right]\sqrt{f'_m} + 0.25\frac{P}{A_n}$$

As (M/Vd) increases, F_{vm} decreases. Because (M/Vd) need not be taken greater than 1.0 (TMS 402-22, Section 8.3.5.1.3), the most conservative (lowest) value of F_{vm} is obtained with (M/Vd) equal to 1.0. The acting shear stress in a 1-ft wide strip is calculated as follows:

$$f_v = \frac{V}{bd} = \frac{192 \text{ lb}}{12 \times 2.87 \text{ in}^2} = 5.6 \text{ lb/in}^2$$

Also, axial load, P, is zero:

$$F_{vm} = \frac{1}{2}[4.0 - 1.75(1.0)]\sqrt{f'_m}$$

$$F_{vm} = 1.13\sqrt{f'_m}$$

$$F_{vm} = 1.13\sqrt{2500} \text{ lb/in}^2 = 56.5 \text{ lb/in}^2$$

This exceeds the calculated shear stress, and our design is satisfactory so far.

Also, according to TMS 402-22, Equation 8-22,

$$F_v \le \left(2\sqrt{f'_m}\right)\gamma_g$$

This does not govern, and the shear design is acceptable without shear reinforcement.

8.3.6 Note on Simplification of Allowable-Stress Design for Flexure

From the above example, it is apparent that the flexural check requires most of the design time. For most practical combinations of f'_m and element dimensions, the values of k and j can be assumed rather than calculated:

$$k \approx \left(\frac{3}{8}\right)$$

$$j \approx \left(\frac{7}{8}\right)$$

This considerably decreases the time required for the flexural check.

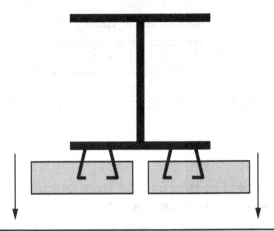

FIGURE 8.19 Anchors holding the ends of curtain wall strips to columns.

8.3.7 Design of Anchors for Curtain Wall

The design of the curtain wall would have to finish with the design of anchors holding the ends of the curtain wall strips, to the columns (Fig. 8.19).

For example, if anchors are spaced at 12 in. vertically, the load per anchor is

$$\text{Anchor load} = \frac{qbL}{2} = \frac{0.6 \times 32 \text{ lb/ft}^2 \times 1 \text{ ft} \times 20 \text{ ft}}{2} = 192 \text{ lb}$$

8.4 Allowable-Stress Design of Reinforced Bearing Walls

8.4.1 Introduction to Allowable-Stress Design of Reinforced Bearing Walls

In this section, we shall study the behavior and design of reinforced masonry wall elements subjected to combinations of axial force and out-of-plane flexure. In the context of engineering mechanics, they are beam-columns. In the context of the *TMS 402*, however, a "column" is an isolated masonry element rarely found in real masonry construction.

Masonry beam-columns, like those of reinforced concrete, are designed using moment-axial force interaction diagrams. Combinations of axial force and moment lying inside the diagram represent permitted designs; combinations lying outside, prohibited ones.

Unlike reinforced concrete, however, reinforced masonry beam-columns rarely take the form of isolated rectangular elements with four longitudinal bars and transverse ties. The most common form for a reinforced masonry beam-column is a wall, loaded out-of-plane by eccentric gravity load, alone or in combination with wind.

For example, Fig. 8.20 shows a portion of a wall, with a total effective width of $6t$ prescribed by Section 5.1.2 of *TMS 402-22*.

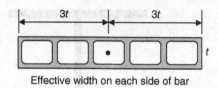

FIGURE 8.20 Effective width of a reinforced masonry bearing wall.

8.4.2 Background on Moment-Axial Force Interaction Diagrams by the Allowable-Stress Approach

Using the allowable-stress approach, we seek to construct interaction diagrams that represent combinations of axial and flexural capacity. This can be done completely by hand, or with the help of a spreadsheet.

8.4.3 Allowable-Stress Interaction Diagrams by Hand

By hand, we can compute three points (pure compression, pure flexure, and the allowable-stress balance point). We then connect those points by straight lines. As with the strength approach, if the balance point does not correspond to the maximum moment, the interaction diagram formed by connecting those points by straight lines may differ considerably from that obtained using more points and calculated by spreadsheet.

8.4.3.1 Pure Compression

For members with slenderness (h/r) less than or equal to 99 (the most common case),

$$P_a = (0.25 f'_m A_n + 0.65 A_{st} F_s)\left[1 - \left(\frac{h}{140r}\right)^2\right]$$

8.4.3.2 Pure Flexure

As before, the possible contribution of compressive reinforcement is small and can be neglected. For most cases, flexural capacity is governed by the allowable stress in reinforcement.

$$jd = d - \frac{kd}{3}$$
$$jd \approx \frac{7}{8}d$$
$$M = A_s F_s jd$$

8.4.3.3 Balance Point

First, locate the neutral axis under allowable-stress balanced conditions, as shown in Fig. 8.21.

Allowable-Stress Design of Reinforced Masonry Elements

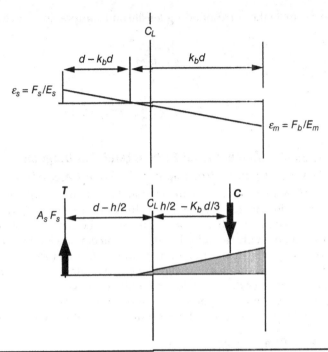

FIGURE 8.21 Location of neutral axis under allowable-stress balanced conditions.

Because strains vary linearly over the depth of the cross-section,

$$\frac{\varepsilon_m}{\varepsilon_s} = \frac{(F_b/E_m)}{(F_s/E_s)} = \frac{k_b d}{d - k_b d}$$

$$\left(\frac{F_b}{E_m}\right)(d - k_b d) = \left(\frac{F_s}{E_s}\right) k_b d$$

$$\frac{E_s}{E_m} \equiv n$$

$$\left(\frac{F_b}{E_m}\right) d - \left(\frac{F_b}{E_m}\right) k_b d = \left(\frac{F_s}{n E_m}\right) k_b d$$

$$k_b \left(\frac{F_b}{E_m} + \frac{F_s}{n E_m}\right) = \left(\frac{F_b}{E_m}\right)$$

$$k_b = \frac{F_b}{F_b + F_s/n}$$

So

$$k_b = \frac{n}{(F_s/F_b) + n}$$

Next, we calculate the corresponding tensile and compressive forces:

$$T = A_s F_s$$
$$C = k_b db F_b/2$$
$$P = C - T$$
$$M = T\left(d - \frac{h}{2}\right) + C\left(\frac{h}{2} - \frac{k_b d}{3}\right)$$

8.4.4 Example: Moment-Axial Force Interaction Diagram by the Allowable-Stress Approach (Hand Calculation)

Construct the moment-axial force interaction diagram by the allowable-stress approach for a nominal 8-in. concrete masonry wall, fully grouted, with $f'_m = 2000$ lb/in² and reinforcement consisting of #5 bars at 48 in., placed in the center of the wall.

Beam-columns with centrally located reinforcement can have moment-axial force interaction diagrams that differ in appearance from those of conventional beam-columns. This is even more so for allowable-stress interaction diagrams. For example, the balance point is located far below the point of maximum moment. Because of this, hand calculations are useful for some reinforced masonry beam-columns, but not all. In particular, they are not useful for most masonry walls loaded out-of-plane.

8.4.4.1 Pure Compression

Neglect slenderness effects (assume $h = 0$). Because reinforcement is not supported laterally, neglect it in compression.

$$P_a = (0.25 f'_m A_n + 0.65 A_{st} F_s)\left[1 - \left(\frac{h}{140r}\right)^2\right]$$

$$P_a = 0.25 \times 2000 \text{ lb/in}^2 \,(7.63 \text{ in.} \times 48 \text{ in.} - 0.31 \text{ in}^2) + 0.65 \times 0.31 \text{ in}^2 \times 0 \text{ lb/in}^2$$

$$P_a = 182{,}965 \text{ lb}$$

The capacity per foot of wall length will be the above value, divided by 4:

$$P_a = 45{,}741 \text{ lb}$$

8.4.4.2 Pure Flexure

Locate the neutral axis

$$\rho = \frac{A_s}{bd} = \frac{0.31 \text{ in}^2}{48 \text{ in.} \times 3.81 \text{ in.}} = 0.00170$$

$$n = \frac{E_s}{E_m} = \frac{29 \times 10^6 \text{ psi}}{900 \times 2000 \text{ psi}} = 16.11$$

$$k = -n\rho + \sqrt{(n\rho)^2 + 2n\rho} = 0.208$$

$$j = 1 - \frac{k}{3} = 0.931$$

$$M = A_s F_s j d$$

$$M = 0.31 \text{ in}^2 \times 32{,}000 \text{ lb/in}^2 \times 0.931 \times 3.81 \text{ in.}$$

$$M = 35{,}175 \text{ lb-in.}$$

The capacity per foot of wall length will be the above value, divided by 4:

$$M = 8794 \text{ lb-in.}$$

8.4.4.3 Balance Point
First, locate the neutral axis.

$$E_s = 29{,}000{,}000 \text{ lb/in}^2$$

$$E_m = 900 \, f'_m = 900 \times 2000 \text{ lb/in}^2 = 1{,}800{,}000 \text{ lb/in}^2$$

$$n = \frac{E_e}{E_m} = \frac{29}{1.80} = 16.11$$

$$F_s = 32{,}000 \text{ lb/in}^2$$

$$F_b = 0.45 \, f'_m = 0.45 \times 2000 \text{ lb/in}^2 = 900 \text{ lb/in}^2$$

$$k_b = \frac{n}{\left(F_s/F_b\right) + n} = \frac{16.11}{(32{,}000/900) + 16.11} = 0.312$$

Now calculate the corresponding axial force and moment:

$$T = A_s F_s$$

$$T = 0.31 \text{ in}^2 \times 32{,}000 \text{ lb/in}^2 = 9978 \text{ lb}$$

$$C = 1/2 \, (k_b d b F_b)$$

$$C = 1/2 \, (0.312 \times 3.81 \text{ in.} \times 48 \text{ in.} \times 900 \text{ psi}) = 25{,}677 \text{ lb}$$

$$P = C - T$$

$$P = 25{,}677 \text{ lb} - 9978 \text{ lb} = 15{,}698 \text{ lb}$$

$$M = T\left(d - \frac{h}{2}\right) + C\left(\frac{h}{2} - \frac{k_b d}{3}\right)$$

$$M = 9978 \text{ lb}\left(3.81 \text{ in.} - \frac{7.63 \text{ in.}}{2}\right) + 25{,}677 \text{ lb}\left(\frac{7.63 \text{ in.}}{2} - \frac{0.312 \times 3.81 \text{ in.}}{3}\right)$$

$$M = 0 + 87{,}784 \text{ lb-in.} = 87{,}784 \text{ lb-in.}$$

The capacities per foot of wall length will be the above values, divided by 4:

$$P = 2925 \text{ lb}$$

$$M = 21{,}946 \text{ lb-in.}$$

8.4.5 Plot of Allowable-Stress Interaction Diagram by Hand
The allowable-stress moment-axial force interaction diagram calculated above is plotted in Fig. 8.22.

As we shall shortly see, the points that we have calculated are correct. The form of the diagram is misleading, however, because the balance point is actually not the point of maximum moment. It is incorrect but very conservative to draw the diagram with a

282　Chapter Eight

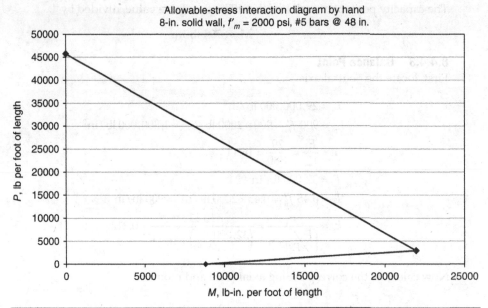

FIGURE 8.22 Plot of allowable-stress moment-axial force interaction diagram calculated by hand.

straight line from the balance point to the pure-compression point. This may not matter in fact because axial loads should generally be below the allowable-stress balance point.

8.4.6　Allowable-Stress Interaction Diagrams by Spreadsheet

To calculate allowable-stress interaction diagrams using a spreadsheet, first calculate the position of the neutral axis corresponding to the balance point (Fig. 8.23).

The location of the neutral axis can be determined:

$$\frac{\varepsilon_m}{\varepsilon_s} = \frac{(F_b/E_m)}{(F_s/E_s)} = \frac{k_b d}{d - k_b d}$$

$$\left(\frac{F_b}{E_m}\right)(d - k_b d) = \left(\frac{F_s}{E_s}\right)k_b d$$

$$\frac{E_s}{E_m} \equiv n$$

$$\left(\frac{F_b}{E_m}\right)d - \left(\frac{F_b}{E_m}\right)k_b d = \left(\frac{F_s}{nE_m}\right)k_b d$$

$$k_b\left(\frac{F_b}{E_m} + \frac{F_s}{nE_m}\right) = \left(\frac{F_b}{E_m}\right)$$

$$k_b = \frac{F_b}{F_b + F_s/n}$$

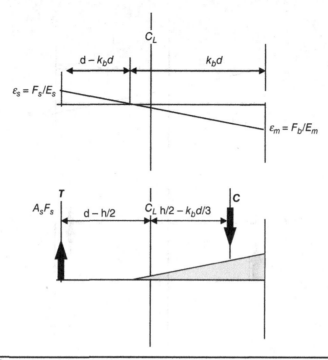

FIGURE 8.23 Conditions of strain and stress at allowable-stress balanced conditions.

So

$$k_b = \frac{n}{\left(F_s/F_b\right)+n}$$

For values of k less than that balanced value, the steel will reach its allowable stress before the masonry reaches its allowable stress. Combinations of axial force and moment can then be calculated, as can the corresponding moment (Fig. 8.24).

$$\varepsilon_m = \varepsilon_s\left(\frac{kd}{d-kd}\right)$$
$$f_b = \varepsilon_m E_m$$
$$C = kd \cdot b \cdot f_b/2$$
$$T = A_s F_s$$
$$P = C - T$$
$$M = T\left(d - \frac{h}{2}\right) + C\left(\frac{h}{2} - \frac{kd}{3}\right)$$

Similarly, for values of kd greater than the allowable-stress balance-point value, the steel will not have reached its allowable stress when the masonry is at its allowable stress. Compute the strain (and corresponding stress) in the steel by proportion, and

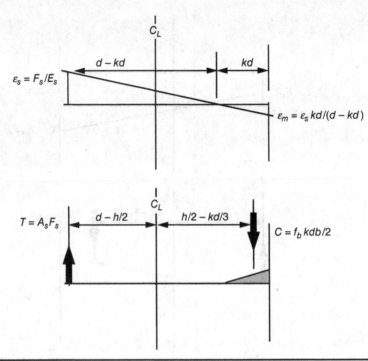

FIGURE 8.24 Conditions of strain and stress for values of k less than the allowable-stress balanced value.

find combinations of axial force and moment corresponding to each position of the neutral axis (Fig. 8.25):

$$\varepsilon_s = \varepsilon_m \left(\frac{d - kd}{kd}\right)$$

$$f_s = \varepsilon_s E_s$$

$$C = kd \times b \times F_b / 2$$

$$T = A_s f_s$$

$$P = C - T$$

$$M = T\left(d - \frac{h}{2}\right) + C\left(\frac{h}{2} - \frac{kd}{3}\right)$$

This calculation is limited by the pure compression resistance, calculated as noted above:

$$P_a = (0.25 f'_m A_n + 0.65 A_{st} F_s)\left[1 - \left(\frac{h}{140r}\right)^2\right]$$

Allowable-Stress Design of Reinforced Masonry Elements

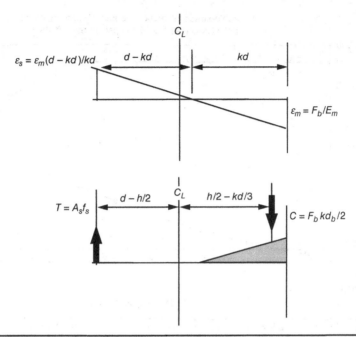

FIGURE 8.25 Conditions of strain and stress for values of *k* greater than the allowable-stress balanced value.

8.4.7 Example: Moment-Axial Force Interaction Diagram by the Allowable-Stress Approach (Spreadsheet Calculation)

Construct the moment-axial force interaction diagram by the allowable-stress approach for a nominal 8-in. CMU wall, fully grouted, with f'_m = 2000 lb/in² and reinforcement consisting of #5 bars at 48 in., placed in the center of the wall.

The effective width of the wall is $6t$, or 48 in. The spreadsheet and corresponding interaction diagram are shown below. As noted previously in this section, the results are interesting. Because the reinforcement is located at the geometric centroid of the section, and because the allowable-stress balance point does not reflect real behavior, the allowable-stress balance-point axial load (about 9000 lb) does not correspond to the maximum moment capacity. The diagram is also valid for partially grouted walls, provided that the neutral axis is within the face shell.

8.4.8 Plot of Allowable-Stress Interaction Diagram by Spreadsheet

The allowable-stress interaction diagram, calculated by spreadsheet, is shown in Fig. 8.26.
   Relevant cells from the spreadsheet are reproduced in Table 8.2.

8.4.9 Example: Allowable-Stress Design of Masonry Walls Loaded Out-of-Plane

Once we have developed the moment-axial force interaction diagram by the allowable-stress approach, the actual design simply consists of verifying that design actions (calculated using allowable-stress load factors) lie within the diagram.

286 Chapter Eight

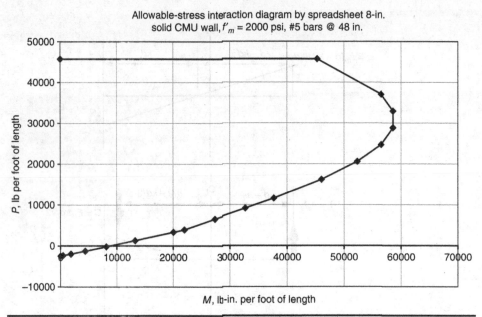

FIGURE 8.26 Plot of allowable-stress interaction calculated by spreadsheet.

TABLE 8.2 Spreadsheet for Calculating Allowable-Stress Interaction Diagram for Wall Loaded Out-of-Plane

Spreadsheet for calculating allowable-stress M-N diagram for solid masonry wall	
Total depth	7.625
f'_m	2000
E_m	1800000
f_b	900
E_s	29000000
F_s	32000
d	3.8125
$K_{balanced}$	0.311828
Tensile reinforcement	0.31
Width	48
because compression reinforcement is not tied, it is not counted	

	k	kd	f_b	C_{mass}	f_s	Moment	Axial Force
Pure compression						0	45711
Points controlled by masonry	2.22	8.46	900	182817	0	45304	45704
	1.8	6.86	900	148230	0	56513	37058
	1.6	6.10	900	131760	0	58606	32940
	1.4	5.34	900	115290	0	58606	28823

(continued)

Allowable-Stress Design of Reinforced Masonry Elements

	k	kd	f_b	C_{mass}	f_s	Moment	Axial Force
	1.2	4.58	900	98820	0	56513	24705
	1	3.81	900	82350	0	52327	20588
	0.8	3.05	900	65880	–3625	46047	16189
	0.6	2.29	900	49410	–9667	37675	11603
	0.5	1.91	900	41175	–14500	32704	9170
	0.4	1.53	900	32940	–21750	27210	6549
	0.311828	1.19	900	25679	–32000	21931	3940
Points controlled by steel	0.311828	1.19	900	25679	–32000	21931	3940
	0.3	1.14	851	23366	–32000	20044	3362
	0.25	0.95	662	15145	–32000	13232	1306
	0.2	0.76	497	9087	–32000	8084	–208
	0.15	0.57	351	4811	–32000	4356	–1277
	0.1	0.38	221	2019	–32000	1861	–1975
	0.05	0.19	105	478	–32000	448	–2360
	0.01	0.04	20	18	–32000	17	–2475

Consider the bearing wall designed previously as unreinforced. It has an eccentric axial load plus out-of-plane wind load of 40 lb/ft². The governing allowable-stress loading combination from the 2022 IBC is 0.6 D + 0.6 W. The eccentric axial load is 1050 lb/ft, of which 700 lb/ft is dead load, and 350 lb/ft is live load.

The wall is as shown in Fig. 8.27.

At each horizontal plane through the wall, the following condition must be met:

- Combinations of axial load and moment must lie within the moment-axial force interaction diagram

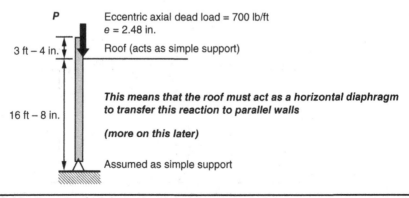

FIGURE 8.27 Example of reinforced bearing wall loaded out-of-plane.

To avoid having to check a large number of loading combinations and potentially critical locations, it is worthwhile to assess them first, and check only the ones that will probably govern.

Due to wind only, the unfactored moment on a 1-ft strip at the base of the parapet (roof level) is

$$M = \frac{wL^2_{parapet}}{2} = \frac{40 \text{ lb/ft} \times 3.33^2 \text{ ft}^2}{2} \times 12 \text{ in./ft} = 2661 \text{ lb-in.}$$

The maximum moment is close to that occurring at midheight. The moment from wind load is the superposition of one-half moment at the upper support due to wind load on the parapet only, plus the midspan moment in a simply supported beam with that same wind load:

$$M_{midspan} = -\frac{2661}{2} + \frac{wL^2}{8} = -\frac{2661}{2} + \frac{40 \text{ lb/ft} \times 16.67^2 \text{ ft}^2}{8} \times 12 \text{ in./ft} = 15{,}343 \text{ lb-in.}$$

The unfactored moment due to eccentric axial dead load is

$$M_{gravity} = Pe = 700 \text{ lb} \times 2.48 \text{ in.} = 1736 \text{ lb-in.}$$

Unfactored moment diagrams due to eccentric axial load and wind are as shown in Fig. 8.28.

Check the adequacy of the wall with 8-in. nominal units, a specified compressive strength, f'_m, of 2000 lb/in^2, and #5 bars spaced at 48 in. All design actions are calculated per foot of width of the wall. The governing loading combination is $0.6D + 0.6W$.

At the midheight of the wall, the axial force due to $0.6D$ is

$$P = 0.6(700 \text{ lb}) + 0.6(3.33 \text{ ft} + 8.33 \text{ ft}) \times 81 \text{ lb/ft} = 987 \text{ lb}$$

At the midheight of the wall, the ASD factored design moment, M, is given by

$$M = P\frac{e}{2} + M_{wind} = \left(\frac{1}{2}\right)0.6 \times 700 \text{ lb} \times 2.48 \text{ in.} + 0.6 \times 15{,}343 \text{ lb-in.} = 9727 \text{ lb-in.}$$

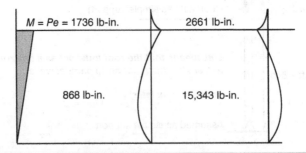

Figure 8.28 Unfactored moment diagrams due to eccentric axial load plus wind load.

In each foot of wall, the design actions are $P = 987$ lb, and $M = 9727$ lb-in. That combination lies within the interaction diagram of allowable capacities (Fig. 8.26), and the design is satisfactory.

In contrast to strength design, allowable-stress design of reinforced masonry walls loaded out of plane is not subject to maximum reinforcement limits, or to a secondary-moment check.

8.5 Allowable-Stress Design of Reinforced Shear Walls

8.5.1 Introduction to Allowable-Stress Design of Reinforced Shear Walls

In this section, we shall study the behavior and design of reinforced masonry shear walls. The discussion follows the same approach used previously for unreinforced masonry shear walls.

8.5.2 Design Steps for Allowable-Stress Design of Reinforced Shear Walls

Reinforced masonry shear walls must be designed for the effects of:

1) Gravity loads from self-weight, plus gravity loads from overlying roof or floor levels
2) Moments and shears from in-plane shear loads

Actions are shown in Fig. 8.29.

Flexural capacity of reinforced shear walls using allowable stress procedures is calculated using moment-axial force interaction diagrams as discussed in the section on masonry walls loaded out-of-plane.

Because this is a reinforced element subject to flexural tension, shearing capacity is calculated using Section 8.3.5.1.1 of *TMS 402-22*. Shear stresses are calculated by

$$f_v = \frac{V}{A_{nv}}$$

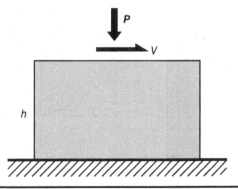

Figure 8.29 Design actions for reinforced masonry shear walls.

The allowable in-plane shear stress, F_v, is the summation of an allowable shear stress in masonry and an allowable stress in shear reinforcement:

$$F_v = (F_{vm} + F_{vs})\gamma_g$$

$$F_{vm} = \frac{1}{2}\left[4.0 - 1.75\left(\frac{M}{Vd}\right)\right]\sqrt{f'_m} + 0.25\frac{P}{A_n}$$

As (M/Vd) increases, F_{vm} decreases. Because (M/Vd) need not be taken greater than 1.0 (TMS 402-22, Section 8.3.5.1.2), the most conservative (lowest) value of F_{vm} is obtained with (M/Vd) equal to 1.0. This is shown in Fig. 8.30.

Just as in the strength design of reinforced masonry, this model assumes that shear is resisted by reinforcement crossing a hypothetical failure surface oriented at 45 degrees, as shown in Fig. 8.31.

The allowable resistance from reinforcement is taken as the area associated with each set of shear reinforcement, multiplied by the number of sets of shear reinforcement

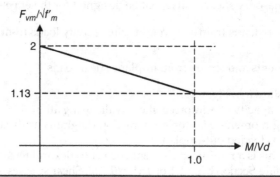

FIGURE 8.30 V_{nm} as a function of $(M_u/V_u d_v)$.

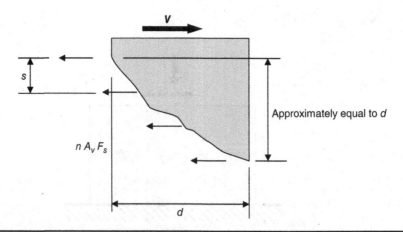

FIGURE 8.31 Idealized model used in evaluating the resistance due to shear reinforcement.

crossing the hypothetical failure surface, multiplied by the allowable stress in the shear reinforcement. Because the hypothetical failure surface is assumed to be inclined at 45 degrees, its projection along the length of the member is approximately equal to d, and number of sets of shear reinforcement crossing the hypothetical failure surface can be approximated by (d/s). The allowable stress corresponding to that allowable resistance divided by the net area of the cross-section

$$\text{Allowable resistance} = A_v F_s \left(\frac{d}{s}\right)$$

$$\text{Allowable stress} = A_v F_s \left(\frac{d}{s}\right)\left(\frac{1}{A_n}\right)$$

The actual failure surface may be inclined at a larger angle with respect to the axis of the wall, however. Also, all reinforcement crossing the failure surface may not yield. For both these reasons, the assumed resistance is decreased by an efficiency factor of 0.5. From *TMS 402-22*, Section 8.3.5.1.4,

$$F_{vs} = 0.5 \frac{A_v F_s d_v}{A_n s}$$

Finally, because shear resistance really comes from a truss mechanism in which horizontal reinforcement is in tension, and diagonal struts in the masonry are in compression, crushing of the diagonal compressive struts is controlled by limiting the total allowable shear stress F_v, regardless of the amount of shear reinforcement (Fig. 8.32).

For $(M/Vd_v) < 0.25$,

$$F_v \leq \left(3\sqrt{f'_m}\right)\gamma_g;$$

and for $(M/Vd_v) > 1.00$,

$$F_v \leq \left(2\sqrt{f'_m}\right)\gamma_g.$$

Interpolation is permitted between these limits (*TMS 402-22*, Section 8.3.5.1.2).

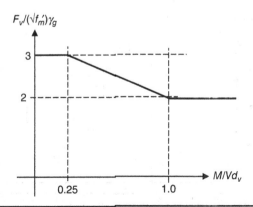

FIGURE 8.32 Maximum allowable shear stress as a function of (M/Vd).

If these upper limits on F_v are not satisfied, the cross-sectional area of the section must be increased.

8.5.3 Example: Allowable-Stress Design of Reinforced Clay Masonry Shear Wall

Consider the masonry shear wall shown in Fig. 8.33.

Design the wall. Unfactored in-plane lateral loads at each floor level are due to earthquake, and are shown in Fig. 8.34, along with the corresponding shear and moment diagrams.

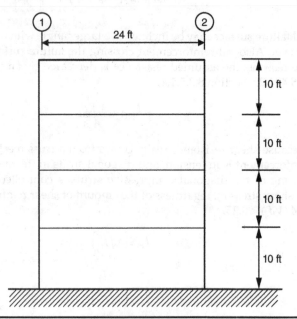

FIGURE 8.33 Reinforced masonry shear wall to be designed.

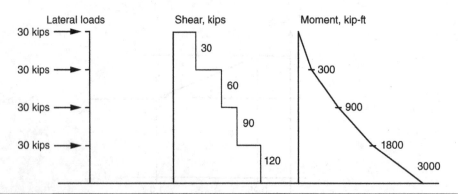

FIGURE 8.34 Unfactored in-plane lateral loads, shear and moment diagrams for reinforced masonry shear wall.

Allowable-Stress Design of Reinforced Masonry Elements

Assume an 8-in. nominal clay masonry wall, grouted solid, with Type S PCL mortar. The total plan length of the wall is 24 ft (288 in.), and its thickness is 7.5 in. Assume an effective depth d of 285 in.

	Clay Masonry
Unit strength	6600
Mortar	Type S
f'_m	2500
E_m	1.75×10^6
n	16.6
Reinforcement = Grade 60; $E_s = 29 \times 10^6$ psi	

Unfactored cumulative axial loads on the wall, including self-weight, are given in the table below:

Level (Top of Wall)	DL, kips	LL, kips
4	90	15
3	180	35
2	270	55
1	360	75

Check shear for the assumed wall thickness.
Use ASD Basic Load Combination 9 from the 2022 *IBC*: $0.6D + 0.7E$

$$V = 0.7 \times 120{,}000 \text{ lb} = 84{,}000 \text{ lb}$$
$$M = 0.7 \times 3000 \text{ kip-ft} = 2100 \text{ kip-ft}$$
$$P = 0.6 \times 360 \text{ kips} = 216 \text{ kips}$$

By *TMS 402-22* Section 8.3.5.1.1,

$$f_v = \frac{V}{A_{nv}} = \frac{84{,}000 \text{ lb}}{7.5 \times 288 \text{ in}^2} = 39.9 \text{ psi}$$

$$\frac{M}{Vd_v} = \frac{3000 \text{ kip-ft} \times 12 \text{ in./ft}}{120 \text{ kips} \times 288 \text{ in.}} = 1.04$$

The value of (M/Vd) need not be taken greater than 1.0.
The allowable in-plane shear stress, F_v, is the summation of an allowable shear stress in masonry and an allowable stress in shear reinforcement:

$$F_v = (F_{vm} + F_{vs})\gamma_g$$

$$F_{vm} = \frac{1}{2}\left[4.0 - 1.75\left(\frac{M}{Vd_v}\right)\right]\sqrt{f'_m} + 0.25\frac{P}{A_n}$$

$$F_{vm} = \frac{1}{2}[4.0 - 1.75(1.0)]\sqrt{2500} + 0.25 \times \frac{216 \text{ kips} \times 1000 \text{ lb/kip}}{7.50 \times 288 \text{ in}^2}$$

$$F_{vm} = 56.25 \text{ lb/in}^2 + 25 \text{ lb/in}^2 = 81.25 \text{ lb/in}^2$$

This exceeds the calculated shear stress of 39.5 lb/in², and no shear reinforcement is required for shear resistance. Shear reinforcement may be necessary to meet prescriptive seismic requirements.

Now consider the flexural design. The spreadsheet for this problem illustrates how to calculate an allowable-stress moment-axial force interaction diagram for this wall (Fig. 8.35). That spreadsheet is first used to check the wall with reinforcement consisting of #5 bars @ 4 ft.

The interaction diagram shows that the wall, as designed above, can resist the combination of axial load and moment (216 kips, 2100 kip-ft).

The design must also satisfy Section 8.3.4.2.1 of *TMS 402-22*:

For members having an *h/r* ratio not greater than 99,

$$P_a = (0.3 f'_m A_n + 0.65 A_{st} F_s)\left[1 - \left(\frac{h}{140r}\right)^2\right] \quad \text{TMS 402-16 Equation 8-16}$$

For members having an *h/r* ratio greater than 99,

$$P_a = (f'_m A_n + 0.65 A_{st} F_s)\left(\frac{70r}{h}\right)^2 \quad \text{TMS 402-22 Equation 8-17}$$

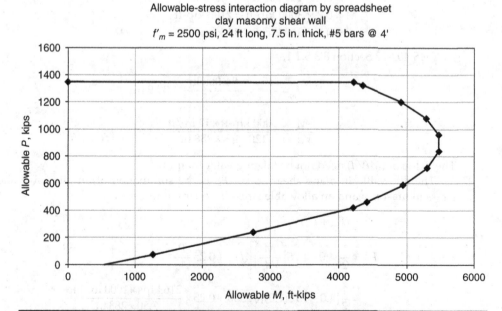

FIGURE 8.35 Plot of allowable-stress moment-axial force interaction diagram calculated by spreadsheet.

To calculate stiffness-related parameters for the wall, we use the average cross-section, corresponding to the gross section.

$$r = \frac{t}{\sqrt{12}} = \frac{7.5 \text{ in.}}{\sqrt{12}} = 2.17 \text{ in.}$$

$$\frac{kh}{r} = \frac{h}{r} = \frac{10 \times 12 \text{ in.}}{2.17 \text{ in.}} = 55.3$$

This is less than the transition slenderness of 99, so Equation 8-16 applies. Neglect the reinforcement because it is not laterally supported.

$$P_a = (0.3 f'_m A_n + 0.65 A_{st} F_s)\left[1 - \left(\frac{h}{140r}\right)^2\right]$$

$$P_a = (0.3 \times 1500 \text{ lb/in}^2 \times 7.5 \text{ in.} \times 24 \text{ ft} \times 12 \text{ in./ft})\left[1 - \left(\frac{10 \text{ ft} \times 12 \text{ in./ft}}{140 \times 2.17 \text{ in.}}\right)^2\right]$$

$$P_a = (972 \text{ kips})[0.843] = 819.6 \text{ kips}$$

This far exceeds the factored axial load (even from the critical combination D+L), and the design is satisfactory.

8.5.4 Minimum and Maximum Reinforcement Ratios for Flexural Design by the Allowable-Stress Approach

The allowable-stress provisions of *TMS 402-22* have no requirements for minimum nor maximum flexural reinforcement, except for a maximum-reinforcement requirement for special reinforced masonry shear walls.

In the provisions of *TMS 402-22*, E_m and F_b are constant multiples of f'_m and F_s ranges from 40% to 53% of f_y. The net result is that the allowable-stress balanced steel area, though having no physical significance of its own, is actually a constant fraction of the strength balanced area:

$$\rho_{bal}^{strength} = 0.85 \beta_1 \left(\frac{f'_m}{f_y}\right)\left(\frac{\varepsilon_{mu}}{\varepsilon_{mu} + \varepsilon_y}\right)$$

$$\rho_{bal}^{allowable} = \left(\frac{1}{2}\right)k_b\left(\frac{F_b}{F_s}\right) = \left(\frac{1}{2}\right)\frac{n}{\left(\frac{F_s}{F_b}\right)+n}\left(\frac{F_b}{F_s}\right)$$

$$= \frac{nF_b}{nF_s\left(n+\frac{F_s}{F_b}\right)}$$

TMS 402-22 replaces the allowable stresses, F_m and F_b with f'_m and f_y in *TMS 402-22*.

$$\rho_{max} = \frac{nf'_m}{nf_y\left(n+\frac{f_y}{f'_m}\right)} \qquad \text{TMS 402-22 Equation 8-18}$$

Using the simplifying assumption that $E_m \approx 800 f'_m$,

f'_m, lb/in²	$\rho_{bal}^{allowable}/\rho_{bal}^{strength}$
1500	0.347
2000	0.347
2500	0.347

Therefore, a design in which flexural reinforcement is kept below the allowable-stress balanced steel area, will coincidentally result in a design in which flexural reinforcement is below the balanced area for strength design as well.

8.5.5 Additional Comments on the Design of Reinforced Shear Walls

Reinforced masonry shear walls, like unreinforced ones, are relatively easy to design by either strength or allowable-stress approaches. Although shear capacities per unit area is small, the available area is large.

With either strength or allowable-stress approaches, it is rarely necessary to use shear reinforcement. In this sense, the best shear design strategy for shear walls is like that for shear design of beams—use enough cross-sectional area to eliminate the need for shear reinforcement. Seismic requirements may still dictate some shear reinforcement, however.

8.6 Required Details for Reinforced Bearing Walls and Shear Walls

Bearing walls that resist out-of-plane lateral loads, and shear walls, must be designed to transfer lateral loads to the floors above and below. Examples of such connections are shown below. These connections would have to be strengthened for regions subject to strong earthquakes or strong winds. Section 1604.8.2 of the 2022 *IBC* has additional requirements for anchorage of diaphragms to masonry walls. Section 12.11 of *ASCE 7-22* has additional requirements for anchorage of structural walls for structures assigned to Seismic Design Categories C and higher.

8.6.1 Typical Details of Wall-to-Foundation Connections

As shown in Fig. 8.36, CMU walls (or the inner CMU wythe of a drainage wall) must be connected to the concrete foundation. Bond breaker should be used only between the outer veneer wythe and the foundation.

8.6.2 Typical Details of Wall-to-Floor Connections

Examples of a wall-to-floor detail are shown in Figs. 8.37 and 8.38. In the latter detail (floor or roof planks oriented parallel to walls), the planks are actually cambered. They are shown on the outside of the walls so that this camber does not interfere with the coursing of the units. Some designers object to this detail because it could lead to spalling of the cover. If it is modified so that the planks rest on the face shells of the walls, then the thickness of the topping must vary to adjust for the camber, and form boards must be used against both sides of the wall underneath the planks, so that the concrete or grout that is cast into the bond beam does not run out underneath the cambered beam.

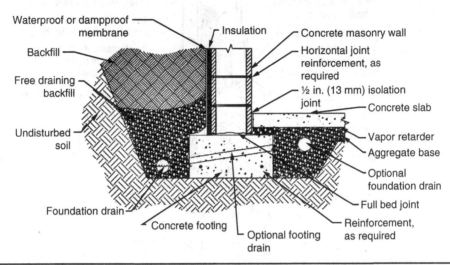

FIGURE 8.36 Example of floor-to-wall connection. (*Source:* Figure 1 of NCMC TEK 05-03.)

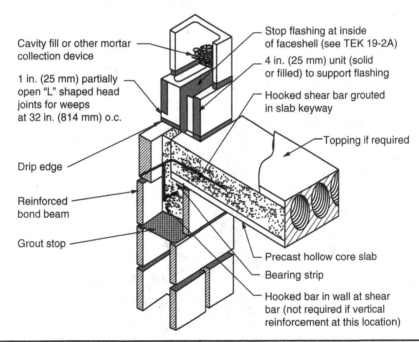

FIGURE 8.37 Example of wall-to-floor connection, planks perpendicular to wall. (*Source:* Figure 14 of CMHA TEK 05-07A.)

8.6.3 Typical Details of Wall-to-Roof Connections

An example of a wall-to-roof detail is shown in Fig. 8.39.

8.6.4 Typical Details of Wall-to-Wall Connections

Typical details of wall-to-wall connections are shown in Fig. 8.40.

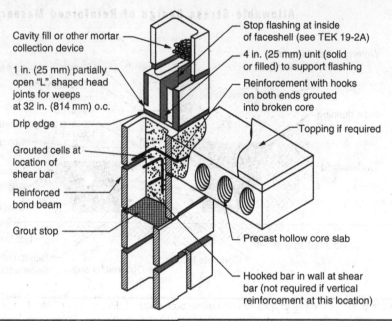

FIGURE 8.38 Example of wall-to-floor connection, planks parallel to wall. (*Source:* Figure 15 of CMHA TEK 05-07A.)

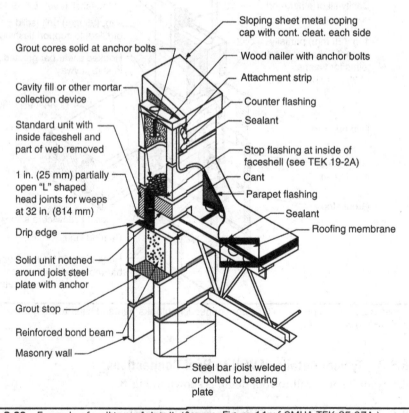

FIGURE 8.39 Example of wall-to-roof detail. (*Source:* Figure 11 of CMHA TEK 05-07A.)

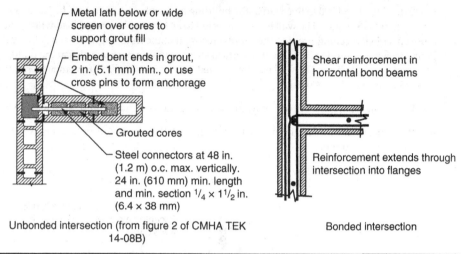

FIGURE 8.40 Examples of wall-to-wall connection details. (*Source:* From Figure 2 of CMHA TEK 14-08B.)

8.7 Problems

8.1 Design a simply supported, fully grouted, reinforced bearing wall subjected to eccentric axial loads of 500 lb dead and 250 lb live load per foot of plan length, combined with out-of-plane wind load of 25 psf. All loads are unfactored. The axial-load eccentricity is 2.5 in. and the story height is 10 ft. Assume a specified compressive strength of masonry of 2000 psi. Use nominal 8-in. CMU and the self-weight from Table 5.6 (81 lb/ft² for fully grouted units). Use the following load conditions.

Part 1 Considering gravity loads only, check the existing design for compliance with *TMS 402-22*.

Part 2 Repeat Part 1 including wind load.

The wall is as shown below:

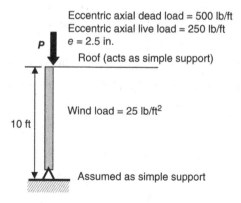

8.2 In the building shown below, the roof is assumed to span longitudinally between the two gable walls. The 1-ft strip of CMU shown below is subjected to unfactored eccentric gravity loads of

800 lb dead load and 200 lb live load at the building apex, whose height is 16 ft. The eccentricity is 3 in. Include self-weight. The wall is also subjected to an out-of-plane wind load whose magnitude is not specified. A ceiling provides horizontal restraint at the mid-height of each gable wall. As an initial design assumption, idealize this vertical strip assuming zero moment at the building apex, the ceiling, and the base. The wall is fully grouted, with 8-in. units, reinforcement consisting of #4 bars at 48 in., and f'_m = 2000 psi.

Part 1 Considering gravity loads only, check the existing design for compliance with *TMS 402-22*.

Part 2 Repeat Part 1 including wind load. Calculate the maximum unfactored wind load the vertical strip can support.

The wall is as shown below:

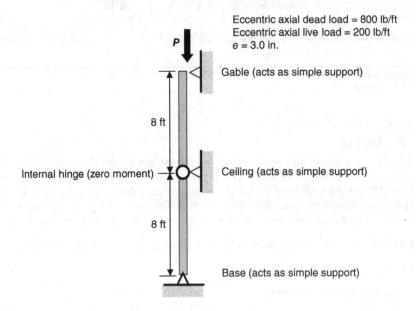

*8.3 Repeat Problem 8.2 using a single two-span beam. This assumes a continuous beam-column at the height of the ceiling and at the base. Comment on how the maximum permissible wind load changes.

Part 1 Considering gravity loads only, check the existing design for compliance with *TMS 402-22*.

Part 2 Repeat Part 1 including wind load. Calculate the maximum unfactored wind load the vertical strip can support.

The wall is as shown below:

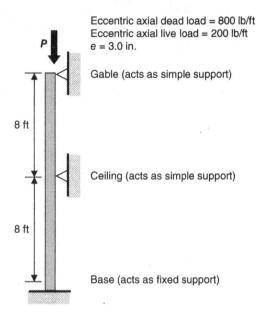

8.4 Extend the problem of Fig. 7.21 to a two-story building. Change the typical story height to 10 ft. Gravity loads on a typical floor are equal to those on the roof. Try a nominal 8-in. CMU wall, ungrouted, with face-shell bedding and Type S PCL mortar. Use a specified masonry compressive strength of 2000 psi. Assume a unit density of 115 lb/ft^3, and use the self-weight from Table 5.4 (33 lb/ft^2). If this does not work, list an alternate way to solve the problem using 8-in. units.

*8.5 Using the design of Problem 6.4, and continuing the same load at each diaphragm level, how many stories could the building have?

---

*Denotes problems intended for graduate students.

CHAPTER 9
Comparison of Design by the Allowable-Stress Approach Versus the Strength Approach

In this chapter, designs carried out by the allowable-stress approach of *TMS 402-22* are compared with those carried out by the strength approach. The masonry code committee has devoted considerable effort to harmonize these two design approaches, so that they give quite similar results. Some differences still exist, however, and it is useful to be aware of them.

In this chapter, designs are compared in general terms by comparing the load side and the resistance side of each set of design equations—strength and allowable-stress.

9.1 Comparison of Allowable-Stress and Strength Design of Unreinforced Panel Walls

Allowable-stress design and strength design for unreinforced panel walls loaded out-of-plane can be compared in tabular form, as shown in Table 9.1. In that table, for allowable-stress design, load effects are denoted by W, and resistances by R. Using strength design, load effects are the unfactored load effects W, multiplied by the load factor for wind (1.0). Nominal resistances are proportional to the same section properties as for allowable-stress design, but the modulus of rupture is about 2.5 times the allowable stress. Design resistances are therefore proportional to $2.5R$, multiplied by the strength-reduction factor of 0.6.

For a given load effect W, the strength design provisions require about 1.1 times as much resistance as the allowable-stress provisions. This difference is not significant for practical purposes.

TABLE 9.1 Comparison of Allowable-Stress and Strength Design for Unreinforced Panel Walls

Allowable Stress Design		Strength Design	
Load Effects	Resistances	Load Effects	Resistances
0.6W	R	1.0W	$\phi(2.5R)$
W	1.67R	1.0W	0.6(2.5R)
		W	1.50R
			1.50R

9.2 Comparison of Allowable Stress Design and Strength Design of Unreinforced Bearing Walls

Allowable-stress design and strength design for unreinforced bearing walls loaded out-of-plane are not as easy to compare as they are for unreinforced panel walls. This is because bearing walls are subjected to combinations of axial load and moment from eccentric gravity load, out-of-plane wind, or both.

For the critical strength loading combination (0.9D + 1.0W) location (mid-height of the wall), and criterion (maximum tensile stress), required resistances are compared in Table 9.2.

TABLE 9.2 Comparison of Allowable-Stress and Strength Design for Unreinforced Bearing Walls

Allowable Stress Design		Strength Design	
Load Effects	Resistances	Load Effects	Resistances
0.6W	R	1.0W	$\phi(2.5R)$
W	1.67R	1.0W	0.6(2.5R)
		W	1.5R
			1.5R

For a given load effect W, the strength design provisions requires about 1.1 times as much resistance as the allowable-stress provisions. This difference is not significant for practical purposes.

9.3 Comparison of Allowable Stress Design and Strength Design of Unreinforced Shear Walls

Assessing the comparative level of safety of strength design and allowable stress design is relatively simple. Assume that the critical loading combination for strength design will be 0.9D + 1.0W, because this gives the smallest shear capacity for the third shear strength criterion, which usually controls. Allowable-stress design for shear uses a peak shear stress equal to (3/2) times the average stress, so the load effect is essentially multiplied by 1.5, or (3/2). Resistances are calculated based on an allowable resistance R. The equations for nominal shear capacity for strength design, divided by the equations for allowable-stress shear capacity, produce capacity ratios varying from 1.5 for the third shear criterion, to 2.5 for the first and second (300/120). This discrepancy will probably be addressed in future editions of TMS 402. Using a ratio of 2.50 for comparison purposes, the net result is shown in Table 9.3:

TABLE 9.3 Comparison of Allowable-Stress and Strength Design for Unreinforced Shear Walls

Allowable Stress Design		Strength Design	
Load Effects	Resistances	Load Effects	Resistances
0.6(1.5)W	R	1.0W	$\phi(2.5)R$
W	1.11R	W	0.80(2.5)R
			2.0R

If allowable stress design and strength design are compared in terms of equal load effects, and if the strength-design resistances are higher than their allowable-stress counterparts by a factor that is usually 2.5, then the final results for strength design require about half as much cross-sectional area as is required by allowable-stress. This discrepancy should be addressed in future editions of TMS 402.

9.4 Comparison of Allowable-Stress and Strength Designs for Anchor Bolts

Allowable-stress design and strength design for anchor bolts are somewhat simple to compare, because the two sets of equations in *TMS 402-22* are harmonized. The resistance (capacity) sides of allowable-stress equations for failure modes governed by masonry are about one-third of the corresponding strength equations. For pullout, the corresponding factor is 0.4. For steel failure, the factor is 0.5.

Because anchor bolts can be subjected to many different loading combinations, a typical load factor for strength design is difficult to establish. For purposes of these course notes, it will be assumed that wind governs (which is often the case), and therefore a typical weighted load factor (representing gravity plus wind loads) is about 1.0 for strength design, and about 0.6 for allowable-stress design.

Because strength reduction factors are different for behavior governed by masonry (0.65) and behavior governed by steel (0.75), they are presented separately in Table 9.4 and Table 9.5, respectively.

TABLE 9.4 Comparison of Allowable-Stress and Strength Design for Anchor Bolts, Masonry Controls

Allowable Stress Design		Strength Design	
Load Effects	Resistances	Load Effects	Resistances
0.6W	R	1.0W	$\phi(1/0.33)R$
W	1.67R	W	0.65(3.0)R
			1.95R

TABLE 9.5 Comparison of Allowable-Stress and Strength Design for Anchor Bolts, Steel Controls

Allowable Stress Design		Strength Design	
Load Effects	Resistances	Load Effects	Resistances
0.6W	R	1.0W	$\phi(1/0.5)R$
W	1.67R	W	0.75(2)R
			1.5R

In each case, we can see that the allowable-stress and strength equations for anchor bolt design have been harmonized so that they give similar results.

9.5 Comparison of Allowable-Stress and Strength Designs for Reinforced Beams and Lintels

1. The design objective that the lintel be deep enough to preclude the need for transverse reinforcement means that the flexural design is governed by stresses in tensile reinforcement in each case. Allowable-stress design for flexure uses $D + L$. Resistances are based on an allowable stress of 32,000 lb/in² for Grade 60 reinforcing bars. Assume that the critical loading combination for strength design is $1.2D + 1.6L$, or about $1.4(D + L)$. Resistances are based on specified yield stress (60,000 lb/in²). There is practically no difference between internal lever arms for the two-design approaches. The net result for tension-controlled specimens is shown in Table 9.6:

TABLE 9.6 Comparison of Allowable-Stress and Strength Design for Reinforced Beams and Lintels (as Governed by Flexure)

Allowable Stress Design		Strength Design	
Load Effects	Resistances	Load Effects	Resistances
$D + L$	32	$1.4(D + L)$	ϕ 60
		$1.4(D + L)$	0.90(60)
		$1.4(D + L)$	54
		$D + L$	38.6

If allowable stress design and strength design are compared in terms of equal load effects, the resistance for strength design is higher than for allowable stress design, by a factor of (38.6/32), or 1.21. While allowable stress design is more conservative, the actual difference in required reinforcement is quite small.

2. The required depth of the lintel can also be compared for each design approach. Allowable-stress design for shear uses $D + L$. Resistances are based on an allowable stress of $\sqrt{f'_m}$. Assume that the critical loading combination for

strength design will be $1.2D + 1.6L$, or about $1.4(D + L)$. Resistances are based on $2.25\sqrt{f'_m}$. The net result is shown in Table 9.7:

TABLE 9.7 Comparison of Allowable-Stress and Strength Design for Reinforced Beams and Lintels (as Governed by Shear)

| Allowable Stress Design || Strength Design ||
Load Effects	Resistances	Load Effects	Resistances
$D + L$	$0.5(2.25)\sqrt{f'_m}$	$1.4(D + L)$	$\phi(2.25)\sqrt{f'_m}$
$D + L$	$1.13\sqrt{f'_m}$	$1.4(D + L)$	$0.80(2.25)\sqrt{f'_m}$
		$1.4(D + L)$	$1.8\sqrt{f'_m}$
		$D + L$	$1.29\sqrt{f'_m}$

If allowable stress design and strength design are compared in terms of equal load effects, the required depth for allowable stress design is essentially equal to that for strength design.

9.6 Comparison of Allowable-Stress and Strength Designs for Reinforced Curtain Walls

Because the design of reinforced curtain walls is almost always governed by flexure, comparison of the results of allowable-stress and strength design approaches is similar to that of beams and lintels governed by flexure.

9.7 Comparison of Allowable-Stress and Strength Designs for Reinforced Bearing Walls

For most masonry walls of practical interest, design is controlled by stresses in tensile reinforcement, and the shape of the compressive stress block (triangular vs. rectangular) does not make much difference. Allowable-stress design for flexure uses $D + L$. Resistances are based on an allowable stress of 32,000 lb/in² for Grade 60 reinforcing bars. Assume that the critical loading combination for strength design is $1.2D + 1.6L$, or about $1.4(D + L)$. Resistances are based on specified yield stress (60,000 lb/in²). There is practically no difference between internal lever arms for the two design approaches. The net result is shown in Table 9.8:

TABLE 9.8 Comparison of Allowable-Stress and Strength Design for Reinforced Bearing Walls (Governed by Flexure)

| Allowable Stress Design || Strength Design ||
Load Effects	Resistances	Load Effects	Resistances
$D + L$	32	$1.4(D + L)$	ϕ 60
		$1.4(D + L)$	0.90(60)
		$1.4(D + L)$	54
		$D + L$	38.6

If allowable stress design and strength design are compared in terms of equal load effects, the resistance for strength design is higher than for allowable stress design, by a factor of (38.6/32), or 1.21. While allowable stress design is more conservative, the actual difference in required reinforcement is quite small.

9.8 Comparison of Allowable-Stress and Strength Designs for Reinforced Shear Walls

1. For design governed by flexure, the comparison is basically similar to what we have seen for beams. Flexural design is governed by stresses in tensile reinforcement in each case. Allowable-stress design for flexure uses 0.6W. Resistances are based on an allowable stress of 32,000 lb/in² for Grade 60 reinforcing bars. Assume that the critical loading combination for strength design is 1.0W. Resistances are based on yield stress (60,000 lb/in²). There is practically no difference between internal lever arms for the two design approaches. The net result is shown in Table 9.9:

TABLE 9.9 Comparison of Allowable-Stress and Strength Design for Reinforced Shear Walls (as Governed by Flexure)

Allowable Stress Design		Strength Design	
Load Effects	Resistances	Load Effects	Resistances
0.6W	32	1.0W	ϕ 60
W	53.3	W	0.90(60)
		W	54

If allowable stress design and strength design are compared in terms of equal load effects, the resistance for strength design is essentially equal to that for allowable stress design.

2. For design governed by shear, the comparison is similar to shear for beams, but the loading combination is different. Allowable-stress design for shear uses 0.6W. Resistances are based on an allowable stress of about $1.13\sqrt{f'_m}$. Assume that the critical loading combination for strength design is 1.0W. Minimum resistances are based on $2.25\sqrt{f'_m}$. The net result is shown in Table 9.10:

TABLE 9.10 Comparison of Allowable-Stress and Strength Design for Reinforced Shear Walls (as Governed by Shear)

Allowable Stress Design		Strength Design	
Load Effects	Resistances	Load Effects	Resistances
0.6W	$1.13\sqrt{f'_m}$	1.0W	$\phi(2.25)\sqrt{f'_m}$
W	$1.88\sqrt{f'_m}$	W	$0.80(2.25)\sqrt{f'_m}$
		W	$1.80\sqrt{f'_m}$

If allowable stress design and strength design are compared in terms of equal load effects, the resistance for strength design is essentially equal to that for allowable stress design.

CHAPTER 10
Lateral Load Analysis of Shear Wall Structures

10.1 Introduction to Lateral Load Analysis of Shear Wall Structures

The preceding chapters contained an introduction to the behavior and design of masonry shear walls by the strength approach and by the allowable-stress approach. In the design examples, it was clear that all walls would resist equal shears. In the design examples with a perforated wall, it was clear that all wall segments would resist equal shears. This, however, is not generally the case.

Consider, for example, the building of Fig. 10.1, with a uniformly distributed wind pressure (wind from the south) of 35 lb/ft^2.

The openings on the east wall introduce two problems:

- How are north-south shears distributed between the two walls oriented in that direction, and what is the resulting building response?
- How is the shear on the east wall distributed among the three segments comprising that wall?

The classical design steps for this problem are as follows:

1) Classify the floor diaphragm as "rigid" or "flexible."
2) Based on that classification, solve for the distribution of shear to walls and to wall segments.

In the following sections, each of those steps is explained in more detail. The steps are then simplified, greatly reducing the required effort for most problems. Finally, readers are encouraged to use the simplified steps for rigid and for flexible diaphragms to bound the answer, eliminating the need to classify the diaphragms as rigid or flexible.

10.2 Classification of Horizontal Diaphragms as "Rigid" or "Flexible"

When a wall-type building is loaded laterally, its response, and the distribution of lateral load to its shear walls, depends on the in-plane flexibility of its horizontal diaphragms with respect to the in-plane flexibility of its walls. Horizontal diaphragms

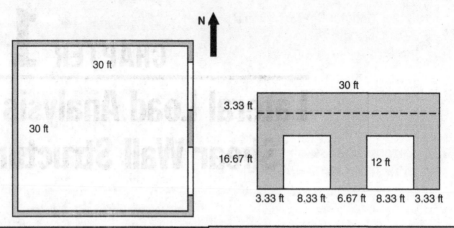

FIGURE 10.1 Example of building with perforated walls.

are classified as "rigid," "flexible," or "semi-rigid" in accordance with Section 1604.4 of the 2024 *IBC*, which also references Section 12.3.1 of *ASCE 7-22*, as modified by Section 1613.5.1 of the 2024 *IBC*.

- Diaphragms whose in-plane diaphragm deformation is less than two times the in-plane wall deformation (average story drift), or which meet certain prescriptive requirements, are required to be considered as "rigid" (Section 12.3.1 of *ASCE 7-22*);
- Diaphragms whose in-plane deformation is greater than two times the in-plane wall deformation (average story drift), or which meet certain prescriptive requirements, are permitted to be considered as "flexible;" and
- Diaphragms not classified as "rigid" or "flexible" according to the above criteria are considered "semi-rigid," and their flexibility must be explicitly considered in distributing wind or seismic forces (Section 12.3.1 of *ASCE 7-22*).

While some computer programs permit analysis of buildings including the effects of in-plane deformations of horizontal diaphragms, this is generally unnecessary. For almost all practical cases, it is sufficient to classify the diaphragm as either "rigid" or "flexible," and then to analyze the building with the help of simplifying assumptions consistent with that classification. For preliminary design, it is even possible to first analyze the building assuming that the diaphragm is "rigid," then analyze it assuming that the diaphragm is "flexible," and take the more critical of the two cases to arrive at design actions for each shear wall.

10.2.1 Prescriptive Characteristics of "Rigid" Diaphragms

In accordance with Section 12.3.1.2 of *ASCE 7-22*, horizontal diaphragms are permitted to be considered as rigid if they can be described as follows:

- Diaphragms of concrete slabs or concrete-filled metal deck with span-to-depth ratios of 3 or less in structures that have no horizontal irregularities.

10.2.2 General Characteristics of "Flexible" Diaphragms

In accordance with Section 12.3.1.1 of *ASCE 7-22*, horizontal diaphragms are permitted to be considered as flexible if they can be described as follows:

- Diaphragms constructed of untopped steel decking or wood structural panels in structures in which the vertical elements are masonry shear walls.

10.3 Lateral Load Analysis of Shear Wall Structures with Rigid Floor Diaphragms

Many possible methods are available for the lateral-load analysis of shear-wall structures with rigid floor diaphragms. These are enumerated below; example analyses are conducted using each numbered method; and the numbered methods are then compared with respect to solution accuracy and time. Finally, based on those comparisons, recommendations are made for the best method for analyzing such structures.

Method 1: The first method (referred to in this section as Method 1) is the linear elastic, finite element analysis of walls with openings (e.g., SAP 2000©), assuming rigid floor diaphragms. This is reasonably quick with modern programs, but it is very difficult to adequately address cracking.

Most computer programs developed for the analysis of buildings consider floor diaphragms to be rigid in their own planes. Each floor level has only three horizontal degrees of freedom (two horizontal displacements and rotation about a vertical axis). This method, while reasonable for frame structures, whose floors are much more rigid in their own planes than the vertical frames, is not correct for wall structures, whose horizontal diaphragms are usually about as rigid as their vertical diaphragms (walls).

Using this method, because all but three horizontal degrees are condensed out at each floor level, in-plane actions in floor diaphragms cannot be calculated. For some loading conditions, in-plane actions can be inferred from differences in shears in vertical elements above and below each floor level. This process is always tedious, however, and is also inaccurate for cases involving multi-modal response to dynamic loads.

Method 2: The second method (referred to in this chapter as Method 2), consists of the approximate analysis of panels with openings, followed by an analysis of the building. In order of increasing complexity, several variations of Method 2 are available:

Method 2a: Consider only shearing deformations of walls. Assume that shearing stiffness is proportional to length in plan. Ignore plan torsion due to eccentricity between center of stiffness of building, and line of application of lateral load.

Method 2b: This is the same as Method 2a, but considers plan torsion.

Method 2c: This is the same as Method 2b, but considers flexural and shearing deformations of wall segments.

In the remainder of this section, evidence will be presented for the following observations:

- Method 1 can be accurate, provided that cracking is correctly addressed. It requires a computer, a suitable finite element program, and considerable work.
- Method 2a gives reasonably accurate results with very little effort and is therefore quite cost-effective for design.
- Method 2b gives almost the same accuracy as Method 2a, and requires significantly more effort. For most buildings, the effects of plan torsion are not significant, and Method 2b is not cost-effective.
- Method 2c generally requires much more effort than Method 2b, is not more accurate than Method 2a and is not justified.

10.3.1 Example Application of Method 1

A reference answer for the example problem of this section is obtained using the finite element method. The roof diaphragm is assumed rigid. A masonry modulus of 1.5×10^6 lb/in^2 is used. The applied lateral load of 35 lb/ft^2 results in a load of 12,600 lb applied through the plan center of the building, at the level of the roof diaphragm. Using the example structure of Fig. 10.1, the solution of Fig. 10.2 is obtained. That solution is also summarized in Tables 10.1 and 10.2.

> *Modeling and analysis time: 30 minutes*

The structure rotates very slightly counter-clockwise. The plan center of the building displaces 0.0070 in. to the north. Shears applied to the tops of the walls, just below the roof, are shown in the left-hand figure above. The right-hand figure shows the distribution of shears in the segments of the east wall.

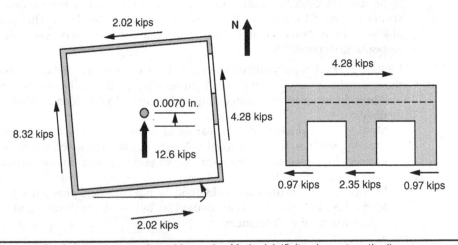

Figure 10.2 Solution to example problem using Method 1 (finite element method).

10.3.2 Simplest Hand Method (Method 2a)

In the simplest hand method (Method 2a), consider only shearing deformations of the walls. Assume that shearing stiffness is proportional to length in plan. Ignore plan torsion due to eccentricity between center of stiffness of building, and line of application of lateral load.

Plan torsion can be ignored if the structure has reasonable plan length of walls in each principal plan direction. The deformation of wall segments can be idealized as due to shearing deformations only provided that the segments have an aspect ratio (ratio of height to plan length) of about 1.0 or less.

10.3.2.1 Shearing Stiffness of Each Wall Segment

The shearing deformation of a wall segment with height H and plan length L is shown in Fig. 10.3.

The lateral deflection at the level of the diaphragm is

$$\Delta = \frac{VH}{A'G}$$

where G = shearing modulus of masonry
H = wall height
A' = effective shear area of the wall, taken for convenience as the product of the wall length in plan, L, and the wall thickness, t

Assume that G, t, and H are uniform. Therefore the deflection is proportional to V and inversely proportional to L:

$$\Delta \propto \frac{V}{L}$$

Finally, the stiffness of the segment is the applied shear divided by the deflection and is simply proportional to the plan length of the wall segment.

$$\text{Stiffness} = \frac{V}{\Delta} \propto L$$

10.3.2.2 Distribution of Shears among Wall Segments

So the stiffness of each wall is proportional to its length in plan. In the elastic range, shears are distributed to the walls in proportion to their stiffnesses; that is, in proportion to their plan lengths.

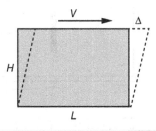

FIGURE 10.3 Shearing deformation of a wall segment.

10.3.3 Example of Simplest Hand Method (Method 2a)

To illustrate the simplest hand method (Method 2a), apply it to the example problem previously considered. The plan lengths of shear walls are shown in Fig. 10.4.

Given the total shear of 12.6 kips, the shear to Wall 2 and Wall 4 are easily computed using the proportions of wall lengths. The shear in each wall is the total shear, multiplied by the ratio of the plan length of that wall divided by the total length of walls in the direction of applied load. Because plan torsion is neglected, there are no shears in the walls oriented perpendicular to the applied load.

$$V_2 = 12.6 \text{ kips} \left(\frac{L_1}{L_{total}}\right) = 12.6 \text{ kips} \left(\frac{30 \text{ ft}}{30 + 3.33 + 6.67 + 3.33 \text{ ft}}\right) = 12.6 \left(\frac{30}{43.33}\right) = 8.72 \text{ kips}$$

$$V_4 = 12.6 \text{ kips} \left(\frac{L_2}{L_{total}}\right) = 12.6 \text{ kips} \left(\frac{3.33 + 6.67 + 3.33 \text{ ft}}{30 + 3.33 + 6.67 + 3.33 \text{ ft}}\right) = 12.6 \left(\frac{13.33}{43.33}\right) = 3.88 \text{ kips}$$

$$V_1 = V_3 = 0$$

The resulting shears in Wall 2 and Wall 4 are shown in Figs. 10.5 and 10.6.

The 3.88 kips applied to the east wall will be distributed to the three segments of that wall in proportion to their plan lengths. The equations for wall shears are provided below, and the calculated shears in each wall segment are shown in Tables 10.1 and 10.2.

$$V_A = V_C = 3.88 \text{ kips} \left(\frac{L_A}{L_{total}}\right) = 3.88 \text{ kips} \left(\frac{3.33 \text{ ft}}{3.33 + 6.67 + 3.33 \text{ ft}}\right) = 3.88 \left(\frac{3.33}{13.33}\right) = 0.97 \text{ kips}$$

$$V_B = 3.88 \text{ kips} \left(\frac{L_B}{L_{total}}\right) = 3.88 \text{ kips} \left(\frac{6.67 \text{ ft}}{3.33 + 6.67 + 3.33 \text{ ft}}\right) = 3.88 \left(\frac{6.67}{13.33}\right) = 1.94 \text{ kips}$$

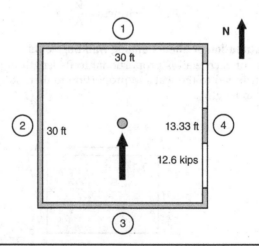

FIGURE 10.4 Plan lengths of wall segments for example problem using simplest hand method (Method 2a).

Lateral Load Analysis of Shear Wall Structures

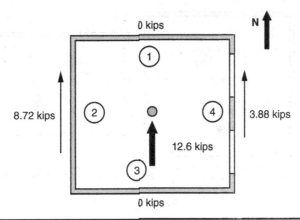

FIGURE 10.5 Shears in Wall 2 and Wall 4 of example using the simplest hand method (Method 2a).

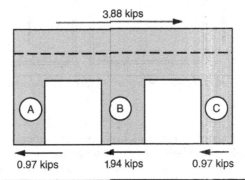

FIGURE 10.6 Shears in wall segments of Wall 4 using the simplest hand method (Method 2a).

These results are close to those obtained by finite-element analysis, but the analysis time is much less. The results are also summarized in Tables 10.1 and 10.2, which are discussed later.

Analysis time: 10 minutes

10.3.4 More Complex Hand Method (Method 2b)

Now modify Method 2a to consider plan torsion due to eccentricity between center of stiffness of building, and line of application of lateral load.

10.3.4.1 Concept of Center of Rigidity

To do this, we must introduce the concept of the center of rigidity, or shear center. The center of rigidity of a building is that plan location through which lateral load must be applied so as not to produce any twisting of the building in plan.

The center of rigidity of a symmetrical building is located at the geometric centroid of the building's plan area. Examples are shown in Fig. 10.7.

316 Chapter Ten

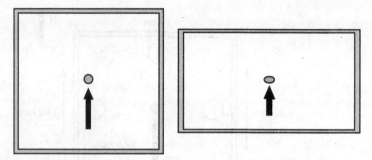

FIGURE 10.7 Examples of location of center of rigidity for symmetrical buildings.

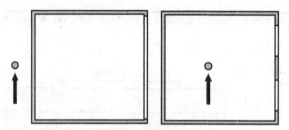

FIGURE 10.8 Examples of location of center of rigidity for unsymmetrical buildings.

If the building is unsymmetrical, however, the center of rigidity is not located at the geometric centroid of the building's plan area. The classic example is the channel section, for which the shear center is actually located outside the plan area. Examples are shown in Fig. 10.8.

To include the effects of plan torsion, it is necessary to locate the center of rigidity of the building. Lateral loading applied through some arbitrary point is then treated as loading through the center of rigidity (which causes no torsional response), plus a plan torsion about the center of rigidity (which produces pure torsional response). This is shown in Fig. 10.9.

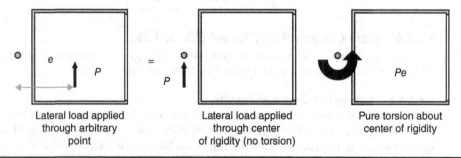

FIGURE 10.9 Decomposition of lateral load into a lateral load applied through the center of rigidity plus pure torsion about the center of rigidity.

10.3.4.2 Location of Center of Rigidity

The location of the center of rigidity along any building axis depends on the relative stiffnesses of the walls of the building that are oriented perpendicular to that axis. Refer to Fig. 10.10.

Define k_{yi} as the stiffness in the y direction of Wall i. If only shearing deformations are considered, the stiffness of each wall is proportional to its plan area. Then if the load P is applied through the center of rigidity (no twist), each wall will deflect laterally an equal amount in the y direction:

$$\Delta_{y1} = \Delta_{y2} = \Delta_y$$

Each wall applies a force on the underside of the roof diaphragm, equal to the wall's stiffness multiplied by that deflection. This is shown by the free-body diagram of Fig. 10.11.

Taking moments about the point of application of the external load P, rotational equilibrium of the roof requires that:

$$k_{y1}\Delta_y \cdot x_1 = k_{y2}\Delta_y \cdot x_2$$

Canceling the common term Δy, and again noting that if only shearing deformations are considered, the forces applied by each wall are proportional to that wall's plan area, the above equation locates the line of action of the applied load P at the geometric centroid of the wall areas.

Along the x axis, the geometric centroid of the wall areas is given by:

$$\bar{x} = \frac{\sum k_{yi} x_i}{\sum k_{yi}} = \frac{\sum \text{Area}_{yi} x_i}{\sum \text{Area}_{yi}}$$

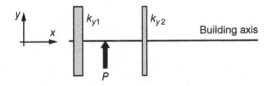

FIGURE 10.10 Location of the center of rigidity in one direction.

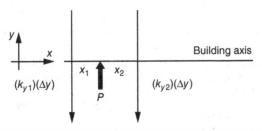

FIGURE 10.11 Free-body diagram of diaphragm showing applied loads and reactions from shear walls.

So the location of the center of rigidity along the x axis is given by

$$\bar{x}_r = \frac{\sum k_{yi} x_i}{\sum k_{yi}} = \frac{\sum \text{Area}_{yi} x_i}{\sum \text{Area}_{yi}}$$

And similarly, if k_{yx} is the stiffness in the x direction of Wall i, the location of the center of rigidity along the y axis is given by:

$$\bar{y}_r = \frac{\sum k_{xi} y_i}{\sum k_{xi}} = \frac{\sum \text{Area}_{xi} y_i}{\sum \text{Area}_{xi}}$$

10.3.4.3 Response to Lateral Load Applied through an Arbitrary Point

As introduced above, once the center of rigidity is located in plan, any lateral load can be treated as the superposition of a load through the center of rigidity (producing no twist), plus a moment equal to the load times its eccentricity, acting about the center of rigidity (producing only twist).

In Fig. 10.12, a load P, acting in the y direction with an eccentricity e_x along the x axis, is decomposed into that same load P, acting in the y direction through the center of rigidity, plus a counter-clockwise moment Pe_x about the center of rigidity. Load in the x direction is handled in an analogous way.

Now let's examine the response of the structure under each of those load cases.

10.3.4.4 Response of the Structure due to Lateral Load Applied through Center of Rigidity

Due only to the lateral load applied through the center of rigidity, the structure does not twist (Fig. 10.13).

Shear forces are produced only in those walls oriented parallel to the direction of applied load. The shear forces are proportional to the shear stiffnesses (plan areas) of the walls:

$$F_{xi} = 0$$

$$F_{yi} = \left(\frac{k_{yi}}{\sum k_{yi}}\right) P = \left(\frac{\text{Area}_{yi}}{\sum \text{Area}_{yi}}\right) P$$

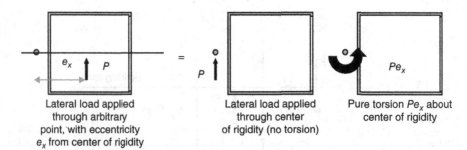

Lateral load applied through arbitrary point, with eccentricity e_x from center of rigidity

Lateral load applied through center of rigidity (no torsion)

Pure torsion Pe_x about center of rigidity

Figure 10.12 Decomposition of lateral load into lateral load through center of rigidity plus torsion about the center of rigidity.

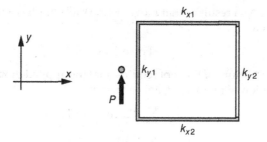

FIGURE 10.13 Lateral load applied through the center of rigidity.

The displacement of the structure in the y direction is:

$$\Delta_y = \frac{P_y}{\sum k_{yi}}$$

Analogous expressions apply for load in the x direction.

10.3.4.5 Response of the Structure due to Torsional Moment Applied at Center of Rigidity

As shown in Fig. 10.14, due only to the torsional moment applied at the center of rigidity, the structure undergoes twist only. The center of rigidity does not translate.

The force in each wall depends on that wall's stiffness and perpendicular distance from the center of rigidity.

Let x_i and y_i be the perpendicular distances from Wall i to the center of rigidity. Then if the roof rotates in plan through some angle θ, the force exerted by each wall on the roof is proportional to that wall's shear stiffness times the displacement of the top of the wall in its own plane. The displacement of each wall in its own plane is the product of the angle θ and the perpendicular distance of the wall from the center of rigidity. To simplify the calculation, forces from each wall can be computed separately in the x and y directions.

For example, in Fig. 10.14, Wall 1 is located at a perpendicular distance y_1 from the center of rigidity. As a result of a counter-clockwise rotation θ of the roof about the center of rigidity, the top of Wall 1 moves to the left (parallel to the x axis) a

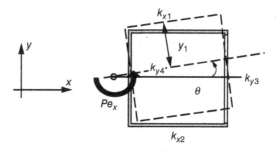

FIGURE 10.14 Pure rotation in plan of a structure with lateral load applied through the center of rigidity.

distance $\theta \cdot y_1$. As a result of that movement, Wall 1 applies a force on the underside of the roof, equal to:

$$\text{Force}_{x1} = k_{x1} \cdot \theta \cdot y_i$$

Rotational equilibrium of the roof requires that the applied moment, Pe_x, be equilibrated by the summation of moments from each wall:

$$P \cdot e_x = \sum (\text{Force}_{xi} \cdot y_i + \text{Force}_{yi} \cdot x_i)$$

$$P \cdot e_x = \sum (k_{xi} y_i^2 + k_{yi} x_i^2) \theta$$

This lets us solve for the plan rotation, θ:

$$\theta = \frac{Pe_x}{J}$$

The shear force applied to Wall 1 is then

$$\text{Force}_{x1} = k_{k1} \cdot \theta \cdot y_i = \frac{Pe_x}{J} y_1 k_x$$

In general,

$$\text{Force}_{xi} = \frac{P_y e_x}{J} y_i k_{xi}$$

$$\text{Force}_{yi} = \frac{P_y e_x}{J} x_i k_{yi}$$

10.3.4.6 Response of the Structure due to Direct Shear plus Plan Torsion

Finally, consider a structure loaded by a combination of direct shear plus the torsional moment applied at the center of rigidity (Fig. 10.15). The structure undergoes displacement as calculated above, and twist as calculated above.

$$\bar{x} = \frac{\sum k_{yi} x_i}{\sum k_{yi}}$$

$$\bar{y} = \frac{\sum k_{xi} y_i}{\sum k_{xi}}$$

$$\Delta_x = \frac{P_x}{\sum k_{xi}}$$

$$\Delta_y = \frac{P_y}{\sum k_{yi}}$$

$$\theta = \frac{P_y e_x + P_x e_y}{J}$$

$$\text{Force}_{xi} = \left(\frac{k_{xi}}{\sum k_{xi}}\right) P_x + \left(\frac{k_{xi} y_i}{J}\right)(P_x e_y + P_y e_x)$$

$$\text{Force}_{yi} = \left(\frac{k_{yi}}{\sum k_{yi}}\right) P_y + \left(\frac{k_{yi} x_i}{J}\right)(P_x e_y + P_y e_x)$$

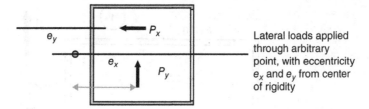

FIGURE 10.15 Structure loaded by a combination of load through the center of rigidity plus plan torsion about the center of rigidity.

10.3.4.7 Example of More Complex Hand Method

Now apply these principles to the structure considered in this section (Fig. 10.16).

The center of rigidity is calculated using the equations below. As shown in Fig. 10.17, the center of rigidity is located at 5.77 ft from the line of action of the applied load.

$$\bar{x} = \frac{\sum k_{yi} x_i}{\sum k_{yi}} = \frac{30(0) + 13.33(30)}{30 + 13.33} = 9.23 \text{ ft}$$

$$e_x = 15 \text{ ft} - 9.23 \text{ ft} = 5.77 \text{ ft}$$

$$e_y = 0$$

$$J = \sum (k_{xi} y_i^2 + k_{yi} x_i^2)$$

$$J = 2(30)15^2 + (30)9.23^2 + 13.33(30 - 9.23)^2$$

$$J = 21{,}806 \text{ kip-ft}$$

Now calculate the shear forces in each wall. Because Wall 2 and Wall 4 are oriented parallel to the direction of the applied lateral force, they experience direct shear plus additional shear due to plan torsion. Because Wall 1 and Wall 3 are oriented perpendicular to the direction of the applied lateral force, they experience only shear due to plan torsion.

Wall 1:

$$\text{Force}_{xi} = \left(\frac{k_{xi}}{\sum k_{xi}}\right) P_x + \left(\frac{k_{xi} y_i}{J}\right)(P_x e_y + P_y e_x)$$

$$\text{Force}_{xi} = \left(\frac{k_{xi} y_i}{J}\right)(P_y e_x)$$

$$\text{Force}_{x1} = \left(\frac{k_{x1} y_1}{J}\right)(P_y e_x)$$

$$\text{Force}_1 = \left(\frac{30 \cdot 15 \text{ ft}}{21{,}806}\right)(P_y \cdot 5.77 \text{ ft}) = 0.12 P_y = 1.50 \text{ kips}$$

322 Chapter Ten

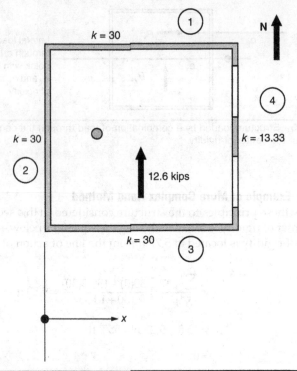

Figure 10.16 Application of rigid-diaphragm analysis to the structure considered in this section (Method 2b).

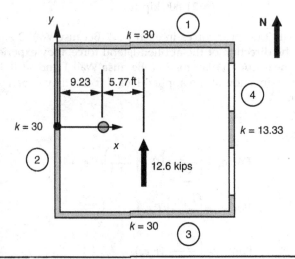

Figure 10.17 Location of center of rigidity for the example of this section (Method 2b).

Wall 3:

$$\text{Force}_{x3} = \left(\frac{k_{x3}y_3}{J}\right)(P_y e_x)$$

$$\text{Force}_3 = \left(\frac{30 \cdot 15\,\text{ft}}{21,806}\right)(P_y \cdot 5.77\,\text{ft}) = 0.12 P_y = 1.50\,\text{kips}$$

Wall 2:

$$\text{Force}_{yi} = \left(\frac{k_{yi}}{\sum k_{yi}}\right) P_y + \left(\frac{k_{yi} x_i}{J}\right)(P_x e_y + P_y e_x)$$

$$\text{Force}_{y2} = \left(\frac{k_{y2}}{\sum k_{yi}}\right) P_y + \left(\frac{k_{y2} x_2}{J}\right)(P_y e_x)$$

$$\text{Force}_{y2} = \left(\frac{30}{30+13.33}\right) P_y + \left(\frac{30 \cdot 9.23 x_2}{21,806}\right)(P_y \cdot 5.77\,\text{ft})$$

$$\text{Force}_{y2} = 0.692 P - 0.073 P$$

$$\text{Force}_{y2} = 8.72\,\text{kips} - 0.92\,\text{kips} = 7.80\,\text{kips}$$

Wall 4:

$$\text{Force}_{yi} = \left(\frac{k_{yi}}{\sum k_{yi}}\right) P_y + \left(\frac{k_{yi} x_i}{J}\right)(P_x e_y + P_y e_x)$$

$$\text{Force}_{y4} = \left(\frac{k_{y4}}{\sum k_{yi}}\right) P_y + \left(\frac{k_{y4} x_4}{J}\right)(P_y e_x)$$

$$\text{Force}_{y4} = \left(\frac{13.33}{30+13.33}\right) P_y + \left(\frac{13.33 \cdot (30-9.23)}{21,806}\right)(P_y \cdot 5.77\,\text{ft})$$

$$\text{Force}_{y4} = 0.308 P + 0.073 P$$

$$\text{Force}_{y4} = 3.88\,\text{kips} + 0.92\,\text{kips} = 4.80\,\text{kips}$$

The final shear forces acting on the walls due to load applied through the center of rigidity, and due to plan torsion about the center of rigidity, are shown separately in Fig. 10.18, and combined in Fig. 10.19.

Finally, distribute the shear of 4.80 kips to the segments of the east wall in proportion to their plan lengths, as shown in Fig. 10.20.

These results are quite close to those obtained by finite-element analysis. The results are also summarized in Tables 10.1 and 10.2, which are discussed later.

> Analysis time: 60 minutes

10.3.5 Most Complex Hand Method (Method 2c)

The most complex hand method (Method 2c) is similar to the more complex hand method (Method 2b) discussed immediately above, with the additional complication

324 Chapter Ten

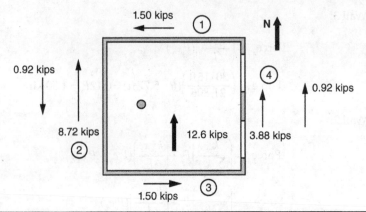

FIGURE 10.18 Shear forces acting on walls due to direct shear and due to torsion (Method 2b).

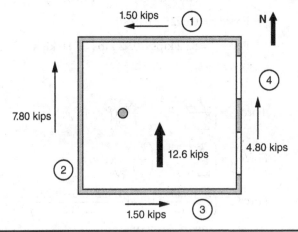

FIGURE 10.19 Combined shear forces acting on walls of example structure (Method 2b).

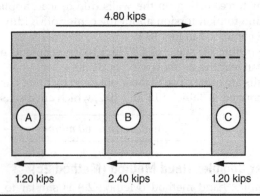

FIGURE 10.20 Distribution of shears to segments of the east wall of example structure (Method 2b).

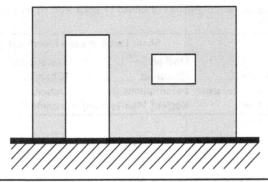

FIGURE 10.21 Example of perforated wall with segments of unequal height.

that the stiffness of each wall segment includes flexural stiffness as well as shearing stiffness. In previously published versions of that method, this is often accomplished by modifying the shearing stiffness of each wall segment by a factor that depends on the aspect ratio of that segment.

Because Method 2c is inherently more complex than Method 2b, the time involved in it must be even greater. This increased time does not always result in increased accuracy, however, because any variant of Method 2 has problems in handling perforated walls in which the wall segments have unequal heights (such as that shown in Fig. 10.21). Such segments cannot simply be idealized as subjected to equal displacements at the diaphragm levels. Some previously published methods for applying Methods 2 to such systems even lead to the counter-intuitive and clearly suspect conclusion that the stiffness of walls is increased by perforating them. As a consequence, Method 2c is not pursued further here.

10.3.6 Comparison of Results from Each Method

In Table 10.1 are compared the results obtained for shear forces in the walls and wall segments of this example structure, using Method 1 (the finite element reference method), and variations on Method 2 (hand methods).

In Table 10.2 are presented the same results, but now organized by method, and including the percent error (compared to the reference solution of Method 1) and the required time.

10.3.7 Comments on Analysis of Shear-Wall Structures with Rigid Diaphragms

1) Using Method 1 (finite element analysis) as a reference, the simplest hand method (Method 2a), which considers wall shearing deformations only, and neglects plan torsion, gives acceptable results for this example and is very efficient in terms of time.

2) Extending Method 2a to include plan torsion (Method 2b), requires much more time, and produces results that are not much more accurate.

3) Although Method 2b might appear more accurate because it correctly predicts shears in perpendicular walls (Walls 1 and 3 in this example) due to plan

TABLE 10.1 Comparison of Results Obtained by Each Method for Calculating Shear-Wall Forces by Each Method

Element	Shear Force in Each Element, kips			
	Method 1 (Finite Element Method)	Method 2a (Shearing Deformations Only, Neglect Plan Torsion)	Method 2b (Shearing Deformations Only, Include Plan Torsion)	Method 2c (Shearing and Flexural Deformations)
Wall 1	2.02	0	1.50	?
Wall 2	8.32	8.72	7.80	?
Wall 3	2.02	0	1.50	?
Wall 4a	0.97	0.97	1.20	?
Wall 4b	2.35	1.94	2.40	?
Wall 4c	0.97	0.97	1.20	?

TABLE 10.2 Comparison of Results Obtained by Each Method for Calculating Shear-Wall Forces by Each Method

Analysis Method	Element	Shear, kips	% Error	Required Time
Method 1 (finite element method)	Wall 1	2.02	Used as reference	30 min, computer required
	Wall 2	8.32		
	Wall 3	2.02		
	Wall 4a	0.97		
	Wall 4b	2.35		
	Wall 4c	0.97		
Method 2a (shearing stiffness only, neglect plan torsion)	Wall 1	0	– (Not critical)	10 min, no computer required
	Wall 2	8.72	5%	
	Wall 3	0	– (Not critical)	
	Wall 4a	0.97	0%	
	Wall 4b	1.94	17%	
	Wall 4c	0.97	0%	
Method 2b (shearing stiffness only, include plan torsion)	Wall 1	1.50	– (Not critical)	60 min, no computer required
	Wall 2	7.80	7%	
	Wall 3	1.50	– (Not critical)	
	Wall 4a	1.20	24%	
	Wall 4b	2.40	2%	
	Wall 4c	1.20	24%	
Method 2c (shearing and flexural stiffness)			Not as accurate as Method 1	Probably 120 min, no computer required

torsion, those calculated shears are not critical for design. Critical shears in those walls occur under lateral loads acting parallel to the wall orientation. In this case, for example, shears in the perpendicular walls are 1.50 kips for a northward lateral load of 12.6 kips. If the same lateral load were applied in the EW direction, Walls 1 and 3 would each have a shear of half that applied load, or 6.3 kips.

4) Further extending Method 2b to include flexural as well as shearing deformations (Method 2c) is not productive. It requires much more time, and produces results that are not necessarily any better. Hand methods following Method 2c present conceptual difficulties for openings of different heights. For example, they can sometimes predict that a wall with irregular openings will have greater in-plane stiffness than an otherwise identical wall with no openings.

10.3.8 Conclusions Regarding the Lateral Load Analysis of Low-Rise Buildings with Rigid Diaphragms

1) For shear wall buildings with rigid diaphragms, the distribution of shears to individual walls can generally be determined efficiently and with sufficient accuracy by considering only shearing deformations of the walls (i.e., by assuming that wall stiffness is proportional to plan area, or simply to plan length if walls are of equal thickness), and by neglecting plan torsion. This method presumes that the building has a reasonable number of shear walls in each principal plan direction.

2) If more accuracy is desired, the distribution of shears to individual walls can be determined efficiently by linear elastic finite element analysis.

3) More sophisticated hand methods (e.g., including plan torsion, or considering flexural as well as shearing deformations) are generally not cost-effective.

10.4 Lateral Load Analysis and Design of Shear Wall Structures with Flexible Floor Diaphragms

10.4.1 Introduction to Lateral Load Analysis and Design of Shear Wall Structures with Flexible Floor Diaphragms

In the previous section, it was noted that the classical approach to analyzing structures including the effect of horizontal diaphragm flexibility, is first classify the horizontal diaphragm as "rigid" or as "flexible" compared to the vertically oriented lateral force-resisting system, and then to evaluate the actions on the shear walls comprising the lateral force-resisting system. The beginning of this section continues with that approach. It finishes, however, with what might be termed "the simplest of all possible worlds." For preliminary design, it is even possible to first analyze the building assuming that the diaphragm is "rigid," then analyze it assuming that the diaphragm is "flexible," and take the more critical of the two cases to arrive at design actions for each shear wall.

10.4.2 "Exact" Approach to Flexible Diaphragms

General-purpose finite element programs, and a few building analysis programs, permit floor diaphragms to be analyzed as elements with in-plane flexibility (e.g., as membrane elements). Effects of in-plane floor flexibility can be included in the analysis, and floor member actions can be evaluated. While this approach appears correct, its accuracy decreases greatly if the floor diaphragm is cracked.

10.4.3 Approximate Approach to Flexible Diaphragms

In cases involving flexible diaphragms, floor actions and structural response can usually be approximated by assuming that the diaphragm is completely flexible compared to the vertical elements that support it. In other words, the diaphragm can be designed as a series of beam elements acting in the horizontal plane, and supported by vertical elements. This approach is adopted in this section. Even more simply, diaphragm reactions (shears on shear walls), can be estimated based on horizontal tributary areas.

10.4.4 Example: Analysis of Shear-Wall Building with Flexible Diaphragms

Consider, for example, the building of the previous section, with a uniformly distributed wind pressure (wind from the south) of 35 lb/ft^2. The building is shown in Fig. 10.22.

Because the left and right supports (Walls 2 and 4) are very stiff compared to the diaphragm, the diaphragm behaves like a simply supported beam, and the reactions on its supporting walls are simply $\frac{1}{2}V$ for each wall. This solution is shown in Fig. 10.23.

As before, the 6.3 kips applied to the east wall is distributed to the three segments of that wall in proportion to their plan lengths.

Analysis time: 5 minutes

10.4.5 Example: Distribution of Shears with Flexible Diaphragm

A flexible horizontal diaphragm with more than two points of lateral support can be analyzed as a continuous beam, as shown in Fig. 10.24. Such a continuous beam could have different cross-sectional properties (in the horizontal plane) in different spans.

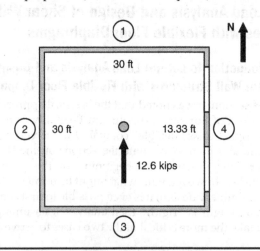

FIGURE 10.22 Plan view of example building with flexible roof diaphragm.

Lateral Load Analysis of Shear Wall Structures

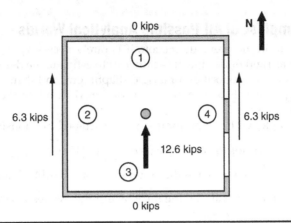

FIGURE 10.23 Results of example problem, assuming flexible diaphragm.

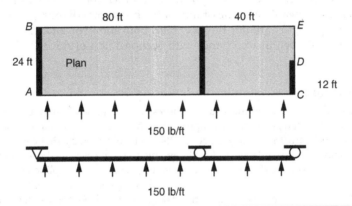

FIGURE 10.24 Example of a flexible horizontal diaphragm with more than two points of lateral support.

It is even simpler to analyze this continuous beam by tributary areas (i.e., according to the tributary length supported by each wall). The left-hand wall has a tributary length of 40 ft; the middle wall, 60 ft; and the right-hand wall, 20 ft.

$$V_{left} = \left(\frac{Area_{left}}{A_{total}}\right) V_{total} = \left[\frac{(80/2)}{120}\right] V_{total} = 0.333\, V_{total}$$

$$V_{middle} = \left(\frac{Area_{middle}}{A_{total}}\right) V_{total} = \left[\frac{(80/2 + 40/2)}{120}\right] V_{total} = 0.50\, V_{total}$$

$$V_{right} = \left(\frac{Area_{right}}{A_{total}}\right) V_{total} = \left[\frac{(40/2)}{120}\right] V_{total} = 0.167\, V_{total}$$

10.5 The Simplest of All Possible Analytical Worlds

As alluded to in the previous section, it is rarely necessary to explicitly categorize a diaphragm as rigid or flexible. It is sufficient to estimate the design actions in each wall based first on the supposition of a rigid diaphragm, and then on the supposition of a flexible diaphragm. Finally, each wall is designed based on the more critical of those two assumptions.

For example, with the perforated wall discussed previously, the assumption of a rigid diaphragm leads to design shears of $\left(\frac{30}{43.33}\right)V$ and $\left(\frac{13.3}{43.3}\right)V$ for the left- and right-hand walls respectively, while the assumption of a flexible diaphragm leads to design shears of $\frac{1}{2}V$ for each wall. Taking the worse of the two results for each wall, we would have design shears of $\left(\frac{30}{43.33}\right)V$, or 0.69 V for the left-hand wall, and $\frac{1}{2}V$, or 0.50 V, for the right-hand wall. In many practical cases, we would easily have sufficient capacity in each wall to resist these design shears, and we could easily finish the design without having to evaluate the flexibility of the horizontal diaphragm. For seismic design, when diaphragms are not flexible, then both inherent and accidental torsion must also be considered in accordance with Section 12.8.4 of *ASCE 7-22*.

10.6 Problems

The preceding sections of this chapter address the lateral load analysis of a particular low-rise shear wall structure, using various approaches. At the end of the chapter, the authors assert that for most such structures, satisfactory results can be obtained by first considering the horizontal diaphragms as rigid, and then as flexible, and by designing each wall segment for the more critical case. They further assert that the rigid-diaphragm case can be simplified by considering shearing deformations only; by considering only those wall segments without openings; and by neglecting plan torsion. The problems of this section ask the reader to repeat those steps using low-rise shear wall structures with another configuration, and to evaluate the validity of the authors' assertions for this other structure, using the same type of tabular comparison.

10.1 Consider a one-story structure that is square in plan, with out-to-out dimensions of 29 ft 4 in. in each plan direction. The north, west, and south sides of the structure have no openings. The east side of the structure has openings as shown below.

The structure is subjected to a lateral load of 100 kips, applied in the northward direction through the center of the roof slab, at a height of 8 ft 0 in. above the foundation.

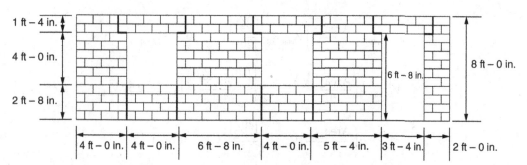

Following the simplified procedures proposed at the end of the body of this chapter, compute the design shears in each wall of the structure, and in each wall segment of the east wall.

Repeat for the lateral load applied in the westward direction through the center of the roof slab, at a height of 8 ft 0 in. above the foundation.

***10.2** Repeat the analysis steps of the body of this chapter to compute the design shears in each wall of the structure, and in each wall segment of the east wall. Compare the results in tabular form as in this chapter. Comment.

Repeat for the lateral load applied in the westward direction through the center of the roof slab, at a height of 8 ft 0 in. above the foundation.

---

*Denotes problems intended for graduate students.

CHAPTER 11
Design and Detailing of Floor and Roof Diaphragms

11.1 Introduction to Design of Diaphragms

The preceding chapter addresses the determination of forces in shear walls of structures subjected to lateral load. Those shear wall forces can be used to calculate shear forces and moments in those diaphragms, and finally to design the diaphragms for those forces. While this procedure is in principle the same for every diaphragm (regardless of whether it is rigid, flexible, or semi-rigid), it is possible to apply it differently for rigid and for flexible diaphragms, because rigid diaphragms are often stronger than flexible ones.

In addition to the general principles set forth here, other code requirements may also apply. For example, for structures assigned to Seismic Design Categories C and higher, Section 12.11.2.2.1 of *ASCE 7-22* imposes requirements for diaphragm connections, and implicitly introduces the concept of diaphragms as composed of sub-diaphragms, linked together by collectors.

11.2 Introduction to Design of Rigid Diaphragms

Rigid diaphragms usually have enough in-plane strength so that they do not have to be explicitly designed. They must, however, be connected to the walls that transfer their shear. The connections must be designed for that shear. Diaphragm chords and collectors also need to be checked, using the same procedures as for flexible diaphragms.

11.3 Introduction to Design of Flexible Diaphragms

Flexible diaphragms should be designed for shear and bending actions, and to transfer those actions to walls. Of particular importance are

- Connections between precast planks (shear transfer)
- Average shear stress in thin topping
- Shear in nailed sheathing

Diaphragm chords and collectors also need to be checked, using the procedures demonstrated later in this section.

11.3.1 Example: Design for Shears and Moments in Flexible Diaphragm

Calculate the distribution of shears to the two walls of the structure shown in Fig. 11.1, and design the roof diaphragm:

Because the diaphragm is flexible, the shear in each wall can be obtained either by idealizing the diaphragm as a simply supported beam, or by distributing the shears applied to each wall according to the tributary diaphragm length associated with each wall. In this case (two walls only), those two approaches give the same result. The shear applied to each wall is 150 lb/ft × 120 ft/2 = 9000 lb.

To make sure that shears acting within the roof diaphragm at a distance from Wall CD be transferred to that wall, it is desirable to put a "drag strut" between Points D and E.

If the roof diaphragm is considered simply supported in the horizontal plane (in view of the insignificant torsional stiffness of the walls), it is possible to calculate bending moments and shears in the roof diaphragm, as shown in Fig. 11.2.

Internal shears must be resisted by the roof diaphragm. The available net area is the area over which shear forces can be transmitted: the net cross-sectional area of the diaphragm for an integral diaphragm; or the cross-sectional area of the topping for a nonintegral diaphragm. Bending moments in the diaphragm are resisted by tensile and compressive forces in the chords of the diaphragm, calculated as illustrated in Fig. 11.3.

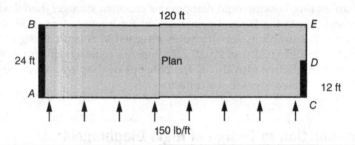

Figure 11.1 Example of a flexible diaphragm.

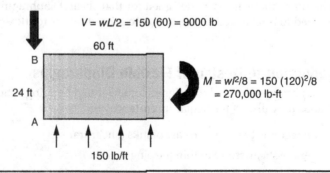

Figure 11.2 Example of design of a flexible diaphragm for shear and moment.

Design and Detailing of Floor and Roof Diaphragms

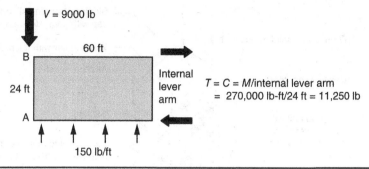

FIGURE 11.3 Example of computation of diaphragm chord forces.

The compression chord is made up of a portion of the roof diaphragm itself, and need not be designed. The tension chord consists of deformed reinforcement, placed either in the slab topping, or directly in the bond beam at the level of the roof diaphragm. The required area can be calculated easily. Using strength design, for example,

$$A_s^{required} = \frac{T}{F_y} = \frac{11,250 \text{ lb}}{60,000 \text{ in}^2} = 0.19 \text{ in}^2$$

This is easily satisfied with one or two #4 bars.

11.4 Typical Connection Details for Roof and Floor Diaphragms

The connections between roof and floor diaphragms and their supporting walls must be designed to transfer the required design forces. In the remainder of this section, necessary connections to walls must be designed. Examples of such connections are shown below. These connections would have to be strengthened for regions subject to strong earthquakes or strong winds.

An example of a connection detail between a CMU wall and a roof or floor diaphragm composed of steel joists is shown in Fig. 11.4. Vertical reinforcement from the CMU wall is continuous through or anchored in a horizontal bond beam, and the base plate for the joists is anchored to the bond beam.

An example of a connection detail between a CMU wall and a roof or floor diaphragm composed of wooden joists is shown in Fig. 11.5. Vertical reinforcement from the CMU wall is continuous through or anchored in a horizontal bond beam, and the base plate for the joists is anchored to the bond beam.

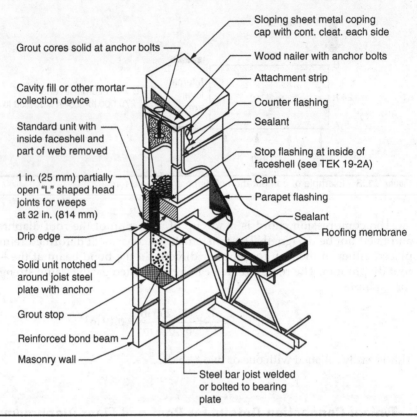

FIGURE 11.4 Example of a connection detail between a CMU wall and steel joists (Figure 11 of CMHA TEK 05-07A).

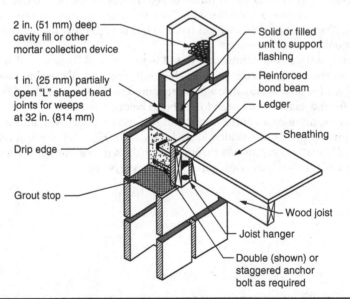

FIGURE 11.5 Example of a connection detail between a CMU wall and wooden joists (Figure 6 of CMHA TEK 05-07A).

CHAPTER 12

Strength Design Example: Low-Rise Building with Reinforced Concrete Masonry

12.1 Introduction

Previous sections of this book have addressed the specification and detailing of masonry buildings requiring little or no structural calculation, and the structural calculation, by strength and allowable stress approaches, of individual masonry elements. Design of those individual masonry elements has included implicit consideration of how they work together to form a structural assemblage. For example, design calculations for masonry bearing walls were related to the required performance of horizontal diaphragms, and to the analysis and design of those diaphragms to obtain that performance.

It is now time to put this information together to carry out the preliminary layout, specification, and structural design of a complete masonry building. The first such design example is a one-story commercial building (a warehouse), located in the outskirts of Austin, Texas. Design loads due to earthquake are neglected for this problem.

This combined example problem is carried out using the strength design approach. Previous comparisons are intended to facilitate estimation of the extent to which the design would change if the allowable-stress approach were used. This will also be commented on at the end of the example.

12.2 Design Steps for One-Story Building

The design steps for this one-story building are enumerated below.

1) Choose design criteria, calculate design loads, propose structural system:
   - Propose plan, elevation, materials, f'_m
   - Calculate D, L, W loads
   - Propose structural systems for gravity and lateral load

2) Design walls for gravity plus out-of-plane loads, using thickened wall sections at points of reaction of long-span joists (if necessary)

3) Design lintels

4) Conduct lateral force analysis, design roof diaphragm

5) Design wall segments for combined shear, flexure and axial loads

6) Design and detail connections

7) Design roof framing (this is not done here—a joist catalog would normally be used)

8) Design interior columns (this is not done here—structural steel tubes would be used)

12.3 Step 1: Choose Design Criteria

The plan and elevation of the building are shown in Figs. 12.1 and 12.2.

12.3.1 Design for Water-Penetration Resistance

A single-wythe barrier wall will be used. The wall will permit the passage of some water.

12.3.2 Locate Control Joints

On the North and South facades, space control joints at 20 ft, as shown in Fig. 12.3.

On the West façade, space control joints at 20 ft, as shown in Fig. 12.4. On the East façade, space control joints at about 20 ft, as shown in Fig. 12.5.

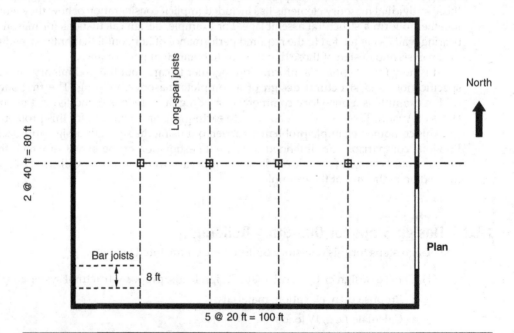

Figure 12.1 Plan of example single-story building.

Strength Design Example: Low-Rise Building with Reinforced Concrete Masonry   339

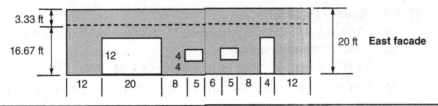

FIGURE 12.2   Elevation of example single-story building.

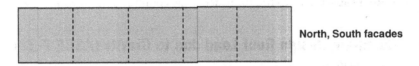

FIGURE 12.3   Locations of control joints on North and South facades.

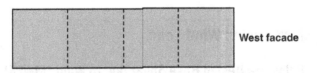

FIGURE 12.4   Locations of control joints on West facade.

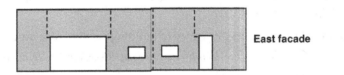

FIGURE 12.5   Spacing of control joints on East facade.

12.3.3   Design for Fire (2024 *IBC*)

Design for fire follows the 2024 *IBC*.

    Use and occupancy: Group F, Division 1 (moderate hazard)

    Use Type I or Type II construction (noncombustible material)

    No area or height restrictions

    2- or 3-hour rating required

    Meet separation requirements of 2024 *IBC* Table 705.2

    Use grouted 8-in. CMU for bearing walls

12.3.4 Specify Materials

8-in. CMU (*ASTM C90*), fully grouted for bearing walls, ungrouted or partially grouted for non-bearing walls

Type S PCL mortar, specified by proportion (*ASTM C270*)

$f_m' = 2000$ lb/in². This can be satisfied using C90 units and Type S PCL mortar.

Deformed reinforcement meeting *ASTM A615*, Gr. 60.

Roof of long-span joists, supporting bar joists spaced at 8 ft.

Corrugated decking with 3-in. lightweight concrete topping.

Roof supported by structural steel tube columns at midspan.

12.4 Calculate Design Roof Load due to Gravity (ASCE 7-22)

$D = 60$ lb/ft²

$L = 20$ lb/ft² for tributary area up to 200 ft²

$L = 12$ lb/ft² for tributary areas greater than 600 ft²

Linear interpolation between those two limits (*ASCE 7-22*, Table 4.3-1).

12.5 Calculate Design Wind Load

12.5.1 Calculate Design Base Shear due to Wind (MWFRS)

A three-dimensional view of the low-rise building is shown in Fig. 12.6.

The critical direction for wind will be NS, because the area is greater on the north and south sides, and the area of shear walls is less in the NS direction. The steps are the same as those followed in the introduction to wind design. Section and figure references here are for *ASCE 7-22*.

Step 1: Determine risk category of building or other structure, see Table 1.3-1.

Assume that the default risk category, Risk Category II, applies to this building.

Step 2: Determine the basic wind speed, V, for the applicable risk category, see Figure 26.5-1A, B, or C.

Because this building is in Risk Category II, use Figure 26.5-1A. For Austin, Texas, the basic wind speed is 100 miles per hour.

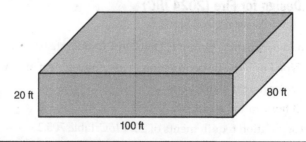

Figure 12.6 Three-dimensional view of low-rise building.

Strength Design Example: Low-Rise Building with Reinforced Concrete Masonry

Step 3: Determine wind load parameters:

- Wind directionality factor, K_d, see Section 26.6 and Table 26.6-1.
$$K_d = 0.85$$

- Exposure category, see Section 26.7.
  Assume a long upwind stretch of Surface Roughness C (Open terrain with scattered obstructions having heights generally less than 30 ft), and corresponding Exposure Category C.

- Topographic factor, K_{zt}, see Section 26.8 and Table 26.8-1.
  Assume $K_{zt} = 1.0$ (no hills, ridges, or escarpments).

- Ground elevation factor, K_e, see Section 26.9.
  Elevation of Austin, TX is 500 ft. Use $K_e = 0.98$ (interpolate between elevations of 0 and 1000 ft).

- Gust Effect Factor, G, see Section 26.11.
  Because this structure's period of vibration is much shorter than the characteristic period of wind gusts, it is considered rigid, and the gust effect factor G can be taken as 0.85.

- Enclosure classification, see Section 26.10.
  Because this structure has few openings, and because glazing is impact-resistant, it is classified as enclosed.

- Internal pressure coefficient, (GC_{pi}), see Section 26.13 and Table 26.13-1.
  Because this structure is enclosed, from Table 26.13-1, the internal pressure coefficient (GC_{pi}) is ±0.18.

Step 4: Determine the velocity pressure exposure coefficient, K_z or K_h using Table 27.3-1 of *ASCE 7-22*.

From Table 27.3-1 of *ASCE 7-22*, for Exposure Category C, relevant table cells are reproduced below as Table 12.1.

Step 5: Determine velocity pressure q_z or q_h using Equation 26.10-1.
$$q_z = 0.00256 K_z K_{zt} K_e V^2$$
$$K_e = 0.98$$
$$V = 100 \text{ mi/h}$$
$$K_{zt} = 0.87$$
$$q_z = 21.83 K_z \text{ lb/ft}^2$$

Note that the above expression for q_z has the velocity pressure exposure coefficient K_z embedded in it.

TABLE 12.1 Velocity Pressure Coefficients for Low-Rise Example Building (Taken from Table 27.3-1 of *ASCE 7-22*)

Height above Ground Level, z	K_h, K_z
1–15	0.85
20	0.90

Step 6: Determine external pressure coefficient, C_p or C_N.

The external pressure coefficients C_p for main wind force resisting systems are given in Figure 27.3-1 of ASCE 7-22 for walls and flat roofs. Note that the title of the figure is in black letters on a white background.

From the plan views in Figure 27.3-1 of ASCE 7-22, the windward pressure is $q_z GC_p$. The leeward pressure is $q_h GC_p$. The difference between the q_z and the q_h is that the former varies as a function of the height above ground level, while the latter is uniform over the height of the building and is evaluated using the height of the building.

For wind blowing in the NS direction, $L/B = 0.5$. From Figure 27.3-1, on the windward side of the building the external pressure coefficient C_p is 0.8. On the leeward side of the building, it is -0.5.

Step 7: Calculate wind pressure, p, on each building surface.

Use Equation 27.3-1 for MWFRS and rigid systems:

$$p = qK_d GC_p - q_i K_d (GC_{pi})$$

where $q = q_z$ for windward walls evaluated at height z above the ground;
$\quad\quad = q_h$ for leeward walls, side walls, and roofs, evaluated at height h;
$\quad q_i = q_h$ for windward walls, side walls, leeward walls, and roofs of enclosed buildings and for negative internal pressure evaluation in partially enclosed buildings;
$\quad\quad = q_z$ for positive internal pressure evaluation in partially enclosed buildings where height z is defined as the level of the highest opening in the building that could affect the positive internal pressure. For buildings sited in wind-borne debris regions, glazing that is not impact-resistant or protected with an impact-resistant covering shall be treated as an opening in accordance with Section 26.12.3. For positive internal pressure evaluation, q_i may conservatively be evaluated at height $h(q_i = q_h)$.
$\quad K_d$ = wind directionality factor from Section 26.6;
$\quad G$ = gust effect factor from Section 26.11;
$\quad C_p$ = external pressure coefficient from Figures 27.3-1, 27.3-2, and 27.3-3;
$\quad GC_{pi}$ = internal pressure coefficient from Table 26.13-1.

q and q_i shall be evaluated using exposure defined in Section 26.7.3. Pressure shall be applied simultaneously on windward and leeward walls and on roof surfaces as defined in Figures 27.3-1, 27.3-2, and 27.3-3.

Because the building is enclosed, the internal pressures on the windward and leeward sides are of equal magnitude and opposite direction, produce zero net base shear, and therefore need not be considered.

On the windward side of the building,

$$p = q_z K_d GC_p$$
$$p = (21.83 K_z) K_d GC_p$$

Because C_p is positive in sign, this pressure is positive in sign, indicating that the pressure acts inward against the windward wall. If the wind comes from the south, for example, the force on the windward wall acts toward the north. These values are shown in the "Windward Side" columns of the spreadsheet (Table 12.2).

TABLE 12.2 Spreadsheet for Computation of Base Shear for Example Low-Rise Building (MWFRS)

Building Floor	Height above Ground	Tributary Area	\multicolumn{7}{c	}{Windward Side}	\multicolumn{7}{c	}{Leeward Side}
			K_z	q_z	K_d	G	C_p	p	Force	K_h	q_h	K_d	G	C_p	p	Force
Roof	16.67	1166.5	0.867	18.92	0.85	0.85	0.8	10.94	12.76	0.867	18.92	0.85	0.85	−0.5	−6.68	−7.97
Ground	0	833.5	0.85	18.56	0.85	0.85	0.8	10.73	8.94	0.867	18.92	0.85	0.85	−0.5	−6.68	−5.70
Total force									21.70							−13.67

On the leeward side of the building,

$$p = q_h K_d G C_p$$
$$p = (21.83 K_h) K_d G C_p$$

Because C_p is negative in sign, this pressure is negative in sign, indicating that the pressure acts outward against the leeward wall. If the wind comes from the south, for example, the force on the leeward wall acts toward the north. These values are shown in the "Leeward Side" columns of the spreadsheet of Table 12.2.

The design base shear due to wind load is the summation of 21.7 kips acting inward on the upwind wall and 13.67 kips acting outward on the downwind wall, for a total of 35.37 kips.

12.5.2 Calculate Design Pressure on Wall Elements due to Wind (Components and Cladding)

The critical region will be at the parapet, near a corner.

Step 1: Determine risk category of building or other structure, see Table 1.5-1.

Assume that the default risk category, Risk Category II, applies to this building.

Step 2: Determine the basic wind speed, V, for the applicable risk category, see Figure 26.5-1A, B or C.

Because this building is in Risk Category II, use Figure 26.5-1A. For Austin, Texas, the basic wind speed is 100 miles per hour.

Step 3: Determine wind load parameters:

- Wind directionality factor, K_d, see Section 26.6 and Table 26.6-1

$$K_d = 0.85$$

- Exposure category, see Section 26.7.
  Assume a long upwind stretch of Surface Roughness C (Open terrain with scattered obstructions having heights generally less than 30 ft), and corresponding Exposure Category C.

- Topographic factor, K_{zt}, see Section 26.8 and Table 26.8-1.
  Assume $K_{zt} = 1.0$ (no hills, ridges, or escarpments).

- Ground elevation factor, K_e, see Section 26.9.
  Elevation of Austin, TX is 500 ft. Use $K_e = 0.98$ (interpolate between elevations of 0 and 1000 ft).

- Gust Effect Factor, G, see Section 26.11.
  Because this structure's period of vibration is much shorter than the characteristic period of wind gusts, it is considered rigid, and the gust effect factor G can be taken as 0.85.

Strength Design Example: Low-Rise Building with Reinforced Concrete Masonry   345

- Enclosure classification, see Section 26.12.
  Because this structure has few openings, and because glazing is impact-resistant, it is classified as enclosed.
- Internal pressure coefficient, (GC_{pi}), see Section 26.13 and Table 26.13-1.
  Because this structure is enclosed, from Table 26.13-1, the internal pressure coefficient (GC_{pi}) is ±0.18.

Step 4: Determine velocity pressure exposure coefficient, K_z or K_h, using Table 26.10-1 of ASCE 7-22.

For Exposure Category C, at a height of 16.67 ft above the ground, K_z equals 0.867.

Step 5: Determine velocity pressure, q_h, using Equation 30.3-1.

$$q_z = 0.00256 K_z K_{zt} K_e V^2$$
$$K_d = 0.85$$
$$V = 100 \, \text{mi/h}$$
$$K_{zt} = 0.867$$
$$q_z = 21.83 K_z \, \text{lb/ft}^2$$

Note that the above expression for q_z has the velocity pressure exposure coefficient K_z embedded in it.

Step 6: Determine external pressure coefficient, (GC_p) for buildings with $h < 60$ ft.

- Walls, see Figure 30.3-1 and Fig. 12.7.
- Flat roofs ($\theta < 10$ degrees), gable and hip roofs, see Figure 30.3-2.
- Arched roofs, see Figure 30.3-8.
- Domed roofs, see Figure 30.3-7.

The external pressure coefficients for components and cladding GC_p are given in Figure 30.3-1 of ASCE 7-22.

In computing the effective area of the cladding element, it is permitted to use an effective area equal to the product of the span and an effective width not less than one-third the span (7-22).

For simplicity and continuity from the chapter dealing with calculation of wind loads, Figure 30.3-1 of ASCE 7-22 will be used, even though this building is less than 60 ft in height to the roof.

Assume a panel with a span equal to the diaphragm height of 16.67 ft. Assume an effective width of one-third of that span, or 5.56 ft. The resulting effective area is 92.7 ft². From Figure 30.3-1, a panel in Zone 5 has a positive pressure coefficient of 0.8, and a negative pressure coefficient of –1.4.

Step 7: Calculate wind pressure, p, Equation 30.3-1

Use Equation 30.3-1 to evaluate the wind pressure, p.

$$p = q K_d (GC_p) - q_i K_d (GC_{pi})$$

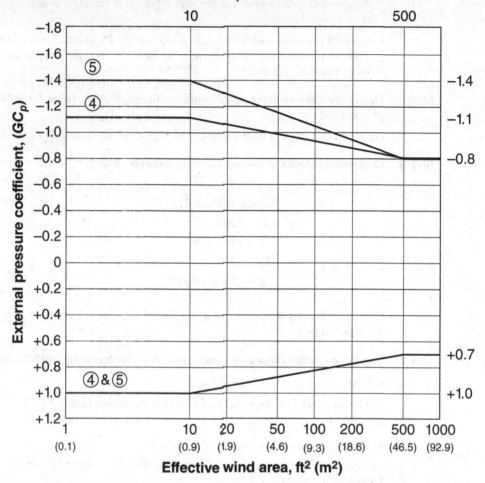

FIGURE 12.7 External pressure coefficient for walls with $h < 60$ ft. Adapted from Figure 30.3-1 of ASCE 7-22.

12.5.2.1 Windward Side of Building

On the windward side of the building, the maximum inward pressure will be produced on the cladding, due to the combination of GC_p acting inward (positive sign) and GC_{pi} also acting inward (negative sign).

$q = q_z$ evaluated at the height of the element, or 16.67 ft
$q_i = q_h$ evaluated at the height of the building, or 16.67 ft
$(GC_p) = 0.85$ (Figure 30.3-1), see Fig. 12.7.
$(GC_{pi}) = \pm 0.18$ (Table 26.13-1).

$$p = qK_d(GC_p) - q_iK_d(GC_{pi})$$
$$p = q_zK_d(GC_p) - q_hK_d(GC_{pi})$$
$$p = (21.83K_z)K_dGC_p - (21.83K_h)K_dGC_{pi}$$

Strength Design Example: Low-Rise Building with Reinforced Concrete Masonry 347

TABLE 12.3 Spreadsheet for Calculation of Wind Pressure on Windward Side of Low-Rise Example Building (Components and Cladding)

Building Height, h	Height above Ground, z	\multicolumn{5}{c	}{Maximum Inward Pressure (Windward Wall)}					Total
		\multicolumn{5}{c	}{External Pressure}	\multicolumn{5}{c	}{Internal Pressure}	
		K_h	q_h	GC_p	K_d	$p_{outside}$	K_h	q_h	GC_{pi}	K_d	p_{inside}	p_{total}
16.67	16.67	0.8667	18.92	0.8	0.85	12.87	0.8667	18.92	−0.18	0.85	−2.89	15.76

These values are shown in the spreadsheet of Table 12.3. The maximum inward pressure is the sum of 12.87 psf on the outside plus 2.89 psf on the inside, for a total of 15.76 psf acting inward.

12.5.2.2 Leeward Side of Building

On the leeward side of the building, the maximum outward pressure will be produced on the cladding, due to the combination of GC_p acting outward (negative sign) and GC_{pi} also acting outward (positive sign).

$$q = q_h, \text{ or } 16.67 \text{ ft}$$
$$q_i = q_h, \text{ or } 16.67 \text{ ft}$$
$$(GC_p) = -1.05 \text{ (Figure 30.4-1)}$$
$$(GC_{pi}) = \pm 0.18 \text{ (Table 26.13-1)}.$$
$$p = qK_d(GC_p) - q_iK_d(GC_{pi})$$
$$p = q_zK_d(GC_p) - q_hK_d(GC_{pi})$$
$$p = (21.83K_z)K_dGC_p - (21.83K_h)K_dGC_{pi}$$

These values are shown in the spreadsheet of Table 12.4. The maximum outward pressure is the sum of −16.89 psf on the outside plus 2.89 psf on the inside, for a total of −19.78 psf acting outward.

Wall elements must therefore be designed for a pressure of 15.76 lb/ft² acting inward, and 19.78 lb/ft² acting outward. The latter governs.

10.5.2.3 Wind Pressures on Roof

Now evaluate the wind pressures on the roof. Those pressures are calculated using Components and Cladding Coefficients, which depend on the tributary area of the roof element under consideration. In this case we are interested in the reactions from the long-span joists. Repeat the above steps, starting with Step 6:

Step 6: Determine external pressure coefficient, (GC_p)
- Walls, see Figure 30.3-1.
- Flat roofs ($\theta < 10$ deg), gable and hip roofs, see Figure 30.3-2.

TABLE 12.4 Spreadsheet for Calculation of Wind Pressure on Leeward Side of Low-Rise Example Building (Components and Cladding)

Building Height, h	Height above Ground, z	\multicolumn{5}{c	}{Maximum Outward Pressure (leeward wall)}					Total
		\multicolumn{5}{c	}{External Pressure}	\multicolumn{5}{c	}{Internal Pressure}	
		K_h	q_h	GC_p	K_d	$p_{outside}$	K_h	q_h	GC_{pi}	K_d	p_{inside}	p_{total}
16.67	16.67	0.867	18.92	−1.05	0.85	−16.89	0.867	18.92	0.18	0.85	2.89	−19.78

- Arched roofs, see Figure 30.3-8.
- Domed roofs, see Figure 30.3-7.

The external pressure coefficients for components and cladding GC_p are given in Figure 30.3-1 of ASCE 7-22.

In computing the effective area of the cladding element, it is permitted to use an effective area equal to the product of the span and an effective width not less than one-third the span.

The long-span joists have a span of 40 ft. Assume an effective width of one-third of that span, or 13.33 ft. The resulting effective area is 533 ft². Figure 30.2-1 of ASCE 7-22 will be used because the building height is less than 60 ft in height to the roof. For simplicity, values from Zone 1 will be used. From Figure 30.3-1, a roof element in Zone 1 has a negative pressure coefficient of −1.0.

Step 7: Calculate wind pressure, p, Equation 30.3-1.

For a building with $h < 60$ ft:

$$p = qK_d(GC_p) - q_iK_d(GC_{pi})$$

On the roof of the building, upward pressure will be critical. The maximum upward pressure will be produced due to the combination of GC_p acting outward (negative sign) and GC_{pi} also acting outward (positive sign).

$q = q_z$ evaluated at the height of the element, or 16.67 ft

$q_i = q_h$ evaluated at the height of the building, or 16.67 ft

$(GC_p) = -1.0$ (Figure 30.3-1)

$(GC_{pi}) = \pm 0.18$ (Table 26.13-1)

$$p = qK_d(GC_p) - q_iK_d(GC_{pi})$$
$$p = q_zK_d(GC_p) - q_hK_d(GC_{pi})$$
$$p = (21.83K_z)K_dGC_p - (21.83K_h)K_dGC_{pi}$$

These values are shown in the spreadsheet of Table 12.5. The maximum outward (uplift) pressure is the sum of 19.08 psf on the outside plus 3.82 psf on the inside, for a total of 22.90 psf acting outward. This is less than the dead load of 60 psf, so net wind uplift does not exist.

TABLE 12.5 Spreadsheet for Calculation of Wind Pressure on Roof of Low-Rise Example Building (Components and Cladding)

Building Height, h	Height above Ground, z	\multicolumn{5}{c	}{Maximum Outward Pressure (Roof)}					
		\multicolumn{5}{c	}{External Pressure}	\multicolumn{5}{c	}{Internal Pressure}	\multicolumn{2}{c	}{Total}
		K_h	q_h	GC_p	K_d	$p_{outside}$	K_h	q_h	GC_{pi}	K_d	p_{inside}	p_{total}
16.67	16.67	0.867	24.94	−0.9	0.85	−19.08	0.867	24.94	0.18	0.85	3.82	−22.90

12.6 Propose Structural Systems for Gravity and Lateral Load

Gravity loads are carried from the corrugated decking to the bar joists, from the bar joists to the long-span joists, and from the long-span joists to the north and south walls, and to the interior steel columns.

Lateral loads are resisted by perpendicular walls (vertical strips), which transfer their loads to the roof diaphragm and the foundation. Loads transferred to the roof diaphragm are carried to shear walls oriented parallel to the load.

12.7 Step 2: Design Walls for Gravity plus Out-of-Plane Loads

12.7.1 Design of West Wall for Gravity plus Out-of-Plane Loads

The west wall carries gravity load from a portion of the tributary area of the roof, plus wind loads.

As in previous design examples, suppose that the load is applied over a 4-in. bearing plate, and assume that bearing stresses vary linearly under the bearing plate as shown in Fig. 12.8.

Then the eccentricity of the applied load with respect to the centerline of the wall is

$$e = \frac{t}{2} - \frac{\text{plate}}{3} = \frac{7.63 \text{ in.}}{2} - \frac{4 \text{ in.}}{3} = 2.48 \text{ in.}$$

Compute the load on the west wall from the roof, based on the tributary area shown in Fig. 12.9.

The tributary area of an entire bar joist is the product of the span (20 ft) and the distance between bar joists (8 ft). The tributary area of bar joist loading the west wall is one-half that, or 80 ft².

The roof dead load is 60 lb/ft². For tributary areas up to 200 ft², the roof live load is 20 lb/ft².

Assume as before that the critical loading combination is $0.9D + 1.0W$. Because wind loads are small and do not produce net uplift, they are neglected for simplicity. The factored gravity load acting on the wall per foot of length is therefore:

$$w_u = 10 \text{ ft} \cdot 0.9(60 \text{ lb/ft}^2) = 540 \text{ lb/ft}$$

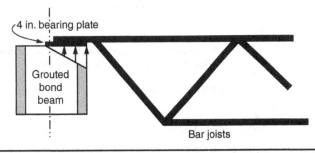

FIGURE 12.8 Assumed variation of bearing stresses under bearing plate.

350 Chapter Twelve

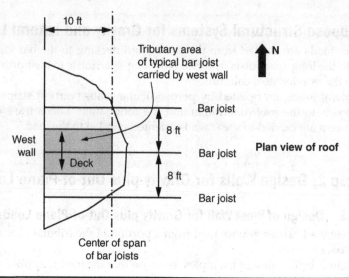

FIGURE 12.9 Tributary area of typical bar joist on west wall.

As in previous example problems, try an initial design of the wall as unreinforced (Fig. 12.10).

At each horizontal plane through the wall, the following conditions must be met:

- Maximum compressive stress from factored axial loads must not exceed the slenderness-dependent values in Equations 9-11 or 9-12 as appropriate, reduced by a ϕ factor of 0.60.

- Maximum compressive stress from factored loads (including a moment magnifiers) must not exceed $0.80\,f'_m$ in the extreme compression fiber, reduced by a ϕ factor of 0.60.

- Maximum tension stress from factored loads (including a moment magnifier) must not exceed the modulus of rupture in the extreme tension fiber, reduced by the ϕ factor of 0.60.

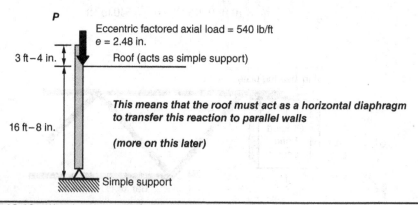

FIGURE 12.10 West bearing wall of example low-rise building.

Strength Design Example: Low-Rise Building with Reinforced Concrete Masonry

For each condition, the more critical of the two possible loading combinations must be checked. Because there is wind load, and because previous examples showed little problem with the first two criteria, the third criterion (net tension) may well be critical. For this criterion, the critical loading condition could be 1.2D + 1.6L, or 0.9D + 1.0W. Both loading conditions must be checked.

We also must check various points on the wall. Critical points are just below the roof reaction (moment is high and axial load is low, so maximum tension may govern); and at the base of the wall (axial load is high, so maximum compression may govern).

To avoid having to check a large number of loading combinations and potentially critical locations, it is worthwhile to assess them first and check only the ones that will probably govern.

Because the eccentric axial load places the outer fibers of the wall in tension, the critical wind condition will be suction, for which the design wind pressure is 19.78 lb/ft². Because we are designing a 1-ft wide strip and the load factor for wind is 1.0, the factored uniformly distributed load will be 19.78 lb/ft.

Due to wind only, the unfactored moment on a 1-ft strip at the base of the parapet (roof level) is

$$M = \frac{w_u L_{parapet}^2}{2} = \frac{19.78 \text{ lb/ft} \times 3.33^2 \text{ ft}^2}{2} \times 12 \text{ in./ft} = 1316 \text{ lb-in.}$$

The maximum moment is close to that occurring at mid-height. The moment from wind load is the superposition of one-half moment at the upper support due to wind load on the parapet only, plus the midspan moment in a simply supported beam with that same wind load:

$$M_{midspan} = -\frac{1316}{2} + \frac{w_u L^2}{8} = -\frac{1316}{2} + \frac{19.78 \text{ lb/ft} \times 16.67^2 \text{ ft}^2}{8} 12 \text{ in./ft} = 7587 \text{ lb-in.}$$

Unfactored moment diagrams due to eccentric dead load and wind are as shown below.

From previous examples, we know that loading combination 1.2D + 1.6L was not close to critical directly underneath the roof. Because the wind-load moments directly underneath the roof are not very large, they will probably not be critical either. The critical location will probably be at mid-height; the critical loading condition will probably be 0.9D + 1.0W; and the critical criterion will probably be net tension, because this masonry wall is unreinforced, as illustrated in Fig. 12.11.

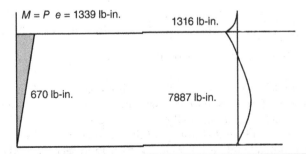

FIGURE 12.11 Unfactored moment diagrams from eccentric dead load and wind load.

Work with a strip with a width of 1 ft (measured along the length of the wall in plan). Stresses are calculated using the critical section, consisting of the bedded area only (TMS 402-22, Section 4.4.1).

Check the net tensile stress. At the mid-height of the wall, the axial force due to 0.9D is:

$$P_u = 0.9(600 \text{ lb}) + 0.9(3.33 \text{ ft} + 8.33 \text{ ft}) \times 48 \text{ lb/ft} = 886 \text{ lb}$$

At the mid-height of the wall, the factored design moment, M_u, is given by:

$$M_u = P_{u\,eccentric} \frac{e}{2} + M_{u\,wind} = \left(\frac{1}{2}\right) 0.9 \times 600 \text{ lb} \times 2.48 \text{ in.} + 1.0 \times 7587 \text{ lb-in.} = 8257 \text{ lb-in.}$$

$$f_{tension} = -\frac{P_u}{A} + \frac{M_u c}{I}$$

$$f_{tension} = -\frac{886 \text{ lb}}{30 \text{ in}^2} + \frac{8257 \text{ lb-in.}(7.63/2) \text{ in.}}{309 \text{ in}^4} = -29.5 \text{ lb/in}^2 + 101.9 \text{ lb/in}^2 = 72.4 \text{ lb/in}^2$$

$$0.60 f_r = 0.60 \times 84 \text{ lb/in}^2 = 50.4 \text{ lb/in}^2$$

The maximum tensile stress exceeds the prescribed value, and the design is not satisfactory. It will be necessary to grout or reinforce the wall. Recheck using a grouted wall.

Check the net tensile stress. At the mid-height of the wall, compute the axial force due to 0.9D. Use a self-weight of 81 lb/ft² for a fully grouted wall.

$$P_u = 0.9(600 \text{ lb}) + 0.9(3.33 \text{ ft} + 8.33 \text{ ft}) \times 81 \text{ lb/ft} = 1390 \text{ lb}$$

At the mid-height of the wall, the factored design moment, M_u, is given by:

$$M_u = P_{u\,eccentric} \frac{e}{2} + M_{u\,wind} = \left(\frac{1}{2}\right) 0.9 \times 600 \text{ lb} \times 2.48 \text{ in.} + 1.0 \times 7587 \text{ lb-in.} = 8257 \text{ lb-in.}$$

For a solid 8-in. wall, $A = (7.63 \text{ in.} \times 12 \text{ in.}) = 91.56 \text{ in}^2$, and $I = (12 \text{ in.} \times 7.63^3 \text{ in}^3)/12 = 444 \text{ in}^4$.

$$f_{tension} = -\frac{P_u}{A} + \frac{M_u c}{I}$$

$$f_{tension} = -\frac{1390 \text{ lb}}{91.56 \text{ in}^2} + \frac{8257 \text{ lb-in.}(7.63/2) \text{ in.}}{444 \text{ in}^4} = -15.18 \text{ lb/in}^2 + 70.9 \text{ lb/in}^2 = 55.7 \text{ lb/in}^2$$

$$0.60 f_r = 0.60 \times 163 \text{ lb/in}^2 = 97.8 \text{ lb/in}^2$$

The maximum tensile stress is less than the nominal factored tensile strength. Although this works, a reinforced wall design with prescriptive reinforcement will be necessary because the effect of openings will require using steel as shown in Section 12.7.2.

Try #5 bars @ 48 in. Assuming a fully grouted wall, the factored axial load and moment per foot of length are 1390 lb and 8257 lb-in. as indicated by the square marker. Because that point falls within the interaction diagram, capped for slenderness effects as shown in Fig. 12.12, the design is satisfactory.

Strength Design Example: Low-Rise Building with Reinforced Concrete Masonry

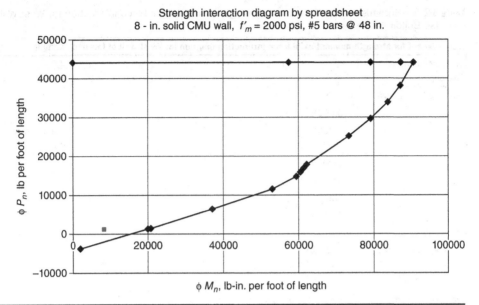

FIGURE 12.12 Design moment-axial force interaction diagram for West wall of example low-rise building.

Relevant cells from the spreadsheet are reproduced in Table 12.6.

The strength is sufficient. Use #5 bars @ 48 in. Because the compressive stress block remains in the face shell for this axial load (refer to the spreadsheet), the wall can be partially grouted, and the interaction diagram is still valid.

12.7.2 Design East Wall for Gravity plus Out-of-Plane Loads

The loads on the east wall are identical to those on the west wall, except for the presence of the openings. This wall is designed for prescriptive reinforcement. Loads on each wall segment are increased by the ratio of the tributary width of the wall segment, to the actual width. The elevation of the east wall is shown in Fig. 12.13.

By inspection, Wall Segment B, with a ratio of tributary width to actual width of (20.5/8), is most critical. At the mid-height of the wall, the factored axial load and factored moment per foot of length, P_u and M_u, are given by:

$$P_u = 1390 \text{ lb}$$

$$M_u = P_{u \text{ eccentric}} \frac{e}{2} + M_{u \text{ wind}} = \left(\frac{1}{2}\right) 0.9 \times 600 \text{ lb} \times 2.48 \text{ in.} + 1.0 \times 7587 \text{ lb-in.} = 8257 \text{ lb-in.}$$

The factored axial load and moment on Wall Segment B are obtained by multiplying those factored design axial loads and moments per foot of length, times the tributary wall length of 20.5 ft, giving a total factored design axial load and moment on the critical Wall Segment B of 28,495 lb (20.5 × 1390 lb) and 169,259 lb-in. (20.5 × 8257 lb-in.), respectively.

As before, the strength moment-axial force interaction diagram for a solidly grouted 8-in. masonry wall loaded out of plane is shown in Fig. 12.12. For vertical reinforcement consisting of #5 bars spaced at 48 in. and an axial load close to zero, out-of-plane design flexural capacity is about 15,000 lb-in. per foot of length. For Segment B, with a plan length of 8 ft, the out-of-plane design flexural capacity is about 120,000 lb-in. (15,000 lb-in. × 8). This corresponds to two #5 bars, or a total area of flexural reinforcement of 0.62 in^2.

TABLE 12.6 Spreadsheet for Calculating Strength Moment-Axial Force Interaction for West Wall of Low-Rise Building

Spreadsheet for strength moment-axial force interaction diagram for West wall of low-rise example									
Reinforcement at mid-depth							h		200
Specified thickness	7.625						r		2.201
emu	0.0025						h/r		90.880
f'_m	2000						Slenderness factor		0.579
f_y	60000								
E_s	29000000								
e_y	0.002069								
d	3.8125								
(c/d) balanced	0.54717								
Tensile reinforcement area	0.31								
Effective width	48								
Because compression reinforcement is not supported, it is not counted									
	c/d	c	C_{mas}	ε_s	f_s	ϕ	ϕMn	ϕPn	
Pure axial load						0.650	0	44011	
Points controlled by masonry	2	7.625	468480	0.00125	0	0.65	58048	44011	
	1.7	6.48125	398208	0.00103	0	0.65	78945	44011	
	1.5	5.71875	351360	0.00083	0	0.65	87071	44011	
	1.3	4.95625	304512	0.00058	0	0.65	90554	44011	
	1.2	4.575	281088	0.00042	0	0.65	90554	44011	
	1	3.8125	234240	0.00000	0	0.65	87071	38064	
	0.9	3.43125	210816	−0.00028	−8056	0.65	83589	33852	
	0.8	3.05	187392	−0.00063	−18125	0.65	78945	29538	
	0.7	2.66875	163968	−0.00107	−31071	0.65	73140	25080	
	0.54717	2.086085	128169	−0.00207	−60000	0.65	62026	17805	
Points controlled by steel	0.54717	2.086085	128169	−0.00207	−60000	0.65	62026	17805	
	0.5	1.90625	117120	−0.00250	−60000	0.69	61255	16894	
	0.45	1.715625	105408	−0.00306	−60000	0.73	60322	15891	
	0.4	1.525	93696	−0.00375	−60000	0.79	59269	14833	
	0.3	1.14375	70272	−0.00583	−60000	0.90	53047	11626	
	0.2	0.7625	46848	−0.01000	−60000	0.90	36972	6356	
	0.10578	0.403286	24778	−0.02113	−60000	0.90	20355	1390	
	0.1	0.38125	23424	−0.02250	−60000	0.90	19290	1085	
	0.01	0.038125	2342	−0.24750	−60000	0.90	2001	−3658	

Strength Design Example: Low-Rise Building with Reinforced Concrete Masonry

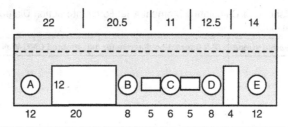

FIGURE 12.13 East wall of example low-rise building.

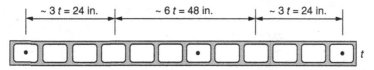

FIGURE 12.14 Trial design Segment B of East wall as governed by out-of-plane wind load.

Continue a trial design using three #5 bars per wall segment (steel area equals 3 × 0.31 in², or 0.93 in²), as illustrated in Fig. 12.14. For the critical Wall Segment B, the effective width is $3t$ on each side of each bar. This is essentially equal to the total segment length of 8 ft. Capacity is insensitive to effective width at low axial loads.

We obtain a moment-axial force interaction diagram (strength) for the trial design of the critical Wall Segment B. This diagram capped for slenderness effects is shown in Fig. 12.15.

The cells of the spreadsheet are shown in Table 12.7.

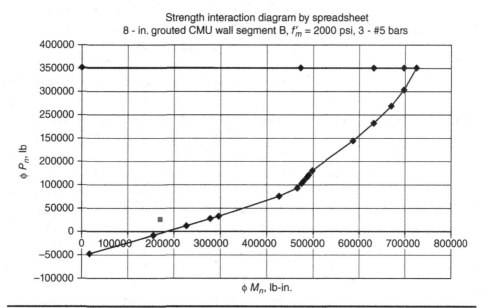

FIGURE 12.15 Design moment-axial force interaction diagram for Wall Segment B of low-rise example building.

TABLE 12.7 Spreadsheet for Calculating Moment-Axial Force Interaction Diagram for Wall Segment B of Low-Rise Example Building

Spreadsheet for calculating strength M-N interaction diagram for fully grouted CMU Wall Segment B, Chapter 12									
Reinforcement at mid-depth							h		200
Specified thickness	7.625						r		2.201
emu	0.0025						h/r		90.880
f'_m	2000						Slenderness factor		0.579
f_y	60000								
E_s	29000000								
ε_y	0.002069								
d	3.8125								
(c/d) balanced	0.54717								
Tensile reinforcement area	0.93								
Effective width	96								
Because compression reinforcement is not supported, it is not counted									
	c/d	c	C_{mas}	ε_s	f_s	ϕ	ϕMn	ϕPn	
Pure axial load						0.65	0	351943	
Points controlled by masonry	1.99	7.586875	932275	0.0012	0	0.65	471300	351943	
	1.7	6.48125	796416	0.0010	0	0.65	631558	351943	
	1.5	5.71875	702720	0.0008	0	0.65	696571	351943	
	1.3	4.95625	609024	0.0006	0	0.65	724434	351943	
	1.2	4.575	562176	0.0004	0	0.65	724434	351943	
	1	3.8125	468480	0.0000	0	0.65	696571	304512	
	0.9	3.43125	421632	−0.0003	−8056	0.65	668708	269191	
	0.8	3.05	374784	−0.0006	−18125	0.65	631558	232653	
	0.7	2.66875	327936	−0.0011	−31071	0.65	585120	194376	
	0.54717	2.086085	256338	−0.0021	−60000	0.65	496205	130350	
Points controlled by steel	0.54717	2.086085	256338	−0.0021	−60000	0.65	496205	130350	
	0.5	1.90625	234240	−0.0025	−60000	0.69	490043	122395	
	0.47	1.791875	220186	−0.0028	−60000	0.71	485679	117127	
	0.43	1.639375	201446	−0.0033	−60000	0.75	479321	109781	
	0.4	1.525	187392	−0.0038	−60000	0.79	474149	103969	
	0.35	1.334375	163968	−0.0046	−60000	0.86	464759	93510	
	0.3	1.14375	140544	−0.0058	−60000	0.90	424373	76270	
	0.2	0.7625	93696	−0.0100	−60000	0.90	295775	34106	
	0.18669	0.711756	87461	−0.0109	−60000	0.90	277689	28494	
	0.15	0.571875	70272	−0.0142	−60000	0.90	226654	13025	
	0.1	0.38125	46848	−0.0225	−60000	0.90	154317	−8057	
	0.01	0.038125	4685	−0.2475	−60000	0.90	16010	−46004	

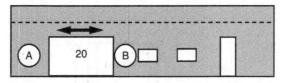

FIGURE 12.16 Design of lintel on east wall for out-of-plane loads.

At an axial load of 28,495 lb, indicated by the square marker, the design out-of-plane flexural capacity of the critical Wall Segment B is 277,689 lb-in. Because the ultimate loads are contained within the interaction diagram, the design is satisfactory.

For simplicity, use three #5 bars vertically in every wall segment of the east wall.

We have completed the design of the wall segments of the east wall. Now consider the design of the horizontally spanning lintel between Wall Segment A and Wall Segment B, against out-of-plane wind. This is shown in Fig. 12.16. The seismic provisions of *ASCE 7-22* would in many cases require that the roof diaphragm be connected to the walls at intervals of about 4 ft. For purposes of this example, the possible constraints imposed by such requirements are ignored in computing the span of the lintel out of plane. As will be seen later in this example, this has the additional advantage of showing that out-of-plane loads do not govern for the design of such lintels, even ignoring intermediate supports that will actually be there.

Again, suction will be critical. The span of the lintel out-of-plane is the distance between connectors to the diaphragm, assumed here as 4 ft. The width, b, of the lintel is 20 ft and 8 in. The factored design out-of-plane moment on the lintel is:

$$w_u = (1.0) \cdot q \cdot b = (1.0)\, 19.78 \text{ lb/ft}^2 \cdot (20.67) \text{ ft} = 408.8 \text{ lb-ft}$$

$$M_u^{\text{out-of-plane}} = \frac{w_u L^2}{8} = \frac{408.8 \text{ lb-ft} \cdot 4^2 \text{ft}^2 \cdot 12 \text{ in./ft}}{8}$$

$$M_u^{\text{out-of-plane}} = 9812 \text{ lb-in.}$$

Conservatively assume an effective depth equal to 90% of one-half the wall thickness.

$$A_s^{\text{required}} = \frac{M_u}{\phi\, d\, f_y} \approx \frac{9812 \text{ lb-in.}}{0.90 \times \left(0.9 \times \dfrac{7.63}{2} \text{ in.}\right) 60{,}000 \text{ lb/in}^2} = 0.053 \text{ in}^2$$

This will easily be satisfied using two #4 bars in a bond beam at the level of the roof, plus two #4 bars at the top of the parapet, plus two #4 bars in the lowest course of the lintel. For out-of-plane loading, one-half the bars will work at a time.

12.7.3 Design North and South Walls for Gravity plus Out-of-Plane Wind Loads

The north and south walls span vertically between the foundation slab and the roof diaphragm. They support gravity loads from self-weight alone, because the long-span joists rest on pilasters (thickened wall sections) that are separated from the north and south walls by vertically oriented control joints. They also support out-of-plane wind loads.

Because the bar joists are oriented parallel to the north and south walls, a bar joist will be placed right next to those walls (Fig. 12.17). The north and south walls will therefore not support any gravity loads except their own weight.

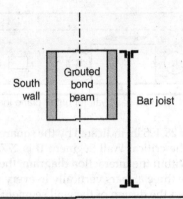

FIGURE 12.17 Placement of bar joists adjacent to North and South walls.

At each horizontal plane through the wall, the following conditions must be met:

- Maximum compressive stress from factored axial loads must not exceed the slenderness-dependent values in Equations 9-9 or 9-10 as appropriate, reduced by a ϕ factor of 0.60.
- Maximum compressive stress from factored loads (including a moment magnifiers) must not exceed $0.80 f'_m$ in the extreme compression fiber, reduced by a ϕ factor of 0.60.
- Maximum tension stress from factored loads (including a moment magnifier) must not exceed the modulus of rupture in the extreme tension fiber, reduced by the ϕ factor of 0.60.

Check midspan moment in the wall. Wind pressures, and corresponding wind moments, will be the same as before.

Check the net tensile stress. At the mid-height of the wall, compute the axial force due to 0.9D. Assume a fully grouted wall, with a self-weight of 81 lb/ft².

$$P_u = 0.9(3.33 \text{ ft} + 8.33 \text{ ft}) \times 81 \text{ lb/ft} = 850 \text{ lb}$$

At the mid-height of the wall, the factored design moment, M_u, is given by:

$$M_u = M_{u\,wind} = 1.0 \times 8257 \text{ lb-in.} = 8257 \text{ lb-in.}$$

For a solid-grouted 8-in. wall,

$A = (7.63 \text{ in.} \times 12 \text{ in.}) = 91.56 \text{ in}^2$, and

$I = (12 \text{ in.} \times 7.63 \text{ in}^3)/12 = 444 \text{ in}^4$.

$$f_{tension} = -\frac{P_u}{A} + \frac{M_u c}{I}$$

$$f_{tension} = -\frac{850 \text{ lb}}{91.56 \text{ in}^2} + \frac{8257 \text{ lb-in.} \left(7.63/2\right)}{444 \text{ in}^4} = -9.29 + 70.9 \text{ lb/in}^2 = 61.6 \text{ lb/in}^2$$

$$0.60 f_r = 0.60 \times 163 \text{ lb/in}^2 = 97.8 \text{ lb/in}^2$$

The maximum tensile stress is less than prescribed value, and the wall design is satisfactory. Regardless use prescriptive steel of #5 bars @ 120 in., at openings, near movement joints, and ends as prescribed by *TMS 402-22*. Vertically spanning strips will react against the diaphragm.

12.7.4 Design Pilasters (Columns) in North and South Walls

Because the north and south walls have vertically oriented control joints at each pilaster, the pilasters really behave like 16- by 16-in. beam-columns. In the specific context of *TMS 402-22*, however, they do not have to meet the prescriptive requirements for columns (including transverse reinforcement), because they are not isolated elements. The cross-section of a typical pilaster is shown in Fig. 12.18.

The load on the pilasters comes from eccentric gravity loads from the long-span joists. Their tributary area is shown in Fig. 12.19.

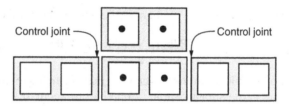

FIGURE 12.18 Cross-section of typical pilaster in north and south walls of example low-rise building.

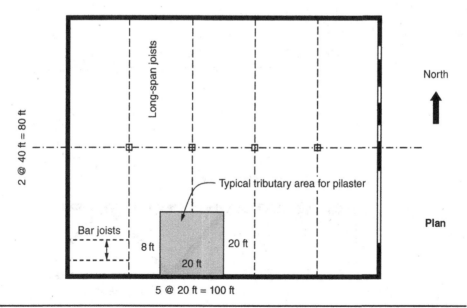

FIGURE 12.19 Tributary area supported by typical pilaster.

The tributary area is 400 ft², which corresponds to a reduced live load of 20 lb/ft² × 0.80 = 16 lb/ft², according to Section 4.8.2 of *ASCE 7-22*. This is irrelevant, however, because as before, axial load significantly increases pilaster capacity below the balance point, and the governing loading combination is $0.9D + 1.0W$.

The factored axial load on each pilaster is therefore:

$$P_u = 0.9 \times 60 \text{ lb/ft}^2 \times 400 \text{ ft}^2 = 21{,}600 \text{ lb}$$

The long-span joists rest on the pilasters through full-width base plates. Assuming a triangular stress distribution under the bearing plates, the eccentricity of gravity load can be calculated, as shown in Fig. 12.20.

The corresponding factored moment at the top of the pilaster due to eccentric gravity load is therefore

$$M_u = P_u e = 21{,}600 \text{ lb} \times 2.61 \text{ in.} = 56{,}376 \text{ lb-in.}$$

Due to wind only, the factored moment at the base of the parapet (roof level) is

$$M_u = \frac{q_u L^2}{2} = \frac{1.0 \times 19.78 \text{ lb/ft}^2 \times 1.33 \text{ ft} \times 3.33^2 \text{ ft}^2}{2} \times 12 \text{ in./ft} = 1750 \text{ lb-in.}$$

The maximum wind-load moment is close to that occurring at mid-height. The moment from wind load is the superposition of one-half moment at the upper support due to wind load on the parapet only, plus the midspan moment in a simply supported beam with that same wind load. Because the north and south walls are separated from the pilasters by control joints, the wind-load moment on the pilasters is due to their frontal area alone:

$$M_{u \text{ midspan}} = -\frac{1750}{2} + \frac{qL^2}{8}$$

$$M_{u \text{ midspan}} = -\frac{1750}{2} + \frac{1.0 \times 19.78 \frac{\text{lb}}{\text{ft}^2} \times 1.33 \text{ ft} \times 16.67^2 \text{ ft}^2}{8} \times 12 \text{ in./ft} = 11{,}840 \text{ lb-in.}$$

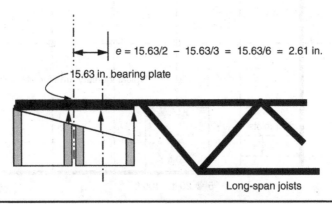

FIGURE 12.20 Distribution of bearing stresses under bearing plates of pilasters.

Strength Design Example: Low-Rise Building with Reinforced Concrete Masonry 361

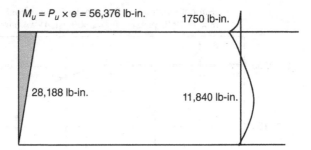

FIGURE 12.21 Factored moment diagrams due to eccentric dead load and wind on pilasters.

Factored moment diagrams due to eccentric dead load and wind are as shown in Fig. 12.21.

Maximum factored design moment is the summation of that due to eccentric gravity load and that due to wind:

$$M_u = 28{,}188 + 11{,}840 = 40{,}029 \text{ lb-in.}$$

Now design the pilaster to have sufficient capacity.

The effective depth, d, of the pilaster is computed based on the specified dimensions of nominal 8-in. CMU (see Fig. 12.22).

Using a spreadsheet as before, a strength-based, moment-axial force interaction diagram can be generated, as illustrated in Fig. 12.23. Because the compressive reinforcement will probably not be supported (tied) laterally, its contribution is neglected.

Because the reinforcement is located a good distance from the geometric centroid of the cross-section, the shape of the interaction diagram is familiar, with the maximum moment capacity corresponding to the balance point.

The spreadsheet cells are reproduced in Table 12.8.

Using four #4 bars, the capacity of the pilaster is much greater than required. Wind uplift will not govern, as shown in Fig. 12.22. Shear is very small and will not govern.

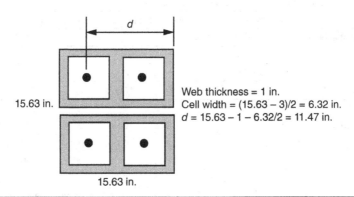

FIGURE 12.22 Effective depth, d, of pilasters.

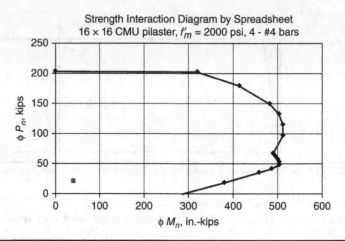

Figure 12.23 Strength moment-axial force interaction diagram for typical pilaster.

Table 12.8 Spreadsheet for Calculating Strength Moment-Axial Force Interaction Diagram for Typical Pilaster

Spreadsheet for calculating strength Mn-Pn interaction diagram for 16-inch CMU pilaster, Chapter 12									
Depth	15.63								
emu	0.0025								ϕ
f'_m	2								
f_y	60								
E_s	29000								
ε_y	0.002069								
d	11.47								
(c/d) balanced	0.54717								
Width	15.63								
Steel layers are counted from the extreme compression fiber to the extreme tension fiber									
Distances are measured from the extreme compression fiber									
Compression in masonry and reinforcement is taken as positive									
Stress in compressive reinforcement is set to zero, because the reinforcement may not be laterally supported									
Row of Reinforcement	distance	Area							
1	4.16	0.40							
2	11.47	0.40							
	c/d	c	C_{mas}	$f_s(1)$	ε_s	$f_s(2)$	ϕ	ϕMn	Pn
Pure axial load							0.65	0.0	202.6
Points controlled by masonry	1.36	15.60	312	0.00	0.0007	0.00	0.65	319.6	202.9
	1.2	13.76	275	0.00	0.0004	0.00	0.65	413.4	179.0
	1	11.47	229	0.00	0.0000	0.00	0.65	481.3	149.2
	0.9	10.32	207	0.00	−0.0003	−8.06	0.65	502.4	132.1
	0.8	9.18	184	0.00	−0.0006	−18.13	0.65	511.8	114.6
	0.7	8.03	161	0.00	−0.0011	−31.07	0.65	510.2	96.3
	0.54717	6.28	126	0.00	−0.0021	−60.00	0.65	489.9	66.0

(continued)

Strength Design Example: Low-Rise Building with Reinforced Concrete Masonry

	c/d	c	C_{mas}	$f_s(1)$	ε_s	$f_s(2)$	ϕ	ϕMn	Pn
Points controlled by steel	0.54717	6.28	126	0.00	−0.0021	−60.00	0.65	489.9	66.0
	0.5	5.74	115	0.00	−0.0025	−60.00	0.69	494.7	62.2
	0.45	5.16	103	0.00	−0.0031	−60.00	0.73	499.0	58.0
	0.4	4.59	92	0.00	−0.0038	−60.00	0.79	503.0	53.6
	0.3494	4.01	80	−2.76	−0.0047	−60.00	0.87	503.5	47.7
	0.32	3.67	73	−9.67	−0.0053	−60.00	0.90	485.7	41.0
	0.3	3.44	69	−15.15	−0.0058	−60.00	0.90	457.9	34.9
	0.25	2.87	57	−32.68	−0.0075	−60.00	0.90	380.2	18.3
	0.2	2.29	46	−58.97	−0.0100	−60.00	0.90	286.2	−1.5
	0.1	1.15	23	−60.00	−0.0225	−60.00	0.90	151.9	−22.5
	0.01	0.11	2	−60.00	−0.2475	−60.00	0.90	16.0	−41.1

The bearing plate dimensions are shown in Fig. 12.24.

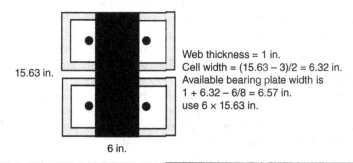

Web thickness = 1 in.
Cell width = (15.63 − 3)/2 = 6.32 in.
Available bearing plate width is
1 + 6.32 − 6/8 = 6.57 in.
use 6 × 15.63 in.

15.63 in.

6 in.

FIGURE 12.24 Bearing plate under long-span joists.

12.7.5 Design Bearing Plate under Long-Span Joists

TMS 402-22 specifies a strength-reduction factor of 0.60 for bearing (Section 9.1.4.1), and provides formulas for nominal bearing capacity (Section 9.1.8):

$$\phi P_{n\,bearing} = \phi 0.8 A_n f'_m = 0.6 \times 0.8 \times 15.63^2 \text{ in}^2 \times 2000 \text{ lb/in}^2 = 234{,}525 \text{ lb}$$

This design capacity is far in excess of the factored axial load. The required area of the bearing plate is about 10% of the cross-sectional area of the pilaster. Use a bearing plate measuring about 6 in. × 15 in.

12.8 Step 3: Design Lintels

Only the lintel over the 20-ft opening will be critical (Fig. 12.25).

As with the previous design of the area over the lintel for out-of-plane flexure in the horizontal plane, the structural span of the lintel is 20 ft, plus one-half of one-half unit on each side, or 20.67 ft. Conservatively, arching action will be neglected.

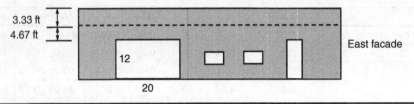

FIGURE 12.25 East façade of low-rise building, showing critical 20-ft lintel.

12.8.1 Calculate Gravity Load on Lintel

The lintel supports some direct gravity load from the roof decking, based on the tributary area shown below.

The tributary area supported by the entire lintel is 10 ft (tributary width from Fig. 12.26), multiplied by the span of 20 ft, or 200 ft². Because this is exactly equal to the upper limit of the tributary area at which live load reduction starts, no live load reduction is applied.

Factored gravity loads per foot of length on the lintel are itemized in Table 12.9. Because the lintel is uncoupled from the wall system by the control joints at each end, gravity loads alone constitute the critical loading case for it, and the governing loading combination is $1.2D + 1.6L$. In calculating the self-weight of the parapet and wall above the opening, the masonry is assumed to be fully grouted, with a self-weight of 81 lb/ft².

As in previous lintel-design examples, the bars in the lintel will probably be placed in the lower part of an inverted bottom course. As shown in Fig. 12.27, the effective depth d is calculated using the minimum cover of 1.5 in. (Section 6.1.4.2 of *TMS 402-22*), plus one-half the diameter of an assumed #8 bar.

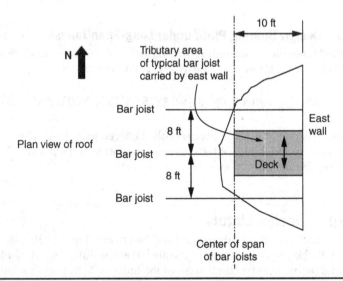

FIGURE 12.26 Tributary area supported by bar joists bearing on lintel of east wall.

Strength Design Example: Low-Rise Building with Reinforced Concrete Masonry

TABLE 12.9 Factored Gravity Loads Acting on 20-ft Lintel of East Wall

Description	Calculation	Load Factor	Factored Load, lb/ft
Roof DL	60 lb/ft² × 10 ft	1.2	720
Roof LL	20 lb/ft² × 10 ft	1.6	320
parapet + wall	8 ft × 81 lb/ft²	1.2	648
Total			1688

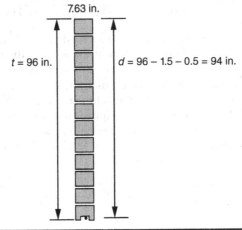

FIGURE 12.27 Section through 20-ft lintel of east wall.

Calculate the factored design moment and shear for the lintel:

$$V_u = \frac{w_u L}{2} = \frac{1668 \text{ lb/ft} \times 20.67 \text{ ft}}{2} = 17{,}445 \text{ lb}$$

$$M_u = \frac{w_u L^2}{8} = \frac{1668 \text{ lb/ft} \times 20.67^2 \text{ ft}^2 \times 12 \text{ in./ft}}{8} = 1081.8 \text{ kip-in.}$$

Because this is a reinforced element, shearing capacity is calculated using Section 9.3.3.1.2.1 of *TMS 402-22*:

$$V_{nm} = \left[4.0 - 1.75\left(\frac{M_u}{V_u d_v}\right)\right] A_{nv} \sqrt{f'_m} + 0.25 P_u$$

As $(M_u/V_u d_v)$ increases, V_{nm} decreases. Because $(M_u/V_u d_v)$ need not be taken greater than 1.0 (*TMS 402-22*, Section 9.3.3.1.2.1), the most conservative (lowest) value of V_{nm} is obtained with $(M_u/V_u d_v)$ equal to 1.0. Also, axial load, P_u, is zero:

$$V_{nm} = [4.0 - 1.75(1.0)] A_{nv} \sqrt{f'_m}$$

$$V_{nm} = 2.25 A_{nv} \sqrt{f'_m}$$

$$V_u = 17{,}445 \text{ lb} \leq \phi V_n = 0.8 \times 2.25 \times 7.63 \text{ in.} \times 94 \text{ in.} \sqrt{2000} \text{ lb/in}^2 = 57{,}735 \text{ lb}$$

and the design is acceptable for shear.

Now check the required flexural reinforcement:

$$M_n \approx A_s f_y 0.9d$$

In our case,

$$M_n^{\text{required}} = \frac{M_u}{\phi} = \frac{M_u}{0.9} = \frac{1{,}081{,}800 \text{ lb-in.}}{0.9} = 1{,}260{,}000 \text{ lb-in.}$$

Solve for the required steel area:

$$A_s^{\text{required}} = \frac{M_u}{\phi f_y 0.9d} = \frac{1{,}081{,}800 \text{ lb-in.}}{0.9 \times 60{,}000 \text{ psi} \times 0.9 \times 94 \text{ in.}} = 0.237 \text{ in}^2$$

Because of the depth of the beam, this can easily be satisfied with two #4 bars in the lowest course. Also include two #4 bars at the level of the roof (bond beam reinforcement). This will be consistent with the requirements of the design of the lintel for out-of-plane bending in a horizontal plane. Finally, to guard against possible cracking of the lintel near the top, use two more #4 bars at the top course of the parapet.

Section 9.3.4.2.2.2 of *TMS 402-22* requires that the nominal flexural strength of a beam not be less than 1.3 times the nominal cracking capacity, calculated using the modulus of rupture from Section 9.3.3.2.2 of *TMS 402-22*. In our case, the nominal cracking moment for the 8-ft deep section is

$$M_{cr} = Sf_r = \frac{bt^2}{6} f_r = \frac{7.63 \text{ in.} \times 96^2 \text{ in}^2}{6} \times 267 \text{ lb/in}^2 = 3.123 \times 10^6 \text{ lb-in.}$$

This value, multiplied by 1.3, is 4.06×10^6 lb-in. The nominal flexural capacity of a lintel with a single bottom layer of reinforcement of $A_s = 0.237$ in² is 1.081×10^6 lb-in. divided by 0.9, or 1.202×10^6 lb-in. With a single bottom layer of reinforcement of two #4 bars, the nominal flexural capacity is approximately that value multiplied by the ratio of 0.40 in²/0.237 in², or 2.029×10^6 lb-in. Using additional reinforcement of two #4 bars near mid-depth (with an area of reinforcement equal to that of the bottom layer, and an internal lever equal to about half that of the bottom layer) will increase this nominal capacity by a factor of about 1.5, to about 3.046×10^6 lb-in. This still does not meet the criterion of Section 9.3.3.2.2.

Under typical circumstances, the area of tensile reinforcement would need to be increased. However, Section 9.3.3.2.2.2 of *TMS 402-22* need not be met if the amount of tensile reinforcement is at least one-third greater than required by analysis (Section 9.3.4.2.2.3 of TMS 402-22). Because in this case $(\phi M_n/M_u) = (3.03/1.134) = 2.67$, we do not need to increase the area of tensile reinforcement further.

12.9 Summary So Far

Thus far in the design, all walls are fully grouted. The west and south walls have #5 bars vertically, at a horizontal spacing of 48 in. The north walls have #5 bars vertically at 10 ft, wall ends, near openings.

As a result of the design of the wall segments of the east wall for out-of-plane bending, the lintel of the east wall for out-of-plane bending, and the design of the lintel of the east wall as a beam, reinforcement in the east wall is as shown in Fig. 12.28. Each wall

Strength Design Example: Low-Rise Building with Reinforced Concrete Masonry

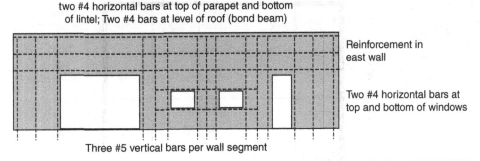

FIGURE 12.28 Reinforcement in east wall of low-rise building.

segment has three #5 vertical bars; and three sets of horizontal reinforcement are provided, in the form of two #4 bars at the top of the parapet and the bottom of the lintel, and two #5 bars at the level of the roof. The #4 and #5 bars are continued around the perimeter of the entire building.

12.10 Step 4: Conduct Lateral Force Analysis, Design Roof Diaphragm

Lateral force analysis will be critical in the north-south direction, because the area normal to the wind is greater, and the area of shear walls is less.

12.10.1 Check Roof Diaphragm

12.10.1.1 Compute Moment and Shear in Roof Diaphragm

From the wind load analysis of Step 1, the unfactored design base shear on the building, due to wind from the north or south (the critical directions), is 35.37 kips.

As shown in Fig. 12.29, some of this is transmitted to the roof diaphragm; the rest is transmitted to the foundation slab. To compute the amount transferred to the roof diaphragm, idealize the 35.37 kips as applied uniformly over either the north or south wall of the building. In reality, it is applied to both, but the simplifying assumption can be used to calculate the diaphragm actions. As before, a simple support is assumed at the base of the wall.

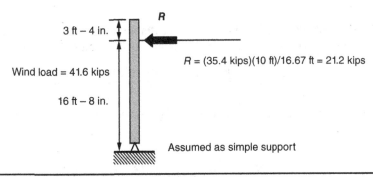

FIGURE 12.29 Wind load transmitted to roof diaphragm.

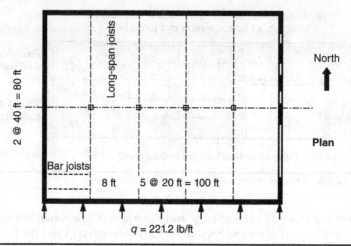

FIGURE 12.30 Plan view of low-rise building showing wind loads transferred to roof diaphragm.

This roof reaction is distributed over the roof length of 100 ft, giving a horizontal load on the diaphragm of 212.2 lb/ft (Fig. 12.30).

12.10.1.2 Design Roof Chords
Next, we need to design the roof chords. The load factor for W is 1.0:

$$M_{u\,roof} = \frac{w_u L^2}{8} = \frac{1.0 \times 212.2 \text{ lb/ft} \times 100^2 \text{ ft}^2}{8} = 265{,}222 \text{ lb-ft}$$

The required chord force is this factored moment, divided by the distance between chords (80 ft), and divided by the ϕ factor for axial tension (0.9). The required steel area is this chord force, divided by the specified yield strength of the reinforcement (60,000 lb/in²):

$$T_{u\,chord} = \frac{M_u}{\phi H} = \frac{265{,}222 \text{ lb-ft}}{0.90 \cdot 80 \text{ ft}} = 3684 \text{ lb}$$

$$A_s^{required} = \frac{T_{u\,chord}}{f_y} = \frac{3684 \text{ lb}}{60{,}000 \text{ lb/in}^2} = 0.061 \text{ in}^2$$

We have already specified two #4 bars around the perimeter of the roof, so that will be fine.

12.10.1.3 Check Shear Capacity of Roof Diaphragm
Next, we need to check the shear capacity of the roof diaphragm. The load factor for W is 1.0:

$$V_{u\,roof} = \frac{w_u L}{2} = \frac{1.0 \cdot 221.2 \text{ lb/ft} \cdot 100 \text{ ft}}{2} = 10{,}609 \text{ lb}$$

Because this is a reinforced element, shearing capacity is calculated using Section 9.3.3.1.2 of *TMS 402-22*:

$$V_{nm} = \left[4.0 - 1.75\left(\frac{M_u}{V_u d_v}\right)\right] A_{nv} \sqrt{f'_m} + 0.25 P_u$$

Strength Design Example: Low-Rise Building with Reinforced Concrete Masonry

As $(M_u/V_u d_v)$ increases, V_{nm} decreases. Because $(M_u/V_u d_v)$ need not be taken greater than 1.0 (TMS 402-22 Section 9.3.3.1.2.1), the most conservative (lowest) value of V_{nm} is obtained with $(M_u/V_u d_v)$ equal to 1.0. Also, axial load, P_u, is zero. In our case, the shearing capacity is given by:

$$V_{nm} = [4.0 - 1.75(1.0)]A_{nv}\sqrt{f'_m}$$
$$V_{nm} = 2.25 A_{nv}\sqrt{f'_m}$$

$V_u = 10{,}609 \text{ lb} \leq \phi V_n = 0.8 \times 2.25 \times 3.00 \text{ in.} \times 80 \text{ ft} \times 12 \text{ in./ft} \times \sqrt{2000} \text{ lb/in}^2 = 231{,}836 \text{ lb}$

For convenience, in the above calculation the specified compressive strength of the lightweight concrete topping has been taken as the same 2000 psi used for masonry, and any reduction in shear capacity due to lightweight aggregate has been neglected. These simplifications are believed to be justified in view of the large excess shear capacity of the roof diaphragm.

Also, according to Equation 9-20,

$$V_n \leq \left(4\sqrt{f'_m} A_n\right)\gamma_g$$

This does not govern, and the shear design is acceptable.

12.10.2 Compute Design Shears on Walls

The total factored design shear applied to the west and east walls due to north-south load is the factored load on the roof diaphragm. This is 1.0 × (21.7 kips + 13.67 kips) (Table 12.2), or 35.37 kips.

Neglect plan torsion. Assume that shear is distributed to walls and wall segments in proportion to the segment lengths on each side. This is consistent with a rigid roof diaphragm, because of the topping on the roof.

On the west side, the total length is 80 ft.
On the east side, the total wall segment length is (12 + 8 + 6 + 8 + 12) ft, or 46 ft.
Calculate the shear in the west and east walls:

$$V_{u\,west} = 35.37 \text{ kips}\left(\frac{80}{80+46}\right) = 20.46 \text{ kips}$$

$$V_{u\,east} = 35.37 \text{ kips}\left(\frac{46}{80+46}\right) = 12.91 \text{ kips}$$

Distribute the shear to the wall segments of the east wall in proportion to their plan length. The results are shown in Table 12.10.

12.11 Step 5: Design Wall Segments

12.11.1 Design West Wall in Plane

The capacity of the west will obviously be governed by shear. This will be no problem. The factored design shear in the west wall, 22.46 kips, is far less than the shear capacity, reduced by the strength-reduction factor for shear.

TABLE 12.10 Design Shear in Each Segment of East Wall due to Design Wind Load

Wall Segment	Plan Length, ft	Design Shear, kips
A	12	3.37
B	8	2.45
C	6	1.68
D	8	2.24
E	12	3.37
Total		12.91

Conservatively neglect the beneficial effects of axial load, and conservatively take $\frac{M_u}{V_u d_v} = 1$.

$$V_{nm} = \left[4.0 - 1.75\left(\frac{M_u}{V_u d_v}\right)\right] A_{nv} \sqrt{f'_m} + 0.25 P_u$$

$$V_{nm} = [4.0 - 1.75(1.0)]\,7.63\text{ in.} \times 80\text{ ft} \times 12\text{ in./ft}\left(\sqrt{2000}\text{ lb/in}^2\right) + 0$$

$$V_{nm} = 737.1\text{ kips}$$

The corresponding design shear capacity is

$$\phi V_n = 0.80 \times 737.1\text{ kips} = 589.6\text{ kips}$$

The design shear capacity far exceeds the factored design shear of 22.46 kips, and the west wall is satisfactory for shear.

12.11.2 Design East Wall in Plane

Because shear has been distributed in proportion to plan length, the nominal in-plane shear stress in each wall segment is equal. Check any wall segment, for example, Wall Segment A. The factored design shear in the wall segment is 3.36 kips.

Assuming a point of inflection at midheight (Fig. 12.31), the corresponding moment is $(VH/2)$, or $(3.36\text{ kips} \times 12\text{ ft}/2) = 20.16$ kip-ft $= 241.9$ kip-in.

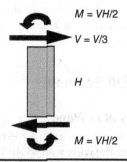

FIGURE 12.31 Assumed variation of shear and moment in each segment of east wall.

Strength Design Example: Low-Rise Building with Reinforced Concrete Masonry

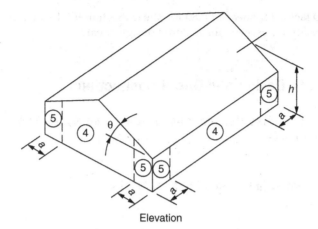

Elevation

12.11.2.1 Capacity of Wall Segment A as Governed by Flexure

Conservatively neglect the effects of axial load and assume an internal lever arm of 90% of the total depth of the wall segment. Compute the flexural capacity of the wall segment with three #7 bars. Neglect the contribution of the compressive reinforcement, and the middle layer of reinforcement:

$$M_n \approx A_s f_y \times 0.9t$$

$$M_n \approx 0.60 \text{ in}^2 \times 60 \text{ kip/in}^2 \times 0.9 \times 144 \text{ in.}$$

$$M_n \approx 4666 \text{ kip-in.}$$

Using a ϕ factor of 0.90 for flexure (TMS 402-22 Section 9.1.4.1), the design flexural capacity of 4666 kip-in. far exceeds the factored design moment of 241.9 kip-in.

12.11.2.2 Capacity of Wall Segment A as Governed by Shear

Now check the capacity of a typical wall segment as governed by shear. All segments have the same nominal shear stress. Check Segment A, with a plan length of 12 ft.

For a single wall segment,

$$V_n = V_{nm} = \left[4.0 - 1.75\left(\frac{M_u}{V_u d_v}\right)\right] A_{nv} \sqrt{f'_m} + 0.25 P_u$$

Conservatively neglect the effects of axial load. Then

$$V_n = \left[4.0 - 1.75\left(\frac{V_u L/2}{V_u d_v}\right)\right] \cdot (12 \text{ ft} \times 12 \text{ in./ft} \times 7.63 \text{ in.}^2)\sqrt{2000 \text{ lb/in}^2}$$

$$V_n = \left[4.0 - 1.75\left(\frac{12 \times 12 \text{ in.}}{2 \times 144 \times 0.9 \text{ in.}}\right)\right] \times 1099 \text{ in}^2 \times 38.73 \text{ lb/in}^2$$

$$V_n = [4.0 - 1.75(0.555)] \times 1099 \text{ in}^2 \times 38.73 \text{ lb/in}^2$$

$$V_n = 3.03 \times 1099 \text{ in}^2 \times 38.73 \text{ lb/in}^2 = 148,812 \text{ lb}$$

Using a ϕ factor for shear of 0.80 for shear (Section 9.1.4.1 of *TMS 402-22*), the design shear capacity far exceeds the factored design shear.

12.12 Step 6: Design and Detail Connections

12.12.1 Wall-Slab Connections for North and South Walls
Use #5 foundation dowels @ 48 in. Use #6 foundation dowels connected to longitudinal reinforcement in pilasters.

12.12.2 Wall-Slab connections for West Wall
Use #5 foundation dowels @ 48 in.

12.12.3 Wall-Slab Connections for East Wall
Use #7 foundation dowels connected to wall segment reinforcement.

12.12.4 Connections between Walls and Roof Diaphragm
Walls will be solid grouted. Bar joists will be embedded into bond beams at roof level. Long-span joists will rest on bearing plates embedded into column (pilaster) sections. Angles at the edge of roof diaphragm will be connected to walls using 1/2-in. anchor bolts spaced at 48 in.

CHAPTER 13

Strength Design Example: Four-Story Building with Clay Masonry

13.1 Introduction

This second example extends the synthesized design principles of the previous chapter, to a multi-story, hotel-type structure. To illustrate the calculation and application of seismic loads from the 2024 *IBC*, seismic loading is included in this example. To emphasize the feasibility of masonry in a zone of significant seismic risk, the building will be located in Charleston, South Carolina. The principal lateral force-resisting elements of the structure are transverse shear walls.

This combined example problem is carried out using strength design. Previous comparisons are intended to facilitate estimation of the extent to which the design would change if the allowable-stress design were used.

13.2 Design Steps for Four-Story Example

1) Choose design criteria, specify materials
   - Propose plan, elevation, materials, f'_m
   - Calculate D, L, W, E loads
   - Propose structural systems for gravity and lateral load
2) Design transverse shear walls for gravity and earthquake loads
3) Design exterior walls for gravity and wind loads
   - Earthquake loads will be carried by longitudinal walls in-plane.
   - Out-of-plane wind loads will be carried by longitudinal walls out-of-plane using vertical and horizontal strips.

13.3 Step 1: Choose Design Criteria, Specify Materials

The plan and elevation of the building are shown in Figs. 13.1 and 13.2.

13.3.1 Architectural Constraints for Four-Story Example Building

Water-penetration resistance: A single-wythe, fully grouted clay masonry wall with through-wall units will be used. The wall will resist water penetration.

Movement joints: Expansion joints will probably not be needed. The building can move. Expansion of clay walls will not be restrained. If needed, use horizontal expansion joints every two bays.

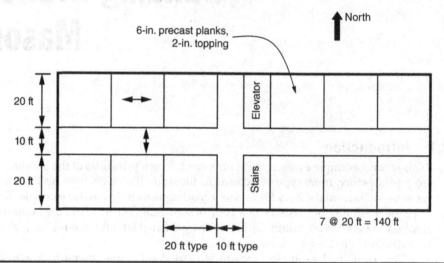

Figure 13.1 Plan view of typical floor of four-story example building.

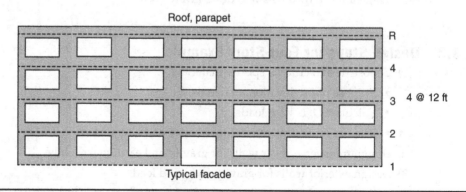

Figure 13.2 Plan view of typical floor of four-story example building.

13.3.2 Design for Fire

Use and occupancy: Group B

Use Type I or Type II construction (noncombustible material)

No area or height restrictions

2- or 3-hour rating required

Must meet separation requirements of Table 705.2 of the 2024 IBC

Bearing walls:	4-h rating	(8-in. nominal grouted masonry OK)
shafts:	2-h rating	(8-in. nominal grouted masonry OK)
floors:	2-h rating	(planks and topping OK)

13.3.3 Specify Materials

8-in. through-wall clay units (*ASTM C652*), fully grouted

Type S PCL mortar, specified by proportion (ASTM C270)

f'_m = 2500 lb/in². Use clay units with a net-area compressive strength of 6600 lb/in², and Type S PCL mortar.

Deformed reinforcement meeting *ASTM A615*, Gr. 60

Cover floors and roof of hollow-core planks with 2-in. topping, reinforced with welded-wire reinforcement.

13.3.4 Structural Systems

Gravity load: Gravity load on roof and floors will be transferred to transverse walls. Gravity load on corridor will be transferred to spine walls.

Lateral load: Lateral load (earthquake will govern) will be transferred by floor and roof diaphragms to the transverse shear walls, which will act as statically determinate cantilevers.

13.3.5 Calculate Design Roof Load due to Gravity

Design roof load due to gravity is calculated below.

Dead load	Planks	60 lb/ft²
	Topping	25 lb/ft²
	HVAC, roofing	30 lb/ft²
		115 lb/ft² total
Live load	Ignore reduction of live load based on tributary area.	20 lb/ft²

13.3.6 Calculate Design Floor Load due to Gravity

Design floor load due to gravity is calculated below.

Dead load	Planks	60 lb/ft²
	Topping	25 lb/ft²
	HVAC, floor finish, partitions	30 lb/ft²
		115 lb/ft² total
Live load	Use weighted average of corridor and guest rooms. Ignore reduction of live load based on tributary area.	60 lb/ft²

13.3.7 Calculate Design Lateral Load from Earthquake

Design earthquake loads are calculated according to Section 1613 of the 2024 *IBC*. That section essentially references *ASCE 7-22*. Seismic design criteria are given in Chapter 11 of *ASCE 7-22*. The seismic design provisions of *ASCE 7-22* begin in Chapter 12, which prescribes basic requirements (including the requirement for continuous load paths) (Section 12.1); selection of structural systems (Section 12.2); diaphragm characteristics and other possible irregularities (Section 12.3); seismic load effects and combinations (Section 12.4); direction of loading (Section 12.5); analysis procedures (Section 12.6); modeling procedures (Section 12.7); and specific design approaches. Four procedures are prescribed: an equivalent lateral force procedure (Section 12.8); a modal response-spectrum analysis (Section 12.9); a simplified alternative procedure (Section 12.14); and a nonlinear seismic response history procedure (Chapter 16). The equivalent lateral-force procedure is described here, because it is relatively simple and is permitted in most situations. The simplified alternative procedure is permitted in only a few situations. The other procedures are permitted in all situations and are required in only a few situations.

Now discuss each step in more detail, following the example of a building in Charleston, South Carolina.

Step 1: Determine S_{MS}, the mapped MCE (maximum considered earthquake), 5% damped, spectral response acceleration parameter at short periods as defined in Section 11.4.3.

Step 2: Determine S_{M1}, the mapped MCE, 5% damped, spectral response acceleration parameter at a period of 1 s as defined in Section 11.4.3.

Determine the parameters S_s and S_1 from the 0.2-s and 1-s spectral response maps shown in Figures 22-1 through 22-7.

For Charleston, South Carolina, $S_{MS} = 2.00$ g, and $S_{M1} = 0.75$ g.

Step 3: Determine the *site class* (*A* through *F*, a measure of soil response characteristics and soil stability) in accordance with Section 20.2 and Table 20.2-1.

Assume Site Class D (stiff soil).

Step 4: Determine the design response acceleration parameter for short periods, S_{DS}, and for a 1-s period, S_{D1}, using Equations 11.4-1 and 11.4-2 respectively.

The design response acceleration is two-thirds of the maximum considered acceleration. Continuing with our example for Charleston, South Carolina, the design response acceleration for short periods is:

$$S_{DS} = \frac{2}{3} \cdot S_{MS} = \frac{2}{3} \cdot 2.00\, g = 1.33\, g$$

and the design response acceleration for a 1-second period is:

$$S_{D1} = \frac{2}{3} \cdot S_{M1} = \frac{2}{3} \cdot 0.75\, g = 0.50\, g$$

Step 5: **If required, determine the design response spectrum curve as prescribed by Section 11.4.5.2.**

Because the equivalent lateral force procedure is being used, the response spectrum curve is not required. Nevertheless, for pedagogical completeness, it is illustrated in Fig. 13.3 and was developed in Section 3.5. Alternatively, an *ASCE* design tool could be used.

Step 6: **Determine the structure's importance factor, *I*, and occupancy category using Section 1.5 and Table 1.5-2.**

Assume that the structure is assigned an Occupancy Category II. This corresponds to an Importance Factor of 1.0.

Step 7: **Determine the structure's Seismic Design Category using Section 11.6.**

Because S_{D1} exceeds 0.20, the structure is assigned to Seismic Design Category D.

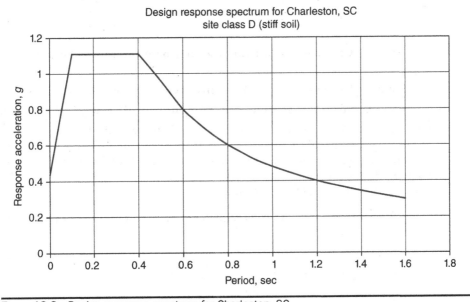

FIGURE 13.3 Design response spectrum for Charleston, SC.

ASCE 7-22 Table 1.5-2 Importance Factors by Risk Category of Buildings and Other Structures for Earthquake Loads

Risk Category from Table 1.5-1	Seismic Importance Factor, I_o
I	1.00
II	1.00
III	1.25
IV	1.50

ASCE 7-22 Table 11.6-1 Seismic Design Category Based on Short-Period Response Acceleration Parameter

	Risk Category	
Value of S_{DS}	I or II or III	IV
$S_{DS} < 0.167$	A	A
$0.167 \leq S_{DS} < 0.33$	B	C
$0.33 \leq S_{DS} < 0.50$	C	D
$0.50 \leq S_{DS}$	D	D

ASCE 7-22 Table 11.6-2 Seismic Design Category Based on 1 s Period Response Acceleration Parameter

	Risk Category	
Value of S_{D1}	I or II or III	IV
$S_{D1} < 0.067$	A	A
$0.067 \leq S_{D1} < 0.133$	B	C
$0.133 \leq S_{D1} < 0.20$	C	D
$0.20 \leq S_{D1}$	D	

Step 8: Calculate the structure's seismic base shear using Sections 12.8.1 and 12.8.2.

Step 9: Distribute seismic base shear vertically using Section 12.8.3.

Step 10: Distribute seismic base shear horizontally using Section 12.8.4.

These last three steps are structure dependent. They depend on the seismic response modification coefficient assigned to the structural system, on the structure's plan structural irregularities, on the structure's vertical structural irregularities, and on the structure's redundancy.

Plan structural irregularities include:

- Plan eccentricities between the center of mass and the center of stiffness
- Re-entrant corners
- Out-of-plane offsets
- Non-parallel systems

These can increase seismic response.

Strength Design Example: Four-Story Building with Clay Masonry

Vertical structural irregularities include:

- Stiffness irregularity
- Mass irregularity
- Vertical geometric irregularity
- In-plane discontinuity in vertical lateral-force-resisting elements
- Discontinuity in capacity—weak story

These can also increase seismic response.

Structures with low redundancy have a higher probability of failure, which is compensated for by increasing design seismic forces.

Step 8: Calculate the structure's seismic base shear using Sections 12.8.1 and 12.8.2.

In accordance with *ASCE 7-22*, Section 12.8.1.1,

$$C_s = \frac{S_{DS}}{\left(\dfrac{R}{I}\right)} \qquad \text{(Equation 12.8-2)}$$

In our case,

$S_{DS} = 1.33$ g

$R = 5$ (meet detailing provisions for special reinforced masonry shear wall)

$I = 1.00$ (*ASCE 7-22*, Table 11.5-1)

$$C_s = \frac{S_{DS}}{\left(\dfrac{R}{I}\right)} = \frac{1.33}{\left(\dfrac{5}{1}\right)} = 0.267$$

The value of C_s computed in accordance with Equation 12.8-2 need not exceed the following:

$$C_s = \frac{S_{D1}}{T\left(\dfrac{R}{I}\right)} \qquad \text{for } T \le T_L \qquad \text{(Equation 12.8-3)}$$

The corresponding equation for $T > T_L$ does not apply. In addition, C_s shall not be less than 0.01.

In our case, the value of C_s given by Equation 12.8-3 is

$$C_s = \frac{S_{D1}}{T\left(\dfrac{R}{I}\right)} = \frac{0.50}{T\left(\dfrac{R}{I}\right)} = \frac{0.50}{5T} = \frac{0.1}{T}$$

And in our case, from Section 12.8.1.1 of *ASCE 7-22*,

$$C_s = \frac{S_{D1}}{T\left(\dfrac{R}{I}\right)} \qquad \text{for } T \le T_L$$

$$C_s = \frac{S_{D1} T_L}{T^2 \left(\dfrac{R}{I}\right)} \qquad \text{for } T > T_L$$

On the left end of the plateau in the design response spectrum, at a period $T = T_0 = 0.075$ s, $C_s = 1.25$, and Equation 12.8-3 doesn't govern. Near the right end of the plateau, at $T = 0.40$ s, $C_s = 0.25$, and Equation 12.8-3 might barely govern. Conservatively assume that the structure is stiff enough that Equation 12.8-3 doesn't govern.

Because the structure is assigned to SDC D, the redundancy factor, ρ, is required to be taken as 1.3 (Section 12.3.4.1) unless certain conditions are met.

Finally, in accordance with *ASCE 7-22*, Section 12.4.2, the design horizontal seismic load effect E_h is

$$E_h = \rho Q_E \qquad \text{(Equation 12.4-1)}$$

Now compute the seismic base shear. In accordance with *ASCE 7-22*, Section 12.8.1, the effects of horizontal seismic forces Q_E come from V. The design seismic base shear is given by:

$$V = C_s W$$
$$V = 0.267W$$

This is multiplied by the redundancy factor of 1.3, giving a product of 0.347. In other words, the building must be designed for 34.7% of its weight, applied as a lateral force.

Step 9: Distribute seismic base shear vertically using Section 12.8.3.

This force is distributed triangularly over the height of the building.

The weight of a typical floor is its area, times the dead load per square foot, plus the interior transverse wall weight, plus the spine wall weight, plus the weight of the exterior walls. For simplicity, assume that the roof weighs the same as a typical floor and ignore the parapet.

Floor weight:	115 lb/ft² × 50 × 140 ft² = 805 kips
Transverse wall weight:	7 × 20 × 12 ft² × 80 lb/ft² = 134.4 kips
Spine wall weight:	2 × 130 × 12 ft² × 80 lb/ft² = 249.6 kips
Perimeter wall weight:	2 × (140 + 50) × 12 ft² × 80 lb/ft² = 364.8 kips

The total weight of a typical floor is 1553.8 kips.

The design base shear is calculated assuming a linear distribution of forces over the height of the structure.

Level	W	H	WH	WH/SUM
R	1553.8	48	74,582	0.40
4	1553.8	36	55,937	0.30
3	1553.8	24	37,291	0.20
2	1553.8	12	18,646	0.10
	6215.2		186,456	

Strength Design Example: Four-Story Building with Clay Masonry

TABLE 13.1 Factored Design Lateral Forces for Four-Story Example Building

Level	F_u, k	H, ft	V_u, k	M_u, k-ft
R	861.8	48	861.8	0
4	646.4	36	1508.2	10,342
3	430.9	24	1939.1	28,440
2	215.5	12	2154.6	51,709
				77,564

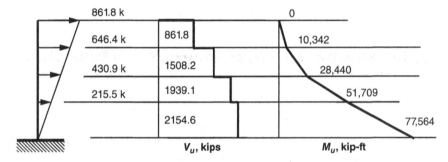

FIGURE 13.4 Factored design shears and moments for four-story example building.

Total design base shear is 6215.2 kips × 0.347 = 2154.6 kips.

At the roof level, the factored design lateral force is the design base shear (2154.6 kips), multiplied by 0.40 (the quotient of WH/SUM) for the triangular distribution, or 861.8 kips. At the next level down, the factored design lateral force is 2154.6 kips, multiplied by 0.30, and so forth.

At each level, the factored design moment is the summation of the products of the factored design lateral forces above that level, each multiplied by its respective height above that level. The load factor for seismic loads is 1.0.

Factored design shear and moment diagrams for the four-story example building are shown in Table 13.1 and Fig. 13.4.

13.4 Step 2: Design Transverse Shear Walls for Gravity plus Earthquake Loads

The transverse direction is critical for this building. The 16 transverse walls are conservatively assumed to be uncoupled, so that each functions as an independent cantilever. As shown in Fig. 13.5, design each transverse wall as an I beam, assuming flange widths of 4 ft. This is less than the limits specified in Section 5.3.2.3 of *TMS 402-22* and is therefore conservative.

382 Chapter Thirteen

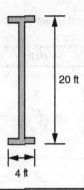

FIGURE 13.5 Effective flange width used for each transverse shear wall.

13.4.1 Shear Design of a Typical Transverse Wall for Earthquake Loads
From *TMS 402-22*, Section 9.3.3.1.2.1,

$$V_n = V_{nm} = \left[4.0 - 1.75\left(\frac{M_u}{V_u d_v}\right)\right] A_{nv} \sqrt{f'_m} + 0.25 P_u$$

Include the effects of axial load, assuming that a typical transverse wall carries its self-weight plus the distributed floor weight on a tributary width of 20 ft:

Self-weight of wall: 19.2 kips/floor
Floor weight: 115 lb/ft² × 20 × 20 = 46 kips/floor

Total unfactored axial dead load at base is 4 × (19.2 + 46) = 260.8 kips.
 Total unfactored axial live load at base is (20 + 3 × 60 psf) × 20 × 20 = 80 kips.
 Then

$$V_n = V_{nm} = \left[4.0 - 1.75\left(\frac{M_u}{V_u d_v}\right)\right] A_{nv} \sqrt{f'_m} + 0.25 P_u$$

$$V_n = \left[4.0 - 1.75\left(\frac{74{,}504 \times 12 \text{ kip-in.}}{2069.6 \times 20 \times 12 \text{ in.}}\right)\right] \times (20 \times 12 \times 7.50 \text{ in}^2)\sqrt{2500 \text{ lb/in}^2}$$

$$+ 0.25 \times 0.9 \times 260{,}800 \text{ lb}$$

$$V_n = [4.0 - 1.75(1.80)] \times 1800 \text{ in}^2 \times 50.0 \text{ lb/in}^2 + 58{,}680 \text{ lb}$$

But the ratio ($M_u/V_u d_v$) need not be taken greater than 1.0. Take it equal to that value.

$$V_n = [4.0 - 1.75(1.0)] \times 1800 \text{ in}^2 \times 50.0 \text{ lb/in}^2 + 58{,}680 \text{ lb}$$
$$V_n = 2.25 \times 1800 \text{ in}^2 \times 50.0 \text{ lb/in}^2 + 58{,}680 \text{ lb}$$
$$V_n = 202{,}500 + 58{,}680 \text{ lb} = 261{,}180 \text{ lb} = 261 \text{ kips}$$

Strength Design Example: Four-Story Building with Clay Masonry

The ϕ factor for shear for reinforced masonry is 0.80 (*TMS 402-22* Section 9.1.4.1).

$$\phi V_n = 0.80 \times 261 \text{ kips} = 209 \text{ kips}$$

This considerably exceeds the design load per each of the 16 walls (1/16 times the factored design base shear (1/16 × 2154.6 kips = 134.7 kips).

The wall must also meet the prescriptive reinforcement requirements and the capacity design requirements corresponding to a "special reinforced shear wall."

In accordance with *TMS 402-22* Section 7.3.2.5(f), the total reinforcement percentage (horizontal and vertical) shall be at least 0.002, with at least one-third of this placed in each direction.

This requirement and capacity design requirements of Section 7.3.2.5.1 will be checked later.

13.4.2 Flexural Design of Transverse Shear Walls for Earthquake Loads

Each transverse shear wall has a plan length of 20 ft. The factored base moment per wall is (1/16) × 77,564 ft-kips, or 4848 ft-kips. The critical load case is $0.9D + 1.0E$. The factored axial load (see above) is 0.9 × 260 kips, or 234 kips. Using a spreadsheet, the interaction diagram for the wall (with #5 bars spaced at 16 in. vertically in the web and flanges) is shown in Fig. 13.6. The spreadsheet is identical to that used previously for shear walls with rectangular cross-section. It is valid only for low axial loads (i.e., axial loads that are low enough to keep the neutral axis within the compression flange).

Selected cells from the spreadsheet are reproduced in Table 13.2.

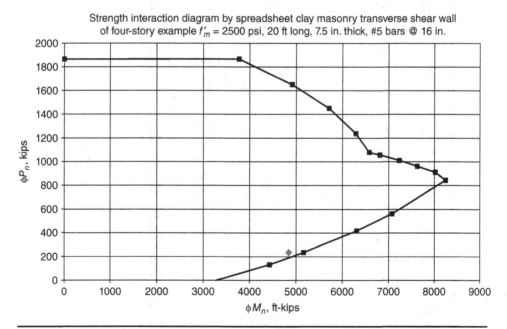

FIGURE 13.6 Strength moment-axial force interaction diagram for transverse masonry shear wall.

TABLE 13.2 Spreadsheet for Calculating Strength Moment-Axial Force Interaction Diagram for Transverse Shear Wall of Four-Story Building Example

Spreadsheet for calculating strength moment-axial force interaction diagram for transverse shear wall of Chapter 13			
Depth	240		
emu	0.0035		
f'_m	2.5		
f_y	60		
E_s	29000		
ε_y	0.002069		
d	237		
(c/d) balanced	0.628483		Mu 4848 kip-ft
Web width	7.5		Pu 234 kip
Abar	0.31		
Steel layers are counted from the extreme compression fiber to the extreme tension fiber			
Distances are measured from the extreme compression fiber			
Reinforcement consists of #5 bars at 16-in. intervals, assumed lumped at 32 in. for this spreadsheet			
Compression in masonry and reinforcement is taken as positive			
Stress in compressive reinforcement is set to zero, because the reinforcement is not laterally supported			
Row of Reinforcement	Distance	Area	
1	3.00	1.55	
2	35.00	0.62	
3	67.00	0.62	
4	99.00	0.62	
5	141.00	0.62	
6	173.00	0.62	
7	205.00	0.62	
8	237.00	1.55	

	c/d	c	C_{mas}	$f_s(1)$	$f_s(2)$	$f_s(3)$	$f_s(4)$	$f_s(5)$	$f_s(6)$	$f_s(7)$	$\varepsilon_y(8)$	$f_s(8)$	ϕ Eqn	ϕ	Mn	Pn	ϕ Mn	ϕ Pn
Pure axial load														0.65	0	2869	0	1865
Points controlled by masonry	1.01	239.37	2872	0.00	0.00	0.00	0.00	0.00	0.00	0.00	0.00003	0.00	0.47	0.65	5805	2872	3773	1867
	0.9	213.30	2560	0.00	0.00	0.00	0.00	0.00	0.00	0.00	-0.00039	-11.28	0.51	0.65	7568	2542	4919	1652
	0.8	189.60	2275	0.00	0.00	0.00	0.00	0.00	0.00	-8.24	-0.00088	-25.38	0.55	0.65	8792	2231	5715	1450
	0.7	165.90	1991	0.00	0.00	0.00	0.00	0.00	-4.34	-23.92	-0.00150	-43.50	0.60	0.65	9673	1906	6288	1239
	0.628483	148.95	1787	0.00	0.00	0.00	0.00	0.00	-16.39	-38.19	-0.00207	-60.00	0.65	0.65	10119	1661	6577	1079
Points controlled by steel	0.628483	148.95	1787	0.00	0.00	0.00	0.00	0.00	-16.39	-38.19	-0.00207	-60.00	0.65	0.65	10119	1661	6577	1079
	0.6	142.20	1706	0.00	0.00	0.00	0.00	0.00	-21.98	-44.83	-0.00233	-60.00	0.67	0.67	10139	1572	6814	1056
	0.55	130.35	1564	0.00	0.00	0.00	0.00	-8.29	-33.21	-58.13	-0.00286	-60.00	0.72	0.72	10108	1409	7239	1009
	0.5	118.50	1422	0.00	0.00	0.00	0.00	-19.27	-46.68	-60.00	-0.00350	-60.00	0.77	0.77	9922	1251	7633	962
	0.45	106.65	1280	0.00	0.00	0.00	0.00	-32.69	-60.00	-60.00	-0.00428	-60.00	0.83	0.83	9618	1092	8022	911
	0.4	94.80	1138	0.00	0.00	0.00	-4.50	-49.47	-60.00	-60.00	-0.00525	-60.00	0.92	0.90	9165	937	8248	843
	0.3	71.10	853	0.00	0.00	0.00	-39.83	-60.00	-60.00	-60.00	-0.00817	-60.00	1.16	0.90	7866	624	7080	562
	0.25	59.25	711	0.00	0.00	-13.28	-60.00	-60.00	-60.00	-60.00	-0.01050	-60.00	1.35	0.90	7004	461	6304	415
	0.1877	44.48	534	0.00	0.00	-51.37	-60.00	-60.00	-60.00	-60.00	-0.01515	-60.00	1.74	0.90	5741	260	5166	234
	0.15	35.55	427	0.00	0.00	-60.00	-60.00	-60.00	-60.00	-60.00	-0.01983	-60.00	2.13	0.90	4931	148	4438	133
	0.01	2.37	28	-26.98	-60.00	-60.00	-60.00	-60.00	-60.00	-60.00	-0.34650	-60.00	29.35	0.90	781	-330	703	-297

Examination of the values in the spreadsheet shows that at a factored axial load of 234 kips, the design moment capacity of the wall is 5166 kip-ft, greater than the required capacity of 4848 kip-ft. The ultimate loads, represented by a diamond marker, fall within the interaction diagram indicating that this design is adequate. The position of the neutral axis is 44.5 in. from the extreme compression fiber.

Flexural reinforcement consisting of #5 bars @ 16 in. is required. Each 4-ft flange has 5 bars, and the web has an additional 12 bars. The total area of reinforcement is 0.31 in² (5 + 5 + 12) = 6.82 in².

Meet minimum reinforcement requirements of TMS 402-22 7.3.2.5(f) using #5 bars at 16-in. vertically. Here, we provide 0.31 in² divided by the web width and spacing. Because compressive stress block extends into the web (0.8c = 0.8(44.5) = 35.6 in. > 7.5 in.), we use b = 7.5 in.

$$\rho_{vertical} = \frac{A_s}{bt} = \frac{0.31 \text{ in}^2}{7.50 \times 16 \text{ in}^2} = 0.00258$$

This exceeds the limit of 0.002 and meets the TMS code requirement.

In addition, this exceeds the required minimum of 0.0007 each way and is satisfactory so far.

Now check ρ_{max}, continuing to consider the wall as a "special" reinforced masonry shear wall ($R = 5$, $\alpha = 4$). The axial load mandated by TMS 402-22 Section 9.3.3.5.6.1(d) is $D + 0.75L + 0.525Q_E$. Because axial loads due to overturning are equal and opposite, they are ignored for this example. Referring to Section 13.4.1,

$$N_u = D + 0.75L + 0.525Q_E = 260.8 \text{ kips} + 0.75 \times 80 \text{ kips} + 0 \text{ kips} = 320.8 \text{ kips}$$

$$\rho_{max} = \frac{0.64 f'_m \left(\frac{\varepsilon_{mu}}{\alpha\varepsilon_y + \varepsilon_{mu}}\right) - \frac{N_u}{bd\phi}}{f_y \left(\frac{\alpha\varepsilon_y - \varepsilon_{mu}}{\alpha\varepsilon_y + \varepsilon_{mu}}\right)}$$

$$\rho_{max} = \frac{0.64 \times 2500 \text{ psi} \left(\frac{0.0035}{4 \times 0.00207 + 0.0035}\right) - \frac{320,800 \text{ lb}}{7.50 \text{ in.} \times 237 \text{ in.} \times 0.9}}{60,000 \text{ psi} \left(\frac{4 \times 0.00207 - 0.0035}{4 \times 0.00207 + 0.0035}\right)}$$

$$\rho_{max} = \frac{1600 \text{ psi}(0.2971) - 200.53}{60,000 \text{ psi}(0.4058)} = \frac{475.36 - 200.53}{24,348}$$

$$\rho_{max} = 0.0113$$

Check the maximum permitted area of flexural reinforcement. Because compressive stress block extends into the web, the effective width, b, is 7.5 in.

$$A_{smax} = \rho_{max} \times b \times d = 0.0113 \times 7.5 \text{ in.} \times 237 \text{ in.} = 20.1 \text{ in}^2$$

We have less than this (6.82 in²), and the design is satisfactory.

Strength Design Example: Four-Story Building with Clay Masonry

Now check TMS 402-22 Section 7.3.2.5.1 (capacity design for shear). We have designed the wall for the calculated design shear, which is normally sufficient. The wall is a special reinforced masonry shear wall, however, as required in areas of high seismic risk, so that the capacity design requirements of Code Section 7.3.5.1 apply.

First try to meet the capacity design provisions of that section. At an axial load of 234 kips, the nominal flexural capacity of this wall is the design capacity of 5166 ft-kips, divided by the strength reduction factor of 0.9, or 5741 ft-kips. The ratio of this nominal flexural capacity to the factored design moment is 5166 divided by 4848, or 1.065. Including the additional factor of 1.25, that gives a ratio of 1.33.

$$\phi V_n \geq 1.68 V_u$$

$$V_n \geq \frac{1.33}{\phi} V_u = \frac{1.33}{0.8} V_u = 1.67 V_u = 1.67 \times 134.7 = 224.3 \text{ kips}$$

Because $V_n = 261$ kips, shear reinforcement is not required for strength. However, prescriptive shear reinforcement is required, we compute the contribution to shear strength as a demonstration.

TMS 402-22 Section 7.3.5.2(f) requires a total steel percentage of 0.002 (summation of horizontal and vertical reinforcement), with at least 0.0007 horizontally and vertically. Vertical reinforcement is 0.00258, greater than the required sum, so horizontal reinforcement must meet only the minimum of 0.0007.

Use #4 bars @ 32 in. horizontally.

$$\rho_{horizontal} = \frac{A_s}{bt} = \frac{0.20 \text{ in}^2}{7.50 \times 32 \text{ in}^2} = 0.000833$$

From TMS 402-13, Section 9.3.3.1.2.2,

$$V_{ns} = 0.5 \left(\frac{A_v}{s} \right) f_y d_v$$

$$V_{ns} = 0.5 \left(\frac{0.20 \text{ in}^2}{16 \text{ in.}} \right) 60 \text{ kips/in}^2 \times 240 \text{ in.}$$

$$V_{ns} = 90 \text{ kips}$$

$$V_n = V_{nm} + V_{ns} = 261 \text{ kips} + 90 \text{ kips} = 351 \text{ kips}$$

This exceeds the required nominal shear from the capacity design (224.3 kips), and the design is satisfactory for shear.

Summary: Use #5 vertical bars @ 16 in.
Use #4 horizontal bars @ 32 in.

13.4.3 Comments on Design of Transverse Shear Walls

- The most laborious part of this design is calculation of the design lateral force for earthquake loads. Once that calculation is done, design of the lateral-force-resisting system is straightforward, even for a region of high seismic risk such as Charleston.

- This structural system would have continued to be feasible up to about six stories.

13.5 Step 3: Design Exterior Walls for Gravity plus Out-of-Plane Wind

This design follows the same steps as in the low-rise building example of Chapter 12. The critical panel will be at the top of the building, where the wind load is highest.

- The panel must be designed for out-of-plane wind. Load effects in vertical jamb strips will be increased by the ratio of the plan length of openings to the total plan length.
- Since the windows occupy at least half the plan length of the perimeter frame, it is possible that the panels will have to be designed as combinations of vertical strips spanning between floor slabs, and horizontal strips spanning between transverse walls.
- The lintels above the windows and door must be designed for in-plane bending and for out-of-plane bending as in the low-rise building example of Chapter 12.

13.6 Overall Comments on Four-Story Building Example

- Although it is located in a region of high seismic risk, this building needs comparatively little reinforcement, because of the large plan area of its bearing walls.
- Considerable simplicity in design and analysis was achieved by letting transverse shear walls resist lateral loads as statically determinate cantilevers.
- Masonry bearing wall construction is inexpensive and straightforward for this type of building.

CHAPTER 14
Structural Design of AAC Masonry

14.1 Introduction to Autoclaved Aerated Concrete (AAC)

Autoclaved Aerated Concrete (AAC) is a concrete-like material with very light weight, obtained by uniformly distributed, closed air bubbles (Fig. 14.1). Material specifications for this product are prescribed in ASTM C 1693.

Because AAC typically has one-sixth to one-third the density of conventional concrete, and about the same ratio of compressive strength, it is useful for cladding and infills, and for bearing-wall components of low- to medium-rise structures. Because its thermal conductivity is one-sixth or less that of concrete, it is energy-efficient. Because its fire rating is slightly longer than that of conventional concrete of the same thickness, it is very fire-resistant. It is not susceptible to mold. Because of its internal porosity, it has very low sound transmission and is acoustically very effective.

14.1.1 Historical Background of AAC

AAC was first produced commercially in Sweden, in 1923. Since that time, its production and use have spread to more than 40 countries on all continents, including North America, Central and South America, Europe, the Middle East, the Far East, and Australia. This wide experience has produced many case studies of use in different climates, and under different building codes. Background material on experience with AAC in Europe is given in RILEM (1993).

In the US, modern uses of AAC began in 1990, for residential and commercial projects in the southeastern states. US production of plain and reinforced AAC started in 1995 in the southeast and has since spread to other parts of the country. Design provisions for AAC are provided in TMS 402-22, and suggested details are provided in ACI 526.1R and in manufacturers' technical manuals.

14.1.2 AAC Elements

AAC can be used to make unreinforced, masonry-type units and also factory-reinforced floor panels, roof panels, wall panels, lintels, beams, and other special shapes (Fig. 14.2). These elements can be used in a variety of applications including residential, commercial and industrial construction. Reinforced wall panels can be used as cladding systems as well as load-bearing and non-load-bearing exterior and interior wall systems. Reinforced floor and roof panels can be efficiently used to provide the horizontal diaphragm system while supporting the necessary gravity loads.

FIGURE 14.1 Close-up view of AAC.

14.1.3 Materials Used in AAC

Materials for AAC vary with manufacture and location. They include some or all of the following: fine silica sand; Class F fly ash; hydraulic cements; calcined lime; gypsum; expansive agents such as finely ground aluminum powder or paste; and mixing water. Details of the mixture designs used by each producer depend on the available

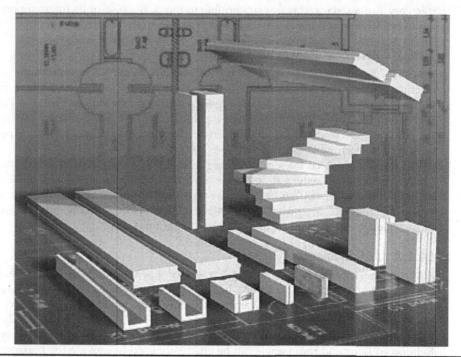

FIGURE 14.2 Examples of AAC elements. (Courtesy of Ytong International.)

materials and the precise manufacturing process, and are not publicly available. The finely ground aluminum power or paste produces expansion by combining with the alkaline slurry to produce hydrogen gas. AAC can be reinforced internally in the manufacturing process with welded wire cages and also at the job site with conventional reinforcement.

14.1.4 How AAC Is Made

Overall steps in the manufacture of AAC are shown in Fig. 14.3, and described below.

Sand is ground to the required fineness in a ball mill, if necessary and is stored along with other raw materials. The raw materials are then batched by weight and delivered to the mixer. Measured amounts of water and expansive agent are added to the mixer, and the cementitious slurry is mixed.

Steel molds are prepared to receive the fresh AAC. If reinforced AAC panels are to be produced, steel reinforcing cages are secured within the molds. After mixing, the slurry is poured into the molds. The expansive agent creates small, finely dispersed voids in the fresh mixture, which increases the volume by approximately 50% in the molds within three hours.

Within a few hours after casting, the initial hydration of cementitious compounds in the AAC gives it sufficient strength to hold its shape and support its own weight.

After cutting, the aerated concrete product is transported to a large autoclave, where the curing process is completed. Autoclaving is required to achieve the desired

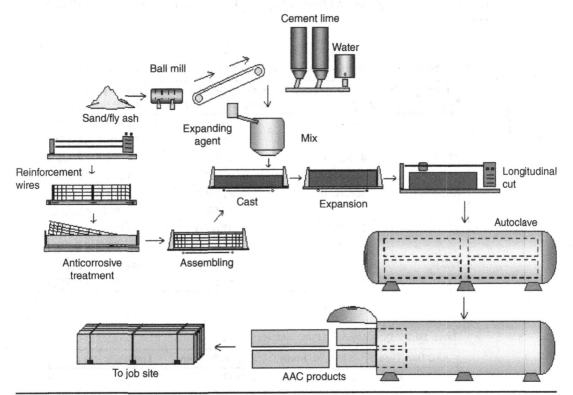

FIGURE 14.3 Overall steps in manufacture of AAC.

structural properties and dimensional stability. The process takes about 8–12 hours under a pressure of about 174 psi (12 Bars) and a temperature of about 360°F (180°C) depending on the grade of material produced. During autoclaving, the wire-cut units remain in their original positions in the AAC block. After autoclaving, they are separated for packaging.

AAC units are normally placed on pallets for shipping. Unreinforced units are typically shrink-wrapped, while reinforced elements are banded only, using corner guards to minimize potential localized damage that might be caused by the banding.

14.1.5 AAC Strength Classes

AAC is produced in different densities and corresponding compressive strengths, in accordance with ASTM C1386 (Precast Autoclaved Aerated Concrete Wall Construction Units). Densities and corresponding strengths are described in terms of "strength classes" (Table 14.1).

14.1.6 Typical Dimensions of AAC Units

Typical dimensions for plain AAC wall units (masonry-type units) are shown in Table 14.2.

Typical dimensions for reinforced AAC panels are 24-in. tall and 20-ft long. Design recommendations for reinforced AAC panels are provided in ACI 526.1R. Because reinforced AAC panels are not addressed by TMS 402, they are not discussed further in this book.

TABLE 14.1 Typical Material Characteristics of AAC in Different Strength Classes

Strength Class	Specified Compressive Strength lb/in² (MPa)	Nominal Dry Bulk Density lb/ft³ (kg/m³)	Density Limits lb/ft³ (kg/m³)
AAC-2	290 (2.0)	25 (400)	22 (350)–28 (450)
		31 (500)	28 (450)–34 (550)
AAC-3	435 (2.0)	31 (500)	28 (450)–34 (550)
		37 (600)	34 (550)–41 (650)
AAC-4	580 (4.0)	31 (500)	28 (450)–34 (550)
		37 (600)	34 (550)–41 (650)
AAC-5	725 (5.0)	37 (600)	34 (550)–41 (650)
		44 (700)	41 (650)–47 (750)
AAC-6	870 (6.0)	37 (600)	34 (550)–41 (650)
		44 (700)	41 (650)–47 (750)

TABLE 14.2 Dimensions of Plain AAC Wall Units

AAC Unit Type	Width, in. (mm)	Height, in. (mm)	Length, in. (mm)
Standard Block	2–15 (50–375)	8 (200)	24 (610)
Jumbo Block	4–15 (100–375)	16–24 (400–610)	24–40 (610–1050)

14.2 Applications of AAC

AAC can be used in a wide variety of structural and non-structural applications (Barnett et al. 2005), examples of which are shown in the following figures. Figure 14.4 shows an AAC residence in Monterrey, Mexico, in which the AAC is used as structure and envelope.

Figure 14.5 shows an AAC hotel in Tampico, Mexico, in which the AAC is again used as structure and envelope.

Figure 14.6 shows an AAC cladding application on a high-rise building in Monterrey, Mexico.

14.3 Structural Design of AAC Elements

14.3.1 Integrated US Design Context for AAC Elements and Structures

Prior to 2003, proposed AAC masonry buildings in the US had to be approved on a case-by-case basis. Beginning in 2003, project approvals could be obtained under the general evaluation-service reports. Beginning in early 2005, project approvals for AAC masonry structures could be obtained through the inclusion of design provisions for AAC masonry in the mandatory-language Appendix A of the 2005 *Masonry Standards Joint Code and Specification*, which was referenced by the International Building Code. Shortly thereafter, AAC masonry shear walls were recognized as a seismic

FIGURE 14.4   AAC residence in Monterrey, Mexico. (Courtesy Xella Mexicana.)

394 Chapter Fourteen

Figure 14.5 AAC hotel in Tampico, Mexico. (Courtesy of Xella Mexicana.)

Figure 14.6 AAC cladding, Monterrey, Mexico. (Courtesy Xella Mexicana.)

Structural Design of AAC Masonry

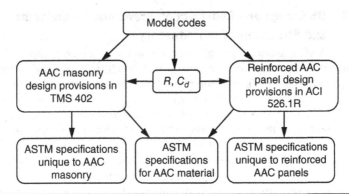

FIGURE 14.7 Integrated US design background for AAC elements and structures.

force-resisting system by ASCE 7. That design framework for AAC masonry remains in effect today. Structural design of AAC masonry is addressed by Chapter 11 of *TMS 402-22*. This design context is shown schematically in Fig. 14.7 and is applied to AAC masonry in the rest of this chapter. Because the basic behavior of structural elements of AAC masonry is quite similar to that of structural elements of clay or concrete masonry, previous sections on basic behavior are not repeated. Design provisions are slightly different, however, and their use is illustrated in detail.

Structural design using AAC is carried out in accordance with the provisions of model codes such as the International Building Code. Those generally reference the structural-integrity requirements and loading provisions, and seismic-design factors (R, C_d, and Ω_0) of ASCE 7. They also reference the appropriate material standards. For AAC masonry, those are TMS 402 (design provisions) and TMS 602 (construction specification). For reinforced AAC panels, those are being developed in ACI 526.1R. Material standards reference ASTM C1693 for the AAC material itself. They can also reference additional ASTM specifications for the manufacture and testing of AAC units, and for nonsafety-related construction specifications.

14.3.2 ASTM Specifications for AAC Construction

ASTM traditionally deals with specifications for materials and methods of test. Standards-development work regarding AAC is addressed by two ASTM committees:

- ASTM Subcommittee C-27.60 (Precast Concrete Elements of AAC) is charged with the development and maintenance of two standards involving reinforced AAC panels. The first of these is the material standard for AAC itself: C 1693, *Standard Specification for Autoclaved Aerated Concrete (AAC)*. The second is C 1694, *Standard Specification for Reinforced Autoclaved Aerated Concrete (AAC) Elements*.

- ASTM Subcommittee C-15.10 (Autoclaved Aerated Concrete Masonry) is charged with the development and maintenance of three standards involving AAC masonry. The first of these is C 1691, *Standard Specification for Unreinforced Autoclaved Aerated Concrete (AAC) Masonry Units*; the second is C 1692, *Standard Practice for Construction and Testing of Autoclaved Aerated Concrete (AAC) Masonry*; and the third is C 1660, *Standard Specification for Thin-bed Mortar for Autoclaved Aerated Concrete (AAC) Masonry*.

14.3.3 US Design and Construction Provisions for Elements and Structures of AAC Masonry

Design of AAC masonry elements is based on the specified compressive strength of the AAC material, f'_{AAC}. Conformance with this specified compressive strength is verified using the manufacturer's reported results for compression testing, during manufacture, of 4-in. cubes of the AAC material only. In contrast to concrete or clay masonry, prism tests are not used. The reason for this is that the compressive strength of AAC masonry elements is close to the compressive strength of the material, because the thin-bed mortar is stronger than the AAC material itself, and the volume of the thin-bed mortar joints is small compared to the total volume of the AAC masonry element. The design equations of TMS 402 are calibrated against this value for f'_{AAC}.

Design of unreinforced AAC masonry elements is similar to design of unreinforced clay or concrete masonry elements, with one exception. Because the tensile strength of the thin-bed mortar used in AAC masonry is required to exceed the tensile strength of the AAC material itself, permissible bond stresses in flexural tension do not govern as often as they do in clay or concrete masonry elements. Nominal capacities in shear can be governed by diagonal tension, crushing of a diagonal strut, or sliding.

Design of reinforced AAC masonry elements is similar to design of unreinforced clay or concrete masonry elements. Flexural resistance of AAC masonry elements is computed assuming yielded flexural reinforcement and an appropriate equivalent rectangular stress block (different from that used for clay or concrete masonry). Maximum reinforcement is limited to ensure tension-controlled behavior. Field-installed reinforcement consisting of deformed bars must be used and must be surrounded by grout. Development and splice requirements are the same as for clay or concrete masonry, except that only the grout is considered. Splitting is further addressed by limiting the bar area as a percentage of the grouted core area. In-plane shear resistance of AAC masonry elements is computed as the sum of resistance from masonry plus deformed reinforcement in intermediate bond beams only. In-plane shear resistance from AAC masonry is checked with respect to web shear, crushing of the diagonal strut, and sliding shear. Out-of-plane resistance of AAC masonry elements is computed using shear equations similar to those used for clay or concrete masonry. Capacity design for shear is required.

The design requirements of TMS 402 mandate the life-safety-related construction requirements in *TMS 602*. Those construction requirements address quality assurance, materials and execution.

14.3.4 Handling, Erection, and Construction with AAC Elements

AAC masonry units are laid with a polymer-modified, thin-bed mortar. AAC panels are lifted and placed using specially designed clamps and are positioned using alignment bars.

When AAC elements are used as a load-bearing wall system, the floor and roof systems are usually designed and detailed as horizontal diaphragms to transfer lateral loads to shear walls. The tops of the panels are connected to the floor or roof diaphragms using a cast-in-place reinforced concrete ring beam.

AAC floor and roof panels can be erected on concrete, steel or masonry construction. All bearing surfaces should be level and minimum required bearing areas (to prevent local crushing) should be maintained. Most floor and roof panels are connected by keyed joints that are reinforced and filled with grout to lock the panels together and provide diaphragm action to resist lateral loads. A cast-in-place reinforced concrete ring beam is normally placed along the perimeter of the diaphragm, completing the system.

14.4 Design of Unreinforced Panel Walls of AAC Masonry

14.4.1 Steps in Flexural Design of Unreinforced Panel Walls of AAC Masonry

Nominal flexural capacity corresponds to a maximum flexural compressive stress of $0.85f'_{AAC}$, or a maximum flexural tensile stress equal to the modulus of rupture. Because the modulus of rupture is much lower than $0.85f'_{AAC}$, it governs. Design actions are factored, and design capacities are computed using those nominal capacities and the appropriate strength-reduction factor.

14.4.1.1 Load Factors

Load factors are as discussed previously. As prescribed in Section 2.3 of the 2022 ASCE 7, the two loading combinations involving wind are:

4a. $1.2D + 1.0W + L + (0.5L_r \text{ or } 0.3S \text{ or } 0.5R)$

5a. $0.9D + 1.0W$

Of these, the second will usually govern. Both combinations have a load factor for W of 1.0.

14.4.1.2 Modulus of Rupture

According to Section 11.1.8.2 of *TMS 402-22*, nominal flexural capacity of unreinforced AAC masonry is computed using a modulus of rupture, f_{rAAC}, equal to twice the splitting tensile strength, f_{tAAC}. According to Section 11.1.8.1 of TMS 402-22, that splitting tensile strength is given as

$$f_{tAAC} = 2.4\sqrt{f'_{AAC}}$$

14.4.1.3 Strength-Reduction Factors

For combinations of flexure and axial load in unreinforced masonry, $\phi = 0.60$ (Section 11.1.5 of TMS 402-22).

14.4.2 Example: Design of a Single-Wythe Panel Wall of AAC Masonry (Solid Units)

Check the design of the panel wall shown in Fig. 14.8, for a wind load, q, of 32 lb/ft², using Class 4 AAC units with a nominal thickness of 8 in., laid using thin-bed mortar.

The panel wall will be designed as unreinforced AAC masonry. The design follows the steps below, using a nominal thickness of 8 in. The panel could be designed as a two-way panel. Nevertheless, because of its aspect ratio, the vertical strips will carry

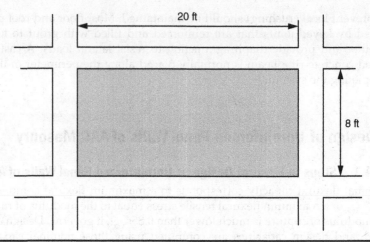

FIGURE 14.8 Example panel wall to be designed using AAC masonry.

practically all the load. Therefore, design it as a one-way panel, consisting of a series of vertically spanning, simply supported strips. AAC masonry units are solid and are fully bedded.

The specified compressive strength, f'_{AAC}, for Class 4 AAC is 580 psi (Table 14.1). The corresponding splitting tensile strength is

$$f_{t\,AAC} = 2.4\sqrt{f'_{AAC}}$$
$$f_{t\,AAC} = 2.4\sqrt{580\ \text{lb/in}^2}$$
$$f_{t\,AAC} = 57.8\ \text{lb/in}^2$$

The modulus of rupture is twice this value, or 115.6 psi.

Calculate the maximum factored design bending moment and corresponding factored design flexural tensile stress in a strip 1-ft wide, with a nominal thickness of 8 in. The specified thickness of the wall is 7.9 in.

$$M_{u\,max} = \frac{w_u \ell^2}{8} = \frac{1.0 \times 32\ \text{lb/ft}\,(8\ \text{ft})^2}{8} \times 12\ \text{in./ft} = 3072\ \text{lb-in.}$$

$$f_t = \frac{Mc}{I} = \frac{3072\ \text{lb-in.} \times \left(7.9/2\right)\ \text{in.}}{\left[12\ \text{in.} \times (7.9\ \text{in.})^3 / 12\right]} = 24.6\ \text{lb/in}^2$$

The factored flexural tensile stress, 26.4 lb/in², is less than the modulus of rupture (115.6 psi), reduced by a strength-reduction factor of 0.6, or 69.4 lb/in². The design is therefore satisfactory. We should also check one-way (beam) shear. An example of this is given below.

14.4.3 Example: Check of Shear Capacity for an Unreinforced Panel Wall of AAC Masonry

Check the effect of shear in the example of Section 14.4.2. From Section 11.2.5 of TMS 402-22, compute the out-of-plane shear capacity using Section 11.3.4.1.2.4. Compute the out-of-plane shear capacity on a 1-ft wide strip:

$$V_{nAAC} = 0.8\sqrt{f'_{AAC}}\, bd$$

$$V_{nAAC} = 0.8\sqrt{580\ \text{lb/in}^2} \times 12\ \text{in.} \times 7.9\ \text{in.}$$

$$V_{nAAC} = 1826\ \text{lb}$$

On a strip 1-ft wide, the factored wind load of 1.0 times 32 lb/ft² produces a factored design shear of

$$V_u = \frac{w_u L}{2} = \frac{1.0 \times 32\ \text{lb/ft} \times (8\ \text{ft})}{2} = 128\ \text{lb}$$

This is far less than the nominal capacity, reduced by the strength-reduction factor for shear in AAC masonry (0.8), and one-way shear does not govern the design.

14.4.4 Overall Comments on Design of Unreinforced Panel Walls of AAC Masonry

- Nonload-bearing masonry, without calculated reinforcement, can easily resist out-of-plane wind loads.
- If noncalculated (prescriptive) reinforcement is included, it will not act until the masonry has cracked.
- Elements such as the ones we have calculated in this section can be designed in many cases by prescription.
- The previous justifications (based on the strip method) for assuming that all load is carried by vertically spanning strips continue to be valid for AAC masonry panel walls.

14.5 Design of Unreinforced Bearing Walls of AAC Masonry

14.5.1 Steps in Design of Unreinforced Bearing Walls of AAC Masonry

In TMS 402-22, design of unreinforced bearing walls of AAC masonry is similar to the design of panel walls, except that axial load must be considered. As stated in Section 11.2.2 of TMS 402-22, the usual assumption of plane sections is invoked, and tensile and compressive stresses in AAC are assumed to be proportional to strain.

Nominal capacities in masonry are reached at an extreme fiber tension equal to the modulus of rupture (Section 11.2.3 of TMS 402-22), and at a compressive stress of $0.85 f'_{AAC}$.

Compressive capacity is given by Equations 11-3 and 11-4 of TMS 402-22:
For $\frac{kh}{r} = \frac{h}{r} \leq 99$,

$$P_n = 0.80 \left\{ 0.85 A_n f'_{AAC} \left[1 - \left(\frac{h}{140r} \right)^2 \right] \right\}.$$

and for $\frac{kh}{r} = \frac{h}{r} > 99$,

$$P_n = 0.80 \left[0.85 A_n f'_{AAC} \left(\frac{70r}{h} \right)^2 \right]$$

The strength reduction factor, ϕ, is equal to 0.60 (Section 11.1.5 of TMS 402-22).

Second-order effects due to combined lateral and axial loads should be checked using an interactive approach or a moment magnifier as prescribed in 11.3.5.5.

14.5.2 Example: Design of Unreinforced AAC Masonry Bearing Wall with Concentric Axial Load

The bearing wall shown in Fig. 14.9 has an unfactored, concentric axial load of 1050 lb/ft. Using AAC masonry, design the wall.

According to the 2022 ASCE 7, and in the context of these example problems (dead load, wind load and roof live load), the following loading combinations must be checked for strength design:

4a. $1.2D + 1.0W + L + (0.5L_r \text{ or } 0.3S \text{ or } 0.5R)$

5a. $0.9D + 1.0W$

The second of these is usually critical, because roof live load must be considered off as well as on.

To apply those loading combinations, let us assume that the total unfactored wall load of 1050 lb/ft represents 700 lb/ft of dead load and 350 lb/ft of live load.

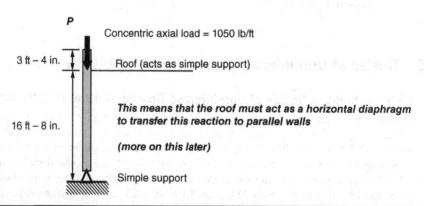

FIGURE 14.9 Unreinforced AAC masonry bearing wall with concentric axial load.

At each horizontal plane through the wall, the following conditions must be met:

- Maximum compressive stress from factored axial loads must not exceed the slenderness-dependent values in Equations 11-3 or 11-4 as appropriate, reduced by a ϕ-factor of 0.60.
- Maximum compressive stress from factored loads (including a moment magnifiers) must not exceed $0.85 f'_{AAC}$ in the extreme compression fiber, reduced by a ϕ-factor of 0.60.
- Maximum tension stress from factored loads must not exceed the modulus of rupture in the extreme tension fiber, reduced by the ϕ-factor of 0.60.

For each condition, the more critical of the two possible loading combinations must be checked. Because there is no wind load, this example will be worked using the loading combination $1.2D + 1.6L$.

In theory, we must check various points on the wall. In this problem, however, the wall has only axial load, which increases from top to bottom due to the wall's self-weight. Therefore, we need to check only at the base of the wall.

Try 8-in. nominal units and Class 4 AAC, with a specified compressive strength, f'_{AAC}, of 580 lb/in² and a unit weight of 40 lb/ft³. Using the specified thickness of 7.9 in., that corresponds to a unit weight of 26.3 lb/ft². Work with a strip with a width of 1 ft (measured along the length of the wall in plan). Stresses are calculated using the critical section, consisting of the entire cross-sectional area (TMS 402-22, Section 4.4.1).

At the base of the wall, the factored axial force is

$$P_u = 1.2(700 \text{ lb}) + 1.6(350 \text{ lb}) + 1.2(20 \text{ ft} \times 26.3 \text{ lb/ft}) = 2031 \text{ lb}$$

To calculate stiffness-related parameters for the wall, we use the average cross-section, corresponding to the fully bedded gross cross-section (TMS 402-22, Section 4.4.1).

$$r = \sqrt{\frac{I}{A}} = \sqrt{\frac{bh^3/12}{bh}} = \frac{h}{\sqrt{12}} = \frac{7.9 \text{ in.}}{\sqrt{12}} = 2.28 \text{ in.}$$

$$\frac{kh}{r} = \frac{16.67 \text{ ft} \times 12 \text{ in./ft}}{2.28 \text{ in.}} = 87.8$$

This is less than the transition slenderness of 99, so the nominal axial capacity is based on the curve that is an approximation to inelastic buckling:

$$\phi P_n = \phi 0.80 \left\{ 0.85 A_n f'_m \left[1 - \left(\frac{h}{140r}\right)^2 \right] \right\}$$

$$\phi P_n = 0.60 \cdot 0.80 \cdot \left\{ 0.85 \times 7.9 \text{ in.} \times 12 \text{ in.} \times 580 \text{ lb/in}^2 \left[1 - \left(\frac{16.67 \text{ ft} \times 12 \text{ in./ft}}{140 \times 2.28 \text{ in}^2}\right)^2 \right] \right\}$$

$$\phi P_n = 22{,}433 \text{ lb} \times 0.607 = 13{,}627 \text{ lb}$$

The factored axial load, P_u, 2031 lb, is far less than this, and this part of the design is satisfactory.

Now check the net compressive stress. Because the load is concentric, there is no bending stress. At the base of the wall,

$$f_a = \frac{P_u}{A} = \frac{1.2(700 \text{ lb}) + 1.6(350 \text{ lb}) + 1.2(20 \text{ ft} \times 26.3 \text{ lb/ft})}{7.9 \times 12 \text{ in}^2} = \frac{2031 \text{ lb}}{30 \text{ in}^2} = 21.4 \text{ lb/in}^2$$

$$f_a = 21.4 \text{ lb/in}^2$$

The maximum permitted compressive stress is

$$0.60 \cdot 0.85 f'_{AAC} = 0.60 \times 0.85 \times 580 \text{ lb/in}^2 = 296 \text{ lb/in}^2$$

The maximum compressive stress is much less than this, and the design is satisfactory for this also.

Clearly, because this example involves concentric axial loads only, the first criterion (axial capacity reduced by slenderness effects) is more severe than the second (maximum compressive stress from axial loads and bending moments).

Because there is no moment, there is no tensile stress, and the third criterion is automatically satisfied. The design is satisfactory.

It would probably be possible to achieve a satisfactory design with a smaller nominal wall thickness. To maintain continuity in the example problems that follow, however, the design will stop at this point.

Although *TMS 402-22* has no explicit minimum eccentricity requirements for walls, the leading coefficient of 0.80 for nominal axial compressive capacity effectively imposes a minimum eccentricity of about 0.1 *t*.

14.5.3 Example: Design of Unreinforced AAC Masonry Bearing Wall with Eccentric Axial Load

Now consider the same bearing wall of the previous example, but make the gravity load eccentric.

As before, suppose that the load is applied over a 4-in. bearing plate, and assume that bearing stresses vary linearly under the bearing plate as shown in Fig. 14.10.

Then the eccentricity of the applied load with respect to the centerline of the wall is

$$e = \frac{t}{2} - \frac{\text{plate}}{3} = \frac{7.9 \text{ in.}}{2} - \frac{4 \text{ in.}}{3} = 2.62 \text{ in.}$$

The wall is as shown in Fig. 14.11.

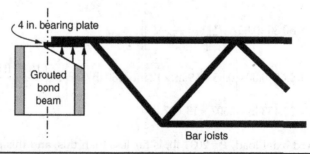

FIGURE 14.10 Assumed linear variation of bearing stresses under bearing plate of AAC masonry wall.

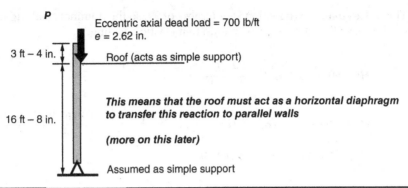

FIGURE 14.11 Unreinforced AAC masonry bearing wall with eccentric axial load.

At each horizontal plane through the wall, the following conditions must be met:

- Maximum compressive stress from factored axial loads must not exceed the slenderness-dependent values in Equations 11-3 or 11-4 as appropriate, reduced by a ϕ-factor of 0.60.
- Maximum compressive stress from factored loads (including a moment magnifiers) must not exceed $0.85 f'_{AAC}$ in the extreme compression fiber, reduced by a ϕ-factor of 0.60.
- Maximum tension stress from factored loads must not exceed the modulus of rupture in the extreme tension fiber, reduced by the ϕ-factor of 0.60.

For each condition, the more critical of the two possible loading combinations must be checked. Because there is no wind load, this example will be worked using the loading combination $1.2D + 1.6L$.

We must check various points on the wall. Critical points are just below the roof reaction (moment is high and axial load is low, so maximum tension may govern); and at the base of the wall (axial load is high, so maximum compression may govern). Check each of these locations.

As before, try 8-in. nominal units, and a specified compressive strength, f'_{AAC}, of 580 lb/in². Work with a strip with a width of 1 ft (measured along the length of the wall in plan). Stresses are calculated using the gross section, because the units are solid and are fully bedded using thin-bed mortar (TMS 402-22, Section 4.4.1).

Just below the roof reaction, the axial force is:

$$P_u = 1.2(700 \text{ lb}) + 1.6(350 \text{ lb}) + 1.2(3.33 \text{ ft} \times 26.3 \text{ lb/ft}) = 1505 \text{ lb}$$

To calculate stiffness-related parameters for the wall, we use the average cross-section, corresponding to the fully bedded gross cross-section (TMS 402-22, Section 4.4.1).

$$r = \sqrt{\frac{I}{A}} = \sqrt{\frac{bh^3/12}{bh}} = \frac{h}{\sqrt{12}} = \frac{7.9 \text{ in.}}{\sqrt{12}} = 2.28 \text{ in.}$$

$$\frac{kh}{r} = \frac{16.67 \text{ ft} \times 12 \text{ in./ft}}{2.28 \text{ in.}} = 87.8$$

This is less than the transition slenderness of 99, so the nominal axial capacity is based on the curve that is an approximation to inelastic buckling:

$$\phi P_n = \phi 0.80 \left\{ 0.85 A_n f'_m \left[1 - \left(\frac{h}{140r} \right)^2 \right] \right\}$$

$$\phi P_n = 0.60 \cdot 0.80 \cdot \left\{ 0.85 \times 7.9 \text{ in.} \times 12 \text{ in.} \times 580 \text{ lb/in}^2 \left[1 - \left(\frac{16.67 \text{ ft} \times 12 \text{ in./ft}}{140 \times 2.28 \text{ in}^2} \right)^2 \right] \right\}$$

$$\phi P_n = 22{,}433 \text{ lb} \times 0.607 = 13{,}627 \text{ lb}$$

Because the factored axial force is much less than slenderness-dependent nominal capacity, reduced by the appropriate ϕ factor, the axial force check is satisfied.

Now check the net compressive stress. Because the loading is eccentric, there is bending stress:

$$f_{compression} = \frac{P_u}{A} + \frac{M_u c}{I}$$

The factored design axial load, P_u, is computed above. The factored design moment, M_u, is given by:

$$M_u = P_u e = (1.2 \times 700 + 1.6 \times 350) \text{ lb} \times 2.62 \text{ in.} = 3668 \text{ lb-in.}$$

$$f_{compression} = \frac{P_u}{A} + \frac{M_u c}{I}$$

$$f_{compression} = \frac{1505 \text{ lb}}{7.9 \times 12 \text{ in}^2} + \frac{3668 \text{ lb-in.} \left(7.9/2 \right)}{12 \times 7.9^3/12 \text{ in}^4} = 15.9 + 29.4 \text{ lb/in}^2 = 45.3 \text{ lb/in}^2$$

$$0.60 \times 0.85 f'_{AAC} = 0.60 \times 0.85 \times 580 \text{ lb/in}^2 = 296 \text{ lb/in}^2$$

The net compressive stress does not exceed the prescribed value. Clearly, because this example involves eccentric axial loads, the first criterion (axial load reduced by slenderness effects) is less severe than the second (maximum compressive stress from axial loads and bending moments).

Now check the net tensile stress. At the mid-height of the wall, the axial force due to $0.9D$ is:

$$P_u = 0.9 \, (700 \text{ lb}) + 0.9 \, (3.33 \text{ ft} + 8.33 \text{ ft}) \times 26.3 \text{ lb/ft} = 906 \text{ lb}$$

At the mid-height of the wall, the factored design moment, M_u, is given by

$$M_u = P_{u \text{ eccentric}} \frac{e}{2} = \left(\frac{1}{2} \right) 0.9 \cdot 700 \text{ lb} \times 2.62 \text{ in.} = 825 \text{ lb-in.}$$

$$f_{tension} = -\frac{P_u}{A} + \frac{M_u c}{I}$$

$$f_{tension} = -\frac{906 \text{ lb}}{7.9 \times 12 \text{ in}^2} + \frac{825 \text{ lb-in.} \left(7.9/2 \right)}{12 \times 7.9^3/12 \text{ in}^4} = -9.56 + 6.61 \text{ lb/in}^2 = -2.95 \text{ lb/in}^2$$

The maximum tensile stress is actually negative, indicating net compression, and the design is satisfactory.

The other critical section could be at the base of the wall, where the checks of all three criteria are identical to those of the previous example. All are satisfied, and the design is therefore satisfactory.

14.5.4 Example: Design of Unreinforced AAC Masonry Bearing Wall with Eccentric Axial Load Plus Wind

Now consider the same AAC masonry bearing wall of the above example, but add a uniformly distributed wind load, q, of 40 lb/ft².

The wall is as shown in Fig. 14.12.

At each horizontal plane through the wall, the following conditions must be met:

- Maximum compressive stress from factored axial loads must not exceed the slenderness-dependent values in Equations 11-3 or 11-4 as appropriate, reduced by a ϕ-factor of 0.60.

- Maximum compressive stress from factored loads (including a moment magnifiers) must not exceed $0.85 f'_{AAC}$ in the extreme compression fiber, reduced by a ϕ-factor of 0.60.

- Maximum tension stress from factored loads must not exceed the modulus of rupture in the extreme tension fiber, reduced by the ϕ-factor of 0.60.

For each condition, the more critical of the two possible loading combinations must be checked. Because there is wind load, and because the previous two examples showed little problem with the first two criteria, the third criterion (net tension) may well be critical. For this criterion, the critical loading condition could be either $1.2D + 1.6L$, or $0.9D + 1.0W$. Both loading conditions must be checked.

We must check various points on the wall. Critical points are just below the roof reaction (moment is high and axial load is low, so net tension may govern); at the mid-height of the wall, where moment from eccentric gravity load and wind load are highest; and at the base of the wall (axial load is high, so the maximum compressive stress may govern). Check each of these locations.

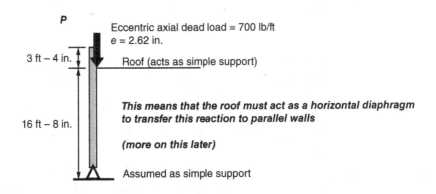

FIGURE 14.12 Unreinforced masonry bearing wall with eccentric axial load and wind load.

To avoid having to check a large number of loading combinations and potentially critical locations, it is worthwhile to assess them first and check only the ones that will probably govern.

Due to wind only, the unfactored moment at the base of the parapet (roof level) is

$$M = \frac{w_u L_{parapet}^2}{2} = \frac{1.0 \times 40 \frac{lb}{ft} \times 3.33^2 \text{ ft}^2}{2} \times 12 \text{ in./ft} = 2661 \text{ lb-in.}$$

The maximum moment is close to that occurring at mid-height. The moment from wind load is the superposition of one-half moment at the upper support due to wind load on the parapet only, plus the midspan moment in a simply supported beam with that same wind load:

$$M_{midspan} = -\frac{2661}{2} + \frac{w_u L^2}{8} = -\frac{2661 \text{ lb-in.}}{2} + \frac{1 \times 40 \frac{lb}{ft} \times 16.67^2 \text{ ft}^2}{8} \times 12 \text{ in./ft} = 15{,}343 \text{ lb-in.}$$

Unfactored moment diagrams due to eccentric axial load and wind are as shown in Fig. 14.13.

From the example of Section, we know that loading combination $1.2D + 1.6L$ was not close to critical directly underneath the roof. Because the wind-load moments directly underneath the roof are not very large, they will probably not be critical either. The critical location will probably be at mid-height; the critical loading condition will probably be $0.9D + 1.0W$; and the critical criterion will probably be net tension, because this AAC masonry wall is unreinforced.

As before, try 8-in. nominal units of Class 4 AAC, with a specified compressive strength, f'_{AAC}, of 580 lb/in². Work with a strip with a width of 1 ft (measured along the length of the wall in plan). Stresses are calculated using the critical section, consisting of the full bedded area (gross area) (TMS 402-22, Section 4.3.1).

Now check the net tensile stress. At the mid-height of the wall, the axial force due to $0.9D$ is:

$$P_u = 0.9 \,(700 \text{ lb}) + 0.9 \,(3.33 \text{ ft} + 8.33 \text{ ft}) \times 26.3 \text{ lb/ft} = 906 \text{ lb}$$

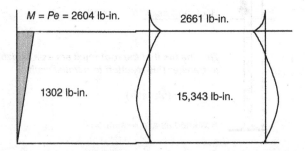

Figure 14.13 Unfactored moment diagrams due to eccentric axial load and wind.

Structural Design of AAC Masonry

At the mid-height of the wall, the factored design moment, M_u, is given by

$$M_u = P_{u\,eccentric}\frac{e}{2} + M_{u\,wind} = \left(\frac{1}{2}\right)0.9 \cdot 700\text{ lb} \times 2.62\text{ in.} + 16{,}673\text{ lb-in.} = 18{,}324\text{ lb-in.}$$

$$f_{tension} = -\frac{P_u}{A} + \frac{M_u c}{I}$$

$$f_{tension} = -\frac{906\text{ lb}}{7.9 \times 12\text{ in}^2} + \frac{18{,}324\text{ lb-in.}\left(7.9/2\text{ in.}\right)}{12 \times 7.9^3 / 12\text{ in}^4} = -9.56 + 146.8\text{ lb/in}^2 = 137.2\text{ lb/in}^2$$

The specified compressive strength, f'_{AAC}, for Class 4 AAC is 580 psi (Table 14.1). The corresponding splitting tensile strength is

$$f_{t\,AAC} = 2.4\sqrt{f'_{AAC}}$$
$$f_{t\,AAC} = 2.4\sqrt{580\text{ lb/in}^2}$$
$$f_{t\,AAC} = 57.8\text{ lb/in}^2$$

The modulus of rupture is twice this value, or 115.6 psi.

The maximum permissible stress is this value, multiplied by the strength-reduction factor of 0.6.

$$0.60 f_r = 0.60 \times 115.6\text{ lb/in}^2 = 69.4\text{ lb/in}^2$$

The maximum tensile stress exceeds the prescribed value, and the design is not satisfactory. It will be necessary to reinforce the wall, as illustrated in the design example of Section 14.9. Thickening the wall, though possible, is probably not a cost-effective option.

14.5.5 Comments on the Above Examples for Design of Unreinforced AAC Masonry Bearing Walls

1) In retrospect, it probably would not have been necessary to check all three criteria at all locations. With experience, a designer could realize that the location with highest wind moment would govern and could therefore check only the mid-height of the wall.

2) The addition of wind load to the second example, to produce the third example, changes the critical location from just under the roof, to the mid-height of the simply supported section of the wall. The wind load, q, of 40 lb/ft² in the third example produces maximum tensile stresses above the allowable values for AAC masonry and makes it necessary to thicken the wall or reinforce it.

14.5.6 Extension of the Above Concepts to AAC Masonry Walls with Openings

AAC masonry bearing walls with openings are handled as in Section 5.2.7. That material is not repeated here.

14.5.7 Final Comment on the Effect of Openings in Unreinforced AAC Masonry Bearing Walls

As the summation of the plan lengths of openings in a bearing wall exceeds about one-half the plan length of the wall, even the higher permissible stresses (or moduli of rupture) corresponding to fully grouted walls will be exceeded, and it will generally become necessary to use reinforcement. Design of reinforced AAC masonry bearing walls is addressed later in this chapter.

14.6 Design of Unreinforced Shear Walls of AAC Masonry

Unreinforced masonry shear walls must be designed for the effects of:

1) Gravity loads from self-weight, plus gravity loads from overlying roof or floor levels.

2) Moments and shears from in-plane shear loads

Actions are shown in Fig. 14.14.

For unreinforced AAC masonry, *TMS 402-22* requires that maximum tensile stresses from in-plane flexure, alone or in combination with axial loads, not exceed the in-plane modulus of rupture from Section 11.1.8.3 of *TMS 402-22*.

Shear must also be checked. According to Section 11.2.5 of *TMS 402-22*, the nominal shear capacity of AAC masonry is the least of the following three equations, related respectively to web-shear cracking, crushing of the diagonal strut, and sliding.

$$V_{n\,AAC} = \min \begin{cases} 0.95 \ell_w t \sqrt{f'_{AAC}} \sqrt{1 + \dfrac{P_u}{2.4\sqrt{f'_{AAC}}\,\ell_w t}} \\ 0.17 f'_{AAC}\, t\, \dfrac{h \cdot \ell_w^2}{h^2 + \left(\dfrac{3}{4}\ell_w\right)^2} \\ \mu_{AAC} P_u \end{cases}$$

The strength-reduction factor for shear is 0.80 (*TMS 402-22*, Section 11.1.5).

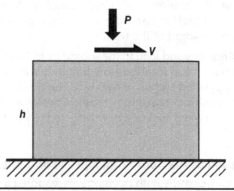

FIGURE 14.14 Design actions for unreinforced shear walls.

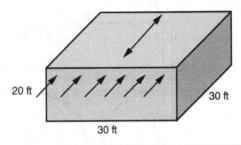

FIGURE 14.15 Example problem for strength design of unreinforced shear wall.

14.6.1 Example: Design of Unreinforced Shear Wall of AAC Masonry

Consider the simple structure of Fig. 14.15, the same one whose bearing walls have been designed previously in this book. Use nominal 8-in. AAC masonry units, Class 4, $f'_{AAC} = 580$ lb/in^2, laid with thin-bed mortar and fully bedded. The roof applies a gravity load of 1050 lb/ft to the walls; the walls measure 16 ft, 8 in. height to the roof, and have an additional 3 ft, 4 in. parapet. The walls are loaded with a wind load of 32 lb/ft.^{2} The roof acts as a one-way system, transmitting gravity loads to the front and back walls. At this stage, all loads are unfactored; load factors will be applied later.

Now design the shear wall. The critical section for shear is just under the roof, where axial load in the shear walls is least, coming from the parapet only.

As a result of the wind loading, the reaction transmitted to the roof diaphragm is as calculated using Fig. 14.16:

$$\text{Reaction} = \frac{32 \text{ lb/ft}^2 \times \left(\dfrac{20^2 \text{ ft}^2}{2}\right)}{16.67 \text{ ft}} = 384 \text{ lb/ft}$$

Total roof reaction acting on one side of the roof is

$$\text{Reaction} = 384 \text{ lb/ft} \times 30 \text{ ft} = 11{,}520 \text{ lb}$$

This is divided evenly between the two shear walls, so the shear per wall is 5760 lb.

In Fig. 14.17, for simplicity, the lateral load is shown as if it acted on the front wall alone. In reality it also acts on the back wall, so that the structure is subjected to pressure on the front wall, and suction on the back wall.

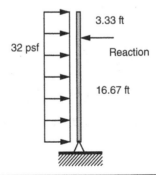

FIGURE 14.16 Calculation of reaction on roof diaphragm, strength design of unreinforced AAC masonry shear wall.

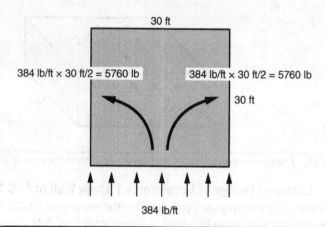

FIGURE 14.17 Transmission of forces from roof diaphragm to shear walls.

The horizontal diaphragm reaction transferred to each shear wall is 240 lb/ft, multiplied by the building width of 30 ft, and then divided equally between the two shear walls, for a total of 5760 lb per shear wall.

Using the conservative loading case of $0.9D + 1.0W$,

$$V_u = 1.0 V_{unfactored} = 1.0 \times 5760 \text{ lb} = 5760 \text{ lb}$$

Compute the axial force in the wall at that level. To be conservative, use the loading combination $0.9D + 1.0W$. The force acting normal to the shear-transfer plane is

$$P_u = 0.9 \times 3.33 \text{ ft} \times 26.3 \text{ lb/ft}^2 \times 30 \text{ ft} = 2365 \text{ lb}$$

The nominal shear capacity at that level, as governed by web-shear cracking, crushing of the diagonal strut, and sliding, respectively, is given in Section 11.3.4.1.2.2 of TMS 402-22. The coefficient of friction between AAC and leveling bed mortar, required in the third equation, is taken as 1.0 in accordance with Section 11.1.8.4 of TMS 402-22.

$$V_{nAAC} = \min \begin{cases} 0.95 \, \ell_w t \sqrt{f'_{AAC}} \sqrt{1 + \dfrac{P_u}{2.4 \sqrt{f'_{AAC}} \ell_w t}} \\ 0.17 f'_{AAC} t \dfrac{h \cdot \ell_w^2}{h^2 + \left(\dfrac{3}{4} \ell_w\right)^2} \\ \mu_{AAC} P_u \end{cases}$$

$$V_{nAAC} = \min \begin{cases} 0.95 \times 30 \text{ ft} \times 12 \text{ in./ft} \times 7.9 \text{ in.} \sqrt{580 \text{ lb/in}^2} \sqrt{1 + \dfrac{2365 \text{ lb}}{2.4\sqrt{580 \text{ lb/in}^2} \times 30 \text{ ft} \times 12 \text{ in./ft} \times 7.9 \text{ in.}}} \\ 0.17 \times 580 \text{ lb/in}^2 \times 7.9 \text{ in.} \times \dfrac{16.67 \text{ ft} \times 12 \text{ in./ft} \times (30 \text{ ft} \times 12 \text{ in./ft})^2}{\left[(16.67 \text{ ft} \times 12 \text{ in./ft})^2 + \left(\dfrac{3}{4} \times 30 \text{ ft} \times 12 \text{ in./ft}\right)^2\right]} \\ 1.0 \times 2365 \text{ lb} \end{cases}$$

$$V_{nAAC} = \min \begin{cases} 65{,}534 \text{ lb} \\ 178{,}842 \text{ lb} \\ 2365 \text{ lb} \end{cases}$$

The design shear capacity is

$$\phi V_n = 0.80 \times 2365 \text{ lb} = 1892 \text{ lb}$$

The design shear capacity is less than the factored design shear of 5760 lb.

This design issue is complex. Some designers might not use the third equation, reasoning that this wall does not have an unbonded interface, because the assumption of unreinforced masonry is consistent with an uncracked condition. If a designer considers the possibility of an unbonded interface, and opts to include the third equation for shear capacity, this design issue would normally be addressed using shear-friction or dowel action across this interface. Additional research of shear friction needs to be completed for AAC masonry. For the time being, the interface is regarded as uncracked, and the third equation is not included. The design capacities associated with the other two limit states (web-shear cracking and crushing of the diagonal strut) greatly exceed the factored design shear, and do not govern.

Now check for the net flexural tensile stress. The critical section is at the base of the wall, where in-plane moment is maximum. Because the roof spans between the front and back walls, the distributed gravity load on the roof does not act on the side walls, and their axial load comes from self-weight only. Again, use the conservative loading combination of $0.9D + 1.0W$:

$$f_{tension} = \frac{M_u c}{I} - \frac{P_u}{A} = \frac{V_u h c}{I} - \frac{P_u}{A} \leq \phi f_r$$

$$f_{tension} = \frac{1.0 \times 5760 \text{ lb} \times 16.67 \text{ ft} \times 12 \text{ in./ft} \left(\frac{30 \text{ ft} \times 12 \text{ in./ft}}{2}\right)}{\left[\frac{7.9 \text{ in.} \times (30 \text{ ft} \times 12 \text{ in./ft})^3}{12}\right]} - \frac{0.9 \times 20 \text{ ft} \times 26.3 \text{ lb/ft}}{7.9 \times 12 \text{ in}^2}$$

$$f_{tension} = 1.0 \times 6.75 \text{ lb/in}^2 - 0.9 \times 5.55 \text{ lb/in}^2$$
$$f_{tension} = 6.75 \text{ lb/in}^2 - 4.00 \text{ lb/in}^2$$
$$f_{tension} = 1.76 \text{ lb/in}^2$$

The specified compressive strength, $f'_{AAC'}$ for Class 4 AAC is 580 psi (Table 14.1). The corresponding splitting tensile strength is

$$f_{t\,AAC} = 2.4\sqrt{f'_{AAC}}$$
$$f_{t\,AAC} = 2.4\sqrt{580 \text{ lb/in}^2}$$
$$f_{t\,AAC} = 57.8 \text{ lb/in}^2$$

The modulus of rupture is twice this value, or 115.6 psi.

The maximum permissible stress is this value, multiplied by the strength-reduction factor of 0.6.

$$0.60 f_r = 0.60 \times 115.6 \text{ lb/in}^2 = 69.4 \text{ lb/in}^2$$

The net tension in the wall is less than this value, and the design is satisfactory.

When the wind blows against the side walls, these walls transfer their loads to the roof diaphragm, and the front and back walls act as shear walls. The side walls must be checked for this loading direction also, following the procedures of previous examples in this book.

14.6.2 Comments on Example Problem with Design of Unreinforced AAC Masonry Shear Walls

Clearly, unreinforced AAC masonry shear walls have large shear capacity because of their large cross-sectional area. Sliding needs to be addressed by the addition of shear-friction provisions in *TMS 402*. If this area is reduced by openings, then shear capacities will decrease, and in-plane flexural capacities as governed by net flexural tension may decrease even faster.

14.7 Design of Reinforced Beams and Lintels of AAC Masonry

Design assumptions (Section 11.3.2 of *TMS 402-22*) are similar to those of strength design for clay or concrete masonry. The maximum usable strain depends on the strength class of AAC; the equivalent rectangular stress block has an intensity of $0.85f'_{AAC}$; and the equivalent rectangular stress block extends two-thirds of the way from the extreme compressive fiber to the neutral axis.

The most common reinforced masonry beam is a lintel. Lintels are beams that support masonry over openings. Strength design of reinforced beams and lintels follows the steps given below:

1) Shear design:
   a) Calculate the design shear, and compare it with the corresponding resistance. Revise the lintel depth if necessary.
2) Flexural design:
   a) Calculate the design moment.
   b) Calculate the required flexural reinforcement. Check that it fits within minimum and maximum reinforcement limitations. Because deformed reinforcement is required to be surrounded by grout, and because AAC masonry units are manufactured solid, it is usually more cost-effective to place deformed horizontal reinforcement for lintels in a bond beam of concrete masonry units.

In many cases, the depth of the lintel is determined by architectural considerations. In other cases, it is necessary to determine the number of courses of masonry that will work as a beam. For example, consider the lintel in Fig. 14.18.

The depth of the beam, and hence the area that is effective in resisting shear, is determined by the number of courses that we consider to comprise it. Because it is not

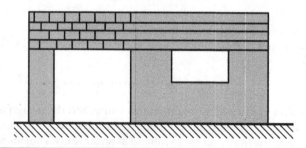

FIGURE 14.18 Example of masonry lintel.

TABLE 14.3 Physical Properties of Steel Reinforcing Bars

Designation	Diameter, in.	Area, in.²
Bars		
#3	0.375	0.11
#4	0.500	0.20
#5	0.625	0.31
#6	0.750	0.44
#7	0.875	0.60
#8	1.000	0.79
#9	1.128	1.00
#10	1.270	1.27
#11	1.410	1.56

very practical to put shear reinforcement in masonry beams, the depth of the beam may be determined by this. In other words, the beam design may start with the number of courses that are needed so that shear can be resisted by masonry alone.

14.7.1 Physical Properties of Steel Reinforcing Bars

Physical properties of steel reinforcing bars are given in Table 14.3.

Cover requirements are given in Section 6.1.4 of TMS 402-22.

14.7.2 Example: Lintel Design Using AAC Masonry

Suppose that we have a uniformly distributed load of 1050 lb/ft, applied at the level of the roof of the structure shown in Fig. 14.19. Design the lintel of Fig. 14.20. Assume AAC masonry with Class 4 AAC units having a nominal thickness of 8 in., a weight of 26.3 lb/ft², and a specified compressive strength of 580 lb/in². Use thin-bed mortar. The lintel has a span of 10 ft, and a total depth (height of parapet plus distance between the roof and the lintel) of 4 ft. These are shown in the schematic figure below. Assume that 500 lb/ft of the roof load is D, and the remaining 250 lb/ft is L. The governing loading combination is $1.2D + 1.6L$.

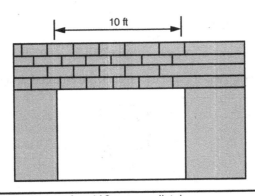

FIGURE 14.19 Example for design of an AAC masonry lintel.

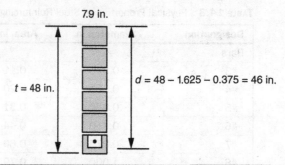

FIGURE 14.20 Example showing placement of bottom reinforcement in lowest course of lintel.

Again, first check whether the depth of the lintel is sufficient to avoid the use of shear reinforcement. Because the opening may have a movement joint on either side, again use a span equal to the clear distance, plus 4 in. on each side. So the span is 10 ft plus 8 in., or 10.67 ft.

$$M_u = \frac{w_u l^2}{8} = \frac{\left[\left(500 + 4\text{ ft} \times 26.3\,\frac{\text{lb}}{\text{ft}}\right) \times 1.2 + 250\,\frac{\text{lb}}{\text{ft}} \times 1.6\right] \times 10.67^2 \text{ ft}^2 \times 12 \text{ in./ft}}{8} = 176{,}163 \text{ in.-lb}$$

$$V_u = \frac{w_u l}{2} = \frac{\left[(500 + 4\text{ ft} \times 26.3\text{ lb/ft}) \times 1.2 + 250\,\frac{\text{lb}}{\text{ft}} \times 1.6\right] \times 10.67 \text{ ft}}{2} = 5503 \text{ lb}$$

The bars in the lintel will be placed in the lower part of AAC masonry.

The effective depth d is calculated using the minimum cover of 1.5 in. (Section 6.1.4 of *TMS 402-22*), plus one-half the diameter of an assumed #6 bar.

The nominal shear capacity is given by Equation 11-14 of *TMS 402-22*.

$$V_{n\,\text{AAC}} = 0.8\sqrt{f'_{\text{AAC}}}\,bd$$
$$V_{n\,\text{AAC}} = 0.8\sqrt{580 \text{ lb/in}^2}\,46 \text{ in.} \times 7.9 \text{ in.}$$
$$V_{n\,\text{AAC}} = 7001 \text{ lb}$$

The design shear capacity is

$$\phi V_n = 0.80 \times 7001 \text{ lb} = 5601 \text{ lb}$$

The factored design shear capacity exceeds the factored design shear of 5503 lb.

$$V_n \le 4\sqrt{f'_{\text{AAC}}}\,A_n$$
$$V_n \le 4\sqrt{580\,\frac{\text{lb}}{\text{in}^2}}\,48 \text{ in.} \times 7.9 \text{ in.}$$
$$V_n \le 36{,}530 \text{ lb}$$

This does not govern, and the shear design is acceptable.

Now check the required flexural reinforcement:

$$M_n = A_s f_y \text{(lever arm)}$$
$$M_n \approx A_s f_y \times 0.9d$$

In our case,

$$M_n^{\text{required}} = \frac{M_u}{\phi} = \frac{M_u}{0.9} = \frac{176{,}163 \text{ lb-in.}}{0.9} = 195{,}737 \text{ lb-in.}$$

$$A_s^{\text{required}} \approx \frac{M_n^{\text{required}}}{0.9\, d f_y} = \frac{195{,}737 \text{ lb-in.}}{0.9 \times 46 \text{ in.} \times 60{,}000 \text{ lb/in}^2} = 0.079 \text{ in}^2$$

Because of the depth of the beam, this can easily be satisfied with a #4 bar in the lowest course (of concrete masonry units). The corresponding nominal flexural capacity is approximately

$$M_n \approx A_s f_y (0.9d)$$
$$M_n \approx 0.20 \text{ in}^2 \times 60{,}000 \text{ lb/in}^2 \times 0.9 \times 46 \text{ in.}$$
$$M_n \approx 496{,}800 \text{ lb-in.}$$

Also include 2-#4 bars at the level of the roof (bond beam reinforcement, again using concrete masonry units). The flexural design is quite simple.

Section 11.3.4.2.2 of *TMS 402-22* requires that the nominal flexural strength of a beam not be less than 1.3 times the nominal cracking capacity, calculated using the modulus of rupture from Section 11.1.8.

The specified compressive strength, f'_{AAC}, for Class 6 AAC is 870 psi (Table 14.1). The corresponding splitting tensile strength is

$$f_{t\,AAC} = 2.4 \sqrt{f'_{AAC}}$$
$$f_{t\,AAC} = 2.4 \sqrt{580 \text{ lb/in}^2}$$
$$f_{t\,AAC} = 57.8 \text{ lb/in}^2$$

The modulus of rupture is twice this value, or 115.6 psi.

In our case, the nominal cracking moment for the 4-ft deep section is

$$M_{cr} = S f_r = \frac{bt^2}{6} f_r = \frac{7.9 \text{ in.} \times 48^2 \text{ in}^2}{6} \times 115.6 \text{ lb/in}^2 = 175{,}341 \text{ lb-in.}$$

This value, multiplied by 1.3, is 227,973 lb-in., which is less than the nominal capacity of this lintel with the provided #4 bar.

Finally, Section 11.3.3 of *TMS 402-22* imposes maximum flexural reinforcement limitations that are based on a series of critical strain gradients. These generally do not govern for members with little or no axial load, like this lintel. They may govern for members with significant axial load, such as tall shear walls.

14.8 Design of Reinforced Curtain Walls of AAC Masonry

Although reinforced curtain walls of AAC masonry are theoretically possible, it is much more cost-effective to use factory-reinforced panels spanning horizontally between columns, rather than field-reinforced AAC masonry. For this reason, the strength design of reinforced curtain walls of AAC masonry is not discussed further here. It is discussed in ACI 526.1R.

14.9 Design of Reinforced Bearing Walls of AAC Masonry

14.9.1 Example: Moment-Axial Force Interaction Diagram for AAC Masonry (Spreadsheet Calculation)

Construct the moment-axial force interaction diagram by the strength approach for a nominal 8-in. AAC masonry wall with Class 4 AAC (f'_{AAC} = 580 lb/in^2) and reinforcement consisting of #5 bars at 32 in., placed in the center of the wall.

The effective width of the wall is the minimum of $6t$ or the bar spacing. In the case the limiting dimension is 32 in. The spreadsheet and corresponding interaction diagram are shown below. As noted in Chapter 6, because the reinforcement is located at the geometric centroid of the section, the balance-point axial load (about 2000 lb) does not correspond to the maximum moment capacity. As required by Section 11.3.2 of *TMS 402-22*, the spreadsheet is similar to that of Chapter 6 (strength design of masonry bearing walls), except that the maximum useful compressive strain in the masonry is 0.003 (rather than 0.0025 or 0.0035); the equivalent rectangular compressive stress block has a height $0.85f'_{AAC}$ (rather than $0.8f'_m$), and β_1 is 0.67 (rather than 0.8). However, the strength reduction factor, ϕ, is constant.

14.9.1.1 Plot of Interaction Diagram for AAC Masonry Bearing Wall by Spreadsheet

The moment-axial force interaction diagram for this AAC masonry bearing wall, plotted by spreadsheet is shown in Fig. 14.21. This diagram does not include slenderness effects.

Relevant cells from the spreadsheet are reproduced in Table 14.4.

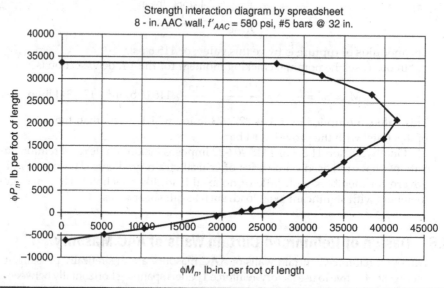

Figure 14.21 Moment-axial force interaction diagram (strength approach), spreadsheet calculation.

TABLE 14.4 Spreadsheet for Computing Moment-Axial Force Interaction Diagram for AAC Bearing Wall

Example of Spreadsheet for Calculating Moment-Axial Force Interaction Diagram for Reinforced AAC Bearing Wall						
Reinforcement at mid-depth						
Specified thickness	7.9					
ε_{mu}	0.003					
f'_m	580					
f_y	60000					
E_s	29000000					
d	3.95					
(c/d) balanced	0.591837					
Tensile reinforcement area	0.31					
Effective width	32					
phi	0.9					
Because compression reinforcement is not supported, it is not counted						
	c/d	c	C_{mas}	f_s	ϕM_n	ϕP_n
Pure axial load					0	33609
Points controlled by masonry	2.387	9.42865	99660	0	26619	33635
	2.2	8.69	91853	0	32205	31000
	1.9	7.505	79327	0	38441	26773
	1.5	5.925	62627	0	41536	21137
	1.2	4.74	50101	0	39941	16909
	1	3.95	41751	0	37014	14091
	0.9	3.555	37576	−9667	34990	11671
	0.8	3.16	33401	−21750	32594	8997
	0.7	2.765	29226	−37286	29825	5963
	0.591837	2.337755	24710	−60000	26410	2062
Points controlled by steel	0.591837	2.337755	24710	−60000	26410	2062
	0.55	2.1725	22963	−60000	24972	1473
	0.5098	2.01371	21285	−60000	23529	906
	0.48	1.896	20041	−60000	22421	486
	0.4	1.58	16700	−60000	19280	−641
	0.2	0.79	8350	−60000	10386	−3459
	0.1	0.395	4175	−60000	5379	−4868
	0.01	0.0395	418	−60000	555	−6137

418 Chapter Fourteen

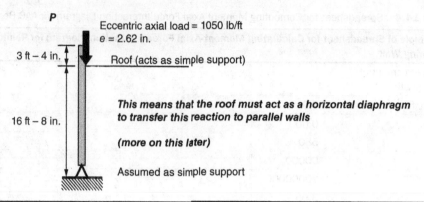

FIGURE 14.22 Reinforced masonry wall loaded by eccentric gravity axial load plus out-of-plane wind load.

14.9.2 Example: Design of AAC Masonry Walls Loaded Out of Plane

Once we have developed the moment-axial force interaction diagram, the actual design simply consists of verifying that the combination of factored design axial force and moment lies within the diagram of nominal axial and flexural capacity, reduced by strength-reduction factors.

Consider the bearing wall designed previously as unreinforced, shown in Fig. 14.22. It has an eccentric axial load plus out-of-plane wind load of 40 lb/ft².

At each horizontal plane through the wall, the following condition must be met:

- Combinations of factored axial load and moment must lie within the moment-axial force interaction diagram, reduced by strength-reduction factors.

Because flexural capacity increases with increasing axial load, the critical loading combination is probably $0.9D + 1.0W$.

From our previous experience, we know that the critical point on the wall is at the midspan of the lower portion.

Due to wind only, the unfactored moment at the base of the parapet (roof level) is

$$M = \frac{w_u L^2_{parapet}}{2} = \frac{40\,\frac{lb}{ft} \times 3.33^2\,ft^2}{2} \times 12\,in./ft = 2661\,lb\text{-}in.$$

The maximum moment is close to that occurring at mid-height. The moment from wind load is the superposition of one-half moment at the upper support due to wind load on the parapet only, plus the midspan moment in a simply supported beam with that same wind load:

$$M_{midspan} = -\frac{2661}{2} + \frac{qL^2}{8} = -\frac{2661}{2} + \frac{40\,\frac{lb}{ft} \times 16.67^2\,ft^2}{8} \times 12\,in./ft = 15{,}343\,lb\text{-}in.$$

The unfactored moment due to eccentric axial load is

$$M_{gravity} = Pe = 1050\,lb \times 2.62\,in. = 2751\,lb\text{-}in.$$

Unfactored moment diagrams due to eccentric axial load and wind are as shown in Fig. 14.23.

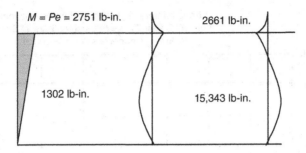

FIGURE 14.23 Unfactored moment diagrams due to eccentric axial load plus wind load.

Check the adequacy of the wall with 8-in. nominal AAC units, Class 4 AAC (specified compressive strength, $f'_{AAC} = 580$ lb/in²), unit weight = 26.3 lb/ft², and #4 bars spaced at 48 in. All design actions are calculated per foot of width of the wall.

At the mid-height of the wall, the axial force due to 0.9D is:

$$P_u = 0.9(700 \text{ lb}) + 0.9(3.33 \text{ ft} + 8.33 \text{ ft}) \times 26.3 \text{ lb/ft} = 906 \text{ lb}$$

At the mid-height of the wall, the factored design moment, M_u, is given by

$$M_u = P_u \frac{e}{2} + M_{u\,wind} = \left(\frac{1}{2}\right) 0.9 \times 700 \text{ lb} \times 2.48 \text{ in.} + 1.0 \times 15{,}343 \text{ lb-in.} = 16{,}124 \text{ lb-in.}$$

The pure compression resistance of the wall is reduced by a slenderness-dependent factor (*TMS 402-22*, Section 11.3.5.4 and Section 11.3.4.1.1). That has the effect of "capping" the moment-axial force interaction diagram.

In each foot of wall, the design actions are $P_u = 906$ lb, and $M_u = 16{,}124$ lb-in. That combination lies within the interaction diagram of design capacities capped for slenderness (Fig. 14.21), and the design is satisfactory. However, P-Δ effects still need to be considered. The ultimate moment on the diagram and the corresponding axial load does include effects of slenderness.

Relevant cells from the spreadsheet of Fig. 14.24 are reproduced in Table 14.5.

Because this out-of-plane wall is checked for magnified moments in accordance with Section 11.3.5.5 of *TMS 402-22*, the slenderness-dependent reduction factor is applied only to the compression capacity under pure axial load, and not to the remaining nominal axial capacities.

Outside of a plastic hinge zone, Section 6.1.3.2.5 of *TMS 402-22* imposes a maximum bar area of 4.5% of the cell. Using a 3-in. grouted core, the area ratio is $(0.625/3)^2$, or 0.043, satisfying the requirement.

TMS 402-22 also requires a check of the possible effects of secondary moments for reinforced walls loaded out of plane, using either the iterative calculation procedure of Section 11.3.5.5.2 or the moment-magnifier procedure of Section 11.3.5.5.3. Initially the moment-magnified procedure is used because of its simplicity.

The cracked moment of inertia I_{cr} for use in *TMS 402* Section 11.3.5.5 is calculated using Section 11.3.5.5.3. Section properties are per foot of plan length. The location of the neutral axis is obtained from the moment-axial force interaction spreadsheet, at an

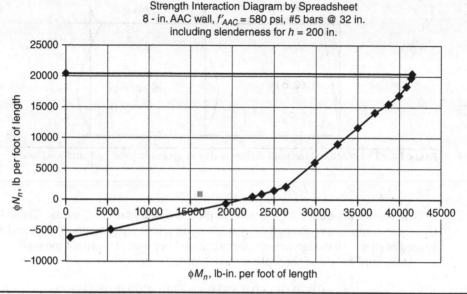

FIGURE 14.24 Moment-axial force interaction diagram for out-of-plane example, including the effects of capping for slenderness.

axial load of 906 lb. The same location could have been obtained using Equation 11-24 of *TMS 402-22*.

$$I_{cr} = n\left(A_s + \frac{P_u}{f_y}\frac{t_{sp}}{2d}\right)(d-c)^2 + \frac{bc^3}{3}$$

$$n = \frac{E_s}{E_{AAC}} = \frac{29 \times 10^6 \text{ lb/in}^2}{6500\left(f'_{AAC}\right)^{0.6}} = \frac{29 \times 10^6 \text{ lb/in}^2}{6500 \times (580)^{0.6} \text{ lb/in}^2} = \frac{29 \times 10^6 \text{ lb/in}^2}{295{,}781 \text{ lb/in}^2} = 98.05$$

$$I_{cr} = 98.05\left(\frac{0.31 \text{ in}^2}{4} + \frac{906 \text{ lb}}{60{,}000 \text{ lb/in}^2} \times \frac{7.95 \text{ in.}}{2 \times \left(\frac{7.95}{2}\right) \text{in.}}\right)\left(\frac{7.95 \text{ in.}}{2} - 2.1037 \text{ in.}\right)^2$$

$$+ \frac{12 \times 2.1037^3 \text{ in}^4}{3}$$

$$I_{cr} = 34.92 \text{ in}^4 + 32.66 \text{ in}^4 = 67.58 \text{ in}^4$$

$$P_e = \frac{\pi^2 E_{AAC} I_{eff}}{h^2} = \frac{\pi^2 E_{AAC} I_{cr}}{h^2} = \frac{\pi^2 \times 295{,}781 \text{ lb/in}^2 \times 67.58 \text{ in}^4}{200^2 \text{ in}^2} = 4933 \text{ lb}$$

$$\psi = \frac{1}{1 - \frac{P_u}{P_e}} = \frac{1}{1 - \frac{906 \text{ lb}}{4933 \text{ lb}}} = 1.225$$

$$M_u = \psi M_{u,0} = 1.225 \times 16{,}124 = 19{,}752 \text{ lb-in.}$$

The moment magnifier gives a simple and satisfactory design moment.

TABLE 14.5 Calculations for Spreadsheet of Out-of-Plane Example, Including Effects of Capping for Slenderness

Example of Spreadsheet for Calculating Moment-Axial Force Interaction Diagram for AAC Masonry						
Reinforcement at mid-depth						
Specified thickness	7.9				h	200
ε_{mu}	0.003				r	2.280534
f'_m	580				h/r	87.69878
f_y	60000				Factor	0.607598
E_s	29000000					
d	3.95					
(c/d) balanced	0.591837					
Tensile reinforcement area	0.31					
Effective width	32					
phi	0.9					
Because compression reinforcement is not supported, it is not counted						
	c/d	c	C_{mas}	f_s	ϕM_n	ϕP_n
Pure axial load					0	20421
Points controlled by masonry	1.44976	5.726552	60529	0	41503	20429
	1.4	5.53	58452	0	41377	19727
	1.3	5.135	54277	0	40846	18318
	1.2	4.74	50101	0	39941	16909
	1.1	4.345	45926	0	38664	15500
	1	3.95	41751	0	37014	14091
	0.9	3.555	37576	−9667	34990	11671
	0.8	3.16	33401	−21750	32594	8997
	0.7	2.765	29226	−37286	29825	5963
	0.591837	2.337755	24710	−60000	26410	2062
Points controlled by steel	0.591837	2.337755	24710	−60000	26410	2062
	0.55	2.1725	22963	−60000	24972	1473
	0.5098	2.01371	21285	−60000	23529	906
	0.48	1.896	20041	−60000	22421	486
	0.4	1.58	16700	−60000	19280	−641
	0.1	0.395	4175	−60000	5379	−4868
	0.01	0.0395	418	−60000	555	−6137

For comparison, the iterative procedure of Section 11.3.5.5.2 will be used. In accordance with that section, code Equation 11-16 is used to calculate the maximum moment, including possible secondary moments. That maximum moment is then compared with the interaction diagram. Equation 11-16 of TMS 402-22 is based on a member simply supported at top and bottom, which is the case here:

$$M_u = \frac{w_u h^2}{8} + P_{uf}\left(\frac{e_u}{2}\right) + P_u \delta_u$$

As calculated above, for each ft of wall length, the first two terms in this equation total 16,124 lb-in., and P_u equals 906 lb. In accordance with Section 11.3.5.5, δ_u is to be calculated using Equations 11-18 and 11-19 of TMS 402-22.

Because the cracking moment used in those equations is calculated without strength-reduction factors, it might exceed the factored design moment. Nevertheless, it is believed prudent to assume that reinforced masonry is cracked at bed joints.

Because the section of AAC has thin-bed mortar joints, $f_{r\,AAC} = 80$ psi (Section 11.1.8.2 of TMS 402-22). Using Equation 11-23 of TMS 402-22,

$$M_{cr} = \left(f_r + \frac{P}{A}\right)\left(\frac{I_g}{t/2}\right) = \left(80\text{ lb/in}^2 + \frac{906\text{ lb}}{12 \times 7.95\text{ in}^2}\right)\left(\frac{12\text{ in.} \times 7.95^3\text{ in}^3}{12 \times 7.95/2\text{ in.}}\right) = 11{,}313\text{ lb-in.}$$

$$\delta_u = \frac{5 M_{cr} h^2}{48 E_{AAC} I_n} + \frac{5(M_u - M_{cr})h^2}{48 E_{AAC} I_{cr}}$$

$h = 200$ in.

$$\delta_u = \frac{5 \times 11{,}313\text{ lb-in.} \times 200^2\text{ in}^2}{48 \times 295{,}781 \times \left(\frac{12 \times 7.95^3\text{ in}^4}{12}\right)} + \frac{5(16{,}124\text{ lb-in.} - 11{,}313\text{ lb-in.}) \times 200^2\text{ in}^2}{48 \times 295{,}781 \times 67.58\text{ in}^4}$$

$\delta_u = 0.317$ in. $+ 0.961$ in. $= 2.076$ in.

$M_{u2} = 16{,}124$ lb-in. $+ 906(2.08)$ lb-in. $= 21{,}633$ lb-in.

Check convergence:

$$\delta_{u2} = \frac{5 M_{cr} h^2}{48 E_{AAC} I_n} + \frac{5(M_{u2} - M_{cr})h^2}{48 E_{AAC} I_{cr}}$$

$h = 200$ in.

$$\delta_{u2} = \frac{5 \times 11{,}313\text{ lb-in.} \times 200^2\text{ in}^2}{48 \times 295{,}781 \times \left(\frac{12 \times 7.95^3\text{ in}^4}{12}\right)} + \frac{5(21{,}633\text{ lb-in.} - 11{,}313\text{ lb-in.}) \times 200^2\text{ in}^2}{48 \times 295{,}781 \times 67.58\text{ in}^4}$$

$\delta_{u2} = 0.317$ in. $+ 2.151$ in. $= 2.47$ in.

Convergence did not occur, so we run a third iteration

$$M_{u3} = 16{,}124\text{ lb-in.} + 906\,(2.47)\text{ lb-in.} = 21{,}998\text{ lb-in.}$$

$$\delta_{u3} = \frac{5 M_{cr} h^2}{48 E_{AAC} I_n} + \frac{5(M_{u3} - M_{cr})h^2}{48 E_{AAC} I_{cr}}$$

$h = 200$ in.

$$\delta_{u2} = \frac{5 \times 11{,}313 \text{ lb-in.} \times 200^2 \text{ in}^2}{48 \times 295{,}781 \times \left(\dfrac{12 \times 7.95^3 \text{ in}^4}{12}\right)} + \frac{5(21{,}998 \text{ lb-in.} - 11{,}313 \text{ lb-in.}) \times 200^2 \text{ in}^2}{48 \times 295{,}781 \times 67.58 \text{ in}^4}$$

$\delta_u = 0.317 \text{ in.} + 2.225 \text{ in.} = 2.54 \text{ in.}$

$M_{u3} = 16{,}124 \text{ lb-in.} + 906(2.54) \text{ lb-in.} = 22{,}055 \text{ lb-in.}$

Because the moment is changing by less than 1%, it can be assumed to have converged.

It is useful to compare the two methods. Because the moment-magnifier procedure is simpler and gives a smaller factored design moment (19.8 vs. 22.06 kip), it is recommended.

The combination of factored axial force and factored moment (including secondary moments) remains within the moment-axial force interaction diagram, and the design is still satisfactory.

Finally, the provisions of *TMS 402-22* also require a check of out-of-plane deflections for reinforced AAC masonry walls loaded out of plane (Section 11.3.5.6).

In accordance with those sections, principles of mechanics are used to calculate the midheight deflection at service loads. The equation below is based on a member simply supported at top and bottom, which is the case here. In this problem, the service-level moment is taken as 0.6 times the strength-level moment because 0.6 is the service-level load factor in the ASCE 7-22 allowable-stress loading combinations. In this problem, service level moments are less than cracking moments.

$$\delta_s = \frac{5 M_s h^2}{48 E_{AAC} I_n} = \frac{5 \times 0.6 \times 16{,}124 \text{ lb-in.} \times 200^2 \text{ in}^2}{48 \times 295{,}781 \times \left(\dfrac{12 \times 7.95^3 \text{ in}^4}{12}\right)} = 0.27 \text{ in.}$$

This deflection is less than $0.007 h$ (equal to 0.007 times 16.67 ft, or 1.40 in.). The out-of-plane deflection requirement is satisfied.

14.9.3 Minimum and Maximum Reinforcement Ratios for Out-of-Plane Flexural Design of AAC Masonry Walls

The design provisions of *TMS 402-22* include requirements for minimum and maximum flexural reinforcement. In this section, the implications of those requirements for the out-of-plane flexural design of AAC masonry walls are addressed.

14.9.3.1 Minimum Flexural Reinforcement by *TMS 402-22*

TMS 402-22 refers designers to Section 11.3.4.2.2 for minimum flexural reinforcement for out-of-plane design of AAC walls.

14.9.3.2 Maximum Flexural Reinforcement for AAC Walls by *TMS 402-22*

Section 11.3.3 of *TMS 402-22* has a maximum reinforcement requirement that is intended to ensure ductile behavior over a range of axial loads. In traditional concrete or clay masonry this is addressed using equation for maximum flexural percentages, ρ_{max}. In those cases, as compressive axial load increases, the maximum permissible reinforcement percentage decreases. For compressive axial loads above a critical value, the maximum permissible reinforcement percentage drops to zero, and design is impossible unless the cross-sectional area of the element is increased. Similar design provisions

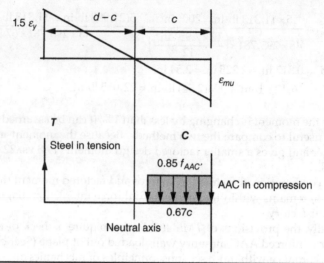

FIGURE 14.25 Critical strain condition for an AAC masonry wall loaded out of plane.

should be developed for AAC masonry based on the derivation shown below and in Section 14.10.1.2.

For walls subjected to out-of-plane forces, for columns, and for beams, the provisions of *TMS 402-22* Section 11.3.3(a) set the maximum permissible reinforcement based on a critical strain condition in which the masonry is at its maximum useful strain, and the extreme tension reinforcement is set at 1.5 times the yield strain.

The critical strain condition for walls with a single layer of concentric reinforcement and loaded out-of-plane is shown in Fig. 14.25, along with the corresponding stress state. The parameters for the equivalent rectangular stress block are the same as those used for conventional flexural design. The height of the equivalent rectangular stress block is $0.85 f'_{AAC}$, and the depth is $0.67c$. The tensile reinforcement is assumed to be at f_y.

Locate the neutral axis using the critical strain condition:

$$\frac{\varepsilon_{mu}}{1.5\varepsilon_y} = \frac{c}{d-c}$$

$$c = d\left(\frac{\varepsilon_{mu}}{1.5\varepsilon_y + \varepsilon_{mu}}\right)$$

Compute the tensile and compressive forces acting on the section, assuming concentric reinforcement with a percentage of reinforcement $\rho = \frac{A}{bd}$, where $d = \frac{t}{2}$.

The compressive force in the masonry is given by

$$C_{masonry} = 0.85 f'_{AAC} 0.67cb$$

The tensile force in the reinforcement is given by

$$T_{steel} = \rho b d f_y$$

Equilibrium of axial forces requires

$$P_n = C - T$$

$$\frac{P_u}{\phi} = C - T$$

$$\frac{P_u}{\phi} = 0.85 f'_{AAC} \, 0.67cb - \rho d b f_y$$

$$\frac{P_u}{\phi} = 0.85 \, f'_{AAC} \, 0.67 d \left(\frac{\varepsilon_{mu}}{1.5\varepsilon_y + \varepsilon_{mu}} \right) b - \rho d b f_y$$

$$\rho = \frac{0.85 f'_{AAC} 0.67 d \left(\dfrac{\varepsilon_{mu}}{1.5\varepsilon_y + \varepsilon_{mu}} \right) b - \dfrac{P_u}{\phi}}{b d f_y}$$

$$\rho = \frac{0.85 f'_{AAC} 0.67 \left(\dfrac{\varepsilon_{mu}}{1.5\varepsilon_y + \varepsilon_{mu}} \right) - \dfrac{P_u}{bd\phi}}{f_y}$$

So

$$\rho_{max} = \frac{0.57 f'_{AAC} \left(\dfrac{\varepsilon_{mu}}{1.5\varepsilon_y + \varepsilon_{mu}} \right) - \dfrac{P_u}{bd\phi}}{f_y}$$

14.10 Design of Reinforced Shear Walls of AAC Masonry

Reinforced shear walls of AAC masonry must be designed for the effects of:

1) gravity loads from self-weight, plus gravity loads from overlying roof or floor levels; and
2) moments and shears from in-plane shear loads

Actions are shown in Fig. 14.26.

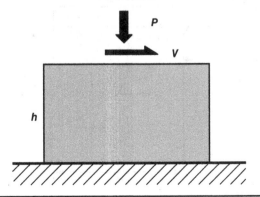

FIGURE 14.26 Design actions for reinforced AAC masonry shear walls.

Flexural capacity of reinforced AAC shear walls is calculated using moment-axial force interaction diagrams as discussed in the section on AAC masonry walls loaded out-of-plane. In contrast to the elements addressed in that section, a shear wall is subjected to flexure in its own plane rather than out-of-plane. It therefore usually has multiple layers of flexural reinforcement. Computation of moment-axial force interaction diagrams for shear walls is much easier using a spreadsheet.

From TMS 402-22, Section 11.3.4.1.2, nominal shear strength is the summation of shear strength from AAC masonry and shear strength from shear reinforcement:

$$V_n = V_{n\,AAC} + V_{ns}$$

According to Section 11.3.4.1.2.1 of *TMS 402-22*, the nominal shear capacity of AAC masonry is the least of the following three equations, related, respectively, to web-shear cracking, crushing of the diagonal strut, and sliding.

$$V_{n\,AAC} = \min \begin{cases} 0.95 \ell_w t \sqrt{f'_{AAC}} \sqrt{1 + \dfrac{P_u}{2.4\sqrt{f'_{AAC}}\,\ell_w t}} \\ 0.17 f'_{AAC}\, t \, \dfrac{h \times \ell_w^2}{h^2 + \left(\dfrac{3}{4}\ell_w\right)^2} \\ \mu_{AAC} P_u \end{cases}$$

The strength-reduction factor for shear is 0.80 (*TMS 402-22*, Section 11.1.5).

Just as in reinforced concrete design, this model assumes that shear is resisted by reinforcement crossing a hypothetical failure surface oriented at 45 degrees, as shown in Fig. 14.27.

The nominal resistance from reinforcement is taken as the area associated with each set of shear reinforcement, multiplied by the number of sets of shear reinforcement crossing the hypothetical failure surface. Because the hypothetical failure surface is assumed to be inclined at 45 degrees, its projection along the length of the member is

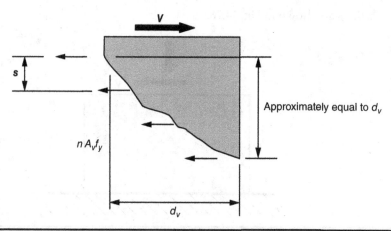

Figure 14.27 Idealized model used in evaluating the resistance due to shear reinforcement.

approximately equal to d_v, and the number of sets of shear reinforcement crossing the hypothetical failure surface can be approximated by (d_v/s):

$$V_{ns} = A_v f_y n$$

$$V_{ns} = A_v f_y \left(\frac{d_v}{s}\right)$$

From *TMS 402-22*, Section 11.3.4.1.2.3, an efficiency factor of 0.5 is used to reflect the fact that not all the shear reinforcement will be yielded:

$$V_{ns} = 0.5 \left(\frac{A_v}{s}\right) f_y d_v$$

In contrast to strength design of clay or concrete masonry, joint reinforcement is not permitted to be used, because it produces local bearing failures of the AAC. Only deformed reinforcement in grouted bond beams is permitted to be included in computing V_{ns} (*TMS 402-22*, Section 11.3.4.1.2.3).

Finally, because shear resistance really comes from a truss mechanism in which horizontal reinforcement is in tension, and diagonal struts in the masonry are in compression, crushing of the diagonal compressive struts is controlled by limiting the total shear resistance V_n, regardless of the amount of shear reinforcement:

For $(M_u/V_u d_v) < 0.25$,

$$V_n = 6 A_n \sqrt{f'_{AAC}}$$

and for $(M_u/V_u d_v) > 1.00$,

$$V_n = 4 A_n \sqrt{f'_{AAC}}$$

Interpolation is permitted between these limits, as shown in Fig. 14.28.

If these upper limits on V_n are not satisfied, the cross-sectional area of the section must be increased.

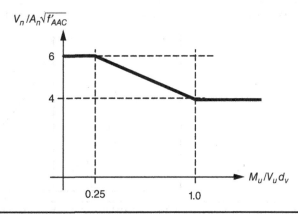

FIGURE 14.28 Maximum permitted nominal shear capacity of AAC masonry as a function of $(M_u/V_u d_v)$.

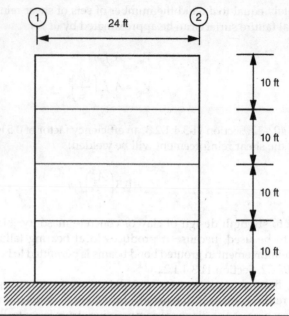

FIGURE 14.29 Reinforced AAC masonry shear wall to be designed.

14.10.1 Example: Design of Reinforced AAC Masonry Shear Wall

Consider the masonry shear wall shown in Fig. 14.29.

Design the wall. Unfactored in-plane lateral loads at each floor level are due to earthquake, and are shown in Fig. 14.30, along with the corresponding shear and moment diagrams.

Assume a 12-in. AAC masonry wall, Class 6 AAC ($f'_{AAC} = 870$ lb/in^2), with thin-bed mortar. The total plan length of the wall is 24 ft (288 in.), and its specified thickness

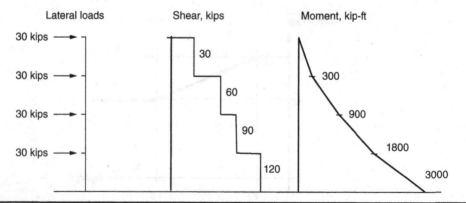

FIGURE 14.30 Unfactored in-plane lateral loads, shear and moment diagrams for reinforced AAC masonry shear wall.

Structural Design of AAC Masonry

is 11.9 in. Assume an effective depth d of 285 in. As is shown later, the reason for the higher strength class of AAC and the greater wall thickness is to increase the shear capacity of the AAC masonry. Shear design and capacity design requirements for shear are critical for this wall.

Unfactored axial loads on the wall are given in the table below.

Level (Top of Wall)	DL (kips)	LL (kips)
4	90	15
3	180	35
2	270	55
1	360	75

Use ASCE 7 strength Load Combination 7: $0.9D + 1.0E$

At the base of the wall, the factored axial load for the critical loading combination is $0.9D$, or 0.9×360 kips $= 324$ kips.

Check shear for assumed wall thickness. By Section 11.3.4.1.2.1 of *TMS 402-22*,

$$V_n = V_{n\,AAC} + V_{ns}$$

$$V_{n\,AAC} = \min \begin{cases} 0.95 \ell_w t \sqrt{f'_{AAC}} \sqrt{1 + \dfrac{P_u}{2.4\sqrt{f'_{AAC}}\,\ell_w t}} \\[2mm] 0.17 f'_{AAC} t \dfrac{h \times \ell_w^2}{h^2 + \left(\dfrac{3}{4}\ell_w\right)^2} \\[2mm] \mu_{AAC} P_u \end{cases}$$

Take the coefficient of friction for the third equation as 1.0 (AAC against mortar).

$$V_{n\,AAC} = \min \begin{cases} 0.95 \times 288 \text{ in.} \times 11.9 \text{ in.} \sqrt{870 \text{ lb/in}^2} \sqrt{1 + \dfrac{324{,}000 \text{ lb}}{2.4\sqrt{870 \text{ lb/in}^2} \times 288 \text{ in.} \times 11.9 \text{ in.}}} \\[2mm] 0.17 \times 870 \text{ lb/in}^2 \times 11.9 \text{ in.} \dfrac{40 \text{ ft} \times 24^2 \text{ ft}^2}{40^2 \text{ ft}^2 + \left(\dfrac{3}{4} \times 24\right)^2 \text{ ft}^2} \times 12 \text{ in./ft} \\[2mm] 1.0 \times 324 \text{ kips} \end{cases}$$

$$V_{n\,AAC} = \min \begin{cases} 146{,}761 \text{ lb} \\ 252{,}914 \text{ lb} \\ 324{,}000 \text{ lb} \end{cases}$$

$$\phi V_n > V_u \quad \phi = 0.80 \quad V_n = V_{n\,AAC} = 146.8 \text{ kips}$$
$$0.80(146.8 \text{ kips}) = 117.4 \text{ kips} < V_u = 120 \text{ kips}$$

Shear design is not satisfactory. Reinforcement will be required. Try horizontal reinforcement consisting of two #4 bars in bond beams at each story level, corresponding to a spacing of 10 ft. The additional nominal capacity due to reinforcement is

$$V_{ns} = 0.5 \left(\frac{A_v}{s}\right) f_y d_v$$

$$V_{ns} = 0.5 \left(\frac{2 \times 0.20 \text{ in}^2}{10 \text{ ft}}\right) 60 \text{ kip/in}^2 \times 24 \text{ ft}$$

$$V_{ns} = 28.8 \text{ kip}$$

$$V_n = V_{n\,AAC} + V_{ns}$$

$$V_n = 146.8 \text{ kips} + 28.8 \text{ kips}$$

$$V_n = 175.6 \text{ kips}$$

$$\phi V_n = 0.8 \, V_n = 140.5 \text{ kips}$$

$$M_u = 3000 \times 12 \times 1000 \text{ lb-in.} = 36.0 \times 10^6 \text{ lb-in.}$$
$$V_u d_v = 120{,}000 \text{ lb} \qquad d_v = 285 \text{ in.}$$

$$M_u / V_u d_v = \frac{36 \times 10^6 \text{ lb-in.}}{120{,}000 \text{ lb } (285 \text{ in.})} = 1.05$$

For $(M_u / V_u d_v) > 1.00$,

$$V_n \leq 4 A_n \sqrt{f'_{AAC}}$$
$$V_n \leq 4 \times 11.9 \text{ in.} \times 288 \text{ in.} \sqrt{870 \text{ lb/in}^2}$$
$$V_n \leq 404{,}351 \text{ lb}$$

This is satisfied, and design for shear is OK so far. Shear capacity design will be checked later.

Now check flexural capacity using a spreadsheet-generated moment-axial force interaction diagram. Try #3 bars @ 4 ft. Neglecting slenderness effects, the diagram is shown in Fig. 14.31.

The corresponding spreadsheet is shown in Table 14.6.

At a factored axial load of 0.9D, or 0.9 × 360 kips = 324 kips, the design flexural capacity of this wall is 3702 kip-ft, and the design is satisfactory for flexure.

We have designed the wall for the calculated design shear. AAC masonry shear walls are required to be designed to meet the capacity design requirements of *TMS 402-22*, Section 7.3.2.8.1

At an axial load of 324 kips, the nominal flexural capacity of this wall is the design capacity of 3702 kip-ft, divided by the strength reduction factor of 0.9, or 4113 kip-ft. The ratio of this nominal flexural capacity to the factored design moment

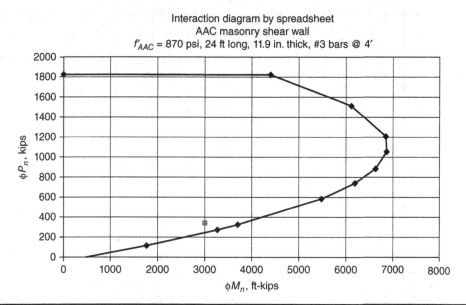

FIGURE 14.31 Moment-axial force interaction for reinforced AAC shear wall, neglecting slenderness effects.

is 4113 divided by 3000, or 1.37. Including the additional factor of 1.25, that gives a ratio of 1.71.

$$\phi V_n \geq 1.71 V_u$$

$$V_n \geq \frac{1.71}{\phi} V_u = \frac{1.71}{0.8} V_u = 2.14 V_u = 2.14 \times 120 = 257.1 \text{ kips}$$

Shear design is not satisfactory. Additional shear reinforcement will be required. We are still under the maximum upper limit for V_n. Use horizontal reinforcement consisting of two #5 bars in bond beams at a spacing of 4 ft. The additional nominal capacity due to reinforcement is

$$V_{ns} = 0.5 \left(\frac{A_v}{s} \right) f_y d_v$$

$$V_{ns} = 0.5 \left(\frac{2 \times 0.31 \text{ in}^2}{4 \text{ ft}} \right) 60 \text{ kip/in}^2 \times 24 \text{ ft}$$

$$V_{ns} = 111.6 \text{ kip}$$

$$V_n = V_{n\,AAC} + V_{ns}$$

$$V_n = 146.8 \text{ kips} + 111.6 \text{ kips}$$

$$V_n = 258.4 \text{ kips}$$

Design for shear is barely satisfactory. The upper limit for V_n has not changed and is still 268,435 kip. The design is just satisfactory and is clearly governed by capacity design requirements.

TABLE 14.6 Spreadsheet for Reinforced AAC Shear Wall

Spreadsheet for Calculating Moment-Axial Force Interaction Diagram for AAC Masonry Shear Wall

Depth	288
ε_{nu}	0.003
f'_m	0.87
f_y	60
E_s	29000
d	285
(c/d) balanced	0.591837
Width	11.9
phi	0.9

Steel layers are counted from the extreme compression fiber to the extreme tension fiber

Distances are measured from the extreme compression fiber

Reinforcement is assumed to be placed at 4-ft intervals

Compression in masonry and reinforcement is taken as positive

Stress in compressive reinforcement is set to zero, because the reinforcement is not laterally supported

Row of Reinforcement	Distance	Area
1	3.00	0.11
2	51.00	0.11
3	99.00	0.11
4	147.00	0.11
5	195.00	0.11
6	237.00	0.11
7	285.00	0.11

	c/d	c	C_{mas}	$f_s(1)$	$f_s(2)$	$f_s(3)$	$f_s(4)$	$f_s(5)$	$f_s(6)$	$f_s(7)$	Moment	Axial Force
Pure axial load											0	1824
Points controlled by masonry	1.205	343.43	2025	0.00	0.00	0.00	0.00	0.00	0.00	0.00	4397	1822
	1	285.00	1680	0.00	0.00	0.00	0.00	0.00	0.00	0.00	6115	1512
	0.8	228.00	1344	0.00	0.00	0.00	0.00	0.00	-3.43	-21.75	6846	1207
	0.7	199.50	1176	0.00	0.00	0.00	0.00	0.00	-16.35	-37.29	6864	1053
	0.591837	168.67	995	0.00	0.00	0.00	0.00	-13.58	-35.24	-60.00	6629	884
Points controlled by steel	0.591837	168.67	995	0.00	0.00	0.00	0.00	-13.58	-35.24	-60.00	6629	884
	0.5	142.50	840	0.00	0.00	0.00	-2.75	-32.05	-57.69	-60.00	6193	741
	0.4	114.00	672	0.00	0.00	0.00	-25.18	-60.00	-60.00	-60.00	5476	585
	0.233	66.41	392	0.00	0.00	-42.70	-60.00	-60.00	-60.00	-60.00	3702	324
	0.2	57.00	336	0.00	0.00	-60.00	-60.00	-60.00	-60.00	-60.00	3269	273
	0.1	28.50	168	0.00	-60.00	-60.00	-60.00	-60.00	-60.00	-60.00	1769	116
	0.01	2.85	17	-4.58	-60.00	-60.00	-60.00	-60.00	-60.00	-60.00	249	-21

Check ρ_{max}, assuming that the wall is classified as an ordinary reinforced AAC masonry shear wall ($\alpha = 1.5$). See derivation and discussion at the end of this section.

$$\rho_{max} = \frac{0.64 f'_m \left(\dfrac{\varepsilon_{mu}}{\alpha \varepsilon_y + \varepsilon_{mu}} \right) - \dfrac{P_u}{bd\phi}}{f_y \left(\dfrac{\alpha \varepsilon_y - \varepsilon_{mu}}{\alpha \varepsilon_y + \varepsilon_{mu}} \right)}$$

$$\rho_{max} = \frac{0.64 f'_m \left(\dfrac{\varepsilon_{mu}}{4\varepsilon_y + \varepsilon_{mu}} \right) - \dfrac{P_u}{bd\phi}}{f_y \left(\dfrac{4\varepsilon_y - \varepsilon_{mu}}{4\varepsilon_y + \varepsilon_{mu}} \right)}$$

In accordance with *TMS 602-22* Section 3.3.3.5.1(d), the governing axial load combination is $D + 0.75\,L + 0.525\,Q_E$, and the axial load is $(360{,}000 + 0.75 \times 75{,}000\text{ lb})$, or 416,250 lb.

$$\rho_{max} = \frac{0.57 f'_m \left(\dfrac{\varepsilon_{mu}}{1.5\varepsilon_y + \varepsilon_{mu}} \right) - \dfrac{P_u}{bd\phi}}{f_y \left(\dfrac{1.5\varepsilon_y - \varepsilon_{mu}}{1.5\varepsilon_y + \varepsilon_{mu}} \right)}$$

$$\rho_{max} = \frac{0.57(870\text{ psi})\left[\dfrac{0.003}{1.5(0.00207) + 0.003}\right] - \dfrac{416{,}250\text{ lb}}{(11.9\text{ in.})(285\text{ in.})(0.9)}}{(60{,}000\text{ psi})\left[\dfrac{1.5(0.00207) - 0.003}{1.5(0.00207) + 0.003}\right]}$$

$$\rho_{max} = 0.103$$

Check maximum area of flexural reinforcement per 48 in. of wall length

$$A_{s\,max} = \rho_{max} b \times 48\text{ in.} = 0.103\,(11.9\text{ in.})\,48\text{ in.} = 58.8\text{ in}^2$$

We have 0.11 in² vertical reinforcement every 48 in., and the design is satisfactory.
Summary: Use #4 @ 4 ft vertically, grouted bond beams with two #5 bars @ 4 ft.

14.10.2 Minimum and Maximum Reinforcement Ratios for Flexural Design of AAC Masonry Shear Walls

14.10.2.1 Minimum Flexural Reinforcement by *TMS 402-22*
TMS 402-22 has no global requirements for minimum flexural reinforcement for AAC masonry shear walls.

14.10.2.2 Maximum Flexural Reinforcement by *TMS 402-22*
TMS 402-22 has a maximum reinforcement requirement (Section 11.3.3) that is intended to ensure ductile behavior over a range of axial loads. As compressive axial load

increases, the maximum permissible reinforcement percentage decreases. For compressive axial loads above a critical value, the maximum permissible reinforcement percentage drops to zero, and design is impossible unless the cross-sectional area of the element is increased.

For walls subjected to in-plane forces, for columns, and for beams, the provisions of *TMS 402-22* set the maximum permissible reinforcement based on a critical strain condition in which the masonry is at its maximum useful strain, and the extreme tension reinforcement is set at a multiple of the yield strain, where the multiple depends on the expected curvature ductility demand on the wall. For "special" reinforced masonry shear walls, the multiple is 4; for "intermediate" walls, it is 3. For walls not required to undergo inelastic deformations, no upper limit is imposed.

The critical strain condition for walls loaded in-plane, and for columns and beams, is shown in Fig. 14.32, along with the corresponding stress state. The multiple is termed "α." The parameters for the equivalent rectangular stress block are the same as those used for conventional flexural design. The height of the stress block is $0.85f'_{AAC}$, and the depth is $0.67c$. The stress in yielded tensile reinforcement is assumed to be f_y. Compression reinforcement is included in the calculation, based on the assumption that protecting the compression toe will permit the masonry there to provide lateral support to the compression reinforcement. This assumption, while perhaps reasonable, is not consistent with that used for calculation of moment-axial force interaction diagrams.

Locate the neutral axis using the critical strain condition:

$$\frac{\varepsilon_{mu}}{\alpha\varepsilon_y} = \frac{c}{d-c}$$

$$c = d\left(\frac{\varepsilon_{mu}}{\alpha\varepsilon_y + \varepsilon_{mu}}\right)$$

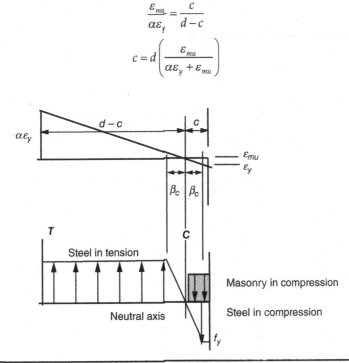

FIGURE 14.32 Critical strain condition for design of AAC masonry walls loaded in-plane, and for columns and beams.

Compute the tensile and compressive forces acting on the section, assuming uniformly distributed flexural reinforcement, with a percentage of reinforcement $\rho = \frac{A}{bd}$. On each side of the neutral axis, the distance over which the reinforcement is in the elastic range is βc, where β is given by proportion as $\beta = \frac{\varepsilon_y}{\varepsilon_{mu}}$.

The compressive force in the AAC masonry is given by

$$C_{masonry} = 0.85 f'_{AAC} 0.67 cb$$

The compressive force in the reinforcement is given by

$$C_{steel} = \rho \beta c b f_y \left(\frac{1}{2}\right) + \rho(1-\beta) c b f_y$$

$$C_{steel} = \rho \left(\frac{\varepsilon_y}{\varepsilon_{mu}}\right) c b f_y \left(\frac{1}{2}\right) + \rho \left[1 - \left(\frac{\varepsilon_y}{\varepsilon_{mu}}\right)\right] c b f_y$$

The tensile force in the reinforcement is given by

$$T_{steel} = \rho \beta c b f_y \left(\frac{1}{2}\right) + \rho(d-c-\beta c) b f_y$$

$$T_{steel} = \rho \left(\frac{\varepsilon_y}{\varepsilon_{mu}}\right) c b f_y \left(\frac{1}{2}\right) + \rho \left[d-c-\left(\frac{\varepsilon_y}{\varepsilon_{mu}}\right) c\right] b f_y$$

Equilibrium of axial forces requires

$$P_n = C - T$$

$$\frac{P_u}{\phi} = C - T$$

$$\frac{P_u}{\phi} = 0.85 f'_{AAC} 0.67 cb$$

$$+ \rho \left(\frac{\varepsilon_y}{\varepsilon_{mu}}\right) c b f_y \left(\frac{1}{2}\right) + \rho \left[1 - \left(\frac{\varepsilon_y}{\varepsilon_{mu}}\right)\right] c b f_y$$

$$- \rho \left(\frac{\varepsilon_y}{\varepsilon_{mu}}\right) c b f_y \left(\frac{1}{2}\right) - \rho \left[d-c-\left(\frac{\varepsilon_y}{\varepsilon_{mu}}\right) c\right] b f_y$$

$$\frac{P_u}{\phi} = 0.85 f'_{AAC} 0.67 cb + \rho \left[1 - \left(\frac{\varepsilon_y}{\varepsilon_{mu}}\right)\right] c b f_y - \rho \left[d-c-\left(\frac{\varepsilon_y}{\varepsilon_{mu}}\right) c\right] b f_y$$

$$\frac{P_u}{\phi} = 0.85 f'_{AAC} 0.67 cb + \rho(2-d) c b f_y$$

$$\frac{P_u}{\phi} = 0.85 f'_{AAC} 0.67 d \left(\frac{\varepsilon_{mu}}{\alpha \varepsilon_y + \varepsilon_{mu}}\right) b + 2 \rho c b f_y - \rho d b f_y$$

$$\frac{P_u}{\phi} = 0.85 f'_{AAC} 0.67 d \left(\frac{\varepsilon_{mu}}{\alpha\varepsilon_y + \varepsilon_{mu}} \right) b + 2\rho d \left(\frac{\varepsilon_{mu}}{\alpha\varepsilon_y + \varepsilon_{mu}} \right) bf_y - \rho db f_y$$

$$\frac{P_u}{\phi} = 0.85 f'_{AAC} 0.67 d \left(\frac{\varepsilon_{mu}}{\alpha\varepsilon_y + \varepsilon_{mu}} \right) b + \rho bd f_y \left[\left(\frac{2\varepsilon_{mu}}{\alpha\varepsilon_y + \varepsilon_{mu}} \right) - 1 \right]$$

$$\rho bd f_y \left[1 - \left(\frac{2\varepsilon_{mu}}{\alpha\varepsilon_y + \varepsilon_{mu}} \right) \right] = 0.85 f'_{AAC} 0.67 d \left(\frac{\varepsilon_{mu}}{\alpha\varepsilon_y + \varepsilon_{mu}} \right) b - \frac{P_u}{\phi}$$

$$\rho = \frac{0.85 f'_{AAC} 0.67 d \left(\frac{\varepsilon_{mu}}{\alpha\varepsilon_y + \varepsilon_{mu}} \right) b - \frac{N_u}{\phi}}{bd f_y \left[1 - \left(\frac{2\varepsilon_{mu}}{\alpha\varepsilon_y + \varepsilon_{mu}} \right) \right]} = \frac{0.85 f'_{AAC} 0.67 \left(\frac{\varepsilon_{mu}}{\alpha\varepsilon_y + \varepsilon_{mu}} \right) - \frac{P_u}{bd\phi}}{f_y \left[1 - \left(\frac{2\varepsilon_{mu}}{\alpha\varepsilon_y + \varepsilon_{mu}} \right) \right]}$$

$$\rho = \frac{0.85 f'_{AAC} 0.67 \left(\frac{\varepsilon_{mu}}{\alpha\varepsilon_y + \varepsilon_{mu}} \right) - \frac{N_u}{bd\phi}}{f_y \left[\left(\frac{\alpha\varepsilon_y + \varepsilon_{mu}}{\alpha\varepsilon_y + \varepsilon_{mu}} \right) - \left(\frac{2\varepsilon_{mu}}{\alpha\varepsilon_y + \varepsilon_{mu}} \right) \right]} = \frac{0.85 f'_{AAC} 0.67 \left(\frac{\varepsilon_{mu}}{\alpha\varepsilon_y + \varepsilon_{mu}} \right) - \frac{N_u}{bd\phi}}{f_y \left(\frac{\alpha\varepsilon_y - \varepsilon_{mu}}{\alpha\varepsilon_y + \varepsilon_{mu}} \right)}$$

So:

$$\rho_{max} = \frac{0.57 f'_{AAC} \left(\frac{\varepsilon_{mu}}{\alpha\varepsilon_y + \varepsilon_{mu}} \right) - \frac{P_u}{bd\phi}}{f_y \left(\frac{\alpha\varepsilon_y - \varepsilon_{mu}}{\alpha\varepsilon_y + \varepsilon_{mu}} \right)}$$

14.10.3 Additional Comments of the Design of Reinforced AAC Shear Walls

Reinforced AAC masonry shear walls have lower shear capacity than otherwise similar shear walls of concrete or clay masonry. They will probably need to be thicker than clay or concrete masonry shear walls and will probably need Class 6 AAC (the highest strength). Capacity design may govern the design for shear, because these walls are required to be ductile.

14.11 Seismic Design of AAC Structures

Because it has been used extensively in Europe for more than 70 years, AAC has been extensively researched there (RILEM 1993). Outside of the US, seismic qualification of AAC components and structures is based on experience in the Middle East and Japan. In the US, it is based indirectly on that experience, and directly on an extensive experimental and analytical research program described further here and in

Tanner et al. (2005a,b), Varela et al. (2006), and Klingner et al. (2005a,b). That research program developed design models, draft design provisions, and seismic design factors (R and C_d). Later work confirmed some of the findings from that research study Costa et al. (2011) and Chen et al. (2013). In the rest of this chapter, the US approach to seismic design of AAC structures is summarized; a design example is presented; and the research background for the design procedure is reviewed.

14.11.1 Basic Earthquake Resistance Mechanism of AAC Structures

Structures whose basic earthquake resistance depends on AAC elements are generally shear-wall structures. Lateral earthquake loads are carried by horizontal diaphragms to AAC shear walls, which transfer those loads to the ground. General response of shear wall structures to lateral loads is discussed in the *Masonry Designers' Guide* (MDG 2022) and is not repeated here.

Earthquake design of AAC shear-wall structures is similar to earthquake design of conventional masonry shear-wall structures. A complete design example is given later in this document.

14.11.2 Seismic Design Factors (R and C_d) for Ductile AAC Shear-Wall Structures in the US

Because AAC structures (whether of masonry units or reinforced panels) in practically all parts of the US must be designed for earthquake loads, it is necessary to develop seismic design factors (R and C_d) for use with ASCE 7, the seismic load document referenced by model codes such as the IBC.

The seismic force-reduction factor (R) is intended to account for ductility, and for structural over-strength. It is based on observation of the performance of different structural systems in previous strong earthquakes, on technical justification, and on tradition. Because AAC is a new material in the US, its seismic design factors (R and C_d) must be based on laboratory test results and numerical simulation of the response of AAC structures to earthquake ground motions. The proposed factors must then be verified against the observed response of AAC structures in strong earthquakes.

Values of R and C_d for ductile AAC shear-wall structures are included in IBC 2015 and ASCE 7 for reinforced AAC masonry shear wall systems Varela et al. (2006).

14.12 Design Example: Three-Story AAC Shear-Wall Hotel

This example illustrates the preliminary design of a three-story AAC shear-wall hotel in Richmond, Virginia, a zone of moderate seismic risk, using the loading provisions of the 2024 IBC and the AAC masonry design and detailing provisions of TMS 402-22 and TMS 602-22. The principal lateral force-resisting elements of the structure are transverse shear walls. Seismic design factors are presented in Table 14.7.

The design proceeds using the following steps:

1) Choose design criteria:
   - propose plan, elevation, materials, f'_{AAC}
   - calculate D, L, W, E loads
   - propose structural systems for gravity and lateral load
2) Design transverse shear walls for gravity and earthquake loads

Structural Design of AAC Masonry   **439**

TABLE 14.7 Seismic Design Factors for Ordinary Reinforced AAC Masonry Shear Walls

Response Modification Coefficient, R	System Overstrength Factor, Ω_0	Deflection Amplification Factor, C_D	\multicolumn{4}{l}{System Limitations and Building Height Limitations (Feet) by Seismic Design Category as Determined in Section 1613.5.6}			
			A or B	C	D	E	F
2	2.5	2	NL	35	NP	NP	NP

3) Design exterior walls for gravity and wind loads
   - earthquake loads will be carried by longitudinal walls in-plane
   - out-of-plane wind loads will be carried by longitudinal walls out-of-plane using vertical and horizontal strips

14.12.1 Step 1: Choose Design Criteria

The plan and elevation of the building are shown in Figs. 14.33 and 14.34. The structure has a story height of 11 ft and a 2-ft parapet, making a total height of 35 ft.

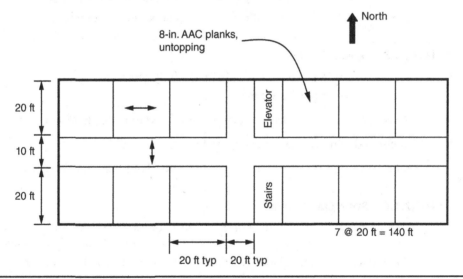

FIGURE 14.33 Plan of three-story hotel example using AAC masonry.

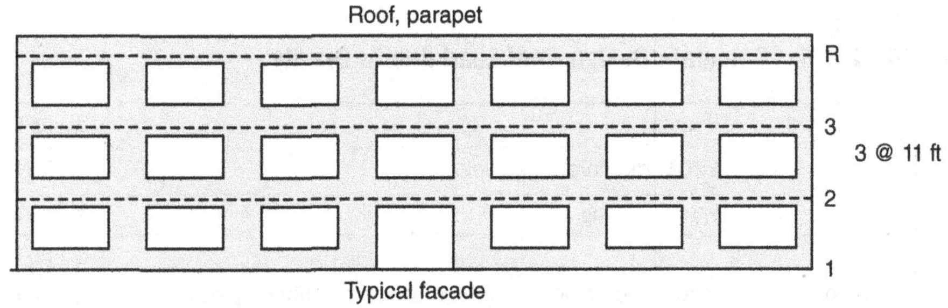

FIGURE 14.34 Elevation of three-story hotel example using AAC masonry.

14.12.1.1 Architectural Constraints

Water-penetration resistance: A single-wythe AAC masonry wall will be used. Exterior protection will be provided by low-modulus acrylic stucco.

Movement joints: To control crack widths from shrinkage of AAC walls, use vertical control joints every bay.

14.12.1.2 Design for Fire

Use and occupancy: Group R-1

Use Type I or Type II construction (noncombustible material)

The building meets the area or height restrictions of Table 503

2- or 3-hour rating required

must meet separation requirements of Table 602 of the 2024 IBC

Bearing walls:	4-hr rating	(8-in. nominal AAC masonry OK)
Shafts:	2-hr rating	(8-in. nominal AAC masonry OK)
Floors:	2-hr rating	(Planks and topping OK)

14.12.1.3 Specify Materials

12-in. AAC masonry units (ASTM C1691), fully mortared

thin-bed mortar (ASTM C1660)

Class 6 AAC (f'_{AAC} = 6 MPa or 870 psi), assumed unit weight 45 pcf

deformed reinforcement meeting ASTM A615, Gr. 60

floors and roof of untopped AAC planks with diaphragm reinforcement

14.12.1.4 Structural Systems

Gravity load: Gravity load on roof and floors will be transferred to transverse walls. Gravity load on corridor will be transferred to spine walls.

Lateral load: Lateral load (earthquake will govern) will be transferred by floor and roof diaphragms to the transverse shear walls, which will act as statically determinate cantilevers.

14.12.1.5 Calculate Design Roof Load due to Gravity

Dead Load	Planks	30 lb/ft²
	EPDM membrane, gravel	20 lb/ft²
	HVAC, roofing	30 lb/ft²
		80 lb/ft² total
Live Load	Ignore reduction of live load based on tributary area.	20 lb/ft²

14.12.1.6 Calculate Design Floor Load due to Gravity

Dead Load	Planks	30 lb/ft²
	HVAC, floor finish, partitions	20 lb/ft²
		50 lb/ft² total
Live Load	Use weighted average of corridor and guest rooms. Ignore reduction of live load based on tributary area.	60 lb/ft²

14.12.1.7 Calculate Design Lateral Load from Earthquake

Design earthquake loads are calculated according to Section 1613 of the 2024 IBC. That section essentially references *ASCE 7-22*. Seismic design criteria are given in Chapter 11. The seismic design provisions of ASCE 7-22 begin in Chapter 12, which prescribes basic requirements (including the requirement for continuous load paths) (Section 12.1); selection of structural systems (Section 12.2); diaphragm characteristics and other possible irregularities (Section 12.3); seismic load effects and combinations (Section 12.4); direction of loading (Section 12.5); analysis procedures (Section 12.6); modeling procedures (Section 12.7); and specific design approaches. Four procedures are prescribed: an equivalent lateral force procedure (Section 12.8); a modal response-spectrum analysis (Section 12.9); a simplified alternative procedure (Section 12.14); and a seismic response history procedure (Chapter 16). The equivalent lateral-force procedure is described here, because it is relatively simple and is permitted in most situations. The simplified alternative procedure is permitted in only a few situations. The other procedures are permitted in all situations, and are required in only a few situations.

The required seismic design steps are summarized below. Section references are to ASCE 7-22.

14.12.1.7.1 Determine Seismic Ground Motion Values

1) Determine S_{MS}, the mapped MCE (maximum considered earthquake), 5% damped, spectral response acceleration parameter at short periods as defined in Section 11.4.3 of *ASCE 7-22*, at the USGS Web site at http://earthquake.usgs.gov/designmaps, or through the ASCE load calculator.

2) Determine S_{M1}, the mapped MCE, 5% damped, spectral response acceleration parameter at a period of 1 second as defined in Section 11.4.3.

3) Determine the *site class* (A through F, a measure of soil response characteristics and soil stability) in accordance with Section 20.2 and Table 20.2-1.

4) Determine the design response acceleration parameter for short periods, S_{DS}, and for a 1-second period, S_{D1}, using Equations 11.4-1 and 11.4-2 respectively.

5) If required, determine the design response spectrum curve as prescribed by Section 11.4.5.

14.12.1.7.2 Determine Seismic Base Shear Using the Equivalent Lateral Force Procedure

1. Determine the structure's importance factor, I, and occupancy category using Sections 1.5.1 and 11.5.

2. Determine the structure's Seismic Design Category using Section 11.6.

3. Calculate the structure's seismic base shear using Sections 12.8.1 and 12.8.2.

14.12.1.7.3 Distribute Seismic Base Shear Vertically and Horizontally

1. Distribute seismic base shear vertically using Section 12.8.3.
2. Distribute seismic base shear horizontally using Section 12.8.4.

Now apply these steps to an example in Richmond, VA:

Step 1: Determine S_{MS}, the mapped MCE (maximum considered earthquake), 5% damped, spectral response acceleration parameter at short periods as defined in Section 11.4.3.

Step 2: Determine S_{M1}, the mapped MCE, 5% damped, spectral response acceleration parameter at a period of 1 second as defined in Section 11.4.3.

Determine the parameters S_{MS} and S_{M1} from the 0.2-second and 1-second spectral response maps shown in Figures 22-1 through 22-7.

With the exception of some parts of the western US (where maximum considered earthquakes have a deterministic basis), those maps correspond to accelerations with a 2% probability of exceedance within a 50-year period. Such an earthquake is sometimes described as a "2500-year earthquake." To see why, let p be the unknown annual probability of exceedance of that level of acceleration.

The probability of exceedance in a particular year is:	p
The probability of non-exceedance in a particular year is:	$(1-p)$
The probability of non-exceedance in 50 consecutive years is:	$(1-p)^{50}$
The probability of exceedance within a 50-year period is:	$[1-(1-p)^{50}]$

Solve for p, the annual probability of exceedance.
Set the probability of exceedance within the 50-year period equal to the given 2%:

$$[1-(1-p)^{50}] = 0.02$$
$$(1-p)^{50} = 0.98$$
$$p = 1 - 0.98^{(1/50)}$$
$$p = 4.04 \times 10^{-4}$$

The return period is the reciprocal of the annual probability of exceedance:

$$1/p = 2475$$

The approximate return period is: 2500 years

The maximum considered earthquake ground motion for 0.2-sec response acceleration (from Figure 22-1 of ASCE7-22) is shown below. For Richmond, Virginia the corresponding contour is 30% g.

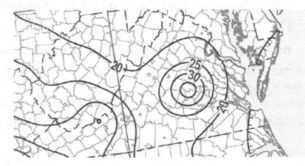

Structural Design of AAC Masonry 443

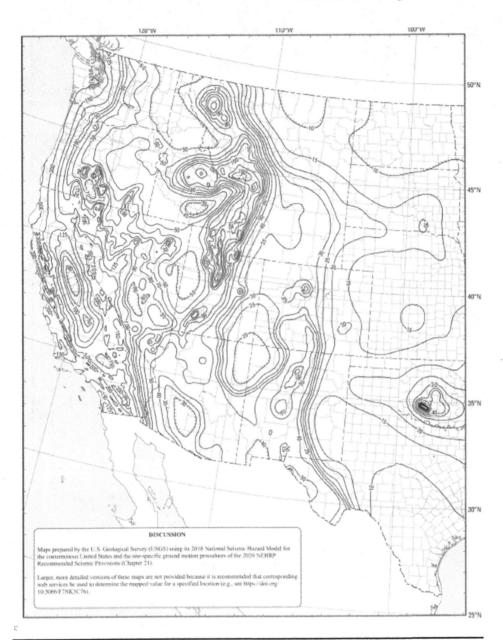

ASCE 7-22 FIGURE 22-1 S_{MS} for the default site conditions for the conterminous United States.

444 Chapter Fourteen

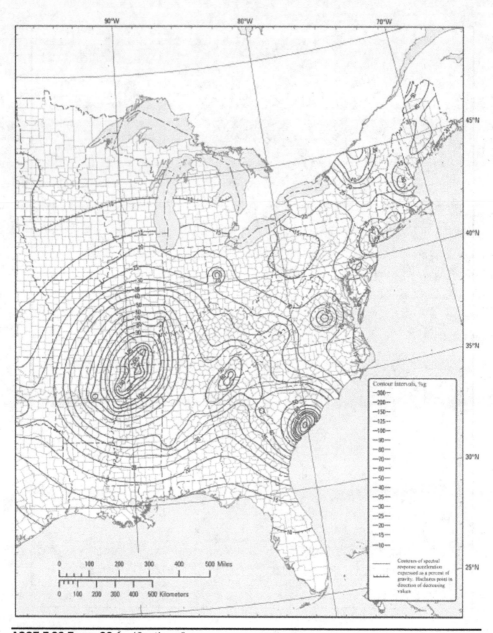

ASCE 7-22 Figure 22-1 (Continued)

Structural Design of AAC Masonry 445

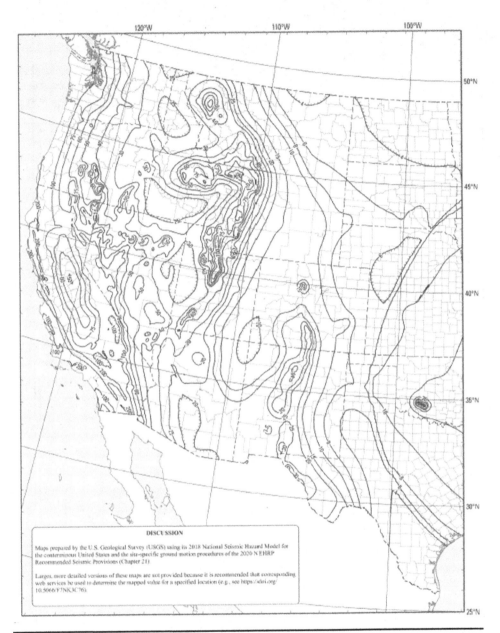

ASCE 7-22 FIGURE 22-1 (Continued)

446 Chapter Fourteen

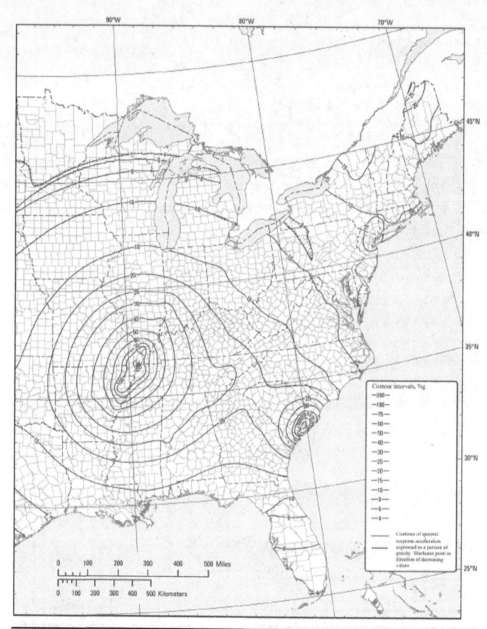

ASCE 7-22 FIGURE 22-1 *(Continued)*

The maximum considered earthquake ground motion for 1-sec response acceleration (from Figure 22-2) of ASCE7-22 is shown below. For Richmond, Virginia the corresponding contour is between 11% g and 12% g. Conservatively use 12% g.

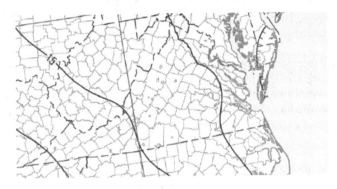

For Richmond, Virginia, therefore, $S_{MS} = 0.30g$ and $S_{M1} = 0.12g$.

Step 3: Determine the *site class* (A through F, a measure of soil response characteristics and soil stability) in accordance with Section 20.2 and Table 20.2-1.

In accordance with Table 20.2-1, site classes are assigned as follows:

ASCE 7-22 TABLE 20.2-1 Site Classification

Site Class	$\bar{v}_s$ Calculated Using Measured or Estimated Shear Wave Velocity Profile (ft/s)
A. Hard rock	>5,000
B. Medium hard rock	>3,000 to 5,000
BC. Soft rock	>2,100 to 3,000
C. Very dense sand and hard clay	>1,450 to 2,100
CD. Dense sand or very stiff clay	>1,000 to 1,450
D. Medium dense sand or stiff clay	>700 to 1,000
DE. Loose sand or medium stiff clay	>500 to 700
E. Very loose sand or soft clay	≥500
F. Soils requiring site response analysis in accordance with Section 21.1	See Section 20.2.1

Note: For SI: 1 ft/s = 0.3048 m; 1 ft/s = 0.3048 m/s.

Assume Site Class D (stiff soil).

Step 4: Determine the design response acceleration parameter for short periods, S_{DS}, and for a 1-second period, S_{D1}, using Equations 11.4-1 and 11.4-2 respectively.

Chapter Fourteen

The design response acceleration is two-thirds of the maximum considered acceleration:

$$S_{DS} = \frac{2}{3} \cdot S_{MS} \quad (11.4\text{-}1)$$

$$S_{D1} = \frac{2}{3} \cdot S_{M1} \quad (11.4\text{-}2)$$

With the exception of some parts of the western US (where design earthquakes have a deterministic basis), these design spectral ordinates correspond to an earthquake with a 10% probability of exceedance within a 50-year period. Such an earthquake is sometimes described as a "500-year earthquake." To see why, let p be the unknown annual probability of exceedance of that level of acceleration:

The probability of exceedance in a particular year is:	p
The probability of non-exceedance in a particular year is:	$(1-p)$
The probability of non-exceedance in 50 consecutive years is:	$(1-p)^{50}$
The probability of exceedance within a 50-year period is:	$[1-(1-p)^{50}]$
Solve for p, the annual probability of exceedance. Set the probability of exceedance within the 50-year period equal to the given 10%:	$[1-(1-p)^{50}] = 0.10$ $(1-p)^{50} = 0.90$ $p = 1 - 0.90^{(1/50)}$ $p = 2.10 \times 10^{-3}$
The return period is the reciprocal of the annual probability of exceedance:	$1/p = 475$
The approximate return period is:	500 years

Continuing with our example for Richmond, Virginia, the design response acceleration for short periods is:

$$S_{DS} = \frac{2}{3} \cdot S_{MS} = \frac{2}{3} \cdot 0.3g = 0.2g$$

and the design response acceleration for a 1-second period is:

$$S_{D1} = \frac{2}{3} \cdot S_{M1} = \frac{2}{3} \cdot 0.12g = 0.08g$$

Step 5: If required, determine the design response spectrum curve as prescribed by Section 11.4.5.2.

Because the equivalent lateral force procedure is being used, the response spectrum curve is not required. Nevertheless, for pedagogical completeness, it will be developed. First, define $T_0 \equiv 0.2 \frac{S_{D1}}{S_{DS}}$ and $T_S \equiv \frac{S_{D1}}{S_{DS}}$.

Then for our case,

$$T_0 \equiv 0.2 \frac{S_{D1}}{S_{DS}} = 0.2 \left(\frac{0.08g}{0.2g}\right) = 0.08 \text{ sec}$$

$$T_S \equiv \frac{S_{D1}}{S_{DS}} = \left(\frac{0.08g}{0.2g}\right) = 0.4 \text{ sec}$$

- For periods less than or equal to T_0, the design spectral response acceleration, S_a, is given by Equation 11.4-3:

$$S_a = S_{DS}\left(0.4 + 0.6 \frac{T}{T_0}\right) \tag{11.4-3}$$

- For periods greater than T_0 and less than or equal to T_S, the design spectral response acceleration, S_a, is equal to S_{DS}.
- For periods greater than T_S and less than or equal to T_L (from Figures 22-15 through 22-20), the design spectral response acceleration, S_a, is given by Equation 11.4-6. In our case, $T_L = 8$ seconds.

$$S_a = \frac{S_{D1}}{T} \tag{11.4-6}$$

- For periods greater than T_L, the design spectral response acceleration, S_a, is given by Equation 11.4-7:

$$S_a = \frac{S_{D1} T_L}{T^2} \tag{11.4-7}$$

The resulting design acceleration response spectrum is given in Fig. 14.35.

Step 6: Determine the structure's importance factor, I, and occupancy category using Sections 1.5.1 and 11.5 based on ASCE 7-22.

ASCE 7-22 TABLE 1.5.1 Importance Factors by Risk Category of Buildings and Other Structures for Earthquake Loads

Risk Category from Table 1.5-1	Seismic Importance Factor, I_o
I	1.00
II	1.00
III	1.25
IV	1.50

Because the building is a hotel, it is assigned to Occupancy Category II in accordance with Table 1604.5 of the 2024 IBC. This corresponds to an Importance Factor of 1.0.

Step 7: Determine the structure's Seismic Design Category using Section 11.6.

Tables 11.6-1 and 11.6-2 must be checked, and the higher seismic design category from those two tables applies.

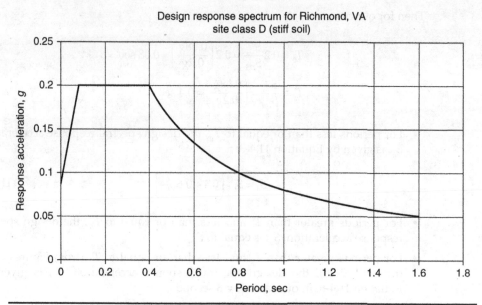

FIGURE 14.35 Design response spectrum for Richmond, VA.

ASCE 7-22 TABLE 11.6-1 Seismic Design Category Based on Short-Period Response Acceleration Parameter

Value of S_{DS}	Risk Category I or II or III	IV
$S_{DS} < 0.167$	A	A
$0.167 \leq S_{DS} < 0.33$	B	C
$0.33 \leq S_{DS} < 0.50$	C	D
$0.50 \leq S_{DS}$	D	D

ASCE 7-22 TABLE 11.6-2 Seismic Design Category Based on 1 s Period Response Acceleration Parameter

Value of S_{D1}	Risk Category I or II or III	IV
$S_{D1} < 0.067$	A	A
$0.067 \leq S_{D1} < 0.133$	B	C
$0.133 \leq S_{D1} < 0.20$	C	D
$0.20 \leq S_{D1}$	D	

In our case, S_{DS} is 0.2, and S_{D1} is 0.08. Because S_{DS} is between 0.1067 and 0.133 (Table 11.6-1), and S_{D1} is also between 0.1067 and 0.133 (Table 11.6-2), the structure is assigned to Seismic Design Category B. Because the structure is less than or equal to

35 ft in height and is assigned to SDC C, it can be designed as ordinary reinforced AAC masonry according to the provisions of the 2024 IBC.

Step 8: Calculate the structure's seismic base shear using Sections 12.8.1 and 12.8.2. In accordance with ASCE 7-22, Section 12.8.1.1 Method 1,

$$C_s = \frac{S_a}{\left(\frac{R}{I}\right)} \quad \text{(Equation 12.8-2)}$$

In our case,

$S_a = 0.2g$ (plateau of response spectra)
$R = 2$ (ordinary AAC masonry shear wall systems)
$I = 1.00$ (ASCE7-22, Table 11.5-1)

$$C_s = \frac{S_a}{\left(\frac{R}{I}\right)} = \frac{0.2}{\left(\frac{2}{1}\right)} = 0.04$$

The value of C_s computed in accordance with Equation 12.8-2 need not exceed the following:

$$C_s = \frac{S_{D1}}{T\left(\frac{R}{I}\right)} \quad \text{for } T \leq T_L \quad \text{(Equation 12.8-4)}$$

The corresponding equation for $T > T_L$ does not apply. In addition, C_s shall not be less than $0.044\, S_{DS} I$, nor less than 0.01.

The approximate period of the building as given by Equation 12.8-7 of ASCE 7-22 is

$$T_a = C_t h_n^x$$

In our case, h_n (the height above the base to the highest level of the structure) is 35 ft. The values of C_t and x are given by Table 12.8-2 of ASCE 7-22 as 0.02 and 0.75, respectively.

$$T_a = 0.02(35)^{0.75}$$
$$T_a = 0.29 \text{ sec}$$

This is less than the transition period $T_s = 0.4$ sec, and the structure is on the plateau of the design spectrum. Equation 12.8-8 governs, and $C_s = 0.2$.

Because the structure is assigned to SDC B, the redundancy factor, ρ, is permitted to be taken as 1.0 (Section 12.3.4.1). The structure has no vertical or horizontal irregularities, and the diaphragms are not flexible.

Finally, in accordance with ASCE 7-22, Section 12.4.2, the design horizontal seismic load effect E_h is

$$E_h = \rho Q_E \quad \text{(Equation 12.4-3)}$$

Now compute the seismic base shear. In accordance with ASCE 7-22, Section 12.8.1, the effects of horizontal seismic forces Q_E come from V. The design seismic base shear is given by:

$$V = C_s W$$
$$V = 0.2W$$

This is multiplied by the redundancy factor of 1.0, giving a product of 0.2. In other words, the building must be designed for 20% of its weight, applied as a lateral force.

Step 9: Distribute seismic base shear vertically using Section 12.8.3.

This force is distributed linearly in an triangle form over the height of the building.

The weight of a typical floor is its area, times the dead load per square foot, plus the interior transverse wall weight, plus the spine wall weight, plus the weight of the exterior walls. For simplicity, assume that the roof weighs the same as a typical floor, and ignore the parapet.

Floor weight: $50 \text{ lb/ft}^2 \times 50 \times 140 \text{ ft}^2 = 350$ kips
Transverse wall weight: $7 \times 20 \times 11 \text{ ft}^2 \times 45 \text{ lb/ft}^2 = 69.3$ kips
Spine wall weight: $2 \times 130 \times 11 \text{ ft}^2 \times 45 \text{ lb/ft}^2 = 128.7$ kips
Perimeter wall weight: $2 \times (140 + 50) \times 12 \text{ ft}^2 \times 45 \text{ lb/ft}^2 = 188.1$ kips

Total weight of a typical floor is 736.1 kips.

The design base shear is calculated assuming a linear distribution of forces over the height of the structure, because the fundamental period of the structure is less than 0.5 sec (ASCE 7-22, Section 12.8.3). Total design base shear is 2208 kips × 0.20 = 441.7 kips.

Level	W	H	WH	WH/SUM
R	736.1	33	24,291	0.50
3	736.1	22	16,194	0.333
2	736.1	11	8,097	0.167
	2208.3		48,582	

At the roof level, the factored design lateral force is the factored design base shear (441.7 kips), multiplied by 0.50 (the quotient of WH/SUM) for the triangular distribution, or 220.9 kips. At the next level down, the factored design lateral force is 441.7 kips, multiplied by 0.333, and so forth.

At each level, the factored design moment is the summation of the products of the factored design lateral forces above that level, each multiplied by its respective height above that level. Because seismic loads based on ASCE 7 are at strength level, the load factor for seismic loads is 1.0. Factored design shear and moment diagrams for the building are shown in the table and figure below.

TABLE 14.8 Factored Design Shears and Moments for three-Story Hotel Example Using AAC Masonry

Level	F_u, k	H, ft	V_u, k	M_u, k-ft
R	220.9	33	220.9	0
3	147.2	22	368.1	2430
2	73.6	11	441.7	6479
				11,338

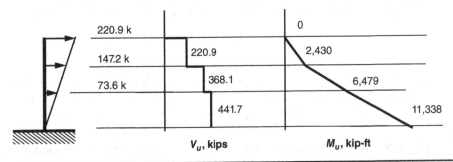

FIGURE 14.36 Graphs of factored design shears and moments for three-story hotel example using AAC masonry.

Step 10: Distribute seismic base shear horizontally using Section 12.8.4.

These last three steps are structure-dependent. They depend on the seismic response modification coefficient assigned to the structural system, on the structure's plan structural irregularities, on the structure's vertical structural irregularities, and on the structure's redundancy.

Plan structural irregularities include:

- plan eccentricities between the center of mass and the center of stiffness;
- re-entrant corners;
- out-of-plane offsets; and
- non-parallel systems.

These can increase seismic response.
   Vertical structural irregularities include:

- stiffness irregularity;
- mass irregularity;
- vertical geometric irregularity;
- in-plane discontinuity in vertical lateral-force-resisting elements;
- discontinuity in capacity – weak story.

These can also increase seismic response.
   Structures with low redundancy have a higher probability of failure, which is compensated for by increasing design seismic forces.
   The building under consideration here has no plan or vertical structural irregularities.

454 Chapter Fourteen

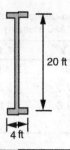

FIGURE 14.37 Typical transverse shear wall of three-story hotel example with AAC masonry.

In general, the effects of torsion must be included. Inherent torsion is a function of the walls and is negligible in this case, because the walls are symmetrically arranged in plan. Accidental torsion is independent of the walls and is prescribed by Section 12.8.4.2 of ASCE 7-22. For the sake of simplicity, torsion is ignored in this example.

14.12.2 Design Transverse Shear Walls for Gravity Plus Earthquake Loads
(All references are to TMS 402-22 and *Specification*.)

The transverse direction is critical for this building. The 16 transverse walls are conservatively assumed to be uncoupled, so that each functions as an independent cantilever. As shown in Fig. 14.37, design each transverse wall as an I beam, assuming flange widths of 4 ft. This is less than the limits specified in Section 5.2.2.3 of TMS 402-22 and is therefore conservative.

14.12.2.1 Shear Design of a Typical Transverse Wall for Earthquake Loads
Check shear for assumed wall thickness. Include the effects of axial load, assuming that a typical transverse wall carries its self-weight plus the distributed floor weight on a tributary width of 20 ft:

Self-weight of wall: 9.9 kips/floor
Floor weight: 60 lb/ft² × 20 × 20 = 24 kips/floor

Total unfactored axial load at base, P, is $3 \times (9.9 + 24) = 101.7$ kips. Assume that the critical load case is $P_u = 0.9D = 91.5$ kips.

By Section 11.3.4.1.2 of TMS 402-22,

$$V_n = V_{n\,AAC} + V_{ns}$$

$$V_{n\,AAC} = \min \begin{cases} 0.95 \ell_w t \sqrt{f'_{AAC}} \sqrt{1 + \dfrac{P_u}{2.4\sqrt{f'_{AAC}}\, \ell_w t}} \\[2mm] 0.17 f'_{AAC} t \dfrac{h \cdot \ell_w^2}{h^2 + \left(\dfrac{3}{4}\ell_w\right)^2} \\[2mm] \mu_{AAC} P_u \end{cases}$$

Take the coefficient of friction for the third equation as 1.0 (AAC against mortar).

$$V_{n\,AAC} = \min \begin{cases} 0.95 \times 240 \text{ in.} \times 11.9 \text{ in.} \sqrt{870 \text{ lb/in}^2} \sqrt{1 + \dfrac{91{,}530 \text{ lb}}{2.4\sqrt{870 \text{ lb/in}^2} \times 240 \text{ in.} \times 11.9 \text{ in.}}} \\ 0.17 \times 870 \text{ lb/in}^2 \times 11.9 \text{ in.} \dfrac{33 \text{ ft} \times 20^2 \text{ ft}^2}{33^2 \text{ ft}^2 + \left(\dfrac{3}{4} \times 20\right)^2 \text{ ft}^2} \times 12 \text{ in./ft} \\ 1.0 \times 91.5 \text{ kips} \end{cases}$$

$$V_{n\,AAC} = \min \begin{cases} 96{,}457 \text{ lb} \\ 212{,}166 \text{ lb} \\ 91{,}500 \text{ lb} \end{cases}$$

$V_{n\,AAC} = 91{,}500$ lb

$\phi V_{n\,AAC} = 0.8 \times 91{,}500 \text{ lb} = 73{,}200 \text{ lb}$

This exceeds (1/16 walls) times the factored design base shear (1/16 × 441.7 kips = 27.6 kips), and the transverse walls are satisfactory for shear thus far. While floor-level bond beams are required, no shear reinforcement is required.

14.12.2.2 In-Plane Flexural Design of Transverse Shear Walls for Earthquake Loads

Each transverse shear wall has a plan length of 20 ft. The factored design base moment per wall is (1/16) × 11,338 ft-kips, or 708.63 ft-kips. The critical load case is *0.9D + 1.0E*. The factored axial load (see above) is 0.9 × 101.7 kips, or 91.5 kips.

Because of the flanges, the effective width of the wall is taken as 48 in. This is valid provided that the compressive stress block does not leave the flange. This will be checked later.

Using a spreadsheet, the interaction diagram for the wall is shown in Fig. 14.38, and the corresponding calculation sheet is shown in Table 14.9. At a factored axial load of 91.5 kips, the factored moment capacity is 19,774 kip-ft, more than satisfactory. The neutral axis is located 7.3 in. from the extreme compression fiber, still in the flange, so the interaction diagram calculated using a 48-in. effective width is valid.

Flexural reinforcement consisting of 1 - #4 bar at each end is required. The bars should be placed in grouted sections at least 12-in. square (at intersections of web and flanges).

Check splice requirements and percent area requirements. Assume a 2000-psi grout strength by the proportion specification of ASTM C476. Based on Section 6.1.6.3.1 of TMS 402-22,

$$l_d = \frac{0.13 d_b^2 f_y \gamma}{K_{AAC}\sqrt{f'_g}} = \frac{0.13 \times 0.5^2 \times 60{,}000 \times 1.0}{\left(\dfrac{12 - 0.5}{2}\right)\sqrt{2000}} = 7.58 \text{ in.}$$

12 inches governs. By Section 6.1.3.2.5 of TMS 402-22, the maximum percent area in a plastic hinge zone is 3%. For a 12-in. square core, a #4 bar easily satisfies this requirement.

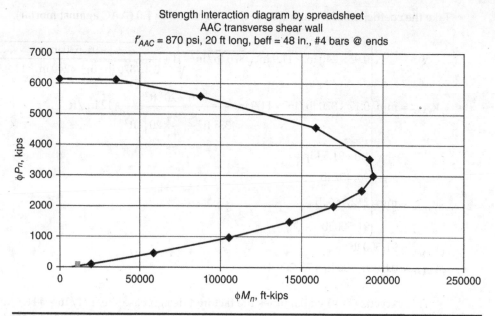

FIGURE 14.38 Strength interaction diagram by spreadsheet, AAC transverse shear wall.

Because the wall is symmetrically reinforced, maximum reinforcement limitations (Section 11.3.3) are satisfied.

Now check capacity design for shear (Section 7.3.2.5.1 of TMS 402-22). At an axial load of 91.5 kips, the nominal flexural capacity of this wall is the design flexural capacity of 1104 ft-kips, divided by the strength reduction factor of 0.9, or 1227 ft-kips. The ratio of this nominal flexural capacity to the factored design moment is 1227 divided by 708.6, or 1.73. Including the additional factor of 1.25, that gives a ratio of 2.16.

$$\phi V_n \geq 2.16 V_u$$

$$V_n \geq \frac{2.16}{\phi} V_u = \frac{2.16}{0.8} V_u = 2.70 V_u = 2.70 \times 27.6 = 74.7 \text{ kips}$$

V_n (governed by sliding shear) is 91.5 kips, considerably greater than this. The wall is satisfactory without shear reinforcement. A nominal 8-in. wall could probably be used instead of 12 in. Horizontal reinforcement will be needed at diaphragm-level bond beams (Section 7.3.2.8 of TMS 402-22).

14.12.2.3 Comments of Design of Transverse Shear Walls for Seismic Loads

- The most laborious part of this design is calculation of the design lateral force for earthquake loads. Once that calculation is done, design of the lateral-force-resisting system is straightforward, even for a region of moderate seismic risk such as Richmond.
- This structural system could be designed for increased capacity. Increased flexural capacity would be quite easy to achieve, but increased shear capacity (to meet capacity design requirements) would probably require intermediate bond beams.

TABLE 14.9 Calculations for Spreadsheet for Typical Transverse Shear Wall of AAC Masonry

Spreadsheet for Calculating Strength Moment-Axial Force Interaction Diagram for Transverse AAC Shear Wall	
Depth	240
ε_{mu}	0.003
f'_m	0.87
f_y	60
E_s	29000
d	237
(c/d) balanced	0.591837
Width	48
phi	0.9

Steel layers are counted from the extreme compression fiber to the extreme tension fiber

Distances are measured from the extreme compression fiber

Reinforcement consists of 2 #4 bars 4 in. and 20 in. from ends, followed by one #4 at 48 in. for this spreadsheet

Compression in masonry and reinforcement is taken as positive

Stress in compressive reinforcement is set to zero, because the reinforcement is not laterally supported

Row of Reinforcement	Distance	Area
1	4.00	0.20
2	20.00	0.20
3	68.00	0.20
4	140.00	0.20
5	172.00	0.20
6	220.00	0.20
7	236.00	0.20

TABLE 14.9 Calculations for Spreadsheet for Typical Transverse Shear Wall of AAC Masonry *(Continued)*

	c/d	c	C_{mas}	$f_s(1)$	$f_s(2)$	$f_s(3)$	$f_s(4)$	$f_s(5)$	$f_s(6)$	$f_s(7)$	ϕM_n	ϕP_n
Pure axial load											0	6133
	1.205	285.59	6792	0.00	0.00	0.00	0.00	0.00	0.00	0.00	35246	6113
	1.1	260.70	6200	0.00	0.00	0.00	0.00	0.00	0.00	0.00	87718	5580
	0.9	213.30	5073	0.00	0.00	0.00	0.00	0.00	-2.73	-9.26	158574	4563
	0.7	165.90	3945	0.00	0.00	0.00	0.00	-3.20	-28.37	-36.76	191781	3539
Points controlled by masonry	0.591837	140.27	3336	0.00	0.00	0.00	0.00	-19.68	-49.46	-59.38	194140	2979
Points controlled by steel	0.591837	140.27	3336	0.00	0.00	0.00	0.00	-19.68	-49.46	-59.38	194140	2979
	0.5	118.50	2818	0.00	0.00	0.00	-15.78	-39.28	-60.00	-60.00	186899	2505
	0.4	94.80	2255	0.00	0.00	0.00	-41.48	-60.00	-60.00	-60.00	169593	1989
	0.3	71.10	1691	0.00	0.00	0.00	-60.00	-60.00	-60.00	-60.00	142449	1479
	0.2	47.40	1127	0.00	0.00	-37.81	-60.00	-60.00	-60.00	-60.00	105267	965
	0.1	23.70	564	0.00	0.00	-60.00	-60.00	-60.00	-60.00	-60.00	58613	453
	0.03082	7.30	174	0.00	-60.00	-60.00	-60.00	-60.00	-60.00	-60.00	19773	91.5
	0.01	2.37	56	-59.84	-60.00	-60.00	-60.00	-60.00	-60.00	-60.00	6259	-25

14.12.3 Design Exterior Walls for Gravity Plus Out-of-Plane Wind

The critical panel will be at the top of the building, where the wind load is highest. The panel must be designed for out-of-plane wind. Load effects in vertical jamb strips will be increased by the ratio of the plan length of openings to the total plan length.

Use factored wind load (components and cladding) on wall $q_u = 50$ lbs/ft²

Reinforcement will be placed in 3-in. grouted cells at 4 ft. on center

The span is 11 ft, and the panel thickness is 12 in.

The plan view of a 4-ft end section of wall is shown in Fig. 14.39.
The wall is considered simply supported at each floor diaphragm.

14.12.3.1 Flexural Capacity of Out-of-Plane Walls

a) Determine design moment

$$w_u = q_u \times \text{width} = 50 \text{ lb/ft}^2 \times 4 \text{ ft} = 200 \text{ lb/ft}$$

$$M_u = \frac{w_u l^2}{8} = \frac{200 \frac{\text{lb}}{\text{ft}} \times (11 \text{ ft})^2}{8} = 3025 \text{ lb-ft} = 36,300 \text{ lb-in.}$$

b) Try a #4 bar, and conservatively neglect axial load

$$T = A_s f_y = 0.20 \text{ in}^2 \times 60,000 \text{ lb/in}^2 = 12,000 \text{ lb}$$

$$a = \frac{T}{0.85 f'_{AAC} b} = \frac{12,000 \text{ lb}}{0.85 \times 870 \text{ lb/in}^2 \times 48 \text{ in.}} = 0.34 \text{ in.}$$

$$M_n = A_s f_y \left(d - \frac{a}{2} \right) = 12.0 \text{ kips} \times \left(6 - \frac{0.34}{2} \right) \text{ in.} = 70,000 \text{ lb-in.}$$

$$M_u = \phi M_n = 0.9 \times 70,000 \text{ lb-in.} = 63,000 \text{ lb-in.} > M_u \quad \text{OK}$$

Use a #4 bar. With the exception of plastic hinge zones, Section 6.1.3.2.5 of TMS 402-22 imposes a maximum bar area of 4.5% of the cell. Using a 3-in. grouted core, the area ratio is $(0.5/3)^2$, or 2.8%, easily satisfying the requirement. This bar size will easily

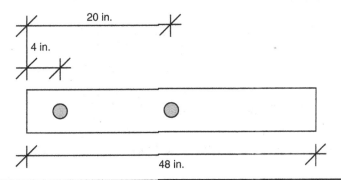

Figure 14.39 Plan view of section of exterior wall, three-story example with AAC masonry.

satisfy the maximum reinforcement limitations of Section 11.3.3.5 of TMS 402-22 for out-of-plane flexure, and the design is satisfactory for flexure.

14.12.3.2 Shear Capacity

a) Determine factored loads and maximum shear force for a single panel.

$q_u = 50$ psf, and because the panel is 4 ft wide $w_u = 200$ lb/ft.

$$V_u = \frac{200 \text{ lb/ft} \times 11 \text{ ft}}{2} = 1100 \text{ lb}$$

b) Determine shear capacity of panel.

$$V_n = V_{n\,AAC} = 0.8\sqrt{f'_{AAC}}\, A_n = 0.8\sqrt{870} \times 48 \text{ in.} \times 6 \text{ in.} = 6796 \text{ lb}$$
$$\phi V_n = 0.8 V_n = 0.8 \times 6796 = 5437 \text{ lb} > V_u = 1100 \text{ lb} \quad \text{OK}$$

14.12.4 Design Floor Diaphragms for In-Plane Actions

Design requirements for AAC floor diaphragms are not given in TMS 402-22 and TMS 602-22, because that can be applied to many different types of floor systems. The design procedure given is based on Tanner 2003, Tanner et al. 2005b, and ACI 526.1R.

$$f'_{AAC} = 870 \text{ psi}$$
$$f'_{grout} = 2000 \text{ psi}$$
$$f_y = 60{,}000 \text{ psi}$$

Ring beam reinforcement 2 #5

Grouted key reinforcement 1 #4

Factored transverse lateral load in each bay, $F_u = 220.9$ kips /16 bays = 13.81 kips.
The plan view and sectional view of the diaphragm are shown in Figs. 14.40 and 14.41, respectively.

a) Design diaphragm for flexure, assuming that load is uniformly distributed along span

$$M = \frac{w_u l^2}{8} = \frac{F_u \times l}{8} = \frac{13{,}810 \text{ lb} \times 240 \text{ in.}}{8} = 414{,}188 \text{ lb-in.}$$

$$T = A_s f_y = 2 \times 0.31 \text{ in}^2 \times 60{,}000 \text{ lb/in}^2 = 37{,}200 \text{ lb}$$

$$a = \frac{C}{0.85 f'_{grout} b} = \frac{37{,}200 \text{ lb}}{0.85\,(2000 \text{ lb/in}^2)(240 \text{ in.})} = 0.09 \text{ in.}$$

d = length of key − ring beam/2 − 2 × U-block thickness = 240 in. − 4 in. − 4 in. = 238 in.

$$\phi M_n = \phi A_s f_y \cdot \left(d - \frac{a}{2}\right) = 0.9 \times 37{,}200 \text{ lb} \times (238 \text{ in.} - 0.09 \text{ in.}) = 7{,}970{,}000 \text{ lb-in.} \geq M_u \quad \text{OK}$$

Structural Design of AAC Masonry **461**

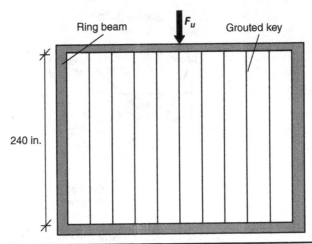

FIGURE 14.40 Plan view of AAC floor diaphragm, three-story hotel example with AAC masonry.

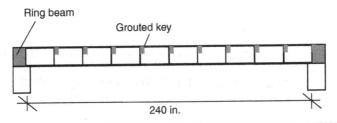

FIGURE 14.41 Section of AAC floor diaphragm, three-story hotel example with AAC masonry.

b) Design diaphragm for shear based on adhesion

   i) Panel-to-panel joint
   A section of the panel-to-panel joint is shown in Fig. 14.42.
   The total resistance is the adhesion of the grouted area plus the adhesion of the thin-bed mortar area.

$$b_{grout} = 3 \text{ in.}$$
$$b_{thin\text{-}bed} = 4.9 \text{ in.}$$
$$V_{grout} = \tau_{grout} \times b_{grout} \times l = 50 \times 3 \times 240 = 36{,}000 \text{ lb}$$
$$V_{thin\text{-}bed} = \tau_{thin\text{-}bed} \times b_{thin\text{-}bed} \times l = 18 \times 4.9 \times 240 = 21{,}168 \text{ lb}$$
$$V_{total} = V_{grout} + V_{thin\text{-}bed} = 57{,}168 \text{ lb}$$
$$\phi V_{total} = 0.6(57{,}168 \text{ lb}) = 34{,}300 \text{ lb} > V_u = \frac{F_u}{2} = 6900 \text{ lb} \quad \text{OK}$$

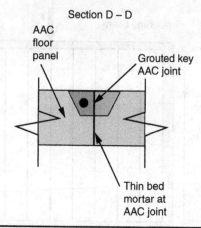

FIGURE 14.42 Section of panel-to-panel joint or typical grouted key between AAC floor panels.

ii) Panel-to-bond beam joint
A section of the panel-to-bond beam joint is shown in Fig. 14.43.

$$b_{grout} = 4.9 \text{ in.}$$
$$V_{grout} = \tau_{grout} b_{grout} l = 50 \text{ lb/in}^2 \times 7.9 \text{ in.} \times 240 \text{ in.} = 94{,}440 \text{ lb}$$
$$\phi V_{total} = 0.6(94{,}440 \text{ lb}) = 56{,}660 \text{ lb} > V_u = \frac{F_u}{2} = 6900 \text{ lb} \quad \text{OK}$$

c) Design diaphragm for shear based on truss model. The nomenclature, capacity-modification factors, and capacity-reduction factors are those of ACI 318-19 Chapter 23 (Strut-and-Tie Models).

Use one # 4 bar in each grouted key. Each plank is 2 ft wide, so there are 10 planks. The load applied to each node is 1/10 of the total load, or 1.38 kips. Refer to Fig. 14.44.

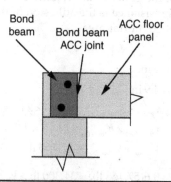

FIGURE 14.43 Section of panel-to-bond beam joint, AAC floor diaphragm.

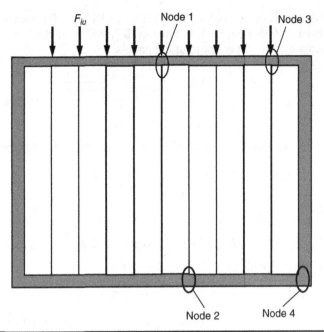

FIGURE 14.44 Truss model for design of AAC diaphragm.

In this model the compression chords act as diagonal compression members. There are two types of nodes: loaded nodes (on the upper side of Fig. 14.45) and unloaded nodes (on the lower side, as shown in Fig. 14.46).

The critical diagonal compression occurs in the panels next to the support. The component of that compression parallel to the transverse walls is one-half the total factored

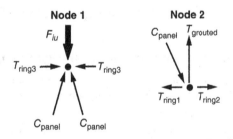

FIGURE 14.45 Loaded nodes for design of AAC diaphragm.

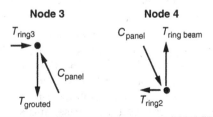

FIGURE 14.46 Unloaded notes for design of AAC diaphragm.

load on the panel, or one-half of 13.81 kips, or 6.91 kips. The total compressive force in the diagonal and also the tension force in the associated tension tie, is essentially that shear, because of the aspect ratio of the panels.

$$C_{panel} = \frac{6.91 \text{ kips} \times l_{strut}}{l_{panel}} = \frac{6.91 \text{ kips} \times \sqrt{20^2 + 2^2}}{20} = 6.94 \text{ kips} = T_{grouted}$$

Check the capacity of the compression strut using the following terms:

W_{strut} = width of the compression strut = 6 in.

T_{panel} = panel thickness = 7.9 in.

β_s = strut factor based on ACI 318-11 Section A.3.2.4 = 0.6

F_{strut} = 6.94 kips/(6 × 7.9) in² = 146 psi < 0.75 β_s (0.85f'_{AAC})

= 0.75(0.6)(0.85)(870) = 333 psi OK

Check the capacity at Node 4, which is the critical node.

β_n = node factor based on ACI 318-11 Section A.5.2 = 0.8

$T_{grouted\ key}$ = 6.94 kips < $\phi \beta_n A_s f_y$ = 0.75(0.8)(0.20)(60,000) = 7200 lb OK

Tension ties in ring beams have already been checked, and are satisfactory. Consider crushing of grouted key at support:

$$f_{grout} = \frac{\text{Reaction}}{h_{grout} \times b_{grout}} = \frac{6910 \text{ lb}}{7.9 \text{ in.} \times 4.9 \text{ in.}}$$

= 178 psi < $\phi \beta_n \times 0.85 f'_g$ = 0.75(0.8)(0.85 × 5000 psi) = 2550 psi

14.12.5 Overall Comments on Seismic Design Example with AAC Masonry

- Although it is located in a region of moderate seismic risk, this building needs comparatively little reinforcement, because of the large plan area of its bearing walls.
- Considerable simplicity in design and analysis was achieved by letting transverse shear walls resist lateral loads as statically determinate cantilevers.
- Design of AAC bearing walls is inexpensive and straightforward for this type of building.
- Many types of floor and roof systems are possible with AAC. To adapt this design to other types of floor or roof elements, the unit weight would have to be changed appropriately; the connection details would have to be changed appropriately; and the diaphragm actions would have to be checked appropriately. For example, if hollow-core prestressed concrete planks were used, the unit weight would increase, and so would the seismic base shear and overturning moment. Shear design of the transverse shear walls would

still govern. Details of the connections between walls and floor or roof would be similar to those used with the AAC planks. Shears in the horizontal diaphragms would be transferred in topping only.

14.13 References on AAC

Because the US code basis for structural design of AAC is relatively new, the references used to develop that code basis are included in the final sections of Chapter 14.

ASTM C 1660 (2024): ASTM C 1660, *Standard Specification for Thin-bed Mortar for Autoclaved Aerated Concrete (AAC) Masonry*, ASTM International, West Conshohocken, Pennsylvania.

ASTM C 1691 (2021): ASTM C 1691, *Standard Specification for Unreinforced Autoclaved Aerated Concrete (AAC) Masonry Units*, ASTM International, West Conshohocken, Pennsylvania.

ASTM C 1692 (2018): ASTM C 1692, *Standard Practice for Construction and Testing of Autoclaved Aerated Concrete (AAC) Masonry*, ASTM International, West Conshohocken, Pennsylvania.

ASTM C 1693 (2017): ASTM C 1693, *Standard Specification for Autoclaved Aerated Concrete (AAC)*, ASTM International, West Conshohocken, Pennsylvania.

ASTM C 1694 (2017): ASTM C 1694, *Standard Specification for Reinforced Autoclaved Aerated Concrete (AAC) Elements*, ASTM International, West Conshohocken, Pennsylvania.

Barnett et al. (2005): Barnett, R. E., Tanner, J. E., Klingner, R. E. and Fouad, F. H. "Guide for Using Autoclaved Aerated Concrete Panels: I - Structural Design," *ACI Special Publication SP 226*, Caijun Shi and Fouad H. Fouad, eds, American Concrete Institute, Farmington Hills, Michigan, April 2005, pp. 17–28.

ICC AC 215 (2003): "Acceptance Criteria for Seismic Design Factors and Coefficients for Seismic-Force-Resisting Systems of Autoclaved Aerated Concrete (AAC)," *Evaluation Report AC215*, ICC Evaluation Service, Inc., Whittier, California, November 1, 2003.

ICC ESR-1371 (2004): "Autoclaved Aerated Concrete (AAC) Block Masonry Units," *Evaluation Report ESR-1371*, ICC Evaluation Service, Inc., Whittier, California, October 1, 2004.

Klingner et al. (2005a): Klingner, R. E., Tanner, J. E., Varela, J. L., Brightman, M., Argudo, J. and Cancino, U., "Technical Justification for Proposed Design Provisions for AAC Structures: Introduction and Shear Wall Tests," *ACI Special Publication SP 226*, Caijun Shi and Fouad H. Fouad, eds, American Concrete Institute, Farmington Hills, Michigan, April 2005, pp. 45–66.

Klingner et al. (2005b): Klingner, R. E., Tanner, J. E. and Varela, J. L., "Technical Justification for Proposed Design Provisions for AAC Structures: Assemblage Test and Development of R and C_d Factors," *ACI Special Publication SP 226*, Caijun Shi and Fouad H. Fouad, eds, American Concrete Institute, Farmington Hills, Michigan, April 2005, pp. 67–90.

MDG (2013): *Masonry Designers' Guide*, 5th edition, Phillip J. Samblanet, ed., The Masonry Society, Boulder Colorado, 2013.

RILEM (1993): Autoclaved Aerated Concrete: Properties, Testing and Design, RILEM Recommended Practice, RILEM Technical Committees 78-MCA and 51-ALC, E & FN Spon, London.

Tanner et al. (2005a): Tanner, J. E., Varela, J. L., Klingner, R. E., "Design and Seismic Testing of a Two-story Full-scale Autoclaved Aerated Concrete (AAC) Assemblage Specimen," *Structures Journal*, American Concrete Institute, Farmington Hills, Michigan, vol. 102, no. 1, January–February 2005, pp. 114–119.

Tanner et al. (2005b): Tanner, J. E., Varela, J. L., Klingner, R. E., Brightman M. J. and Cancino, U., "Seismic Testing of Autoclaved Aerated Concrete (AAC) Shear Walls: A Comprehensive Review," *Structures Journal*, American Concrete Institute, Farmington Hills, Michigan, vol. 102, no. 3, May–June 2005, pp. 374–382.

Varela et al. (2006): Varela, J. L., Tanner, J. E. and Klingner, R. E., "Development of Seismic Force-Reduction and Displacement Amplification Factors for AAC Structures," *EERI Spectra*, vol. 22, no. 1, February 2006, pp. 267–286.

Refereed Journal Publications

Barnett, R. E., Tanner, J. E., Klingner, R. E. and Fouad, F. H. "Guide for Using Autoclaved Aerated Concrete Panels: I - Structural Design," *ACI Special Publication SP 226*, Caijun Shi and Fouad H. Fouad, eds, American Concrete Institute, Farmington Hills, Michigan, April 2005, pp. 17–28.

Chen, Y., Peng, M., Zhang, Y. and Liu, Y., 2013, "Mechanical Properties of Autoclaved Aerated Concrete with Different Densities," *Advances in Civil Engineering Materials*, vol. 2, no. 1, pp. 441–456.

Costa, A. A., Penna, A. and Magenes, G. (2011). "Seismic performance of autoclaved aerated concrete (AAC) masonry: from experimental testing of the in-plane capacity of walls to building response simulation." *Journal of Earthquake Engineering*, vol. 15, no. 1, pp. 1–31.

Getz D. and Memari D., (2006) "Static and Cyclic Racking Performance of AAC Cladding Panels," *ASCE Journal of Architectural Engineering*, vol. 12, no. 1, pp. 12–23.

Klingner, R. E., Tanner, J. E., Varela, J. L., Brightman, M., Argudo, J. and Cancino, U., "Technical Justification for Proposed Design Provisions for AAC Structures: Introduction and Shear Wall Tests," *ACI Special Publication SP 226*, Caijun Shi and Fouad H. Fouad, eds, American Concrete Institute, Farmington Hills, Michigan, April 2005, pp. 45–66.

Klingner, R. E., Tanner, J. E. and Varela, J. L., "Technical Justification for Proposed Design Provisions for AAC Structures: Assemblage Test and Development of R and C_d Factors," *ACI Special Publication SP 226*, Caijun Shi and Fouad H. Fouad, eds, American Concrete Institute, Farmington Hills, Michigan, April 2005, pp. 67–90.

Tanner, J. E., Varela, J. L. and Klingner, R. E., "Design and Seismic Testing of a Two-story Full-scale Autoclaved Aerated Concrete (AAC) Assemblage Specimen," *Structures Journal*, American Concrete Institute, Farmington Hills, Michigan, vol. 102, no. 1, January–February 2005, pp. 114–119.

Tanner, J. E., Varela, J. L., Klingner, R. E., Brightman, M. J. and Cancino, U., "Seismic Testing of Autoclaved Aerated Concrete (AAC) Shear Walls: A Comprehensive Review," *Structures Journal*, American Concrete Institute, Farmington Hills, Michigan, vol. 102, no. 3, May–June 2005, pp. 374–382.

Varela, J. L., Tanner, J. E. and Klingner, R. E., "Development of Seismic Force-Reduction and Displacement Amplification Factors for AAC Structures," *EERI Spectra*, vol. 22, no. 1, February 2006, pp. 267–286.

CHAPTER 15

References

15.1 General References

ACI 318-22: ACI Committee 318, *Building Code Requirements for Reinforced Concrete (ACI 318-22)*, American Concrete Institute, Farmington Hills, Michigan, 2022.

ACI 526.1R: ACI Committee 526, Design Guide for the Use of Autoclaved Aerated Concrete Precast Panels (ACI 526.1R), American Concrete Institute, Farmington Hills, Michigan, 2019.

AISC LRFD 2022: *Manual of Steel Construction, Load and Resistance Factor Design*, American Institute of Steel Construction, Chicago, Illinois, 2022.

ASCE 7-22: *Minimum Design Loads for Buildings and Other Structures (ASCE 7-22)*, American Society of Civil Engineers, Reston, Virginia, 2022.

ATC 3-06: *Tentative Provisions for the Development of Seismic Regulations for Buildings (ATC 3-06)*, Applied Technology Council, National Bureau of Standards, 1978.

Beall, Christine, *Masonry Design and Detailing*, 5th edition, McGraw Hill, New York, 2003.

Brandow, Gregg E., Ekwueme, Chukwuma, and Hart, Gary C., *2015 Design of Reinforced Masonry Structures*, Concrete Masonry Association of California and Nevada, Citrus Heights, California, 2015.

Drysdale, Robert and Hamid, Ahmad, *Masonry Structures: Behavior and Design*, 4th edition, The Masonry Society, Longmont, Colorado, 2023.

Hillerborg, Arne, *Strip Method Design Handbook*, Taylor & Francis, New York, 1996.

IBC 2022: *International Building Code*, 2022 Edition, International Code Council, Washington, DC, 2022.

MDG 2022: Masonry Designers' Guide, The Masonry Society, Boulder, Colorado, 2022.

NEHRP 2022: *NEHRP (National Earthquake Hazards Reduction Program) Recommended Provisions for the Development of Seismic Regulations for New Buildings (FEMA 450)*, Building Seismic Safety Council, Federal Emergency Management Agency, Washington, DC, 2022.

SBC: *Standard Building Code*, Southern Building Code Congress International, Birmingham, Alabama.

Taly, Narendra, *Design of Reinforced Masonry Structures*, McGraw Hill, New York, 2010.

TMS 402 2022a: *Building Code Requirements for Masonry Structures* (TMS 402-22), The Masonry Society, Boulder, Colorado, 2022.

TMS 602 2022b: *Specification for Masonry Structures* (TMS 602-22), The Masonry Society, Boulder, Colorado, 2022.

UBC 1997: *Uniform Building Code*, 1997 Edition, International Conference of Building Officials, Whittier, California, 1997.

15.2 ASTM Standards

All ASTM standards are published by the American Society for Testing and Materials, West Conshohocken, Pennsylvania.

ASTM A153 (2023): Zinc Coating (Hot-Dip) on Iron and Steel Hardware.

ASTM A193 (2024): Alloy-Steel and Stainless Steel Bolting Materials for High Temperature or High Pressure Service and Other Special Purpose Applications.

ASTM A416 (2024): Low-Relaxation, Seven-Wire Steel Strand for Prestressed Concrete.

ASTM A480 (2024): Flat-Rolled Stainless and Heat-Resisting Steel Plate, Sheet, and Strip.

ASTM A615 (2024): Deformed and Plain Carbon-Steel Bars for Concrete Reinforcement.

ASTM A641 (2019): Zinc–Coated (Galvanized) Carbon Steel Wire.

ASTM A653 (2023): Steel Sheet, Zinc-Coated (Galvanized) or Zinc-Iron Alloy-Coated (Galvannealed) by the Hot-Dip Process.

ASTM A706 (2024): Low-Alloy Steel Deformed and Plain Bars for Concrete Reinforcement

ASTM A951 (2022): Steel Wire for Masonry Joint Reinforcement.

ASTM A996 (2024): Rail-Steel and Axle-Steel Deformed Bars for Concrete Reinforcement.

ASTM A1008 (2024): Steel, Sheet, Cold-Rolled, Carbon, Structural, High-Strength Low-Alloy, High-Strength Low-Alloy with Improved Formability, Solution Hardened, and Bake Hardenable.

ASTM A1022 (2022): Deformed and Plain Stainless Steel Wire and Welded Wire for Concrete Reinforcement.

ASTM A1064 (2024): Steel Wire, Plain, for Concrete Reinforcement.

ASTM C55 (2023): Concrete Building Brick.

ASTM C62 (2023): Building Brick (Solid Masonry Units Made from Clay or Shale).

ASTM C67 (2023a): Sampling and Testing Brick and Structural Clay Tile.

ASTM C90 (2024): Loadbearing Concrete Masonry Units.

ASTM C91 (2023): Masonry Cement.

ASTM C129 (2023): Nonloadbearing Concrete Masonry Units.

ASTM C139 (2023): Concrete Masonry Units for Construction of Catch Basins and Manholes.

ASTM C140 (2023): Sampling and Testing Concrete Masonry Units and Related Units.

ASTM C144 (2018): Aggregate for Masonry Mortar.

ASTM C207 (2024): Hydrated Lime for Masonry Purposes.

ASTM C216 (2023): Facing Brick (Solid Masonry Units Made from Clay or Shale).

ASTM C270 (2024): Standard Specification for Mortar for Unit Masonry.

ASTM C410 (2023): Industrial Floor Brick.

ASTM C426 (2023): Linear Drying Shrinkage of Concrete Masonry Units.

ASTM C476 (2023): Grout for Masonry.

ASTM C652 (2022): Hollow Brick (Hollow Masonry Units Made from Clay or Shale).

ASTM C744 (2021): Prefaced Concrete and Calcium Silicate Masonry Units.

ASTM C902 (2022): Pedestrian and Light Traffic Paving Brick.

ASTM C936 (2024): Solid Concrete Interlocking Paving Units.

ASTM C1006 (2020a): Splitting Tensile Strength of Masonry Units.

ASTM C1019 (2024): Sampling and Testing Grout.

ASTM C1072 (2022): Measurement of Masonry Flexural Bond Strength.

ASTM C1180 (2024): Standard Terminology of Mortar and Grout for Unit Masonry.

ASTM C1232 (2024): Standard Terminology of Masonry.

ASTM C1272 (2022): Heavy Vehicular Paving Brick.

References

ASTM C1314 (2023): Compressive Strength of Masonry Prisms.
ASTM C1319 (2023b): Concrete Grid Paving Units.
ASTM C1372 (2023): Dry-Cast Segmental Retaining Wall Units.
ASTM C1611 (2021): Slump Flow of Self-Consolidating Concrete.
ASTM C1660 (2024): Thin-bed Mortar for Autoclaved Aerated Concrete (AAC) Masonry.
ASTM C1691 (2021): Unreinforced Autoclaved Aerated Concrete (AAC) Masonry Units.
ASTM C1692 (2021): Construction and Testing of Autoclaved Aerated Concrete (AAC) Masonry.
ASTM C1717 (2019): Conducting Strength Tests of Masonry Wall Panel.
ASTM E514 (2020): Water Penetration and Leakage Through Masonry.
ASTM E518 (2022): Flexural Bond Strength of Masonry.
ASTM E519 (2022): Diagonal Tension (Shear) in Masonry Assemblages.
ASTM F3125 (2023): High Strength Structural Bolts, Steel and Allow Steel, Heat Treated, 120 and 105 ksi Minimum Tensile Strength.

Index

Note: Page numbers followed by *f* indicate figures; *t* indicate tables.

A

AAC. *See* Autoclaved aerated concrete (AAC)
AAC cladding, 393, 394*f*
AAC elements, 389, 390*f*
AAC hotel, 393, 394*f*. *See also* Three-story AAC shear-wall hotel
AAC masonry beams and lintels, 412–415
    example (lintel design), 413–415
    flexural design, 412
    modulus of rupture, 415
    shear design, 412
    steel reinforcing bars, 413, 413*t*
AAC masonry panel walls, 397–399
    design by prescription, 399
    load factors, 397
    modulus of rupture, 397
    noncalculated (prescriptive) reinforcement, 399
    shear capacity, 399
    single-wythe panel wall, 397–398
    strength-reduction factors, 397
    vertically spanning strips, 399
AAC residence, 393, 393*f*
AAC strength classes, 392, 392*t*
AACPA. *See* Autoclaved Aerated Concrete Products Association (AACPA)
Acceleration response spectrum, 80, 80*f*, 88, 88*f*
Accessory materials. *See* Masonry accessory materials
Accidental torsion, 454
ACI. *See* American Concrete Institute (ACI)
Actual dimensions, 7
Adjustable pintle ties, 30, 32*f*
Adjustable ties, 31, 33*f*
Allowable flexural capacity, 263–265
Allowable in-plane shear stress, 269, 275

Allowable-stress balanced reinforcement, 265–267
Allowable-stress balanced steel area, 265, 266
Allowable-stress design:
    anchor bolts, 241–248
    beams and lintels, 267–271
    bearing walls (reinforced), 277–289
    bearing walls (unreinforced), 220–235
    curtain walls, 272–277
    generally, 103
    linear elastic range, 255. *See also* Cracked, transformed sections
    loading combinations, 95–96
    panel walls, 207–220
    probability of failure, 103
    required details, 248–251, 296–299
    shear walls (reinforced), 289–296
    shear walls (unreinforced), 235–241
    strength design, compared. *See* Comparison of strength/allowable-stress designs
    TMS 402-22, 95–99
Allowable-stress design of curtain walls, 272–276
    allowable in-plane shear stress, 275
    clay masonry, 273, 273*f*
    concrete masonry, 273, 274*f*
    example, 274–276
    flexural check, 275
    maximum bending moment, 275
    maximum shear, 275
    structural action, 274
Allowable-stress design of reinforced beams and lintels, 267–271
    allowable in-plane shear stress, 269
    arching action, 271
    depth of bottom reinforcement, 269, 269*f*

471

Allowable-stress design of reinforced beams and lintels (*Cont.*):
  design steps, 97*t*, 267–268
  equilibrium of force, 270, 270*f*
  example, 268–271
  flexural design, 267
  maximum/minimum reinforcement requirements, 270
  shear design, 267
  unit strength method, 268
Allowable-stress design of reinforced bearing walls, 277–289
  balance point, 278, 281
  moment-axial force interaction diagram (hand calculation), 278–282
  moment-axial force interaction diagram (spreadsheet calculation), 282–285, 286*t*, 287*f*
  neutral axis, 278, 279*f*, 282
  out-of-plane load, 285–289
  pure compression, 278, 280
  pure flexure, 278, 280–281
  required details, 296–299
  unfactored moment diagram, 288, 288*f*
Allowable-stress design of reinforced shear walls, 289–296
  allowable in-plane shear stress, 290, 293
  allowable-stress balanced steel area, 295
  best design strategy, 296
  clay masonry shear wall, 292–295
  design steps, 99*t*, 289–292
  failure surface, 290, 291
  minimum/maximum reinforcement ratios, 295–296
  (M/Vd_c), 291, 291*f*, 293
  required details, 296–299
  seismic requirements, 296
  unfactored in-plane lateral loads, 292, 292*f*
Allowable-stress design of unreinforced bearing walls, 220–235. *See also* Bearing walls
  concentric axial load, 222–224
  design steps, 97*t*, 221–222
  eccentric axial load, 225–228
  eccentric axial load plus wind, 228–233
  Euler buckling equation, 222
  examples, 222–233
  extreme-fiber tensile stress, 221
  inelastic buckling, 229
  moment magnifier, 222
  openings, 233–235
  required details, 248–251
  stability equation. *See* Stability equation

Allowable-stress design of unreinforced bearing walls (*Cont.*):
  unfactored moment diagram, 229, 229*f*
  unity equation. *See* Unity equation
Allowable-stress design of unreinforced panel walls, 207–220. *See also* Panel walls
  design steps, 96*t*
  factoids, 215
  flexural design, 208
  load factors, 210
  one-way shear, 214–215
  out-of-plane load, 217–218, 218–220
  section properties for masonry walls, 215, 215*t*, 216*t*
  shear stress, 215
  single-wythe (hollow units), 211–212
  single-wythe (hollow units, face-shell bedding only), 212–213
  single-wythe (hollow units, fully grouted), 213
  single-wythe (solid units), 210–211
  strength-reduction factors, 112
  strip method, 216–217
  two-wythe panel (hollow units, face-shell bedding only), 213–214
Allowable-stress design of unreinforced shear walls, 235–241
  design steps, 97*t*, 236–237
  example, 237–239
  free body of one wall segment, 240, 241*f*
  openings, 240, 240*f*
  required details, 248–251
  wall buildings, generally, 239–240
Allowable-stress loading combinations, 91, 95–96
Allowable tensile capacity, 241
American Concrete Institute (ACI), 48, 99
American National Standards Institute (ANSI), 47, 100
American Society for Testing and Materials (ASTM), 48, 100. *See also* ASTM specifications
American Society of Civil Engineers (ASCE), 49, 99
Anchor. *See* Anchor bolts
Anchor bolts:
  allowable-stress design - loaded in combined tension and shear, 248
  allowable-stress design - loaded in shear, 245–248
  allowable-stress design - loaded in tension, 241–245
  allowable tensile capacity, 241
  comparing allowable-stress/strength design, 305–306, 305*t*, 306*t*

Anchor bolts (*Cont.*):
  conical breakout cones, 141, 142*f*, 241, 242*f*
  curtain walls, 167, 167*f*
  horizontally oriented bolts, 141, 141*f*, 241, 241*f*
  nominal tensile capacity, 141
  pryout failure, 145, 145*f*, 245, 245*f*
  reduction of breakout area by void areas/adjacent anchors, 142, 142*f*, 242–243, 242*f*
  shear breakout failure, 145, 145*f*, 146*f*, 245, 245*f*, 246*f*
  straightening-of-bent-portion failure, 141, 241
  strength design, 141–148
  strength design - loaded in combined tension and shear, 148
  strength design - loaded in shear, 145–148
  strength design - loaded in tension, 141–145
  tension breakout failure, 141, 241
  uses, 141, 141*f*, 241, 241*f*
  vertically oriented bolts, 141, 141*f*, 241, 241*f*
ANSI. *See* American National Standards Institute (ANSI)
ANSI consensus rules, 47
Arching action, 162, 271
ASCE. *See* American Society of Civil Engineers (ASCE)
ASCE 7-22, 49, 54, 79. *See also* Earthquake loading
ASTM. *See* American Society for Testing and Materials (ASTM)
ASTM C62, 25*t*
ASTM C216, 25*t*
ASTM specifications:
  AAC masonry, 395
  ASTM standards, listed, 468–469
  clay or shale masonry units, 19
  concrete masonry units, 20
  masonry assemblages, 20
ATC 3-06, 50
Autoclaved aerated concrete (AAC), 389–466
  AAC cladding, 393, 394*f*
  AAC elements, 389, 390*f*
  AAC hotel, 393, 394*f*
  AAC residence, 393, 393*f*
  AAC strength classes, 392, 392*t*
  ASTM specifications, 395
  beams and lintels, 412–415
  bearing walls - reinforced, 416–425
  bearing walls - unreinforced, 399–408
  curtain walls, 415
  dimensions of AAC units, 392, 392*t*
  handling, erection and construction, 396–397
  historical background, 389
  integrated US design, 393, 395, 395*f*

Autoclaved aerated concrete (AAC) (*Cont.*):
  manufacture of AAC, 391–392, 391*f*
  materials, 390–391
  panel walls, 397–399
  professional organization (AACPA), 99
  project approvals for AAC structures, 393
  seismic design, 437–438
  shear walls - reinforced, 425–437
  shear walls - unreinforced, 408–412
  structural design, 393–397
  three-story building. *See* Three-story AAC shear-wall hotel
  US design and construction provisions, 396
  what is it?, 389, 390*f*
Autoclaved Aerated Concrete Products Association (AACPA), 99

B

Balanced reinforcement percentage, 157, 157*f*
Balanced steel percentage, 266
Barrier wall, 8, 9*f*
Base shear due to wind (MWFRS), 340–344
  basic wind speed, 340
  enclosure classification, 341
  exposure category, 341
  external pressure coefficient, 342
  ground elevation factor, 341
  gust effect factor, 341
  internal pressure coefficient, 341
  risk category, 340
  topographic factor, 341
  velocity pressure, 341
  velocity pressure exposure coefficient, 341
  wind directionality factor, 341
  wind pressure, 342–344
Basic allowable-stress loading combinations, 91
Beam-columns, 167. *See also* Allowable-stress design of reinforced bearing walls; Strength design of reinforced bearing walls
Beams and lintels. *See also* Lintel
  AAC masonry, 412–415
  allowable-stress design, 272–276. *See also* Allowable-stress design of reinforced beams and lintels
  comparing allowable-stress/strength design, 306–307, 306*t*, 307*t*
  east wall/out-of-plane loads, 357, 357*f*
  low-rise building, 363–366
  reinforcement, 103, 104*f*
  strength design, 165–172. *See also* Strength design of reinforced beams and lintels

Index

Bearing walls:
    AAC masonry - unreinforced walls, 399–408
    allowable-stress design - reinforced walls, 277–289
    allowable-stress design - unreinforced walls, 220–235
    design issues to be considered, 122, 220
    effective length coefficient, 122, 220
    effective width of masonry beam-column, 168, 168f, 277, 278f
    four-story building, 388
    most common form of masonry beam-column, 168, 277
    slenderness, 122, 123f, 220, 221f
    strength design - reinforced walls, 167–185
    strength design - unreinforced walls, 122–135
    terminology (beam-column), 167, 277
    vertically spanning strips, 122, 123f, 220, 220f
Bed joint reinforcement, 29, 30f
Bent-bar anchor bolt, 141, 241. *See also* Anchor bolts
BIA. *See* Brick Industry Association (BIA)
BOCA. *See* Building Officials and Code Administrators International (BOCA)
Boiling-water absorption, 22–23, 25t
Bond patterns, 7, 8f
Brick Industry Association (BIA), 49, 99
BSSC. *See* Building Seismic Safety Council (BSSC)
Building codes, 47–100
    ANSI consensus rules, 47
    ASCE 7-22, 79. *See also* Earthquake loading
    governmental organizations, 50, 100
    IBC. *See* 2024 IBC
    industry organizations, 49, 99–100
    legacy model codes, 48f, 50
    model code organizations, 50–51, 100
    overview, 47–48, 48f
    specification development organization, 100. *See also* American Society for Testing and Materials (ASTM); *specific named specifications*
    technical speciality organizations, 48–49, 99
    TMS 402. *See* TMS 402-22
Building Officials and Code Administrators International (BOCA), 50
Building Seismic Safety Council (BSSC), 50, 100

C

c/b ratio, 23, 25t
Cantilever beam-column, 2
Capping for slenderness, 419, 420f, 421t
Capping the moment-axial force interaction diagram, 179, 419
Cavity wall, 9, 9f
C&C. *See* Components and Cladding (C&C)
Cement-lime mortar, 13–14, 13t, 17–18
Center of rigidity:
    defined, 315
    geometric centroid of wall areas, 317
    location, 317–318
    plan torsion, 316, 316f
    symmetrical building, 315, 316f
    unsymmetrical building, 316, 316f
Centroidal moment of inertia, 256
Chippage:
    clay masonry, 23, 25t
    concrete masonry, 26
Clay masonry, 21–26
    adobe, 6t
    appearance, 23
    ASTM C62, 25t
    ASTM C216, 25t
    chemistry, 21
    chippage, 23, 25t
    coefficient of thermal expansion, 26
    color, 25
    compressive strength, 25t
    curtain walls - allowable-stress design, 273, 273f
    curtain walls - strength design, 164, 164f
    design criteria, 23, 25t
    dimensional tolerances, 22, 25t
    durability, 22, 25t
    efflorescence, 23, 25t
    freeze-thaw expansion, 26
    freeze-thaw resistance, 22–23
    geology, 21
    initial rate of absorption (IRA), 26
    manufacturing of, 21–22
    mechanical characteristics, 23
    modulus of elasticity, 26
    saturation coefficient (c/b ratio), 23, 25t
    section properties, 118t, 215t
    shear walls - allowable-stress design, 292–295
    shear walls - strength design, 188–197
    specification, 24–25
    strength design. *See* Four-story building with clay masonry
    tensile bond strength, 26
    tensile strength, 25
    weathering index, 24, 24f
Clay wythe, 38, 42, 42f
CMHA. *See* Concrete Masonry Hardscapes Association (CMHA)
CMU wythe, 38, 42, 42f

Index

Coarse grout, 18
Coatings, 7, 28t, 34
Code basis for structural design. *See* Building codes
Coefficient of thermal expansion:
  clay masonry, 26
  concrete masonry, 27
Cold-water absorption, 22
Columns, 105. *See also* Pilasters (columns)
Comparison of strength/allowable-stress designs, 303–308
  anchor bolts, 305–306, 305t, 306t
  beams and lintels, 306–307, 306t, 307t
  bearing walls (reinforced), 307–308, 307t
  bearing walls (unreinforced), 304, 304t
  curtain walls, 307
  panel walls, 303, 304t
  shear walls (reinforced), 308, 308t
  shear walls (unreinforced), 304–305, 305t
Components and Cladding (C&C)
  example (wind loading), 73–78
  external pressure coefficient, 74f, 77f
  general procedures, 55
  leeward side of building, 78, 78t, 347, 347t
  pressure on wall elements due to wind, 344–348. *See also* Pressure on wall elements due to wind (C&C)
  windward side of building, 76, 78, 78t, 346, 347t
Compression chord, 335, 335f, 463
Compressive capacity, 101
Compressive strength:
  clay masonry, 25t
  concrete masonry, 27
  masonry assemblages, 28
  mortar, 16–17
Concentric axial load:
  allowable-stress design - unreinforced bearing walls, 222–224
  strength design - unreinforced bearing walls, 124–127
  unreinforced AAC masonry bearing walls, 400–402
Concrete masonry:
  AAC. *See* Autoclaved aerated concrete (AAC)
  absorption, 27
  adobe, 6t
  beams and lintels, 271
  chippage, 26
  coefficient of thermal expansion, 27
  color, 26
  compressive strength, 27
  curtain walls - allowable-stress design, 273, 274f

Concrete masonry (*Cont.*):
  curtain walls - strength design, 164, 165f
  dimensional tolerances, 26
  initial rate of absorption (IRA), 27
  materials and manufacturing, 26
  mechanical characteristics, 27
  modulus of elasticity, 27
  section properties, 118t, 216t
  shrinkage, 27
  tensile bond strength, 27
  tensile strength, 27
  type I/II units, 27
  visual and serviceability characteristics, 26
  warehouse. *See* One-story commercial building - reinforced concrete masonry
Concrete Masonry Hardscapes Association (CMHA), 49, 100
Confined masonry, 105
Conical breakout cones, 141, 142f, 241, 242f
Connections. *See* Required details (connections)
Connectors, 6, 28t, 29–31, 32f, 33f
Construction joints, 31, 35
Control joints:
  cracking, 31, 35, 36f
  low-rise building, 338, 339f
Corrugated tie, 32f
Cracked, transformed sections, 255–267
  allowable flexural capacity, 263–265
  allowable-stress balanced reinforcement, 265–267
  allowable-stress balanced steel area, 265, 266
  axial equilibrium of compressive block, 259
  balanced steel percentage, 266
  bond behavior, 260–261
  centroidal moment of inertia, 256
  equilibrium between bond force and difference in tensile force, 261f
  equilibrium between shear forces and difference in shear forces, 258f
  equilibrium of compressive and tensile portions, 259, 259f
  equilibrium of difference in compressive force and difference in tensile force, 260f
  flexural behavior, 255–257
  kinematics, stress-strain relationships, statics, 255, 256f
  modular ratio, 263
  moment equilibrium, 256
  neutral axis, 257–258, 261–263
  shear behavior, 258–259
  states of stress and strain, 256f
  steel reinforcing wire and bars, 261, 262t

Cracked, transformed sections (*Cont.*):
 triangular compressive stress blocks, 258*f*
 unit strength method, 261
Critical diagonal compression, 463–464
Critical strain condition, 424, 424*f*
Crushing strength, 101
Crypto-forescence, 23
Curtain walls
 allowable-stress design, 272–276. *See also* Allowable-stress design of curtain walls
 anchors, 167, 167*f*
 comparing allowable-stress/strength design, 307
 flexural tensile strength, 163, 272
 flexural tensile stresses, 163, 272
 gravity load, 163, 272
 horizontal span, 163, 272
 nonlead-bearing masonry, 163, 272
 number of stories, 163, 272
 out-of-plane load, 163, 272
 reinforcement, 104
 single-wythe, 163, 272
 strength design, 163–167. *See also* Strength design of curtain walls
 typical curtain wall construction, 163*f*, 272*f*

D

Deformed reinforcement, 29, 29*f*
Degree-of-freedom system, 79, 79*f*
Design acceleration response spectrum, 449, 450*f*
Design codes, 47. *See also* Building codes
Design response acceleration parameter, 447–448
Design response spectrum curve, 448–449
Details. *See* Required details
Diaphragm:
 classification, 310
 connections - CMU wall-to-diaphragm (steel joists), 335, 336*f*
 connections - CMU wall-to-diaphragm (wooden joists), 335, 336*f*
 connections - roof and floor diaphragms, 335, 336*f*
 design and detailing, 333–336
 flexible. *See* Flexible diaphragm
 low-rise building (roof diaphragm), 367–369
 rigid. *See* Rigid diaphragm
 semi-rigid, 310
 three-story building, 460–464. *See also* Floor diaphragm - three-story AAC masonry hotel
Diaphragm chords and collectors:
 flexible diaphragm, 334, 335, 335*f*
 rigid diaphragm, 333

Dimensional tolerances:
 clay masonry, 22, 25*t*
 concrete masonry, 26
Dog-legged control joint, 35, 36*f*
Drag strut, 334
Drainage wall, 9, 9*f*
Drip edge, 3*f*
Dry press process, 21
Durability, 22, 25*t*

E

Earthquake loading, 79–90. *See also* Seismic design
 acceleration response spectrum, 80, 80*f*
 design acceleration response spectrum, 88, 88*f*
 equation for equilibrium, 79
 equivalent lateral force procedure (ELFP), 80
 500-year earthquake, 87
 four-story building, 376–388
 importance factor, 88
 occupancy category, 88
 plan structural irregularities, 89, 378, 453
 redundancy, 90
 seismic base shear, 80–90
 seismic design category, 89, 89*t*
 seismic ground motion values, 80
 single-degree-of-freedom system, 79, 79*f*
 transverse shear walls, 381–388
 2500-year earthquake, 81, 442
 vertical structural irregularities, 89–90, 379, 453
East of Denver, 106
Eccentric axial load:
 allowable-stress design - unreinforced bearing walls, 225–228
 strength design - unreinforced bearing walls, 127–130
 unreinforced AAC masonry bearing walls, 402–405
Eccentric axial load plus wind:
 allowable-stress design - unreinforced bearing walls, 228–233
 strength design - unreinforced bearing walls, 130–132
 unreinforced AAC masonry bearing walls, 405–407
Efflorescence, 23, 25*t*
Efflorescence testing, 23
ELFP. *See* Equivalent lateral force procedure (ELFP)

Index

Enclosed building, 60t, 71
Enclosure classification:
   base shear due to wind (MWFRS), 341
   MWFRS, 56, 60t
   pressure on wall elements due to wind (C&C), 345
Equivalent lateral force procedure (ELFP), 80, 441
Escarpment, 59
ESCSI. See Expanded Shale Clay and Slate Institute (ESCSI)
Euler buckling equation, 222
Expanded Shale Clay and Slate Institute (ESCSI), 49
Expansion joints, 31, 35, 35f
Exposure category:
   base shear due to wind (MWFRS), 341
   MWFRS, 57, 69
   pressure on wall elements due to wind (C&C), 344
Exposure Category C, 57
External pressure coefficient:
   base shear due to wind (MWFRS), 342
   C&C, 74f, 77f
   MWFRS, 60, 62–63f, 73
   pressure on wall elements due to wind (C&C), 345, 346f
Extreme-fiber tensile stress, 221

F

Factored design lateral force, 381
Factored moment diagram, 361, 361f
Factors of safety, 103
Failure, probability of, 103
Fastest mile wind speed, 56
Federal Emergency Management Agency (FEMA), 50
FEMA. See Federal Emergency Management Agency (FEMA)
Field mortar, 15
Fine grout, 18
Finite element analysis, 328. See also Method 1 (finite element analysis)
Fire:
   four-story building, 375
   low-rise building, 339
   three-story AAC shear-wall hotel, 440
Fired clay masonry, 6t. See also Clay masonry
500-year earthquake, 87
Fixed lintel, 42, 42f, 43f
Flashing, 3f, 7, 28t, 32, 34, 34f
Flemish bond, 7, 8f

Flexible diaphragm:
   characteristics, 311
   compression chord, 335, 335f
   defined, 310
   design, 333–335
   drag strut, 334
   lateral load analysis. See Shear wall structures with flexible floor diaphragms
   tension chord, 335, 335f
Flexural design:
   beams and lintels - AAC masonry, 412
   beams and lintels - allowable-stress design, 267
   beams and lintels - strength design, 158
   curtain walls, 166
   panel walls, 109, 111
   TMS 402-22, 109, 111, 208, 210
   transverse shear walls, 383–387, 455–456
Floor diaphragm - three-story AAC masonry hotel, 460–464
   compression chords, 463
   critical diagonal compression, 463–464
   loaded/unloaded nodes, 463, 463f
   panel-to-bond joint beam, 462, 462f
   panel-to-panel joint, 461, 462f
   plan and sectional view of AAC floor diaphragm, 460, 461f
   truss model, 462, 463f
Floor live load, 51–52, 52t
Floor live load reduction, 52–53
Floor slab-wall connection. See Wall-to-foundation connection
Flow, 15
Foundation-wall detail. See Wall-to-foundation connection
Four-story building with clay masonry, 373–388
   bearing wall construction, 388
   design steps, listed, 373
   diagram, 374f
   earthquake loads, 376–388
   exterior walls for gravity plus out-of-plane wind, 388
   fire, 375
   floor load due to gravity, 376, 376t
   gravity load, 375
   lateral load, 375
   materials, 375
   movement joints, 374
   principal lateral force-resisting elements, 373
   reinforcement requirements, 388
   roof load due to gravity, 375, 375t
   simplicity in design and analysis, 388

478 Index

Four-story building with clay masonry (Cont.):
   transverse shear walls, 381–388. See also Transverse shear walls
   water penetration resistance, 374
Freeze-thaw expansion, 26
Freeze-thaw resistance, 22–23
Fresh grout, 18
Fresh mortar, 15–16
Fully reinforced masonry, 107

G

Geometric centroid of wall areas, 317
Glass-block masonry design, 103
Governmental organizations, 50, 100
Grade MW brick, 22–24
Grade NW brick, 22–24
Grade SW brick, 22–24
Gravity:
   dead load, 51
   floor live load, 51–52
   floor live-load reduction, 52–53
   four-story building (floor load), 376, 376t
   four-story building (roof load), 375, 375t
   roof live load, 53, 54f
   three-story building (floor load), 441
   three-story building (roof load), 440
   wall live-load reduction, 53
Gravity plus out-of-plane loads:
   four-story building, 388
   low-rise building (east wall), 353–357
   low-rise building (north and south walls), 357–359
   low-rise building (west wall), 349–353
Ground elevation factor:
   base shear due to wind (MWFRS), 341
   pressure on wall elements due to wind (C&C), 344
Gust effect factor:
   base shear due to wind (MWFRS), 341
   MWFRS, 59, 70
   pressure on wall elements due to wind (C&C), 344
Gypsum, 11–12

H

Hardened grout, 18
Hardened mortar, 16–17
Hill, 59
Hollow-core prestressed concrete planks, 464
Horizontal diaphragm, 309–310. See also Diaphragm
Horizontal reinforcement, 2, 3f, 105

Horizontally oriented expansion joint, 35f
Hotel-type structure. See Four-story building with clay masonry
Hurricane zone, 57
Hydraulic-cement mortar, 11–12
Hydrostone, 11

I

IBC. See International Building Code (IBC)
ICBO. See International Conference of Building Officials (ICBO)
ICC. See International Code Council (ICC)
IMI. See International Masonry Institute (IMI)
Importance factor, 88, 377, 378t
Industry organizations, 49, 99–100
Inelastic buckling, 229
Inherent torsion, 454
Initial rate of absorption (IRA):
   clay masonry, 26
   concrete masonry, 27
Interaction diagram. See Moment-axial force interaction diagram
Internal pressure coefficient:
   base shear due to wind (MWFRS), 341
   MWFRS, 56
   pressure on wall elements due to wind (C&C), 345
International Building Code (IBC), 50. See also 2024 IBC
International Code Council (ICC), 50, 51, 100
International Conference of Building Officials (ICBO), 50
International Masonry Institute (IMI), 49, 100
IRA. See Initial rate of absorption (IRA)

J

J-bolt, 141, 241
Joint reinforcement, 29, 30f

K

K-bolt, 141, 241

L

Laboratory-mixed mortar, 15
Lateral load analysis of shear wall structures, 309–332
   classification of diaphragms, 309–311
   flexible floor diaphragms. See Shear wall structures with flexible floor diaphragms
   resisting lateral loads, generally, 135, 135f, 235–236, 235f

Lateral load analysis of shear wall structures (*Cont.*):
    rigid floor diaphragms. *See* Shear wall structures with rigid floor diaphragms
    seismic design, 330
    simplest of all possible analytical worlds, 330
Leeward side:
    wind loading (C&C), 78, 78*t*
    wind pressure (C&C), 347, 347*t*
Legacy model codes, 48*f*, 50
Linear elastic finite element analysis. *See* Method 1 (finite element analysis)
Linear elastic range, 255. *See also* Cracked, transformed sections
Lintel. *See also* Beams and lintels
    clay masonry, 104*f*
    CMU, 104*f*
    fixed, 42, 42*f*, 43*f*
    loose, 42, 42*f*, 43*f*
    schematic illustration, 158*f*
    strength design, 159*f*
Little structural calculation. *See* Masonry structures (little structural calculation)
Live load:
    floor, 51–52, 52*t*
    floor live load reduction, 52–53
    roof, 53, 54*f*
    wall live load reduction, 53
Load-bearing masonry, 102, 122, 220. *See also* Bearing walls
Loaded/unloaded nodes, 463, 463*f*
Loading combinations:
    allowable-stress, 91, 95–96
    1/3 stress increase, 91
    strength, 90, 92
Loose lintel, 42, 42*f*, 43*f*
Low-rise masonry buildings:
    basic structural behavior, 1, 1*f*
    basic structural configuration, 2, 3*f*
    basic structural design, 2–3
    fundamental design premise, 2
    starting point for reinforcement, 3, 3*f*
    warehouse. *See* One-story commercial building - reinforced concrete masonry

M

Main Wind-Force Resisting System (MWFRS):
    base shear due to wind, 340–344. *See also* Base shear due to wind (MWFRS)
    directional procedure, 54, 55–63
    enclosure classification, 56, 60*t*
    example, 63–73
    exposure category, 57, 69

Main Wind-Force Resisting System (MWFRS) (*Cont.*):
    external pressure coefficient, 60, 62–63*f*, 73
    general procedures, 54–55
    gust effect factor, 59, 70
    internal pressure coefficient, 56
    risk category, 56, 57*f*
    surface roughness category, 57
    topographic factor, 57, 59
    velocity pressure, 59–60, 71, 73
    velocity pressure exposure coefficient, 59, 61*t*, 71
    wind directionality factor, 57, 58*t*
    wind load parameters, 56
    wind pressure, 60, 62–63, 73
Mason Contractors' Association of America (MCAA), 49, 100
Masonry:
    AAC design, 103. *See also* Autoclaved aerated concrete (AAC)
    accessory materials. *See* Masonry accessory materials
    allowable-stress design. *See* Allowable-stress design
    architectural applications, 5
    assemblages. *See* Masonry assemblages
    bond patterns, 7, 8*f*
    classification of masonry elements, 101
    classification of masonry units, 5, 6*f*
    composite material, 101
    compressive capacity, 101
    concrete. *See* Concrete masonry
    confined, 105
    crushing strength, 101
    dimensions, 7
    East of Denver/West of Denver, 106–107
    factors of safety, 103
    fired clay. *See* Clay masonry
    fully reinforced, 107
    glass-block masonry design, 103
    grout, 18–19
    load-bearing, 102, 122, 220
    mechanical behavior, 101–102
    mortar. *See* Masonry mortar
    nonload-bearing, 102, 399
    orientation of masonry units, 7, 8*f*
    partially reinforced, 106
    reinforced. *See* Reinforced masonry
    strength design. *See* Strength design
    tensile capacity, 101
    terminology, 7

Masonry (*Cont.*):
    types of walls, 8–9
    unreinforced. *See* Unreinforced masonry
    veneer design, 103
    water penetration resistance, 43–45
Masonry accessory materials, 6–7, 28–36
    coatings, 7, 28*t*, 34
    connectors, 6, 28*t*, 29–31, 32*f*, 33*f*
    flashing, 7, 28*t*, 32, 34, 34*f*
    moisture barriers, 7, 28*t*, 35
    movement joints, 35, 35*f*, 36*f*
    sealants, 7, 28*t*, 31–32
    vapor barriers, 7, 28*t*, 34–35
Masonry assemblages:
    ASTM specifications, 20
    compressive strength, 28
    shear strength, 28
    tensile bond strength, 28
    water permeability, 28
Masonry-cement mortar, 14–15, 14*t*, 15*t*
Masonry Designers' Guide, 49, 438
Masonry dimensions, 7
Masonry grout, 6, 18–19
Masonry lintel. *See* Lintel
Masonry mortar, 10–18
    air content, 16
    cement-lime mortar, 13–14, 13*t*, 17–18
    cementitious systems, 12–13
    characteristics, 15–18
    choices to be made by designer, 10
    compressive strength, 16–17
    flow, 15
    fresh mortar, 15–16
    hardened mortar, 16–17
    hydraulic-cement mortar, 11–12
    masonry-cement mortar, 14–15, 14*t*, 15*t*
    mortar-cement mortar, 15, 16*t*, 17–18
    Portland cement, 12
    retentivity, 15
    sand-lime mortar, 10–11
    tensile bond strength, 17
    types, 13
    workability, 15
Masonry-related organizations:
    governmental organizations, 50, 100
    industry organizations, 49, 99–100
    model code organizations, 50–51, 100
    specification development organization, 100
    technical speciality organizations, 48–49, 99
Masonry Standards Joint Committee (MSJC), 48, 49

Masonry structures (little structural calculation), 36–43
    clay wythe, 38, 42, 42*f*
    CMU wythe, 38, 42, 42*f*
    control joints, 42, 42*f*
    expansion joints, 42, 42*f*
    floor-wall connections, 38, 39*f*, 40*f*
    overall modularity, 38, 39*f*
    overall starting point for reinforcement, 38, 38*f*
    steps in design process, 36–37
    wall-roof connections, 38, 40*f*, 41*f*
    wall sections at doors, 43
    wall sections at windows, 42–43, 43*f*
Masonry veneer, 103
Masonry walls, 8–9
MaSoNwOrK, 13
MCAA. *See* Mason Contractors' Association of America (MCAA)
Metallic flashing, 34
Method 1 (finite element analysis):
    cracking, 311, 312
    example, 312
    generally, 311, 312
    in-plane actions, 311
    inaccuracy of method (multi-modal response to dynamic loads), 311
    other methods, compared, 326*t*
    tediousness of process, 311
Method 2a (shearing stiffness):
    distribution of shears among wall segments, 313
    example, 314–315
    generally, 311, 312
    other methods, compared, 326*t*
    shearing stiffness of each wall segment, 313, 313*f*
Method 2b (shearing stiffness plus plan torsion), 315–323
    center of rigidity. *See* Center of rigidity
    direct shear plus plan torsion, 320, 321*f*
    example, 321–324
    generally, 311, 312
    lateral load applied through arbitrary point, 318
    lateral load applied through center of rigidity, 318–319
    other methods, compared, 326*t*
    torsional moment applied at center of rigidity, 319–320
Method 2c (shearing and flexural stiffness):
    example, 323, 325
    generally, 311, 312
    other methods, compared, 326*t*
    time commitment, 325

Index   481

Minimum Design Loads for Buildings and Other Structures (ASCE 7-22), 54
Model code organizations, 50–51, 100
Moderate weathering regions, 24, 24f
Modular ratio, 263
Modulus of elasticity:
    clay masonry, 26
    concrete masonry, 27
Modulus of rupture:
    AAC masonry beams and lintels, 415
    AAC masonry panel walls, 397
    panel walls, 111, 111t
    unreinforced AAC masonry bearing walls, 407
Moisture barriers, 7, 28t, 35
Moment-axial force interaction diagram:
    capping the diagram, 179, 419
    low-rise building (east wall/segment B), 353, 355, 355f, 356t
    low-rise building (west wall), 352, 354t
    pilaster, 361, 362t, 363f
    reinforced bearing wall - AAC masonry, 416f, 417t, 419, 420f, 421t
    reinforced bearing wall - allowable-stress design (hand calculation), 278–282
    reinforced bearing wall - allowable-stress design (spreadsheet calculation), 282–285, 286t, 287f
    reinforced bearing wall - strength design (hand calculation), 168–172
    reinforced bearing wall - strength design (spreadsheet calculation), 172–176, 177t
    reinforced shear wall - AAC masonry, 430, 431f
    reinforced shear wall - strength design, 190, 190f, 193, 193f
Moment equilibrium, 256
Moment magnifier:
    AAC masonry - reinforced bearing wall, 420
    AAC masonry - unreinforced bearing wall, 400
    allowable-stress design - unreinforced bearing wall, 222
    strength design - reinforced bearing walls, 182
    strength design - unreinforced bearing wall, 123, 129, 130, 132, 139
Mortar. *See* Masonry mortar
Mortar-cement mortar, 15, 16t, 17–18
Movement joints:
    construction joints, 35
    control joints, 35, 36f
    expansion joints, 35, 35f, 440
    four-story building with clay masonry, 374
    three-story AAC shear-wall hotel, 440
MSJC. *See* Masonry Standards Joint Committee (MSJC)

Multi-story structures. *See* Four-story building with clay masonry; Three-story AAC shear-wall hotel
Multi-wythe barrier wall, 8
Multi-wythe drainage wall, 9

N

National Building Code (NBC), 50
National Concrete Masonry Association (NCMA), 49
National Earthquake Hazard Reduction Program (NEHRP), 50
National Fire Protection Association (NFPA), 51, 100
National Institute of Building Sciences (NIBS), 50
National Lime Association (NLA), 49
NBC. *See* National Building Code (NBC)
NCMA. *See* National Concrete Masonry Association (NCMA)
Negligible weathering regions, 24, 24f
NEHRP. *See* National Earthquake Hazard Reduction Program (NEHRP)
NEHRP *Recommended Provisions*, 50
NFPA. *See* National Fire Protection Association (NFPA)
NFPA 5000, 51
NIBS. *See* National Institute of Building Sciences (NIBS)
NLA. *See* National Lime Association (NLA)
Nominal dimensions, 7
Nominal flexural capacity, 161
Nominal in-plane shear stress, 161
Nominal tensile capacity, 141
Nonload-bearing masonry, 102, 399
Nonmetallic flashing, 34

O

Occupancy category, 88, 377
One-story commercial building - reinforced concrete masonry, 337–372
    base shear due to wind, 340–344. *See also* Base shear due to wind (MWFRS)
    bearing plate under long-span joists, 363, 363f
    connections, 366
    control joints, 338, 339f
    design steps, listed, 337–338
    diagram of building, 338f, 339f, 340f
    fire, 339
    gravity, 349–359. *See also* Gravity plus out-of-plane loads
    lintel (east wall/out-of-plane load), 357, 357f
    lintel (low-rise building), 363–366

One-story commercial building - reinforced concrete masonry (*Cont.*):
  materials, 340
  pilasters (columns), 359–363
  pressure on wall elements due to wind, 344–348. *See also* Pressure on wall elements due to wind (C&C)
  roof diaphragm, 367–369
  roof load due to gravity, 340
  wall segments, 369–372. *See also* Wall segments
  water penetration resistance, 338
1/3 running bond, 7, 8*f*
1/3 stress increase, 91
Open building, 60*t*, 70
Openings:
  allowable-stress design of unreinforced bearing walls, 233–235
  allowable-stress design of unreinforced shear walls, 240, 240*f*
  strength design of unreinforced bearing walls, 133–135
  strength design of unreinforced shear walls, 140–141
  unreinforced AAC masonry bearing walls, 407, 408
Organizations. *See* Masonry-related organizations
Orientation of masonry units, 7, 8*f*
Out-of-plane load:
  allowable-stress design of reinforced bearing walls, 285–289
  allowable-stress design of unreinforced panel walls, 217–218, 218–220
  curtain walls, 163, 272
  four-story building, 388
  low-rise building, 349–359
  strength design of reinforced bearing walls, 176–184
  strength design of unreinforced panel walls, 119–120, 120–122
  three-story building, 459–460
Overall modularity, 38, 39*f*

P

Paint, 34
Panel-to-bond joint beam, 462, 462*f*
Panel-to-panel joint, 461, 462*f*
Panel walls:
  AAC masonry, 397–399
  allowable-stress design, 207–220. *See also* Allowable-stress design of unreinforced panel walls
  comparing allowable-stress/strength design, 303, 304*t*

Panel walls (*Cont.*):
  connecting panel wall to column, 109, 110*f*, 207, 208*f*
  inner wythes, 109, 110*f*, 207, 209*f*
  multiwythe noncomposite wall, 109, 207
  nonload-bearing masonry, 163
  outer wythes, 109, 110*f*, 207, 209*f*
  strength design, 109–122. *See also* Strength design of unreinforced panel walls
  vertical and horizontal crossing strips, 109, 110*f*, 207, 209*f*
Partially enclosed building, 60*t*
Partially open building, 60*t*
Partially reinforced masonry, 106
Participating elements, 102
PCA. *See* Portland Cement Association (PCA)
PCI. *See* Prestressed Concrete Institute (PCI)
Pilasters (columns):
  defined, 105
  hollow units, 105, 106*f*
  low-rise building, 359–363
  solid units, 105
Plan structural irregularities, 89, 378, 453
Plaster of Paris, 11
Portland cement, 12
Portland Cement Association (PCA), 49, 100
Posttensioning tendons, 29, 31*f*
Pozzolanic cement, 11, 12
Pressure on wall elements due to wind (C&C), 344–348
  basic wind speed, 344
  enclosure classification, 345
  exposure category, 344
  external pressure coefficient, 345, 346*f*
  ground elevation factor, 344
  gust effect factor, 344
  internal pressure coefficient, 345
  risk category, 344
  topographic factor, 344
  velocity pressure, 345
  velocity pressure exposure coefficient, 345
  wind directionality factor, 344
  wind pressure (leeward side), 347, 347*t*
  wind pressure (roof), 347–348, 348*t*
  wind pressure (windward side), 346, 347*t*
Prestressed Concrete Institute (PCI), 100
Probability of failure, 103
Pryout failure, 145, 145*f*, 245, 245*f*

Q

Quartz, 11
Quicklime, 10

Index

R

Rectangular tie, 32f
Redundancy, 90, 379
Reinforced AAC masonry bearing walls, 416–425
Reinforced beam-column, 2
Reinforced beams and lintels. *See* Beams and lintels
Reinforced bearing walls:
    AAC masonry, 416–425
    allowable-stress design, 277–289. *See also* Allowable-stress design of reinforced bearing walls
    comparing allowable-stress/strength design, 307–308, 307t
    required details, 201–203, 296–299
    strength design, 167–185. *See also* Strength design of reinforced bearing walls
Reinforced curtain walls. *See* Curtain walls
Reinforced masonry:
    AAC masonry - beams and lintels, 412–415
    AAC masonry - bearing walls, 416–425
    AAC masonry - curtain walls, 415
    AAC masonry - shear walls, 425–437
    allowable-stress design - beams and lintels, 267–271
    allowable-stress design - bearing walls, 277–289
    allowable-stress design - curtain walls, 272–277
    allowable-stress design - shear walls, 289–296
    comparing allowable-stress/strength design, 303–308
    defined, 102
    linear elastic range, 255. *See also* Cracked, transformed sections
    nomenclature, 105–107
    strength design - beams and lintels, 155–162
    strength design - bearing walls, 167–185
    strength design - curtain walls, 163–167
    strength design - shear walls, 185–200
    warehouse. *See* One-story commercial building - reinforced concrete masonry
Reinforced shear walls:
    AAC masonry, 425–437
    allowable-stress design, 289–296. *See also* Allowable-stress design of reinforced shear walls
    comparing allowable-stress/strength design, 308, 308t
    strength design, 185–200. *See also* Strength design of reinforced shear walls

Reinforcement:
    AAC masonry panel walls, 399
    balanced reinforcement percentage, 157, 157f
    beams and lintels, 103–104, 104f
    clay masonry lintels, 104f
    CMU lintels, 104f
    columns and pilasters, 105, 106f
    curtain walls, 104
    deformed, 29, 29f
    four-story building, 388
    horizontal, 2, 3f, 105
    joint, 29, 30f
    posttensioning tendons, 29, 31f
    three-story AAC shear-wall hotel, 464
    unreinforced masonry, 105
    uses, 29, 29f, 30f, 31f
    vertical, 2, 3f, 105
    walls, 104–105, 105f
    welded wire, 29, 30f
Required details (connections). *See also named connections*
    CMU wall-to-diaphragm (steel joists), 335, 336f
    CMU wall-to-diaphragm (wooden joists), 335, 336f
    low-rise building, 372
    reinforced bearing walls and shear walls, 201–203, 296–299
    roof and floor diaphragms, 335, 336f
    unreinforced bearing walls and shear walls, 149–151, 248–251
Response spectrum:
    acceleration, 80, 80f, 88, 88f
    four-story building, 377, 377f
    three-story building, 448–449, 450f
Retentivity, 15
Ridge, 59
Rigid diaphragm:
    defined, 310
    design, 333
    lateral load analysis. *See* Shear wall structures with rigid floor diaphragms
    prescriptive characteristics, 310
Risk category:
    base shear due to wind (MWFRS), 340
    MWFRS, 56, 57f
    pressure on wall elements due to wind (C&C), 344
Risk Category II buildings, 56, 57f, 68, 69f
Roof:
    chords, 368
    external pressure coefficients (MWFRS), 62f

Roof (*Cont.*):
  factored design lateral force, 381
  live load, 53, 54*f*
  low-rise building (roof diaphragm), 367–369
  shear walls - horizontal roof diaphragm, 135–136
  wooden roof truss, 41*f*
Running bond, 7, 8*f*

S

Sailor orientation, 8*f*
Sand-lime mortar, 10–11
Saturation coefficient (c/b ratio), 23, 25*t*
SBC. *See* Standard Building Code (SBC)
SBCCI. *See* Southern Building Code Congress International (SBCCI)
Sealants, 7, 28*t*, 31–32
Section properties:
  clay masonry, 118*t*, 215*t*
  concrete masonry, 118*t*, 216*t*
Seismic base shear, 80–90, 441, 451–453
Seismic design. *See also* Earthquake loading
  AAC masonry, 437–438
  seismic design factors of reinforced AAC masonry shear walls, 438*t*
  shear wall structures, 200, 296, 330
  zone of moderate seismic risk. *See* Three-story AAC shear-wall hotel
Seismic design category, 89, 89*t*, 377, 378*t*, 449–451
Seismic force-reduction factor, 438
Seismic ground motion values, 80, 441
Self-adhering flashing, 34
Self-consolidating grout, 19
Self-weights:
  fully grouted CMU walls, 132*t*, 231*t*
  hollow CMU walls, 125*t*, 223*t*
Semi-rigid diaphragm, 310
Severe weathering regions, 24, 24*f*
Shear breakout failure:
  unreinforced masonry - allowable-stress design, 245, 245*f*, 246*f*
  unreinforced masonry - strength design, 145, 145*f*, 146*f*
Shear capacity, 460
Shear center. *See* Center of rigidity
Shear design:
  AAC masonry beams and lintels, 412
  beams and lintels, 158
  curtain walls, 166–167
  transverse shear walls, 382–383, 454–455

Shear strength, 28
Shear wall:
  AAC masonry, 425–437
  allowable-stress design - reinforced walls, 289–296
  allowable-stress design - unreinforced walls, 235–241
  cantilever beam-columns, 2
  horizontal roof diaphragm, 135–136, 236
  lateral loads. *See* Lateral load analysis of shear wall structures
  seismic design factors of reinforced AAC masonry shear walls, 438*t*
  strength design - reinforced walls, 185–200
  strength design - unreinforced walls, 135–141
  transverse. *See* Transverse shear walls
Shear wall structures with flexible floor diaphragms, 327–329
  approximate approach, 328
  continuous beam, 328–329
  exact approach, 328
  example (analysis of building with flexible diaphragms), 328, 328*f*
  example (distribution of shears with flexible diaphragm), 328–329, 329*f*
Shear wall structures with rigid floor diaphragms, 311–327
  comments/conclusions, 325, 327
  comparisons of methods 1, 2a, 2b, and 2c, 326*t*
  cost effectiveness of methods, 327
  finite element analysis. *See* Method 1 (finite element analysis)
  shearing plus flexural stiffness. *See* Method 2c (shearing and flexural stiffness)
  shearing stiffness. *See* Method 2a (shearing stiffness)
  shearing stiffness plus torsion. *See* Method 2b (shearing stiffness plus plan torsion)
Shearing plus flexural stiffness. *See* Method 2c (shearing and flexural stiffness)
Shearing stiffness. *See* Method 2a (shearing stiffness)
Shearing stiffness plus torsion. *See* Method 2b (shearing stiffness plus plan torsion)
Shrinkage control joint, 31, 35, 36*f*
Single-degree-of-freedom system, 79, 79*f*
Single-story building. *See* One-story commercial building - reinforced concrete masonry
Single-wythe AAC masonry panel wall, 397–398
Single-wythe barrier wall, 8, 9*f*
Single-wythe curtain wall, 163
Single-wythe drainage wall, 9
Single-wythe panel wall, 112–116, 210–214

Index

Site classification, 447
Slag cement, 12
Slenderness:
    capping the interaction diagram, 419, 420f, 421t
    reinforced AAC masonry bearing walls, 419
    reinforced shear walls, 193, 193f
    unreinforced bearing walls, 122, 123f, 220, 221f
Slenderness-dependent factor, 175
Soft mud process, 21
Soldier orientation, 7, 8f
Southern Building Code Congress International (SBCCI), 50
Specification development organization, 100. See also American Society for Testing and Materials (ASTM); *specific named specifications*
Specified dimensions, 7
Stability equation:
    allowable-stress design - concentric axial load, 224
    allowable-stress design - eccentric axial load, 227
    allowable-stress design - eccentric axial load plus wind, 230, 233
Stack bond, 7, 8f
Standard Building Code (SBC), 50
Steel joists, 335, 336f
Steel prestressing strand, 29
Steel reinforcing wire and bars:
    AAC masonry beams and lintels, 413, 413t
    beams and lintels, 159, 159t
    cracked, transformed sections, 261, 262t
Stiff mud process, 21
Straightening-of-bent-portion failure, 141, 241
Strength design:
    allowable-stress design, compared. *See* Comparison of strength/allowable-stress designs
    beams and lintels, 155–162
    bearing walls (reinforced), 167–185
    bearing walls (unreinforced), 122–135
    curtain walls, 163–165
    generally, 103
    loading combinations, 92
    multi-story hotel-type structure. *See* Four-story building with clay masonry
    panel walls, 109–122
    probability of failure, 103
    required details, 149–151, 201–203
    shear walls (reinforced), 185–200
    shear walls (unreinforced), 135–141
    strength-reduction factors, 92, 92t
    TMS 402-22, 92–95

Strength design (*Cont.*):
    warehouse. *See* One-story commercial building - reinforced concrete masonry
Strength design of curtain walls, 163–167
    clay masonry, 164f
    concrete masonry, 164, 165f
    example, 165–167
    flexural design, 166
    shear design, 166–167
    strength-reduction factor, 163
    structural action, 165
Strength design of reinforced beams and lintels, 155–162
    arching action, 162
    balanced reinforcement percentage, 157, 157f
    basic assumptions, 155, 156f
    depth of bottom reinforcement, 160, 160f
    design steps, 94t, 158–159
    equilibrium of internal stresses and external nominal moment, 156f
    example, 159–162
    flexural design, 158
    nominal flexural capacity, 161
    nominal in-plane shear stress, 161
    shear design, 158
    steel reinforcing wire and bars, 159, 159t
    tensile reinforcement index, 157
    unit strength method, 160
Strength design of reinforced bearing walls, 167–185. *See also* Bearing walls
    balance point, 168f, 169–170, 171–172
    cracked moment of inertia, 180
    critical strain condition, 184, 184f
    maximum flexural reinforcement, 183–185
    minimum flexural reinforcement, 183
    moment-axial force interaction diagram (hand calculation), 168–172
    moment-axial force interaction diagram (spreadsheet calculation), 172–176, 177t
    moment magnifier, 182
    out-of-plane load, 176–184
    pure compression, 168f, 169, 170
    pure flexure, 168f, 169, 170–171
    required details, 201–203
    service level moments, 182
    slenderness-dependent factor, 175, 179
    unfactored moment diagram, 178, 178f
Strength design of reinforced shear walls, 185–200
    best design strategy, 200
    clay masonry shear wall, 188–197
    critical strain condition, 198, 198f
    design steps, 95t, 185–188

Strength design of reinforced shear walls (*Cont.*):
   maximum flexural reinforcement, 197–200
   minimum flexural reinforcement, 197
   moment-axial force interaction diagram, 190, 190f, 193, 193f
   prescriptive seismic reinforcement, 196
   required details, 201–203
   seismic requirements, 200
   slenderness, 193, 193f
Strength design of unreinforced bearing walls, 122–135
   concentric axial load, 124–127
   design steps, 93t, 122–123
   eccentric axial load, 127–130
   eccentric axial load plus wind, 130–132
   examples, 124–133
   factoids, 133
   moment magnifier, 123, 129, 130, 132, 139
   openings, 133–135
   required details, 149–151
   unfactored moment diagram, 131, 131f
Strength design of unreinforced panel walls, 109–122. *See also* Panel walls
   double-wythe (hollow units, face-shell bedding only), 116
   flexural design, 109, 111
   load factors, 111
   modulus of rupture, 111, 111t
   one-way shear, 116–117
   out-of-plane load, 119–120, 120–122
   overview, 93t, 109, 117
   section properties for masonry walls, 118, 118t
   shear capacity, 117
   single-wythe (hollow units), 113–114
   single-wythe (hollow units, face-shell bedding only), 114–115
   single-wythe (hollow units, fully grouted), 115–116
   single-wythe (solid units), 112–113
   strength-reduction factors, 112
   strip method, 118–119
Strength design of unreinforced shear walls, 135–141
   design steps, 94t, 136
   example, 137–139
   free body of one wall segment, 140, 140f
   openings, 140–141
   required details, 149–151
   wall buildings, generally, 139–140
Strength loading combinations, 90, 92
Strength-reduction factor:
   AAC masonry panel walls, 397
   curtain walls, 163

Strength-reduction factor (*Cont.*):
   reinforced AAC masonry shear wall, 426
   strength design, 92, 92t
   unreinforced AAC masonry bearing walls, 400
   unreinforced AAC masonry shear walls, 408
   unreinforced bearing walls, 123
   unreinforced panel walls, 112
   unreinforced shear walls, 136
Stretcher orientation, 7, 8f
Strip method, 118–119, 399
Structural behavior:
   AAC masonry, 393–397
   curtain walls, 164
   low-rise masonry buildings, 1, 1f
Structural irregularities:
   plan, 89, 378, 453
   vertical, 89–90, 379, 453
Surface Roughness B, 57, 69
Surface Roughness C, 57, 69
Surface roughness category, 57
Surface Roughness D, 57, 69

T

Technical speciality organizations, 48–49, 99
Tensile bond strength:
   clay masonry, 26
   concrete masonry, 27
   masonry assemblages, 28
   mortar, 17
Tensile capacity, 101
Tensile reinforcement index, 157
Tensile strength:
   clay masonry, 25
   concrete masonry, 27
Tension breakout failure, 141, 241
Tension chord, 335, 335f
Terminology:
   beam-column, 167, 277
   sides of masonry unit, 7
The Masonry Society (TMS), 49, 99
Three-story AAC shear-wall hotel, 438–465
   accidental torsion, 454
   design acceleration response spectrum, 449, 450f
   design of AAC bearing walls, 464
   design response acceleration parameter, 447–448
   design response spectrum curve, 448–449
   design steps, 439
   diagram, 439f
   distributing seismic base shear vertically and horizontally, 442, 452, 453–454
   exterior walls - gravity plus out-of-plane wind, 459–460

Index   487

Three-story AAC shear-wall hotel (*Cont.*):
  factored design shears and moments, 453*f*, 453*t*
  fire, 440
  flexural capacity - out-of-plane walls, 459–460
  floor diaphragm, 460–464. *See also* Floor diaphragm - three-story AAC masonry hotel
  floor load due to gravity, 441
  gravity load, 440
  hollow-core prestressed concrete planks, 464
  inherent torsion, 454
  lateral load, 440
  mapped MCE (maximum considered earthquake), 442
  materials, 440
  maximum considered earthquake ground motion, 442, 447
  movement joints, 440
  principal lateral force-resisting elements, 439
  reinforcement requirements, 464
  roof load due to gravity, 440
  seismic base shear, 441, 451–452
  seismic design category, 449–451
  seismic ground motion values, 441
  shear capacity, 460
  simplicity in design and analysis, 464
  site classification, 447
  transverse shear walls, 454–459
  types of floor and roof elements, 464–465
  water penetration resistance, 440
3-s gust speed, 56
TMS. *See* The Masonry Society (TMS)
TMS 402, 49, 395
TMS 402-22:
  AAC masonry, 395. *See also* Autoclaved aerated concrete (AAC)
  allowable stress design provisions, 95–99
  eccentricity requirements for walls, 224
  flexural design, 109, 111, 208, 210
  flexural design of transverse shear walls, 387
  maximum flexural reinforcement, 183–185, 197–200
  minimum flexural reinforcement, 183, 197
  modulus of rupture, 111*t*
  panel walls, 109, 111, 208, 210
  strength design provisions, 92–95
TMS 602, 49, 101, 102, 395
Topographic factor:
  base shear due to wind (MWFRS), 341
  MWFRS, 57, 59
  pressure on wall elements due to wind (C&C), 344

Transverse shear walls:
  flexural design, 383–387, 455–456
  four-story building with clay masonry, 381–388
  moment-axial force interaction diagram, 383, 384–385*t*
  most laborious part of design, 387
  resisting lateral loads as statically determinate cantilevers, 388
  shear design, 382–383, 454–455
  structural system feasible up to about six stories, 388
  three-story AAC shear-wall hotel, 454–459
Triangular compressive stress blocks, 258*f*
Trough units, 104
2024 IBC:
  allowable-stress loading combinations, 91
  dead load, 51
  earthquake loading. *See* Earthquake loading
  floor live load, 51–52, 52*t*
  floor live load reduction, 52–53
  generally, 51
  gravity loads, 51–53
  loading combinations, 90–91
  roof live load, 53, 54*f*
  strength loading combinations, 90
  wall live load reduction, 53
  wind loading. *See* Wind loading
2500-year earthquake, 81, 442
Type FBS brick, 22, 24
Type FBX brick, 22, 24
Type I concrete, 27
Type II concrete, 27
Type K mortar, 13
Type M mortar, 13, 13*t*, 14*t*, 15*t*
Type N mortar, 13, 13*t*, 14*t*, 15*t*
Type O mortar, 13, 13*t*, 14*t*, 15*t*
Type S mortar, 13, 13*t*, 14*t*, 15*t*

U

UBC. *See* Uniform Building Code (UBC)
Unfactored moment diagram:
  AAC masonry - reinforced bearing walls, 418, 419*f*
  allowable-stress design - reinforced bearing walls, 288, 288*f*
  allowable-stress design - unreinforced bearing walls, 229, 229*f*
  low-rise building, 351, 351*f*
  strength design - reinforced bearing walls, 178, 178*f*
  strength design - unreinforced bearing walls, 131, 131*f*

Uniform Building Code (UBC), 50
Unit strength method:
   advantage of, 101
   allowable-stress design - beams and lintels, 268
   cracked, transformed sections, 261
   strength design - beams and lintels, 160
Unity equation:
   allowable-stress design - concentric axial load, 224
   allowable-stress design - eccentric axial load, 227
   allowable-stress design - eccentric axial load plus wind, 230–232
   combinations of axial force and bending, 221
Unloaded/loaded nodes, 463, 463f
Unreinforced AAC masonry bearing walls, 399–408
   authors' comments, 407
   compressive capacity, 400
   concentric axial load, 400–402
   eccentric axial load, 402–405
   eccentric axial load plus wind, 405–407
   location with highest wind moment, 407
   modulus of rupture, 407
   openings, 407, 408
   second-order effects, 400
   strength-reduction factor, 400
Unreinforced bearing walls:
   AAC masonry, 399–408. *See also* Unreinforced AAC masonry bearing walls
   allowable-stress design, 220–235. *See also* Allowable-stress design of unreinforced bearing walls
   comparing allowable-stress/strength design, 304, 304t
   required details, 149–151
   strength design, 122–135. *See also* Strength design of unreinforced bearing walls
Unreinforced masonry:
   AAC masonry - bearing walls, 399–408
   AAC masonry - panel walls, 397–399
   AAC masonry - shear walls, 408–412
   allowable-stress design - anchor bolts, 241–248
   allowable-stress design - bearing walls, 220–235
   allowable-stress design - panel walls, 207–220
   allowable-stress design - shear walls, 235–241
   comparing allowable-stress/strength design, 303–308
   defined, 102
   reinforcement, 105
   strength design - anchor bolts, 141–148
   strength design - bearing walls, 122–135
   strength design - panel walls, 109–122
   strength design - shear walls, 135–141

Unreinforced panel walls. *See* Panel walls
Unreinforced shear walls:
   AAC masonry, 408–412
   allowable-stress design, 235–241. *See also* Allowable-stress design of unreinforced shear walls
   comparing allowable-stress/strength design, 304–305, 305t
   required details, 149–151
   strength design, 135–141. *See also* Strength design of unreinforced shear walls

V

Vapor barriers, 7, 28t, 34–35
Velocity pressure:
   base shear due to wind (MWFRS), 341
   MWFRS, 59–60, 71, 73
   pressure on wall elements due to wind (C&C), 345
Velocity pressure exposure coefficient:
   base shear due to wind (MWFRS), 341
   MWFRS, 59, 61t, 71
   pressure on wall elements due to wind (C&C), 345
Veneer design, 103
Veneer ties, 30, 32f
Vertical reinforcement, 2, 3f, 105
Vertical strip, 2
Vertical structural irregularities, 89–90, 379, 453
Vertically oriented expansion joint, 35f
Vertically spanning strips:
   AAC masonry panel walls, 399
   bearing walls, 122, 123f, 220, 220f

W

Wall buildings, 139–140, 239–240. *See also* Shear wall
Wall live load reduction, 53
Wall sections at doors, 43
Wall sections at windows, 42–43, 43f
Wall segments:
   capacity of segment A (flexure), 371
   capacity of segment A (shear), 371–372
   east wall in plane, 370–372
   west wall in plane, 369–370
Wall-to-floor connection:
   reinforced bearing walls, 201, 202f, 296, 297f, 298f
   reinforced shear walls, 201, 202f, 296, 297f, 298f
   unreinforced bearing walls, 149, 150f, 248, 249f, 250f
   unreinforced shear walls, 149, 150f, 248, 249f, 250f

Wall-to-foundation connection:
   little structural calculation, 38, 39f, 40f
   reinforced bearing walls, 201, 201f, 296, 297f
   reinforced shear walls, 201, 201f, 296, 297f
   unreinforced bearing walls, 149, 149f, 248, 249f
   unreinforced shear walls, 149, 149f, 248, 249f
Wall-to-roof connection:
   little structural calculation, 38, 40f, 41f
   reinforced bearing walls, 201, 203f, 298, 299f
   reinforced shear walls, 201, 203f, 298, 299f
   unreinforced bearing walls, 149, 151f, 248, 250f
   unreinforced shear walls, 149, 151f, 248, 250f
Wall-to-wall connection:
   reinforced bearing walls, 203, 203f, 297, 297f
   reinforced shear walls, 203, 203f, 297, 297f
   unreinforced bearing walls, 151, 151f, 248, 251f
   unreinforced shear walls, 151, 151f, 248, 251f
Water penetration resistance:
   construction, 44–45
   four-story building, 374
   low-rise building, 338
   specification and design, 43–44
   three-story AAC shear-wall hotel, 440
Water permeability, 28
Water-repellent coatings, 34
Weathering index, 24, 24f
Welded wire reinforcement, 29, 30f
West of Denver, 107

Wind directionality factor:
   base shear due to wind (MWFRS), 341
   MWFRS, 57, 58t
   pressure on wall elements due to wind (C&C), 344
Wind load parameters, 56
Wind loading, 54–78
   ASCE 7-22, 54
   C&C. *See* Components and Cladding (C&C)
   generally, 54
   MWFRS. *See* Main Wind-Force Resisting System (MWFRS)
Wind pressure:
   base shear due to wind (MWFRS), 342–344
   MWFRS, 60, 62–63, 73
   pressure on wall elements due to wind (C&C), 346–348
Wind speed:
   base shear due to wind (MWFRS), 340
   fastest mile, 56
   pressure on wall elements due to wind (C&C), 344
Windward side:
   wind loading (C&C), 76, 78, 78t
   wind pressure (C&C), 346, 347t
Wooden joists, 335, 336f
Wooden roof truss, 41f
Workability, 15

Z

Z tie, 32f

ENGINEERING RELATED PUBLICATIONS

Reinforced Masonry Engineering Handbook
Clay and Concrete Masonry, 9th Edition

Reinforced Masonry Engineering Handbook, 9th Edition, is based on the requirements of the 2021 *International Building Code* and The Masonry Society (TMS) 402/602-16 *Building Code Requirements and Specification for Masonry Structures*. This book is useful to designers of reinforced masonry in eliminating repetitious and routine calculations. This handbook will increase the understanding and reduce the time required for masonry design.

This book addresses essential information on:
- Materials
- Masonry Assemblage, Strengths and Properties
- Distribution and Analysis for Lateral Forces.
- Design of Structural Members by Allowable Stress Design
- Design of Structural Members by Strength Design

Price $139.95
+ Tax and S&H

Reinforcing Steel in Masonry, 5th Edition

This 140-page handbook presents details and construction practices for the use of reinforcing steel in masonry based on Code requirements.

Connections are shown, specifications are provided and Code design tables are included for the benefit and convenience of the user.

Based on the 2009 IBC and the 2008 TMS 402/602

The handbook Includes information on:
- Function of Reinforcing Steel
- Types of Reinforcements
- Shear Walls
- Spacing of Steel in Masonry Walls
- Anchorage of Reinforcing Steel in Masonry
- Anchor Bolts
- Beams

Price $21.95
+ Tax and S&H

Reinforced Concrete Masonry Construction Inspector's Handbook, 11th Edition

This publication is the most recognized information source written exclusively for structural masonry inspection. This book covers all aspects of reinforced concrete masonry construction and inspection. Every inspector, designer and contractor should have a copy of this most important publication.

448 Pages

The handbook Includes information on:
- Responsibilities and Duties
- Materials
- Quality Control
- Inspection
- Construction in Severe Weather
  ....and more

Based on the 2021 IBC and the TMS 402/602-16

Price $49.95
+ Tax and S&H

ORDER ONLINE NOW!
www.masonryinstitute.org

MASONRY INSTITUTE OF AMERICA